Perception and Identity

A Study of the Relationship between the Ethiopian Orthodox Church and Evangelical Churches in Ethiopia

Seblewengel Daniel

© 2019 Seblewengel Daniel

Published 2019 by Langham Academic (Previously Langham Monographs)
An imprint of Langham Publishing
www.langhampublishing.org

Langham Publishing and its imprints are a ministry of Langham Partnership

Langham Partnership
PO Box 296, Carlisle, Cumbria, CA3 9WZ, UK
www.langham.org

ISBNs:
978-1-78368-634-6 Print
978-1-78368-635-3 ePub
978-1-78368-637-7 PDF

Seblewengel Daniel has asserted her right under the Copyright, Designs and Patents Act, 1988 to be identified as the Author of this work.

All rights reserved. No part of this publication may be reproduced, stored in a retrieval system or transmitted, in any form or by any means, electronic, mechanical, photocopying, recording or otherwise, without the prior written permission of the publisher or the Copyright Licensing Agency.

Requests to reuse content from Langham Publishing are processed through PLSclear. Please visit www.plsclear.com to complete your request.

All Scripture quotations, unless otherwise indicated, are taken from the Holy Bible, New International Version®, NIV®. Copyright ©1973, 1978, 1984, 2011 by Biblica, Inc.™ Used by permission of Zondervan.

British Library Cataloguing-in-Publication Data
A catalogue record for this book is available from the British Library

ISBN: 978-1-78368-634-6

Cover & Book Design: projectluz.com

Langham Partnership actively supports theological dialogue and an author's right to publish but does not necessarily endorse the views and opinions set forth here or in works referenced within this publication, nor can we guarantee technical and grammatical correctness. Langham Partnership does not accept any responsibility or liability to persons or property as a consequence of the reading, use or interpretation of its published content.

This book by Seblewengel Daniel is a well-researched, thoughtful and sympathetic study offering a new approach to an age-old problem in Ethiopia – engaging the uneasy relationship between the diverse Christian traditions that have taken root in Ethiopia over many centuries through the twin lenses of perception and identity.

As an important yardstick for understanding the Ethiopian church predicament, she employs three key themes in the dynamics of Christian history identified by Andrew Walls – the essential continuity of Christianity, the indigenizing principle and the pilgrim principle.

Weaving together in a historical survey the perceptions of each other's traditions and what constitutes the heart of their identity, she analyzes the root causes of the divergence, and identifies commonalities and pointers to convergence, with a view to fostering a greater mutual understanding within the diverse body of Christ in Ethiopia. This is a timely aim, given the many existential challenges facing the church and country today.

Gillian Mary Bediako, PhD
Deputy Rector,
Akrofi-Christaller Institute of Theology, Mission and Culture,
Akropong-Akuapem, Ghana

Perception and Identity: A Study of the Relationship between the Ethiopian Orthodox Church and Evangelical Churches in Ethiopia by Seblewengel Daniel, eloquently synthesizes the notion of perception and identity among members of the Ethiopian Orthodox Church and Evangelical churches in Ethiopia. It offers a thoroughly researched analysis of the nature of relationship between the Ethiopian Orthodox Church and Evangelical church on multiple fronts: theological, missional, cultural, etc., tapping on secondary and primary sources. It is a distinct contribution to a subject of seminal importance that has been overlooked by scholars. Seble has ably and engagingly explored the cartography of encounters between the two Christian faith traditions by situating the varied elements in the country's unique historical contexts. Ethiopia is a non-colonized nation, having an indigenous church with a powerful presence. The Evangelical church is growing alarmingly, gaining increasing visibility, despite its recency. Seble offers a nuanced inquiry of the troubled engagements by tracing its origin mainly to the theological and cultural misunderstandings on Mary and the Bible.

The book is highly relevant in the context of contemporary Ethiopia where the need for mutual dialogue and unity is vitally felt. This rich and brilliantly presented book deserves a place in serious scholarly instructions and libraries promoting the field of Christianity and mission studies.

Tibebe Eshete, PhD
Visiting Professor of History,
Michigan State University, East Langsing, Michigan, USA,
Calvin College, Grand Rapids, Michigan, USA

This is a valuable study, sensitive and well-researched, of culture clash and the interactions of tradition, identity and renewal. It enlarges our understanding of Ethiopia's modern religious history, gives insights into both ancient and recent Christian developments, and transmits messages both of warning and of hope.

Andrew F. Walls, PhD
Emeritus Professor, History of Missions,
University of Edinburgh, UK
Liverpool Hope University, UK

Contents

English Abstract ix

Kambatisa Abstract...xi

Amharic Abstract..xiii

Acknowledgements xv

Abbreviations xix

Chapter 1 1
Introduction
    1.1. Motivation..1
    1.2. Intellectual Framework 3
    1.3. Methodology 6
    1.4. Historical Background to the Study 7

Chapter 2.. 11
The Formation of Ethiopian Christian Identity
    Introduction 11
    2.1. The Aksumite Period..13
        2.1.1. The Role of the Monarchy 13
        2.1.2. The Alexandrian Connection 18
        2.1.3. The Role of the Nine Saints and the Vernacular
              Scriptures...22
        2.1.4. Judaic Influences..25
    2.2. The Move into the Interior...27
        2.2.1. The Rise of Islam and Its Coastal Presence 27
        2.2.2. The Long Process of Westward Expansion and the
              Role of Amharic..28
        2.2.3. The Process of Christianization 34
        2.2.4. Development of Learning 47
        2.2.5. Advance and Recession 51
        2.2.6. The Great Jihad and the Arrival of Western Christianity ...52
        2.2.7. The Nineteenth-Century Revival of Ethiopia –
              Including New European Interest 62
        2.2.8. The Nineteenth-Century Expansion of the
              Monarchy and the Integration of the South 66

  2.2.9. Haile Sellassie (1930–1974) and the Italian War
     and Recovery 70
  2.2.10. Revolution and the Derg 76
  2.2.11. The Post-Revolutionary Settlement 85
 Conclusion 85

Chapter 3 89
Protestant Missions and the Emergence of Evangelical Churches
 Introduction 89
 3.1. Lutherans 90
 3.2. New Evangelical Missions and Churches 96
  3.2.1. Eastern Mennonite Board of Missions 97
  3.2.2. Baptist Missions 98
 3.3. Indigenous Initiatives in the South Prior to the Coming of
   Missionaries 99
 3.4. The Establishment of the Ethiopian Kale Heywet Church
   (EKHC) 103
 3.5. Pentecostals 112
 3.6. Transformation and Polarization: The Outcomes of
   Pentecostal Movement 119
 3.7. The Sufficiency of Scripture in Vernacular 124
 Conclusion 125

Chapter 4 127
The Anglican-Orthodox Encounter: An Attempt to Revitalize the Church of Ethiopia
 Introduction 127
 4.1. An Overview of Evangelicalism in England and the
   Establishment of the Church Missionary Society 128
 4.2. The Political and Spiritual Condition of Ethiopia in the
   Nineteenth Century 134
 4.3. The Missionaries' Interlude in Egypt 139
 4.4. Firsthand Experience of Abyssinian Christianity 148
  4.4.1. Kugler in Tigray 154
  4.4.2. Gobat in Gondar 165
 4.5. The Deaths of Kugler and Sabagadis 177
 4.6. The Aftermath 180
 4.7. Conclusion of the First Attempt to Revitalize the Church
   of Ethiopia 187
 4.8. New Recruits, Greater Challenges 189
 4.9. CMS in Shewa 192

    4.10. The End of CMS Mission to Ethiopia 203
    4.11. Renewed Efforts of Samuel Gobat 208
    Conclusion 211

Chapter 5 225
Evangelical–Ethiopian Orthodox Church Encounter: A Story of Mutual Antagonism and Misunderstanding
    Introduction 225
    5.1. Brief History of the Encounter between Ethiopian Orthodox Church and Evangelicals 226
        5.1.1. "We Are the Church in Ethiopia" 231
        5.1.2. The *Tsere-Mariam* Accusation against the Evangelicals through the Centuries 237
        5.1.3. The Depiction of Evangelicals as *Mete* (Foreign) 243
        5.1.4. Longstanding Doctrinal Differences between EOC and Evangelicals: The Depiction of Evangelicals as *Menafiq* and "Thieves" 251
        5.1.5. The Ethiopian Orthodox Church's Perception of Pentecostals 262
        5.1.6. Concluding Remarks 266
    5.2. The Evangelicals' Perceptions of the EOC 268
        5.2.1. The Evangelicals' Perception of Themselves as Believers "አማኞች" 269
        5.2.2. The Evangelical View of the Ethiopian Orthodox Church as Authoritarian and Discriminatory 272
        5.2.3. The Evangelical Depiction of the Orthodox as *Ahzab*/without Christ 278
    5.3. The Two Great Battle Grounds and One of the Consequences 283
        5.3.1. The Mother of God, the Mother of Jesus 283
        5.3.2. Sola Scriptura and the Mother-Tongue Translations of the Bible 304
        5.3.3. The Issue of Burial 320
    Conclusion 327

Chapter 6 335
Contemporary Reformation Impulses in the Ethiopian Orthodox Church
    Introduction 335
    6.1. An Overview of Reformation in the Church 336
    6.2. The Controversy over the Term *Tehadiso* 346

  6.3. An Overview of Reformation Movements 350
    6.3.1. Aba Estifanos, the "Ancestor" of Modern Reformers 351
    6.3.2. Expelled Insiders 355
  6.4. Tension between Reforming and Preserving the Tradition
    of the Church 359
    6.4.1. The In-Between Reformers 360
    6.4.2. "Silent" Reformers 364
    6.4.3. Popular Preachers and Singers 366
    6.4.4. Mahbere Kidusan: The "Watchdog" of Ancient
      Tradition 369
  6.5. The Evangelicals and Reformation Movements 376
  Conclusion 378

Chapter 7 385
 Conclusion

Appendix 405
 Early Attempts at Ecumenism

Glossary 411

Bibliography 415

Index of Names 439

Index of Subjects 443

English Abstract

The Church Missionary Society came to Ethiopia in 1830 with strong desire to revitalize the church of Ethiopia as a sister national church. The missionaries disseminated large quantities of Bibles, in the conviction that the Ethiopians would be able to renew their own church through the reading of the Bible in the vernacular. However, the tactless approach of later missionaries resulted in the expulsion of the CMS in 1843. The CMS legacy was that of a growing interest in Bible reading, but it stirred up a fear of jeopardizing the ancient tradition to such an extent that the Bible readers were expelled from the church. The nineteenth- and twentieth-century mission organizations departed from the vision of the Church Missionary Society for a number of reasons. Their work among the peripheral groups, however, brought forth believers whose Christian consciousness significantly differed from that of the Orthodox adherents and the Orthodox Church rejected them as unauthentic. The relationship between Orthodox and Evangelicals further deteriorated with the rise of the Pentecostal movement, which spread in the urban centres, drawing in members of the Orthodox Church, as well as new believers. Despite the contrasting styles of Evangelical religion and theology, there was continuity in the Orthodox response to the Evangelical presence in the country because the Orthodox Church considered itself as *the* church in Ethiopia. The status of Mary as the *shibboleth* of Ethiopian orthodoxy and the Evangelicals' vehement rejection of it made peaceful dialogue between the Orthodox and Evangelicals difficult. Evangelicals were perceived as Enemies of Mary, while they perceived the extensive devotion of the Orthodox to Mary as idolatry. Archival sources, interviews, unpublished literature and popular media indicate that the cardinal battleground between Orthodox and Evangelicals remained the status of Mary and the Bible; Mary being the strong identity marker for the Orthodox, and the

Bible for Evangelicals. Reform impulses have been evident in the Orthodox Church, but many reformers and Evangelicals seem to view the centrality of the Bible as an identification with the Protestant tradition. However, the threat of fanatic Islamists, the rise of Orthodox groups which are committed to Bible reading with adequate respect for the saints, the Evangelicals' growing regret over sheep-stealing, and the effort of the Bible Society to bring the two bodies together seem to be bringing steady improvement in the relationship. In addition, theological schools and the Christian media could further mutual understanding and trust by providing a platform for dealing with the past hurt and dialogue on matters of difference and common Christian identity. Both Orthodox and Evangelical Christians uphold the ultimate significance of Christ and use the Bible, and so belonging to the one faith, both groups need to refrain from perceiving each other as rivals and attempting to impose their tradition on one another in the name of promoting an authentic Christian identity.

Kambatisa Abstract

ፈረንጃ ጀቾ ዋሊሻ ሳቢን 1830 ማረቶ ዋጋን ቸርቾ ሚሺነሪ ሶሳይቲ(ሲ ኤም ኤስ) ያመነት ገአንታ ሚስዮኑ ሂዘጋ ቱዳኢ ኦርቶክሲ ቤተ ክርስታና ባዲ አፊኤን ክታበንቴ መገኒ ላጋን ቃርሲ ከጀልት ቶጺታ ዋልቴኢ። ሚሲዮኑስ በትናሻ መጠፋ ቅዱሳ አፋ ዋልት ኬሶ ሆለማ መኒሃ ቤከንያን ዋዘናተሳ ቃሩ አመዕነቱ ዮሳ ኢኬ፣ ሂኩንሲን ጀቾንተስ ዮኢ መጠፋ ቅዱሳ ክንቲት ቤኤን በትናኙ መኑ መገኒ ላጋታ አፊኤንተስ አነበባዳ ባዳሲ መኑንኩ ቤተ ክርስታናስ ዶርሃ ደንደዋ ያፄ። ሚሲዮኒሲ ዊዳን ዋልቶ ፈረንጃቾ መመቲሳን ዊዳን በሬዱ ሰዋቱ ቆርመቲ ኩቴያን ሚሲዮኑስ ፈረንጀ ጀቾ ዋሊሻ ሳቢን 1843 ማረቶ ዋጋን ቶጼቾ ሸረሞ። ኦርቶክሲ ቤተ ክርስቲያና ቄሳዋ ዋዘናን መገኒ ላጋታ አነቢ ቁልቱ ገሉንተኒ ሚሲዮኑስ አብሸ ካዕሌኢ ኢኩዲኒ ላጋስ አነበ ኬኑ ቤተ ክርስታና አዘኒ በሺላ ዶላ ኤጌሬ ዋጊቾ ጥሮዕጵ ይቶን ሰዋቱ አቁት ቤተ ክርስታኔት ሸረቴሶ። ዘኪ ዶላን ዋልቶ ሚስዮኑ ሲ ኤም ኤስ ያመሞ ሆሪቾን ቢርሲ ዋሎ ሚሲዮን ሰዋቴቾ አነገታ ዓላማን ዋንዘሳ ሰበኪ ሆለማ መና አመዕነስን ገጊሳ ቤተ ክርስታና ፈዎንተሳ ኦርቶክሲ ቤተ ክርስቲያንቾት አብስ አመዕረቶ። ሂቲ አሙሪቲ ሲጊቶናቶ ከተማዛ ሄጌየን ወንዝላ ሰበከ ኬሶ በትናፊ ኦርቶክስ ቢርጊቴ ቤተ ክርስቲያናሳ ቃርሲቶ ጌንቴቆስጌ አመዕቴቱ ኬኡስ፣ ኦርቶክሱ ወንዝላ አመዕናኑ አብስ ቀራሰቀንቴንታ አሴኤ ኢኬ። አነና አነና ዊዳን ኦርቶክሲ ቤተ ክርስቲያንቾን ሜጦማታ ቆጭሃ ከጀልቴ አመዕናኑ አነታ ጀቾን ኬአደኒ ኦርቶክሲ ቤተ ክርስቲያንቾት ሆሪንከሳ ሚኒታ ከንቴዕ ኢኬ። ኦርቶክሳከት ወንዝላ አመዕናኑ ሃዳ ባዲ ሚጋ ቱዳሲ መሽኩት ኦርቶክሲ ቤተ ክርስቲያንቾት ገገሴ ጠላ ቶጼ ቤተ ክርስቲያንቾጋ ቱዳተኘፋት። መቱ መንጅ ማርያሜ ተነሃ ዮሲ አመዕነቱ ጠሉ፣ ኩ መንቾ ገዌ ኦርቶክስቾ ኢሃሃንስ ኬነንቻ ይት ኦርቶክሱ ሰዋታአ፣ ወንዝላ አመእናኑ አሞንቺሲ ሂቲና አመዕነቱ ቃርሲታ ጊባአ። ሂትጎኑ ሰዋቱ ለሜንክ ቤተ ክርስቲያና አመዕናኒ ሜሬርን ኬዕማሻ ነምበቀንቻ ቆጨእኒ ቱሚን ሃሳዋንበጋ አሴሳኒ። ኦርቶክሱ ወንዝላ አመዕናን "ማርያሜ መሲቻካታ" ይት ገእታሳ፣ ወንዝላ አመእናኑ አሞንቺሲ ኦርቶክስ ማርያም ተነሃ ዮሳ አመዕነቱ ወንዝላቾ ሃዳታ ይት ኬዕ ዲኪሻታ ይታእ። ኪታበንቱምቡ ቱሁፋከቲ፣ መመቶ መኒን አሴማ ሃሳዊሁ፣ ምኒ ሰዋታ ቱዲሲ መቆ ዮሳ ቱሁፋጌቲ ቱዲሳፋ ሄአዳ ኦርቶክሲና ወንዝላ አመዕናኒ ሜሬርን ዮኢ ጊበቀንቾ ቡዱስ ማርያሜ ተነ ዮሳ አመዕነቱ፣ ማርያም ኦርቶክሲ ኬነሃ ዋና አመዕነቲ ሸሆ ደረጃ ኢሊቴኢ። ወንዝላ አመዕናኑ አሞንቺሲ መጠፋ ቅዱሲቾ በጋን ዋሉ አመዕነቱሃ አቁናምበኪሳ ይታእ። ተሃዲሱታ ያመንት ገአንታ ኬኑ አሞንቺሲ ኦርቶክሲቾ አባ ወንዝላ አመዕናኒ ሰዋቲጊን መረንታእ አጉጀ ለለዮስ። ጠሁ ኢኩዲኒ እስላሚ ሃይማኖታ ቃርሲታ ኬኑ በተኡስ፣ ዋዶ አመዕነቱሃ

መጣፍ ቅዱሳሃ ሜጦማን አፍ መረሚ ከጀልታ ኦርቶዶኪሱ በተኣን ዋሉሳ፤ ወንጌሊ አሞዕናኮ ኦርቶዶክሲ አሞእናኮ ገጋሰ ዉዱ ዋሾ አጉሪ ቁልጣቱታ ቡዲሱሳ፤ ጤዼ መጣፍ ቅዱሲ ማህበሩ ሥላሴ አሞዕናኒ ሜሬሮን ሜጦመታ ቆጨሃ ቃር ሁጀቱስ ላሉታ ላሾኢ፡፡ ሂከኒ አሌን ቲዋሎጀ ትምህርቲ ሚናከት፤ ሚናደበ ጣዝ ሃሳዊሳ መጣፋት ለሜንከ ቤተ ክርስቲያኒ አሞዕናኒ ሜሬሮን ሜጦማቲ፤ አሞዕነቀንቹሁ ቆጨሙንታ፤ ከኒች ቢሬ ሂዕላንቻ አጉዕረንት ኬአ ሜሬሮንተሳ ዮኢ አነኖመታ አገቀንቺ ሃሳዊን ሂርቱንታ ዎቃሃ ፈኒ ደንዲታእ፡፡ ለሜንከ ዉዲ አሞዕናኮ ክርስትኒ ቡዳ ኢከ ክርስቶሳሃ መጣፍ ቅዱሳሃ ጡቃሲት ዋና አሲት አፉሳ፤ ለሜንከ አሞዕነቲ ሜሬሮን ቃረት ሜጦማት ዮጋ ለሊሰኖቢኪሃ አኮንከኮ አኮንከኮ ገገጌ ዎጋ መገኒች አሰሜ ሂጊጋ አሲት ቡዱሃ ኢስ ኢሶአ አሞዕነቱ ሺጊግ ዩሃ አጉሩ ሀስሰኖሳ።

Amharic Abstract

እንደ አውሮፓውያኑ አቆጣጠር በ 1830 ቸርች ሚሽነሪ ሶሳይቲ (ሲ ኤም ኤስ) የተሰኘው ድርጅት እንዲ እህት ቤተ ክርስቲያን የሚመለከታትን የኢትዮጵያ ኦርቶዶክስ ቤተ ክርስቲያንን በሀገርኛ ቋንቋ መጽሐፍ ቅዱስን በመጠቀም የማነቃቃትን ዓላማ ሰንቆ ወደ ኢትዮጵያ መጣ። ሚስዮናውያኑ መጽሐፍ ቅዱስን በብዛት ሲያከፋፍሉ በወቅቱ የነበሩት ክፍተኛ የመጽሐፍ ቅዱስ እጥረት ተቀርፎ ኢትዮጵያውያን ክርስቲያኖች በሚገባቸው ቋንቋ ቃሉን ማንበብ የቻሉ እንደው ቤተ ክርስቲናፋውን የማደስ ብቃት እንዳላቸው ተማምነው ነበር። ነገር ግን ከአንዳንድ ጥብቀ የጎደላቸው ሚስዮናውያን አሉታዊ አካሄድ የተነሳ በ 1843 ሲ ኤም ኤስ ከሀገር የመባርር ዕጣ ደረሰው። በኦርቶዶክስ ቤተ ክርስቲያን ቀሳውስት ዘንድ መጽሐፍ ቅዱስን የማንበብ ጥማትን በማሳደግ ረገድ ሲ ኤም ኤስ ጉልህ ሚና የተጫወተ ቢሆንም ቅሉ አንባቢዎች የተከተሉት የአተረጓገም አካሄድ የጥንታዊቷን ቤተ ክርስቲያን ትውፊት እንዳላገናዘብ ፍራቻ በማሳደሩ የመጽሐፍ ቅዱስ አንባቢዎች ከቤተ ክርስቲያኗ እንዲሰደዱ ሆነ። ከተለያዩ ምክንያቶች የተነሳ በ19ኛው እና በ20ኛው ክፍለ ዘመናት የመጡት ሚስዮናውያን ሲ ኤም ኤስ አንግቦት የነበረውን ራዕይ ወደ ጎን በመተው በአብዛኛው ባህላዊ እምነት ተከታይ በነበሩት አናሳ ብሔሮች መካከል መስራት ጀመሩ፤ ይህም ራሳቸውን ከኦርቶዶክስ ትውፊት ጋር ሳላዛመዱ የክርስትና እምነት ተከታዮች መፈጠር ምክንያት ከመሆኑ በላይ የኦርቶዶክስ ቤተ ክርስቲያንን በአያሌው አስከፋታል። በተጨማሪም የኦርቶዶክስ ግዛት ተደርገው ይታሰቡ የነበሩት ከተሞች በማጥለቀልቀ ኦርቶዶክስ የነበሩውንም ሆነ ሌላውን ከተሜ ወደራሱ ያፈለሰው የጴንጤቆስጤአዊ ትቅናት መነሳት በወንጌላውያን አማኞችን በኦርቶዶክስ መካከል የነበረውን ግንኙነት ይበልጥ እንዳሻከረው ይታመናል። ምንም እንኪን የተለያያ አመለካከትና አቀራረብ ያነገቡ ወንጌላውያን አማኞች በየዚዜው ቢነሱም የኦርቶዶክስ ቤተ ክርስቲያን ምላሻና ለእነሱ የነበራት አመለካከት ግን ተመሳሳይነት ነበረው። ይህም የሆነው ቤተ ክርስቲያኗ የራሷን ትውፊት እንደ ብቸኛ የኢትዮጵያዊ ክርስትና መገለጫ የመቁጠር አዝማሚያ ስላለት ነው ማለት ይቻላል። አንድ ሰው ስለማርያም ያለው አመለካከት እንደ እውነተኛ ኦርቶዶክሳዊነት መለኪያ ተደርጎ መወሰዱና ወንጌላውያን አማኞች ደግሞ ለዚህ መሰሉ አቋም ያላቸው ብርቱ ተቃውሞ በሁለቱ አብያተ ክርስቲያናት መካከል ጤናማ የሃሳብ ልውውጥ እንዳይኖር እንቅፋት ሆኖ ቆይቷል፤ : ከዚህም የተነሳ ወንጌላውያን አማኞች "ጸረ-ማርያም" የሚል ቅጽል ስም ሲሰጣቸው እነርሱ ደግሞ ኦርቶዶክሳውያንን ለማርያም ያላቸው ከፈታ ክልክ በላይ በመሆኑ ጣዖት እንደማምለክ ይቆጥራል ይላሉ። የተሃድሶ ንቅናቄዎች በተለያየ መልኩ ቢነሱም አካሄዳቸው ግን የመጽሐፍ

ቅዱስን ማዕከላዊነት የፕሮቴስታንትን ዶክትሪን ሙሉ ለሙሉ ከመቀበል ጋር የማያያዝ አዝማሚያ ይታይበታል። ያልታተሙ መዘግብት፣ ጽሁፎች፣ ቃለ መጠይቆች፣ የሀብረተሰቡ አመለካከት ከሞላ ጎደል የሚንጸባረቅባቸው በተለያዩ የመገናኛ ዘዴዎች የሚሰራጩና በዝብ መንጋን ተሽክሪካሪዎች ላይ የሚለጠፉ ጽሁፎች በኦርቶክሳውያንና በወንጌላውያን አማኞች መካከል ዋነኛ የሰልፍ ሜዳ የሆነው ጉዳይ ለማርያም የሚሰጠው ሥፍራ እንደሆነ ያመለክታሉ። ማርያም የኦርቶክሳውያን ማንነት መገለጫ እስከመሆን የደረሰች ሲሆን ወንጌላውያን አማኞች ደግሞ መጽሐፍ ቅዱስን የሚጥኝ ይላሉ። ዳሩ ግን የአክራሪ እስልምና መስፋፋት፣ ጥንታዊውን እምነትና መጽሐፍ ቅዱስን አጣጥሞው ለመንዳዝ ቁርጠኛነት ያላቸው ኦርቶክሳውያን መነሳት፣ ወንጌላውያን አማኞች የኦርቶክስን መንጋ ከማፍለስ ለመቆጠብ ያላቸው ፍላጎት እያደገ መሔዱ፣ እና የኢትዮጵያ መጽሐፍ ቅዱስ ማህበር የሥላሴ አማኞችን ለማቀራረብ የሚያደርገው ያላሰለሰ ጥረት ፍሬ እያፈራ እንዳለ ይመስላል። በተጨማሪም የሥነ መለከት ተቋማትና መገናኛ ብዙሃን በአብይቱ ክርስቲያናት መካከል አሜኔታን ለመፍጠርና መከባበርን ለማሳደግ፣ ያለፈውን ቅይማት በይቅርታ ዘግተው በልዩነቶቻቸውና አንድነቶቻቸው ላይ ጤናማና ገንቢ የሃሳብ ልውውጦችን እንዲያደርጉ አዎንታዊ ተጽዕኖ የማሳደር ሚና ሊጫወቱ እንደሚችሉ ይታመናል። ሁሉቱም ወገኖች የክርስትና እምነት ማዕከል ለሆነው ለክርስቶስና ለመጽሐፍ ቅዱስ ከፍተኛ ግምት መስጠታቸው በእምነታቸው መካከል ያለውን ጥብቅ ትስስር ስለሚያመለክት፣ የየራሳቸውን ልምምድ ከእግዚአብሔር እንደተሰጠ እንደ ብቸኛው የክርስትና ትውፊት አድርገው ከማቅረብ የመቆጠብ፣ የሌላውን ከማንቋሸሽ የገረጥ ከመተያየት የመታቀብ ኃላፊነት አለባቸው።

Acknowledgements

An academic work hardly comes to fruition with the sole effort of one person and this book is no exception. Its successful completion came about with the support of family members and countless friends. I will not be able to name everyone who supported me in one way or another but acknowledge the help of few people.

I like to begin by expressing my gratitude to the EGST Faculty Council for putting my name forward for the scholarship offered by the late Rev Prof Kwame Bediako when he came to Ethiopia in 2001 for Frumentius lectures. Thank you EGST Faculty Council for believing in me. I am also deeply grateful to the ETC administration for releasing me for studies and supporting me with prayer. I thank the ACI for the financial support and Langham Partnership for the generous scholarship payment and continuous encouragement, which made this study possible.

How did I come to the finishing lines with young children? One of the answers is God's gift of Tamiru, a kind head, a cheerful companion and partner in ministry. He took upon himself the difficult task of managing the house and minding the boys while I was away several times. I also thank my children Sebhat, Leul and Bamlak for giving me immeasurable joy. With their love, they helped me relax despite the demands of academic research. I promised Sebhat and Leul (Bamlak was not born then) a trip to Ghana for my graduation if they let me finish my work. They continued to ask me, have you finished yet? Sebhat was exasperated and asked, "Are you going to finish when I grow up?" Leul told me with his childlike innocence, "I do not love you anymore" each time I asked him to stop distracting me while I was working at home. Bamlak asked me not to bring my laptop home. This among many things made me work hard. I would also like to thank

Worknesh, who joyfully helped Tamiru look after the children and assumed the burden of cooking and cleaning while I was busy with my work.

My parents, Daniel and Abebech, minded Leul during the day until he turned one and entertained the children when I was away. I have counted on their prayers since I was a young girl. They exemplified Christ-likeness in such a powerful way that I decided to follow and serve their God who has become mine. My sisters Ruth and Tizita and my brothers Biruk, Tewolde and Dink along with their families supported me with their prayers and provisions immensely. Thank you so much my family members. My best friends Engidu and Gash Bezu were always there for me with prayer and emotional support. They cheered me up when I progressed in my work and encouraged me not to give up when I was torn between family responsibilities and research demands. God bless you my friends.

I am also deeply grateful to the staff, faculty members and students at Akrofi-Christaller Institute, Ghana. The late Rev Prof Kwame Bediako impacted my life immeasurably with christlike humility and respect for his students. He exemplified reliance on the Lord and rigorous scholarship. I will never forget his enthusiasm over his students' work, and how he valued each of us. I miss you Prof!

Special thanks to Ms Beatrice of Akosombo who entertained us in her home while we awaited Sebhat's birth and Rev Dr Solomon and Sister Beatrice Sule-Saa along with their family members who helped us adjust with life with a new baby in Ghana. I am utterly grateful to them. Korkulu Laryea and Gertrude Baiden too helped us care for Sebhat and did all the shopping for us. What sisters!

In my research on the Orthodox Church, Daniel Seife-Michael provided the information I needed with great interest in my work. He was willing to answer my questions in person, through telephone and email. Thank you, Daniel. Aba Daniel Assefa of the Capuchin Franciscan Institute allowed me to use the Institute's library and encouraged me a lot. I thank you Aba. Agizachew Tefera and brothers "T" and "D" provided me with valuable materials and answered my questions tirelessly. I am deeply grateful to you brothers.

Dr Staffan Grenstedt gave me every book I wished to borrow from his library and cheered me up with mother-tongue greetings each time I saw him; *maganu asu staffan*. Dr Paul Balisky sent me material from Canada even read part of my work and inspired me to research more and I would like to thank him. I am also thankful to Dr Steve Bryan who took interest in my work and gave me valuable comments as the academic mentor of JSM. Mikiyas Belay provided me with a digital recorder while doing my interviews and allowed me to keep it until I was done with the interviews. Thank you so much Miki. Moreover, I am deeply grateful to all of my informants who made time from their busy schedules, answered my questions and inspired me to reflect more.

I am thankful to the librarians of Akrofi-Christaller Institute, Evangelical Theological College, Ethiopian Graduate School of Theology, Institute of Ethiopian Studies, Holy Trinity Theological College and National Archives of Ethiopia for their cheerful assistance in my endeavour to locate resources. I am also grateful to the librarians of Liverpool Hope University, and archivists of the University of Birmingham. I am indebted to Dr John and Mrs Grace Azumah, Prof Daniel and Rev Sheila Jeyaraj, Ms Sue Harwood, Zuriash Adnew and her siblings, Genet and Yodit for making my stay in the UK bearable. I would also like to thank those in charge of the guest houses of Africa International University and Daystar University for joyfully hosting me while in Nairobi. My deep gratitude to pastor Zenaw Deneke and Dr Habtamu Kedir for allowing me to borrow the back issues of *Gesame* and Kale Heywet magazines.

I was blessed with the legendary supervisor Emeritus Prof Andrew Walls who gladly stepped in to help when Professor Kwame Bediako went to be with the Lord. Professor Walls was never intimidating, but very kind and encouraging. He happily covered my expenses while in Nairobi and told me that he would come to Ethiopia if needed in order to help me finish sooner. He also warned me ahead that there will come a day when my work will feel like a burden to me, and even more so to my husband. Sure enough, I was weary of going forward but his words of wisdom helped me to stay on course while passing through the inevitable valley of academic research. You have been more than an academic supervisor, Professor. The words "Thank you" are inadequate to express my gratitude to you. እግዚአብሔር ይስጥልኝ! (May the Lord reward you on my behalf!) That is how we say it in Amharic. I also thank Professor Mary Bediako, my secondary advisor, for her inspiration, patience and gentle spirit while reading my work and giving me feedback with an amazing efficiency. Aunty Mary, *medase*!

Last but not least, I give glory to God. Doctoral studies at times becomes a lonely journey through dark valleys of mental blockade and emotional struggles. My work has been an itch for the past six years; many times salutary, but at times burdensome. I carried a deep sense of guilt each time I travelled, but in all of this, the Lord has sustained me with his grace and surprised me with unexpected blessings. The one who called me has been faithful in providing for me and my family, keeping us all safe and seeing me through. He has not let me down. The long journey brought home the words of Jesus that apart from him, I can do nothing, and with God, all things are possible. To him be glory both now and forever more, Amen!

Abbreviations

AFM: Abyssinian Frontiers Mission
AUPM: American United Presbyterian Mission
CMS: Church Missionary Society
ECFE: Evangelical Churches Fellowship of Ethiopia
ECWA: Evangelical Churches of West Africa
EECMY: Ethiopian Evangelical Church Mekane Yesus
EKHC: Ethiopian Kale Heywet Church
EOC: Ethiopian Orthodox Church
Eth. C: Ethiopian Calendar
HAM: Heart of Africa Mission
HM: Hermannsburg Mission
MKC: Meserete Kristos Church
MWBC: Mulu Wongel Believers Church
RCC: Roman Catholic Church
SEM: Swedish Evangelical Mission
SIM: Sudan Interior Mission (now known as Serving In Mission)
UB SC: University of Birmingham Special Collections
WCC: World Council of Churches

CHAPTER 1

Introduction

1.1. Motivation

My own personal journey provides the background to the motivation for this study. I was born and raised in a rural area near Durame, southern Ethiopia, in the former Sudan Interior Mission (SIM)[1] compound. The area was dominated by members of Kale Heywet Church[2] with a considerable number of Mekane Yesus[3] members not too far from us. There are a few Ethiopian Orthodox churches far from my village which I never visited. They are mostly built on hills and also in small towns. A number of Orthodox priests (mostly northern/Shewan settlers who married local women) and their families lived at the edge of our big compound and they walked to their church which was at least four kilometres away in Durame town and further up at Qetta hill. People identified themselves as Kale Heywet, Mekane Yesus or Orthodox, but there appeared to be no major animosity between them.

When I moved to Addis at the age of fourteen it did not take long for the students at the school I joined to know that I was from the countryside because of my Amharic accent which amused them. I told them where I was from but they did not have a clue about my area. They asked me, "What is your religion "ሃይማኖት?" I was a bit baffled and said, "My religion? I am

---

1. Sudan Interior Mission, which is now called Serving in Mission, is a non-denominational organization which entered to Ethiopia in 1927. It primarily worked among people groups of southern Ethiopia.

2. This is the largest Evangelical Church in Ethiopia which was established by SIM.

3. Ethiopian Evangelical Church Mekane Yesus (EECMY) was established by Lutheran missionaries from Europe who entered Massawa in 1866.

Kale Heywet." Most of them did not know what it was and asked, "What is that?" Another one replied that it is a mission church and the first inquirer said, "Aha! You are Pente." They told me that Orthodox are Christians and I am "Pente/mission." However, very soon, I found myself right in the middle of the controversy when my friend invoked the angel Michael before we walked into an exam hall. I asked her, "Why do you pray to Michael instead of God?" This encounter stirred up a new dimension of thought in my religious consciousness and an interest to explore the differences.

However, even though moving from my local universe into a complex urban religious setting entailed some disorientation I do not remember feeling any resentment against those who came from a different Christian tradition. I even went to the Orthodox Church with my friend and accompanied her as she kissed the gate and the ground. I did not understand why one had to kiss the gates, the ground and pictures, but I never said anything to her. I also learned that some Evangelicals would not partake in feasts dedicated to angels and that the Orthodox would not eat the meat of an animal killed by Evangelicals. None of it made sense to me then because I had two Muslim uncles on my father's side and each time they visited us they killed a sheep or a goat and we all ate. I never came from a rigid religious background that affected my interaction with others.

After I joined theological school I learned about religious paradigms and their significance, methods of interpretation of the Bible, the canon of the Scriptures, and the fathers of the church, among other things. Even though my theological study broadened my perspective, the tension between Evangelicals and the Orthodox in the past twenty years which gained momentum caught my attention. Why do the Orthodox seem to dislike us so much? Why do we come so near to considering them as non-Christians? What is the history behind such negative perceptions of one another? While I was entertaining such questions, my experience at the ACI strengthened my desire to study the history of Orthodox and Evangelical traditions. Fellow students were proud of Ethiopia's history of independence and longed to visit the Ethiopian Orthodox Church (EOC) and learn more about its indigenous Christianity. They asked me, "Are you from the Orthodox Church?" It seemed that Ethiopia and the EOC were inseparable in their minds. I wondered, "How do they even think Evangelicals and Orthodox would study together?" Such questions gave me all the more reason to study the encounter between the indigenous Ethiopian Orthodox Church and Evangelical Christianity, the Evangelicals coming from the reformed tradition. Thus, I was interested in exploring the consequent tensions, misunderstandings and conflicts that had arisen between these two distinct Christian traditions.

1.2. Intellectual Framework

In this work the complex subject of perceptions and identity is approached from different angles and mainly historical and theological frameworks are used to explain the dynamics at play. The contemporary discussion about identity is quite broad and complex. However, Kwame Bediako's approach in his book entitled *Theology and Identity: The Impact of Culture upon Christian Thought in the Second Century and Modern Africa* provides one with an excellent framework for the discussion of identity in the African religious and cultural setting. Bediako discusses the hurdles involved in seeking to understand Christian identity in view of African cultural heritage and religious consciousness.[4] He uses the struggle of the second-century Christians to define their identity as a helpful model to understand the twentieth-century African theological discussion concerning African Christian identity. The second-century Christians struggled to come to terms with their Christian identity in a context where their faith, which failed to comply with the traditional religion, was considered superstitious and even atheistic.[5] The response of Christian thinkers of the time towards the cultural heritage ranged from a desire to sift through it and make a positive use of the Hellenistic philosophical tradition, to utter rejection of all of it as demonic.[6] This thesis discusses the similar approach of both Ethiopian Orthodox and Protestant missionaries towards the culture and religious heritage of the people they were attempting to convert and interprets the history of the engagement in view of their perceptions towards themselves and the people they were trying to reach.

---

4. Kwame Bediako, *Theology and Identity: The Impact of Culture upon Christian Thought in the Second Century and Modern Africa* (Oxford: Regnum Books, 1992), 1–10.

5. Bediako, *Theology and Identity*, 15–29.

6. Bediako, 64–222.

Bediako observes that the response of the missionaries to the tradition and culture they found in Africa was that of rejection. Such an approach resulted in an identity crisis in African Christian understanding where the Western value setting which did not resonate with that of Africa was rejected but an indigenous theological model was not built.[7] In their quest for identity, therefore, African theologians struggled to come to terms with their primal past in the face of the new-found faith. Bediako discusses the range of responses represented by some African theologians: an argument for the full continuity between primal religion and the biblical revelation, a call for interaction between the gospel and culture, and an argument about the discontinuity between the biblical revelation and Africa's primal religion.[8] Bediako's analysis enhances the discussion of this thesis about aspects of continuity and discontinuity of Christian faith with the primal worldview and the ensuing difficulty in areas where religious quests are not properly catered for by the church.

Bediako suggests four points which are helpful in the quest of Africans to assert their Christian identity: first, studying the fathers (especially the African fathers) enhances the task of doing an authentic African theology. Second, since the African context is pluralistic other religions need to be taken into consideration. Third, there is the need to indigenize in view of the reality that the God of Christianity is the one God of all humankind. Fourth, the pre-Christian heritage is to be seen as a tradition of response related to the question of identity.[9]

Bediako's response to the identity discussion is very helpful. It shows that there is similarity between second-century Christians' and African theologians' search for Christian identity. They were to define their Christian identity in comparison or contrast to their tradition and cultural heritage. Bediako suggests that in the discussion of Christian identity using the model of the fathers with adequate attention to the contemporary pluralistic context with no compromise on the universality of the God of Christianity, is vital.

This theological paradigm is decisive for this study which attempts to discuss the encounter of indigenous Christianity which gives room to the

---

7. Bediako, 225–252.
8. Bediako, 267–416.
9. Bediako, 426–441.

fathers, with Evangelical Christianity, which appears to have little consciousness of the fathers because mostly it came out of reformed and Evangelical traditions. Bediako's careful study of the background of second-century and African theologians in their own context, therefore, urges a similar approach to be used in considering other aspects of the African Christian story, instead of judging people from the past by using imported models from the twenty-first century.

For its assessment of the question of identity and the rationale behind the negative perceptions of Ethiopian Orthodox and Evangelical Christians, this work uses Andrew Walls' insights from his book entitled, *The Missionary Movement in Christian History: Studies in the Transmission of Faith*. Walls' models are immensely helpful to understand the dynamics of Christian history and recommend ways of promoting better relations. In his discussion Walls discerns three significant aspects in the transmission of Christian faith: an essential continuity in Christianity, the "Indigenizing" Principle, and the "Pilgrim" Principle.[10]

These three aspects challenge Christians in their perceptions of themselves and of other Christian traditions. The fact that Christianity did not have a fixed geographical centre and a sacred language, challenges the perceptions of Christians towards one another. However, the definite signs of continuity in Christian faith despite its having different centres and media over the years points to a presence of shared Christian identity.[11] What Walls calls the "Indigenizing Principle" asserts that God accepts people along with their good and bad cultural orientations on the ground of the sacrificial death of Christ. Thus the attempt to impose one's culture or tradition as *the* correct one has no biblical ground.[12]

However, what Walls calls "Pilgrim Principle" asserts that God accepts people in order to transform their minds towards Christ. Thus, Christians are to demonstrate Christlikeness and this puts them out of step with the society they are in.[13] These three principles are quite helpful in the discus-

---

10. Andrew Walls, *The Missionary Movement in Christian History, Studies in the Transmission of Faith* (Maryknoll, NY: Orbis Books, 2004), 3–9.

11. Walls, *Missionary Movement*, 6–7.

12. Walls, 8.

13. Walls, 8–9.

sion of perceptions and identity. They remind Ethiopian Christians that there is no perfect tradition which is to be imposed on others, God accepts them as they are but likes to transform them, and finally their commitment to Christ puts them out of step with their society and will create kinships across cultural boundaries.

As a final major resource for the discussion of perceptions and identity in the Ethiopian context, Lamin Sanneh's *Translating the Message: The Missionary Impact on Culture* is important. Sanneh discusses how the translation of the Scriptures into African mother-tongues limited the transmission of "Western cultural presuppositions" and enabled indigenous Christianity to emerge.[14] The Ethiopian situation is not exactly the same as other African countries, which often read the Bible in foreign languages prior to the availability of mother-tongue Scriptures. The early presence of the Ge'ez translation of the Bible helped the survival of Christianity in Ethiopia. But eventually Ge'ez ceased to be a vernacular and it was the translation of the Bible into Amharic and its wide distribution that initiated renewal impulses in the Ethiopian Orthodox and Evangelical churches alike. The use of mother-tongues in the preaching of the gospel resulted in the conversion of multitudes in southern and south-western Ethiopia and so helped to engender the present situation where there are plural cultural identities within Christianity in Ethiopia.

1.3. Methodology

In the course of this study I made extensive use of primary material. Nearly all of the CMS story is extracted from handwritten letters and journals I found at the Special Collections of the University of Birmingham. I also used a number of unpublished manuscripts, and conducted interviews with thirty-one people. Eleven of my interviewees were from the EOC, fifteen from Evangelical churches, and five current and former leaders of reformation movement. The participants were chosen through purposive sampling and presented with three kinds of semi-structured interview questions consecutively. All interviews were conducted in Amharic and most responses were recorded, transcribed and translated. For two years I closely observed,

---

14. Lamin Sanneh, *Translating the Message: The Missionary Impact on Culture* (Maryknoll, NY: Orbis Books, 1989), 200–203.

collected and analyzed the newly emerging phenomenon of what can be described as "slogan theology" most of which was found on public transportation. I also consulted numerous secondary materials pertinent to the topic.

However, there were a number of limitations to the work. First, the study was primarily conducted while in Ethiopia and this limited my access to up-to-date secondary materials published elsewhere. Second, some of the informants did not allow me to record the interview, neither to take notes, so I had to rely on my memory to recall what they said. Finally, given the sensitivity of the nature of my work, a number of informants who could have shed further light on the issue were not willing to give me an interview and some who did make it clear that they did not wish most of their views to appear in my work. Hence, I could not fully utilize in the thesis the information supplied to me, though I abstracted the essential thoughts.

1.4. Historical Background to the Study

Ethiopia is an ancient, historic country with a rich written tradition. With more than eighty-five ethnic groups and a population over ninety million,[15] it is the second largest country in Africa. In addition to the pre-existent primal religion, Ethiopia has accommodated all three monotheistic faiths: Judaism, Christianity, and Islam for a long time. According to the 2008 census, Muslims comprise 33 percent, Ethiopian Orthodox Church (EOC)[16] 43.5 percent, and Evangelical believers 18 percent of the total population.

Religious groups tend to be concentrated in certain areas of the country. Roughly, the northern part (Tigray and Amhara), part of the central Ethiopia (Shewa) and Oromiya are dominated by the Orthodox Church, whereas in southern and part of central Oromiya and eastern areas Islam is dominant. The southern and south-western parts of Ethiopia are inhabited by Evangelicals.

Ethiopia's unique history of independence, ancient Christian identity and rich religious heritage has made it an icon of freedom and indigenous

---

15. Sources like the UN set the population at 84.9 million, cited by www.bbc.com, country profile, Ethiopia. Accessed May 2011.

16. www.uselectionatlas.org, accessed 17 April 2010.

Christianity among fellow Africans. As for the high regard of many Africans towards Ethiopia and the Orthodox Church,[17] Staffan Grenstedt remarks:

> Ethiopia, through its unique political independence and its venerable indigenous Ethiopian Orthodox Church, represents an impressive continuity in the history of the church in Africa. Moreover, familiar texts in the Bible like the story in the Acts of the Apostles about the baptism of the Ethiopian eunuch (Acts 8:26–39) and the promise proclaimed in the Psalms ". . . Ethiopia shall soon stretch out her hands unto God" (Ps 68:31), offered points of identification for African Christians.[18]

Consequently, African Christians included "Ethiopia" in the name of their churches both "as historical example of independence and as a biblical symbol in Africa."[19] The Ras Tafarians of Jamaica in the Caribbean went even further. They adopted the Amharic language as the "only true tongoe (sic) spoken by man," recognized Haile Sellassie I as the black, reincarnated Christ, and elevated the national colours of Ethiopia as heavenly colours.[20]

Christianity in Ethiopia spread by means of assimilation and also forceful conversions. The country entertained Catholic and Protestant missions alike which responded in various ways to the indigenous Christianity they found in the country. Some of them were tolerant and respectful of the Orthodox tradition, others extremely judgemental. When their message was rejected, both Protestant and Catholic missionaries were sometimes tempted to revert to what Sven Rubenson calls "the disastrous alliance between gospel and guns."[21] Such a reaction was not unique to the missionaries. The Orthodox Church also converted pagans and Muslims on pain of execution. Thus,

---

17. In this work, the Orthodox Church will be referred to as Ethiopian Orthodox Church (EOC) unless quoting.

18. The Ethiopian churches in South Africa which are led and controlled by Africans is one of the examples. Staffan Grenstedt, *Ambaricho and Shonkolla: from Local Independent Church to Evangelical Mainstream in Ethiopia, the Origins of the Mekane Yesus Church in Kambata Hadiya* (Stockholm: Elanders Gotab, 2000), 17.

19. Grenstedt, *Ambaricho and Shonkolla*, 17.

20. Claudia Rogers, "What's a Rasta," *Caribbean Review* 7, no. 1 (1975): 9–12.

21. Sven Rubenson, "Consequences of a Colonial Context," in *The Missionary Factor in Ethiopia* (Frankfurt: Peter Lang, 1998), 69.

impatience and disregard for the Ethiopians' former way of life was evident in the missionary strategies of Protestants, Catholics and the Orthodox alike.

The Ethiopian Orthodox Church is noteworthy for many reasons, including the fact that it preserved Christianity in spite of being surrounded by the Islamic forces which managed to extinguish Nubian Christianity and reduce Alexandrian Christianity to a remnant. The church, however, survived the worst of the storms and maintained a vibrant Christianity, incorporating the so-called Judaic elements such as food taboos and the myth of the ark of the covenant as core marks of Orthodox Christian identity.

As for the Orthodox-Evangelical[22] interactions, Evangelical convictions have always been looked at suspiciously in the history of the church, but when the faith was institutionalized with the establishment of Mekane Yesus Church in 1959, the opposition grew. The presence of other forms of Christianity was not welcome and this opposition resulted in severe persecution and ostracism. The rift between the two bodies grew from time to time with the harsh treatment of Evangelicals during Haile Sellassie's regime and the Orthodox Church's depiction of Evangelicals as opposed to Mary. The coming of the Derg[23] with its atheistic ideology, affected all forms of Christianity but Evangelicals received the worst blow, as the Derg made things worse for them by portraying their faith as foreign.

In the post-communist era there was relative peace and stability in the country, but Evangelicals were not as free to exercise their faith as were Orthodox adherents. Mindful of their constitutional rights, they started to fight back and gained unprecedented religious freedom which opened the way for them to worship with relative freedom in many parts of the country. However, among other factors, their indiscriminate attacks on the Orthodox Church and the uncritical accommodation by the Orthodox of traditions with no biblical foundation caused the two bodies to grow still further apart.

This thesis explores the notion of perception and identity among the Orthodox and Evangelicals beginning with the earliest organized Protestant

---

22. This work uses the term Evangelical to include Pentecostals because they are part of the Evangelical tradition which has been evident in Western Christianity since the Reformation.

23. The Derg, officially the Provisional Military Government of Socialist Ethiopia, was a military junta that ruled Ethiopia from 1974 to 1987.

missionary engagement with the Orthodox Church and examines the contemporary self-consciousness and perception of each other. Thus, chapters 2 and 3 give background information about the development and spread of Orthodox and Evangelical Christianity. Chapter 4 explores the efforts of the Church Missionary Society (CMS), which embodied the first organized attempt to revitalize the Orthodox Church as a strategy to reach "heathen" all around it. Chapter 5 discusses the perceptions of Orthodox and Evangelicals of each other and explores how they developed. Chapter 6 discusses the contemporary reformed movements in the church and their relationship with the Evangelicals churches.

Chapter 7, which is the final chapter, integrates the dynamics at play in the discussion of Christian identity and the perceptions of other Christian traditions. It also highlights major areas of conflict and offers some recommendations as to how the relationship could be improved and points out that Christian identity is not confined to a particular tradition.

CHAPTER 2

The Formation of Ethiopian Christian Identity

Introduction

Ethiopia's geographical position enabled the people in the northern plateau to have meaningful trade relationships with nations along the coast of the Red Sea and across the Mediterranean with Aksum as the centre of trade. Most importantly, the regular encounter with foreigners resulted in the coming of Christianity making Ethiopia one of the ancient nations which accepted Christianity early on.

The strategic location of the country attracted the attention of foreign explorers and writers so that the name Ethiopia was widely known. The foreign interest was based on commerce and uncovering the source of the Nile. Ethiopia meant different things at different times in history. The Greek term Αἰθιοπία was used by ancient historians in reference to a wider geographical location than the present Ethiopia. It referred to the whole region from East Africa to people who were living to the south of Egypt.[1] The Christian kingdom which was located on the northern plateau of present Ethiopia, on the other hand, was referred to as Abyssinia by external writers. The inhabitants, however, called themselves *Habesha*[2] perhaps after "Habashat,"

---

1. Sergew Hable Sellassie, *Ancient and Medieval Ethiopian History to 1270* (Addis Ababa: United Printers, 1972), 45.

2. Mekuria Bulcha, *The Making of the Oromo Diaspora: A Historical Sociology of Forced Migration* (Minneapolis, MN: Kirk House, 2002), 11–13.

one of the tribes which migrated from South Arabia.³ The indigenes of the northern plateau were Cushitic. People groups whose language belonged to the same group (Cushitic) and shared similar culture and lifestyle continue to live scattered in the present East and horn of Africa.⁴

In the case of Ethiopia, the immigrants did not come as colonizers thus they peacefully assimilated with the indigenous population. Their superior way of life, however, influenced the natives and brought lasting change including the introduction of Sabean alphabets.⁵ The immigrants practised different forms of pagan worship, the core deities being the sun god, moon god and the serpent.⁶ Thus, the Semitic people gradually intermingled with the Cushites and took the political upper hand and in the millennium that followed Aksum emerged as such a powerful centre of culture and trade that a Persian writer in the third century counted it among the four kingdoms of the world.⁷

The commercial centeredness of Aksum came to a close in the tenth century. However, Aksum lived on because of its citizens' self-consciousness as followers of historic Christianity and their act of spreading the faith in the interior along with the territorial expansion of the monarchs. In addition, the church of Ethiopia brought together Judaism and Christianity in a unique way and made an intriguing claim about the presence of the ark of the covenant at Aksum. This among many things continued to attract the attention of the world to Ethiopia. This chapter tells the story of the beginning of Christianity in Aksum and its concurrent expansion in the hinterland.

---

3. Sergew Hable Sellassie, *Ancient and Medieval Ethiopian History*, 27.

4. Bahru Zewde, *A History of Modern Ethiopia (1855–1991)* (Addis Ababa: Addis Ababa University Press, 2002), 4–5.

5. Taddesse Tamrat, *Church and State in Ethiopia, 1270–1527* (Oxford: Clarendon, 1972), 5–9.

6. Archbishop Yesehaq, *The Ethiopian Tewahedo Church: An Integrally African Church* (New York: Vantage, 1989), 3.

7. Sergew Hable Sellassie, *Ancient and Medieval Ethiopian History*, 81–82.

2.1. The Aksumite Period
2.1.1. The Role of the Monarchy

Perhaps with the influence of Arabian immigrants who brought in their developed culture and trade system, Aksum rose to prominence in the third century. It extensively traded with China and India and even served as the channel between the Greco-Roman world and India. This was possible because of the Aksumites' economic strength which enabled them to make the expensive and long journey to India. The prominence of Aksum lived on into the fourth and fifth centuries as well.[8]

As in Pharaohnic Egypt, rock-hewn obelisks stand to this day as reminders of the legacy of Aksumites' greatness. The cemeteries, which are marked with rock-hewn stelae or obelisks were most likely erected prior to the adoption of Christianity by the royal court.[9] The Aksumite population, which consisted of Semitic, Cushitic, and Nilo-Saharan speaking people was collectively known as *Habesha* and its monarch as King of kings. As will be discussed below, there appears to have been rivalry between the Cushitic, Judaic and Semitic dynasties between the fourth and the eleventh centuries.[10]

Until the tenth century, Aksum remained more or less a centre of power and exerted influence over the peoples all around it. The most important thing which gave Aksum lasting prominence even after the fall of its economy was Christianity. Traditional sources and archival evidence indicate that prior to the coming of Christianity, paganism and Judaism were practised side by side[11] but there is no evidence to suggest that Judaism was the official

---

8. Sergew Hable Sellassie, 84–89

9. Department of Arts of Africa, Oceania, and the Americas. "The Monumental Stelae of Aksum (3rd–4th century)," in *Heilbrunn Timeline of Art History* (New York: Metropolitan Museum of Art, 2000). http://www.metmuseum.org/toah/hd/aksu_2/hd_aksu_2.htm (October 2000), accessed 31 July 2011.

10. The status of Christianity was affected in the process of expansionand power struggle between anti-Christian (Judaic), indigenous (Cushitic) and Semitic ("Solomonic Dynasty"). Upon the defeat of the Judaic monarchy, Cushitic and Semitic Christian royalties rivalled over the right to the throne. The question seems to have been whether the extension of "Solomonic Dynasty" or the local Cushitic (Agaw) royal lineage was to be considered as divine appointment. In the power struggle which lasted for some time, monasteries and the church of Alexandria played significant role in supporting and endorsing a particular Dynasty.

11. Sergew Hable Sellassie et al., "The Establishment of the Ethiopian Church," in *The Church of Ethiopia: A Panorama of History and Spiritual Life* (Addis Ababa: The Ethiopian Orthodox Church, 1997), 1.

religion of the royal court.¹² The probable sources of Judaic influences will be discussed later.

As for the origins of Christianity in Aksumite kingdom, there are different accounts. One of the claims, endorsed by Eusebius, traces Christianity to the evangelistic activity of Philip who preached to the Ethiopian eunuch who then came back home and spread Christianity.¹³ The church historians Rufinus and Socrates are cited as claiming that following the preaching of the Ethiopian eunuch who is mentioned in the Bible (Acts 8:26–40), the apostles Matthew, Nathaniel, Bartholomew and Thomas had preached the gospel in Ethiopia and Nubia.¹⁴ Ethiopian representation at the day of Pentecost is another assumption.¹⁵

The strongest of all is the account of Rufinus, who claims to have got it from Edesius, which traces Christianity to the fourth century.¹⁶ According to the story, young boys Frumentius and Edesius who were from Tyre, accompanied their uncle Merophius¹⁷ on his journey to India. On their way back to Tyre they stopped for provisions of water but were attacked by barbarians who drowned some and took the others captive. Frumentius and Edesius were among the captives who were taken to the king where they found favour in his eyes because of their intelligence. The king died, but the young men stayed with [Ezana] the son of the king for a long time at the request of the

---

12. Sergew Hable Sellassie, *Ancient and Medieval Ethiopian History*, 44.

13. Hawaze Birhan Wolde Michael et al., eds., መጽሐፈ ሚስጥር ዘጎባ ጊዮርጊስ ዘጋስጫ፤ (Aba Giorgis of Gascha's Book of Mysteries) (Addis Ababa, Ethiopian National Archives and Library, 2001 Eth. C), 87; Sergew Hable Sellassie et al., eds., *The Church of Ethiopia Past and Present* (Addis Ababa: Ethiopian Orthodox Church, Commercial Printing Enterprise, 1997), 11; Gorgorios, የኢትዮጵያ ኦርቶዶክስ ተዋህዶ ቤተ ክርስቲያን ታሪክ፣ (*The history of the Ethiopian Orthodox Tewahdo Church*) (Addis Ababa: 1974 Eth. C), 18; Isaac Boyle, trans., *The Ecclesiastical History of Eusebius Pamphilus* (Grand Rapids, MI: Baker, 1989), 50.

14. Sergew Hable Sellassie et al., eds., *Church of Ethiopia Past and Present*, 12.

15. Ephraim Isaac, *The Ethiopian Church* (Boston: Henry Sawyer Co., 1967), 18, 20; Sergew Hable Sellassie, *Ancient and Medieval Ethiopian History*, 97.

16. Philip Schaff and Henry Wace, "Conversion of the Indians," in *A Select Library of the Nicene and Post-Nicene Fathers of the Christian Church III Theodoret, Jerome, Gennadius, Rufinus* (Grand Rapids: Eerdmans, 1979), 58.

17. Philip Schaff and Henry Wace, "Some Indian Nations Received Christianity at That Time through the Instrumentality of Two Captives, Frumentius and Edesius," in *A Select Library of the Nicene and Post-Nicene Fathers of the Christian Church II: Socrates, Sozomenus* (Grand Rapids: Eerdmans, 1979), 274.

queen until her son grew up.[18] They agreed and were promoted to greater power. As they had been brought up in the true religion, they exhorted the merchants who visited the country to assemble, according to the custom of Romans, to take part in the divine liturgy." After a long time they asked the king to allow them to return to their country as a reward for their service, and the king permitted them to go.[19]

Edesius went to Tyre but Frumentius headed to Alexandria and informed Bishop Athanasius about Aksum and that "the Indians[20] were deeply anxious to obtain spiritual light." Athanasius decided to appoint Frumentius bishop (*Abun*)[21] and sent him back to Aksum.[22] Frumentius's ministry thrived[23] that he was referred to as *Kesate Birhan* (Revealer of Light) and *Abba Selama* (Father of Peace). He is considered a reformer of the Sabean scripts and introduced the way of writing from left to right.[24]

Christianity was accepted by Ezana and the royal family and gradually made its way into the lives of the common people, not as swiftly as often assumed but with significant resistance in the kingdom. Former pagan temples were converted into churches and new worship centres erected.[25] Christianity's expansion in ancient Ethiopia thus came about not as a result of evangelistic activity, but because it was the desire of the King. The inscriptions which imply Ezana's conversion raised a number of questions.

---

18. Schaff and Wace, "Some Indian Nations," 274.

19. Sozomen's account of Rufinus says that the king liberated them before he died. Schaff and Wace, "Some Indian Nations," 274.

20. The term "India" was used widely to refer to Africa and Asia. In this context it refers to Abyssinians. Schaff and Wace, "Conversion of the Indians," fn. 1, 58.

21. *Abun* is a title of the head of the Ethiopian Orthodox Church.

22. Later when he was exiled by Arians, the Ethiopian church, deeply rooted in the teaching of Frumentius, stood firm on the Nicene faith and would not give in to the command of Constantius to depose Frumentius. Sergew Hable Sellassie et al., eds., *Church of Ethiopia: A Panorama*, 6.

23. "Therefore having the grace of God to labour with him, he cheerfully and successfully played the husbandman, catching those who sought to gainsay his works by works of apostolic wonder, and thus, by these marvels, confirming his teaching, he continued each day to take many souls alive." Schaff and Wace, "Conversion of the Indians," 58.

24. Gorgorios, የኢትዮጵያ ኦርቶዶክስ ተዋህዶ ቤተ ክርስቲያን ታሪክ፣ 19–23. There is also an argument for the presence of Christianity long before Frumentius through merchants from the Roman Empire. According to this view Frumentius did not introduce Christianity, but rather established its organized form as a state religion. Sergew et al., *Church of Ethiopia Past and Present*, 3.

25. Taddesse Tamrat, *Church and State*, 23, 196.

In his early inscriptions Ezana dedicates his victory to pagan gods and further evidence of his pagan beliefs is found in the coins which bear the symbols of crescent and the disc. In the earliest discoveries which point to a change in his religious convictions Ezana ascribes his victory over Noba people to "the might of the Lord of Heaven who has created me, of the Lord of all by whom the King is beloved." This inscription raised questions as to the character of Ezana's conversion. The question was resolved with the publication of a new inscription of Ezana in 1970 in which he explicitly states his Christian convictions. Ezana wrote, "In the faith of God and the Power of the Father, and the Son, and the Holy Ghost who have saved my kingdom. I believe in your son Jesus Christ who has saved me."[26] The inscriptions proved not only his Christian convictions but also anti-Arian christological position.[27]

However, two questions were raised: why Ezana chose to express his conversion in an ambiguous manner, and whether his conversion was politically motivated. Kaplan argues that Ezana's use of "the Lord of Heaven" was not politically motivated to hide his conversion from his subjects. Rather it implies his "authentic interest in the Christian view of the cosmology" in view of the traditional African worldview which attributes bigger activities to the supreme being and local things to lesser divinities. Kaplan also notes that the fact that Ezana introduced changes to his Ge'ez inscriptions which could not be read by foreigners shows that he was not converted for political reasons.[28] "The prosperity and power of Aksum reached its peak during the time of Ezana. The king's dominion extended to both sides of the Red Sea and into the Sudan. More than any of the previous Aksumite rulers, Ezana was involved in the world of international politics and long-distance trade. The religious change which the king underwent must be viewed against this background."[29]

---

26. Steven Kaplan, "Ezana's Conversion Reconsidered," *Journal of Religion in Africa* 13, no. 2 (1982): 103.

27. Black, Stephanie, "In the Power of God Christ: Greek Inscriptional Evidence for the Anti-Arian Theology of Ethiopia's First Christian King," *Bulletin of SOAS* 71, no. 1 (2008): 93–110.

28. Kaplan, "Ezana's Conversion," 106.

29. Kaplan, 107.

The long-lasting prominence of Aksum came to a close with its conflict with pagans and Jewish migrants in the hinterland. The monarchs of Aksum sought to convert the pagans and Jewish migrants to Christianity which led them to rise against the Christian kingdom. The Jewish queen Judith (Yodit) managed to incite pagans to join hands to overthrow Aksum. In the battle that followed, she overtook Aksum and converted many of the citizens to Judaism. According to traditional sources, Judith ruled for forty years and her descendants stayed in power until 1137 in which the last king of her dynasty was overthrown by the Agew (Cushitic) Marha Tekle Haymanot, the son-in-law of Dil Na'od, the last king of Aksum. This was the origin of the *Ze-Agew* dynasty, which in Ge'ez meant "of Agew," popularly known as the Zagwe Dynasty. The best known of the Zagwe kings was Gebre Meskel Lalibela who is credited with the construction of the world-renowned rock-hewn churches of Lalibela.

With the rise of the Zagwe Dynasty, pilgrimage to Jerusalem grew and the building of churches furthered the dominance and prestige of Christianity. The church which we can now begin to call the Ethiopian Orthodox Church (EOC) flourished once again. Monastic life was strengthened, religious books were translated from Arabic to Ge'ez and many church books were written by native scholars.[30] Tekle Haymanot of Shewa was the most influential figure of this period.[31]

However, there was one major problem. The Zagwe Dynasty was not of Semitic and "Judaic" origin for it was Cushitic. Its monarchy's devout Orthodox adherence did not seem to have counted. The dissatisfaction over the Zagwe dynasty led to significant opposition in Tigray and Amhara who strongly believed in the divine appointment of the "Solomonic Dynasty" which according to tradition was inaugurated with Menelik I. In 1270, Yikunno-Amlak, who claimed descent from a prince of the "Solomonic Dynasty" who had managed to escape Judith's rage, was assisted by Shewa[32] to overthrow the Zagwe dynasty and establish the long-lasting "Solomonic"

---

30. Sergew et al., *Church of Ethiopia Past and Present*, 14–15.
31. Brian Fargher, *The Origins of the New Churches Movement in the Southern Ethiopia 1927–1944* (Leiden: Brill, 1996), 8.
32. There was a large Amhara settlement in the first half of the thirteenth century in the still pagan Shewa.

dynasty.³³ This story illustrates the vital role of monarchs in expanding Christianity and the importance of the "Solomonic" dynasty in uniting the country and protecting the faith. The reestablishment of the "Solomonic Dynasty" meant not only continued territorial expansion but the imposition of Christianity as well.

In addition, from its inception, the Ethiopian church was strongly attached to the church of Alexandria which provided it with bishops until autocephaly in 1951. The ancient creeds and councils which were accepted by the church of Alexandria thus were accepted by the Ethiopians. The strong reliance on Alexandria, therefore, defined the doctrine of the church of Ethiopia and connected it to ancient historical Christianity.

2.1.2. The Alexandrian Connection
a. Strongly Nicene Christology

The EOC was the passionate champion of the great councils which were accepted by the Alexandrian church, of which the Council of Nicaea is outstanding. It was the first ecumenical council of the church that was held in Nicaea in 325 AD through the initiative of Roman Emperor Constantine I to settle doctrinal controversies over the relationship between Jesus Christ and God the Father. It is generally accepted that 318 bishops attended the council which went on for a month listening to the arguments of Arius and his opponent Alexander both of whom were from Alexandria.³⁴ The Council declared Father and Son co-equal and consubstantial and has been generally adopted by the churches of both East and West.

The Ethiopian church, which took its patriarch from Alexandria, adopted the Nicene Creed (የኒቂያ ጉባኤ) and remained its rigorous guardian in Ethiopia. The outworking of the divine and human in the person of Christ,

---

33. The anti-Zagwe feelings in Amhara and Tigre grew especially when the Kibre-Negest which clearly states that the non-Israelite kings are transgressors of the law was translated from Coptic into Arabic in 1225. "Yikunno-Amlak founded a new Christian Dynasty in the kingdom. Common resentment of the Lasta domination probably bought him much support in Tigre, where the Amhara tradition of Tigre origin strengthened his position as against the Zagwe. The predominantly Agaw rulers of the Christian kingdom were deposed, and the throne was once again occupied by a Semitic-speaking monarch. Only in this sense was the advent of Yikunno-Amlak a *restoration*." Taddesse Tamrat, *Church and State*, 64–68.

34. Kevin Knight, ed., "Council of Nicaea" http://www.newadvent.org, 2 August 2011.

however, became the next heated topic of controversy which, among other things, eventually caused a split in the church.

b. Non-Chalcedonian, Anti-Diophysite Christology ("ተዋህዶ" Tewahdo)

The controversy regarding the person of Christ was heated between two rival schools of thought, Antioch and Alexandria represented by two prominent patriarchs of the church: Nestorius of Constantinople and Cyril of Alexandria respectively. Nestorius expressed reservations towards the usage of "*theotokós*" (God-bearer) which appeared to endanger the true humanity of Christ.[35] Cyril on the other hand strongly defended "theotokós" and accused Nestorius of driving apart the divine and human natures so much so that the person of Christ was divided.[36]

The argument led to another Council in 431 at Ephesus and Nestorius was anathematized for dividing up the person of Christ. The attempts to keep the unity of the person of Christ and avoid Nestorianism at all cost, however, resulted in the opposite controversy Eutychianism. Eutyches, who was the president of a monastery outside Constantinople supported by Dioscurus, patriarch of Alexandria, proposed a one nature Christology in which the divine nature absorbed the human. When Eutyches's teaching was known, he was summoned to the Synod of Constantinople in AD 449. His views that Christ's human nature was not of the same essence with the human race, led to his deposition.[37]

---

35. George Kretschmar, "The Councils of the Ancient Church," in *The Councils of the Church: History and Analysis*, ed. Hans Jochen Margull (Philadelphia: Fortress, 1966), 69–76.

36. In AD 431 St Cyril of Alexandria wrote: "If anyone will not confess that the Emmanuel is very God, and that therefore the Holy Virgin is the Mother of God (Θεοτόκος), inasmuch as in the flesh she bore the Word of God made flesh [as it is written, "The Word was made flesh"] let him be anathema." Philip Schaff and Henry Wace, "Excursus on the Word Θεοτόκος," in *A Select Library of Nicene and Post-Nicene Fathers of the Christian Church XIV, the Seven Ecumenical Councils* (Edinburgh: T&T Clark; Grand Rapids: Eerdmans), 1998, 206. There was a dispute over the translation "Mother of God" fearing that it implied that the God-head had its origin in Mary. "All that every child derives from its Mother that God the Son derived from Mary, and this without the co-operation of any man, but by the direct operation of the Holy Ghost, so that in a fuller, truer, and more perfect sense, Mary is the Mother of God the Son in his incarnation, than any other earthly mother is of her son." Schaff and Wace, "Excursus on the Word Θεοτόκος," 208–210.

37. Eutyches appealed both to emperor Theodosius II and Pope Leo I. His appeal resulted with a Council of Ephesus in 449 AD to look into the matter. Dioscurus overruled

After the sudden death of emperor Theodosius II, Marcian, who was opposed to Eutyches came to power and called the Council which was held near Constantinople in the city of Chalcedon in 451. Unprecedentedly, more than six hundred bishops assembled together at the Council of Chalcedon. Despite his initial reservation about the calling of the Council, Leo the Great, bishop of Rome, played a significant role in the Chalcedon formulation. The Council deposed Dioscurus for endorsing the heresy of Eutyches and declared Christ one and the same. Chalcedon did not give a precise formula for the relationship of divinity and humanity in Christ, but indicated the areas which were "safe" and christological positions that were "off limits." Therefore, the period following Chalcedon needed conceptual clarification just like that of Nicaea and the struggle over Chalcedon lasted for centuries.[38]

While it appeared that all bishops agreed on the creed of Chalcedon, upon their return to their respective sees and the translation of the statement into other languages, Oriental churches (Alexandria being the chief) raised questions. They were concerned that the unity of the two natures as asserted by Cyril was not emphasized and that the Chalcedon formulation would revive Nestorianism. The majority of Greek and Latin speaking churches accepted Chalcedon. The Egyptian church split; most Greek speakers, but not all, accepted Chalcedon, and most Copts objected to it. A split occurred in Syria where again most Greek speakers accepted Chalcedon and most Syriac speakers objected. In the footsteps of Coptic Egypt, the church of Ethiopia upheld one nature Christology.[39]

The attempt to unite the churches continued for several years, but crisis came in the sixth century as successive Roman emperors tried to impose Chalcedon by force, making the split permanent. When the Muslims took over Egypt and Syria from Byzantine Empire, it was a relief for anti-Chalcedonians in the two provinces which were embittered by oppression and

---

in the Council to the effect that only Eutyches's supporters were allowed to vote. He ignored the delegates of the Pope and refused to read his letter on the assembly. The Council declared Eutyches Orthodox and deposed two opponent bishops. The emperor supported the decisions of the Council but the Pope strongly opposed that he called it "Robber Synod" and asked for another Council to be called but the emperor was not willing. www.newadvent.org. Accessed 2 August 2011.

38. Kretschmar, "The Councils of the Ancient Church," 73.
39. Kretschmar, 73.

persecution. Generally speaking, most of the Greek and Latin churches, that is, the European, adhere to Chalcedon whereas those of Asia and Africa did not.

c. Continued Dependence on Alexandria

The Ethiopian church maintained a very strong relationship with the Alexandrian church and remained loyal to it even in times when they could no longer depend on Alexandria to appoint bishops and they had the great difficulty of bringing bishops from Egypt. After 641 AD Islam had the upper hand in Egypt and Christians were increasingly marginalized. Islamic influence over the coast of Ethiopia grew from the seventh century to the point where it became impossible to bring bishop from Egypt without the permission of Muslim authorities in Egypt and those on the coast of Ethiopia for passage to the interior. These difficulties often meant that there were times when there was no bishop in Ethiopia and the spiritual condition deteriorated. Especially when the country was weakened through internal strife, the faith was affected greatly because the princes/monarchs served as the protectors of Christianity as well.

The church of Alexandria played a significant role in endorsing or refusing to acclaim a particular monarch of Ethiopia. For example, in the tenth century, there was an internal power struggle between two brothers in which Petros, the Alexandrian bishop of Ethiopia, took sides and eventually was banished and died in exile. Alexandria held the king responsible for the death of the bishop and refused to send a substitute. This resulted in low morale among Christians and both the kingdom and Christianity were weakened. The Christians were able to revive when through the intercession of Nubia, the relationship with Alexandria was restored and a new Abun appointed.[40]

However, the Ethiopian church was not a mere follower of Alexandrian Christianity, but firmly stood by the Nicene Creed and was passionately anti-Chalcedonian. A case in point is its refusal to send Frumentius back to Egypt for reconsecration by an Arian bishop when King Constantine I demanded it after he banished Athanasius. One of the reasons for such a strong stand was their familiarity with the works of the Alexandrian fathers. For instance in the sixth century, a book known as "Qerlos" which has works

---

40. Taddesse Tamrat, *Church and State*, 39–41.

of Cyril and other fathers as well, was translated from Greek into Ge'ez. Sergew notes, "It is on this book that the doctrine of the Ethiopian Church is largely based."[41] Attacking the Alexandrian church thus meant attacking the Ethiopian church.

However, there was often a sense of dissatisfaction among the most learned members of clergy as to why Egyptians, who did not know the language or the culture, should remain heads of the Ethiopian church.[42] But the church of Ethiopia patiently waited until the Alexandrian church was willing to let it go. The loyalty thus continued until the autocephaly of the Ethiopian church was granted in 1951. According to Gorgorios, over the one thousand and six hundred years of dependence of the Ethiopian church on the Alexandrian church, one hundred and eleven Egyptian bishops came as heads of the Ethiopian church.[43]

2.1.3. The Role of the Nine Saints and the Vernacular Scriptures

In addition to Ethiopia's connection to historic Christianity through Alexandria, the early vernacular translation of the Bible gave Ethiopians a strong Christian self-consciousness. The Ge'ez translation of the Bible which played a vital role in the preservation and expansion of Christianity, is traditionally attributed to a group of monks referred to as the Nine Saints and *tsadiqan* who came to Ethiopia in the year AD 480.

Their exact origin is disputed. Sergew notes that their names imply that they were of different places in the Roman Empire but shared one faith.[44] The argument in favour of their familiarity with the Syriac tradition is based on: the adaptation of Syriac words in their translation of the Bible into Ethiopic (e.g. "ሃይማኖት" haimanot, "ገሃነም" gehanem, "ጣዖት" ta'ot, "ምሥዋት" miswat, "ቁርባን" qurban[45]), the similarity of the liturgy of the Orthodox Church to

---

41. "In spite of the title, this book is not exclusively devoted to the dogmatic homilies of St Cyril, Patriarch of Alexandria, but also contains those of other church fathers of the fourth and the first half of the fifth century." Sergew Hable Sellassie, *Ancient and Medieval Ethiopian History*, 121.

42. Taddesse Tamrat, *Church and State*, 245–247.

43. Gorgorios, የኢትዮጵያ ኦርቶዶክስ ተዋህዶ ቤተ ክርስቲያን ታሪክ፣ 9.

44. Sergew Hable Sellassie, *Ancient and Medieval Ethiopian History*, 116.

45. Sergew Hable Sellassie, 120. Here is the English probable translation of the Amharic words which are taken from Syriac: Faith (religion), hell, idol, offering (giving),

the Syriac rite, and the evidence of Syriac style in the church music and the architecture of the old churches in Ethiopia.[46]

It is believed that the Nine Saints rejected Chalcedon and faced persecution at the hands of Byzantine emperors and eventually fled to Ethiopia. Their names were Abba Pantelewon, Abba Gerima (Issac, or Yeshaq), Abba Aftse, Abba Guba, Abba Alef, Abba Yem'ata, Abba Liqanos, Abba Aragawi (Ze-Mika'él), and Abba Sehma. Traditionally, the monastic order these saints followed was connected to the order of St Pacomius of Alexandria.[47] Ze-Mika'él Aregawi is said to have been the first to come to Ethiopia. The others came upon his invitation.

The monks were warmly welcomed in Aksum and after they all enjoyed a twelve-year stay at the court of the Emperor Al'ameda, and later of his successor, they decided to part ways in order to spread Christianity beyond the seat of the emperor.[48] The saints were not able to spread Christianity as far as they hoped, because of the rampancy of paganism in the hinterland of Aksum. They were committed to eradicating paganism and spreading monasticism. However, they did not always demolish pagan temples, but transformed them into churches or built churches on the ruins of former pagan temples.[49] Despite their attempts to eradicate paganism the monks did not suffer persecution because they enjoyed the full support and protection of the king.[50]

In addition to converting pagans, the Nine Saints developed Ge'ez liturgy and literature with the introduction of Syriac expressions and vocabulary. Most importantly, they are credited with the completion of the translation of the Bible, which was started in part during the time of Frumentius.

Eucharist, consecutively.

46. Sergew Hable Sellassie, 120–121.

47. Taddesse Tamrat, *Church and State*, 108.

48. "Ze-Mika'él and Edna, with a disciple called Mattéwos, went to Eggala, Tegré, where the hill Damo was chosen for a monastery and he established the Pachomian or coenobitic monastic life. In Ethiopian iconography Ze-Mika'él Aregawi is often portrayed with a serpent, for, when unable to find a path up the rocky site, he held fast to the tail of a serpent and was pulled up to the summit." *Za-Michael Aragawi*, Dictionary of African Christian Biography, Electronic Source, accessed April 2007.

49. Sergew et al., *Church of Ethiopia*, 8; Sergew Hable Sellassie, *Ancient and Medieval Ethiopian History*, 117.

50. Sergew et al., *Church of Ethiopia*, 8.

Moreover, they translated a number of basic religious works into Ge'ez such as the "Life of Saint Antony," and contributed greatly to the art and architecture in the Orthodox Church.[51]

Michael Knibb questions the long held opinion that it was Syriac missionaries who translated the Bible from Greek in the fourth/fifth century. According to him, there is a greater possibility that the Ge'ez Bible was revised in the fourteenth century with the help of Arabic texts which were influenced by the Syriac version. Knibb does not rule out the possibility of influence from Syriac sources, but given that Greek was used in the Aksumite court, the translators might not necessarily be monks who came from outside. Although there seem to be "numerous instances of agreement" between the Syriac and Ethiopic versions of the Old Testament, which clearly show an influence of the Syriac version, such influences cannot be attributed with certainty to the fifth or sixth century. Most likely the influence belongs to the fourteenth-century revision which was made with reference to Arabic texts which were in turn strongly influenced by the Syriac version.[52]

Sergew credits the Nine Saints with the Christianization of the culture, daily life, expressions, architecture and the language itself. "In the whole function of life, Christianity penetrated. It changed the whole life of the Ethiopians from that time on."[53] Thus, it is almost impossible to utter words of thanks or wish others well without invoking the name of God. According to him, the Nine Saints are the ones who contributed the most in missionary field.[54]

By the beginning of the sixth century there were churches all over Tigray, the whole of the Eritrean plateau and the coastal settlements. The active expansion was also felt in the interior.[55] Although there is no scientific

---

51. The indigenization of the music of the church inaugurated by St Yared one of the disciples of the Nine Saints and a great Ethiopian composer played its own role in making the faith Ethiopian. Sergew et al., *Church of Ethiopia*, 8–9.

52. Michael Knibb, *Translating the Bible: The Ethiopic Version of the Old Testament* (Oxford: Oxford University Press, 1999), 23–35.

53. Sergew Hable Sellassie, "The Religious Life in Ethiopia with a Special Emphasis on the Church of Ethiopia," in *Education and Culture in Eastern Africa* 1, C. C. Cheseldine Memorial Edition, Report to Institute of International Studies Office of Education, Department of Health, Education and Welfare, Washington, DC (18 June 1870), 11.

54. Sergew et al., *Church of Ethiopia*, 7.

55. Taddesse Tamrat, *Church and State*, 25–29.

documentation, Taddesse Tamrat writes, "[T]he essential doctrinal and liturgical traditions were securely established in the first four centuries of the history of Aksumite church. It is indeed due to the strength of these traditions that the Ethiopian church was able to survive a long period of only intermittent contacts with Alexandria."[56]

2.1.4. Judaic Influences

Ethiopian Christianity was influenced by not only Alexandrian and Syrian Christianity but also uniquely accommodated Judaic features into its tradition, so much so that they serve as its identity markers. Despite evidences of strong Judaic influence, there is no evidence that it was the official faith of Ethiopians prior to the coming of Christianity.[57] Traditional sources such as Kibre Negest[58] trace Judaism to the affair between King Solomon of Israel and the Queen of Sheba.

The Sabean queen visited King Solomon who tricked her into sleeping with him. Upon her return to her land she bore Menelik I, who as a young man travelled to Jerusalem to visit his father. When it was time for Menelik to return to his mother, Solomon sent along with him the son of Zadok the high priest, numerous Levites and the replica of the ark of the covenant, or so he thought. However, the son of Zadok instead of the replica took with him the actual ark of the covenant which to this day is claimed to have been kept in the northern part of Ethiopia, at the Church of Zion in Aksum.[59] Another suggestion is that the Felasha,[60] (the Jews who took refuge in Ethiopia during the first destruction of Jerusalem in AD 70) spread Judaism.

---

56. Taddesse Tamrat, 30.

57. Sergew Hable Sellassie, *Ancient and Medieval Ethiopian History*, 44.

58. Literally means "glory of kings." Its translation from the Arabic to the present form dates to the fourteenth century but the original one could be traced to the sixth century. Taddesse Tamrat, *Church and State*, 64, 250; Adrian Hastings, *The Church in Africa 1450–1950* (Oxford: Clarendon Press, 1994), 12–13.

59. Sergew et al., *Church of Ethiopia*, 9.

60. They are also referred to as "*Bete Israel*" (house of Israel). Felasha means exile. It is said that they derived their name from the decree of king Yishaq (1413–1430). He decreed that those who refuse to be baptized in the Christian religion would be "Falasi" but those who are baptized into Christianity would inherit the land of their ancestors. Taddesse Tamrat, *Church and State*, 196–201. Felasha could have its roots in the Amharic verb "Felese" which means to migrate. Perhaps, they are called Felasha because they are migrants.

Some writers believe that Ethiopians were influenced to integrate Judaic elements into their faith by their neighbouring Jews who were spread over Yemen and Egypt. Also some suggest that during the destruction of Jerusalem by the Babylonians many Jews fled and were scattered all over the desert. Some of them came to Ethiopia and were able to spread their faith.[61]

Another view is that Egyptian Christian tradition was far more Judaic than usually thought, and that was passed on to the Ethiopian church. Or perhaps during their isolation from the rest of the Christian world Ethiopians themselves felt the impact of the Old Testament more, which led to the development of Judaic forms of worship.[62] Observation of the dietary laws of the Old Testament, the dressing code of the clergy and male circumcision on the eighth day after birth are among the practices which underline the influence of Judaism in pre-Christian Ethiopia.[63] As stated earlier, the Ethiopian church claims to have the ark of the covenant (*Tabot*) in its custody in the Aksum Zion Church. Each Orthodox church has the replica of *Tabot* dedicated to saints and angels which is carried by priests in an intriguing procession during Epiphany. The Judaic attachment and the Solomonic descent, therefore, encouraged the regional princes and the later monarchy to painstakingly trace their roots to King Solomon of Israel.[64] Such a claim gave them a divine mandate to rule and they were considered appointees of God. The common Orthodox adherents, therefore, nurtured the idea of Ethiopia as "the promised land."[65] This notion was widely accepted even by

---

61. Gorgorios, የኢትዮጵያ ኦርቶዶክስ ተዋህዶ ቤተ ክርስቲያን ታሪክ፣ 13–14.

62. Hastings, *Church in Africa*, 11.

63. Gorgorios, የኢትዮጵያ ኦርቶዶክስ ተዋህዶ ቤተ ክርስቲያን ታሪክ፣ 14–15.

64. While the CMS missionaries were in Adigrate in 1830, messengers of Dejazmach Wubie came with a present and Sabagadis ordered his clerk to bring the large book which traced his genealogy back to Solomon. The clerk sat up late into the evening reading out the genealogy as Sabagadis was attentive. The two messengers commented that they did not understand the book because it was in Ethiopic. Part of Rev C. Kugler's Journal, February 25 to April 24, 1830, University of Birmingham, Special Collections, CMS/ B/ OMS/ C M O46/24, 16; Emperors of the nineteenth and twentieth centuries claimed to be descendants of Solomon and boldly added the title "ሞዓ አንበሳ ዘአምነገደ ይሁዳ" (the conqueror Lion of the tribe of Judah) before their names.

65. The claim was not only supported by the Solomonic story but by the presence of the name Ethiopia and allusion to Ethiopians in the Bible. Some even claim that Keturah, Abraham's later wife was Ethiopian. Abraham sent away her children to the land of East and they are the fathers of several tribes in Ethiopia. Passages such as Numbers 12:1–2 are also romanticized because God judged the Israelite Miriam on account of her attitude to

the later Protestants who modified the claim, supporting it with contemporary and ancient prophecies.[66]

2.2. The Move into the Interior

2.2.1. The Rise of Islam and Its Coastal Presence

Ethiopian Christianity adopted different features from Christian traditions elsewhere, and also from Judaism but through its journey of over seventeen centuries, it added its own unique features which are deeply rooted the faith in the heart of its adherents. As noted earlier, Christian expansion into the interior was accompanied by the territorial expansion of Solomonic kings. However, the rise of Islam in Arabia, in a place which was closely connected to Aksum, eventually affected Christianity and contributed to the weakening of the Aksumite kingdom. Initially the relationship between Arabian Muslims and Aksumites was peaceful. Aksum even received favourably those who fled persecution in Arabia beginning from AD 615. The provision of refuge for his followers resulted in Mohammed strictly ordering his followers to spare Ethiopia from the Jihads. The steady migration of Muslims resulted in the spread of Islam among the local people. The eventual upper hand of Islam over Arabia and the coast of Red Sea, however, had serious repercussions, including cutting off Ethiopia from the rest of the world.[67]

The orders of Muhammad seem to have been ignored, and Ethiopian Christian communities in Arabia were eventually hard pressed. More devastating was Islamic control of the coastal lands and taking over of the

---

the Ethiopian Zipporah! The writer comments that this story shows us "how much God is concerned for Ethiopians." Menelik Mered Alemu, መጽሐፍ ቅዱስና ኢትዮጵያ፣ (The Bible and Ethiopia) (Addis Ababa: n.p., 1999 Eth. C): 72–77.

66. Bekele Wolde Kidan, senior pastor of Mulu Wongel, the largest Pentecostal church in Ethiopia wrote two books which discuss the divinely appointed call of Ethiopia to take the gospel to the nations. In one of the books even the famine of the early 1990s is presented as a sign from God to the world. Bekele Wolde Kidan, ለዚህ ጊዜ፣ *(For such a time as this)* (Addis Ababa: Bekele Wolde Kidan, 2001 Eth. C), 52ff. The writer gives an extensive testimony of prophecies uttered by both Ethiopians and non-Ethiopians about the upcoming trial and the subsequent unfolding of God's great plans for Ethiopia. Also see Bekele Wolde Kidan, ርህይሳ ኢትዮጵያና የመጨረሻው መጨረሻ (Revival, Ethiopia, and the End of Ends), (Addis Ababa: Addis Ababa Mulu Wongel Church, 1994 Eth. C). Needless to say such perceptions have helped Ethiopian Christians persevere despite immense poverty and famine, the regrettable identity badges of Ethiopians throughout the world.

67. Sergew Hable Sellassie, *Ancient and Medieval Ethiopian History*, 181–191.

maritime trade from Aksum. The conversion of local people in the trade centres added to the difficulty of the Christian kingdom of Aksum. This resulted in the weakening of Aksum economically, and made the coming of Egyptian patriarchs extremely difficult.[68] The force of Islam was felt in the interior as well. In the second half of the tenth century, the inhabitants of Awash Valley, who were probably Muslims, resisted the attempts of the Amhara to expand into their territory.[69] In southern Ethiopia, Islam and Christianity were contending to gain dominance and Taddesse Tamrat writes that the long history of Christianity's presence in that region gave it prestige and power over Islam.[70]

2.2.2. The Long Process of Westward Expansion and the Role of Amharic

The ninth century was marked by the expansion of Christianity and shift of the seat of the kingdom towards Lake Hayiq. The enlargement of both political and spiritual territory further added Amhara and Shewa to the kingdom with a definite program for Christian settlement and evangelism. Furthermore, the Church developed its own Ge'ez commentary on biblical and patristic texts which is known as *Andemta*.[71]

---

68. Taddesse Tamrat, *Church and State*, 41–50.

69. Taddesse Tamrat, 42–43. When Egypt became independent the steady growth of Islam in the coastal lands and trade centres took a different shape. The Muslims wanted to exercise the same freedom of worship as was afforded to the Copts in Egypt. When the king and priests in Ethiopia were not willing to give them freedom they appealed to Egypt to exert pressure on the Alexandrian patriarch to order the Ethiopian church to give them freedom. Towards the end of the eleventh century the whole thing took a different form when upon the death of the Patriarch of Ethiopia, the Egyptian authorities were lured into twisting the arms of the Alexandrian Patriarch to validate the "appointment" of a Muslim imposter as patriarch of Ethiopia. Although such attempt was reversed, the position of the bishops in Alexandria became increasingly difficult as they were pressured to command the king of Ethiopia to pay tribute, look after the welfare of the Muslims there and also build mosques, lest the Amir threatened to demolish the churches in Alexandria. The Ethiopians, on the other hand maintained strong anti-Muslim policies and exempted the patriarch from direct public involvement. Taddesse Tamrat, *Church and State*, 46– 49.

70. Taddesse Tamrat, *Church and State*, 51–52.

71. *Andemta* comes from the Amharic term *Andem* which means *also, or, on one hand, on the other hand*. However, currently the term it is widely used to give an equivalent meaning for the English term *implication*. Abraham Mengesha, "An Evaluation of the Position of the Ethiopian Orthodox Tewahido Church on the Eternal High Priesthood of Jesus Christ" (MTh thesis, Ethiopian Graduate School of Theology, 2005), 3. Regarding the *Andemta* commentary please also see Roger W. Cowley, *The Traditional Interpretation of the Apocalypse*

Steady migration of the Amhara people further semiticized the new territories. This as well must have given a platform for Amharic to be widely spoken and serve as the vehicle of Christianity. In addition to monarchy and monastery, Amharic played significant role in both the expansion of the kingdom and spread of Christianity. It served as a tool of communication between people of different ethnic groups. The emergence of Amharic which made communication possible also contributed to the fading of Ge'ez from public life. However, the church continued to use Ge'ez even though it gradually ceased to serve as means of communication and was limited to the church service.

Although the eighth and ninth centuries in Ethiopia were not major periods for original authorship or the translation of foreign works, the manuscript evidence proves that it was a time of intellectual enquiry and expansion of church education, as the number of manuscripts produced greatly increased in these periods.[72]

The expansion of Christianity was marked by not only military upper hand but gradual assimilation too, as illustrated by the act of the Balaw princes of the Eritrean region adopting not only the faith but Tigrigna as well.[73] The role of monarchs and rulers in promoting and protecting the faith has often been decisive because church and state were like two sides of the same coin. During the periods when the kingdom was relatively weak the church was often also weakened; the weakness of the church, arising from internal theological disputes, also affected the emperors. As a result of this interdependence, church and emperors sought to protect each other's interest.

This meant that the rulers and kings sought the conversion of their new subjects often for political reasons. They also closely watched and guided spiritual affairs by getting involved in resolving theological controversies through dialogue which was followed by the imposition of the position of the "winner."[74] Political instability meant religious instability and vice versa,

---

of St. John in the Ethiopian Orthodox Church (Cambridge: University of Cambridge Oriental Publications, 1983), 3.

72. Abraham Mengesha, "Evaluation of the Position," 3.

73. Taddesse Tamrat, *Church and State*, 80.

74. Haile Sellassie I vividly expressed the interdependence between the two: "The Church is like a sword, and the government is like an arm; therefore, the sword cannot cut

and both made the country vulnerable to outside forces or internal struggles between governors of different regions.[75]

The kings, therefore, attempted to integrate new territories through Christianizing them by all means. Although it appears that the monarchy's idea of reform was converting their subjects and maintaining uniformity of doctrine, many monarchs also had a genuine zeal for the expansion and preservation of Christianity. The commitment of monarchs to both territorial advancement and Christianization of the newly conquered provinces was powerfully illustrated in the reigns of Amde Tsion and Zer'a Ya'iqob.

Amde Tsion (1314–1344)

Amde Tsion was the grandson of Yikunno-Amlak[76] and came to power in the fourteenth century. His reign created a conducive environment for the growth of Ethiopian Orthodox Christianity because he promoted the faith to the new conquered territories and restrained Islam's expansion. Amde Tsion sought to ensure that the Christian kingdom of Ethiopia had the political, religious and economic upper hand.

Consequently, he conquered Hadiya, Damot and Gojjam and subjugated the governor of Intarta who had grown more and more independent of the "Solomonic Dynasty" during the internal struggle for power, and consequently posed a threat to the unity of the Christian kingdom. Moreover, Amde Tsion was concerned about the spread of Islam in the South and in Eritrea as well, and won a campaign against the powers in the coastal land of Eritrea.[77]

He ascribed his victory to the help of God. "God delivered into my hands the ruler of Intarta with all his army, his followers, his relatives, and all his country as far as the Cathedral of Aksum."[78] The king grew stronger and his kingdom larger.[79] He incorporated the present southern Ethiopia, which was known for its fertility, into his kingdom. He subjugated the powerful

---

by itself without the use of the arm." Tibebe Eshete, *The Evangelical Movement in Ethiopia* (Waco, TX: Baylor University Press, 2009), 38.

75. Hastings, *Church in Africa*, 167.
76. Taddesse Tamrat, *Church and State*, 19.
77. Taddesse Tamrat, 72–77.
78. Taddesse Tamrat, 73.
79. Taddesse Tamrat, 80–86.

dynasties of Sidama and Hadiya[80] and also reinstituted his dominance over the Muslim king of Yifat who had rebelled against him with a plan to conquer the whole of Ethiopia and Islamize the nation.[81]

It was the territories of Amde Tsion that Zer'a Ya'iqob wanted to stabilize and in which he conducted religious reform.[82] The expansion of Menelik II in the nineteenth century was also aimed at reintegrating the territories ruled by Amde Tsion. Once again Christianity expanded not only through its imposition upon the new colonies, but also through the assimilation of the settlers from the Christian kingdom with the local people. Amde Tsion expanded his territories to include the Muslim dominated area in the east beyond Awash. His expansion was followed by the expansion of the Orthodox Church.

The impact of Amde Tsion's reform was immense, both politically and spiritually. His campaigns expanded the territories of Ethiopia and unified the country under one king. Most importantly in view of this work, it was Amde Tsion who conquered what is now south Ethiopia and opened the way for Orthodox Christianity to take the gospel to these new frontiers. Unlike the situation in the northern and central Ethiopia, Orthodox Christianity did not thrive in these areas.

Zer'a Ya'iqob (1434–1468)

Zer'a Ya'iqob was the son of King Dawit (1380–1412), who had a great affection for Mary. He was dedicated to the service of Mary as a baby because he was a miracle child born in response to his mother's vow to Mary.[83] Zer'a Ya'iqob was known for his devotion to the promotion of the cult of Mary and also his zeal for the annihilation of "idol worship" of any kind. He even

---

80. Taddesse Tamrat, 106, 122.

81. Amde Tsion said to him, "Of a truth, did you not burn the churches of God and kill the Christians? And those who survived, did you make them turn to your religion, which is not as the religion of Christ, but (is) that of the Devil your father?" G. W. B. Huntingford, trans. and ed., *The Glorious Victories of Amde Seyon* (Oxford: Clarendon, 1965), 54, as quoted by Paul Balisky, *Wolaitta Evangelists: A Study of Religious Innovation in Southern Ethiopia, 1937–1975* (Eugene, OR: Pickwick, 2009), 5.

82. Taddesse Tamrat, *Church and State*, 20

83. Afework Hailu, "A Survey of the Ethiopian Orthodox Church Mariology: An Attempt to Understand the Origin, Development, and Teaching Regarding Mary in the EOC," (MTh thesis, Ethiopian Graduate School of Theology, 2002), 63–68.

ordered the killing on the spot of anyone who was seen sacrificing to Satan.[84] He required all of his citizens to bow at the mention of the names of Mary, Jesus and himself.[85] As noted earlier, he wanted to stabilize the territories of Amde Tsion and have them demonstrate their commitment to Christianity by external signs.[86]

Zer'a Ya'iqob required that people go to the nearest church on Saturdays and Sundays and if a church was too far away, a priest was to travel there on weekends to instruct them. He also established libraries in the churches. He required all Christians to carry the sign of the cross tattooed on their foreheads, their dress, instruments of wars and ploughs.[87] Zer'a Ya'iqob further supported his views with the production and translation of literature for which he claimed divine inspiration. These include hagiographies of different saints ገድል (*gedel*), books bearing the name of angels ድርሳን (*dirsan*) and narratives of miracles performed by the saints and angels ታምር (*tamir*).[88] When his strict rule resulted in much bloodshed, some of his own chiefs and clergy conspired to overthrow him but the patriarch of Alexandria, who strongly supported Zer'a Ya'iqob, sent an official letter of excommunication against those who opposed him and wished to depose him.[89]

His commitment to upholding the political and religious dominance of the Christian kingdom led him to contemplate alliance with the Western church because he feared Islam. He also wanted military, material and spiritual assistance from the Western world. The Egyptian church as the overseer of the Ethiopian church, was not opposed to the proposal. Consequently, two missions were sent to Rome and a painting, which is preserved in the Vatican, captures the only evidence of their embassy.[90] Budge notes that Zer'a

---

84. Taddesse Tamrat, *Church and State*, 240.

85. Getatchew Haile, *Religious Controversies and the Growth of Ethiopic Literature in the Fourteenth and Fifteenth Centuries* (Addis Ababa: Ethiopian Studies, Miscellanea 1, n.d.), 196.

86. Taddesse Tamrat, *Church and State*, 20

87. Taddesse Tamrat, 239.

88. Eshete, *Evangelical Movement*, 47.

89. Taddesse Tamrat, *Church and State*, 241.

90. James Bruce, *Travels to Discover the Source of the Nile, in the Years 1768–1773* (Edinburgh: George Ramsey & Co., 1813), 117–118; E. A. Wallis Budge, *A History of Ethiopia, Nubia and Abyssinia vol. 1* (Netherlands: Anthropological Publications Oosterhout N. B., 1966), 304; E. A. Wallis Budge, *The Legends of Our Lady the Perpetual Virgin and Her Mother Hanna* (Oxford: Oxford University Press, 1933), LXIV, xliii–xlv.

Ya'iqob signed a treaty that united the Orthodox Church with the Catholic Church and as a result the Pope allowed him to establish an Abyssinian monastery in Rome.[91]

Ethiopian church historians, however, oppose this story. According to them, the purpose of the presence of the Ethiopian envoy at the Council of Florence along with those of other Oriental Orthodox churches and the Roman Catholic Church was to create ecumenism and combat Muslim expansion. In fact, some of the delegates were so displeased with the Pope's ambition to act as the leader of the churches around the world that they left the meeting abruptly.[92]

Zer'a Ya'iqob's commitment to the promotion of Mariology was articulated in writings such as, ታምረ ማርያም (*Miracles of Mary*) which calls for sons of Adam to praise Mary, "the saviour for sinners."[93] In one of the miracles, Mary says that she would cleanse people from all of their sins.[94] Tamre Mariam also stated that anyone who refuses to honour the feast of Mary and hear her miracles was to be anathematized.[95]

Under the supervision of Zer'a Ya'iqob the liturgy of the church was rewritten. Additions were made and local liturgical books were produced to replace books of Egyptian origin. The clergy were required to use these newly produced liturgies. The additions were meant to refute the teachings of the "heretic" Estifanosites, who refused to bow down for the king, Mary and the cross.[96] The Egyptian Horologium was replaced by the local Masehafe Berhan composed by Abba Giyorgis, a devout supporter of Zer'a Ya'iqob's "reforms."[97]

---

91. Budge, *History of Ethiopia*, 311. Cf. Merid Wolde Aregay, "The Legacy of Jesuit Missionary Activities in Ethiopia from 1555 to 1632," in *The Missionary Factor in Ethiopia*, ed. Getatchew Haile et al.(Frankfurt: Peter Lang, 1998), 31.

92. Abba Gorgorious, የኢትዮጵያ ኦርቶዶክስ ተዋህዶ ቤተ ክርስቲያን ታሪክ፣ 49–50; Lule Melaku, የቤተ ክርስቲያን ታሪክ፣ *(The history of the church)* (Addis Ababa: Tinsae Publishing, 1986 Eth. C), 133.

93. ታምረ ማርያም፣ Tamre Mariam (Addis Ababa: Tinsae Zegubae Printing, 1989 Eth. C), 4.

94. Getatchew Haile, *On the Writings of Abba Giyorgis Saglawi from Two Unedited Miracles of Mary* (Addis Ababa: Institute of Ethiopian Studies, Miscellanea 1, n.d.), 189–190.

95. Tamre Mariam, 5, 8–11.

96. Getatchew Haile, *Religious Controversies*, 135.

97. Getatchew Haile, *Fikare Haymanot of the Faith of Abba Giyorgis Saglawi* (Addis Ababa: Institute of Ethiopian Studies, Miscellanea 1, n.d.), 135.

Contemporaries of Zer'a Ya'iqob wrestled with the question, is equal reverence and worship due to Mary and Jesus as Zer'a Ya'iqob prescribed in his statement: "Honour and glory for her and worship and prostration for her, together with her Son"? In a manner fitting the ancient church's resistance against innovations, the churches in the north, Aksum, discarded the phrase "together with her Son," but those in Gojjam retained the Zer'a Ya'iqob formula. The Council of Boru Meda dealt with the controversy by discarding the phrase "together with her Son" and replacing it with "and for her Son."[98] In addition, those who claimed that Mary's death was salvific were anathematized by the archbishop of Alexandria.[99]

Zer'a Ya'iqob, therefore, is notable in the history of Christianity in Ethiopia for several reasons. Some of them are his acts of strengthening monasteries economically and turning them into centres of learning, culmination of religious nationalism towards independence from Alexandria and bringing Mary to the centre of the worship of the church in an unprecedented way. Later reform attempts mostly aimed at contending the orthodoxy of his arguments.

2.2.3. The Process of Christianization
Tekle Haymanot, One of the Key Figures of the Monastic Revival
In the expansion of Christianity and the effort to reform the church, the indigenous monastic movement played a vital role. Indigenous monks built on the foundation laid down by Frumentius and organized by the Nine Saints. From the middle of the thirteenth century the monastic revival in the church of Ethiopia followed two traditions: the houses of Tekle Haymanot and Ewostatéwos. Tekle Haymanot's influence was felt in Shewa where he followed the expansion of the kingdom, whereas Ewostatéwos carried out intensive monastic activity in the northern plateau.[100]

---

98. Getatchew Haile, trans., *A Third Supplication for the Reading of the Miracles of Mary: The Cause of Estifanosites, a Fundamental Sect in the Church of Ethiopia*, appendix V (Addis Ababa: Institute of Ethiopian Studies, Religion Miscellanea 3, n. d.): 127–128.

99. Getatchew Haile, *Cause of Estifanosites*, 128.

100. Taddesse Tamrat, *Church and State*, 109. There was internal theological conflict among the house of Tekle Haymanot and that of Ewostatéwos over the interpretation of Acts 10:38 where Peter declares that God anointed Jesus of Nazareth with the Holy Spirit and with power. If as in Western doctrine two natures exist in Christ, it seemed easier to say that God anointed the human nature of Christ. But the church rejected two natures

In the beginning of the thirteenth century, Tekle Haymanot returned to Shewa, his birthplace, from his monastic activities in the North. His coming was inspired by a sense of responsibility to preach the gospel to his countrymen who, surrounded by pagans, developed complacency towards Christianity. "He revived the religious consciousness of his fellow Christians and realized the relative degree of Christian learning among them." Nearly all of the future leaders of the church at the time "derived their origin from Tekle Haymanot's new community."[101]

Prior to his coming to prominence, for ten years, Tekle Haymanot had studied under Yesus Mo'a, the Abbot of St Estifanos monastery at Hayq in the islands of Tana. His stay with Yesus Mo'a gave him an opportunity to study the lives of the Nine Saints which interested him so much that he decided to visit the monasteries they established. Of the monasteries he visited he decided to settle at Debre Damo where he learned under Aba Yohanni who led him through the four stages of monastic vows: "the qamis, qenat, quob and askema."[102]

According to tradition Tekle Haymanot returned to Shewa when he was about sixty years old along with Yikunno Amlak, the rightful occupant of the throne who was hiding in the monastery of Hayq.[103] The monk continued preaching the gospel to pagans in Shewa. However, he was distressed at the fact that the Christian settlers were being absorbed by the pagan influence all around them. He therefore sought to instruct them in the faith and send

---

Christology so the question "what was anointed?" remained. Hastings writes that Peter Heyling, a German Lutheran missionary who accompanied Abuna Marqos in 1637, may have diverted the form of the controversy by focusing attention on the meaning of the term "anointed" which underlies the meaning of "Christ." "Ewostathians held that the anointing was the divinization of the humanity, identical with the union of the two natures into one. This was known as Kebat. The House of Takla Haymanot, on the other hand, held that the anointing had nothing to do with the union itself, which it presupposed, but instead made Jesus into the Messiah or second Adam. This became known as Tewahdo. The Kebat was more rigorously Monophysite, the Tewahdo approximating more to Western views." Hastings, *Church in Africa*, 163. Gorgorios, however, writes that the "Kebat" were branches of the Roman Catholic Church. Gorgorios, የኢትዮጵያ ኦርቶዶክስ ተዋህዶ ቤተ ክርስቲያን ታሪክ፣ 57.

101. Taddesse Tamrat, *Church and State*, 168–173. There is a venerable tradition about him that he prayed for seven years standing on one leg. He was the first Ethiopian to be appointed as the chief administrator of the Church with the title *Echage*. Fargher, *Origins of New Churches*, 8.

102. Taddesse Tamrat, *Church and State*, 164.

103. Taddesse Tamrat, 168.

them out for evangelism.¹⁰⁴ His strategy for evangelization was to build a centre as a monastery. He chose the most strategic area among the pagan population. According to his hagiography, he obtained the site of his monastery Debre Asbo (Debre Libanos) with the help of a local chief whom he converted to Christianity. It is believed that Tekle Haymanot deliberately chose high ground which was tucked into a cliff and surrounded by Muslims as a strategic place to be safe from Muslim insurgency. Second, he wanted the small community to gradually spread its influence in the local people.¹⁰⁵

While at Debre Asbo (Debre Libanos) monastery, Tekle Haymanot attracted many students by his life and teaching. They joined his monastery from different parts of Ethiopia. The monastery was not only a place of learning but also a launching pad for evangelism to the pagan societies in southern and western Ethiopia. The new community of Tekle Haymanot lived on wild fruits of the forest and it took them a long time to establish trust among the local people. According to his hagiography Tekle Haymanot performed numerous miracles which attracted the pagans to Christianity. He is even credited with converting the notorious pagan King Motolomi of the Wolaitta Dynasty.¹⁰⁶ The account of Tekle Haymanot shows a vigorous confrontation and charismatic evangelism – much more in line with Protestant evangelists than with the modern EOC.¹⁰⁷

---

104. Taddesse Tamrat, 168.
105. Taddesse Tamrat, 170.
106. Taddesse Tamrat, 168–169. Zewde, *History of Modern Ethiopia*, 17–18.

107. Here are some of the miracles attributed to him: He chased Satan, who had deceived the inhabitants of Katata, Shewa into worshipping him as their god, he cut the tree down and built church with the wood, while he was praying for the resuscitation of men who were stricken by Satan, men who died during the reign of Abreha and Asbeha and were buried on the ground the stricken ones fell, came to life, while in Damot, he smote the face of the magician king and threw him to the ground, he caused the earth to swallow multitudes of magicians who hardened their heart against the gospel, etc. Tekle Haymanot courageously faced demonic and human forces alike, who were against the kingdom of God. In the hands of evil spirits and their human counterparts, his bones were crushed and was put to death several times, but he came to life by God's power and continued his power encounter courageously. Thousands believed in Christ as the result of his ministry accompanied with signs and wonders. E. A. Wallis Budge, *The Life of Takla Haymanot in the Version of Dabra Libanos and the Miracles of Takla Haymanot in the Version of Dabra Libanos and the Book of the Riches of Kings*, (London: Privately Printed for Lady Meux, 1906), 75–82, 88–91, 101–106, 129–132.

He was the first *Echege*[108] of the Church of Ethiopia after the death of the Egyptian Abune Qerlos in 1250 and it became impossible to have a replacement for a long time because of the unwillingness of Muslim authorities in Egypt. The leaders of the Ethiopian church resolved that they needed to assign an acting person until the coming of a Coptic bishop and Tekle Haymanot was chosen to fill the gap.[109]

Tekle Haymanot used his position to reform the church and help the clergy to remain close to the people they served. He helped to build more monasteries as centres of learning and influenced the kings to support the church financially. In addition, Tekle Haymanot played a significant role in restoring the "Solomonic Dynasty" by using his influence to bring Yikunno Amlak to power.[110] Because of the absence of Alexandrian Abun, Tekle Haymanot even crowned Yikunno Amlak emperor of Ethiopia.[111]

Tekle Haymanot, therefore, was instrumental in the revival of both Christianity and the "Solomonic Dynasty." He came to prominence at a time of the decline of Christianity through pagan influence and the rising of Islam towards the North of Ethiopia. Tekle Haymanot is credited with the spread of Christianity in the South, revival of monasticism which focused on evangelism, instruction of Christians and the use of monasteries as centres of education. The revival of monasticism thus served as an effective vehicle for the expansion of the church in the kingdom.

Militant Monks and the Role of Monasteries in Preserving Christianity

The monastic communities which were instrumental in the spread of Christianity into the interior used not only preaching but also force in their attempt to convert pagans. The story of Ewostatéwos is a case in point.

---

108. This is a title of an Ethiopian monk next in rank to the Egyptian patriarch.

109. Sergew, *Ancient and Medieval Ethiopian History*, 282.

110. As to how the transition was made there are different accounts one of which was that Tekle Haymanot persuaded the last of the Zagwe kings to give up the throne. It is also maintained that a war broke out between the rival dynasties in which the Zagwe Dynasty was weakened and Tekle Haymanot intervened and drafted a peace treaty between the two to the effect that Solomon's descendants would sit on a golden throne, whereas the Zagwe ones on a silver throne ruling over Lasta. Richard Pankhurst, *The Ethiopians* (Oxford: Blackwell, 2001), 53–55.

111. Sergew, *Ancient and Medieval Ethiopian History*, 286.

Unlike Tekle Haymanot who sought to attract people, Ewostatéwos followed a militant approach towards Muslims and pagans by exerting force on those who were not willing to give up their religion.[112] A similar attitude was evident in the ministry of the fifteenth-century Abot of Debre Libanos, Aba Merha-Kristos. He was entrusted by king Zer'a Ya'iqob with visitation of the churches and preaching of the gospel, and was given an army to protect him and enforce his reform and preaching. He confronted traditional religion head on by burning books of magic. At the same time, another monk, Aba Tekle Hawaryat also burned books of magic, flogged a witchdoctor publicly and even expelled opponents by burning their houses down. In doing so, the monks sought to demonstrate the powerlessness of paganism at the face of Christianity.[113]

The monks did not limit their activities to banishing and flogging agents of paganism, but also challenged emperors and even the Patriarch when they deviated from Christian principles or when a given doctrine was not upheld. For example Aba Anorios and Aba Filipos confronted king Amde Tsion when he married his father's concubine and he had them flogged, made them walk naked publicly and then exiled them.[114] Also Betselote Mikael of Amhara, openly challenged Abune Yohannis over corruption, and emperor Amda Tsion about his polygamy. The emperor had him beaten and exiled to Tigray.[115]

Emperors appreciated the missionary role of the monks. However, at times, they considered the monks' admonishment and expression of their opinion on doctrinal matters divisive, and they paid dearly.[116] The fourteenth-century monk Aba Estifanos and his followers, whose story will be discussed later, are a case in point. They stood for what they believed was true and were tortured and put to death for their refusal to prostrate before Emperor Zer'a Ya'iqob, pictures of St Mary and the cross. Thus, monks not only promoted Christianity, but also tried to protect it from perversion even by the monarchy.

---

112. Taddesse Tamrat, *Church and State*, 109.
113. Taddesse Tamrat, 239–240.
114. Getatchew Haile, *Dekike Estifanos: Behig Amlak*, 2nd edition (Addis Ababa: AAU Press, 2010), 23.
115. Taddesse Tamrat, *Church and State*, 114–117.
116. Taddesse Tamrat, 107–118, 208.

Monasteries also served as centres for producing and copying religious manuscripts, thereby contributing significantly to the preservation of Christianity. Especially during the attempts of the ninth/tenth century Queen Yodit (Judith) and the sixteenth-century Gragn Mohammed to annihilate Christianity, monasteries served as hiding places for monks and also large amounts of Christian literature. Thus the monastic movement played a crucial role in the expansion, interpretation and preservation of Christianity. Monasteries served as centres of Christian learning for the leaders of the country such as Zer'a Ya'iqob, who changed the course of Christianity in the country. In other words, monasteries rooted the faith in the culture and impressed the faith deeper in the hearts of the Christians as part of their identity and kept it vibrant from generation to generation.

Continuity with African Traditional World View

In addition to the role of monks and monarchs, Ethiopian Christianity bears marks of African traditional religion. The Orthodox Church was believed to be for the whole nation. People who are born to it are expected to keep it and die in it. In a typical African traditional fashion, people refer to Orthodoxy as the faith of their ancestors. Converting to other Christian traditions, therefore, is considered as rejection of the community. In other words, individuals do not have the right to leave the faith while dependent on their family. When they do so, they might be asked to leave the house of their parents. Individualism, therefore has little place in the communal living. A person is baptized into the church and when he or she dies, burial rites are very important because proper burial rites are believed to guarantee the person's eternal destiny.

Another aspect of traditional religion which appears to be strong in the church is the function of divination, magic and charms. Although the church teaches against it and there seems to be consciousness that it is contrary to Christianity, Christians are still strongly tempted towards magic, divination and sorcery. They tend to seek help from traditional medicine men and diviners in times of deep trouble. Members of clergy take part in providing traditional cures and charms as means of protection.[117]

---

117. A mother took her daughter to the sacred fountain (*tsebel*) for healing, when it did not work, she went to consult a diviner who ordered her to give her daughter goat meat and butter. The mother begs the diviner to reassign another day for the meat and butter because

Even though it is not practised in daylight, Christians still go to consult *Awaqi* (literally knowledgeable) also called *qalicha* under the cover of darkness about their future and for retribution against those who have wronged them. The number of prominent people who allegedly go to consult mediums under the cover of darkness is believed to be high.[118] The use of both black magic and white magic is common.[119] People visit traditional medicine men or herbalists for cures from illnesses, but such visits are not considered as evil necessarily, and therefore are done during the day. However, the herbalists chant prayers while administering the medicine to their customers and such prayers are associated with supernatural forces.

The diviners who are visited in the night or early in the morning are many times associated with demons, but traditionally, they too were considered as *Awaqi*. They are consulted for things like protection from evil forces, success in profession, prediction of the future, to win a lover, gaining more children or in cases of barrenness.[120] The same person also practices black magic (sorcery) to manipulate evil forces towards bringing harm on people. People consult *qalicha* and do what they ask them to do to stop a rival from success, usually by placing strangled poultry with features of a particular colour at his/ her doorstep, or burying objects on his or her property or other things as suggested by the diviner.

---

the day was a fasting day. Fanose Geda, *Hiwot*, no. 12 (Meskerem 1986), 27. Hailu Letta, a former member of Orthodox Church tells how his parents went to the Orthodox Church regularly, but also believed in ancestral spirits and took care of the "beads" of the ancestors. The priests themselves played two roles: they were "*qedash*" (ministers in the church) and at the same time "*tenquway*" (diviners). There were little boundaries marked out so people led their lives anyhow. What stood for adherence to EOC was observing the fasts, going to church and dancing and celebrations during holidays specially timket (epiphany). Apart from participating in the holidays and external marks of Christianity, there was little instruction given to Christians. Hailu Letta, Elder of Ketta Genet Church, O.i, 18 February 2011.

118. Two years ago a crime committed by Tamrat Geleta, a person believed to be "Tenquway" (medium of spirits) was investigated by the police and the person detained with no bail. Subsequent to his arrest the names of prominent people who allegedly visited him came out and some of the artists were at pains to prove that they were devout Orthodox and had never visited the man. አየንጋለ, *Enqu* 2, no. 19 (Miyazia 2001 Eth. C); Cf. *Enqu* Megabit 2001 Eth. C. Following Tamrat's arrest many "mediums" fled their residences in Addis Ababa.

119. Richard J. Gehman, *African Traditional Religion in Biblical Perspective* (Kenya: Kesho Publications, 1989), 67–96.

120. Gehman, *African Traditional Religion*, 69, 94–95.

Black and white magic appear to be so intertwined with Christianity that names of angels and the saints are used. Some persons who claim to have been servants of such diviners observe that the spirit appeared in the form of female and male. And those who appeared in the form of female appeared under the disguise of St Mary, or other, indigenous, female saints of the church.[121] When a request is granted, people are encouraged to give gifts to the church, successfully blending Christian and pagan practices. Therefore, persons who practise magic and divination appear to be Christians, and can wear a cross around their necks. They also act as *Awaqi* for Muslims and Christians in different occasions by changing their names and attire accordingly.[122]

Ancestral worship is another aspect of traditional worldview which governs people's decisions. There still is a visible fear of ancestral spirits, *wuqabi*, who might choose to dwell on a particular person in a family. This might take place unexpectedly when a member of the family suddenly begins acting in a strange way. He or she might show preference for a particular food or request the slaughter of an animal and even a particular kind of traditional attire to be given to him or her.[123] Family members will usually take the person to the church especially to places which are famous for the healing power of their consecrated fountain. Priests will touch the forehead

---

121. Fantu, who claims to have been immersed in traditional worship while a devout Orthodox notes that the feminine spirit which is known as Yearusiwa Emebet has caused holy water to flow and sends people to drink from it and be freed from demonic oppression. The spirit also commands people to respect "tabot," and pay tithes for St Michael and St Gabriel. According to her interpretation, this was done to deceive people into believing that what they were doing was in fact acceptable in the faith. Hiwot, Tir/Yekatit, no. 4 (1986 Eth. C), 19–21. According to the testimony of Tesfaye, a former servant of Tenquway, the spirit who possessed the man accepted adoration as "bale arba tabot" (master of the forty tabots), Yegebriel Geta (lord of Gabriel). Tesfaye claims that in Ethiopia in the name of Gabriel, Michael, Mary etc. evil spirits are being worshipped. The spirits claim to be male and female, the female ones are worshipped under the disguise of St Mary, St Hannah, St Kristos Samra, Kidane Mihret, etc. ቤተ መንግስቴ የተቃለለበት ጥንቁላ, Testimony of Tesfaye Gebre, 15–17, *Gesame* 2, no. 5 (Ginbot, 2000 Eth. C); *Gesame* 2, no. 7 (Meskerem, 2001), 12–14; *Kale Heywet*, no. 15 (1990 Eth. C), 21–23. Hastings cites the experience of Marha Kristos (1462–96), the Abbot of Dabra Libanos in the later fifteenth century who encountered people who were "possessed" by the three persons of the Trinity. He also described a woman "speaking in the spirit of Satan" who claimed that Mikael and Gabriel spoke with her. In one instance she told the priests in her village that Mary wanted them to administer the Eucharist at noon on Wednesday and Friday and the priests succumbed. Adrian Hastings, *Church in Africa*, 26.

122. Cf. እያንዳላ, *Enqu* 2, no. 19 (Miyazia 2001 Eth. C).

123. Gehman, *African Traditional Religion*, 158–160.

of the person with a cross and immerse the person in consecrated water and make him or her drink it. This might last for several days. When the desired deliverance does not come about, *Awaqi* will be consulted who will give family members specific instructions as to how to appease the spirit or even claim to deliver the person.[124]

People are also possessed when they are requested to set themselves aside for the spirit. This usually means taking up *Chelle* (beads) dedicated to ancestral spirits, which used to be taken care of by their parents or even distant members of the family. The person chosen by the spirit might willingly set aside themselves for the spirit or suffer the consequences. There is a tremendous apprehension about harm brought by ancestral spirits who may kill all of the family members until their request is fulfilled. Family members tend to rely on the counsel of the ancestral spirits and strive to appease them, lest everyone in the family die in a horrible way.

At times the needed way out of such fearful situation may not be found in the clergy members. A story is told about a young man whose family members were killed by an ancestral spirit even after he went bankrupt trying to meet the spirit's demands. Exasperated, he contemplated discarding the *Chelle* and consulted his father confessor. The father confessor told him, "if this is the spirit of your ancestors, how can you discard its objects. If you decide to do that do not ask for my advice and do not make me part of your plans."[125] There is a common belief that if people do not retain the faith of their ancestors they will be cursed and doomed to unsuccessfulness in life.

---

124. Begashaw Desalegn, የመስቀሉ ሥር ቁማርተኞች (Gamblers under the cross) (Addis Ababa: n.p., 1998 Eth. C), 47.

125. Dawit W/Yohannes, "ምሥክርነት" (Testimony). *Gesame* 1, no. 9 (Meskerem–Tikimpt 1995 Eth. C), 7. Stories of people tormented by ancestral spirit regardless of their membership at the EOC did not make sense to Evangelicals. Thus, those who torment and demand sacrifices were believed to be evil spirits and they were to come out in the name of Jesus, period! They are not to be prayed to, or appeased through sacrifice to have mercy on the people they possessed. The deliverance of those upon coming to Evangelical churches made Evangelicals question whether there was real deliverance at EOC. ቀዳሚዋ ዘሪ - የሂሪዋ ዘማሪ፣ *Kale Heywet* 29 (1996 Eth. C): 23–24. One of the most romanticized stories of the EOC in which Aba Ze-Mika'él Aregawi was believed to have been pulled up the rocky church by a huge serpent does not seem to fit the theology of some Evangelical preachers. In his sermon which was considered provocative, pastor Dawit Molalegn mocked, "How can a serpent pull a saint up the church? The Bible says that you crush the head of the serpent, so we will crush its head for you!" Dawit Molalegn, ቀሉ ስላመጣ አይቅላልባችሁ (Do not take [the humble gospel] for granted), Audiovisual Sermon (VCD), n.d. The Orthodox seemed to wish to address his

There also is fear of evil eye so women put a piece of charcoal or metal over grain put out in the sun. The bedroom of a mother who has given birth is kept dark and she takes metal with her while going out of the house to the toilet. A metal object (usually a knife) is believed to keep bad spirits away from people and their grain. The Bible is also used as an object of protection. Mothers will put the New Testament or other religious books under the pillow of their children for protection.[126] Adults too will place the Bible under their pillows while going to sleep or even press it against the chest/body of possessed people for deliverance.

In addition, charms are used as protection from evil spirits. It is not uncommon to see Christians wearing charms on their bodies and that of their children or tied on the horns of their cattle. CMS missionaries wrote about being asked for paper for the purpose of writing charms on and were even asked to wear them for protection. Christians did not see much incongruence between their faith and traditional practices. In fact, they were astonished when the CMS missionaries told them that such practices lead people to hell.[127] Having visible objects for protection, therefore, was such a strong temptation that even the Scriptures were used as tools of protection.[128]

Clearly, there is tremendous fear of the involvement of demonic forces in people's lives and also a desire to manipulate them for one's advantage. The infiltration of such pagan practices implies that traditional worldviews are powerfully at work. Power encounter, however, was part of the ministry of monks who spread Christianity among pagans. In the footsteps of the Nine Saints, who attempted to eradicate paganism, indigenous monks such as Tekle Haymanot confronted witchcraft head on. Endorsed by Zer'a

---

ridicule by hanging a huge poster at the junction of his church with words of Psalms 31:18, "Let the lying lips be put to silence; which speak grievous things proudly and contemptuously against the righteous." 19 January 2011.

126. Nigusse Bulcha, Director of Scripture Union, Interview, 30 September 2010, Addis Ababa.

127. Kugler's Journal, 25 February – 24 April 1830, University of Birmingham Special Collections, CMS/B/OMS/ C M/ O46/24, 13; Gobat's Journal from 25 February 1830 – 16 February 1833, UB SC, CMS/B/OMS/C M/O28/113, 137–139.

128. Kugler's Journal, 25 February – 24 April 1830, UB SC, CMS/B/OMS/ C M/ O46/24, 14–15.

Ya'iqob,[129] the fifteenth-century evangelists such as Aba Merha Kristos and Aba Tekle Hawaryat publicly challenged witchdoctors, burnt their books of magic and flogged them. They even expelled people from highland districts on the basis of their involvement in pagan worship. The aim of such violent measures was to demonstrate "the powerlessness of the pagan gods and their human agents."[130]

Unfortunately, as time went by, it seems that the vastness of the church made it possible for the revival of traditional practices in the structures of the church. People used the name and the priestly office of the church in order to make money in the name of healing and bringing good fortune.[131] Even though the church teaches against such practices, it is slow in confronting its clergy members who allegedly practice magic and divination.[132] Apparently, old practices are recognized (if not officially endorsed from the top) by the priests who serve at the grass root level. Christianity and traditional practices thus are not presented as mutually exclusive.

However, there is consciousness that such practices are unacceptable to God so that Christians who are involved in ancestor worship and divination dare not partake in the Holy Communion fearing God's wrath may overtake them on the spot. When they want to celebrate the Eucharist, they will discard their objects of worship. However, the fact that the practice has a long history and has been transferred from generation to generation and blended into the culture makes it difficult to deal with. In addition, little theological engagement is done by the theologians of the church to provide church authorities with tools to deal with the practice.

---

129. Emperor Zer'a Ya'iqob is depicted as ruthless person, who did not spare his critics even Aba Tekle Hawaryat died out of torture for confronting the king about the massive shedding of blood. Zer'a Ya'iqob also remained polygamous and ruthless in his judgements "which convey very little of the sense of justice of a deeply religious man." Taddesse Tamrat, *Church and State*, 243.

130. Taddesse Tamrat, *Church and State*, 239–240.

131. Daniel Seife Michael, Teacher at Holy Trinity Theological College, Interview, 8 September 2010, Addis Ababa.

132. Mekonnen Workneh, Teacher at Holy Trinity Theological College, Interview, 14 November 2010, Addis Ababa.

Moreover, the people who practice it are referred to as *awaqi* and this title safely disguises the evil works which are going on behind the scenes.[133] The long history of the practice also enabled prominent people who were immersed in it to assume high ecclesiastical positions. This of all the other factors, has made it most difficult for the church to expose the practice and denounce people who are involved in it.[134] The widespread presence of such practices despite the seventeen-century-long existence of Christianity, however, indicates that there is a vacuum in the spiritual life of the people which the church is not yet filling.

In addition to magic and ancestral spirits, prophecies through dreams and visions have played a significant role in the background, shaping people's perceptions, arousing their expectations and informing their decisions. One example was the decision to put aside doctrinal differences and welcome the Portuguese soldiers in 1520, which was based on a prophecy "which said that Christians were to come to this port, that they would open a well in it, and when this well was opened there would be no Moors there." The bishop Abune Marqos related another prophecy to Father Francisco Alvarez who accompanied the Portuguese army, that an alliance between Christian Ethiopians and Europeans would bring an end to Islam.[135] Emperor Libne Dingil took the prophecy so seriously that he proposed a lasting military alliance to be established with Portugal.[136] Although the Portuguese army was in any case welcome because of its coming to the rescue of Ethiopians

---

133. A former *debtera* who practised black and white magic tells his story that he did not see much problem with what he was doing. He used to give the money he made to the church and to the needy. He considered what he does as wisdom and not as the work of Satan. "እንደእኔ ያለ ክርስቲያን ያለ ሁሉ አይመስለኝም ነበር፡፡ ጠንቋዬ የማገኘውን ገንዘብ ላጦቤት እሰጣለሁ . . . የሚደርጉትን ድግምት የሰይጣን ስራ ሳይሆን የጥበብ ስራ አድርጌ ነበር የምቆጥረው፡፡" Mussie Menberu, የመስተፋቅር ሌላው መጥፎ ገጽ (The other side of magic), *Trinity* 9, (2003 Eth. C), 20.

134. Bezabih Workneh, Minister in the Mulu Wongel Church, Interview, 25 February 2011, Addis Ababa. Such tendencies evident in the Orthodox Church are looked at as syncretistic, but at times Evangelicals are accused of them too. Birhanu Wolde cited examples of Christians being influenced by their society around and taking up harmful practices such as tying charms on their cows, babies, etc. The writer lamented that Christians are practicing Christianity and traditional beliefs side by side. Birhanu Wolde, "መጽሐፍ ቅዱስ ወይስ ባህል? ይታሰብበት" (Priority to the Bible or tradition?), *Kale Heywet* 25 (1994 Eth. C): 14.

135. Merid Wolde Aregay, "Legacy of Jesuit Missionary," 31–32.

136. Aregay, 33.

from the jihadist Gragn's raids, the prophecy must have played a role in facilitating the warm welcome.

In a situation where state and ecclesiastical matters were not separated, the importance of oracles and visions sometimes surfaced in the way monarchs assumed power or the names they decide to take as their crown names. The coming to power of Emperor Tewodros illustrates this. His arrival became legendary because the name Tewodros, belonged to a widespread myth. "At a time of devastating wars, extensive famine and great moral corruption, Christ himself would raise up Teodros, a prince of bygone days, and send him back to restore peace, prosperity and justice and extend empire far as Jerusalem."[137] The source of the prophecy is not specified but it appeared to govern the expectation of people. Tewodros lived up to the expectation of the oracle in his initial years and perhaps as the result of the prophecy surrounding his crown name, he entertained a desire to free Jerusalem from the hand of the Turks.[138]

The coming of Menelik was also surrounded with oracles.[139] His mother, Ejigayehu who was captured in war was a servant in the house of Aleqa Melat, the chief priest of Ankober. One night she saw in her dream a sun coming out of her private parts. Stunned by the dream, she related it to her friends and very soon the news reached her master, who sent her to the royal court. The queen mother arranged for one of her sons to sleep with the slave girl and she gave birth to a baby boy. The king was angry at the news and named the baby boy, Minyeleh-Shewa, literally, "what would Shewa say?' and sent the mother and the baby far from the royal court.[140] But in his dream the king saw himself standing with the little boy and the shadow

---

137. Gustav Aren, *Evangelical Pioneers in Ethiopia: Origins of the Evangelical Church Mekane Yesus* (Stockholm: EFS Forlaget, 1978), 85–86.

138. Zewde, *History of Modern Ethiopia*, 28, 33, 43.

139. Paulos Gnogno, *Ate Menelik*, 3rd edition (Addis Ababa: n.p., 1999 Eth. C), 11–12.

140. When Bezabish, the wife of king Sahle-Sellassie, heard the news she arranged for her favourite son Seifu to sleep with Ejigayehu to make sure that the "sun" came forth by him. But Seifu had a woman he loved so he persuaded his brother Haile-Melekot to sleep with Ejigayehu instead. When the king found out his son slept with a slave girl he was very upset and sent Ejigayehu to another place where she bore a baby boy. The king named him Minyeleh-Shewa. This implied the shamefulness of having a baby from a slave girl. Shewa was the kingdom of Sahle-Sellassie.

of the boy was bigger than his and also the footsteps of the boy were larger than the king's. King Sahle Sellassie decided to rename the boy, Menelik.

There were oracles about the rise of a king by the name Menelik who would make the country great. Sahle Sellassie formerly took the name Menelik as his crown name, but a monk told him that the name was not meant for him and would bring bad fortune upon him if he insisted in taking it. The prophecy seemed to find fulfilment in Emperor Menelik whose reign was relatively peaceful. He secured the boundaries of Ethiopia, defeated European power and introduced modern technology and artefacts to Ethiopia.

People's fear of ancestral spirits and attachment to them, the desire to manipulate the spirit world through the use of white and black magic, and the role of oracles and visions provide us with examples of continuity between African traditional worldview and Ethiopian Christianity. Guidance was provided not only by the tradition of the fathers and the Scriptures, but also with consultation with mediums of the supernatural. Traditional medicine was not limited to providing cure and protection but was extended to education. Even in the context of church education, the use of traditional medicine was believed to help students remember their lessons, so that some of the teachers gave a "medicine" to the students in order to help them remember well.[141]

2.2.4. Development of Learning

The church is the pioneer of indigenous education in the country and prepared people for spiritual as well as civic services. In fact, in ancient times no distinction was made between church education and civic education, so church educated people became clergy and government officials as well. Thus it was common to find government officials who were deacons or priests of the church.

The school system of the EOC dates back to the fourth century, the likely date of the introduction of Christianity to Aksum. As Christianity and the kingdom expanded, the school system underwent some changes and

---

141. Richard Pankhurst, "The Foundations of Education, Printing, Newspapers, Book Productions, Libraries and Literacy in Ethiopia," *Ethiopia Observer* 6, no. 3 (1960), 242. Cf. Gehman, *African Traditional Religion*, 95.

reforms. The current form of the schools was developed during the golden ages of the church (thirteenth – sixteenth century), when the literature of the church reached its peak. The school system has not changed much since.[142] However, literary and cultural activities declined when the church was weakened with wars and internal strife.

Until the mid-thirteenth century the monasteries continued to provide religious and literary educational facilities for the Ethiopian Christian highlands. Young men travelled all the way to northern Ethiopia to acquire serious literary and religious training. Upon returning to their respective regions some of these men opened small schools where they taught children how to read and write. "But until the middle of the thirteenth century, it seems that none of these small local schools in the south attained any particular significance beyond providing very elementary educational services for a handful of local children."[143]

The Traditional School System of the Ethiopian Orthodox Church

The traditional school of the church has three levels of education: *Nebab Bet* (the school of reading), *Qiddase Bet* (the school of the holy mass), and higher schools. The higher schools have three divisions: *Zema Bet* (the school of the hymns), *Qene Bet* (the school of poetry), and *Metshaf Bet* (the school of scriptures).[144]

Nebab Bet primarily teaches children how to read religious books which are written in Ge'ez. Children master the 238[145] letters of Ge'ez and learn how to read. Traditionally writing is not taught because it is not needed in everyday life, but reading is vital for daily prayers and participation in the service of the church. The texts used for the exercise of reading were the

---

142. Sergew et al., *Church of Ethiopia*, 82.

143. Sergew et al., 20.

144. Sergew et al., 81–97; Haile Gabriel Dagne, "Non-Government Schools in Ethiopia," in *Language in Ethiopia*, eds. M. L. Bender et al. (London: Oxford University Press, 1976), 339–370; Haile Gabriel Dagne, "The School System in Ethiopia," in *Zeitschrift fur Kulturaustausch* (Sonderausgabe, 1973), 100–106.

145. This figure includes "ሽ" the letter which represents the "v" sound which is not usually counted along with the main letters.

epistles of John, Paul and writings such as *Miracles of Mary*. The fact that the texts are in Ge'ez makes comprehension nearly impossible.[146]

The next level is *Qiddase Bet* which prepares students as altar priests whose function is limited to carrying out the rituals of the Mass and the Sacraments. The rest, including teaching the traditions and service of the church, is learned through daily experience in the parish itself.[147]

When a student who had completed *Nebab Bet* and *Qiddase Bet* wished to further his studies, he would join the legendary wandering students (*yeqolo temari*) who travel from monastery to monastery and parish to parish in search of a good school and an instructor.[148] The community where the students live supports them with food and grains as the students beg them saying, "in the name of the Lord who provides."[149]

The higher school of the Church has three levels: *Zema Bet*, (school of music), *Qene Bet* (School of Poetry and Composition), and *Metsehaf Bet* (School of Commentaries). The school of music is based on the composition of one of the disciples of the Nine Saints, St Yared, who lived in the sixth century.[150] Unlike the former levels of education, students learn *Qene* with enthusiasm because of its challenging and interesting nature which incorporates free creative activities such as writing poems and singing them with a suitable musical instrument.

Metshaf Bet, on the other hand has four branches: *Beluy* – the 46 books of the Old Testament, *Haddis* – the 35 books of the Ethiopian New Testament, *Liqawent* – writings of the church fathers such as St Cyril.[151] In addition to that, *Liqawent* includes the study of *Fetha Negest* (the canon law) and *Bahre Hasab* (calendar reckoning). The last branch of *Metshaf Bet* is *Menekosat*

---

146. Sergew et al., *Church of Ethiopia*, 85.

147. Teshome Zerihun, "የኢትዮጵያ ቤተ ክርስቲያን ዕድገት," (The growth of the Church of Ethiopia), *Tinsae* (10 Miazia 1960 Eth. C), 31.

148. Such a student is called *yeqolo temari* (literally a student of *Qolo*) to imply the kind of difficult life the student endures; eating *Qolo* and drinking water. *Qolo* is roasted grain which is very dry in character and easy to carry around. *Qolo* connotes poverty, thus the name signifies the kind of lowly life the student is following.

149. Kidane Mariyam Getahun, "ጥንታዊው የቆሎ ተማሪ" (The ancient wandering student) (Addis Ababa: Birhanena Selam Printing, 1954 Eth. C), 15–17, 24.

150. Haile Gabriel, "School System in Ethiopia," 101.

151. St Cyril is referred to as "Qerlos" in the EOC.

(monastic literature).¹⁵² This is the highest stage of the church's education where the *Andemta*¹⁵³ Commentary is studied. "The commentary is all memorized and seems to be passed from professor to professor, partly with the help of books, but chiefly by word of mouth."¹⁵⁴

A graduate of *Metshaf Bet* who has successfully memorized all four branches along with their commentary is traditionally referred to as *Arat Ayna* literally "four-eyed." Such men exist though they are not many in number. It is estimated that the whole study including time of reflection, learning the history of the church, how to make artefacts, copy and bind manuscripts takes no less than thirty years.¹⁵⁵ Johnny Bakke, a Lutheran missionary in Ethiopia however, argues that given the massive number of books that need to be studied, no one can claim a complete and full mastery of them all because it would take more than a lifetime to study by heart all eight hundred of them along with different interpretations.¹⁵⁶

As to why the study takes such a long time, the possible reasons include the massiveness of the subject matter that needs to be covered, the scattered location of the teachers, poor method of teaching, shortage of qualified teachers and time and environmental restraints. In addition, Qes Mekbib, Atnaw¹⁵⁷ argues that the study takes so long mostly because of the methodology used and the attitude of the teachers who take pride in making knowledge inaccessible.¹⁵⁸ With little or no critical reflection and

---

152. Haile Gabriel, "School System in Ethiopia," 101.

153. According to tradition in 832 Eth. C, emperor Dagnazan appointed Abba Yedla chief over hundred and fifty scholars and set them to preach and teach the faith all over the country. While residing at a place called Selales (Etissa) they served as itinerant teachers and eventually developed their teaching material into a commentary in his palace. Roger W. Cowley, *The Traditional Interpretation of the Apocalypse of St. John in the Ethiopian Orthodox Church* (Cambridge: University of Cambridge Oriental Publications, 1983), 22.

154. Douglas O'Hanlon, *Features of the Abyssinian Church* (London: SPCK, 1946), 19.

155. Mekbib Atnaw, "የጥንታዊው የሀገር ትምህርት የአማማር አቅድ" (The ancient country education) *Tinsae* (10 Miazia 1960 Eth. C), 32.

156. Johnny Bakke, *Christian Ministry: Christian Patterns and Functions within the Ethiopian Evangelical Church Mekane Yesus* (Oslo: Solum Forlag A. S. 1987), 89.

157. Mekbib Atnaw served as preacher of the gospel in the General Patriarchate Department of Evangelism and Apostolic Mission for a long time. His current title is መጋቢ አእላፍ (Megabe A'elaf) which means pastor of multitudes.

158. Mekbib Atnaw, "የጥንታዊው የሀገር ትምህርት የአማማር አቅድ," 33.

understanding but memorization, it is very difficult to accurately reproduce the core content of the subject matter in a way that satisfies the teacher.[159]

In fact, any student who dared to question the interpretation of the *Andemta* Commentary would be declared a heretic.[160] Thus the *Andemta* is the authoritative commentary of the church which is regarded as the key to understanding the Bible; its writers as possessing higher knowledge of the ancient languages[161] and illuminated in a way which is unattainable to the modern mind. In addition, there appears to be a fear of corrupting the content of *Andemta* if critical evaluation is allowed. However, this does not mean that students did not learn anything. Justin de Jacobis, the Italian missionary of the nineteenth century, commented "Many a humble *debtera*, had nonetheless more real knowledge than the most learned professors in our European Schools."[162]

With the centuries-old tradition of studying for years in order to reproduce the teaching of the fathers, the idea of renovation might sound like an unsafe path to take. It could also be argued that isolation and resistance to change has enabled the church to formulate and maintain its unique traditions. Sergew argues that the church alone should not be blamed for resistance to change. Even when the clergy wanted to introduce new ways of doing things the Christians themselves resisted.[163]

2.2.5. Advance and Recession

In the middle of the ninth century, the ambition of Aksumite kings for expansion northwards was halted by the kings of Bete Israel (Jewish settlers in Ethiopia) who were against Christianity. In the major conflict which ensued in the middle of the ninth century, the Jewish king Gideon IV was killed and his daughter Yodit (Judith) assumed the throne. Queen Judith managed to join forces with the pagan Agew tribes, who no doubt resented the Christian expansion on to their territories. Around AD 960, the tribal

---

159. Sergew et al., *Church of Ethiopia*, 96.

160. Habte-Mariam Worqneh, ጥንታዊ የኢትዮጵያ ትምህርት (The ancient Ethiopian education) (Addis Ababa: Birhanena Selam Printing, 1970 Eth. C): 217–218.

161. Abraham Mengesha, "Evaluation of the Position," 11.

162. Lady Herbert, *Abyssinia and Its Apostle*, 1867, quoted by Richard Pankhurst, "Foundations of Education," 241.

163. Sergew Hable Sellassie, "Religious Life in Ethiopia," 24, 29.

confederation under the leadership of Judith conquered Aksum and ransacked the city destroying churches, religious manuscripts and massacring clergy and laity. In addition, Judith destroyed the Debre Damo monastery which was the treasury of Aksum and killed all of the potential heirs of the throne who were kept in the monastery. The Queen must have followed in the footsteps of her ancestors who resisted Christianity on their land for a long time.[164] Following the fall of the Aksumite kingdom, the champion of Christianity, and the destruction of priceless literature and the clergy, the Christian faith was significantly weakened.

Christianity spread along with the kings' establishment of military colonies for which they also built churches. The ambitious expansion of the Christian kingdom suffered successive setbacks because of internal strife and external resistance. The pagan Queen of Sidama halted the expansion of the Christian kingdom in the tenth century and weakened it further by killing many Christians and their king.[165]

The development of any religions other than the Orthodox triggered bitter memories of the recession of ancient Christianity. The most painful memory is that of the rise of Mohammed Gragn in the sixteenth century who waged Jihad against the Christian kingdom of Ethiopia and came near to exterminating Christianity. The effort to halt the expansion of Islam, on the other hand, brought Latin Christianity to the scene. Rome's attempt to replace Orthodox with Latin rites resulted in much bloodshed.

2.2.6. The Great Jihad and the Arrival of Western Christianity

Islam, the Principal Threat to the Survival of Christianity

As discussed earlier, Islamic expansion was connected with trade along the coasts of Ethiopia. One important factor was that the need for the Christian

---

164. Tadesse Tamrat, *Church and State*, 192–193, 199–200.

165. At the time, there was internal strife for power between two brothers in which Petros, the Alexandrian bishop, took sides and eventually got banished and died in exile. Alexandria held the king responsible for the death of the bishop and refused to send a substitute. This resulted in low morale among Christians who apparently lost confidence to withstand the anti-Christian activities of the Queen of Sidama. Consequently, both the kingdom and Christianity were weakened. The Christians were able to revive when through the intercession of Nubia, the relationship with Alexandria was restored and a new Abun appointed. Taddesse Tamrat, *Church and State*, 39–41.

state to obtain its single bishop from Egypt meant intermittent contact with its rulers.[166] "This situation strengthened the hand of the Muslims in Ethiopia."[167] However, Islam was resisted by some of the Cushitic people such as Hadiya and Dawaro.[168] Grenstedt notes that according to the tradition of Oromo Muslims in Bale, Sheik Husayn who is their favourite saint, was the first Muslim missionary to Ethiopia in the thirteenth century.[169]

At any rate, Islam in Ethiopia has a long history, even longer than many Ethiopians care to admit. "The single most decisive advance came through the "Jihad" waged by Imam Ahmad b. Ibrahim al-Ghazi of Harar . . . who conquered and ruled most of the Ethiopian state from 1529 to 1543."[170] This period marked the most severe and systematic attack on Christianity in Ethiopian history. Ahmed b. Ibrahim al-Ghazi was called "Gragn" by Ethiopians because he was left handed.[171] The historian Richard Pankhurst notes that Ahmed Gragn was brought up as a family slave who was later liberated. He resented the humiliation and the demand for a tribute by the Christian state. He had been a soldier formerly, but also assumed the position of religious leader, adopting the title "Imam." Moreover, his marriage to the daughter of Mahfuz, a well-known warrior who had made about twenty-five annual raids against the Christian strong hold of Shewa, gave him prominence.

After several raids, Gragn declared a major war in 1529 against Emperor Libne Dingil and decisively defeated him. Gragn's army also suffered such great losses that they retreated for several months to recuperate. In 1531, he fought a great battle.[172] This time, thoroughly equipped by the Ottomans, Gragn's army came upon the emperor of Ethiopia as a "terrible blow and

---

166. J. Spencer Trimingham, *The Influence of Islam upon Africa* (London; Beirut: Longman Group; Librairie du Liban, 1968; 1980), 26.

167. Mervyn Hiskett, *The Course of Islam in Africa* (Edinburgh: Edinburgh University Press, 1994), 138.

168. Trimingham, *Influence of Islam*, 26.

169. Staffan Grenstedt, Ambaricho and Shonkolla, *From Local Independent Church to the Evangelical Mainstream in Ethiopia: The Origins of the Mekane Yesus Church in Kembata Hadiya* (Stockholm: Elanders Gotab, 2000), 53.

170. Nehemia Levtzion and Randall L. Pouwels, eds., *The History of Islam in Africa* (Athens, OH: Ohio University Press, 2000), 229.

171. Fargher, *Origins of the New Churches*, 12.

172. Pankhurst, *The Ethiopians*, 86.

for his people a traumatic shock."[173] In his distress, Emperor Libne Dingil appealed for help to the Portuguese, but it took a long time for the desired help to come to the rescue of the Christian state. Emperor Libne Dingil died as a fugitive.[174]

When the Portuguese finally came to the aid of the Christian state, his son Gelawdewos was in power. The Portuguese troops arrived at Massawa in 1541 led by "Dom Christovao da Gama, a son of the famous mariner Vasco." When the rumour of the coming of a mighty army spread all over the country, many soldiers abandoned Gragn and joined the Christian state. Gragn was initially challenged and wounded and he retreated for a while, but strengthened with the aid of the Ottomans, he defeated the Portuguese and their commander was captured and beheaded. Gragn was overcome with such a feeling of false security that he did not attempt to stop his Turkish allies from returning back home.[175]

In 1541, Emperor Gelawdewos along with his mother and the survivors of Dom Christovao's army confronted Gragn and killed him and his army fled. "The fourteen-year Muslim ascendancy thereupon crumpled almost overnight."[176]

In his attempt to wipe out the Christian faith, Gragn killed many clergy all over the country not to mention the monks some of whom out of desperation threw themselves into the blazing fire, as historic monasteries such as Debre Libanos (dedicated to the memory of the great Saint Tekle Haymanot) were set on fire.[177] "It took Gragn only twelve[178] short and terrible years to destroy most of the Christian culture built up over hundreds of years."[179] In addition to destroying masses of Orthodox literature, Gragn also succeeded in converting a considerable number of Christians to Islam. Conversion to Islam did not always come through force. A multitude of opportunists and

---

173. Bengt Sundkler and Christopher Steed, *A History of the Church in Africa* (Cambridge: Cambridge University Press, 2000), 75.
174. Sundkler and Steed, *History of the Church in Africa*, 88.
175. Pankhurst, *The Ethiopians*, 92.
176. Pankhurst, 93.
177. Sundkler and Steed, *History of the Church in Africa*, 74.
178. Pankhurst says fourteen years. Pankhurst, *The Ethiopians*, 93.
179. Sundkler and Steed, *History of the Church in Africa*, 74.

even staunch Christians adopted Islam out of desperation, thinking that the Christian kingdom which had been laid waste would never be restored.[180]

In addition to its impact of winning numerous converts to Islam, Gragn's conquest also contributed in large measure to the weakening of the Christian state of Ethiopia. Both Ottomans and the Portuguese desired to gain control over the state of Ethiopia. The Portuguese had an agenda of maintaining the political and religious upper hand in Ethiopia. The Ottomans on the other hand sought to Islamize the country state and in 1555 and 1576 they declared war against Ethiopia. The Ethiopian state had to resist the attempt of each power and this weakened the state still further[181] coupled with internal troubles.[182] This opened the door for the massive migration of Oromo which overwhelmed both the Christian state and the Muslim principalities.[183]

Christians did not immediately take revenge on Muslims which gave Islam time to spread to the extent of that "In c. 1630, the Portuguese missionary Manoel d'Almeida believed that one-third of the population of the Ethiopian state was Muslim."[184]

The early presence of Islam and its encounter with Christianity appears to have left its mark on the tradition of the ancient church of Ethiopia. The insistence on Ge'ez as the sacred language and *Andemta* as the infallible commentary, the intolerance towards reform through fear of corruption, and the striking similarity between the traditional school systems makes one wonder whether such influences were exerted by the long-standing presence of Islam in Ethiopia.[185]

Latin Christianity

As hinted earlier, Ethiopians came into contact with Catholicism when they requested military assistance during the raid of Ahmed Gragn in 1529. Rome, however, had received information about Ethiopia and the kind of Christianity it adhered to from the small community of monks who resided

---

180. Pankhurst, *The Ethiopians*, 88–90.
181. Levtzion and Pouwels, eds., *History of Islam*, 230.
182. Trimingham, *Influence of Islam*, 27.
183. Levtzion and Pouwels, eds., *History of Islam*, 230.
184. Levtzion and Pouwels, 230.
185. Cf. Haile Gabriel Dagne, "School System in Ethiopia," 101–102; Haile Gabriel Dagne, "Non-Government Schools in Ethiopia," 349–353.

near the Vatican as early as the 1480s.[186] Their presence led to the printing of the Ethiopian Psalter in 1553 and the arrival of Tesfa Tsion who was known as "Petrus Aethiops" in Rome, the "most remarkable monk from Debre Libanos." He had the Ge'ez New Testament and Eucharistic liturgy printed in 1548. The arrival of the Jesuit Oviedo in 1557 in the era of Emperor Gelawdewos and his desire to ensure the primacy of Roman order over the Alexandrian one caused tension.[187] Ethiopian Christians appreciated the sacrifice made by Portuguese soldiers to bring about physical liberation from Gragn's raid. However, their respect for Catholicism as the religion of the Portuguese and willingness to acknowledge it as a Christian tradition different from theirs was not reciprocated.[188]

By the time of the arrival of Catholic missionaries Ethiopia had already been Christian for over ten centuries. ". . . the holy Scripture being translated into the language of the country and its ancient praxis of the Christian faith and the celebration of the Christian mysteries expressed in its own calendar and rite. This means that the long mutual interaction between the Christian faith and Ethiopian culture had already created a strong local Christian tradition."[189] Turning the hearts of the people away from such indigenous Christian tradition to Rome was virtually impossible.

In 1603 a group of Catholic missionaries (Jesuits) led by Pedro Paez arrived. Because of his favourable attitude towards the Jesuits, there was a wide spread rumour that Emperor Zedingil had accepted Catholicism and

---

186. Hastings, *Church in Africa*, 139–140.

187. Hastings, 140–141.

188. Gelawdewos expressed his disappointment in writing to Pedro Mascarenhas, the governor of Portuguese soldiers who decided to remain in Ethiopia. Gelawdewos was deeply offended by Goncalo Rodriguez, a Jesuit priest's designation of him as unbeliever and a heretic. He argued that adherents of Alexandrian faith should not be regarded as non-Christians. The way he ended his letter was moving, "I believe, I believe, I believe until I die and as long as I live and throughout the time of times, Amen." Aregay, "Legacy of Jesuit Missionary," 39. Emperor Gelawdewos was willing to recognize Andres Oviedo as the patriarch of the Portuguese but Oviedo was extremely offended and declared the king "an irredeemable heretic" and banned all Portuguese soldiers from serving the emperor and having any communications with him on pains of excommunication. The outcome was the death of the emperor overwhelmed by Muslim hordes. Aregay, "Legacy of Jesuit Missionary," 40–41.

189. Ayele Teklehaymanot, "The Struggle for the "Ethiopianization" of the Roman Catholic Tradition," in *The Missionary Factor in Ethiopia* (Frankfurt: Peter Lang, 1998), 136.

he was killed, accused of abandoning the faith of his ancestors.[190] Paez,[191] however, displayed, humility and respect for the Ethiopian Orthodox *Tewahdo* Church. "He was cautious, tactful, and tolerant, and the success of the Jesuits, culminating in the conversion to Catholicism of the Emperor Susinyos was largely due to him."[192] The Emperor's motives may not have been purely religious but political as well, for Paez connected him with the Roman Pope Clement and Philip III, the emperor of Spain.[193] Gorgorios notes that Paez was not as stubborn as Andres Oviedo; instead, he studied Ge'ez and did teaching and the mass in Ge'ez and within seven years the emperor accepted Catholicism,[194] was baptized along with his family and gave land for the Catholics to build a church.[195] Aba Paez died of fever six weeks after the king's acceptance of Catholicism in 1622.[196]

Rome consecrated the Spanish-born Alphonse Mendez as patriarch and sent him to Ethiopia along with eighteen priests and two bishops, one of whom died on the way. Mendez was everything that Paez was not. He "lacked all the qualities of tact and tolerance which Paez had so amply possessed. He treated Ethiopians as infidels rather than Christians . . ."[197] He was so zealous to enforce the Roman Catholic church's ways of doing things that upon his arrival the emperor decreed the Ethiopian church subject to Rome.

---

190. Aregay, "Legacy of Jesuit Missionary," 45.

191. Aba Gorgorios thinks of him as shrewd. Gorgorios, የኢትዮጵያ ኦርቶዶክስ ተዋህዶ ቤት ክርስቲያን ታሪክ፣ 51. Hastings notes that Paez was enslaved for six years during his first attempt to enter Ethiopia and when he was freed he came. He belongs to a generation of top universitymen who volunteered for missionary work in the Society of Jesus. Hastings, *Church in Africa*, 148.

192. Edward Ullendorff, *The Ethiopians: An Introduction to Country and People* (London: Oxford University Press, 1965), 6.

193. Hastings writes that Paez was alarmed by the Emperor's quick announcement of allegiance to Rome and recommended caution but it was disregarded. Ze Dengel's unwise issue of "upgrading Sunday and downgrading Saturday" resulted in his excommunication and eventually a rebellion in which he was killed. Hastings, *Church in Africa*, 149.

194. The Emperor wrote a letter under the pretence of asking for arms to Don Filipos, the Emperor of Spain and Portugal and to Paul IV, the Pope of Rome. However, it is suspected that he might have stated his acceptance of the Catholic dogma. Gorgorios, የኢትዮጵያ ኦርቶዶክስ ተዋህዶ ቤት ክርስቲያን ታሪክ፣ 51.

195. Gorgorios argues that the decision of the emperor was motivated by Paez's assurance that if he accepted Catholicity the Portuguese would give him many rifles. Gorgorios, የኢትዮጵያ ኦርቶዶክስ ተዋህዶ ቤት ክርስቲያን ታሪክ, 51.

196. Hastings, *Church in Africa*, 152–153.

197. Ullendorff, *The Ethiopians*, 7.

Among many other changes, Mendez[198] required all who were baptized under the EOC order to be re-baptized in the Roman Catholic order, the clergy to be re-ordained, and abandonment of circumcision.[199]

Such an attempt resulted in a major religious war between Orthodox and Roman Catholic followers.[200] In the 1617's uprising of peasants against Susinyos, the Egyptian patriarch at the time, Abune Semeon, declared that those who sided with Emperor Susinyos had changed the religion of their ancestors and excommunicated them. The conflict went on for about fifteen years. "When the king realized how serious the problem was, he again reinstated the Orthodox faith as the state religion and he himself resigned the throne."[201] He died soon after but the cause of his sudden death was not known. Ethiopian sources claim that he was stricken by God for shedding

---

198. Gorgorios refers to him as the "bloody man." Gorgorios, የኢትዮጵያ ኦርቶዶክስ ተዋህዶ ቤተ ክርስቲያን ታሪክ, 53.

199. Merid Wolde Aregay disputes the widely held opinion that Paez was tactful and tolerant. According to him, Paez is responsible for "complete Latinization of the beliefs and rites of Ethiopian Christians. . ." and Mendez is unduly criticized. Aregay, "Legacy of Jesuit Missionary," 44–50.

200. Upon his conversion, Susinyos attempted to enforce Latin Christianity upon the people. With the conversion of Si'ele Kristos, his younger maternal brother, however, public rebaptism started. The king presided as judge over debates between Si'ele Kristos and Orthodox clergy. He rewarded those who converted and flogged clergy who argued "with conviction and zeal." Most of the tenets of Orthodoxy were condemned one by one as heresies and practices which were depicted as Judaic (circumcision, observance of Saturday, food taboos, etc) were banned and the Chalcedonian formula was imposed. The Alexandrian ordination was revoked and clergy required to be re-ordained and re-baptized after the Latin order. Paez and Susinyos understood the peasant uprising of 1617 as incited by rivals to the throne. The Jesuits went to the extent of forcing people to eat Pork. Si'ele Kristos and his followers used excessive force to bring about the desired change of order but resistance was building throughout the kingdom. The Orthodox hermits responded by burning pictures and books distributed by the Jesuits. The hermits explained to the peasants that Latin Christianity sympathized with Nestorianism. They accused Catholics of denying that Mary is the mother of God "theotokos" but the mother of the human Jesus. This resulted with the Catholics being referred as *tsere Mariam* (enemies of Mary). Consequently, the peasant uprising spread across the kingdom and members of elite and heads of churches who were forced to give up their positions joined the revolt. The opponents organized themselves under a leader of Solomonic descent. The war that followed caused a lot of bloodshed that Susinyos abdicated his throne for his son Fasiledes in June 1632 and soon after died. Aregay, "Legacy of Jesuit Missionary," 44–56.

201. Sergew Hable Sellassie, "Religious Life in Ethiopia," 18.

the blood of Christians.[202] His son Fasiledes[203] came to power and expelled the Jesuits. Ethiopian Catholics were killed and imprisoned.

In a dramatic turn of events, the Portuguese, whose help was much sought for and who had been celebrated "as saviours of the country and its Christian religion," were now considered "a source of danger to its independence."[204] However, they had achieved several things: helped the country gain its independence from Islamic insurgence, expanded education and provided information about the country by exploring it extensively. "Yet the damage was almost equally great: by religious intolerance and narrow-mindedness, . . . they implanted in the people a deep-seated suspicion of Europeans, . . . and threw them back into an isolation and aloofness which lasted for centuries."[205]

The attitude of Catholic missionaries towards Ethiopian Christian tradition has also troubled the church's historians. Taddesse Tamrat observes that such an attitude was evident even in de Jacobis, the most respected Catholic missionary.[206] The fact that the Ethiopian Orthodox church never

---

202. After seven years of civil war the emperor got seriously sick and could not talk. His son, Fasiledes presumed that God inflicted his father because he shed the blood of Christians. He then quickly sent for prominent clergy in the EOC assuring them that he would do all necessary to appease the wrath of God. The EOC men came to his aid. After fasting and praying for three days they sprinkled the "apostate" emperor with holy water and he was able to speak. He immediately asked his son to take over the kingdom, reinstate the Alexandrian faith and renounce the Roman Catholic faith. The decree enabled the EOC's clergy to come out of hiding and the "apostates" were allowed to repent and rejoin the Church. Soon after, Susinyos died and his son took over. The people were all the more happy with the news of the death of the "apostate" Emperor. Gorgorios, የኢትዮጵያ ኦርቶዶክስ ተዋሀዶ ቤተ ክርስቲያን ታሪክ, 51–52. Hastings does not write anything about the bloody war. Hastings, *Church in Africa*, 154ff.

203. On another account Fasiledes is recorded as having such a high regard for Peter Heyling, a Lutheran missionary that he raised him to the office of special advisor but sent him away from Gondar later on because of the opposition he faced from the clergy of the EOC. Johannes Launhardt, *Evangelicals in Addis Ababa 1919 – 1991* (London: Münster LIT, 2004), 22–23.

204. Aregay, "Legacy of Jesuit Missionary," 42–43.

205. Ullendorff, *The Ethiopians*, 7.

206. When he got hold of an ancient manuscript that had an apparent quotation from the Nicene Creed about the procession of the Holy Spirit from the Father, de Jacobis did not hesitate to take out his pen and add *and the Son*. Taddesse remarked that such an act comes from the inner conviction of Catholic missionaries that the Ethiopian church was "the lost sheep" and that it needed to return to its mother, the Roman Catholic Church. Taddesse Tamrat, "Evangelizing the Evangelized: The Root Problem between Missions and the Ethiopian Orthodox Church," in *The Missionary Factor in Ethiopia*, ed. Getatchew Haile, et al. (Frankfurt: Peter Lang, 1998), 26–28.

associated itself with Rome and saw little or no connection with it but with Alexandria did not matter.

In all this, it was as if the Ethiopian Africans themselves did not count. They were mere recipients of whatever faiths were transmitted to them from Egypt or Rome! The protest of the Ethiopians, and the explanations of their ecclesiastical historians regarding their continuous links with Alexandria from the very beginning, were completely disregarded as ignorant assertions. Essentially, it is this basic lack of meaningful dialogue and the generally arrogant attitude towards local Ethiopian scholarship and traditional learning that will continue to limit the impact of the missionary on the wider body-politic of the Ethiopian Church.[207]

However, the church of Ethiopia does not seem to be free from Roman Catholic influence in her Mariology. It is important to discover the origin of the Cult of Mary if we are to understand the current ever growing trends of exalting Mary as "Co-redeemer" There has been a growing question of whether the Ethiopian Orthodox church's heavy attachment to Mary was influenced by Latin Christianity.

Roman Catholic influence was exerted perhaps in the time of Zer'a Ya'iqob's fear of an Islamic invasion, and also the connection of some EOC monks with the church in Rome.[208] It was noted that Zer'a Ya'iqob preferred the Roman style of paintings of Mary and Jesus which portrayed Mary holding Jesus with her left arm, to the Ethiopian traditional painting which portrays Mary holding Jesus in her right arm.[209] However, there still is a difference between the Mariology of the Roman Catholic Church and that of the EOC. The EOC maintains that Mary was born from human parents, but the Catholics call her "አርያማዊት' "*Areyamawit*," heavenly, as though she had heavenly flesh.[210]

---

207. Taddesse Tamrat, "Evangelizing the Evangelized," 28. Paez is also accused of collecting as many non-chalcedonian creeds as he could find and having them corrected or replaced.

208. James Bruce, *Travels to Discover the Source of the Nile, in the Years 1768–1773* (Edinburgh: George Ramsey & Co., 1813), 117–118.

209. Afework, "Survey of the Ethiopian," 83; Bruce, *Travels*, 117–118; Budge, *History of Ethiopia, Nubia and Abyssinia vol. 1*, 304; Budge, *Legends of Our Lady*, xliii–xlv.

210. Mekonnen, Interview, 15 November 2010.

Moreover, the seventeenth-century attempt of the Jesuits to Latinize the EOC may have further strengthened the Roman Catholic footmarks on the Mariology of the Orthodox Church thereby further reinforcing the legacy of Zer'a Ya'iqob. Thus, the shape of Mariology got stronger and stronger over the years to the extent of exalting her as "saviour of the world" "ቤዛዊት ዓለም" (or "ቤዛዊተ-ኩሉ" [saviour of all]). Daniel Mekonnen, teacher of theology at Holy Trinity Theological College, strongly argues that these titles are to be looked at in the context of her motherhood of Jesus.[211]

The Orthodox Church's Council of Scholars denies any influence from Catholicism in any of the teaching, culture or traditions of the church. According to them the church does not equate Mary to the creator. Rather, the honour attributed to her is in accordance with the teaching of the Bible regarding Mary and Zion.[212] However, the fact that such teachings created disagreement between the leaders of the EOC indicates that the implications had to do with more than her motherhood. Moreover, the emphasis on Mary, even more than Christ, is to be accounted for.

Ethiopia's interaction with Latin Christianity appears to have left its mark on the tradition of the church, especially that of Mary. Whether it was mediated through Zer'a Ya'iqob or the Catholic missionaries, the exalted status of Mary inclined more to Catholicism than Orthodoxy elsewhere. Moreover, the civil war which was caused by the harsh measures taken by the Jesuits and their Ethiopian counterparts' attempts to Latinize the nation, have left a permanent scar on the Ethiopian Orthodox Church which had led to suspicion and scepticism towards foreign missionaries. This has discouraged the church from interacting with other Christian traditions in a meaningful and brotherly manner. After its bitter encounter with the Jesuits, the country closed its doors against foreigners.

---

211. Daniel, Interview, 8 September 2010.

212. ዑቁ ኢያስሕቴክሙ እንዳያስቷችሁ ተጠንቀቁ, መናፍቁ ጌታቸው "ገድል ወይስ ገደል" በማለት ለጻፈው የኩደት ትምህርት ከኢትዮጵያ ኦርቶዶክስ ተዋሕዶ ቤተ ክርስቲያን ሊቃውንት ጉባዔ የተሰጠ መልስ (Beware lest you will be led astray: A reply from the Council of Scholars of the Ethiopian Orthodox Tewahdo Church to apostasy writing of the *menafiq*), Getachew, "Gedil Weys Gedel" (Addis Ababa: Tinsae Zegubae Printing Press, 1996 Eth. C), 10.

When Europe's interest towards Ethiopia was renewed,[213] Ethiopians too were eager to get acquainted with the technology of the time and to interact with the world. However, they maintained reservations. The coming of Europeans, therefore, was met with both caution and eagerness.[214]

2.2.7. The Nineteenth-Century Revival of Ethiopia – Including New European Interest

There was a renewed European interest in Ethiopia in the nineteenth century because of four interrelated reasons which Bahru Zewde identifies as: "the commercial, the official, the missionary and the scientific."[215] The Church Missionary Society was the first to make an organized encounter with the church of Ethiopia. Its missionaries Christian Kugler and Samuel Gobat, arrived in Ethiopia in 1829 with an aim of revitalizing the ancient church with the reading of the vernacular Bible so that it might reach the Muslims all around it.

Amharic Scriptures

Bible translation, literacy and the use of Amharic have played a major role in the expansion of Christianity in Ethiopia. Ever since the translation of the Bible into Ge'ez, the vernacular of the fifth century, vernacular Scriptures have been a significant factor in expanding Christianity. They also provided clergy members and monks with moral values with which to instruct the people. In the Orthodox Church's traditional schools, portions of the Scriptures in Ge'ez played a vital role as instruments of education. For example in the first stage of the traditional school which is the school of reading ንባብ ቤት (*Nibab Bet*), New Testament books were used to teach students to read. These books include the Gospel of John, selected epistles of John, Paul, James and Peter, and the book of Acts.[216] The impact of such passages on the reader perhaps was limited because Ge'ez ceased to be the language of communication and was limited to the service of the church.

---

213. C. E. Bosworth, "Henry Salt, Consul in Egypt 1816–1827 and Pioneer Egyptologist," in *Bulletin of the John Rylands Library* 57 (1974): 73–76.
214. Bahru Zewde, *History of Modern Ethiopia*, 24.
215. Bahru Zewde, 25.
216. Sergew et al., *Church of Ethiopia*, 81–88.

Since Peter Heyling's effort[217] in the seventeenth century to translate part of the New Testament into Amharic, missionaries have highlighted the key role of vernacular translation to reform the church and evangelize pagans.[218] The first Amharic translation of the New Testament did not appear until 1824. The translation of the whole Bible which was done by Aba Abraham, a monk from Gojjam, (northern Ethiopia)[219] was purchased and handed to the British and Foreign Bible Society by William Jowett, the literary representative of the Church Missionary Society in Malta. "After due examination

---

217. Heyling was a physician, lawyer and gifted linguist who was influenced by the famous historian and theologian Hugo Grotius to become a missionary with an aim to "rejuvenate the ancient Churches of the Orient and infuse them with new evangelical life." He travelled to Egypt in 1633 and after spending a year in the desert monastery of Makarios, accompanied Abune Markos to Ethiopia. Markos was deeply impressed by Heyling and introduced him to emperor Fasil upon their arrival. The emperor too was so won by Heyling's personality and learning that he ordered him to stay in his court and soon after appointed him as his special advisor. The king even gave him his close relative in marriage. With a deeper conviction that study of the Scripture "would engender spiritual life" Heyling engaged in translating the Bible into the common language, Amharic. His translation of the Gospel of John was published and there was a greater demand for it. In 1652 Heyling left Ethiopia and was beheaded by a Turkish pasha at the coast who demanded him to convert to Islam. There are opposing views on his status as missionary and the reasons for his departure. Aren writes that Heyling went for a vacation and disputes the conclusion that he was expelled because of engaging in christological controversy. Launhardt, a Lutheran missionary to Ethiopia, however, supports the Catholic sources. Launhardt, *Evangelicals in Addis Ababa*, 22–24; Hasting, *Church in Africa*, 163; Aren, *Evangelical Pioneers*, 35–36. Donald Crummy argues that Heyling did not have any impact on the Ethiopian church so he should not be called a missionary. Donald Crummey, *Priests and Politicians: Protestant and Catholic Missions in Orthodox Ethiopia* (Oxford: Clarendon, 1972), 10. Aren, however, calls him a missionary and argues that Heyling's teaching inspired scholars in the EOC and caused priests and *debtera* to turn away from "the traditional legends of the saints." Aren, *Evangelical Pioneers*, 409.

218. A case in point is the vision of Church Missionary Society which aimed to revitalize the Orthodox Church through vernacular Scriptures and equip it reach the "heathen" all around it. For full discussion see chapter 4.

219. He is also referred to as Abu Rumi, Abu Ruhh, or Abu Rukh. Aren, *Evangelical Pioneers*, fn. 71, 43. Aba Abraham made a pilgrimage to Jerusalem and from there to Egypt, Syria, Armenia, Persia and even India before he went back to Ethiopia. Aba Abraham met Asselin de Cherville, the French vice-consul in Cairo, on his second visit to Egypt while he was seriously ill. Asselin "snatched [Abraham]from the arms of death" and befriended him. When Asselin discovered that Aba Abraham was not only a linguist but "a true scholar and master of Ethiopian literature" he set him to translate the entire Bible into Amharic. "For ten years the two men spent every Tuesday and Saturday at their task, translating the sacred text verse by verse with great care. Asselin assisted his friend by explaining difficult words and phrases with the aid of "the Hebrew original, the Syriac version, or the Septuagint as well as a few glossaries and commentaries" unless Abraham himself could find the explanation in Ge'ez." Aren, *Evangelical Pioneers*, 42–43.

by language experts in Great Britain the Gospels were published in 1824," the New Testament in 1829 and the whole Bible in 1840.[220]

Aba Abraham's translation which is usually referred to as "Abu Rumi's Bible" was highly welcomed by the church when it was distributed by the CMS missionaries as will be discussed in detail in chapter 4. "Yet the Bible remained virtually unknown to most of Ethiopian society, intriguingly so in the highland regions of Ethiopia, considered to be bastion of Christianity."[221] This enabled traditional writings to assume higher status and resulted in a general decline of morality. Members of the Church of England desired to help a sister church of Ethiopia. They believed that the vitality of the church of Ethiopia would be restored and the church would reach the "heathen" all around it if the Scriptures in vernacular were available. With such a strong conviction, they sent missionaries.

Anglicans

Three missionaries of the Church Missionary Society Samuel Gobat, Christian Kugler and the carpenter Aichinger arrived in the country in 1829. The prevailing attitude of the EOC clergy was one of suspicion regarding the intentions of the CMS missionaries. The missionaries in turn were frustrated by the lack of Scripture knowledge and what they saw as rampant superstition among the clergy and the people at large. It was their hope to renew the church through the distribution of the Ge'ez and Amharic translations of the Bible.

The rulers on the other hand showed great interest in the coming of the missionaries hoping to use them as channels to connect with Europe. Especially in the person of Sabagadis, the governor of Tigray who received them warmly in 1830, the missionaries found genuine affection and a deep desire for his people to learn new things, but he examined them on the very day of their arrival at his court with regard to the nature of Christ. Once he had ascertained that they held to the two births of Christ and not three, their friendship was sealed. The CMS missionaries distributed numerous copies of the Scripture and tried their best to engage the clergy in theological discussions. The change they desired to see did not materialize because

---

220. Aren, *Evangelical Pioneers*, 42–44.
221. Eshete, *Evangelical Movement*, 126.

the country was plunged into civil war upon the execution of Sabagadis by the "Galla" in 1831.

Later missionaries Carl Wilhelm Isenberg and Johann Ludwig Krapf who arrived in the country in 1835 and 1837 respectively, appeared to show little respect for the indigenous Christianity and as a result did not enjoy the same love and acceptance as their predecessors. Krapf was able to stay in Shewa from 1839–1841 and was able to instruct a number of young boys. However, the missionaries' attitude of disrespect put the clergy on high alert and their fierce opposition led by Aleqa Kidane Mariam of Adwa resulted in the expulsion of the missionaries in 1843.

The desired revitalization of the Ethiopian church in order to give rise to an Orthodox mission to non-Christians thus appeared to come to nothing. The impulses to reform which arose out of the reading of Scriptures in various places faced strong opposition from the leading clergy who believed the reform would alter the cherished tradition of the church. The end result was a gradual but steady exodus of people Aren refers to as, "the would-be reformers"[222] from the church to form an independent Evangelical church as will be shown below. The massive distribution of Abu Rumi's Amharic Bible, however, was successful in giving rise to an Evangelical movement among the Felasha (the Ethiopian Jews).[223]

During the time of the ministry of the CMS missionaries, the emperor in Gondar, the imperial capital established by Fasiledes, was weak and the church was not united. The missionaries therefore relied on regional lords to protect them. The fear that mission involvement would result in alteration of the ancient faith was evident. However, because the CMS worked when the country was relatively smaller, they did not have to deal with complex ethnic and language issues which came with the integration of the South[224] with greater Ethiopia.

---

222. Aren, *Evangelical Pioneers*, 123.

223. Aren, 123.

224. South is used in reference to the peripheral people groups who live in the Southern part of the country who after significant resistance were integrated into Ethiopia by Menelik II.

2.2.8. The Nineteenth-Century Expansion of the Monarchy and the Integration of the South

The Era of the Princes came to a close when Kassa, head of bandits from Quara in Gondar fought his way to defeating all of the princes with the purpose of uniting the country. He was of a noble background but when denied legitimate access to power he turned into a rebel. Kassa controlled Quara with military power and won the love of the people with his simplicity and concern for social justice. He even distributed to the peasants what he acquired through robbery. Alarmed at his growing prominence, Ras Ali, a prominent prince of Yejju, gave Kassa his daughter in marriage, but Kassa refused to submit. In a series of battles, he defeated major regional princes one after the other, bringing the long era of the princes to a close. In 1856 he was crowned king of kings by Abune Selama with a crown name Tewodros II (1855–1868).[225]

During the coming to power of Tewodros, the church was divided along doctrinal lines. Abune Selama thus gave his blessings to Tewodros under the condition that the king would enforce "*Tewahdo*" doctrine. Tewodros introduced some reforms in the country including establishing a national army and replacing the system of billeting with payment of salaries. His desire to display absolute power over the clergy brought him into head on collision with them. He felt that the church held excessive land and took part of it and distributed it among tribute paying peasants.[226]

Tewodros was so painfully aware of his country's backwardness and the danger of the Egyptian presence at the coast that he sought the assistance of European Christian nations, especially that of Britain. He was openly affectionate towards the British perhaps because of his relationship with two Protestant British gentlemen: the traveller John Bell and the first British consul Walter Plowden. Tewodros was even accused of abandoning the Orthodox faith because of his close association with the pilgrim missionaries.[227] The missionaries were skilled people sent after the failure of CMS as

---

225. Bahru Zewde, *History of Modern Ethiopia*, 27–30.

226. Bahru Zewde, 35.

227. Donald Crummey, "The Politics of Modernization: Protestant and Catholic Missionaries in Modern Ethiopia," in *The Missionary Factor in Ethiopia*, eds. Getatchew Haile et al. (Frankfurt: Peter Lang, 1998), 98.

will be discussed in chapter 4. Tewodros's favourable attitude towards the missionaries, however, was motivated by his deep desire for the introduction of European technology to Ethiopia.

Tewodros looked up to Christian Britain as a natural ally to Christian Ethiopia and must have been shocked by the news that Christian Britain and France sided with the Muslim Turkey against the Orthodox Russia.[228] European countries, however, seemed to pay attention to countries which provided them with opportunities for trade and investment regardless of their religious convictions.

When his request for assistance was ignored by Britain, Tewodros was so exasperated that he imprisoned the British consul along with European missionaries. At the time of their imprisonment he was also faced with mounting rebellion nationwide so that Britain's military expedition to free the Europeans was fully supported by internal enemies of Tewodros, Kassa Mercha of Tigray being the chief. Unwilling to be humiliated by the British force, Tewodros committed suicide in 1868.

The British army, however, withdrew upon freeing European prisoners because Britain had no interest in Ethiopia. Kassa was rewarded with modern arms for his assistance and with it he was able to defeat strong aspirants to the throne and emerge as the next king with the crown name Yohannes IV (1872–1889). Unlike Tewodros, he allowed regional autonomy but demanded recognition as the emperor. Rebels were subjugated but those who were aware of his power including the future Menelik II then ruling in Shewa, submitted to him.

However, Yohannes's tolerance was limited to the political sphere and did not extend to religion. He was intolerant towards paganism, Islam and other Christian traditions and sought to unite the whole country under OrthodoxChristianity. Consequently he expelled missionaries, banned the reading of the vernacular Scriptures[229] and denounced any attempt at ecclesiastical reform as a "Western heresy."[230] He sought to restore the unity of the

---

228. Bahru Zewde, *History of Modern Ethiopia*, 36.

229. The Bible readers in the EOC were accused of abandoning the tradition of the church by some of the clergy who appealed to Yohannes. Although Yohannes initially refused to respond to the allegations, he relented after some time. Aren, *Evangelical Pioneers*, 179.

230. Aren, *Evangelical Pioneers*, 183.

church and called a Council at Boru Meda. He then declared the *Tewahdo* doctrine as the binding one and required others to conform to it. Those who refused were persecuted.[231] Yohannes's policies were meant to imply that the Orthodox *Tewahdo* marked Ethiopian identity: one nation – one faith. Towards this end, for the first time in the history of the country, he managed to bring four bishops from Egypt.

As for his relationship with European countries, Yohannes requested British military advisors, but his request was turned down with a note that Britain was not interested. Just like Tewodros, Yohannes hoped to get help from Christian Britain to protect Christian Ethiopia from Egyptian attack. "Baffling as their reactions must have appeared to Yohannes, the European powers did not find the theme of Christian solidarity very convincing. To them, Muslim though it was, Egypt offered more opportunities for trade and investment than Ethiopia did, for in economic terms Ethiopia was a relatively unknown quantity."[232]

Although the help he hoped for did not come from Europe, Yohannes managed to decisively defeat the Egyptian forces twice. The British intervention which he had sought for so long finally came when their interest was at stake with the rising of Mahdists in Sudan against Egypt. Unfortunately, the treaty mediated by Britain which benefited Egypt and bound Yohannes to facilitate the movement of its troops turned the Mahdists against him. The result was successive bloody battles with Mahdists which claimed his life.[233]

Menelik II (1889–1913), succeeded Yohannes. His reign coincided with the European scramble for Africa and he is portrayed as having a scramble of his own. In the footsteps of his ancestors, Menelik had been making steady expansion south and southeast toward Shewa before his crowning as king of

---

231. Bahru Zewde, *History of Modern Ethiopia*, 48.

232. Bahru Zewde, 51.

233. The rising of Mahadists in Sudan who emerged out of revivalism of Islam and were strongly against Egyptian upper hand in Sudan, caused Britain to mediate a peace treaty between Egypt and Ethiopia. Accordingly the Hewett (Adwa) Peace Treaty was signed on 3 June 1884 between Egypt and Ethiopia facilitated by the British negotiator Rear Admiral Sir William Hewett. Among other things, the treaty stated that Egypt was to facilitate the coming of bishops for Ethiopia whereas Ethiopia was to facilitate the evacuation of Egyptian troops from Sudan. It also stated that Massawa was to remain under British Protection. Although Yohannes faithfully carried out his obligation of the treaty, which eventually turned Mahadists against him, Britain breached the treaty and handed over Massawa to Italy. Bahru Zewde, *History of Modern Ethiopia*, 54–59.

kings. His expansion even surpassed territories formerly conquered by Amde Tsion. He subjugated the Oromo ("Galla") all around Shewa and moved to the Gurage people groups, Arsi (southeast) and from there to Harar in the eastern part of the country. He also subjugated powerful dynasties such as Wolaitta and Kaffa and with the collapse of Mahadist upper hand in the region, Menelik expanded westward in 1897.[234]

Unlike his predecessors, Menelik refrained from forcibly converting Muslims, and tolerated reform impulses in the church. Neither did he take away power from traditional kings/chiefs. Once he seized a territory, he restored the former chief/king with a demand to pay an annual tribute to the central government. Apart from that he did not interfere in internal matters, unless there were complaints of injustice. He was affectionately called "Emiye Menelik" literally "motherly Menelik" to indicate his kindness towards his people. However, he fought bloody battles while expanding his territories, and his army ruthlessly crushed civilians in the process. It is even accused of ripping open pregnant women. Among the people groups conquered by Menelik, therefore, there was a deep resentment towards him.[235]

Menelik is credited with abolishing slavery from his kingdom and introducing modernization and technology such as electricity, indigenous currency, hotels, banks, running water (tap water), and a postal system.[236] He broke the superstitious fear of technological products such as the telephone and automobiles by publicly using them.[237] Despite fierce opposition from the clergy, Menelik opened a modern school.[238] As a way of dealing with

---

234. Zewde, *History of Modern Ethiopia*, 60–68.

235. Mekuria Bulcha, *The Making of the Oromo Diaspora: A Historical Sociology of Forced Migration* (Minneapolis, MN: Kirk House, 2002), 51–85.

236. Menelik declared war against Aba Jifar, the king of Kaffa and subdued him because he refused to stop slave trading. He wrote to him, "There is no such thing as a human slave. All of us are God's slaves." "የሰው ባርያ የለውም፡፡ ሁላችንም የአግዚአብሔር ባርያዎች ነን፡፡" There is a famous saying attributed to him "It is forbidden to sell a human being even 'Galla.'" (By "Galla," he was referring to pagans because it was already prohibited to enslave or sell a fellow Christian.) Paulos, *Ate Menelik*, 32–33, 242–384.

237. Paulos, *Ate Menelik*, 259. He also started a printing press and a newspaper. When he was given a typewriter as a present by an American man, he marvelled at it and asked why not an Amharic one as well? Then ordered for an Amharic typewriter to be made. Paulos, *Ate Menelik*, 326, 336. He even took off his royal cloak and tried to ride the first ever bicycle in Ethiopia and remarked, "I don't get it. If it does not give rest to the feet, what is the benefit of it?" "ያለገሰኝ ነገር እግር ከመወዘወዝ ካላረፈ ደካሙ ምን ቀረለት," Paulos, *Ate Menelik*, 355.

238. Pankhurst, "Foundations of Education," 252.

the concern of the clergy that with the opening of modern schools foreign teachers would come and obliterate the ancient faith, Menelik recruited Egyptian teachers.[239]

When Italy declared war against Ethiopia Menelik immediately wrote to the European nations. "Quoting from the Bible, he concluded: 'Ethiopia stretches her hands to God.'" When he learned that war was inevitable Menelik knew how to mobilize Ethiopians to join the battle to defend their country.

> An enemy trespassed our God-given Sea border and has now come upon us to ruin our country and change our faith. By the help of God, I will not hand over my country to [it]. If you are physically fit, join me but if you are weak, help me by sympathizing with me for *the* sake of your child, wife and faith. If you fail to join me out of laziness, as Mary lives, I will not spare you. No intercession will stop me from dealing with you.[240]

The victory of Ethiopians over Italy in 1896 marked an important date in African history both politically and religiously as a black Christian nation had managed to withstand European invasion. In spite of continued problems of all sorts and the loss of some northern territory, Menelik established a coherent Christian state whose sovereignty was recognized even by Europeans.[241]

2.2.9. Haile Sellassie (1930–1974) and the Italian War and Recovery

Menelik named his grandson, Iyassu (1913–1916), as his successor. Iyassu, a son of king Michael, an ex-Muslim, was not repulsed by Islam like the other monarchs. He therefore, took radical measures to bring Christianity

---

239. Paulos, *Ate Menelik*, 242–244. Menelik also had foreigners working for him in different capacities. Richard Pankhurst, "Menelik and the Utilization of Foreign Skills in Ethiopia," *Journal of Ethiopian Studies* 1 (January 1967): 29–86.

240. Translation by the researcher. "አሁንም አገር የሚያጠፋ፣ ሃይማኖት የሚለውጥ ጠላት፣ እግዚአብሔር የወሰነልንን የባሕር ቦር አልፎ መጥቷልና . . . በእግዚአብሔር ረዳትነት አገሬን አሳልፌ አልሰጠውም፡፡ ያገሬ ሰው፣ . . . ጉልበት ያለህ በጉልበትህ እርዳኝ፡፡ ጉልበት የሌለህ ለልጅህ፣ ለምሽትህ፣ ለሃይማኖትህ ስትል በሀዘን እርዳኝ፡ ፡ ወስለትህ የቀረህ ግን ኋላ ትጣላኛለህ፡፡ አለተውህም፡፡ ማርያምን ለሁ አማላጅ የለኝም፡፡" Paulos Gnogno, *Ate Menelik*, 159.

241. Hastings, *Church in Africa*, 236–237.

and Islam together. He married a number of daughters of both Muslim and Christian chiefs. He built churches and mosques alike. His actions were considered to be an abomination against the Christian state and brought about his deposition.[242]

Zawditu (1916–1928), the daughter of Menelik, was crowned as Queen and Tafari Mekonnen regent. Tafari took the reins of administration into his hands though he did not hide his actions from her.[243] He grew more and more powerful. Zawditu's short-lived reign is significant in the history of the Church because the repeated request of the Ethiopian church for an Ethiopian bishop was finally answered. On 21 May 1921 four Ethiopian bishops were consecrated by Yohannes XIX at St Mark's Cathedral and when he visited Ethiopia a year later, he consecrated one more bishop, increasing the number of Ethiopian bishops to five; but the archbishop was still Egyptian.[244] In 1930, Zewditu died of an illness and Tafari was crowned as Haile Sellassie I that same year. Haile Sellassie I, the last emperor of the "Solomonic Dynasty," continued in the footsteps of his predecessors in his attempts to reform the country. Despite strong opposition from the established Church, Haile Sellassie I successfully took up Menelik's legacy of thirst for Western technology and promoting tolerance of people of other faiths.

Educated under French Catholics, he was more open to missionaries. The emperor assumed many responsibilities as patron of different organizations, such as the Ministry of Education, the Empress Zewditu Hospital (which was established by Seventh Day Adventists), and even the renewal movement Haymanote Abew (literally the faith of the fathers), in order to guarantee that institutions/groups would remain under his wing. Haymanote Abew, was established in 1958 by university students with a concern that the teaching of the church ought to be made relevant to the educated and dynamic generation.[245]

---

242. Zewde, *History of Modern Ethiopia*, 120–128.

243. He was the great grandson of King Sahle Sellassie of Shewa, the grandfather of Menelik. Thus both Zewditu and Tafari were great grandchildren of king Sahle Sellassie. Zewde, 128–129.

244. Sergew et al., *Church of Ethiopia Past and Present*, 15–16.

245. Eshete, *Evangelical Movement*, 57–58; Melaku Baweke, ስውር አደጋ (The subtle danger) (Los Angeles: n.p., 2005), 135.

Where the church was opposed to modern education, Haile Sellassie named schools after himself to protect and promote them. He was also painfully aware of the inadequate training of the clergy. He desired that the clergy be well trained in the traditional church education and "exposed to modern religious thought and foreign languages."[246]

Towards this end, he established the Holy Trinity Theological College, which was inaugurated in 1960 with H. G. Bishop Trenig Poladian of the Armenian Church as Dean. With the inauguration of the Haile Sellassie I University in December 1961, the theological college was incorporated as one of the charter units of the university and the University assumed its administration.[247] Haile Sellassie did not refrain from supporting schools out of his personal funds. He even donated five thousand Maria Theresa thalers to a Jewish school, which educated Felasha of Ethiopia in Addis, and they were able to purchase land.[248]

The emperor was eager to have at least an elementary school in every town and village. However, his Ministry of Education could not begin to cope with the great demand. Although the remote communities did not awaken to the need for a school, others petitioned the Ministry of Education. The missionaries came to the scene because the government was not able to meet the need for schools and teachers.[249] The coming of Protestant mission organizations will be discussed in chapter 3. Haile Sellassie allowed missions to operate in the country not because he did not have strong Orthodox convictions, but simply because of his strong desire to spread education in the whole country. In addition, he desired the Christianization of southern peoples who had proved largely unresponsive to Orthodox Christianity.

The emperor also encouraged gifted individuals to continue in their work regardless of the church's sentiments against them. For example, when he came across Aleqa Meseret Sebhat Leab's book entitled *Seme'a Tsidq Beherawi*, he summoned him. When he found out that Aleqa had been expelled from

---

246. Calvin Earl Shenk, "The Development of the Ethiopian Orthodox Church and Its Relationship with the Ethiopian Government from 1930–1970" (PhD thesis, New York University, 1972), 241.

247. K. C. Joseph, "Theological College of the Holy Trinity," *The Ethiopian Herald* (5 May 1966): 20, 30.

248. Launhardt, *Evangelicals in Addis Ababa*, 21.

249. Hege, *Beyond Our Prayers*, 67–68.

the church because he taught the Bible, he expressed his disappointment and after hearing how he prepared the book, he asked him, "What do you wish us to do for you?" Aleqa Meseret was asked to choose between working at the special office of the emperor or the Ministry of Education and he chose the latter.[250]

Beside literacy, Haile Sellassie also took a personal interest in the translation and distribution of the Amharic Bible because he believed that people should have an informed basis for their faith.[251] To this end, he brought together a team of eighteen scholars; (twelve Ethiopians and six expatriates) to translate the Bible into Amharic in the 1930s. The work of translation, which was interrupted during Italy's conquest, was completed in 1962. The Bible was sold at a very cheap price and even given freely to ensure its wide distribution.[252] The former requirement of special permission from the patriarch to sell Amharic Scriptures was abandoned when Haile Sellassie encouraged the Bible Society to open an office in Ethiopia and personally attended its opening ceremony. This opened the way for a large number of Scriptures to be available to the public.[253]

However, the availability of the Scriptures in Amharic did not ensure its wider usage, primarily because the church did not make use of it "as a basis of its teachings and as an effective tool to transmit the gospel to the Ethiopian people at large."[254] The general feeling of the priests was that the Bible was a sacred tradition which should not be left for the common people to interpret and apply for themselves. If revealed to the public it would "grow profane."[255] Such an attitude recalls the feeling of Muslims towards the Qur'an and makes one wonder if it is derived from the long Islamic presence among the Orthodox. In the Orthodox evangelistic endeavours, baptism into the church has been given prominence over the teaching and preaching of the Bible. In other words, baptism is synonymous with conversion

---

250. Interview, "ከአለቃ መሠረት ስብሐት ለአብ ጋር በየጊዜው ተደርጎ ከነበረው ቃለ ምልልስ የተወሰደ" (Taken from interview held with Aleqa Meseret Sibhat Leab over a period of time), 14–16.

251. Hege, *Beyond Our Prayers*, 67.

252. Eshete, *Evangelical Movement*, 125–127.

253. Eshete, 127–128.

254. Eshete, 126.

255. Eshete, 127.

to Christianity and instruction from the Bible is not as emphasized in the way it is in the Evangelical tradition.[256]

The church flourished during Sellassie's reign, but Italy had not forgotten its humiliation at Adwa. It attacked Ethiopia in 1936 using modern weapons and chemical warfare. Italy conquered Ethiopia for five years and the emperor was exiled. The church played a significant role in the resistance movement.[257] The Protestant churches also resisted the occupation.[258] Ethiopian patriotic forces, with the help of the British army, defeated Italy in 1941, the emperor returned, and peace was restored in the land. When

---

256. There is a report of baptism of four hundred converts from Gumuz people grou Upon their baptism in the hands of Abune Barnabas, they were given crosses to wear over their neck. Cf. Berihun Tefera, "ከ400 የሚበልጡ የጉምዝ ብሔረሰብ አባላት ተጠመቁ" (More than 400 people from Gumuz Ethnic Group were baptized), www.eotc-mkidusan.org, accessed 25 February 2011. Evangelical churches too mark baptism as a very important event in the life of a believer. For instance, in his account of the establishment of the Kale Heywet Church, Peter Cotterell reports the baptism of several individuals and does not use the usual Evangelical terminology, "came to Christ" or "received Christ as his/her Saviour." However, baptism is preceded by rigorous instruction from the Bible and in many cases, an interview to ensure abandonment of habits such as drinking alcohol, as well. Peter Cotterell, *Born at Midnight* (Chicago: Moody Press, 1973), 97–98. Cf. Fargher, *Origin of New Churches*, 139–149.

257. One of the five Ethiopian bishops, Abune Petros, was executed by Italians and his monument stands in Addis Ababa. He directly took part in encouraging patriots on the battle field. Upon the defeat of the Ethiopian army, he joined the patriots who were fighting a guerrilla war against Italians came back to Addis later on. He was caught as the patriots were fighting in Addis Ababa and brought to Graziani who asked him to confess that he is subject to the king of Italy. Abune Petros replied, "my king is Jesus Christ and Ethiopia belongs to Ethiopians, not to fascists." Graziani got so angry that he ordered his execution. Just before he was executed, he looked around at the crowd gathered and said, "Do not listen to the fascists who call the patriots rebels. A rebel is the one who takes away a country which is not its own and sheds the blood of its citizens, burns churches, takes away people's land and property. Thus, Italy is the rebel, and not the patriots who are fighting for their country." Lule Melaku, የቤተ ክርስቲያን ታሪክ (Church history) (Addis Ababa: Tinsae Publishing, 1986 Eth. C), 136.

258. The Catholic clergy who accompanied the Italian fascists during the conquest of Ethiopia tried to impose Catholicism on Evangelicals. They took over their worship places and turned them into Roman Catholic Churches and asked the Evangelicals to join them by being rebaptized. The Evangelicals refused to join the Catholics and worshipped under trees and in private residences. Many were imprisoned and tortured because of their resistance to the imposition of Roman Catholicism. Evangelical faith was declared a heresy and banned, so the Evangelicals started to worship in secret. EOC priests took advantage of the situation by accusing the Evangelicals and having them imprisoned by the fascists. Gustav Aren, *Envoys of the Gospel* (Stockholm: EFS Forlaget, 1999), 510ff. Cf. Ali Wondiye, በመከራ ውስጥ ያለፈች ቤተ ክርስቲያን (The church out of tribulation) (Addis Ababa: The Ethiopian Kale Heywet Church Literature Department, 1998), 147; Dawit Garoma, "Evangelical Movements in Ethiopia," (unpublished MTh dissertation, Ethiopian Graduate School of Theology, Addis Ababa, 2007), 54.

a coup was attempted against Haile Sellassie in 1960, it did not succeed because, among many other factors, the church denounced it.

The emperor also desired to protect the interests of the church. Thus, he was very careful in his policies towards mission organizations – he decreed areas in which Islam and traditional religions were dominant open for mission work, but Orthodox-dominated areas such as Gojjam, Begemeder, northern Shewa, parts of Tigray and Wollo were declared closed except for limited philanthropic work.[259]

In the history of the country, the suspicious attitude towards both Protestants and Catholics made it difficult for Haile Sellassie to use them to bring about reforms in the country. One of the charges brought against him before his enthronement, was that he favoured Catholicism.[260] Such a charge could have seriously affected the support of the church for him. His later favour towards the Protestants, was also not appreciated by the church on the grounds that it might pose a threat to the existence of the ancient faith. Crummey notes that much of the old church made no distinction between the modernity represented by the West and the religion of Western people. The desire of the emperor to adopt modernity thus implied adopting European religion as well.[261]

In his speech on the occasion when the Alexandrian church granted autocephaly to the EOC in 1951, the emperor declared, "When we say religion, it is not restricted to the professed faith. In this connection no one should question the faith of others for no human being can be a judge of the ways of God."[262] The emperor maintained openness and his famous saying, "Religion is the affair of the individual and the nation the affair of all people" "ሃይማኖት የግል፣ ሀገር የጋራ" is quoted to this day.[263]

---

259. Negarit Gazetta, 3rd year, no. 12 (1944): 158–161.

260. Donald Crummey, "The Politics of Modernization: Protestant and Catholic Missionaries in Modern Ethiopia," in *The Missionary Factor in Ethiopia* (Frankfurt: Peter Lang, 1998), 99. Haile Sellassie was educated "under the guidance of" the Capuchin priest Father André Jarosseau (Aba Endriays). Bahru, *History of Modern Ethiopia*, 130.

261. Crummey, "Politics of Modernization," 98–99.

262. *The Ethiopian Herald*, 11 May 1971, 4.

263. Tormod Engelsviken, "Pentecostal Revival in Ethiopia" (Unpublished manuscript, Oslo, Norway, 1997), 154, fn. 5. Cf. Eshete, *Evangelical Movement*, 181.

Haile Sellassie's story, therefore, is very important for the reformation of the church and spread of Christianity throughout the kingdom. Unlike his predecessors, he did not encourage forced conversions, but was concerned about the smooth integration of southern peoples who resisted Orthodox Christianity. Pragmatic church reformer as he was, he came up with a new plan for the people groups of the south, who paid lip service to Orthodox faith. He allowed Protestant missionaries to work among them.

The success story of missionaries, therefore, is to be attributed to the measures taken by Haile Sellassie, amid great opposition from the established church. Moreover, he personally got involved in the process of Bible translation, the opening of modern theological colleges and protected the reform impulses among progressive Ethiopians. His efforts did not satisfy the youth, so that opposition to imperial rule arose throughout the country with a special intensity in the urban centres and among university students.

2.2.10. Revolution and the Derg

In 1974, Haile Sellassie was overthrown and a communist regime, the Derg, took over, bringing the centuries-old "Solomonic Dynasty" to a dramatic close. Many Ethiopians who felt oppressed both economically and spiritually under the imperial regime hoped for a better life at the dawn of the Derg, because it did not show its true colours for some time.

Those who had suffered under the feudal system which took their land and turned them into poor tenants were happy to hear the slogan "land for the tiller." In fact, such a change of system had been foretold by some of the prophets (Esa for example)[264] who got in trouble for their message and suffered at the hands of Haile Sellassie's officials. In addition, the initial rhetoric of the Derg, which appeared to ensure justice, equality and religious freedom, sounded biblical. Thus the Evangelicals, whose emergence will be discussed in chapter 3, were initially supportive of the political change and even openly praised God for the change of government.[265]

The Derg acted as a peacemaker in the beginning. It even made an effort to bring together Muslims and Christians. Its agenda toward uniting the two faiths was initiated by Libya, which hosted the first meeting towards unity

---

264. His story is discussed in chapter 4.
265. Eshete, *Evangelical Movement*, 212–213.

in 1976. Delegates from both faiths attended and the meeting reached a climax with one of the Muslim scholars reading from the Gospel of Matthew 25:31–46 and a Christian scholar "beautifully" crying out "Allah Akbar," to which the assembly are said to have responded with an emotional applause.[266] The Derg thus was not explicit about its anti-religious sentiments. In fact, in some areas Christians held prominent positions and actively supported the "Power to the masses" theme of the regime.[267] They were further assured that there would be religious freedom for all and that Socialism and religion could co-exist.[268]

The Derg wanted so much to win the support of religious bodies, that it organized a committee to look into the grievances of churches against its leadership and called the religious bodies to a consultation in which the Evangelical churches were well represented. Representatives of the Orthodox church, Ethiopian Catholic Church and Evangelical churches strongly expressed their opposition to an essay presented by an Ethiopian Orthodox theologian trained in Russia, arguing that Socialism was the fulfilment of the future promises of hope and prosperity in the Bible. The Derg, however, did not give up. It modified the agenda for unity and ordered the churches to register as members of a committee called በሀገር ጉዳይ ሃይማኖት አይለያየንም (In matters concerning the nation, religion will not divide us) and to nominate delegates for it. According to Getachew, the supposed alliance between religious bodies was part of a subtle plan to restrain the expansion of Christianity.[269]

Abune Theophilos, the patriarch at the time, tried his best to influence the communist cadres, especially regarding the land and houses for rent which were taken away from the church. He also tried to persuade the government to include articles in the new constitution guaranteeing that the rights of the Orthodox Church would be respected.[270] But he was deposed and replaced by a less educated monk from the South, Tekle Haymanot. The new regime

---

266. Getachew Belete, *Agonies*, 139.
267. Fargher, *Origins of New Churches*, 303.
268. Cumbers, *Living with the Red Terror*, 65.
269. Getachew Belete, እልህና ሃሌሉያ *(Agonies and Hallelujah)* (Addis Ababa: Kale Heywet Church Literature Department, 2000), 144–151.
270. Abune Paulos, *Brief Life History of His Holiness Patriarch Theophilos: Before and After His Visit to the Western Hemisphere* (Addis Ababa: 1987), 198.

allowed the church to operate, but systematically weakened it by reducing religious holidays, depriving the church of its influence in the educational system, replacing moral education with the secular philosophy of dialectical materialism and instructing its members not to attend church or participate in any religious festivals.[271]

Eshete notes, "Most of all, the nationalization of land in 1975 drastically undermined the economic base of the Church, for it was an institution with significant land holdings on which it also depended."[272] Showing its disregard for religious authority, the Derg imprisoned many clergyand in 1976, even the patriarch Abune Theophilos.[273] In 1978 the atheist philosophy of the Derg, copied from China, was openly declared but before that time Christianity was systematically condemned through the state-owned media, bringing the initial alleged honeymoon between Christianity and Socialism to a close.

The usual greeting and expression of good wishes, which was nearly impossible without invoking the name of God, was discouraged and substituted by a new kind of greeting and expression of best wishes devoid of the name of God. The Derg further changed the names of places and educational institutions that bore religious undertone. For example the "መስቀል አደባባይ"[274] (Cross Square) was renamed as "አብዮት አደባባይ" (Revolutionary Square). Accordingly, names of schools were changed. For example upon confiscation the SIM-owned Grace Christian Academy was renamed "የአብዮት ቅርስ" (Heritage of the Revolution).

The Derg declared the separation of the state from the church in its first draft constitution in 1974, and the church believed that the new constitution

---

271. The Derg members who for the most part had EOC background used to perform the baptism of their infants secretly, or would be absent from the ceremony under the pretence of work, or else pretending that they knew nothing about it as their wives performed it at home, all the while with their full knowledge. "There are even reports that some members of the Derg, including the former president, visited seers or wise men (*Awaqki*) and acted on their advice in making certain political decisions." Eshete, *Evangelical Movement*, 221.

272. Eshete, *Evangelical Movement*, 210–211.

273. Abune Paulos, *Brief History of His Holiness Patriarch Theophilos: Before and After His Visit to the Western Hemisphere* (Addis Ababa: 1987), 202.

274. This place which is in the heart of Addis Ababa city was used by the EOC to celebrate the founding of the true cross annually on 27 September. The Derg prohibited the EOC from using the "Mesqel Square" anymore and the EOC was forced to celebrate it elsewhere.

drafted by the government would undermine its uniqueness and give "leeway to other non-Ethiopian and non-African religions to have a firm foothold in the country."[275] The Derg did not listen to the church. In fact it corporately blamed it and the monarchical system for the backwardness of the country, and pointed its finger at the church as the source of the problems in the country. "The conservatism, traditionalism, fatalism and political quietism of the Ethiopian masses can be traced without difficulty to the dominating role of the Ethiopian Church in the various aspects of organised life."[276]

Such accusations were only the beginning of more trouble for the established church. After suffering some years of imprisonment, the patriarch was strangled to death by commandos of the Derg in 1979.[277] The Derg was indifferent to the hopes of its leaders that the Orthodox Church would maintain its unique status in Ethiopia, and indeed, cared little for any religious organization, nationalized all land, including that of the church, closed the Holy Trinity Theological College and confiscated its property in 1974.

The Ethiopian revolution, unlike the Russian revolution, was not accompanied by strong hatred for the clergy, but a considerable amount of indignation towards the church was evident because of its support of the imperial government. Opposition or indifference to church and missions was demonstrated by the university and senior high school students and teachers who were sent all over the country as a result of the decree for "Development Through Cooperation" campaign primarily to teach literacy in 1975.[278]

But as will be discussed below, the impact of the persecution was felt more by the Evangelicals than the Orthodox Church. The Derg did not target individual members of the Orthodox Church but the church as an institution. The minority Evangelical churches, however, were easy prey and suffered as institutions, while their members were also targeted as individuals.

---

275. "In Draft Constitution Church Deplores Some Provisions," *The Ethiopian Herald* (18 August 1974), 1, 4.

276. Gashu, "Looking Back: The Decayed Monarchical System," *The Ethiopian Herald* (2 October 1974), 3.

277. Abune Paulos, *Brief History of His Holiness*, 205.

278. Eshete, *Evangelical Movement*, 205. According to critics the prime reason for the campaign, however, was to remove the youth from the scene of politics, because the Derg knew well that it was the youth who had brought down the emperor and if they stayed in the city they would join forces against the Derg as well. Getachew Belete, *Agonies*, 84–85.

Evangelicals and the Derg

Evangelicals were not adequately prepared to resist the regime's oppressive measures. Many of them who had been deceived through the preaching about harmony between socialism and Christianity were confused. Church leaders took the initiative to pray together and discuss how to respond to the growing antagonism around them. Most of all they wanted to promote interdenominational harmony and join forces to educate the people and speak against the injustice in the country. To this end in 1975, two conferences were held sponsored by the EKHC-SIM and EECMY-LWF respectively.[279]

From February 1975 through October 1976 a series of seminars were conducted which brought leaders of different Evangelical churches and delegates from both Orthodox and Catholic churches together.[280] Mekane Yesus Church also took part in various activities to educate and equip the youth in the face of Communist ideology.[281]

The Derg was not pleased with the participation of the EECMY in promoting Christianity which was championed by Qes Gudina Tumsa. In 1979 Qes Gudina was detained by security forces and charged with joining hands with the Oromo Liberation Front (OLF).[282] It was later confirmed that he was strangled to death.[283] In 1977 the Derg confiscated the "Radio Voice of the Gospel" and the Evangelical College in Debre Zeit which was run by the Ethiopian Evangelical Church Mekane Yesus (EECMY).[284]

---

279. Eshete, *Evangelical Movement*, 220ff.

280. Eshete, 232, 259–261.

281. EECMY highly supported the fellowship of the Christian students in the universities and secondary schools by employing a full-time coordinator to "galvanize and direct the various youth initiatives." During the Derg's campaign which involved young students from all over the country, the Mekane Yesus Church used creative ways in which to help the Christian students remain in the faith in the midst of heavy Marxist propaganda. To this end the Mekane Yesus Church invited Mildred Young, a Korean-American missionary who facilitated the preparation and circulation of Bible study materials and newsletter which has multiple testimonies of perseverance and exchanged information among the students. Leaders of student fellowships were allowed to organize seminars at the EECMY compounds. Eshete, *Evangelical Movement*, 232–240.

282. The former president of Ethiopia, Negasso Gidada confirmed that Qes Gudina was indeed a member of OLF. Daniel Tefera, ዳንዲ የነጋሶ መንገድ (The way of Negaso) (Addis Ababa: 2003 Eth. C) 109–110.

283. Launhardt, *Evangelicals in Addis Ababa*, 248–250. Cf. Abune Paulos, *Brief History of His Holiness*, 205.

284. Launhardt, 243.

Members of the established church used the platform set by the Derg to express their disdain towards the relatively new Evangelical churches. An official plea was made in 1978 by delegates from clergy and professionals of different sorts. The primary accusation against Evangelicals was that they were instruments of foreigners and their faith posed a threat to national security. As a result of such a plea, the Derg set up a committee to investigate the matter. The committee came to the conclusion that the *Pentes* were indeed dangerous and should be eradicated.[285]

Upon the recommendation of the committee set up by the Derg, open persecution started against Evangelical Christians everywhere beginning from 1978. Many churches were closed and believers thrown into prison. Singing and carrying the Bible were punishable by torture.[286] The Derg replaced the doctrinal and ecclesiastical opposition towards Evangelicals with ideological antagonism where Evangelicals were depicted as *mete* (foreign). As the real atheist identity of the Derg was revealed the Evangelicals were labelled as spies of imperialist countries, especially the USA. More churches were closed and schools and properties of missions nationalized. More distressingly, the seven-storey central office building of EECMY was confiscated in 1981.[287]

Mulu Wongel, Meserete Kristos and churches of Baptist General Conference and Southern Baptist were confiscated.[288] The bank account of Meserete Kristos Church was frozen.[289] Meserete Kristos Church served as a refuge for Pentecostals who were primary targets of fierce persecution in the urban centres. Kale Heywet churches in Addis Ababa and the South were closed and believers imprisoned. Kale Heywet churches in Kembatta and

---

285. Eshete, *Evangelical Movement*, 220ff.

286. Getachew Belete, *Agonies*, 219ff. Immediately after some of the Derg cadres stormed a worship service and imprisoned members of Kolfe Kale Heywet Church in Addis Ababa a heavy rain storm with hail stones poured down, covering the whole area. The cadres reasoned that it was the prayer of the believers which caused the unprecedented icy rain fall. Thus they ordered the believers to clean the icy heap from the compound of the prison and the vicinity in their bare feet. Getachew Belete, *Agonies*, 227.

287. Launhardt, *Evangelicals in Addis Ababa*, 243.

288. Mulu Wongel is an indigenous Pentecostal church whereas Meserete Kristos was established by Mennonite missionaries.

289. Hege, *Beyond Our Prayers*, 25ff. Meserete Kristos Church was planted by Mennonite Missionaries in the beginning of the 1950s.

Hadiya region were spared because of the vibrant development work and the relative consideration of the cadre in charge. Similarly two Kale Heywet local churches in Addis which ran elementary schools were not closed.

Speaking of those times Hege noted, "It was indeed a fearful time. The Western reader in a democratic society can hardly grasp the extent of the ridicule heaped on Evangelical believers. Radio programs and newspaper articles constantly called them foreigners, CIA agents, anti-progress people, reactionary elements, even dogs. Their experiences were like those of the early Christians . . ."[290]

The Mekane Yesus Seminary and Ourael Mekane Yesus Church in Addis Ababa which were closed in the morning of 25 January 1982 were reopened the same day after the intervention of the Ambassador of Germany. Local authorities were encouraged to confiscate Evangelical churches with no written order, but in case of an international outcry, they were blamed.[291] It seems that the intervention of European diplomats was behind the opening of Mekane Yesus churches. The local churches of Mekane Yesus in Addis Ababa served all Evangelical Christians whose churches were closed. Believers gathered there for worship, weddings and religious holidays such as Christmas and Easter.[292]

The officials of the Derg, who for the most part were former adherents of the EOC, and thus hated evangelicals all the more, were determined to wipe out evangelical faith from the nation. The church's association with the SIM was taken as a link with CIA agents providing the Derg with ideological argument to annihilate the faith from the South. The Derg came up with villagization and resettlement programs and removed many people from their villages and resettled them in the Western part hoping to achieve Marxist re-educating by uprooting them from the land of their ancestors. "Weakening

---

290. Hege, *Beyond Our Prayers*, 178. The accusation in the case of Meserete Kristos Church leaders was based on misinterpretation. The Eastern Mennonite board corresponded with the Church about their loan funds through Church Investment Associates and the letters referred to this fund simply as CIA. Although the name was changed by the request of the missionaries the old correspondences retained the former name which was taken as evidence of the church leaders' political connections with the USA. Hege, *Beyond Our Prayers*, 24.

291. Launhardt, *Evangelicals in Addis Ababa*, 264–265.

292. Eshete, *Evangelical Movement*, 232–240.

the faith at the place where its constituency was strongest seemed to be an effective strategy of rendering it impotent."[293]

The cadres of the regime were irritated because Evangelicals were absent from the compulsory meetings for Marxist indoctrination.[294] The Marxist-Leninist forum was deliberately scheduled on Sunday mornings. These were aimed to educate the society to adopt socialist consciousness. The antagonistic propaganda of the Communist regime with its very dark portrayal of the Western missionaries affected the perception of the Evangelicals themselves towards the missionaries. To the shock of the missionaries the usually silent Ethiopians came up with strong grievances which were not always seen by the missionaries as legitimate.[295]

However, there were instances in which missions received support from the people they were serving. A case in point is the intervention of parents of pupils of the German Church School in Addis Ababa. When the cadres made several attempts to close the school in 1978 and 1979 parents argued with them and put pressure on the local leadership, so that the school was spared from confiscation.[296]

On a more positive note, Socialism as a common enemy was causing Evangelical Christians to draw closer together.[297] The tension between the Pentecostals and the other Evangelical churches that had been caused by "sheep-stealing" by the Pentecostals decreased in the face of the external pressure and persecution both from the EOC and the Derg.[298] Evangelicals from all walks of faith flooded the open churches to worship and encourage

---

293. Eshete, 250.

294. Hege, *Beyond Our Prayers*, 22.

295. John Cumbers, *Count It All Joy: Testimonies from a Persecuted Church* (Kearney, NE: Morris Publishing, 1995), 33–37. Upon the confiscation of its four-storey building and the ban in its radio programs, the Mekane Yesus Church dismissed the workers in the audio visual and literature section of Yemisrach Dimts. The workers took the church to court and won. The Church had to pay the salaries of the dismissed workers who refused the offer of the church to give them work elsewhere. Launhardt, *Evangelicals in Addis Ababa*, 244.

296. Launhardt, *Evangelicals in Addis Ababa*, 250, 51.

297. John Cumbers, *Living with the Red Terror* (Kearney, NE: Morris Publishing, 1996), 36.

298. Engelsviken, "Pentecostal Revival," 168.

one another.[299] The persecution was considered to be refinery. Christians who passed through the fire believed that their faith grew as a result of it.[300]

The suffering of Evangelicals at the hands of the alleged "adherents" of atheism was not as difficult to bear as that directed from EOC, the supposedly Christian church. The Catholic Church of Ethiopia was not exempt either. Especially at the time when international bodies were pressuring the Derg to stop the persecution, the representatives of both the Orthodox and Catholic churches supposedly held press conferences on their way back from a meeting of the World Council of Churches and strongly denied the allegation that there was no religious freedom in Ethiopia.[301]

Evangelicals, therefore, ended up suffering more, paying with their lives and enduring much antagonism and stigmatization. The Derg authorities were against Evangelical Christianity more through patriotism than ideology. It is doubtful whether most of them understood Marxism or had such convictions apart from memorizing the ideology. Rather, because the majority of them came from the Orthodox Church they exhibited the hatred towards Evangelicals which was evident in the former regime as propagated by the church. In addition, they resented the sheep-stealing carried out by Evangelicals and their lower opinion towards the Orthodox Church.

The difference between the persecution of the Derg against the Orthodox and Evangelicals was that Derg attacked the Orthodox Church as an institution but Evangelicals were personally targeted. The Orthodox Church lost land, status, power and wealth but since most people were Orthodox, the full weight of persecution was not felt by them directly. Evangelicals on the other hand were much divided and exposed so they suffered directly and personally and were vulnerable to the charge of being "foreign." Those who for whatever reason disliked features of Evangelical life, therefore, joined the persecution without being necessarily convinced Marxists.

---

299. Getachew Belete, *Agonies*, 219.

300. Getachew Belete, 304.

301. Getachew Belete, 171. This was reported in *Addis Zemen* one of the state newspapers. The media of the Derg had no problem fabricating lies, thus, if it was not heard from the representatives live it was hard to trust what the papers printed as news.

2.2.11. The Post-Revolutionary Settlement

State-sponsored persecution was halted at the fall of the Derg in 1990, and at the dawn of the Ethiopian Peoples' Revolutionary Democratic Front (EPRDF) there was a degree of compassion from the Orthodox people at large because of the suffering Evangelicals had endured.[302] With the new constitution, which granted freedom of worship, open persecution became punishable by law, but as Evangelicalism was more and more institutionalized its spread appeared to be a threat to the existence of Orthodoxy. The Evangelicals' unrestrained act of converting Orthodox followers was adding fuel to the conflict. In addition, a more than 150-year-old controversy over burial places was not fully resolved, as we will discuss later on.

After the establishment of the constitution, which allowed religious freedom, believers brought to the attention of government legislators legitimate grievances and asked for protection. Thus, fighting for the right to practice (or for the constitutional rights to be respected) faith grew over time. The Evangelicals' perception of the perpetuators of the persecution, however, was affected; leading them to question the legitimacy of their claim to be Christians. As Evangelicalism became more and more institutionalized with the emerging of numerous Protestant churches, an organized effort to keep members of the Orthodox from flocking to Evangelical churches increased. The later developments of mass crusades on traditional Orthodox sites such as the "*Mesqel* Square" in Addis Ababa, were perhaps provocative and most annoying to the Orthodox Church.[303]

Conclusion

Ethiopia's ancient history of greatness in the horn of Africa and its early acceptance of Christianity is a source of pride for Ethiopian Christians. The expansion of Christianity was inseparable from the monarchy and monks and its doctrinal position from the church of Alexandria. Amharic served as

---

302. Nigusse Bulcha, Director of Scripture Union Ethiopia, Interview, 30 September 2010, Addis Ababa.

303. The Reinhardt Bonkee Crusade which was planned to be held at Mesqel Square in the early 1990s was disrupted by Orthodox opposition. There were also attempts to disrupt the global video crusade of Billy Graham which was displayed in the Addis Ababa stadium. Such big events were looked at as Protestant invasions on Orthodox identity.

a vehicle of Christianity and mark of Ethiopian identity and speaking it was seen as synonymous to civilization. However Ge'ez remained the language of the Scripture.

The upper hand of Islam in the coastal land and the Middle East significantly weakened the Aksumite Empire and created difficulty for the church in bringing patriarchs from Egypt. However, Ethiopia remained emphatically a Christian state despite the strong presence of Islam all around it and its spread into the interior. Christian expansion into the interior faced significant opposition both from pagans and Jewish immigrants and would not have succeeded without the help of the monarchs. Besides forceful conversions, large settlements of Semitic peoples in the newly conquered territories enhanced the spread of Christianity. Through centuries of integration, therefore, Orthodox Christianity took hold of the whole of the northern plateau and Shewa as part and parcel of the people's identity. However, the efforts of the church to Christianize people groups in the South and southwestern parts of the country were not as successful as the North and Shewa although the people seemed to pay lip service to Christianity.

In addition to resistance from pagan peoples, the Christian kingdom faced challenges from outside forces. Islam and Latin Christianity attempted to alter the ancient faith, whereas Italy tried to take away the nation's independence. The nineteenth century brought renewed interest of Christian Europe in Ethiopia however the focus was on the commercial benefits and not on Christian allegiance as Ethiopian monarchs had hoped.

Unlike other nineteenth- and twentieth-century monarchs of Ethiopia, Tewodros, Menelik and Haile Sellassie showed great openness towards Europeans, including Protestant missionaries. Haile Sellassie's willingness to receive missionaries and provide protection for them was faced with fierce opposition from the established church. Motivated by his great desire to promote education and modernism in the whole country, Haile Sellassie supported mission work. He also hoped for the Christianization of southern peoples who resisted the Orthodox Church for a long time. With his permission, missionaries did philanthropic work, opened schools and preached the gospel concurrently. Their preaching resulted in the emergence of a solid Christian body other than the Orthodox Church which was uncalled for, at least as far as Haile Sellassie was concerned.

As will be discussed below, the majority of Evangelicals in southern Ethiopia emerged out of the preaching of North American missionaries. Among many things, because of their background, the missionaries did not consider working with the national church, neither were they ready to acknowledge Orthodox Christianity as authentic. Their preaching, therefore, was directed to all, including the Orthodox members who lived in the "open" areas and when they found converts from the Orthodox Church, they did not refrain from baptising them.

CHAPTER 3

Protestant Missions and the Emergence of Evangelical Churches

Introduction

During the reign of the innovator Haile Sellassie, several mission organizations came to Ethiopia from Germany, the United Kingdom, Sweden and the United States. The failure of the Anglican attempt to revitalize the Orthodox Church, however, discouraged missions from attempting further activities in the Orthodox Church.[1] The Orthodox Church was not pleased with the coming of mission organizations and its members continued to resist the Evangelical movement. Moreover, as stated earlier, Haile Sellassie restricted the work of missions to areas unreached by the Orthodox Church.

A number of Lutheran mission organizations and the Sudan Interior Mission (SIM) turned their face towards non-Christian people groups in the south and south-west regions of Ethiopia. With the preaching of the gospel, and the alienation of the Orthodox Church, the emergence of independent bodies was inevitable. The response of people who were in physical and spiritual distress led to the emergence two large Evangelical churches in Ethiopia: Ethiopian Evangelical Church Mekane Yesus (EECMY) and Ethiopian Kale Heywet Church (EKHC). The mission organizations played a major role in delivering peripheral people from physical, spiritual and economic bondage through literacy and the translation of the Bible into the mother-tongue.

---

1. Bible Churchmen's Missionary Society which entered the country in 1932, however, continued to work with the Orthodox Church with no intention of establishing other church.

The relevance of the whole Bible was further enforced and the spirituality of the people found legitimate platform through the ground-breaking revival led by Pentecostals in the 1960s. The movement later formed Pentecostal denominations of which the Mulu Wongel Church was the largest and most influential. As was mentioned in chapter 2 and will be discussed later on, the persecution of Christians under the communist regime (1974–1991) brought the denominations together and served as a catalyst for mutual acceptance, unity and greater similarity of worship style among churches of different traditions.

This chapter discusses the roles of Lutheran missions, SIM and indigenous Pentecostal movements in the expansion of Christianity and hints their interaction with the established church. An extensive treatment of their interaction with the Orthodox Church, however, will be presented in chapter 5.

3.1. Lutherans

The desire of the CMS to reach the "Galla" (Oromo) people was taken up by the Hermannsburg Mission (HM) and the Swedish Evangelical Mission (SEM). The Hermannsburg Mission was established in Germany in 1849 prior to the reign of Emperor Tewodros by Louis Harms with the aim of evangelizing the Oromo tribes. His vision was influenced by the German version of Krapf's account of his travels which was published in 1858 in which Krapf gave vivid description of the Oromo as "the Germany of Africa."[2] The conviction was that by reaching the Oromo people the whole of eastern Africa would be reached.[3] Enthusiastic about mission work, Harms opened a school for missionary candidates in 1849 in Hermannsburg and acquired partial recognition from his church. Like the CMS he sought to recruit trained and ordained missionaries to preach the gospel. After the model of the monastic communities of the Middle Ages in which monks converted the heathen and lay people provided for their material need, Harms sought

---

2. Aren, *Evangelical Pioneers*, 72–74.

3. The Protestants were not alone in attempting to reach Oromo as a gateway to other parts of the continent; Capuchins within the Catholic tradition shared a similar hope that the conversion of the Oromo would open the way to central Africa. Donald Crummey, *Priests and Politicians* (Oxford: Clarendon Press, 1972), 148.

to send out groups of people. He wished to plant a Lutheran church among the Oromo.[4]

HM made two unsuccessful attempts to reach the "Galla" in 1853 and 1858. The first group of missionaries who sailed to Zanzibar and the second group who followed the Somali coast were not allowed to go into the interior by the Arabs and British consul respectively. When the board of HM was on the verge of giving up, Krapf intervened and persuaded them to make another attempt in 1873. It too came to nothing.[5]

Meanwhile, Swedes were motivated by a similar vision of reaching the "Galla." The Swedish Evangelical Mission (SEM) came into being as a result of an Evangelical revival movement in Sweden. In 1835 the Swedish Evangelical Society was formed through the efforts of Rev George Scott, a Methodist preacher from Britain, in Stockholm, who played an active role towards revival in Sweden and in stimulating an interest in foreign missions and distributing Scriptures. Initially the Society did not send out missionaries of its own but supported similar societies abroad. It played a significant part in stimulating Swedish mission interest. In 1856 through the inspiration of Rev Hans Jakob Lundborg a group of like-minded people formed *Evangeliska Fosterlands-Stiftelsen*. The literal translation is Evangelical Fatherland Foundation, but in Ethiopia for the sake of convenience it was known as The Swedish Evangelical Mission (SEM). The founders of SEM were committed to a nation-wide revival and to stimulating Christians to engage in voluntary activities to promote the kingdom of Christ.[6]

After four years of prayer for clear guidance and considering a number of possible mission fields, including West Africa, the board of SEM sought the advice of Samuel Gobat on the matter. Gobat's detailed and informative reply arrived in August 1863. Gobat first suggested a mission to the Oromo, only to strongly advise against it in March 1864, on the grounds that Ethiopia's "religio-political climate" had changed and that two missionaries, Henry A. Stern and H. Rosenthal, had been arrested.[7] The board of SEM was not totally discouraged and sought the advice of Krapf, who was

---

4. Aren, *Evangelical Pioneers*, 107–110.
5. Aren, 110–114.
6. Aren, 114–120.
7. Aren, 101–102, 120–121.

now retired. Krapf replied promptly with a long letter giving them various alternatives and urged them to seek to reach the Oromo people groups. On the strength of Krapf's proposal the SEM board sent out three missionaries: Lars-Johan Lange, Per-Eric Kjellberg and Carl Johan Carlsson in 1865 with a similar goal as that of the CMS[8] ". . . to encourage Bible study through a wide distribution of the Holy Scriptures and thus promote a reform of the ancient Ethiopian Orthodox Church and eventually give rise to an Orthodox mission to Muslim and non-Christian groups."[9]

On 15 March 1866 the missionaries arrived at the Red Sea port of Massawa, part of what is now Eritrea, but because of political problems they were not able to proceed to the interior and started working among the Kunama people, where they stayed for four years. During their stay there they endured tremendous difficulties and paid a high price: five of them died from disease and two were murdered on their way to Massawa.[10]

The presence of missionaries in Kunama displeased the Egyptians who desired to Islamize and colonize the borderland. Nor were the Ethiopian authorities in Adwa happy about the growing mission work among the Kunama. The missionaries were caught in the middle of fighting between tribes who refused to pay tribute and the Egyptians who exerted force. Thus, making peace and preventing fights claimed significant time and energy of the missionaries and resulted in misunderstandings which made it difficult for them to stay in Kunama.[11]

The vision to reach the Oromo was not fully abandoned, but was rekindled at a time when the door in Kunama was closed in 1870. More missionaries were recruited, and old and new missionaries settled in Hamasen and were surprised to find in Tseazega priests of the EOC who were diligent Bible readers and committed to reforming the church. Hamasen was the place where the CMS missionaries had distributed the Scriptures during their very last attempt to re-enter Adwa in 1843.[12]

---

8. Aren, 121–123.
9. Aren, 123.
10. Aren, 127–148.
11. Aren, 133–148.
12. C. W. Isenberg and J. L. Krapf, *The Journals of C. W. Isenberg and J. L. Krapf* (London: Frank Cass & Co., 1968), 110.

Onesimos Nesib,[13] a freed Oromo slave, was the first convert and he was baptized on 18 March 1872.[14] Lundahl, the missionary in charge, conducted a communion service for the new converts. In so doing, he took the first step towards founding an independent Evangelical church.[15] Establishing an independent church had not been part of the plan of the SEM. Lundahl stated it when he first celebrated Holy Communion with Onesimos and three other students.[16] Those who came from the Orthodox Church were not baptized but offered instruction and confirmation.[17] In line with the tradition of the European Reformation, which sought to reform the existing church, the SEM recognized the Orthodox Church as the national church and desired to reform it. This formed part of its strategy for reaching the Oromo. The mission desired to work with the Ethiopian church rather than establishing a new church.[18]

The repeated efforts of the agents of renewal to remain in the Orthodox Church[19] and of the missionaries to avoid establishing a new church, proved futile because the Orthodox priests grew intolerant of the Bible readers.[20] In fact, they accused them of heresy and a greater persecution broke out in 1874 in Hamasen, "Everyone who possessed a copy of the printed Scriptures was imprisoned and his property confiscated."[21] EOC priests who were

---

13. Onesimos later on translated the Bible into Oromifa with the help of Aster Ganno. Aren, *Evangelical Pioneers*, 383.

14. Aren, *Evangelical Pioneers*, 164–165.

15. Aren, 166–167.

16. Aren, 222.

17. Aren, 224.

18. E. Forslund, *The Word of God in Ethiopian Tongues: Rhetorical Features in the Preaching of the Ethiopian Evangelical Church Mekane Yesus* (Uppsala: International Tryk AB., 1993), 65.

19. Aren, *Evangelical Pioneers*, 182.

20. Getatchew Haile deeply resents the attempt of the missionaries to "Christianize the Christians" or to proselytize because according to him the apostle Paul forbids it; in his view there was no need to open new churches. He feels that true missionaries come to help the Church and not to "steal sheep." He argues that the EOC members are devoted to their church because it forms their identity. But he does not discuss the official and non-official persecution that members of the Orthodox Church suffered simply because they possessed a copy of the Bible and wanted to read it for themselves. Getatchew Haile, "The Missionary's Dream: An Ethiopian Perspective on Western Missions in Ethiopia," in *The Missionary Factor in Ethiopia*, Getatchew Haile, et al (Frankfurt: Peter Lang, 1998), 1–8.

21. Aren, *Evangelical Pioneers*, 180.

accused of violating the decree were severely flogged and placed in solitary confinement. The missionaries were tolerated but the Orthodox reformers were seriously dealt with.[22]

In Wollega those Orthodox with Evangelical convictions considered themselves reformers and not separatists. They tried to remain in the church but the intolerance and isolation grew to the extent that they were eventually denied the sacrament and burial place for their dead.[23] For those who were isolated and excommunicated it was difficult to obtain permission from the government to establish their own churches. When congregations founded by Lutherans located in different parts of Ethiopia got closer to securing the permit to establish a church, they encountered resistance which was championed by the Orthodox Church. The leaders of the church tried to prevent them from including the adjective "Ethiopian" in the name of the new church.[24] Even after the church was established as independent from the Orthodox Church, the persecution of members of the Evangelical church continued. The Evangelicals were isolated from their communities and ridiculed by priests and ordinary EOC members with little sympathy from government officials."[25]

Both the Evangelical Church of Eritrea and the Ethiopian Evangelical Church Mekane Yesus thus derive their origin from the persecution of the Bible readers by the EOC and the conscious acts of some missionaries to establish a church separate from the EOC.[26] Such acts included worshipping

---

22. Aren, 225.

23. Bakke, *Christian Ministry*, 112.

24. Johnny Bakke, "Models of Leadership in Ethiopia: The Missionary Contribution," in *The Missionary Factor in Ethiopia*, Getatchew Haile et al. (Frankfurt: Peter Lang, 1998), 156. When the students who later took on the name "Mulu Wongel" applied for permission with a proposed name "Tintawit Yegziabher Mahber" (God's Ancient Association) for their new church, they were denied permission because the term "old-time" (ancient) could only refer to the EOC. Nathan B. Hege, *Beyond Our Prayers: An Amazing Half Century of Church Growth in Ethiopia (1948–1998)* (Scottdale, PA: Herald Press, 1998), 151–52.

25. Debela Birri, "History of the Evangelical Church Bethel 1919–1947" (ThD thesis, Chicago: Lutheran School of Theology, 1995), 147.

26. The attitude of the Protestant missionaries was not always the best and unfortunately, it is this darker side of their dealings which is usually picked up by Ethiopian historians. Some missionaries supported foes of Ethiopians: Egypt and later Italy. Rubenson writes that Krapf tried to convince Egyptians to occupy "a portion of Abyssinia" in the early 1870s. Later on when Italy was defeated in 1896, Rubenson quotes the words of Anders Svensson, the field director of SEM who was in Eritrea, "The defeat at Adwa on 1 March,

in an ordinary house[27] and conducting Holy Communion there, both practices abhorrent to the EOC.[28]

Lutheran missions that eventually joined the EECMY brought together diverse ecclesiastical traditions including some of those of the EOC.[29] In matters such as following the EOC calendar, adapting some of the EOC's religious vocabulary, conducting infant baptism and upholding ordained ministry, EECMY maintained continuity with the Orthodox Church. On the other hand, in rejecting some of the most deeply venerated traditions of the EOC such as the intercessory role of Mary and the saints, views on fasting, and the authority of tradition, EECMY showed discontinuity with the Orthodox Church. Moreover it allowed lay people to preach and also local languages to be used in church services, which has further distinguished it from the EOC.[30]

As for continuity with primal religion, the story of Scandinavian Missionaries in Bale illustrates the crossroad the missionaries stood at during the formative years of the church.[31] They faced a dilemma as to how

---

which was unexpected by all of us, has caused distress and grief all around . . . I visited the dear General Baratieri, who has now been so severely humiliated . . ." His colleague who was in Harar at the time expressed similar feelings of resentment over the victory of Ethiopians. Rubenson comments that the reactions of the missionaries as all other Europeans imply their feelings of superiority. Rubenson, "Consequences of a Colonial Context," 68.

27. It is not the type of the architecture that makes a building a church in the EOC, but the presence of "Tabot" in it. Thus, the Evangelical ecclesiology which has little regard for rituals and the presence of sacred objects was not acceptable to the EOC.

28. Isenberg one of the CMS missionaries was also accused of administering the sacraments and conducting church services at home. Aren, *Evangelical Pioneers*, 66.

29. While SEM was the pioneer Lutheran mission organization with a burden to reform the Orthodox Church, other sister Lutheran missions worked in different parts of Ethiopia. The congregations throughout the country which were established by missionaries of different origins: Swedish Evangelical Mission (1904), German Hermannsburg Mission (1927), Norwegian Lutheran Mission (1948) and Ethiopian reformers agreed to merge into Ethiopian Evangelical Church Mekane Yesus in 1954. Swedish Mission Bible-True Friends (1921) withdrew from the effort of establishing an Ethiopian church because of the exclusion of Luther's name from the name of the new church. Fekadu Gurmessa, *Evangelical Faith Movement in Ethiopia* (Minneapolis, MN: Lutheran University Press, 2009), 231–254. The churches planted by American United Presbyterian Mission (1922) merged with Mekane Yesus in 1972.

30. Cf. Forslund, *The Word of God*, 72–73.

31. Danish Evangelical Mission (1951) and Bible True Friends (1925) worked in the area. Henrik Peterson, ed., *Stories of Bale: Religious Development and Evangelical Christianity* (Addis Ababa: n.p., 2005), 67.

to instruct first converts with regard to their traditions. They feared that demanding a complete break from traditional practices would cut off people from their society and create a serious problem for the convert's identity. On the other hand, allowing some of the practices to continue could lead the people to syncretism. The missionaries made their choice. The converts were to make a complete break from their traditions. This meant that they were no longer able to live in their communities, because in the village, there appeared to be no room for two religions to co-exist. "And then the choice was clear: leave your village and culture, or reject Christianity."[32] People made the difficult choice of becoming Christians by leaving behind nearly all that was dear to them. But not all came out of conviction, some wanted education and still others were lured with material gain in exchange for becoming Christians.[33]

Generally speaking, Lutherans were more sensitive towards traditions of the Orthodox and even of followers of primal religion. For example, they did not rebaptize former Orthodox members, neither did they require abstinence from alcohol and the eradication of polygamy. In carrying out the social mandate of the church, which is sometimes regarded as "secular," the Lutheran missions pioneered development work in rural areas which promoted Mekane Yesus Church's acceptance by the public.

3.2. New Evangelical Missions and Churches

Besides Lutheran missions a number of mission organizations were active in the country. The Pentecostal ones which founded Ethiopian Hiwot *Birhan* and Ethiopian Genet churches and contributed to the revival movement which later organized itself under Mulu Wongel Church will be discussed under the Pentecostal section later. The Ethiopian Kale Heywet Church which was planted by SIM will be discussed in much more detail than the others simply because it is the largest Evangelical church in the country. Moreover, its story is vital for the understanding of indigenous Evangelical development because it thrived among 90 percent illiterate peripheral people

---

32. Peterson, *Stories of Bale*, 69–70.
33. Peterson, 106, 128.

groups after the evacuation of missionaries during the Italian occupation of Ethiopia.

There was a fundamental difference between European and American mission organizations. One of the main differences was that American missionaries came out of American Christianity which did not favour tight hierarchical bodies. Input from individuals therefore, was welcome and people were free to leave and join another church or even start a new one when a disagreement occurred. The idea of a national church was missing because like-minded people established a church. In this the American churches were similar to European voluntary societies.[34] Such a background, among many things, informed the decisions of American missionaries on the mission field and affected their perception of the Ethiopian Orthodox Church.

3.2.1. Eastern Mennonite Board of Missions

The Eastern Mennonite Board of Missions entered the country in 1947. Prior to their coming Mennonites connected to Anabaptists had already started philanthropic and medical work in 1945 based in Nazareth. They were given a five-year contract by the government for relief and medical work. Haile Sellassie was aware of the Mennonite work in Nazareth and even visited the hospital they were running which was called Haile Mariam Mamo hospital, so when they expressed to him their desire to do evangelical mission as well he suggested that they work in the eastern part of the country and in 1951 they were granted permission for mission work.[35]

The mission started medical and educational work in three places in the east including Addis. The missionaries were allowed to teach the Bible to students in the hospital they founded at Nazareth but when they baptized young people, including former EOC members, Haile Sellassie was quite annoyed and they had to apologize and promise not to do that again. However, the baptism marked the beginning of a church in Nazareth. The mission work in the east produced Muslim converts and together with the employees of the mission a church was established in Dire Dawa.[36]

---

34. Walls, *Missionary Movement*, 221–240. Cf. Fargher, *Origins of the New Churches*, 60–126.
35. Eshete, *Evangelical Movement*, 106–107.
36. Hege, *Beyond Our Prayers*, 49ff.

In Addis Ababa as well, a fellowship was started by people who relocated to Addis from the Mennonite churches in the east and their number grew as new people joined them. The first baptism of ten people in 1951 which was held in Addis Ababa marked the beginning of the church. Members of the Mennonite church sought to form a national church and in 1959 the General Church Council which was comprised of delegates from all Mennonite congregations changed the name of the church to "Meserete Kristos Church" (MKC) and gradually took over the leadership of the church from the missionaries. The mission established a high school which was called Nazareth Bible Academy. It served as the centre for annual fellowship of Evangelicals from all over the country.[37]

3.2.2. Baptist Missions

The Baptist General Conference (BGC) came to Ethiopia in 1949 and worked mainly in Shewa. They operated a hospital and were involved in education programs in Ambo and Kachisi towns. Globe Publishing House was their prominent ministry in Addis Ababa. The spiritual and developmental activities in their stations resulted in the establishment of Berhane Wongel Baptist Church in Addis Ababa in 1954 and more than thirty congregations mainly in Jibat and Mecha region in Shewa. When the Derg came to power nearly all of the Birhane Wongel churches were closed.[38]

Besides the BGC, a number of Baptist missions were active in the country one of which was Baptist Bible Fellowship. It started its activities in 1960. The other Baptist-established church is Emmanuel Baptist Church which was founded by Glen Cain, former SIM missionary in 1962. In 1965 the mission built a facility with classrooms and sanctuary and the church was growing, but the facility was confiscated by the Derg.[39] Upon the fall of the Derg the leadership of the church requested its restoration but already a split had occurred in the church in which another group formed, called Beza Baptist Church, and this group approached the government with a similar request. The splinter groups maintained the Baptist doctrine of cessationism, namely that the so-called charismatic gifts of the Holy Spirit (such as

---

37. Hege, 78–84, 128–146.
38. Launhardt, *Evangelicals in Addis Ababa*, 154–155.
39. Launhardt, 155–156.

prophecy, healing and speaking in tongues) had ceased to function upon the canonization of the Bible.

Finally, Southern Baptists were active in the country. Their work was based in Addis Ababa and northern Shewa among the Amhara. They attempted to bring renewal among the Orthodox in Menz and Geshen regions by encouraging priests and the youth to read the Bible. Towards this end they used development projects and tried to exert influence through their lifestyle. The youth who were interested in reading the Bible in these "closed" areas faced opposition and eventually established Addis Kidan (New Covenant) Baptist Church.[40] It must be noted that the story of the Baptist missions in Ethiopia is not as well documented as the other missions; hence the gaps in the story and absence of dates.

3.3. Indigenous Initiatives in the South Prior to the Coming of Missionaries

The Orthodox Church as the state faith attempted to Christianize peoples of the South through various methods, including force. However, Orthodox Christianity did not enjoy the kind of success it encountered in northern Ethiopia and Shewa. In the period 1920s–1940s, some of the practitioners of indigenous religion in southern Ethiopia heard a radical message and a call for repentance from individuals who were believed to be under the influence of a supernatural power. Among these are Esa Lale of Gamo, Abuye of Kembatta and Cheleke of Gofa.

Esa Lale[41] was believed to function under the influence of a spirit but his clan was not among those that were usually associated with the spirit world. Nevertheless Esa strongly opposed the evil ways and works of such people. In fact, some people testified that his teaching echoed the Ten Commandments. He went from place to place preaching loudly and clearly. Esa's teachings emphasized moral uprightness, worshipping the only God who is in heaven

---

40. Eshete, *Evangelical Movement*, 51–52.

41. Lale means the one who releases to freedom from bondage. Paul Balisky, "Esa Lale: A Prophet of Religious Innovation in Southern Ethiopia," in *Proceedings of the XIVth International Conference of Ethiopian Studie*, ed. Baye Yiman et al., (6–11 November 2000), 568.

and renouncing the worship and works of Satan.[42] Moreover, he delivered prophetic messages which came to pass. In one of his prophecies he declared, "God who created the heaven and the earth has given me a revelation that after some time white people will come with a book . . . listen to the book which these white people bring and follow it." Esa's tragic end came because of his prophecy which was not limited to religious reformation but incorporated political change as well.

On one occasion Esa reportedly prophesied, "[T]he Amhara will one day be driven from the South and the land once again be given back to us." This particular prophecy got Esa into trouble with the district governor who was appointed by the emperor. The governor feared that Esa's preaching might incite the local people against the Northerners who occupied the land forcefully and imprisoned and sent him to Addis Ababa and he never returned home.[43] According to Balisky the lasting impression of Esa's teaching upon the hearts and minds of his hearers had three components: first, "the people were to worship the creator God, *Tosa* and offer him that which was sweet and expensive." Second, "Families were to worship together with the head of the household acting as the intercessor . . . The third component of Esa's teaching which made a lasting impression was to foster better relationships one with another."[44]

Some people were disappointed because some of Esa's prophecies did not come to pass. Dana Maja, who reverted to his traditional worship of the ancestors, was asked why he fell back and he said, "no cows came out from the ground as Esa promised."[45] The unfulfilled prophecy of Esa was similar to that of the Xhosa girl in South Africa that a great number of cattle would come out of the ground. Her prophecy brought about the great cattle killing among the Xhosa.[46] It appears that just like the Xhosa girl Nongqawuse, who felt burdened by the colonial yoke upon her people, Esa "felt burdened

---

42. Balisky, "Esa Lale," 577.
43. Balisky, 569.
44. Balisky, 577.
45. Balisky, 577.
46. J. B. Peires, *The Dead Will Arise: Nongqawuse and the Great Xhosa Cattle-Killing Movement of 1856–7* (Bloomington: Indiana University Press, 1989), 78–138.

for his compatriots" because they "were socially and economically harassed by the Northerners."⁴⁷

Eshetu Abate compares Esa's ministry with the ministry of John the Baptist and argues that the Lord sent Esa ahead of the missionaries to prepare the heart of the people. When the missionaries came people were able to relate their teaching with the prophecies and teachings of Esa and consequently, the gospel thrived.⁴⁸

Abuye was the contemporary of Esa and he claimed to have received a revelation from *Magano*, the High God of Kembatta. He was a known *qalicha*⁴⁹ in his area. While Abuye preached he would hold up the palm of his hand and appear to be reading from it and say, "This is what God says" and go on to urge his hearers to stop worshipping Satan and worship only Christ. His teaching was said to be similar to the teachings of the missionaries, so Aba Gole, one of the "Jesus Men" (as the believers were referred to then), went to hear for himself. Upon hearing the preaching of Abuye, Aba Gole was astonished and said, "What you taught previously was Satan's work.⁵⁰ Now teach the truth. Pull down your old house. Build a new one. Have your hair cut off. Drink water⁵¹ and eat your food with gladness."⁵²

The third noteworthy man was Cheleke, a prominent *qalicha* in the Gofa region. He rose to prominence in a time when the missionaries were driven out during the occupation of Ethiopia by Italy. Prior to the Italian invasion, he prophesied that "men would fly and that the mountains would shake. The prophecy was fulfilled when the Italian planes flew over and dropped bombs on Wolaitta and Gofa in 1936."⁵³ Cheleke was considered as "god"

---

47. Balisky, "Esa Lale," 576; Cf. 580.

48. Wondiye Ali, በመከራ ውስጥ ያበበች ቤተ ክርስቲያን *(Church out of tribulation)*, 68–70.

49. Rightful person to do the rituals and communicate with spirits in the context of traditional religion.

50. Such a conclusion appears to have come from the conviction that anything that has to do with traditional religion was demonic. Even with the clear teaching of Abaye against Satan's worship, Aba Gole still called his teaching "Satan's work."

51. "Pull down your old house" refers to the house used for worship, "Have your hair cut." It was customary for spirit-possessed people to have their hair long, "Drink water" this is to imply that Abaye should not drink alcoholic beverages any longer.

52. Peter Cotterell, *Born at Midnight* (Chicago: Moody Press, 1973), 114.

53. Balisky, "Esa Lale," 571.

by his people.[54] He proved able to overpower all of the traditional mediums there, so that the others sought empowerment from him. In fact, there were rumours that he sat on a serpent, a tiger was at his service, and that a snake obeyed him just like a person. When people from Cheleke's district heard the gospel somewhere else they asked, "Is your God mightier than our Cheleke?"

Such was the prominence of Cheleke in the whole area. But he prophesied, "I see a Lord who is mightier than us coming from the rising of the Sun. The soul of those who believe in him will be saved. Messengers who witness the greatness of this Lord will come with a walking stick and a golden book in their hands. They will stand under the tree in my yard, open the golden book and teach. They will build a house which is bigger than all of our houses. The soul of the person who enters that house will be delivered."[55] Cheleke admonished the *qalichas* in his area to worship only *Tosa*[56] and forsake worshipping the clan deities and ancestors.[57] After seventeen years an evangelist went to that area with a golden book but he did not dare yet to go into Cheleke's house so he stood under the tree and sent for Cheleke. When Cheleke came he shared the gospel with him.

Cheleke listened to the evangelist attentively, rose to his feet and said, "Many years ago, when I was seated under this tree, my god told me 'a man like you will come with a golden book and talk to you.' Are you that man?" The evangelist told him that he was a minister of God and gave Cheleke the golden book. Cheleke went home, put the golden book on the back of a black goat and prayed over it and then slaughtered the goat. After examining the entrails he attested that all that was preached to him was true. At that point in front of his servants and wives he declared, "I have believed in the God named Jesus."[58]

Even though the usual stories told about the involvement of supernatural forces are of destruction and manipulation of others, they also played John the Baptist's role as the forerunner to the gospel. As for the southern

---

54. Ali Wondiye, የእኩለ ሌሊት ወገጋታ *(Awakening at midnight)*, (Addis Ababa: Ethiopian Kale Heywet Church Literature Department, 2000), 164.

55. Wondiye, *Church Out of Tribulation*, 71–72.

56. *Tosa* is the Wolaitta equivalent for God.

57. Balisky, "Esa Lale," 573.

58. Wondiye, *Awakening at Midnight*, 161–168.

peoples, the evangelistic attempts of the Orthodox Church were coupled with indigenous oracles which played a significant role in opening them up to the gospel.

3.4. The Establishment of the Ethiopian Kale Heywet Church (EKHC)

In 1927 Sudan Interior Mission (SIM) which was established in 1893 in Toronto, Canada by three men: Walter Gowans, Rowland Bingham and Thomas Kent, entered Ethiopia. The aim of the mission was specified in its title, "to abandon the coastlands which were already well provided with missionaries, and to press on into the interior."[59] Walter Gowans and Thomas Kent died in West Africa in 1895 and Rowland Bingham was so seriously ill that he went back to Canada. Bingham established the first Council of SIM in 1898.

After several attempts, SIM succeeded in entering Patigi in 1902 and their work led to the formation of the Evangelical Churches of West Africa (ECWA), one of the largest Evangelical churches in Nigeria. SIM desired to expand its work to east Africa and to this end Bingham travelled through New Zealand and Australia late in 1926 to recruit missionaries and raise funds for them. On his way back to Canada he read about the establishment of Abyssinian Frontiers Mission (AFM) and sought to convince the founding members Dr Thomas Lambie and George Rhoad to join hands with SIM.[60]

Dr Lambie was already acquainted with the interior of Ethiopia having worked under the American United Presbyterian Mission (AUPM), which he joined in 1907. He worked in the Sudan until 1919. In the same year, he was invited by Dejazmach Birru, governor of Qelem in south-eastern Ethiopia to come to Sayo (Western Wollega) and provide medical care for his soldiers. At the time a deadly influenza which was referred to as *Yehidar Beshita* spread across the country killing thousands of people. It is not stated how the governor got to know about the medical skills of Dr Lambie, but upon his invitation Lambie went to Sayo along with his family and started medical work there in July 1919. He treated patients, and also prayed and

---

59. Cotterell, *Born at Midnight*, 15.
60. Fargher, *Origins of New Churches*, 32.

read Bible passages with them and those around, but encountered no opposition from the authorities or the people. That was the beginning of the first station of AUPM. Some of the men Lambie treated were prominent government people who became his friends. Ras Nadew, a governor of Illubabor region was one such person. He wrote to the regent that Lambie saved his life and that particular letter gained Lambie access to Ras Tafari on his way to the United States for furlough.[61] Tafari expressed his desire for a hospital to be established and administered by AUPM and promised to grant the land. The initial conversation was followed up with several meetings and finally an agreement was signed on terms of co-operation on 25 February 1922.

AUPM did not have ready funds so Lambie raised support from individuals and by the time he returned in 1923, he had all the funds and full support from his mission. In addition, AUPM provided two builders, one nurse and a secretary. The construction of the hospital (the present Pasteur Institute and Central Medical Laboratory) was completed in 1924, equipped and staffed by AUPM and started work in 1925. In order to protect the hospital and the mission from trouble with local authorities, the hospital was named after the regent. The surrounding people, however, called it "Dr Lambie's hospital." The hospital provided access to modern medical care for all. Formerly such care was reserved for the nobility and diplomats in Addis. In addition to medical care, people were assigned to read the Bible and attend to spiritual needs of patients in the wards and the waiting room. The mission had no intention of starting extensive evangelistic work in Addis which was designated as "closed" area. The headquarters of AUPM in Pittsburgh, PA, therefore, had the idea of strengthening the Orthodox Church. Dr Lambie, however was not happy that most of the resources of the missions were invested in medical work in Addis Ababa. He felt a burden for mission among southern people and proposed this to the board of AUPM but the mission was not interested.[62]

In 1926, while Lambie was on furlough in the United States, he was approached by the American committee for Heart of Africa (HAM). The

---

61. Cotterell, *Born at Midnight*, 11–12.
62. Launhardt, *Evangelicals in Addis Ababa*, 48–51.

committee was looking for new mission opportunities for their missionaries who were not on good terms with C. T. Studd, the founder of HAM. The HAM committee learnt about Lambie from the son-in-law of Studd, Alfred Buxton, who read Lambie's article entitled "The Importance of Abyssinia" which was published in World Dominion magazine. Convinced that Lambie was the person to contact, Buxton and his wife travelled to the United States from Britain and along with the HAM committee, they held consecutive meetings with Lambie. Buxton introduced to the Lambies Rev and Mrs George Rhoad, missionary couple of Africa Inland Mission (AIM) in Kenya, who expressed willingness to go to Ethiopia if Lambie left AUPM and joined the new project. In 1926, after twenty years of service, Lambie decided to leave AUPM and joined hands to form a new mission which was called Abyssinian Frontier Mission (AFM).[63]

Things were moving far too slowly in the new mission with regard to securing support. In what seemed like a providential arrangement, Lambie met Rowland Bingham at Stony Brook. Bingham was aware of the formation of AFM and when the two men met they immediately began discussing the possibility of working together. Buxton joined the discussion and in 1927 they folded up AFM and joined SIM.[64]

From the beginning the goal of the first missionary party of SIM was to reach Southern Ethiopia. Dr Lambie sought to follow the outline which he had formerly proposed to the board members of AFM. He suggested that the pioneer missionaries were not only to gather information by travel and study but also to establish one or two mission stations. Once they reached Addis Ababa they were to travel ". . . to the south of its frontiers and finding out where the densest areas of population are, where Mohamedan [sic] advance is most threatening, where slave raiding is most prevalent and where the people live who are most receptive to the gospel message, and from due consideration of these and many others, determine the strategic points."[65]

At the time that the first SIM missionaries arrived in Ethiopia, which was 1927, Zawditu, the daughter of Menelik II, a staunch supporter of the EOC, had been proclaimed empress while Tafari Mekonnen (the future Haile

---

63. Cotterell, *Born at Midnight*, 13–15.
64. Cotterell, 15–16.
65. Cotterell, 16–18.

Sellassie I), who had the reputation of being "progressive and innovative,"[66] was regent. The tremendous political tension in the capital meant the request of SIM missionaries for permission to proceed to the South was delayed. Moreover, the EOC was not happy with SIM's presence in Ethiopia and the *Echege* Gebre Menfes Qiddus summoned the missionaries to question them regarding their doctrine.[67]

Dr Lambie, Mr Rasmussen and Mr Rhoad presented their document to a gathering of fifty or more priests under the leadership of the *Echege*. The argument developed along the lines of the tenets of the Orthodox Church which the missionaries did not uphold, such as the need for fasting, beliefs about the canon, the place of baptism, mediation of angels, and the status of Mary. The discussion extended over several days.[68]

After four meetings the priests said that further discussion was not possible because of the approaching Lenten season. They offered to continue after the forty-days fast was concluded. The missionaries were concerned that by the time Lent was over the rainy season would start, making travel difficult. But the foreign minister Bilaten Geta Hiruy Wolde Selassie intervened and gave them permission to "take the air" with no specific permission for missionary activity. In fact, he advised them not to ask for written permission because he did not think it would be granted to them.[69] So the missionaries were given permission to leave Addis Ababa in the name of refreshing themselves by travelling to the country-side.

The missionaries headed to Jimma but lost their way soon after they left Addis and ended up in Hosanna, the chief town of Kembatta. They were warmly welcomed by the governor Dejazmatch Meshesha, who to Dr Lambie's astonishment was his former patient from Wollega. He told Lambie that Dejazmatch Yigezu, another of his former patients from Wollega, was governor of Wellamo, so the caravan proceeded to Sodo. By this time the rainy season had already begun and the flooded rivers barred them from crossing to Jimma.

---

66. Cotterell, 22.
67. Cotterell, 22.
68. Cotterell, 22.
69. Cotterell, 23–24.

The missionaries were now less concerned about crossing to Jimma and decided to investigate the situation further before settling anywhere. So they went on to Sidamo. In what seemed like a providential arrangement, they found out that Lambie's former friend in Wollega Dejazmatch Birru was the new governor. The missionaries were assured by all three governors that they were welcome to open mission stations at Kembatta, Soddo, and Sidamo consecutively. They even entertained a request to open a mission station in the most unlikely places of all in Ethiopia, Lalibela. In 1934, Ras Kassa, a governor of Lasta who "was anxious to have the mission in the north as well as in the south . . ." wrote to Dr Lambie asking him to open a station in Lalibela, northern Ethiopia. Similar openness of governors was witnessed in Debre Tabor, and Debre Markos.[70]

This proves that the missionaries were welcomed in several places despite the opposition from the Orthodox Church. Therefore, the general perception that missionaries imposed themselves is not always true. Apparently they also responded to invitations from local governors. Securing written agreements prior to opening stations was not always easy. However, this was generally true of all foreign properties. Dr Lambie took a radical measure to solve the problem of securing land for the mission, he forfeited his American citizenship in 1934 and his decision enabled him to finalize the land contract even in Lalibella.[71]

Later on, large churches were planted in Kembatta, Soddo and Sidamo districts but with great opposition, mainly from the Orthodox Church.[72] The converts also faced opposition from adherents of traditional religion. However, they seemed to maintain an unfavourable attitude towards their former religion. Perhaps desiring to magnify the freedom they received from the gospel, they presented their past state as completely dark and strove to

---

70. Lalibela is highly notable for its magnificent churches carved out of the sandstone rock and its reputation as "a shrine of Orthodoxy." Cotterell, *Born at Midnight*, 75–76.

71. Cotterell, *Born at Midnight*, 78–79. However, upon the entrance of Italians to Addis Ababa in 1935, Lambie felt bound by Rom 13:1 which commanded everyone to be subject to higher powers and went to surrender to Italian authorities. His action was understood by the Ethiopians as an offer of friendship with the enemy. The emperor was not willing to meet with Lambie in Khartoum. Cotterell, *Born at Midnight*, 87.

72. Cotterell, *Born at Midnight*, 24–25.

avoid any traces of it whatsoever.[73] Using traditional music instruments, clapping of hands and dancing during worship was not allowed in the Kale Heywet Church for a long time. Many of the converts who actively participated in the traditional rites claimed that noise and dancing reminded them of their former state of darkness. Now that they were worshipping the God of peace, they wanted to worship him solemnly, in a dignified manner.[74]

This appears to be an extension of the "fundamentalist theology of conversion"[75] adopted by the missionaries and the evangelists who followed in their footsteps; that they sought to scrutinize the conversion of people by requiring profession of Christ as Lord, behavioural changes, and separation from worldly practices (polygamy, alcohol, dancing and ancestral worship). Such changes were expected of the baptismal candidates. The expatriate evangelists claimed they did not legislate right and wrong but they left no doubt in the minds of the converts what they considered to be sinful. They felt obligated to teach the necessity of radical separation from any association with such things as intoxicating drink and dancing because they believed that "separation was an integral part of true Christianity."[76]

The missionaries persevered, in spite of enormous difficulty. Within two years of their coming to Ethiopia there were twenty-two missionaries on five

---

73. Alemu Himbaru, ወንጌል ነጻ ያወጣል (The gospel sets free), n.d: 10–12.

74. Segaro Selato, one of the leaders of the Kembatta Subjects: Kale Heywet Church was previously responsible in the house of the chief to restrain him from running away when a spirit came on him violently. He also was in charge of men and women who used to sing and dance all day long for the spirit. They used to clap their hands, jump, beat drums and sing as an act of invoking the spirit to come upon the chief. Segaro did not take the responsibility of the chief's house gladly, but only after the spirit killed two of his sons upon his refusal. When he heard the preaching of the missionaries and saw the power encounter, he gladly surrendered his life to Jesus. (The researcher heard Segaro share his testimony in the late 1980s.) Segaro was strongly opposed to charismatic/Pentecostal movement in the church. In fact, he along with others with a similar background banned for a long time clapping, making joyful cries, using drums and making any sort of body movement during worship in the church. He strongly argued that the church was not to follow the old style of Satanic worship in her worship of the Lord. Intermarriage with people of Charismatic/Pentecostal Churches like Mulu Wongel believers was prohibited accordingly because they were considered to be heretic. As a young adult, the researcher remembers being sternly warned not to go to Mulu Wongel's revival meetings in Kembatta area and when found guilty of participating, strong chastisement followed.

75. Fargher, *Origins of the New Churches*, 27.

76. Fargher, 29.

mission stations.[77] However, the number of believers greatly increased after they left Ethiopia during the Italian conquest of 1936. Italy did not expel any of them, but took over one station after the other and compensated SIM with a payment of £18,870. The missionaries left behind about one hundred and fifty believers, but when they returned after five years they were stunned to find more than two hundred vibrant churches with approximately twenty-five thousand believers.[78]

In the absence of the missionaries, the believers had organized themselves into manageable units. To take one example, believers in Wolaitta divided up the area into fifteen sections with one ruling elder for each. Each local church had at least four elders who administered the church and dealt with minor issues. When difficult issues arose, they referred them to the ruling elder of the district who tried to resolve the matter but if unable to, he took it to the council of ruling elders. The ruling elders held monthly meetings in different places to discuss issues and decide on matters. At these monthly meetings, at least four delegates from each church were present. The district elders held a meeting in a different hut and joined the delegates of churches and communicated their decision. Such an organized form of leadership was not taught by the missionaries, rather, it was an indigenous development.[79]

During the time of the presence of the missionaries the conversion of those who worked for the missionaries was often viewed with scepticism, as a device to protect their jobs, but when the workers continued to follow the new faith in the absence of the missionaries, interest was stirred up and many people were converted.[80] The movement was led by indigenous Ethiopian Christians[81] who had been given limited instruction and literacy but most importantly, a few copies of the Amharic Bible and portions of the Bible in their mother-tongues.

The converts were referred to as "Jesus-men" or derogatively "water-people" an allusion both to baptism with water and abstinence from alcoholic

---

77. Cotterell, *Born at Midnight*, 36.
78. Cotterell, 97–106.
79. Cotterell, 103–106.
80. Cotterell, 27ff; 101, 120, 170; Wondiye, *Church Out of Tribulation*, 146–147.
81. Staffan Grenstedt, *Ambaricho and Shonkolla: From Local Independent Church to Evangelical Mainstream in Ethiopia* (Stockholm: Elanders Gotab, 2000), 19.

beverages.[82] They endured enormous persecution from the clergy of the Orthodox Church, state authorities who were members of EOC and neighbours and family members who were followers of traditional religion. Many believers were uprooted from their villages by force and their houses were demolished and property confiscated.[83]

Despite the persecution, the number of believers grew from time to time. Even though the missionaries did not teach them to pray for and expect miracles, the conversion of many was accompanied by healing and deliverance. Some testified to encountering Jesus himself.[84] Sorsa Sumamo, one of the evangelists in the South at the time, comments that the evangelists did not include healing from physical sickness in their preaching. "People believed on the basis of the message they heard and were encouraged to pray about everything once they believed."[85]

Not all believers became Christians because of crisis or sickness; rather they heard the gospel and responded because they used to live in fear and the gospel offered them freedom from fear.[86] In some cases unbelievers did not oppose the decision of the first converts but waited and watched them very closely fearing that they would die or something bad might happen

---

82. Ali Wondiye, የእኩለ ሌሊት ወግጋታ *Awakening at Midnight*, 198.

83. Wondiye, *Awakening at Midnight*, 191–197.

84. Alemu Arshe was one of such people. He was the only son of his parents but later in his life he was possessed by a spirit who claimed authority over the whole family. Alemu lost his mind and started to live in a cemetery. He grew his hair, walked around naked and ate wild fruits and leaves. One day to the surprise of his relatives and neighbours he returned to the house of his parents and stayed indoors for the whole day. In the middle of the night he started crying out loud as though he was being strangled. After some time his neighbours who thought he was dead went to the house weeping and wailing to bury his body, but they found Alemu with a sober mind. He related to them what happened to him. "He took him by his neck, pulled him out of me and threw him away. As if skinning a sheep he took something off me and then he told me, 'I am Jesus. I have cast down the one who buried you alive. Believe in me. Go to Ocholo to the house of evangelist Genbo. He would explain to you who I am. Listen to what he would tell you. I will show you the way. I am Jesus' Wondiye, *Awakening at Midnight*, 184–187.

85. Sorsa Sumamo, *Bivocational Missionary-Evangelist: The Story of an Itinerant Preacher in Northern Sidama* (Canada: Enterprise Publications, 2002), 127.

86. Sorsa, *Bivocational Missionary*, 80. Some of the converts in South Omo, however, reverted to traditional religion when crisis struck. Going back and forth was a major problem among the few Hamar and many Ari converts in South Omo. Hamar converts would even go back to traditional religion and do the rituals they missed while in church, then they come back. Ermias Mamo, Dean of Students, Ethiopian Graduate School of Theology, Interview, 1 October 2010, Addis Ababa.

to them, their family, or cattle as a result of their embracing the new faith. When the life of the new converts was transformed and nothing bad happened to them others were encouraged to believe as well.[87] The Evangelical faith, therefore, was asserted with many more signs and wonders; there were stories of some persons being raised to life and numerous healings.[88]

The evangelistic activities of the churches had three centres: Wolaitta, Kembatta and Sidamo. The Wolaitta church expanded southward and westward into Gamu-Gofa and Kulo-Konta respectively. The Kembatta church westward and eastward into Janjero and Arussi, whereas the Sidamo church expanded southward to Gedeo and Burji. The explosive church growth was witnessed among people of two large groups: Omote in which Wolaitta is the larger group, and Sidama which includes Kembatta, Hadiya and Gedeo.[89] The "Galla" and Kaffa families, however resisted.[90]

Upon the eviction of Italy, leaders of SIM-planted churches throughout the country worked hard to join hands with churches established by Lutheran missions in order to establish together an Ethiopian Evangelical church. However, their attempt did not succeed partly because of the return of missionaries who introduced the sharp denominational barriers of Western churches.[91]

Leaders of the church also came into conflict with the mission regarding the status of the new churches. Getachew notes that the leaders wished for the church to have an indigenousname and autonomous leadership instead of being linked with SIM and run by the mission as the head. The mission was not happy with the question of independence, suspecting that the request had its origin in the sentiments of the revolution and that the church would

---

87. Sorsa, *Bivocational Missionary*, 77, 88, 137–138, 150–151.

88. Wondiye, *Awakening at Midnight*, 206, 215–218.

89. The Omote group consisted of Gofa, Wolaitta, Gamo, Kullo, Dorze and Koyra. The Sidama group consisted of Hadiya, Kembatta, Timbaro, Alaba, Sidamo and Darassa (Gedeo). The ethnic groups under each family shared common vocabulary. Cotterell, *Born at Midnight*, 108–109.

90. Cotterell, *Born at Midnight*, 107–111.

91. The return of the missionaries served for the better as well, because the clinics and schools they opened demonstrated to the public that "activities of Evangelicals were permitted in the country." Launhardt, *Evangelicals in Addis Ababa*, 118. Cf. Fekadu Gurmessa, *Evangelical Faith Movement in Ethiopia* (Minneapolis, MN: Lutheran University Press, 2009).

disintegrate.[92] Peter Cotterell, however, argues that the church had always been independent, and missionaries acted as advisors but not as masters.[93] In the late 1950s the name Kale Heywet was approved as the official name of SIM-related churches. The question of establishing an independent head office for the churches, however, was delayed for nine years because of the disagreement of the mission. Finally on 14 March, 1974 the establishment of the head office was approved by the general assembly which was held in Addis Ababa.[94]

Unlike the founders of Mekane Yesus Church the founders of the Kale Heywet Church had neither the permission nor the vision to work with the EOC. EKHC thus is an outcome of a deliberate break from the Orthodox Church. In the 2009 census Kale Heywet Church was declared the largest Evangelical church in Ethiopia. With 6.5 million members it comprises about 8.4 percent of the total population of the country.

3.5. Pentecostals

Eshete notes that the earliest recorded Pentecostal movement in Ethiopia was introduced by Bertha Dommemuth, Ruth Shippey, and Ellen French, missionaries of the Assemblies of God in March 1934. They started offering weekly English classes along with Bible study and prayer at their residence. Their classes were attended by young Ethiopians whose number grew from time to time and the missionaries turned it into a language school called American Grade School and Mission. Eventually the missionaries started Sunday services and gave series of lessons on the person and work of the Holy Spirit and the interest of the youth to know about miracles and healing grew, so did their number.[95]

The Italian invasion in 1936 made it so difficult for the missionaries to hold their meetings that they moved to the Swedish mission station (the present Entoto Mekane Yesus Church). The missionaries reported that the

---

92. Getachew Belete, ኢቃያና ሃሌሎያ (*Agonies and Hallelujah*), 34–42.
93. Cotterell, *Born at Midnight*, 164.
94. Getachew Belete, *Agonies*, 34–42.
95. They encountered opposition from Ethiopians and SIM who referred to the Pentecostals as "tongues people" and discouraged their members from attending their services. Eshete, *Evangelical Movement*, 149–150, 176.

youth who were coming to their religious meetings demonstrated character transformation which attracted others to join them. The report of the missionaries in 1937 included not only news of conversion but also of the converts' experiencing baptism of the Spirit. However, the Italians suspected the youth of working in disguise for the patriotic forces, and they arrested many of them as they distributed gospel tracts and killed them. Some of the Pentecostals joined the patriotic forces and died while resisting the Italians. When the restrictions placed upon them became unbearable, the missionaries left the country in May 1938, trusting God to bring up the "precious treasure" to resurrection life in due time.[96]

The connection between the work of the three missionaries and the 1960s Pentecostal movement is not established. Eshete notes that the movement of the 1930s must have died out with the execution of many of the youth and the impossibility of keeping steady fellowship among the survivors.[97]

Eshete refers to two events prior to the 1960s revival, as deeply impacting the Addis Ababa populace. One was a healing service and preaching of the gospel held in the Addis Ababa stadium in 1952 by Mrs J. C. Jane Daoud. The healing ministry which had wide media coverage touched the attendants so deeply that she is remembered as "Cambologi Mariam." Finnish and Swedish Pentecostal missionaries who arrived in the country in 1951 and 1959 respectively affected the rise of Pentecostal revival in the Haile Sellassie I University in Addis Ababa.[98] The revival resulted with the establishment of Mulu Wongel Church, the largest Pentecostal church in Ethiopia.

The church had its origin in the 1960s revival movements among students in the urban areas. The Pentecostal movement which is characterized by speaking in tongues, boldness in evangelism, exorcism and physical healing was pioneered by the Finnish Pentecostal Mission which arrived in Ethiopia in 1951. In addition, the Philadelphia Church Mission which arrived in 1959 and the Mennonite Mission which was granted permission in 1948 played significant roles in the development of the movement.[99] However,

---

96. Eshete, *Evangelical Movement*, 150–151.
97. Eshete, 151.
98. Eshete, 153.
99. Engelsviken, "Pentecostal Revival," 50.

the movement spread and took shape in the hands of Ethiopian agents predominantly in urban settings.

The Pentecostal movement did not have a single source, rather, both the Finnish Pentecostal Mission and the Swedish Philadelphia Mission played large roles in initiating it in Addis Ababa and Awassa (Southern Ethiopia) respectively. The Swedish Philadelphia Mission initially worked with Christians of other denominations but the Finnish Pentecostal Mission worked with high school students who belonged to the EOC.[100] The movement spread like wildfire influencing students in higher institutions throughout the country. Eventually four groups emerged: Hallelujah group, Yesemay *Birhan* group,[101] Harar Teachers Training Institute group, and Haile Sellassie I University group.

Tamiru Zeleke believes that sociological, spiritual and political reasons were behind the Pentecostal movement in Ethiopia which eventually led the youth into opening a church of their own.[102] According to Tamiru, the youth were not active participants in the affairs of the Orthodox Church so their dissatisfaction with the way the church was operating and the fact that there was no platform for voicing their dissatisfaction turned them away from the ancient church. The second factor was spiritual. The youth had many questions and were not ready to be silenced by an appeal for a blind faith as their fathers had been. In addition to that, their spiritual hunger was not adequately catered for by the church. The Pentecostal movement on

---

100. Engelsviken, 32–53.

101. Yesemay Birhan was initiated by students of local government secondary school in Nazareth town in 1962 as a Bible study group in the compound of the Mennonite established hospital. A number of young men asked Dr Rohrer Eshleman, the Mennonite missionary to teach them English and he used the Gospel of John as the text book. Eventually the message of the book became so attractive to them that they made a commitment to follow Jesus, but not wanting to be identified with foreigners, they started to meet in a small rented house outside the hospital. The students learned about the baptism of the Holy Spirit and diligently prayed for the experience. The experience bonded them together and they shared their experience more and more. Their number grew tremendously. Eventually many of them came together to establish the Mulu Wongel Church. Those who were in Nazareth continued to use "Yesemay Birhan" as their name until they merged with the Mennonite established Meserete Kristos Church as a result of both government pressure to eradicate the movement and the openness of the MKC to support the group in any way they could. Hege, *Beyond Our Prayers*, 147ff.

102. Tamiru Zeleke, "The Mission Strategy of the Mulu Wongel Church" (MTh diss., Ghana, Akropong, Akrofi-Christaller Institute, 2008), 41–49.

the other hand presented them with a simple faith giving them all an equal standing in Christ and seemed to cater to their spiritual hunger.

The final factor was political. The new movement was not associated with the Orthodox Church which was closely identified with the corrupt government of Haile Sellassie. The educated people in the 1960s blamed the Orthodox Church for the ignorance and backwardness of the people, and the youth were part of the wave which desired to see change in the country.[103]

In addition, the distribution of Pentecostal/Charismatic literature in English by the missionaries and freely ordered from publishers in the USA by the students themselves, influenced the thinking of the energetic youth. Although the influence of some could be greater than the others, the teachings and writings of five Pentecostal revivalists overseas made an impact on the thinking of the young Ethiopian: Oral Roberts, Gordon Lindsay, T. L. Osborn, David Nunn, and Joseph Mattsson-Boze.[104] Engelsviken notes that the strong emphasis of all other Protestant missions on the inerrancy and authority of the Scriptures had a strong influence on the Pentecostal movement. "Without hesitation or embarrassment [they] expect all aspects of New Testament Christianity to become a reality today. And their experiences seemed to confirm it!"[105]

Members of the movement read the Bible day and night and prayed and fasted fervently and expectantly for the coming of revival. When Mattsson-Boze, one of the above-mentioned Pentecostal evangelists, who was known as the "missionary evangelist," visited Ethiopia in 1963, his ministry gave focus to the youth. He followed the direct and simple commandment of Jesus, "Preach the Gospel – Baptize – Teach – and Heal the sick."[106] He looked at other Christians as ". . . a vast group of good Christian people that never know anything about an abundant life."[107] Such a view was extended by the young members of the movement to depict other Christians as "spiritually dry" at best and "unsaved" at worst.

---

103. Tamiru Zeleke, "MissionStrategy," 47–49.
104. Engelsviken, "Pentecostal Revival," 66ff.
105. Engelsviken, 79–80.
106. Engelsviken, 84.
107. Engelsviken, 87.

Mattsson-Boze introduced Chacha Omahe, the Kenyan evangelist, who had a still greater impact on the Ethiopians. "It was Chacha Omahe who was instrumental in communicating the Pentecostal *experience* that really marked the beginning of the Pentecostal revival in Ethiopia. . ."[108] In the summers of 1963, '64 and '66, Omahe participated in the Bible course which was annually run by the Swedish Philadelphia Mission in Awassa. Young people from different parts of the country attended the course and during his prayer afterwards many were baptized in the Holy Spirit. The following reflection of the experience by one of the participants is very interesting:

> He was an African. It may have had some psychological effect. Probably many of the brothers and sisters may have thought that this baptism in the Holy Spirit was begun by white people, or fabricated by them, and may therefore have been suspicious of it. However, when they saw a black man coming and preaching about it with more strength and power than the missionaries, many of them were very much affected.[109]

Those who did not receive the experience in Omahe's first visit received it in his second visit. "Evangelism was an integral part of the Bible courses, and the participants were sent out in the districts around Awassa during the weekends."[110] This gave them an opportunity to preach what they had been taught and experience and practise the power of the Holy Spirit which they had just received.[111] Most importantly, they "took the fire with them" to their villages and hometowns and the movement spread. The Philadelphia Church Mission through their representatives in Addis Ababa stayed in close contact with the emerging Mulu Wongel Church. Their work in Awassa "eventually led to the formation [of] (sic) an Ethiopian Pentecostal Church called Heywet *Birhan*."[112]

The youth in Addis were rather dissatisfied with the slow pace of the Finnish missionaries. Chacha Omahe visited them on his way back from Awassa in 1963, and held a prayer meeting. All young people who attended the prayer meeting received the experience of ecstasy as being filled by the

---

108. Engelsviken, 88.
109. Informant A, Transcripts 1973, 2, quoted by Engelsviken, "Pentecostal Revival," 90.
110. Engelsviken, "Pentecostal Revival," 91.
111. Engelsviken, 90, 92.
112. Engelsviken, 95.

Holy Spirit. The experience clothed the youth with a new boldness to witness and pray for the demon-possessed. The Finnish ladies were not at ease with the ramifications of the experience. They feared that it would upset the government and warned the students that they must take full responsibility in case of a government inquiry. In what seemed like a mixture of racist and chauvinist attitude Omahe admonished them openly, "You must keep quiet; this is the work of God. I speak to you as I speak to my wife. I am doing the work of God and you should not interfere."[113]

Engelsviken observes, "The white missionaries had not been able or willing to convey this blessing . . . while the black Kenyan evangelist had been instrumental in leading a large number of young people into the experience. There is no wonder that this fact would greatly enhance the self-confidence of the Ethiopian believers."[114] In 1965 they left the mission and joined an independent group working around the Addis Ababa University led by Ethiopians, and the two groups were joined by a group of people coming from "Yesemay *Birhan* in Nazareth. These three groups came together to officially establish "a new local Pentecostal Church."[115]

The fourth group was established in the Haile Sellassie I (HIS) University, when in 1965 four Evangelical Christian students decided to rent a house in which to live and conduct prayer and fasting on Wednesday and Friday afternoons. Their number grew because of the students' active witness accompanied by healing and deliverance and the small house could not contain them all. Members of Yesemay *Birhan* and Hallelujah groups joined the HSI University fellowship. Many students were converted because of the active preaching of the gospel, prayer for healing and for the filling of the Spirit. People brought the sick and demon possessed for deliverance and healing. The number of members grew greatly but services were held only on weekdays and the students attended mission related Evangelical churches on Sunday mornings. As for the way forward, some individuals suggested that it would be best to remain in their respective churches, including the EOC, in order to enhance the spread of the revival.[116] However, in a national

---

113. Engelsviken, 99.
114. Engelsviken, 101.
115. Engelsviken, 102.
116. Eshete, *Evangelical Movement*, 171.

conference held in the summer of 1966 in which nine different regions including Addis Ababa were represented the idea of establishing their own church emerged.[117]

On 1 January 1967, the Swedish missionaries Allan Wedin and Wallberg[118] laid their hands on seven Ethiopian elders elected by the group and ordained them.[119] The next important step was to secure registration with the government and in April 1967 they completed the paper work required for official registration with the government as "ጥንታዊት የእግዚአብሔር ማህበር" (literally God's Ancient Association), but their application was rejected on the grounds that the term "ጥንታዊት" (ancient) applied only to the Ethiopian Orthodox Church. The group then adopted "Mulu Wongel" (Full Gospel) as their name.[120] However, their request was turned down because they were not considered to be worthy of being registered as an independent Ethiopian Christian association.[121] Pending the official grant of registration, they continued to worship and open new churches.

Engelsviken notes two characteristics which made the Mulu Wongel Church different from the other Evangelical churches: "*The Pulpit was reserved almost exclusively for Ethiopians and the church was financially self-supporting.*"[122] The self-supporting factor soon became "a matter of principle and pride" and enabled the church to grow tremendously compared with the other churches which depended on mission input. The Pentecostal movement was at times criticized as harbouring an "anti-white" attitude. Engelsviken, however, argues that although the general critical attitude towards the West was felt in Ethiopia, the movement was not anti-white as such, it was "more an assertion of African and Ethiopian identity and independence."[123]

---

117. Harar, Nazareth, Assela, Awassa, Jimma, Debre Birhan, Mekele, Asmara, and Debre Zeit. Engelsviken, "Pentecostal Revival," 133.

118. His first name is not given. He is referred to as "brother Wallberg." Engelsviken, "Pentecostal Revival," 150.

119. Engelsviken, 142–150.

120. Hege, *Beyond Our Prayers*, 147–152.

121. Engelsviken "Pentecostal Revival," 154.

122. Englesviken, 119.

123. Engelsviken, 119–120.

3.6. Transformation and Polarization: The Outcomes of Pentecostal Movement

The Pentecostal revival led to religious renewal in the mainline Evangelical churches and at the same time created internal conflict and tension. Engelsviken notes that the youth in the mainline churches who were touched by the Pentecostal movement were critical of the leaders of the churches they belonged to, and often with good reason (immorality, lust for power, corruption). The leaders, however, considered the attitude of the youth as disrespectful because it was culturally inappropriate to openly criticize an elderly person, and especially the leader of the church. Moreover, the leaders regarded the youth as fanatical, self righteous[124] and arrogant.

On an organized and unprecedented scale, the Mekane Yesus Church of Addis Ababa held open and official discussion with the leaders of the Mulu Wongel Church in 1967. There was apprehension on both sides. The Lutherans were not happy with the Pentecostals' rejection of the validity of infant baptism and their practice of re-baptizing members of Mekane Yesus Church. The Pentecostals believed that their views were dismissed as emotional and not based on solid teaching of the Scriptures. However, they both agreed that the church should not divide over the movement and that the youth should remain in the Mekane Yesus Church. With respect to worship styles, the Pentecostals favoured spontaneous and dynamic worship rather than a liturgical form. To accommodate both groups a proposal was made that there should be two services in the church: one liturgical and one "free."[125]

SIM, on the contrary, considered the new movement as abnormal and openly discouraged its members from taking any part in it. This view was successfully communicated to the Kale Heywet churches.[126] Both the mission

---

124. The "Yesemay Birhan" group in Nazareth which comprised youth who were fruit of the revival had a similar attitude. They were critical of the members of the Mennonite affiliate Meserete Kristos Church because they did not have the baptism of the Holy Spirit, they did not tithe, and depended heavily on overseas funds to run their ministries. Hege, *Beyond Our Prayers*, 154.

125. Engelsviken, "Pentecostal Revival," 198–202.

126. Kenneth Oglesby, one of SIM's missionaries in 1930s, had a Pentecostal experience while in the USA and was banned from serving upon his return to Ethiopia. He returned to Ethiopia in April 1956 after receiving permission from Haile Sellassie during his first visit to the USA. Oglesby preached and held prayer meetings in his residence. He even organized home church service and was waiting for permission from the government to make it public.

and the indigenous leaders thus had difficulty in accepting the movement and they were not alone. As Engelsviken observes, by its very nature, the movement posed a challenge to all Christian churches because of its "sheep stealing" or "fishing in others' waters." With its doctrine of speaking in tongues as initial evidence of the baptism of the Spirit it sought to reach all peoples regardless of their religious background. Pentecostals thought that it would be wrong to stop those who would join them from other churches and Christian backgrounds.[127]

The Pentecostals appropriated the teaching of the New Testament on the gifts of the Holy Spirit thereby showing the relevance of the charismatic experiences to Ethiopian society. Communicating with the Spirit (instead of the traditional seeking the mediums of spirits) was provided as the proper substitute and a sacred option for people's inborn yearning for maintaining contact with the supernatural. Thus, they paved the way for people to live out their spirituality in a better, godly, safe and lasting way by making use of the biblically supported ongoing aspect of the gifts of the Holy Spirit.

This does not mean that miracles were foreign to the older churches. There are numerous testimonies of the dead rising, the sick being healed, and demons being exorcised in both the Kale Heywet and Mekane Yesus churches. The difference with the Pentecostals was that the miracles were explained as the result of the ongoing work of the Holy Spirit. Thus, the Pentecostals strongly encouraged people to pray for and expect a miracle. The mass prayer, the loud crying and walking about the room as people prayed, seems to have had its beginning with Pentecostals. In addition, encouraging all to pray in tongues loudly and the public annunciation of words of knowledge and prophecy were new experiences, and they were carried forward. "The persecution experience, which led to the dispersal of the young Pentecostals into the various denominations of the Evangelical churches, was one of the first major events that opened the way for the wave of the Pentecostal movement to spread in what could be considered mainline Evangelical churches."[128]

He also served as advisor to the government on tourism and hotel management. Eshete, *Evangelical Movement*, 153–154.

127. Engelsviken, "Pentecostal Revival," 45.

128. Eshete, *Evangelical Movement*, 188.

The Pentecostals did not restrain the manifestation of their charismatic experiences in spite of the uneasiness of the leaders of the mainline churches. The inevitable happened. As believers from all kinds of backgrounds worshipped together, the worship style became more and more spontaneous as the Pentecostals/Charismatics suddenly brought "words of knowledge" and "prophecy." Many prayed in tongues very loudly. The manifestation of demons and exorcism was a common phenomenon. Worship songs were sung with deeper emotion and tears were shed in prayer for the closed churches and dispersed believers throughout the country. People shared experiences, asked questions and desired to experience the so-called charismatic gifts of the Holy Spirit for themselves.

The more conservative churches could not maintain their predictable worship services. The usual order and solemn worship was disrupted. At times the whole service appeared to be chaotic. "Our God is the God of peace and order," cried out some leaders in their endeavour to keep things in check.[129] In all this there grew a tremendous sense of solidarity and unity among believers of all traditions. The suffering of the believers in a certain denomination was felt by all. The fervour of the prayer was great and the faith of believers grew in spite of their suffering.[130] They prayed for deliverance from the hands of their aggressors but at the same time acknowledged the sovereignty of the Lord in the face of tremendous suffering and developed compassion towards the persecutors.

When the persecution was halted for the most part, and churches reopened in 1990, the unity that had developed underground became evident to all. Sharing speakers and choirs became a common phenomenon. The initial negative attitude[131] of Charismatics towards members of the so-called mainline churches decreased. The conservative churches on the other hand

---

129. 1 Corinthians 14:33 was often quoted.

130. John Cumbers, *Living with the Red Terror* (Kearney, NE: Morris Publishing, 1996), 36.

131. Members of other churches were depicted as spiritually dry, not baptized with the Holy Spirit and even not saved. For passionate Pentecostals, there appeared to be no evidence of the fullness of the Holy Spirit without speaking in tongues. Also the solemn and not so emotional worship style of the mainline churches was widely criticized by fiery Pentecostals. Such a view created a lot of friction and nearly destroyed the overall unity of Evangelicals in Ethiopia.

made room for the charismatic experiences.[132] For example, the Kale Heywet Church revised its faith statement, abandoning her cessationist[133] doctrine and lifting the ban on body movement, clapping of hands and making of joyful cries during worship.[134] In addition, Pentecostals emphasized the person and work of the Holy Spirit and demonstrated tremendous passion for the salvation of others.

The influence of the Mulu Wongel Church went beyond those who actually joined it. Many people in other churches, especially among the young, were challenged by the evangelistic zeal and spiritual lifestyle of the Mulu Wongel believers, and even though many did not actually leave their own churches, they experienced a spiritual renewal which often transformed their lives and Christian testimony. So as time went by, the influence of the Mulu Wongel Church was increasingly felt in almost all the other protestant churches.[135]

The coming and subsequent growth of Pentecostalism had both positive and negative effects on the lives of believers and on the the perception of the public towards Evangelical Christians in Ethiopia. It provided Ethiopian Evangelicals with a richer spiritual experience and certainly with a new name, thereby significantly changing the face of Ethiopian Evangelical Christianity. In other words, Pentecostalism brought Evangelical Christianity, which formerly was considered as insignificant movement among peripheral peoples, to the centre.

On the other hand, the sharp dichotomy between worldly citizenship and heavenly citizenship as propagated by Pentecostalism influenced Evangelicals to the extreme so that they isolated themselves from "worldly affairs."[136] However the atheistic ideology of the ruling Communist party

---

132. This was done not only out of conviction but also to keep their members. The initial not so helpful portrayal of Pentecostals as merely based on emotion and fabricating signs and wonders gradually faded away.

133. This view holds that the so-called Charismatic gifts of the Spirit (tongues, miracles, prophecy and healing) were foundational for the establishment of the church and ceased to function upon the establishment of the first-century church. In addition, with the closing of the canon of the Bible, there is no need for such gifts.

134. Eshete, *Evangelical Movement*, 177.

135. Engelsviken, "Pentecostal Revival," 169.

136. Such tendency was greatly resented by onlookers of the time. The followers of "Pentecoste" were accused of being obstacles of the revolution and weakening the patriotism

also is to blame for such isolation.[137] The implications of such a tendency were immense even after the fall of the Derg; that Evangelicals who dared to take part in "non-Christian" activities such as sports or leading "secular" groups were expected to spiritualize it all or make a clear and clean distinction between their faith and what they were leading.[138]

Even public holidays such as "the Victory at Adwa" were used to conduct worship services or hold a prayer and fasting program in their churches. Rarely would they join the great crowd that goes to public squares to commemorate the victory of Adwa. Such isolation of oneself from national events must have contributed to the accusations of Evangelicals as being "unpatriotic, or foreign."

Moreover, the already troubled relationship between the EOC and Evangelicals was further strained with mass evangelism usually conducted by Pentecostal/Charismatic preachers both from Ethiopia and overseas. The unwise and provocative publicity for mass evangelism was often insensitive in the Ethiopian context. Moreover, intolerance towards EOC's traditions and experiences increased with the spread of Pentecostalism and more and more Evangelicals appeared to tell EOC members outright that they were not saved.

In addition "the shouting and screaming during prayer times and healing services"[139] which is a common phenomenon of Pentecostalism, has affected many Evangelical churches and is assumed to represent Evangelicals as a whole. With the spread of charismatic experiences and the subsequent superior feeling of Evangelicals over the Orthodox Church, new ways of polarizing the relationship between the Orthodox and Evangelicals have

---

of the youth. Yirga Haile Mariam, በሃይማኖት ስም የሚነግዱ ወጣቶን ከትግል መድረክ ለማዘናጋት በጻረ አብዮተኞች የሚደረግ ይህ፣ *Addis Zemen* (Ginbot 12, 1971 Eth. C), 3.

137. Many Christians came to fear politics because of its closer association with the Communist regime. Thus, they stayed as far from it as possible. After the fall of the Derg, there was an effort to convince Evangelicals to take part in the politics of the country and to this effect a book was published by an Evangelical writer, Elias Bekele entitled: ክርስቲያንና ፖለቲክ (Politics and the Christian). The generally held notion was that "the whole world was under the control of the evil one," 1 John 5:19. Sime Taddesse in the *Kale Heywet* magazine argued that Christians should participate in politics and show in work their lightness and saltness. Sime Taddesse, ምረጡኝ (Vote for me), *Kale Heywet* 30 (1997 Eth. C), 23–24.

138. Solomon Tilahun, student of Peace and Reconciliation Department at Mennonite Seminary, USA, Interview, 2 September 2010, Addis Ababa.

139. Eshete, *Evangelical Movement*, 175.

emerged. One such example is to perceive some of the sacred traditions of the EOC such as *tabot*, as idol worship.

Moreover, traditional dances during wedding and initiation (circumcision) were interpreted as demonic. The radical view of conversion which was started by the missionaries was further strengthened by Pentecostals. They laid heavy stress on dress codes, banned the use of ornaments for women and introduced terminologies peculiar to Evangelicals.[140] The polarization led to refusing to have table fellowship with the Orthodox on feast days held as commemoration of the angels and saints. There was fear that such commemoration was idolatry, therefore, the food could not be consumed in good conscience. With the spread of the Pentecostal movement sharp distinctions were made between the Orthodox and Evangelicals and the depiction of the Orthodox as *ahzab* which connoted people who do not know God, resulted with intensified "proselytism" widening the rift between the Orthodox and Evangelicals.[141]

3.7. The Sufficiency of Scripture in Vernacular

As discussed above, the first Evangelical church in Ethiopia (EECMY) came into existence as a result of revival caused by the reading of the Bible in Amharic. In line with the reformed tradition, Evangelicals in Ethiopia have depended on the Bible and accepted it as sufficient for instruction in Christian living and witness. Although such a conviction does not rule out the ongoing function of the gifts of the Spirit, in principle, they are not given equal status to the Bible.

The exaltation of the Bible has affected the Evangelicals' perception of the fathers and the tradition of the church as upheld by the Orthodox Church. Generally speaking, Evangelicals show little attachment to the fathers and ancient church tradition. In fact, there is a tendency to trace the origin of

---

140. For example, the usual Christian way of showing gratitude, "Egziabher Yistelegn" (God reward you on my behalf) was nearly abandoned for "Geta Yibarkih/sh" (the Lord bless you).

141. The noisy worship services resulted in discrimination against Evangelicals, making it difficult for them to rent a house in urban areas. Needless to say, the crying and shouting during worship is not always helpful to the Evangelicals themselves. Cf. Eshete, *Evangelical Movement*, 163–168.

Evangelicalism to the Reformation in Europe. In addition, they limit themselves to the sixty-six books and do not seem to accept the apocryphal books.

The Bible they use, therefore, comprises only the sixty-six books and is the main identity mark of Evangelicals. In addition, the Ge'ez Scripture is not used in Evangelical churches as it is in the Orthodox Church. Rather, Amharic and mother-tongue translations are widely used. Evangelicals seek to base their arguments on the Bible and show little sympathy for traditions which do not have strong support from the Bible. Upon joining Evangelical churches, people are strongly encouraged to acquire their own copies of the Bible. Once they are led through the basic doctrines and have received discipleship instructions and baptism, converts are usually expected to read the Bible for themselves. The ramifications of such convictions in the relationship between Evangelicals and the Orthodox Church will be discussed in chapter 5.

Conclusion

After the incident of the Jesuits which led to much bloodshed among brethren, the Orthodox Church closed its door against foreigners. In the nineteenth century, however, European interest towards Ethiopia was renewed and Ethiopia showed increasing openness with the coming of Tewodros, Yohannes, Menelik and Haile Sellassie to power. The coming of foreign missions greatly increased during the reign of Haile Sellassie who desired to make use of their skills to spread education and Christianize the resistant people groups of southern Ethiopia.

The work of mission was mostly limited to areas which were not dominated by the Orthodox Church. Sudan Interior Mission undertook mission work in the south and was successful in converting traditional religion followers and nominal Orthodox adherents to Evangelical Christianity. The question of why the Orthodox Church did not succeed in the south like it did in the northern plateau and parts of Shewa needs further investigation. Perhaps the rising of Gragn which weakened the church hindered it from intensive evangelistic activity. At any rate people groups in the south and south-west identified themselves with the Bible and emerged as strong Christian bodies.

The Orthodox Church, however, was not happy with the growth of Evangelical churches and continued to exert force to hinder their growth. The missionaries tried to avoid collision with the state church and for the most part their work remained among the peripheral peoples with limited involvement in the urbancentres. The rise of the Pentecostal movement in the 1960s, however, challenged the Orthodox Church in the urban centres and Pentecostals suffered intense persecution as a result.

The coming of the Derg affected all churches, but Evangelicals suffered more because they were targeted as individuals and their churches as institutions. With the closing of most of the churches the Pentecostals flocked to the few open churches and this spread Pentecostalism and resulted in a greater similarity of worship styles among Evangelical churches. With the influence of Pentecostals, evangelistic activities targeted all including the Orthodox and the numbers of converting Orthodox members increased. Even though Evangelicals never had the political upper hand their activities were looked at as part of a subtle plan of Western missions to weaken the church by taking its members.

It seems that the nineteenth-century mission organizations were aware of the Orthodox resistance to their involvement and they tried to avoid contact with it, except for the attempts of Hermannsburg Mission and Swedish Evangelical Society which tried to follow in the footsteps of the Church Missionary Society to revitalize the Orthodox with the reading of the Bible in the vernacular. The SEM encountered groups of priests who were expelled from the church because they were committed to the reading of the Bible in Amharic, which was distributed by the CMS.

The CMS story as will be discussed below is important because it shows the early Orthodox-Evangelical encounters at a time when the country was divided and the church did not have central administration. In addition the CMS was instrumental in printing the Amharic Bible which in the hands of indigenous evangelists resulted in the conversion of "pagans" and commitment of nominal Orthodox. Moreover, the success story of the SEM in evangelizing the "Galla" had its origins in the vision of CMS.

CHAPTER 4

The Anglican-Orthodox Encounter: An Attempt to Revitalize the Church of Ethiopia

Introduction

The Church Missionary Society (CMS) channelled the first organized Protestant effort to work with the church of Ethiopia and marked the coming of Evangelicals on the scene of Ethiopian Christianity. Its efforts are important for the story of Christianity in Ethiopia for a number of reasons. At the time of the coming of the CMS the country was smaller and the kingdom of Abyssinia had its seat in the northern highlands and the Orthodox faith was held by the Northern people. It seems that the CMS missionaries did not have to deal with ethnic factors. In other words, the resentment that the "Amhara culture" and Orthodoxy was imposed on other people groups does not appear to have been an issue in the late 1820s.

Second, the CMS, like other later mission agencies, was insistent on the Bible as the sole guide for the church, but unlke some later Protestant missions, it acknowledged the ancient Abyssinian Christian identity as a valid one and did not desire to establish a separate church. The Society saw the Abyssinian church as another national church, like itself, rooted in the early church, especially the Bible and with valid sacraments. The existence of the national church was not a problem to the CMS. In fact, when they came from the church of England to the church of Abyssinia, they came to a sister church. Hence, their concern for the revitalization of the Abyssinian church. With the significance of the study of CMS in Ethiopia stated, we shall now briefly study the background of the mission.

4.1. An Overview of Evangelicalism in England and the Establishment of the Church Missionary Society

In the seventeenth century the higher clergy of the Church of England were wealthy, being well provided for by the people who were under their pastoral care. The bishops were required to be present in the House of Lords in London and left pastoral care to the lower clergy who were sometimes relatively ignorant, extremely poor and struggled to provide for their families. In general church life declined after 1660, and the administration of the Eucharist became infrequent.[1]

Evangelicals believed that the clergy lacked "converting zeal." They were in need of passion for the formation of Christ in people's lives. In other words, they did not take extraordinary pains to improve the spiritual state of their parishners. The Evangelical revival, therefore, attempted to return the church and its clergy to the doctrine of the Bible but its efforts were considered disturbing to the church and thereby, the country. The spiritual state of the church was in decline. "In the desire for a quiet life emotion and feeling had been banished from their proper place in religion and a vigorous personal faith had been replaced by a prudential morality."[2] Zealous Evangelicals thus were not given high office in the Church of England. The church was suspicious of their doctrine, methods, and personal character. They were called, "Enthusiasts" because unlike the clergy as a whole they were passionate for conversion of people.

Evangelicals were committed to bringing back the lost fervour of personal faith, but they did not desire to disturb the Church of England, nor did they contemplate leaving it. Instead, they set out to appeal to the conscience of

---

1. Michael Hennell, *John Venn and the Clapham Sect* (Cambridge: Lutterworth Press, 1958), 11–13.

2. Hennell, *John Venn*, 12.

people, to awaken it to a sense of sin against God, not by combating errors, but by laying down the truth.[3]

The CMS came to existence among such Evangelicals of the Church of England. It was meant to hold to two firm principles at once: an Evangelical doctrine of salvation and an Anglican doctrine of the church. Here are five Evangelical perceptions of the Church of England about the identity of the church. First, the church is ancient. The church did not start with the Reformation; it is continuous from the early church. Thus the creeds and the fathers are regarded highly, though not considered as equal with the Scripture. Unlike the tendency of some continental Protestants, the fathers were not downgraded in order to exalt the Scriptures.

Second, the church was national. Constitutionally it was the church of the nation and citizens were considered members. Although in the view of Evangelicals they might not be regenerate, they still belonged to the church. Third, the church was Protestant. The English Reformation raised issues such as vernacular Bible, rejection of the papacy and the sole mediatorship of Christ. On the other hand, it retained respect for saints although it rejected clerical celibacy and monasticism. But destroying images, abolishing clerical hierarchy and rejecting fasting as works of righteousness, which were part of reformation movements in Scotland and Switzerland, caused little aggression in England.[4]

Fourth, the church was Evangelical. Original sin, justification by faith, regeneration by the Holy Spirit, and the efficacy of the atonement of Christ were preached by the Evangelicals who made calls for conversion. But the preaching was done in the context of the church. The official formularies of the church (the Prayer Book, the thirty-nine Articles of Religion and the Book of Homilies) were regarded by Evangelicals as containing Evangelical doctrine. Anglican Evangelicals argued that no matter how corrupt or "dead" the church might be at any given time and place, separation is wrong; it is a Christian duty to work and pray for reformation and renewal.

Fifth, the Bible was at the centre of the teaching and preaching and the Old Testament apocryphal books were profitable, though not given

---

3. Hennell, 14–17.

4. Destroying images became a feature of the Puritan tradition of the 1640s, which adopted a more radical view of Reformation.

equal status with the Bible. It was believed that the Bible was to spread widely. As noted above the Evangelicals who were passionate to see people commit their lives to Christ were not only concerned about the spiritual state of the Church of England but also preaching the gospel to "heathen." The discussion among friends who were like-minded eventually led to the formation of the Church Missionary Society which was committed to the Church of England and desired to reach the "heathen," that is, those in the non-Christian world.

The Church Missionary Society for Africa and the East (CMS) was established in London on 12 April 1799 with Africa and India in mind as its primary mission fields.[5] The founders[6] were committed to three things: abolition of slavery,[7] bringing social change in their own country and taking the gospel across new frontiers.[8] The mission partnered with Basel Mission

---

5. Eugene Stock, *The History of the Church Missionary Society* (London: Church Missionary Society, 1899), 64.

6. The Venns were prominent in the Church of England as generation of churchmen. Henry Venn (1796–1873) was secretary of the Church Missionary Society for thirty-two years from 1841 to 1873. He was "one of the key figures of the nineteenth-century missionary and evangelical movement. He is known as the father of the indigenous church principle – self-supporting, self-governing and self-propagating." He had two sons, John Venn (1834–1923) and Henry Venn (b1838) and one daughter, Henrietta (1832–1902). His father, John Venn (1759–1813) was Rector of Clapham and member of the Clapham Sect and one of the founders of the CMS. His grandfather, Henry Venn (1725–1797), was a member of the first-generation Evangelicals. John was coached by his father Henry into ministry and developed deeper desire for it. To the delight of his father, he told him that he would rather "be a minister of Christ than a prince." Before he died John charged his cousin who was training for ministry, "Give yourself wholly to it. . . . You have a holy work before you, Christ to help you, the Holy Spirit to enlighten you, heaven for your home, the Bible for your guide. Travel with these companions through this world as a pilgrim and a stranger seeking one above and may you bring many sons to glory." Hennel, *John Venn*, 32–33, 254. Cf. Church Missionary Society: Section III, Part 19, www.ampltd.co.uk/digital_guides/cms_section/, accessed 30 August 2011.

7. In 1806 before the abolition of slave trade, John Venn referred to the need for making reparation for Africa hope of better times, when the true knowledge of God will more generally prevail. "They will look to the infant Church of Africa, and will watch with anxious desire its progress. Africa expects from you some reparation for her wrongs." Hennel, *John Venn*, 244.

8. The committee emphasized the power of the Word of God which changes lives. CMS missionaries thus were never to take the lead, nor to introduce denominational distinctions. Although CMS was fully committed to the Church of England, it desired to enable native churches to be able to modify the ceremonies according to the standard of the Bible to resonate their own national taste. William Knight, *The Missionary Secretariat of Henry Venn, B. D.* (London: Longmans, Green, & Co., 1880), 286.

and other continental societies to train its candidates and sought ordination for them. When the Society was in the making it was influenced by Charles Simeon, an Anglican priest in Cambridge who "gave a threefold definition of the task of the preacher: to humble the sinner, to exalt the Saviour, and to promote holiness."[9]

The Society greatly hoped for the revitalization of the Eastern churches as the means to reach the Muslims and "heathen" all around them. CMS was confident that such awakening would come through the study of the Scriptures ". . . it is by bringing back these churches to the knowledge and love of the sacred Scriptures, that the blessing from on high may be expected to descend on them."[10]

One might wonder why the Society thought of reviving Eastern churches and not the Roman Catholic Church. The society considered the Roman Catholic Church as beyond reformation.

> The Roman Catholic Church is entangled in a snare from which it cannot be freed, while it holds the Infallibility and Universal Headship of the Bishop of Rome. The Greek, Armenian, Syrian, Coptic and Abyssinian churches, though in many points far gone from the simplicity and purity of the truth, are not so entangled; and also possess within themselves the principle and the means of reformation.[11]

These ancient churches were recognized as national churches in their respective countries and CMS had no agenda of proselytizing them. The committee underlined the need for "wisdom and fidelity while serving among the outward members of Christian churches who hold the main truths of the gospel but with mixture of error."[12]

Although the Eastern churches were believed to have mixed the truth with error, CMS greatly hoped that they would be renewed with the power of the Bible, ". . . that wonderful book which alone is suited to every race of

---

9. Andrew F. Walls, "English Neo-Calvinism and the Early Protestant Missionary Movement," in *Calvinism on the Peripheries: Religion and Society in Europe*, ed. Ábrahám Kovács (Budapest: L'Harmattan, 2009), 5.

10. Stock, *History of the Church Missionary Society*, 226.

11. Stock, 226–227.

12. Stock, 226.

mankind, and which comes home to every individual of our race when received in faith, as the well-known voice of a parent speaking to children. . ."[13]

To this end the Society sought ordained missionary candidates with deep conviction and high moral values, "Spiritual men for spiritual work."[14] However, finding English clergymen to send out as missionaries proved to be difficult.[15] If the CMS had not been committed to the Church of England and determined to recruit ordained people, it would have found more candidates. However, the society did not wish to change its principles and opted to send out other nationals.

As stated earlier, in preparation for mission to Eastern churches, the CMS actively engaged in literary and translational work and partnered with the Basel Mission to provide trained men.[16] Gustav Aren notes, "The Basel Mission . . . was international, ecumenical and interconfessional. Its 'confession' was Scripture. The mission combined Lutheran teaching with Reformed principles for forming congregations and Pietistic ideas of worship and conduct."[17] Consequently, the Basel trainees exhibited "a quality in their approach to evangelism and pastoral care that differed from that of their British colleagues in that it was at once more robust and energetic and yet more intimate."[18]

However, the CMS was not a passive recipient of Basel trainees. Instead it sought to ensure that the Basel Mission offered rigorous academic training and its leaders upheld orthodox views. The trainees were not always able to express themselves in English simply and accurately which raised questions in London about the theological orthodoxy of the teaching given at

---

13. Knight, *Missionary Secretariat*, 287.

14. Stock, *History of the Church Missionary Society*, 71.

15. Kevin Ward and Brian Stanley, eds., *The Church Mission Society and World Christianity 1799–1999* (Grand Rapids, MI: Eerdmans, 2000), 44.

16. Paul Jenkins noted, "The contacts between the CMS and the Basel Mission were neither distant nor superficial, but close, vital to both sides, and remarkably intimate, given the communications of the time." Ward and Stanley, *Church Mission Society*, 58.

17. Aren, *Evangelical Pioneers*, 53, 56

18. Ward and Stanley, *Church Mission Society*, 56. The landmark contribution of Basel trainees in the study of the language of indigenous people mitigated the racist thinking of the time that regarded African cultures and languages as primitive (unlike European cultures and languages), and as incapable of expressing deeper thoughts and emotion. Ward and Stanley, 56–55.

Basel Mission. Most of all, what Jenkins calls "the ecclesiological question about the enforcement of Anglican discipline on people with a non-Anglican background" remained a matter of conflict between the two societies.[19] The traditional difference between the two bodies was well reflected on the mission field in Ethiopia, as will be discussed shortly, for example the inflexibility of the Lutheran CMS missionaries over Lenten observances perplexed the Ethiopian Christians for whom fasting was part and parcel of Christian identity.

For the agenda of revitalizing the oriental churches, ". . . assisting in the recovery from their long sleep . . ."[20] vernacular Scripture was vital. To this end, the scripture in Ethiopic[21] was edited and printed and Samuel Lee, a young man who knew Latin, Greek, Hebrew, Syriac and Arabic, Persian and Hindustani was trained in Cambridge at the Society's expense and employed as "the Society's Orientalist."[22] In the report of 1818 the position of the Society was surveyed. ". . . On these Missions it will be seen that the Society has to deal with man in almost every stage of civilization; from the noble but uncultivated New Zealander, upward through the more civilized African, and the still more refined Hindoo, the acute and half enlightened Mohammedan, and the different gradations in which Christianity is enjoyed by the Abyssinian, the Syrian, and the Greek churches."[23]

The Society sent William Jowett to the Mediterranean ". . . as 'Literary Representative' to inquire into the state of religion in the Levant, and to suggest methods of translating and circulating the Scriptures, and other ways of influencing the Oriental churches."[24] Subsequently, a printing press was established in Malta. It was observed that the clergy of the Oriental churches used ancient ecclesiastical languages which were not understood by the people and that often the priests did not possess printed copies of the Scripture. In collaboration with the Bible Society editions of Scripture in the ecclesiastical languages were made for the use of the clergy. The plan

---

19. Ward and Stanley, *Church Mission Society*, 58–61.
20. Stock, *History of the Church Missionary Society*, 121.
21. Ethiopians refer to it as Ge'ez.
22. Stock, *History of the Church Missionary Society*, 118–121.
23. Stock, 121.
24. Stock, 224.

was to enlighten the priests so that they might translate the Scripture into vernaculars. In the case of Ethiopia, as discussed in chapter 2, Jowett purchased for the Bible Society Abu Rumi's translation of the Bible in Amharic.[25] While the Society was preparing to send missionaries to Ethiopia, rulers of the country were attempting to make contact with European countries.

4.2. The Political and Spiritual Condition of Ethiopia in the Nineteenth Century

As the Society was making preparations to work towards the revival of Orthodox churches, the governors of different parts of northern Ethiopia, who considered themselves protectors of the Orthodox faith, were trying to maintain friendly relationship with Great Britain as a Christian nation. One of such rulers was Ras Wolde Sellassie[26] of Tigray – a powerful governor of his time. His letter to George III, king of Great Britain was delivered in February 1811 by Henry Salt.[27] Earlier in 1805 Salt had made what is rated as the first modernProtestantattempt to establish a relationship with Ethiopia[28] but Ras Wolde Sellassie was more interested in assistance to bring an Alexandrian bishop from Egypt than a trade relationship with Britain.[29]

---

25. Stock, 227–228.

26. The letter spells his name as Welleda Selassé. For the sake of consistency with previous citations, unless quoting, I will maintain the usual Ethiopian way of spelling his name as it sounds.

27. In a letter to Rev E. Bickersteth, Christian Kugler, one of the CMS missionaries to Ethiopia, writes that Mr Salt provided them with vital wisdom in their plans to proceed into the interiors of Ethiopia. Kugler to Rev E. Bickersteth, 12 April 1828, University of Birmingham Special Collections, CMS/B/OMS/ C M O46.

28. Salt brought back a letter and a present of fine cloth from Emperor Egwala Tsion to King George III. C. E. Bosworth, "Henry Salt, Consul in Egypt 1816–1827 and Pioneer Egyptologist," in *Bulletin of the John Rylands Library* 57 (1974), 74–75.

29. Bosworth, "Henry Salt," 69–91. Wolde Sellassie saw a dream about Salt in which he was sitting on the brow of a hill and Salt was in a plain below sowing grain with both hands. The corn sprung up instantaneously round Salt in great profusion; while at the same time Wolde Sellassie's lap was full of gold. The impact of the dream was so great that Wolde Sellassie kept Salt near him and was not happy when Salt announced that he was leaving. The ruler continuously asked him if he would come back. When Salt left Wolde Sellassie saw him off with tears running down his face. Henry Salt, *A Voyage to Abyssinia and Travels into the Interior of That Country* (London: F. C. and J. Rivington, St Paul's Church-Yard, 1814), 383–384.

Aren notes that Salt's attempt was significant because it was connected with a deliberate attempt to translate and distribute the Bible.[30]

Salt returned to Ethiopia in January 1809, "charged with the opening of diplomatic relations and with making detailed reports on the state of the country and on the Red Sea coastlands, and especially on their potential as ports of entry for trade." He also brought official presents to Ras Wolde Sellassie and Salt's official visit established the first diplomatic communications between Britain and Ethiopia.[31] Ras Wolde Sellassie's letter of 1811 to King George III shows that he looked at Great Britain as a Christian ally. The governor indicated that Gougousa, the king of Abyssinia at the time, was not Orthodox in faith and that he had gone to war with him. He expressed his gratitude for the gift of spears, knives and artillery which were sent to him.[32] He wished to receive more weapons for the following reason. For before me are heathens and behind me are heathens, on my right hand and my left are heathens, and I am in the middle of them that are all heathens, and all that is on the shore of the Red Sea is heathen, wherefore if thou shalt station one of thy ships along or on the sea that will be good for my messenger and thy messenger that they may meet together voice to voice. And my faith is as thy faith affirms, that the Son has two nativities, a nativity from the Father from eternity, and a nativity from the Virgin in these latter days. This is what I maintain and the doctrine of my faith is written in the Scriptures.[33]

In addition to weapons Ras Wolde Sellassie also asked for help to bring Abun from Egypt.[34] According to his letter, those who called him apostate

---

30. Aren, *Evangelical Pioneers*, 40.

31. Bosworth, "Henry Salt," 75.

32. The king referred to the letter and presents which Salt brought. Salt noted that the king was very happy and ordered that "a prayer should be offered up weekly for the health of his Majesty, the King of Great Britain." Salt also noted, "The effect produced by the present on the minds of all classes became very apparent. The purity of our religion ceased to be questioned, our motives for visiting the country were no longer doubted, and our importance, in consequence, so highly rated." Salt, *A Voyage to Abyssinia*, 297.

33. University of Birmingham Special Collections, CMS/B/OMS/CM E2/67.

34. Beginning from the eighth century, Muslims overpowered and took control of the coastal lands thereby cutting the Church of Ethiopia from the rest of the Christian world. Thus, the need for the Christian state to obtain its single bishop from Egypt meant intermittent contact with its rulers. J. Spencer Trimingham, *The Influence of Islam upon Africa* (London; Beirut: Longman Group Limited; Librairie du Liban, 1980), 26.

were actually the deserters of the Orthodox faith because they believed in three nativities of the Son.[35] The letter made clear the kind of Christianity which was officially practiced at the king's court. In the Ethiopian context a mere proclamation of Christianity was no more enough but a certain understanding of Christology was required in order to be accepted. As we shall discuss in a short while, the very first question the CMS missionaries were faced with was christological.

Salt was aware of Wolde Sellassie's perceptions of Britain as the most powerful Christian nation of the time, a nation which could help him protect his Christian region from Muslim insurgents and Ethiopian nationals who had deserted the true doctrine of the church. The response to his earlier letter must have encouraged him to expect more help. However, it seems that the above cited letter of Wolde Selassie was ignored perhaps because at the time Britain was weary of maintaining its own colonies let alone attempting to help a Christian governor far away.[36] Upon his return to Britain, however, Salt tried to turn the attention of the Prince Regent to Ethiopia.[37]

---

35. Based on the doctrine of Christ, there were four theological parties in the Orthodox Church and the upper hand of each depended on their wining wider acceptance by the people, especially the king/ruler in power at a given time. Upon the monastic revival of the thirteenth and fourteenth centuries two orders emerged. One of them which was prominent in Gojjam (North) was referred to as "*Qebat*" (unction) because of its emphasis on the anointing of Christ. The adherents of *Qebat* believed that the two natures of Christ were united when Christ was anointed by the Holy Spirit and power. This position is based on Acts 10:38. "By this anointing with the Holy Spirit the two natures of Christ had been completely united and he had fully taken upon himself his office as Son." Monks of Debre Libanos strongly opposed the *Qebat* position and championed the traditional Alexandrian position *Tewahdo* (union, made one). *Tewahdo* was in line with the Eastern churches who rejected the Chalcedonian formula. *Tewahdo* expressed the inseparable union of the God-head and manhood in the person of Christ effected in the incarnation. Thus, after the incarnation Christ is one person with one nature. A third party "*Yetsega Lij*" (Son of Grace) emerged in Begemeder and exerted strong influence on the clergy of Shewa. "*Yetsega Lij*" maintains that Christ was not co-eternal with the Father but was adopted Son of God by grace at his baptism. "While on earth he was nothing but the Son of Mary . . . His divine nature was later infused into him by God." The fourth position was *Sost Lidet* (Three Births). "It maintained that Christ was born three times: by the Father before all time, by the Virgin Mary in the incarnation, and by the Holy Spirit in her womb at the annunciation, or possibly, in the river Jordan; both opinions occur." Aren, *Evangelical Pioneers*, 76–78.

36. Even the treaty that was signed later on between King Sahle Sellassie and Britain was revoked because the "The new Tory government in England was unfavourable to British involvement in Ethiopia." Aren, *Evangelical Pioneers*, 79–82.

37. The letter of Salt written on 9 July 1814 is printed in the first pages of his book. "Should it succeed in attracting your notice to the present forlorn and distracted state of Abyssinia, so far as to induce YOUR ROYAL HIGNESS to promote the welfare of that

Although the country had a conducive climate, it did not grab the attention of European explorers of the time with a display of minerals like West African countries, nor did it seem to have agricultural potential like India. It seems that Great Britain was not interested in protecting Christianity where the country did not have much to offer in return.[38]

Moreover, it is obvious from Wolde Sellassie's letter and many other sources that at the time the doctrine of Christ divided the church of Ethiopia. Ethiopian history refers to this period as ዘመነ መሳፍንት *Zemene Mesafint* (the Era of the Princes) where religious and political conditions were unstable and Islam was spreading with the help of Oromo lords and travelling merchants. Moreover, there was no Abun from Alexandria to look after the spiritual condition of the people. "The Church was ravaged through bitter disputes on the natures of Christ. Its morale was low. The various factions fought each other by both spiritual and temporal means."[39]

Twelve years after his first attempt to distribute the Scriptures, Salt came on the scene once more. In March of 1817 he wrote to Jowett from Cairo that the Psalter in Ethiopic was safely delivered to Nathaniel Pearce to be distributed among chiefs and priests in Ethiopia.[40] Salt also reported the death of Ras Wolde Sellassie and the subsequent unrest caused by the chiefs in contest for supreme power and that Sabagadis, a younger chief controlled most of Tigray. Sabagadis is important for our discussion because he was the one who welcomed the first CMS missionaries to Ethiopia.

It was clear from the correspondence that the Abun who entered the country shortly before the death of Ras Wolde Sellassie showed great hostility towards Pearce and his companion William Coffin.[41] He even threatened

---

country, by the introduction of useful arts together with a judicious advancement of the true tenets of the Christian Religion among its inhabitants, I shall feel that my exertions in this cause have not been in vain . . ." Salt, *Voyage to Abyssinia*, no page number.

38. Cf. Aregay, "Legacy of Jesuit Missionary," 35.

39. Aren, *Evangelical Pioneers*, 54–55.

40. Nathaniel Pearce accompanied Salt to Ethiopia in 1809 and was persuaded by Salt to remain in the court of Wolde Sellassie. His journal which has the details of his stay from 1910–1819 was published. J. J. Halls, ed., *The Life and Adventures of Nathaniel Pearce: Written by Himself, during a Residence in Abyssinia, from the Year 1810–1819 Together with Mr. Coffin's Account of His Visit to Gondar, Vol. 1* (London: Henry Colburn & Richard Bentley, 1831).

41. Coffin accompanied Salt in his first journey to Abyssinia in 1805 and decided to remain there. In 1824, he travelled to Cairo as the messenger of Sabagadis. Bosworth, "Henry Salt," 90. In his letter to Pratt Kugler refers to Coffin as a messenger between Ethiopia

to torture and drive them "out of the dominion of his children." The letter does not say why the Abun was hostile towards the two Europeans; could it be because of their attempt to distribute the Scriptures? Regarding the spiritual condition of the people, Salt observed that they were exceedingly attached to their religion and the Scriptures but because of unfortunate circumstances they were led astray into error.[42]

This observation that the Abyssinians were "led astray into error" governed the perception of European Christian explorers of the time. Needless to say the kind of Christianity they found in Ethiopia was different from what they were used to. This was the kind of information the CMS missionaries and their senders had in mind concerning the spiritual state of the nation.[43]

As mentioned above the Bible in Ge'ez was available, but by then Ge'ez was a liturgical language which was no longer understood by the common people anymore. Although Ge'ez had been spoken and understood in earlier years, as time went by, it ceased to function as the lingua franca and was limited to the royal court and the church. Eventually Ge'ez was confined to serving the church as a sacred language suitable for expressing the divine mystery in readings and song.

As few people spoke it, Ge'ez grew incomprehensible among the public and its usage in the church had a counter effect of concealing divine revelation. When Amharic emerged as the language of communication, the need to translate the Bible into the language of the people was not given much

---

and Great Britain. Kugler refers to Coffin as "Abyssinian in his character" and "completely Abesh in his character." In another letter Gobat refers to him as "a good man but not pious" and Kugler was trying to keep him from bad company. Perhaps, Coffin had a bad temper, because when Coffin broke his promise of taking the Ethiopian Ali to Europe, Ali was very upset and Kugler refers to Ali's reaction as, "the violent Abyssinian demonstrations." (Much later on, on two occasions, Gobat writes that he took refuge in the house of "our Egyptian Ali"); earlier Kugler and Gobat note that Ali had prejudices against Coffin. Kugler to Rev Mr Bratt, Alexandria, 8 October 1827, UB SC, CMS/B/OMS/ C M O46; Kugler to Rev E. Bickersteth, 12 April 1828, UB SC, CMS/B/OMS/ C M O46; Kugler to Jowett, 1 October 1827, UB SC, CMS/ B/ OMS/ C M O73/13; Gobat to his parents, Behate, 25 February 1831, UB SC, CMS/B/OMS/ C M/O28/13; Gobat to the Rev E. Bickersteth, Adigrate, 27 February 1832, UB SC, CMS/B/OMS/ C M O73/60; Gobat to Schlienz, 12 March 1828, Alexandria, CMS/B/OMS/C M O73/18; Kugler and Gobat to D. Coates, Cairo, 21 May 1829, CMS/B/OMS/C M/ O28/7.

42. UB SC, CMS/B/OMS/CM E2/66.
43. Ethiopia and Abyssinia are used interchangeably.

consideration. Perhaps this centuries-old experience of having to hear the mass in a language they could not comprehend led the Ethiopian Christians into an understanding that divine revelation was a mystery which was to be understood and interpreted only by the clergy.[44] However, the Amharic Bible (Abu Rumi's Bible), was in great demand and warmly welcomed by the church, the clergy and the people when it was distributed by the CMS missionaries whose coming to Ethiopia was inspired by the Evangelical revival in Europe.[45]

4.3. The Missionaries' Interlude in Egypt

The first CMS missionaries to Ethiopia were the Swiss Rev Samuel Gobat, the German Rev Christian Kugler and the German carpenter Aichinger.[46] They arrived in Alexandria in 1826 and met with Henry Salt, British consul to Egypt whose name was attached to the first Protestant encounter in Ethiopia in 1805. Salt told them that Abyssinia was peaceful and offered to write a letter to Mr Coffin in Abyssinia asking him to come to Alexandria and accompany the missionaries back to Abyssinia. The missionaries had hoped to travel to Ethiopia sooner, but ended up staying in Egypt for three years. In their extended stay in Egypt they learned Amharic with the help of

---

44. Eshete, *Evangelical Movement*, 53.
45. Aren, *Evangelical Pioneers*, 42–44.
46. Kugler wishes to marry "a truly pious European female" and applies to the committee. In addition to avoiding temptation, his reasons include to have a companion in order to face Abyssinians "with licentious habits and with very insinuating manners," he believes that the damage caused by the Jesuits was not forgotten so it is better to have a European female to work as a missionary than a man, because women pose no threat to the organized religion of the Ethiopians, who know no woman teacher of religion. Kugler further reasons that Abyssinians are accustomed to single men as hermits who live in the woods secluded from people. A European single upright man, thus, can only appear to them as a saint from other nation, so his influence would be limited; perhaps giving the wrong impression that it is only saints who can lead an upright life. Kugler urges the Committee to let him know of their decision and adds that he would respect the decision of the Committee either way. Kugler to the CMS Committee, 25 July 1828, Islington, UB SC, CMS/ B/ OMS/ C M O46/10.

their Ethiopian friend Girgis[47] and Ludolf's Lexicon.[48] They also gathered both political and religious information about Ethiopia and continued to look for safe routes and a person to accompany them on their journey.[49]

The news of political and religious instability[50] in Ethiopia troubled them. From what they learnt, the other governors were not on good terms with Sabagadis, the governor of Tigray, who supposedly refused to allow any European to pass beyond his territory.[51] Such news informed the missionaries of the power struggle between princes in Ethiopia, the moral state of the Christians and the head of church at the time and also the importance Sabagadis attached to having the Egyptian Abun on his side.

---

47. Girgis (perhaps Giorgis) was one of the Ethiopians the CMS missionaries met in Egypt. He was sent there to bring Abuna to Ethiopia. In the meantime he fell seriously ill and the CMS missionaries took him into their house and looked after his needs. He ended up developing great attachment to them. They described him as eager to learn. Journal of Gobat and Kugler, 20 August 1827, UB SC, CMS/ B/ OMS/ C M O73/13. His affection for them grew after Gobat spent a whole afternoon with him reading the Ethiopic Psalter and the Amharic Gospels. That was the turning point of the attitude of Girgis who asked Gobat to accompany him to Abyssinia and promised to recommend Gobat and stay with him while in Abyssinia. Remarkably, Girgis referred to Gobat as Abune Samuel. Moreover, Gobat and Kugler noticed the natural ability of Girgis to teach, and the status of the Muslim Ali (who was sent along with Girgis to bring Abuna) as Hadji which would be of great help on their travel to Ethiopia; thus, they invited Girgis and Ali to live with them. Initially they were not impressed with the character of Ali, but later on he proved to be very supportive of them. Kugler and Gobat to the CMS Secretary in London, 26 January 1827, UB SC, CMS/ B/ OMS/ C M O28/3.

48. Kugler and Gobat to the CMS Secretary in London, 26 January 1827, UB SC, CMS/ B/ OMS/ C M O28/3. During their stay in Egypt they had Ethiopian servant called Malo who later came with them to Ethiopia. But much later on Gobat says that he had to send him away "for his idleness and pride." Kugler and Gobat to D. Coates, 19 February 1830, UB SC, CMS/ B/ OMS/ C M O28/8; Gobat to his parents, Behate, 25 February 1831, UB SC, CMS/B/OMS/C M/O28/13.

49. A Greek man, Nasser Allah, who according to Girgis was loved and respected by all of the great men in Abyssinia, offered to accompany the CMS missionaries to wherever they like to go in Abyssinia and bring them back to Egypt safely after two to four years of stay for a payment of two thousand dollars. Journal of Gobat and Kugler, 20 August 1827, UB SC, CMS/ B/ OMS/ C M O73/13.

50. Marou, Imam, and Haile Mariam, the governors of Dembea, Godjam, and Samen consecutively were all in good terms with each other and expelled the "drunkard" Abun from their regions. But Sabagadis was against all three of the governors and took in the Abun. Kugler and Gobat to the CMS Secretary in London, 26 January 1827, UB SC, CMS/ B/ OMS/ C M O28/3.

51. Kugler and Gobat to the CMS Secretary in London, 26 January 1827, UB SC, CMS/ B/ OMS/ C M O28/3.

However, the missionaries had a great hope of reviving the church through vernacular translations of the Bible and communicated to the printing press in Malta about the need for the translation of the whole of the New Testament in Amharic. Gobat wrote "It is difficult to prove everything by the four Gospels only, and the Abyssinians do not accept of anything, but what is in the Bible."[52] This impression was very important and encouraging to the missionaries and helped them to focus on acquiring copies of portions of the Bible in the vernaculars because they judged that all they needed was to prove what they had to say from the Bible to the scripture-loving Abyssinians. Perhaps they were not aware of the extent of the dependence of the church of Ethiopia on traditional sources and on Alexandria whose clergy did not have adequate knowledge of the Bible, and as a result the spiritual state of the church was weak at the time.[53] The story of Orthodox churches elsewhere appeared to be similar. In their joint journal, Gobat and Kugler made similar observations regarding the ignorance of priests and lay people they encountered from Orthodox churches.[54]

---

52. Gobat to Schlienz, 17 October 1829, UB SC, CMS/ B/ OMS/ C M O73/38. Mr. Schlienz was engaged in translation and printing work in Malta.

53. An anonymous journal which appears to be written in the same period sheds light on the condition of the Coptic Church at the time. The person wrote that he enjoyed friendly conversations with a Coptic priest who was initially extremely mistrustful towards him which was the condition of Coptic priests in general. The writer blamed the Catholic missionaries who "insinuated themselves among the Copts with their notorious and exercised craftiness and afterwards reduced to popery a great number of their families." The writer described the enormous reverence of the Copts towards their Patriarch, the ignorance of the clergy, their acceptance of the apocryphal books as authoritative, the poor condition of the schools owned by the church and zero opportunity for girls' education. He added, "Great is the ignorance in which the priesthood of the Copts live: and how great therefore must be the ignorance of the common people." Journal from Cairo to the Faioum in Western Egypt, UB SC, CMS/ B/ OMS/ C M O73/13. Gobat and Kugler seem to have similar concerns about the involvement of Catholics. Kugler learned about the acquaintance of Mr Coffin with a Catholic physician whom Gobat described as "one of the greatest enemies of missionaries." This person had a greater desire to be sent to Ethiopia and goes to England to offer his services. Kugler, thus, accompanied Mr Coffin to England "to keep him from bad company" and make sure that someone with bad character would not be sent to Ethiopia. Gobat to Schlienz, 12 March 1828, Alexandria, UB SC, CMS/ B/ OMS/ C M O73/18; Kugler to Jowett, 14 February 1828, UB SC, CMS/ B/ OMS/ C M O73/17.

54. In Cairo, they read one of the epistles to Timothy with a Greek Orthodox priest. The priest did not recognize it and asked them whether it was a new book from an English author. When they told him that it was Paul's letter to Timothy he replied, "Why then does our Church teach otherwise?" They also noted that the Greek Orthodox church in Beirut excommunicated those who visited missionaries and that the Sultan forbade distribution of Scriptures. It was the Catholics who served as watch-dogs against the missionaries closely

Kugler and Gobat decided to travel to Jerusalem to be acquainted with the Ethiopian community there and they met twenty-five Abyssinians. Little did they know that their travel to Jerusalem would win them favour among the members of the church of Abyssinia who considered pilgrimage to the Holy Land as a sanctifying experience. The CMS missionaries' experience in Jerusalem validated their former perception of the church of Abyssinia in general and the missionary method they were to pursue in particular. They wrote that the Abyssinians in Jerusalem were "superstitious as the others, but when they see already, that the word of God contradicts their opinions, they are ready to leave them. We are almost sure that if some of them had the whole of the New Testament, they would prove more faithful than many Christians in Europe."[55] This is one of the evidences that the missionaries came to Ethiopia with a high hope about what the reading of the Bible in the vernacular could effect.

Furthermore, based on what they learned about the spiritual state of Abyssinians including the divisive christological debates, they felt strongly that the country was well prepared to receive Christian missionaries.

> But may it not just be in that very low condition that the Lord will display the power of his grace, having once declared that he has chosen the poor of this world, the ignorant, and things that are despised? Now the Abyssinians are all this, &, as far as we have been able to get information, it seems as if they were aware of it themselves; & as if they felt that without some help coming to them from another country, they could not get out of the labyrinth in which they are bewildered.[56]

---

and reported to the Sultan. Gobat and Kugler also noted the widespread rumour among the Maronites that the English had no religion and that their books were full of error. Thus, Maronites would not read the Bible and those who did were called "English." They also noted that the Christians in Damascus beat their wives but would not taste milk during lent which appeared to the missionaries to be hypocritical. However, they were soon to witness striking similarities between the church of Abyssinia and the other Orthodox churches. Journal of Gobat and Kugler, 20 August 1827, UB SC, CMS/ B/ OMS/ C M O73/13.

55. Journal of Gobat and Kugler, 20 August 1827, UB SC, CMS/ B/ OMS/ C M O73/13.

56. Journal of Gobat and Kugler, 20 August 1827, UB SC, CMS/ B/ OMS/ C M O73/13.

It appeared to the missionaries that the time was ripe for their ministry in the church of Abyssinia. While in Egypt they discovered that their former information about Abyssinians' deifying Mary did not appear to be true. However, their subsequent conversation with the Abyssinian Girgis was revelatory about Mariology among the Abyssinians. On one occasion Girgis asked the CMS missionaries whether Mary had ever been married. When they replied in the affirmative he told them, "if you would say so in Abyssinia they would kill you."[57] The missionaries were yet to find out for themselves the extent of the devotion of the Orthodox adherents to Mary.

Another account of their conversation with Girgis revealed their perceptions of the spiritual condition of the church of Ethiopia. When he shared with them his desire of getting an English bishop for Abun in Abyssinia they objected and told him that an English bishop would not make the vow of celibacy, would not ordain "ignorant and vicious priests," nor have anything to do with the invocation of saints and images. Girgis replied, "that is all according to the Gospel, but my countrymen do not see it, that cannot be."[58] This, perhaps, was the most revealing statement about the determination of the Abyssinians to keep their tradition, but it does not seem to have been noticed by the CMS missionaries, instead, they blamed the ignorance of the clergy and the scarcity of Bibles in the vernaculars, for the spiritual problem of the people.

The missionaries' attitude at this point was shaped by what they had learned about the weak state of the church of Abyssinia and its people, especially the character of the Egyptian patriarch who, from what they had learnt, was a drunkard and bad tempered – he even beat up the governor. Gobat and Kugler lamented, "Now if the life of the head of the church be such, what must be the spiritual condition of the people. Our Girgis has told us so much of the corruption of the people, that it is shocking even

---

57. He then asked them whether Jesus was the real son of Joseph, when they told him "no" he replied, "if she was virgin till the birth of Christ it is of no consequence whether she had children afterwards or not." Girgis's reply which focused on the nature of Christ rather than the place of Mary was remarkable in view of his Orthodox background. Journal of Gobat and Kugler, 20 August 1827, UB SC, CMS/ B/ OMS/ C M O73/13.

58. Journal of Gobat and Kugler, 20 August 1827, UB SC, CMS/ B/ OMS/ C M O73/13.

to think of it."⁵⁹ However, they were encouraged by the character of Girgis whom they described as very humble in every respect; but he would not give up a single error unless proven wrong by the Scriptures. They also testified about his diligence in nearly learning the Gospels by heart. Their encounter with Girgis cemented their expectations that if only they could engage the Abyssinians with the Scriptures in their own tongues, the church would be revitalized.

Gobat and Kugler thus greatly desired to see the entire New Testament in Amharic. The following conviction was reflected repeatedly in their letters and journals: "The Abyssinians are apt to suppose that those who speak with them about religion are deceivers. But when they see themselves, a passage of the Bible contrary to their opinions they believe it immediately."⁶⁰ The missionaries themselves were seeking a change of heart and not mere utterance of correct doctrine.⁶¹ This was the important aspect to Gobat and Kugler, just as it was to Evangelicals of the Church of England. They were not seeking to promote mere knowledge of the Scriptures and the tradition of the church, but a change of heart. There was no hidden agenda or proselytism or disturbing the national church in any way. The missionaries put their hopes on the distribution of Scripture in vernacular to enable them to engage with the Abyssinians and result in the desired change of heart.

When Gobat and Kugler learned that Ethiopic was not understood by the people and consequently the Ethiopic psalter was not liked, they expressed their desire to see the New Testament translated into the language of the people, which was Amharic. At this point they mentioned the existence of a copy of the Amharic translation of the Old Testament by "Abou Roumi."⁶²

---

59. Journal of Gobat and Kugler, 20 August 1827, UB SC, CMS/ B/ OMS/ C M O73/13.

60. Journal of Gobat and Kugler, 20 August 1827, UB SC, CMS/ B/ OMS/ C M O73/13. Cf. Gobat to Schlienz, 17 October 1829, UB SC, CMS/ B/ OMS/ C M O73/38.

61. Some of their correspondences shed further light on their convictions. For example Gobat remarks about a rich merchant he met in Alexandria who claimed to be a Protestant, that this person struck him as a Protestant as far as understanding went, but did not show evidence of the renewalof his heart by grace. Gobat to Jowett, March 1828, UB SC, CMS/ B/ OMS/ C M O73/18.

62. Journal of Gobat and Kugler, 20 August 1827, UB SC, CMS/ B/ OMS/ C M O73/13.

To their dismay, when the time for their entering Abyssinia came, new concerns emerged – Girgis was not willing to take with him more than two people, fearing that a greater number would cause suspicion.[63] In addition to that Coffin arrived in Egypt, sent by Sabagadis, among other things to take four bishops to help the Coptic patriarch in Abyssinia and to ask for artisans of all kinds. Coffin broke the disheartening news that Sabagadis wanted tradesmen, artisans and especially physicians, but no missionaries. Kugler feared that Sabagadis might detain him to make use of his skills as a physician.[64] The missionaries were confused because the latest information appeared to contradict with the earlier, which assured them that Abyssinian Christians were aware of the great spiritual need they had and looked forward to outside help.[65]

To make matters worse Henry Salt, who was the champion of their missionary calling to Abyssinia all along, had an excellent relationship with prominent people in Abyssinia and knew all the safe routes for them to get there, fell seriously ill. Although the missionaries continued to hope and pray for his recovery, he died. At this point the challenges mounted. They received news that they were not welcome in Ethiopia.[66] On top of that their own health was not in good condition: Kugler repeatedly suffered from malignant fever and Gobat from opthalmia. The missionaries were discouraged.[67]

But Jowett encouraged them to keep up hope, "Your proposed mission to Abyssinia is felt to be, & really is, one of such singular importance, that we cannot but anxiously hope in submission to the divine will, that your past and constant increasing acquirements will be employed for the glory of God in behalf of that interesting people."[68]

---

63. Gobat to Jowett, 14 September 1827, UB SC, CMS/ B/ OMS/ C M O73/13.

64. Kugler to Jowett, 1 October 1827, UB SC, CMS/ B/ OMS/ C M O73/13.

65. Journal of Gobat and Kugler, 20 August 1827, UB SC, CMS/ B/ OMS/ C M O73/13.

66. Kugler to Jowett, 2 November 1827, UB SC, CMS/ B/ OMS/ C M O73/13.

67. Kugler to Jowett, 15 November 1827, UB SC, CMS/ B/ OMS/ C M O73/13. In a following letter Kugler defends his plans to go to England. Among many things he wanted to persuade the committee to send pious Christian tradesmen to Abyssinia and prevent as much as possible the government from sending out a physician of bad principle. Kugler to Jowett, 14 February 1828, UB SC, CMS/ B/ OMS/ C M O73/17.

68. He also informed them that the printing of the book of Acts and the Epistles in Amharic was in progress. He further asked them to send neatly written short Bible stories

Shortly after that, Gobat and Kugler received intelligence from Girgis that the country was in civil war and that they were not to attempt entry to Abyssinia within one year. He also urged them not to separate from Coffin, "who knows all things."[69] After a month, what Gobat learnt from Coffin appeared to cast greater doubt over the whole plan of reviving the church of Abyssinia with vernacular Scriptures. The news was that they could not penetrate into the interior of Abyssinia with books, lest they be killed or sent back in chains. Worse still, they learned that word was left in Massawa not to let any white person enter the country.[70]

The missionaries stayed in Egypt hoping and praying for the door to open, closely following the instructions of Jowett in Malta.[71] Jowett wanted them to approach the church of Ethiopia with great care and humility. However, he had strong feelings about what he suspected to lead into image worship. Although they did not fully know at the moment how far this was going to be a battle on the church of Ethiopia, images provided one of the main issues of conflict between Protestant and Eastern Christianity.

In a letter to CMS missionaries, Jowett strongly objected to the missionaries' adoption of images of the saints in school books. Jowett wrote that such images imitated the French and repeated the errors of the Greek church and the Latin church. He called the images "species of idolatry, and corruption of the pure Gospel." He further reasoned that tolerating the use of images

---

in Amharic for printing and that Mr Schlienz in Malta wanted them to send him an able, morally upright Abyssinian to work in the printing press. Jowett to Kugler and Gobat, 11 January 1828, UB SC, CMS/ B/ OMS/ C M O73/16. When Gobat and Kugler read the further requirements written by Schlienz himself, they despaired, thinking such an upright and able person would not be found in the whole of Abyssinia let alone among the few Abyssinians in Jerusalem and Egypt. Gobat to Schlienz, 12 March 1828, Alexandria, UB SC, CMS/ B/ OMS/ C M O73/18.

69. Gobat to Jowett, 14 February 1828, UB SC, CMS/ B/ OMS/ C M O73/17.
70. Gobat to Jowett, March 1828, UB SC, CMS/ B/ OMS/ C M O73/18.
71. Gobat reported to Jowett in detail what he was doing and how he was going about it, and added, "If you should have other views than I have, I shall always be thankful to receive and follow your advice." Gobat to Jowett, March 1828, UB SC, CMS/ B/ OMS/ C M O73/18. We find a similar statement in an earlier joint letter of Kugler and Gobat, ". . . we shall be very thankful for all your good advices, and follow all your direction; for we feel we are but children in Knowledge and understanding . . ." Kugler and Gobat to the CMS Secretary in London, 26 January 1827, UB SC, CMS/ B/ OMS/ C M O28/3. In a letter of Kugler we read that he remembered the advice of Mr Jowett "not to accompany, or to be accompanied by worldly men . . ." Journal of Gobat and Kugler, 20 August 1827, UB SC, CMS/ B/ OMS/ C M O73/13.

would only foster the tastes, prejudices and ancient habits of people who say, "What harm in a picture? does it not remind the memory, and touch the feelings? Is not this good?" [72] From Jowett's point of view, no room was to be left for such leniency.[73]

According to Jowett the two appointed means of grace were the Bible and prayer.[74] Thus, in addition to their Reformation background, the missionaries' strong views against image worship and the authoritative status of traditional books as expressed in their ministry in Abyssinia, reflected the conviction of the CMS leadership. In addition to the CMS missionaries' concern about the spiritual state of the church of Ethiopia as a whole, their perception of the character of individual Abyssinians from what they were able to gather and experience in Cairo, did not give them high expectations.[75]

The missionaries were thus surprised to find virtues in an Abyssinian. However, the status of the Scriptures among Abyssinians still gave them

---

72. Jowett to Messrs Korck, Jetter and Hildner, Malta, 10 August 1830, UB SC, CMS/ B/ OMS/ C M O73/48.

73. Jowett explained why he was against the use of images. "I would answer, this, according to nature, seems good. But what does the Scripture reveal concerning what is good and what is not good? God has not only revealed Himself, and his Son Jesus Christ, as proper objects of worship: but he has also revealed *how* he will be worshipped: and he has condensed to state the reason why he will not be worshipped by the help of outward visible representations. He has rested that reason upon one of the strongest passions of our nature, Jealousy . . . Now by the use of images & pictures the heart is drawn from God and his ordinances, and not *to* them . . . the habit of meditating on a picture, draws away the mind from self-examination, and consequently from growth in grace. It may excite pathos, but it hinders knowledge . . . The arguments, also, on your side are so strong, that they must wound many an individual both among the priests and the laity, unless they are applied with meekness & (sic) gentleness. Be mindful too, that it is our business, not merely to resist and condemn error, but to exhibit and recommend the Truth. Let them see, in your examples what is really meant by study of the Word of God, by mediation, prayer, edifying conversation, and preaching the gospel to the poor." Rev W. Jowett to Messrs Korck, Jetter and Hildner, Malta, 10 August 1830, UB SC, CMS/ B/ OMS/ C M O73/48.

74. Jowett to Messrs Korck, Jetter and Hildner, Malta, 10 August 1830, UB SC, CMS/ B/ OMS/ C M O73/48.

75. Writing about the moral uprightness of Girgis, Kugler commented, ". . . he is more in every respect than I should ever have expected from an Abyssinian. I would almost say, that he is not far from the kingdom of God . . . we have not yet discovered a single lie. He is even polite more than it should have been expected and thankful." Kugler and Gobat to the Secretary of CMS, 26 January 1827, Cairo, UB SC, CMS/ B/ OMS/ C M O28/3. Perhaps, such a low opinion about Ethiopians sprung from what they have heard regarding the loose moral life of Ethiopian men and women as mentioned in Kugler's letter to the Committee. Kugler to the CMS Committee, 25 July 1828, Islington, UB SC, CMS/B/ OMS/ C M O46/10.

confidence. They also gathered that Abyssinian Christians were aware of the spiritual pit they were in. Against all odds, the missionaries fanned the little flame of hope that remained in their hearts and kept believing that with a copy of the Scriptures in the vernacular they could have a meaningful dialogue with the Abyssinian Christians.

4.4. Firsthand Experience of Abyssinian Christianity

At last, on 20 October 1829, the CMS missionaries were on their way to Abyssinia accompanied by Ali[76], who was sent to Egypt by the governor of Tigray to bring artisans and physicians. Kugler wrote, "He also has settled with the Naib in Arkiko (more commonly Dochono) everything so that we can now proceed in the name of the Lord without obstacles to Abyssinia."[77] In what appeared to be a providential arrangement, Gobat and Kugler had cared for Ali in Egypt while he was very ill.[78] Ali had stayed with them and helped them in their effort to learn Tigrigna.[79] He treated them well all along

---

76. It appears to be the same Ali who stayed with them in Egypt and helped Kugler in his study of Tigri language. Kugler writes that upon their arrival to the shore of Massawa a great crowd (partly Abyssinians and partly inhabitants of Massawa) surrounded Ali and kissed his hands. When they proceeded to the interior of Ethiopia they learned from people the extent of physical danger they had escaped and Kugler and Gobat were all the more grateful for Ali's care for them. Kugler comments, "Ali's conduct has surpassed even our most sanguine expectations." Kugler refers to Ali as "the Mohammedan" and yet in one occasion mentions that both Ali and Wolde Michael (Sabagadis's son) were fasting. Kugler and Gobat to D. Coates, 21 May 1829, Cairo, UB SC, CMS/B/OMS/C M/O28/7; Kugler to Rev C. F. Schlienz in Malta, 6 January 1830, Massowa, UB SC, CMS/ B/ OMS/ C M O73/43; Kugler to D. Coates, Adigrate, 19 February 1830, UB SC, CMS/ B/ OMS/ C M O28/8. Part of Rev C. Kugler's Journal, 25 February to 24 April 1830, UB SC, CMS/ B/ OMS/ C M O46/24.

77. Kugler to Rev C. F. Schlienz in Malta, 6 January 1830, Massowa, UB SC, CMS/ B/ OMS/ C M O73/43. On their way to Ethiopia they stayed for some time in Jeddah and met three Abyssinians one of which Kugler describes as quite a young man from Gojam. The young Ethiopian came to Kugler begging for an Amharic copy of the gospels and rejoiced upon reading the Gospels in his own vernacular. Gobat and Kugler spoke to him about "applying the truths of the gospels to his own heart." They saw that such an application of the Gospels was new to him. The following day the young man came back to the CMS missionaries to confess his sins and ask for absolution.

78. Kugler to the Rev C. F. Schlienz in Malta, 6 January 1830, Massowa, UB SC, CMS/B/OMS/C M 073/43.

79. Gobat and Kugler to D. Coates, UB SC, CMS/ B/ OMS/ C M O28/7.

and upon their arrival in Massawa on the 28 December 1829 he spoke very highly of them to the Naib in Massawa.[80]

They left Massawa on 15 January and arrived to Adigrate on the 15 February. They enjoyed native hospitality on their way and some theological discussion with a priest at Dera who asked for gifts for his church and particularly wanted to know whether they had brought with them some water from the river Jordan.[81]

Ethiopian Christians had a great respect for Jerusalem as the city of the Promised Land. Anyone who had been to Jerusalem was considered to have received a special blessing. Thus pilgrims would bring with them some water from river Jordan and objects from Jerusalem. Especially for the clergy, having been to Jerusalem added credibility to their teaching. The fact that the first CMS missionaries had actually been to Jerusalem must have given them credibility among Ethiopian Christians.[82]

Kugler used the opportunity to discuss the Gospels with an old priest. They read together the Gospel of John chapter 3 and Kugler proved from the passage that baptism would not save.[83] He then went on to argue that neither fasting nor alms were absolutely necessary for salvation. Right from the start, Kugler met the issue head on. More, he was discrediting some of the beliefs the people had held dear for centuries. The priest tried to bring the authority of the fathers in to his arguments but Kugler told him that

---

80. The Naib initially expected a great sum of money as a present, reasoning that even the British Consul Mr. Salt on his way to Shewa had given him one thousand dollar as a present. But Ali argued that the Naib ought not to look at Gobat and Kugler as other Franks but as brethren and convinced him not to demand a present from them. Kugler to Rev C. F. Schlienz in Malta, 6 January 1830, Massowa, UB SC, CMS/ B/ OMS/ C M O73/43.

81. Kugler overheard a priest telling the people that St Gabriel was the Holy Spirit claiming to have read it in the books. Kugler told him that it was only Mohammedians who made such a statement.

82. Krapf wrote how people from all walks of life kept asking for his blessing assuming that he was a priest and had been to Jerusalem. The soldiers were quick to kneel down before him, confident that his blessing would protect them from swords, spears and gun balls. Realizing the importance attached to pilgrimage to Jerusalem, Krapf, one of the latter CMS missionaries, decided not to correct the erroneous assumption of the Ethiopians that he had been to Jerusalem. Isenberg and Krapf, *Journals*, 476–480, 486.

83. While they were waiting at Bechat, Ali's dwelling place, for word of Sabagadis's return Sabagadis sent a messenger to Ali to leave everyone behind and come to him at once. It was resolved that Gobat should accompany Ali to Antalo and that Kugler and Aichinger should stay with the luggage until Ali returned. Gobat and Kugler to D. Coates, Adigrate, 19 February 1830, UB SC, CMS/B/OMS/ C M/ O28/8.

the Gospel was the foundation of the Christian faith and admonished the priest to teach the people the truth he understood from the Scripture lest God hold him accountable. Convinced that Kugler was a priest the priest asked for absolution from him. Kugler told him that true absolution can only be obtained from God through Jesus Christ our mediator.[84]

Kugler's choice to begin his discussion with the priest by pointing out the faulty teaching of his church that baptism and almsgiving had salvific effect, was to serve as his strategy throughout his ministry among the Christians of Ethiopia. Such an approach seen over and over in the encounters between the missionaries and the Ethiopians, tended to make the people defensive towards their traditional practices by quoting the fathers as authoritative.[85] From the point of view of the missionaries, dealing with these issues from the beginning was vital for the revival of the church. The authority of the Scriptures, the sufficiency of the redemptive work of Christ on the cross and the inadequacy of human work for salvation were the core values of the Reformation.

The reaction of the priest is also revealing. When he realized that he could not combat Kugler's informed and authoritative arguments, he asked for absolution but did not find it. Kugler's approach was foreign to the Ethiopian Christians. The priest must have been confused by what he heard and experienced. What kind of Christianity was this? A priest refuses to give absolution!

On their way to meet Sabagadis they stayed overnight in Dagaber, a village full of priests who were hesitant about hosting them. It is not unlikely

---

84. Gobat and Kugler to D. Coates, Adigrate, 19 February 1830, UB SC, CMS/B/OMS/ C M/ O28/8.

85. The EOC at times was criticized as though it was the only church who wanted to keep its traditions. One very good example from the twentieth-century history of missionaries in Ethiopia is that of the Mennonite mission which strictly required its male missionaries to wear a plain coat and not wear a tie. The missionaries followed the regulations and tried to pass it on to the new believers but when they found out that the regulation was creating a gap between clergy and laity, they decided to defer. When the secretary of the mission board along with the Lancaster board visited Ethiopia, "they were met at the airport by men wearing lapel suits and ties. The agenda for the following week was overshadowed by this issue, considered by the visitors to be a breach of trust. The inability of the home church to bring its missionaries 'into line' was a factor in the request of five bishops and a number of ministers and deacons to be released from the Lancaster Mennonite Conference in 1968. They organized the Eastern Pennsylvania Mennonite Church, with its own mission projects." Hege, *Beyond Our Prayers*, 66.

that word about the white priests who would not give absolution had preceded them. While the missionaries were on their way to see Sabagadis, he sent a messenger asking them to visit his seriously ill son first. Perhaps the governor wanted to put to test the skills of the missionaries. Fortunately, Kugler gave him medication and the man recovered.[86]

Consequently when they arrived at the court of Sabagadis, he received them "with greater warmth of love and regard" and invited them to eat breakfast with him sitting on his left side with carpet spread for them. He at once wanted to know why they had come and they told him, "We are come to see the country, to get better acquainted with the people, and knowing the ignorance of the Abyssinians, we shall like to instruct them in some branches of useful knowledge . . . we and our friends at home had the welfare of Habesh[87] at our hearts since many years & that we now should like to try what we can do in behalf of the welfare of Habesh."[88]

Their response was carefully worded. They avoided talking directly about their real purpose of revitalizing the church. Interestingly Sabagadis did not inquire further. He was pleased with their answer and told them that he was a descendant of Solomon by Menelik,[89] thereby asserting his divine mandate to assume the leadership position. He then asked whether they believed in two or three births of Christ. They stated that the Bible speaks of two births of Christ and that is what they believed. Sabagadis was overjoyed to hear

---

86. Gobat and Kugler to D. Coates, Adigrate, 19 February 1830, UB SC, CMS/B/OMS/ C M/ O28/8.

87. Gobat and Kugler at times refer to both the country and the people as Habesh. "Habesha" or "Abesha" is a common way in which Ethiopians refer to themselves. Arabs are credited with introducing the term. At this point I am not sure what it connoted in the nineteenth century.

88. Gobat and Kugler to D. Coates, Adigrate, 19 February 1830, UB SC, CMS/B/OMS/ C M/ O28/8.

89. Also later on while they were in Adigrate two messengers arrived from Dejazmach Wube with a horse and a mule as a present and Kugler observed that Sabagadis ordered his clerk to bring the large book which traced his genealogy up to Solomon. The poor clerk sat up late into the evening reading out the genealogy as Sabagadis was attentive. The two messengers commented that they did not understand the book because it was in Ethiopic. They remarked that they loved the Amharic gospels which were brought to their country. Kugler's Journal, 25 February – 24 April 1830, 16.

their position and told them that they were his brethren and that he will be happy to know and satisfy their wishes.[90]

Their reply to the christological question had cemented Sabagadis's favour towards them. He then told them about his plan to build a new church which they could have under one condition, that they were not to marry. He gave them three days to think about his offer and added that he loved white people because they spoke the truth and did not change their words.[91] Whether he genuinely meant what he said about them in his compliments is hard to tell at that point. He certainly used different methods to test their integrity.[92]

Kugler noted that Sabagadis developed a special liking for Aichinger, the carpenter. Aichinger's and Kugler's skills along with their christological position played a major role in winning Sabagadis's favour for them, so that Sabagadis allowed Kugler to have six or seven boys to whom to teach English as he requested, and agreed to Gobat's desire to go to Gondar. But they had to make a solemn promise that Gobat would come back to Tigray; Sabagadis then agreed to let him go and gave him one of his men to guide and protect him. It is to be recalled that Sabagadis was known for not allowing foreigners to pass beyond his territory into the interior. Thus, his act of permitting Gobat to travel further was remarkable.[93]

Sabagadis' reluctance was understandable, because there was no central government in Ethiopia at that time. The governors of different regions

---

90. In Ethiopia there was a fierce doctrinal controversy over the births of Christ in which proponents of a given position held upper hand according to the favour of the governor/king in power. For example in Shewa in 1842, the CMS missionaries were denied re-entrance partly because proponents of three births were in power. Aren, *Evangelical Pioneers*, 81–82.

91. Gobat and Kugler to D. Coates, Adigrate, 19 February 1830, UB SC, CMS/B/ OMS/ C M/ O28/8.

92. Sabagadis put to the test Kugler's commitment to his fiancée by offering to give him a fine young lady of his choice from Tigre instead. Kugler replied that he loved his fiancée and had already given her his word and that he did not intend to change it. Sabagadis was quite pleased to hear that. He also offered to marry Aichinger to a beautiful young lady. To the amusement of everyone in the court of Sabagadis at the time, Aichinger, who was aware of Sabagadis's liking for him and did not dare to reject his proposal head on, literally ran away and his reaction resulted in a hearty laugh by Sabagadis and the clergy who were with him. Kugler's Journal, 25 February – 24 April 1830, 17.

93. Kugler and Gobat to the CMS Secretary in London, 26 January 1827, UB SC, CMS/ B/ OMS/ C M O28/3. When Henry Salt, wanted to visit Gondar, Wolde Sellassie did not allow him. Salt, *Voyage*, 265.

were rivals and sought to overpower one another. The presence of Europeans under one's protection could mean greater power and access to modern weapons and gave technological superiority over the others. Regardless of their vocation, Europeans were usually considered as representatives of their nations and they did not attempt to refute this perception. At least the local governors suspected that the missionaries would use their connection with Europe against them.[94]

Gobat and Kugler had two reasons in mind for Gobat's travelling to Gondar, ". . . that we may be known in all the country as far as possible before we have enemies. Second, to distribute the Amharic gospels in the Amhara country."[95] We shall come back to the experiences of Gobat in Gondar later.

During meals, Ali spoke up on behalf of the missionaries and told Sabagadis that they did not fast "knowing from the Gospel that knowing, fearing and loving God through Jesus Christ was sufficient to salvation and [their] hope for eternal salvation was founded on the word of God alone." At this point the clergy who were in the court of Sabagadis must have abhorred what they heard. In a country where all Christians observed fast, what they heard about the CMS missionaries appeared to liken them to Muslims. To the surprise of everyone, including the missionaries, Sabagadis declared the CMS missionaries free from fasting[96] and gave orders for provision of meat for them without consulting the priests on the matter. He also gave them three good mules and promised to build them a house.[97]

---

94. Isenberg and Krapf, *Journals*, 267–269; Hastings, *Church in Africa*, 225–226; J. Lewis Krapf, *Travels, Researches and Missionary Labours* (London: Frank Cass & Co., 1968), 108.

95. Gobat and Kugler to D. Coates, Adigrate, 19 February 1830, UB SC, CMS/B/OMS/ C M/ O28/8.

96. Henry Salt and his companions were also declared free from fasting by priest Guebra Mariam, but Ras Wolde Sellassie was not aware of it. One of the Ethiopian companions of Salt was ashamed of not observing fasting that he tried to hide it. Salt, *Voyage to Abyssinia*, 331. Traditionally a priest declares people who are unable to fast for different reasons such as sick people, people who are about to take a long journey, etc., free from fasting.

97. Gobat and Kugler to D. Coates, Adigrate, 19 February 1830, UB SC, CMS/B/OMS/ C M/ O28/8.

Such an extraordinary gesture on the part of Sabagadis revealed his authority both in political and ecclesiastical matters.[98] There was little distinction between state and church affairs. Sabagadis was the one to decide what to enforce and what to tolerate with regard to the missionaries, without consulting the priests. He was willing to put aside treasured and centuries' old traditions, such as fasting, in order to make room for his new friends from Europe. On the other hand he sounded stern in his views on the births of Christ and it is doubtful whether he would have accepted them if they had held a different view on the matter; especially in view of his active effort to bring about unity among the clergy regarding the two births of Christ.[99]

With regard to fasting, however, Sabagadis's tolerance was not shared by all of his people and wherever they went the CMS missionaries were repeatedly asked why they were not fasting. While away to treat Sabagadis's son, Kugler was asked why he was not fasting, and noted that to their satisfaction, he spoke freely "of the true way of salvation by Jesus Christ."[100] Whereever they went, people were curious and asked them why, as Christians, they were not fasting and as priests, why they did not wear a turban and a cross.[101]

4.4.1. Kugler in Tigray

Kugler remained in Tigray while Gobat travelled to Gondar. Sabagadis was pleased to have his service. He felt free to send Kugler to different places to treat prominent people as he saw the need, and made sure that both Kugler and Aichinger were well provided for with whatever they needed, including

---

98. He required his people to build churches by contributing wood from their land and personally punished those who failed to do so. Kugler's Journal, 25 February– 24 April 1830, 8–9.

99. Kugler noted that Sabagadis summoned the chief priest Gebre Mariam, the next priest in rank Gebre Mesich (who believed in three births of Christ), and Girgis (so that he would state the latest position of Alexandria on the matter) in the presence of the Abun to convince Gebre Mesich that Jesus had two births. The Abun of the time did not want to excommunicate the three-births adherents but convinced them through discussion. Kugler to D. Coates, 2 October 1830, Quila, UB SC, CMS/B/OMS/ C M/O46/23A.

100. Kugler's Journal, 25 February – 24 April 1830, UB SC, CMS/B/OMS/ C M/ O46/24.

101. Isenberg and Krapf, *Journals*, 144. Even when all the people were abstaining from food for prayer during the three days of "Kenona" and "those who receive their maintenance" from the king's table were given dry bread. Krapf noted, "However, I received my portion from the King's table as at other times." Isenberg and Krapf, *Journals*, 234.

meat, despite the Lenten season.[102] Very soon Kugler found himself quite occupied with treating patients of all kinds charging the rich and giving free treatment to the poor. He was usually paid with an animal (e.g. a goat) for his service.[103] He attended to patients in the morning and devoted the afternoons and the evenings to study and missionary work.[104] Kugler treated prominent people such as Wolde Michael, Shum[105] Agami, the son of Sabagadis. This perhaps helped him to gain acceptance and appreciation.

He used every opportunity to discuss spiritual matters and point out the pitfalls of Abyssinian Christianity. The principal topics which stood out in his discussion with the clergy and lay people were: fasting, alms giving, the status of Mary, the use of charms as objects of protection, and the issue of images. He tried to engage priests and monks in the discussion as much as possible and attempted to challenge their views on these issues.

Of all the topics, the issue of fasting came up repeatedly because the missionaries openly ate meat during the church-prescribed fasting days or season.[106] Priests and common people alike were quite surprised to see that the missionaries did not fast. While in Gundagundi to visit the church, Kugler took out the Gospels and read in Tigrigna and that sparked a lively discussion with the inhospitable priests.[107]

Their first question was why they were not observing the great fast. Kugler replied that Jesus Christ did not command it. The priests argued that it was commanded in the Gospels but when Kugler demanded that they show him, they looked at each other and smiled. Finally an old monk produced a large

---

102. Kugler's Journal, 25 February – 24 April 1830, 12.

103. Kugler's Journal, 25 February – 24 April 1830, UB SC, CMS/B/OMS/ C M/ O46/24.

104. Kugler noted that venereal disease was a very common complaint in Adwa revealing the wayward lifestyle of the people and the presence of perpetual sin among Christians. Gobat and Kugler to D. Coates, Adigrate, 19 February 1830, UB SC, CMS/B/OMS/ C M/ O28/8.

105. "Shum" literally means appointee.

106. While the missionaries were on tour of churches with Sabagadis, though himself fasting, Sabagadis continually ordered food or grapes for the missionaries. Kugler's Journal, 25 February – 24 April 1830, 12.

107. Kugler's knowledge of Tigrigna was an asset among inhospitable priests at Gundigundi who were not happy to see him and Aichinger with no prior notice of their coming. They had never seen white people before and were astonished all the more when they heard Kugler speak to them in Tigrigna. Kugler's Journal, 25 February – 24 April 1830, UB SC, CMS/B/OMS/ C M/ O46/24.

book of St Ideris to argue about fasting and almsgiving. Kugler declared that "the Holy Scriptures were the only standard in matters of religion, that we must distinguish the word of God from the words of men." He told them that the fathers were not infallible. He recounted, "In short I declared Jesus Christ to be the way the truth and the life in this place as well as I could do it in the Tigri."[108] Each time people took offence at the missionaries' eating meat while Ethiopian Christians fasted, Kugler looked at it as opportunity for speaking of fasting.[109]

The argument of Kugler reveals a fundamental difference between his conviction and that of the priests. As far as Kugler was concerned his teaching focused on the authority of the Bible and in accordance to the tenets of the Reformation. Besides, while in Egypt the missionaries heard a great deal about the love and commitment of Ethiopians to the Bible, hence, his effort to prove everything from the Bible for the Bible-loving Ethiopians. For the Orthodox priests on the other hand, accepting the authority of the fathers, and fasting and almsgiving were so much part and parcel of genuine Christianity that they could not envision Orthodoxy apart from them.[110] Kugler was concerned that fasting and alms giving, the external adherences to faith, led the people away from the true gospel and he wanted to address them head on. Perhaps because the priests could not come up with a prescription from the Bible for compulsory fasting, Kugler referred to his reply to their question regarding fasting and almsgiving as "silencing" them.[111]

---

108. Kugler's Journal, 25 February – 24 April 1830, UB SC, CMS/B/OMS/ C M/ O46/24.

109. Kugler's Journal, 25 February – 24 April 1830, 11. Perhaps if Kugler belonged to the Church of England he would have little problem observing the fast.

110. In passing we may note that the twentieth-century Ethiopian Evangelicals were seriously assaulted when the rumour about them killing a sheep on the eve of Easter was heard. Engelsviken, "Pentecostal Revival," 162. This illustrates the extent of the offensiveness of failing to fast especially in EOC's strongholds. The Orthodox Church, therefore, showed amazing tolerance for the CMS missionaries at this point.

111. However, not all priests were easily "silenced." While Kugler and Aichinger were invited for breakfast to the house of Memhir Gebre Mesih, the head priest of the Church, a knowledgeable priest engaged them in theological discussion. Kugler remarked, "I was much pleased to find that this man was well acquainted with the Holy Scriptures." While they were discussing about prayer the priest quoted Luke 11:11 and commented that the Scorpion represented a fruit called Aqrab, which was full of dust that hurt the eye of the person who dared to cut it. Kugler then told him that the Greek word signified a real Scorpion. He added that he did not believe the Abyssinian plant mentioned grew in Palestine where Jesus told

Besides, in Swiss Reformation, deliberate violation of the Lent by publicly eating sausages on Ash Wednesday marked a stage in the Protestant movement and the reformers strongly argued against compulsory fasting.[112] Thus, in refusing to observe the fast, the missionaries were trying to make a point in their own way. Perhaps just like the Reformers in Europe, the CMS missionaries wanted to challenge the issue of fasting head on, and then use the opportunity to speak about "the freedom of the Christian as taught in the New Testament"[113] and hoped to bring change. Like the Reformers in Europe Kugler was after change of views as evidence of change of heart. Thus, he rejoiced over the change of Girgis and remarked that he held clear views on fasting and other erroneous practices.[114] The New Testament shows that fasting was an early Christian practice, but it was the conviction of the sixteenth-century Reformers in Europe that led the missionaries to make this stand.

Kugler also expressed his disapproval of images. When a monk proudly showed him the picture of the Holy Trinity, he denounced the picture as "strange representation" and told the priest that it was sinful to make such

---

this parable. It is not hard to imagine how the head priest must have felt at the seemingly insensitive and rude replies of Kugler. The anxiousness of Kugler to get his message across limited his ability to appreciate a genuine indigenous interpretation of the Scripture. Kugler's Journal, 25 February – 24 April 1830, UB SC, CMS/B/OMS/ C M/ O46/24, 10.

112. "The first open challenge to ecclesiastical authority took place on Ash Wednesday, 1522," when a circle of friends including a priest "dared to eat sausage in defiance of church restrictions against eating meat during lent." Zwingli was there but refrained from eating in order not to offend others but in the controversy that followed he argued from Acts 10:10–16 "that dietary restrictions ran counter to the freedom of the Christian as thought in the New Testament." Lewis W. Spitz, *The Rise of Modern Europe: The Protestant Reformation 1517 – 1559* (New York: Harper & Row, 1985), 154–155.

113. Spitz, *Rise of Modern Europe*, 155.

114. He also befriended the chief priest Gebre Mariam and the Governor Sabagadis which resulted in many priests seeking his friendship. Kugler also had a golden opportunity to witnessing theological discussions between prominent clergy who were respective of the two births and the three births of Christ and how they settled their differences. Kugler to D. Coates, 6 August 1830, Quila, UB SC, CMS/B/OMS/ C M/O46/22. Kugler writes that the next priest in rank, Gebre Mesich, held to three births of Christ. On 28 September Sabagadis wanted Gebre Mariam, Gebre Mesich and Girgis to discuss the matter in his presence and settle it. After hours of discussion, Gebre Mesich, was convinced, on the basis of their arguments and the fact that Girgis had returned from Egypt, and thus, knew the position of the church of Alexandria. The Coptic patriarch suggested that instead of rude excommunication they should try their best to convince the clergy who held to three births of Christ. Kugler to D. Coates, 2 October 1830, Quila, UB SC, CMS/B/OMS/ C M/O46/23A.

pictures.[115] Kugler used every opportunity to point out traditions of the church which he thought were against the Scriptures. Many times, his critical approach did not allow him to appreciate indigenous Christianity or even the architecture of the church. For instance when Sabagadis asked him to describe what the churches in Europe looked like Kugler bluntly told him that the European churches were meant for preaching the gospel but the Ethiopian ones were principally for the ceremonies of the priests.[116]

Alarmed, Sabagadis wanted to know if there were pictures inside the European churches. When he heard that there were none, he was surprised and directly asked Kugler whether the picture of the Virgin Mary was not in their churches. Kugler thought this a golden opportunity to speak against image worship. He told Sabagadis that Mary and all the saints were creatures and should not be an object of worship. People who worshipped them were guilty of idolatry; Christians are to worship God and him alone. Perhaps noticing the displeasure of the governor, Kugler added that if any of the priests of Sabagadis showed him from the Scriptures a command to worship the Virgin Mary and the saints, he would certainly worship them. The *Aleqa*[117] sitting with them safely confirmed that Mary and the saints were indeed creatures, but he did not speak about their role. Kugler observed, "Sabagadis had never heard such arguments against image worship and this single conversation was quite enough for him, that he took good care of avoiding everything in our conversations which might lead to such like arguments."[118]

---

115. In their discussion of many issues Kugler was quite impressed and noted, "he was not in the least offended when I even told him that the bishops in our country were married according to the word of God." The monk bought the Gospels for one dollar and as he was leaving he declared that they were brethren by faith. Kugler told him that he had "no objection to it, provided his faith rested on the pure Gospel ground." Perhaps, Kugler was anxious to get things right from the beginning by clearly marking the boundaries which defined true brotherhood in the faith. However, at times he appeared to be too cautious. Part of Rev Christian Kugler's Journal, 25 February – 24 April 1830, UB SC, CMS/B/OMS/ C M/ O46/24.

116. Kugler's Journal, 25 February – 24 April 1830, UB SC, CMS/B/OMS/ C M/ O46/24, 11.

117. "Aleqa" in Amharic means chief, head, leader. In the context of the church, it is used in reference to priests who have graduated from the higher traditional schools of the church.

118. Kugler's Journal, 25 February – 24 April 1830, UB SC, CMS/B/OMS/ C M/ O46/24, 11. It is unlikely that Sabagadis thought the missionaries got the doctrine wrong.

It is not hard to imagine what must have gone on in the mind of Sabagadis. Tolerating fasting was one thing, but the issue of Mary and the saints was something else; the core of Orthodox faith. Although Sabagadis was able to somehow tolerate the missionaries' strange practices, they did not reciprocate in making room for Abyssinian practices because they thought that the gospel was at stake. The teaching of the missionaries thus appeared to contradict the teaching of the clergy. The church taught people to work towards their salvation by giving, fasting, pilgrimages, etc.[119]

Ali scolded Kugler for his handling of the issue. Kugler wrote, "[Ali] observed further that people would soon declare us to be Mohammedans, if we would speak more in this manner. My answer to Ali was that I was first asked on the subject & was therefore obliged to give the answer I had given."[120]

Kugler noted that he held discussions with *Echege* Philipos on different topics, particularly regarding the worship of Mary; he said that he spoke his mind as freely as he would do in England against all that he believed was contrary to the teaching of the Bible. Earlier while visiting the church at Gundagundi, the priest proudly showed Kugler a silver cross, a gift of

---

Perhaps, he simply was not ready for change. In another occasion when Wolde Haimanot, Sabagadis's interpreter, spoke highly of dreams, Sabagadis told him that dreams were unreliable. Wolde Haimanot then brought up Pharaoh's dream and Joseph's accurate interpretation and narrated the story up to Isaac's sons and concluded asserting that Jacob was Christian and Esau a Muslim. Kugler's initial delight to hear the story of the Bible turned into disappointment "when it was mixed with fable." He corrected him saying that there were no Christians before Christ and no Mohammedans before Mohammed. When Wolde Haimanot attempted to argue further, Sabagadis rebuked him not to argue with Kugler but to tell the story right. Kugler's Journal, 25 February – 24 April 1830, UB SC, CMS/ B/ OMS/ C M O46/24, 17.

119. Kugler encountered a monk who begged him for a piece of his Arab dress. Kugler scoffed, "What, you are a monk and now you want a fine dress? is your skin not enough for you?" He went on to accuse the monk of his ignorance of the Gospels. The monk cleverly replied that giving would benefit Kugler himself because alms and fasting effected righteousness. Kugler explained that it was possible for a wicked man to fast and give alms with no change of heart, and told the monk that if people's hearts are not renewed by the truth of the gospel they would perish; because good works could not effect any change of heart. Kugler noticed that many people were listening in but the message they had just heard appeared to be strange to them. A priest sitting next to him, however, confirmed that Kugler's teaching was true. Kugler's Journal, 25 February – 24 April 1830, UB SC, CMS/B/OMS/ C M/ O46/24: 13, 14.

120. While Sabagadis was giving a tour of one of his half-finished churches to the missionaries, a soldier attempted to show Kugler the picture of Mary above the door; Sabagadis lashed out, "Kugler does not like such conversations!" The issue of Mary was thus never to be discussed in the presence of Sabagadis. Part of Rev Christian Kugler's Journal, 25 February – 24 April 1830, UB SC, CMS/B/OMS/ C M/ O46/24, 11.

Sabagadis to the church. Kugler read the inscriptions on the cross which read, "in remembrance to the Virgin Mary." Kugler's journal entry reads, "I observed to them that this was a very improper inscription and asked when she was crucified? and (sic) said of whom & of what the cross reminds us. They showed me then to the representation of the crucifixion on this cross & declared that I was in the right."[121]

Kugler held that any kind of representation was contrary to the Scriptures and it turned the attention of the people away from the Saviour. His open criticism might appear to the reader tactless, but he was acting according to his Reformation views. There was no tolerance for images, which were referred to as "idols" in Protestant Europe. Following Zwingli's persuasive arguments in Zurich, all images, pictures and relics were removed from the church and the walls painted white.[122] The Ethiopian context, in which Islam and Christianity co-existed, however, was different. Ali's prediction that attacking the veneration of Mary would liken the missionaries with Muslims was in due time to be proved correct.

As far as Sabagadis was concerned, it felt safer to avoid the topic of images all together, rather than engaging Kugler and finding out more about his convictions. Perhaps he feared that more intolerable revelations of the European religious convictions would surface and make it difficult for him to keep the missionaries in his kingdom.[123] Moreover, Ethiopian Christianity was so strongly tied to the Virgin Mary that attacking representations of her sounded like perversion of Christianity because in Ethiopian Christianity, the mother and the Son are inseparable.

However, the missionaries did not encounter difficulty in their distribution of Scripture. Even some of the chief priests were happy to help. Kugler gave Gebre Mariam, the chief priest of Tigray, fifty copies of the Amharic Gospels and several in Ethiopic for distribution, asking him to give them exclusively to people who understood their contents.[124] To Kugler's surprise

---

121. Kugler's Journal, 25 February – 24 April 1830, UB SC, CMS/B/OMS/ C M/ O46/24.

122. Spitz, *Rise of Modern Europe*, 157.

123. Kugler's Journal, 25 February – 24 April 1830, UB SC, CMS/B/OMS/ C M/ O46/24, 11.

124. Kugler to D. Coates, 26 August 1830, Quila, UB SC, CMS/B/OMS/ C M/ O46/22.

Gebre Mariam distributed them within one day and Kugler promised to give him fifty more copies. The priest also received Kugler's Tigrigna spelling book and the translation of the Gospel of Luke to make corrections. Kugler remarked, "I am exceedingly glad to observe that the people love our books so much with out (sic) the least prejudice. It was a very false representation which was made to us, that the Abyssinians do not like the Ethiopic Psalter, for people ask it always from me."[125]

In addition to images, good works and fasting as means of attaining righteousness, Kugler observed that Abyssinian Christianity did not challenge the superstitious practice of the use of charms for protection. People asked him for paper wherever he went for the purpose of writing charms. He demanded to know the purpose before he gave them a piece of paper. If it was for charms he refused to give it, telling them that charms were objects of idolatry. Kugler noted in his journal, "I have told men of whom I knew that they were in the habit of writing charms that their impostures would finally drag them to hell and they were astonished when I showed them that they draw the hearts of the people away from God by means of those charms, but I can not say with certainty that any one has been induced to give up this bad practice."[126]

Perhaps the fact that some of the priests themselves were involved in providing the charms gave it prominence and acceptance. The governor was not exempt from this practice either. In fact, Sabagadis brought four pieces of charms with him for Kugler and Aichinger, but Kugler politely explained to him that it was sin to put their trust for protection in anything other than God. Kugler then told Sabagadis that in order to please him, he decided to carry his New Testament with him all the time though he knew very well that the New Testament would not protect him from harm. Sabagadis responded with a smile acknowledging that the missionaries were well acquainted with everything in their country but here they were strangers and ought not reject the advice of friends. Kugler replied, "We by no means reject the advice of friends in secular affairs, but we could not follow the advice of men in matters where faith & conscience & the word of God

---

125. Kugler to D. Coates, 2 October 1830, Quila, UB SC, CMS/B/OMS/ C M/ O46/23A.

126. Kugler's Journal, 25 February – 24 April 1830,13.

were the head points. . . . I shall not die except by the will of God . . ." He added that he was ready to die wherever and however God was pleased to call him but he did not fear the devil, much less evil people, because they all were under the control of God almighty. When he saw the concern of Sabagadis for his well being Kugler asked him if the charms had any writing on them and Sabagadis assured him that it was just roots of a certain plant. Then Kugler agreed to accept them but never wore them over his head.[127]

Kugler's reply gives us one of the keys to their actions which at times appeared to be disrespectful and inconsiderate. When the missionaries felt that their faith, conscience and the word of God were at stake, they were not willing to budge. But even then they showed genuine willingness to try to find ways around difficult issues. Kugler's experience also illustrates the fact that the people were aware of the spirit world and looked for ways of protection. At the deeper level they did not feel protected as Christians. This again reflects inadequate teaching regarding the biblical perspective of the spirit world and how to find protection.

However, at times the missionaries' tendency to label practices as "superstitious" was indiscriminate.[128] On one occasion, at Sabagadis's request, Kugler went to treat Dejas[129] Hagos, Sabagadis's son, and observed that there was a fountain at Mai Theloot which is renowned for its healing power. Kugler remarked that people stayed there and left the place with no healing. "I have seen the water and know that it is pure well=water, (sic) & all the report of its miraculous power is the result of superstitions and ignorance."[130]

Kugler thus tried to convince Dejas Hagos to leave the fountain and return to his house where he could give him medication. The head priest at the fountain was quite unhappy about Kugler's remarks regarding the power

---

127. Kugler's Journal, 25 February – 24 April 1830, 14–15.

128. Kugler also noted what he called "syncretistic attitude" of the people. For instance he wrote that he witnessed a strange practice which was very common there, "Christians swear by God in the Mohammedan way (i.e. in Arabic) in their transactions with Mohammedans." Kugler's Journal, 25 February – 24 April 1830, UB SC, CMS/B/OMS/ C M/ O46/24. This is difficult to understand because Salt wrote in the period 1809–1810 that there was a sharp distinction made between Christians and non-Christians. Thus, Christians would not eat with "Galla" (pagans), nor with Muslims. Salt and his companions, therefore, were careful not to eat with Muslims or even hire a Muslim cook. Salt, *Voyage to Abyssinia*, 369, 402.

129. The full title is Dejazmach.

130. Kugler's Journal, 25 February – 24 April 1830, 18.

of the water to heal, and insisted that Hagos should stay for the whole of the seven days, which are usually appointed as needed days for the healing to take effect. Kugler tried to persuade Hagos telling him that he would stay with him at his house for a week and give him the treatment if he went with Kugler right away. Dejas Hagos found himself in a difficult position of choosing between two "charms," that of the European and the traditional Ethiopian which was practised by his ancestors. The prince chose to stay behind and Kugler wrote, ". . . his superstitious belief in the salutary power of this water[131] strengthened by the persuasion of the head priest, prevailed on him to reject my advice." Kugler had some conversation with the head priest and says, he ". . . showed to the people, that the poor man did not know the Gospel correctly. He related something of the Gospel to Dejas Hagos and made several blunders, which I instantly corrected. I spoke then freely of the blessing of the Gospel."[132] Such a public "instant correction" was belittling the head priest and created unpleasant feeling.

Kugler sounded arrogant and impatient but he felt that he had a responsibility to correct erroneous teaching. He believed that his role was to point out unbiblical traditions in order to reform the views of the clergy so that they would be able to teach their people according to the gospel. His condemnatory approach was not different from that of the Reformers back in Europe. His genuine concern and love for the people, however, was illustrated on a number of occasions.[133] On the other hand, he sounded merciless on the clergy who had tried to teach the faith where the Bible was scarce. His calling them ignorant, vicious and their teaching full of fables was offensive. He was too anxious to correct the wrongs and did not seem to be ready to listen and learn before he passed on judgements.

Perhaps his experience provides us with a picture of the clash between European and Ethiopian worldviews. In the Ethiopian world view age,

---

131. Krapf recorded a similar experience. On his way from Shewa to Massawa in a place called Amad Washa, he saw a spring and attempted to drink from it. The people told him that the spring was "*tsebel*" (holy water) and was not to be drunk from unless on the day of the anniversary of the saint who blessed the water, lest the serpent who watched over the spring would bite him. As the people watched him with fear Krapf drank from the spring and demanded, "Where is the serpent?" The people not ready to give in told him, "the serpent does not bite good people." Isenberg and Krapf, *Journals*, 313.

132. Kugler's Journal, 25 February – 24 April 1830, 19.

133. Kugler's Journal, 25 February – 24 April 1830, 20.

experience and background matter as much as, if not more than the ideas a person has. It is also rude to correct people publicly and directly, especially elderly and prominent people. It is customary to use proverbs, stories, implications, and ask questions to point out the fault of others. More importantly perhaps, in the Ethiopian thinking there appears to be little dichotomy between the person and his/her ideas. Thus, opposing one's ideas could as well be taken as opposing the person altogether. In other words, winning people over is not necessarily about how logical and engaging an argument is, but who the speaker is and also how respectful his/her approach proves to be.

Most of all, Kugler was looking for godly teaching and way of life. His heart seems to be fired up to see the Bible brought to the centre of Christian living and witness in Ethiopia. That seems to be the reason behind his harsh address towards the priests. Learning for Kugler meant, knowing and applying the Scriptures. Thus, while praising Girgis, he remarked, "The word of God is his treasure." The letter of Girgis to the CMS in London which was translated by Kugler implies that Girgis met Kugler's expectations on faith matters.[134] In the letter Girgis praises Gobat and Kugler and attests his faith in Christ: "Your son Wolde Girgis believes in Jesus, that he can do all things. Without Him the world could not be saved, & we are saved by his blood. Our Lord has given us the holy spirit, (sic) that we all may praise Christ . . . ."[135]

Contrary to the intelligence the CMS missionaries had received, the Christians did not seem to look forward to spiritual help from outside, at least not their ruler and the clergy. Rather, Sabagadis was more interested in the skills of Aichinger to build churches after a European model and anxious to see the plants from the seeds that Kugler brought from Europe.[136]

However, Kugler continued to distribute the Bible and strive to point out practices which were not supported by it. He was hopeful that their mission would be a success. He wrote, "As for myself, I am very happy here in this country, though I have at present nothing, what would deserve the

---

134. Kugler to D. Coates, 2 October 1830, Quila, UB SC, CMS/B/OMS/ C M/O46/23A.

135. Wolda Girgis to the Christian Society which is in England, 1 October 1830, UB SC, CMS/B/OMS/ C M/O46/23B.

136. Kugler to D. Coates, 10 July 1830, Quila, UB SC, CMS/B/OMS/ C M/O46/21.

name of comfort in Europe, but I enjoy good health and have much work in my hands, the prosperity of which fills my soul with delight . . . Thus we can now say by the mercy of our God, that the work of missions is now commenced and is daily increasing in this country. Pray with us for its prosperity from on high."[137]

4.4.2. Gobat in Gondar

While Kugler remained in Tigray practising medicine and trying to address the vital spiritual problems as much as he could, Gobat was over in Gondar winning the affection of the princes and the people with his humble heart and genuine love for the people. He was well received in Gondar. He referred to Aleqa Estifanos, the head of the church in Gondar, as his friend. The Aleqa arranged to have all of the forty-four churches of Gondar supply Gobat with everything he needed but Gobat declined because of the great scarcity of food.[138]

Gobat adopted a lifestyle which was similar to the localpeople and was cautious not to engage in doctrinal controversy unless it was absolutely necessary. This gives us a striking contrast with Kugler, who almost looked for controversy as a means of making his point. Regarding Gobat Aren observes, "Through upbringing and training he was firmly convinced that every Christian who received the Bible as the word of God with a sincere heart and made it the lodestar of his faith and life was a true disciple of Christ irrespective of his confessional background."[139]

Consequently, Gobat was more tactful in his approach and refrained from addressing sensitive issues head on. As much as possible he sought to avoid engaging in controversy. He was aware of the influence and power of the governors over the church.[140] Therefore, he maintained a friendly relationship

---

137. Kugler to D. Coates, 10 July 1830, Quila, UB SC, CMS/B/OMS/ C M/O46/21.

138. Gobat to his sisters (translation), Gondar, 24 June 1830, UB SC, CMS/B/OMS/ C M/O28/9. The hunger Gobat mentions appears to have been caused by regular conflict among war lords and not draught. The area was unstable with plundering and war. Cf. David Chapple, "Protestant Missionary Attitudes in Ethiopia: Gobat, Isenberg and Krapf," in *Preceedings of the Third Annual Seminar of the Department of History* (Addis Ababa: Addis Ababa University, 1986), 37–39.

139. Aren, *Evangelical Pioneers*, 55–56.

140. He described that the town was in turmoil with wars and that more than once he had to take refuge in a church. The interior was disturbed as well and says that the king

with all of the governors he knew, though the governors were not on good terms with one another. He avoided taking sides, and so the rival governors were willing to protect him. Gobat knew it was not safe for him to stay in Gondar, but he refused Wubie's offer to escort him back to Tigray because he did not want to return without learning about the religious condition of Gondar, the capital of Abyssinia.[141]

Most importantly, Gobat wanted to distribute the copies of the New Testament he had brought with him. He remarked, ". . . we can hardly have any hopes of the people until we are enabled to give them the Bible in their vernacular language."[142] When Wubie learnt that Gobat had decided to stay in Gondar despite the mounting danger, he instructed the priests to take Gobat to *Echege* for protection. Wubie added, "Tell E'Etchigué that if any evil happens to this man at Gondar, I shall not fail to revenge it."[143] This statement shows how valuable the friendship between Wubie and Gobat had been.

Gobat's principle was simple; it was wiser to make friends with everyone, and there was no need to hide it from the others. When people he described as "the greatest enemies of Oubie who have authority at Gondar," asked him if he was a friend to Wubie, Gobat replied "Yes" and added that it was his interest to be the friend of everyone. They did not attack him for that.[144]

In his stay in Gondar from 26 March to 4 October (a little over six months) he distributed sixty copies of the Gospels in all the provinces. He even sent the Gospels and Acts along with a letter to the king of Shewa.[145] He remarked, "I have reason to believe that whenever we multiply copies of the Bible in Abyssinia, it will soon effect a great change in the country: for those

---

did not have much control over the country. Gobat to his sisters, Gondar, 24 June 1830, UB SC, CMS/B/OMS/ C M/O28/9.

141. Wubie was the governor of Semen, and a foe of Marie.

142. Gobat to his parents, Behate, 25 February 1831, UB SC, CMS/B/OMS/ C M/O28/13.

143. Gobat to his sisters, Gondar, 24 June 1830, UB SC, CMS/B/OMS/ C M/O28/9.

144. Gobat to his sisters, Gondar, 24 June 1830, UB SC, CMS/B/OMS/ C M/O28/9.

145. Gobat to the Rev E. Bickersteth, Behate, 24 February 1831, UB SC, CMS/B/OMS/ C M/O28/11.

who are instructed a little, particularly admire the writings of St Paul, while the other tribes that I have seen in the east, scarcely know their names."[146]

The Abyssinians were delighted to see copies of the Scriptures in the vernacular. Gobat remarked, "The Gospel in Amharic has been received with the greatest avidity; and the desire has been equally great to receive the epistles of the Apostles, whose names only are in general known in this country. After the winter in the month of September people from all the provinces of the interior came to see the foreigner who had brought the Gospel in the mother tongue."[147] The warm reception of the Scriptures encouraged Gobat to try to do some translation himself. He started translation with someone whom he described as "one of the best informed men of the country." This person translated Matthew 5–7 and Luke chapters 1 to 11 to the satisfaction of Gobat.[148]

However, Gobat was continuously faced with strong traditions which got in the way of affirming the authority of the Scriptures alone. The issues he was faced with were not different from those which Kugler encountered in Tigray. These included fasting, image worship, Mary's status, the authority of the Bible and the use of charms for protection. Gobat spoke against adoring the saints, but in favour of imitating them. When the governor of Aksum related to him the greatness of the church of Aksum and the unspeakable treasures stored within, Gobat replied, as forty people listened, that in comparison to the vital knowledge of Christ, the earthly things were vanity.[149]

Gobat approached the issue of fasting in a similar manner to that of Kugler, arguing that it was not commanded in the Bible. A monk reasoned with him that Gobat and his people were enlightened by the knowledge of God to do good and avoid evil but "we are wicked . . ." noted the monk, "and this is why we find fasting necessary; in order to mortify our bodies."

---

146. Gobat to his sisters, Gondar, 24 June 1830, UB SC, CMS/B/OMS/ C M/O28/9.

147. Gobat to his parents, Behate, 25 February 1831, UB SC, CMS/B/OMS/ C M/O28/13.

148. Gobat to his parents, Behate, 25 February 1831, UB SC, CMS/B/OMS/ C M/O28/13. He is most likely referring to the Greek man born in Abyssinia who agreed to translate the New Testament for 200 dollars. Gobat to the Rev E. Bickersteth, Behate, 24 February 1831, UB SC, CMS/B/OMS/ C M/O28/11.

149. Gobat's Journal from 25 February 1830 – 16 February 1833, UB SC, CMS/B/OMS/C M/O28/113.

The monk added that the wickedness was a result of the ignorance of the people of God's commandments.[150]

This was the strongest argument Gobat was presented with about the role of fasting for a spiritual life. Most of all, however, the monk made an extraordinary diagnosis of the real problem. Gobat must have waited for such a confession, and asked the monk why they did not instruct the people. The monk sadly replied that they did not have the Scriptures. He told him further that he travelled all the way from Welkayt to Tigray because he heard that there is an Amharic Gospel being distributed there. Gobat was quick to hand him a copy of the New Testament. Upon receiving it the monk replied that he would study it first for himself and then instruct the people.[151]

Gobat's encounter answered one of the questions as to why the clergy did not instruct the people. We can see that for one thing the clergy were inadequately trained and second, they did not have access to the Scriptures in Amharic or Tigrigna. Having a copy of the Scriptures was quite rare in those days because the books were made out of parchment which made them expensive and quite big in size, "thus impairing mobility."[152] In addition to that the Scripture was considered to be a sacred object which was to be kept in the church and not carried around. Eshete notes, "Except for theologians who would often delve into hair-splitting controversies, the ordinary Ethiopian had neither the access to religious books nor the privilege of engaging in public debate for a personal search and enrichment of the basis of one's spiritual convictions. By and large, for the ordinary person, religion was *mester* (mystery) something given, beyond reach and interpretation."[153]

The monastic community was no exception. Gobat wrote that he found them to be self-righteous. While in Debre Damo, Gobat encountered a monk who never came out of the tomb in which he lived and proudly told Gobat how people brought him all he needed without his ever asking them for anything. The monk was highly reputed for his sanctity. Gobat remarked,

---

150. Gobat's Journal from 25 February 1830 – 16 February 1833, UB SC, CMS/B/OMS/C M/O28/113.

151. Gobat's Journal from 25 February 1830 – 16 February 1833, UB SC, CMS/B/OMS/C M/O28/113.

152. Eshete, *Evangelical Movement*, 53.

153. Eshete, 53.

". . . but I found him full of self righteousness and ignorant of the righteousness of Christ. He could only speak to me of himself. . ." Gobat told the monk that his life was "in direct opposition to the Gospel." The monk listened to Gobat intently; astonished that Gobat could doubt his sanctity. When Gobat was finished, the monk asked him for a copy of the Gospels.[154]

Another monk visited Gobat wrapped with a sheep skin. He too, appeared to be proud of his righteousness. He was feared by even the Echege and the king too because he was not afraid of reproving them. He referred to Gobat as a friend of God, and related to him his self-inflicted illness.[155] Gobat proved to him from the Scriptures about justification by faith and not human works.[156] All of the above encounters of Gobat with the monks proved that they had inadequate knowledge of the teachings of the Scripture but diligently pursued good works and mortifying of their bodies in order to attain righteousness. These kinds of experiences and many more were painful for Gobat to witness. He was immensely grieved by the spiritual condition of the people and the clergy.[157] He wrote to his parents:

> When once comes to the article of justification by faith, all the Abyssinians, without exception, content themselves with saying in a very vague manner, that as works are of no avail without faith, so faith is of no avail without works. They believe that faith with baptism is sufficient for the justification of a man who was not a Christian before; but that God demands from the sinner satisfaction for the sins which he has committed after baptism; as fasting, alms and there are some who believe in absolute predestination, not only of the future lot of the just and of sinners; but also of all the actions which are committed in the world. All believe that the moment of the death of

---

154. Gobat's Journal from 25 February 1830 – 16 February 1833, UB SC, CMS/B/OMS/C M/O28/113, 189.

155. He tied his body with a chain so tight that he broke one of his hips, then he beat himself with a stick and bruised all of his body. Then he fasted continually and that ruined his health.

156. Gobat's Journal from 25 February 1830 – 16 February 1833, UB SC, CMS/B/OMS/C M/O28/113, 131–132.

157. Kugler's Journal, 25 February – 24 April 1830, 20.

individuals is decreed from a long time ago, and that there is no means of escaping it.[158]

There was a tremendous desire to please God and attain righteousness through good works and the mortification of the body. There also was fear of the evil and traditional ways of protecting oneself and one's property from the attack of evil. One of the ways was wearing amulets. Similar to Kugler's experience in Tigray, Gobat too was begged to take seriously the traditional protection and medication.

Such a concern was powerfully illustrated when Gobat fell ill. His Ethiopian friends were convinced that he was internally devoured by an evil eye of the *Aleqa* who visited him and tried to persuade him to tie amulets around his neck. The argument took such a long time that Gobat felt like driving them all out of his house. His friends, however, insisted that his impatience with those who wished his deliverance was evidence of the power of the evil eye at work within him. Gobat vividly describes the scene: ". . . they took me by force; and whilst some endeavoured to tie my hands and feet others brought large packets of amulets to tie them round my neck. . . . 'What!' I said to them, 'can I suffer that? I who tell everybody that amulets are the work of the devil, and a heathen invention?' Seeing that I gained nothing, I said to Malo . . . if you let them put amulets in my bed I will turn you away."[159]

Fearing that he might lose his job, Malo, one of the servants of Gobat, stopped Gobat's friends from trying to pin Gobat down to his bed and tie the amulets around his throat. Gobat's friends feared that something dreadful might happen to him and continued to beg Gobat to take other remedies. Out of respect for them he consented. They made him take a certain powder and sprinkled the juice of a certain herb into his nostrils. Gobat wrote that often his eyes were filled with tears as he watched his friends perform these arts, at the same time he could not but smile within

---

158. Gobat to his parents, Behate, 25 February 1831, UB SC, CMS/B/OMS/C M/O28/13.

159. Gobat's Journal from 25 February 1830 – 16 February 1833, UB SC, CMS/B/OMS/C M/O28/113, 137–139.

himself. He concluded, "Certainly the Abyssinians are not less skilled in art than the Parisian Physicians!"[160]

His experience hints why even Gobat, the most tolerant of all the CMS missionaries in Ethiopia, referred to the Ethiopian Christians as superstitious.[161] In addition to the charms and amulets, his reference to the Ethiopian Christians as superstitious was in line with his Reformed views which considered veneration of images and prayer before them as superstitious.[162] The issue of charms, therefore, further proved to the missionaries that Orthodox Christianity did not provide the people with an adequate assurance against their fears of evil forces.

For protection from the evil eye and the like, people wore amulets and charms. Such practices did not seem to be contrary to their Christian faith again because the clergy members were the chief providers of such traditional "remedies" and "protecting" objects. The missionaries endeavoured to address such issues throughout their ministry. However, it was frustrating for them to see that no one was ready to give up such a practice, regardless of their teaching against it. The issue of dependence on traditional remedies was more deep rooted than the missionaries had imagined, and they continued to refer to Abyssinian Christianity as superstitious.

Gobat's letters and journal express both great hope of the success of their mission and utter despair in the face of opposition. It is very clear from his correspondence that he enjoyed a great deal of "angel like" acceptance and appreciation by the people of Gondar including the Echege. He approached theological discussions more tactfully than Kugler, and it is no wonder that he enjoyed wider acceptance and respect among prominent people. Gobat wrote:

> At first, when they questioned me on critical points, I spoke with much caution; but the Abyssinians have much less prejudice against Europeans, than I expected after reading the works of Bruce and Salt. I have almost always my house full of people,

---

160. Gobat's Journal from 25 February 1830 – 16 February 1833, UB SC, CMS/B/OMS/C M/O28/113, 137–139.

161. Gobat's Journal from 25 February 1830 – 16 February 1833, UB SC, CMS/B/OMS/C M/O28/113, 196.

162. Spitz, *Rise of Modern Europe*, 157.

and every day some priests come, with whom I speak freely as I should speak in England, for, to the shame of my country, I must own that up to this time the Abyssinians are more tolerant than the Swiss. I do not conceal a single opinion, nor keep lack any information, and now I find myself respected by all the priests, and, I may say, beloved by many others. The Governor of Gondar, Cantiba=Cassai,[163] is above all particularly attached to me, and, like many *others*, he is not yet quite certain, whether I am a man or an angel.[164]

In a letter to his parents he added,

> During the latter months of my stay at Gondar almost everyone would have considered it blasphemy, if they had heard evil spoken against me, There were even many who, to the last could not persuade themselves that I was any other than an angel, in the form of a man. The more severely I reproved every one, even the King and the Echegua, so much the more every one was persuaded that I only desired the real benefit of the country, I was generally called the Apostle of Abyssinia; and the day that I departed I was followed by a host of men, women, and children, for a quarter of a league from the city. All the marks of friendship which have been shown me in the interior might perhaps lead me to hope more of the people than I ought, if I did not know that at first Jesus was honored by all, Luke IV as also the first Christians, Acts II. 47 For when any soul escape the snares of the devil, persecutions are sure to be excited, thus we must expect."[165]

In a letter to his sisters he wrote, "They talk very generally, of requesting me to become Abouna or Bishop of Abyssinia."[166] Gobat remarked that even the Echege had similar opinions until he had extended discussions

---

163. Probably Kentiba Kahssay. Kentiba stands for mayor.

164. Gobat to his sisters, Gondar, 24 June 1830, UB SC, CMS/B/OMS/ C M/O28/9.

165. Gobat to his parents, Behate, 25 February 1831, UB SC, CMS/B/OMS/ C M/O28/13.

166. Gobat to his sisters, Gondar, 24 June 1830, UB SC, CMS/B/OMS/ C M/O28/9.

within which Gobat expressed his opinion regarding auricular confession, absolution given by the priests, image worship, and the vow of celibacy. Gobat spoke against all four of them.

No doubt Gobat made an impression on the people. The respect and the love must have been real for someone like Gobat who learned the people's language and showed a great respect in his discussions with them would be easy to win the love of the people. Taddesse Tamrat argues that the offer to make Gobat head of the church was mere flattery, an impossible mock offer which Gobat was naïve to take seriously.[167] However, Gobat did not mention the offer in his letter to the CMS, nor to his parents. Taddesse's suggestion that Gobat reported the offer "with apparent exhilaration," therefore, carries little weight.[168] Perhaps the offer to make Gobat head of the church was a casual remark made by Gobat's friends and Echege as a way of appreciating him by affirming that he would make a wonderful Abun. On the other hand, given the desire of Girgis to have an English Abun for the church of Ethiopia,[169] the desire of different princes to have the Abun on their side regardless of his character,[170] and also the notes of Krapf about Armenian priest in Shewa, who won wide acceptance,[171] it is possible that the offer was genuine.

Unfortunately for Gobat his dialogue with the *Echege* was cut short, because he touched a sensitive nerve by stating that Mary was a sinner just like everybody else. The Echege became furious. There was apparent

---

167. Taddesse, "Evangelizing the Evangelized," 25. Gobat seems to have had an idea of the character of Ethiopians. In his "General Remarks on Abyssinia" he observed that Abyssinians would talk about only the good character of the person they like without ever mentioning his weakness, whereas they would speak of only the faults of the person they disliked, with no regard for his virtues. Upon hearing of the death of Ras Ali later on, Gobat remarked, ". . . but in Abyssinia it is impossible to ascertain the truth." Gobat, General Remarks on Abyssinia, UB SC, CMS/B/OMS/C M/028/114; Gobat's Journal from 25 February 1830 – 16 February 1833, UB SC, CMS/B/OMS/C M/028/113, 187.

168. Taddesse, "Evangelizing the Evangelized," 25.

169. Journal of Gobat and Kugler, 20 August 1827, UB SC, CMS/ B/ OMS/ C M O73/13.

170. Sabagadis took in the drunkard Abun whom the princes expelled from their regions. Kugler and Gobat to the CMS Secretary in London, 26 January 1827, UB SC, CMS/ B/ OMS/ C M O28/3.

171. Isenberg and Krapf, *Journals*, 220.

misunderstanding between the two. Perhaps Gobat had in mind the Roman controversy about exalting Mary in her own merit and attempted to refute it.

For the Ethiopians, however, Mariology was an extension of Christology and not a new subject altogether. In other words, affirming the place of Mary was affirming the divinity of the person of Christ. When the *Echege* insisted on her sinlessness, perhaps he was trying to protect the divinity of Jesus Christ her son. Any statement which appeared to belittle or lower the position of Mary thus raised serious christological questions. Perhaps the Echege got very angry thinking that Gobat's attack on Mariology would naturally extend to Christology as well. On the other hand, it is also possible that the Echege was protecting the perception of Mary as propagated since Zer'a Ya'iqob's reign. Gobat's servants realized how upset the Echege was and came in to beg the Echege according to custom, to let Gobat go.[172] Most likely, they wanted to avoid further irritation which might jeopardize Gobat's stay in the country.

As for Gobat's discussion with lay people, he wrote that he was so busy in Gondar that he hardly had time to eat during the day. People came and went continuously. He even acted as a physician.[173] His "miracle working" came to a climax in the healing of an insane person who was put in heavy chains, hands and feet. The healing came as a result of bleeding the person and talking to him closely. Gobat wrote to his sisters, "From that time, when any one attempt to speak against me, the others say to him 'Be silent, is not this the man who drove out the demons which the Priests could not drive out?'"[174] His experience illustrates an important aspect of Ethiopian Christianity. Propositional truth accompanied by reason and philosophy was not persuasive, but words accompanied with deeds or demonstrations were powerful.

---

172. Gobat to his sisters (translation), Gondar, 24 June 1830, UB SC, CMS/B/OMS/ C M/O28/9.

173. He rubbed the hand or the leg with warm water or oil and bled patients. He wrote that the people did not attribute their cure to his medicine but a miracle. They looked at him as a miracle worker and believed that if he touched them or even laid eyes on them, they would be healed. Gobat to his sisters (translation), Gondar, 24 June 1830, UB SC, CMS/B/OMS/ C M/O28/9.

174. Gobat to his sisters, Gondar, 24 June 1830, UB SC, CMS/B/OMS/ C M/O28/9.

However, change as he imagined it was so far from being achieved that at times, Gobat was at the verge of giving up and suggested the use of different means if the work was to be pursued. He suggested that training young people up to the age of nineteen or twenty in order to make them schoolmasters would be preferable.[175] He wrote to his parents, "Schools under the immediate superintendence of missionaries, or of any true Christian, promise more than any other means, because the Abyssinian children are in general, more docile and better than those of every other country in which I have sojourned. People of a certain age so firmly retain all their habits, that we can hardly look for a change except among the young people."[176]

Another possibility that crossed Gobat's mind was attempting to reach the pagan "Galla"[177] people groups.[178] Gobat came to this conclusion for a number of reasons. In addition to their reluctance for change, the habitually wayward lifestyle of Abyssinian adults was a great concern for the missionaries.[179] He lamented that he could not see commitment in Abyssinians because they changed their mind so easily. "One day I am all joy, with the hope that in a short time the Abyssinian Mission will be crowned with glorious success; the following day I am cast down to the very dust by the idea that all attempts will be useless; for the Abyssinians very quickly yield to the truth, but it is only for a while, they cannot make up their minds

---

175. Gobat to his sisters, Gondar, 24 June 1830, UB SC, CMS/B/OMS/ C M/O28/9.

176. Gobat to his parents, Behate, 25 February 1831, UB SC, CMS/B/OMS/ C M/O28/13.

177. The term "Galla" was also used to refer to what is currently known as the "Oromo" people group. The term is considered to be improper and in many cases even derogatory. Gustav Aren writes that the term "Galla," like the terms "Amhara" and "Muslim" referred to faith and not race. "Therefore an Ethiopian is traditionally called Amhara if he is a Christian, Muslim if he is of the Islamic faith, and 'Galla' if he practices the traditional Oromo faith or is animist." Aren, *Evangelical Pioneers*, 29.

178. He notes, "The country of the Gallas is a vast field, which demands the attention of Christians, and which offers, perhaps, fewer difficulties to the messengers of Christ than the people who have more complete systems of idolatry and anti-christian superstitions; but I do not conceive how it can be entered upon without the aid of one or two missionary stations in Christian Abyssinia." Gobat's Journal from 25 February 1830 – 16 February 1833, UB SC, CMS/B/OMS/C M/O28/113, 196.

179. Gobat observed that married men tended to be unfaithful to their wives and have more than one concubine. The women tended to be virtuous as long as they stayed married to their first husband but when they divorced they went into prostitution. He wrote that he met a young woman who was not yet fifteen and yet she was about to be separated from her fifth husband. Gobat to his sisters, Gondar, 24 June 1830, UB SC, CMS/B/OMS/ C M/O28/9.

to (sic) quick so much as one of their customs."[180] These remarks of Gobat help us interpret his actions during his stay in the country.

The Orthodox, who seemingly were slow in accepting any kind of change, were known for their unwavering stand once they accepted a given doctrine. The same thing applied when it came to their commitment to friends. Gobat remarked that they respected men who once held superior position even after they lost their position. "In this respect, they are superior to Europeans."[181] He made use of such a worldview from the very start. He wrote, "my chief aim in coming to Gondar was to secure friends, in order that eventually, if we should have enemies in Tigre,[182] there might be here a right view of our faith; and that, if we should be persecuted in Tigre, we might find an asylum in the interior. And I think that I have sufficiently succeeded. – The Abyssinians very seldom contradict me, because I prove every thing I say by the Bible, for which they have much greater respect than Papists and Greeks."[183]

Regarding Christianity in Ethiopia, Gobat wrote:

> Although the Christian Religion of Abyssinia is entirely degenerated into superstition, yet there is still left sufficiently of it to attach us to the christians (sic) of that country, and to engage us to consider them as brethren, who have alienated themselves from our common Father and have riped (sic) as fruits of their errors, misery and degradation. We may still congratulate them for the little they have preserved of christianity (sic); for it is, after all, to this principle that the Christian traveler is obliged to attribute all the traces in the character of the Abyssinians which, in many respects, renders them superior to all the other nations of Africa. Indeed, it is a great advantage for Abyssinia

---

180. Gobat to his sisters, Gondar, 24 June 1830, UB SC, CMS/B/OMS/ C M/O28/9. Krapf complained in a similar manner. "The deadness of Abyssinians casts me down very often. They hear with one ear, and let it pass through the other." Isenberg and Krapf, *Journals*, 173, 175.

181. Gobat to his sisters, Gondar, 24 June 1830, UB SC, CMS/B/OMS/ C M/O28/9.

182. In their correspondence, the missionaries referred to the region as "Tigre" and the language as "Tigri." The usual way of referring to the place is "Tigray" and the language is "Tigrigna" and these renderings are maintained in the thesis unless quoting.

183. Gobat to his sisters, Gondar, 24 June 1830, UB SC, CMS/B/OMS/ C M/O28/9.

to have had, till now, none but Christian governors: this is acknowledged even by the musulmans of that country themselves. It is in their religion itself that the seed is to be found for the regeneration of the people of Abyssinia. It will not be necessary for their civilization to demoralize them, as many who labored for the civilization of Turkey, have believed, but unjustly, to be obliged completely to demoralize the people in order to ameliorate both men & their circumstances. It would doubtless be much easier to take every moral and religious principle away from the Abyssinians than to restore them again to the truth and to the pure light of Christianity.[184]

The above statement might sound offensive to the Orthodox reader, but it appears to be Gobat's honest reflection of what they found on the ground. It also revealed his intentions and willingness to try to maintain Ethiopian Christianity and conviction that there were enough ingredients left for them to make the connection.

4.5. The Deaths of Kugler and Sabagadis

Kugler's higher expectations about the prosperity of the work of missions in Ethiopia were not realized, for he did not live to see the fruits of his labour materialize. While hunting with Gobat for medical purposes, his gun burst and severely wounded his arm. Exactly a year after setting foot in Massawa and ten months of stay in Tigray, on the evening of 29 December 1830 Rev Christian Kugler died. Gobat and Kugler had hoped to achieve a lot together, and they had a great burden for the church of Ethiopia. Sadly they did not spend much time together in the interior. The sum of the time they spent together in Ethiopia is a little over two months.

Gobat vividly describes Kugler's last moments. Shortly before he died Kugler prayed in Tigrigna and German thanking Jesus and asking him to have mercy upon him and receive him. In his last breath he asked Gobat to

---

184. Gobat, Samuel, "General Remarks on Abyssinia," UB SC, CMS/B/OMS/C M/028/114.

tell the people not to have *tezkar*[185] nor lament for him because he belonged to Jesus.[186]

Crummey notes that Kugler's burial brought an early outward opposition to the Protestant faith. The priests refused to have Kugler buried in the sacred grounds of the church because he was not their member.[187] Gobat commented that the objection of the priests had to do with saying masses for the soul of the deceased.[188] ". . . the priests refused to receive the remains of Kugler in the church, because I would not permit them to pronounce the absolution upon him. . ."[189] The priests knew that Sabagadis and all the rest of Gobat's friends had gone to war and there was no one to support Gobat. Perhaps, they were surfacing their long-hidden disapproval of the presence of CMS. From Gobat's account though, it appears that the priests were hoping to make money out of it.[190]

Gobat called the priests "hypocrites" accusing them of hoping to make money out of Kugler's burial which the priests emphatically denied in front of a large gathering of people, but according to Gobat, they later secretly

---

185. "Tezkar" is a table fellowship held after the death of EOC member to pray for his soul to enter eternity with God. Priests, family members, neighbours and friends would be invited to eat and drink and pray for the soul of the deceased. Tezkar is held on day 12, day 40, day 80, on the sixth month, after a year, and on the seventh year. Then every seven years for those who desire.

186. Extract of a letter from Mr Gobat, Behate, February 1831, UB SC, CMS/B/OMS/ C M/O28/10. Gobat also writes that those who witnessed the death of Kugler (including a Muslim) were impressed at his faith and full confidence in the Saviour. The Muslim remarked that "he had never seen true faith until that day." Gobat to the Rev E. Bickersteth, Behate, 24 February 1831, UB SC, CMS/B/OMS/ C M/O28/11.

187. Donald Crummey, *Priests and Politicians* (Oxford: Clarendon Press, 1972), 38. Taddesse Tamrat notes, "The chronic problem of granting appropriate burial grounds, which is still with us more than one-hundred-sixty years later, was apparently being inaugurated then and there!" Taddesse, "Evangelizing the Evangelized," 25.

188. Extract of a letter from Mr Gobat to Miss Hebler, 25 February 1831, UB SC, CMS/B/OMS/ C M/O28/12.

189. Gobat to the Rev E. Bickersteth, Behate, 24 February 1831, UB SC, CMS/B/OMS/ C M/O28/11.

190. Gobat to the Rev E. Bickersteth, Behate, 24 February 1831, UB SC, CMS/B/OMS/ C M/O28/11. In another story Gobat related the death of the woman of the house in which he lived. She suddenly died stung by an insect which the Ethiopians identified as "damotra." The priests took the little she had as a payment for the absolution. Moreover, because she did not confess before she died they imposed forty days of fasting on all of her relatives. Such actions must have appeared ludicrous to the CMS missionaries. Gobat's Journal from 25 February 1830 – 16 February 1833, UB SC, CMS/B/OMS/C M/O28/113, 165.

sent messengers asking him for money. It took the intervention of Sabagadis to have Kugler buried in the compound of the church.[191]

Unfortunately for Gobat, he was now left without Kugler, his European companion and most importantly Sabagadis, an Ethiopian dear friend. The timing at which he was separated from these two important men was extremely bad. Gobat met Sabagadis alone before the former went to war in which he died. Here is Gobat's account of their last time together.

> When I left Gondar, all was a cry for war against the Tigre. When I arrived at Adowa on the 17 of October I found Saba – Gadis, who was then going to war. He received me in every respect as his equal; we passed two evening (sic) together alone. The last evening he wept almost all the time. When we separated he said to me: "I love you, not because you are a great man, not because you are a white man, but because you love the Lord whom I wish to love with all my heart. I pray you to be my brother and to consider me as your brother." No said I, I will be your son and you shall be my father. At this he kissed my hand crying and said: "I am not worthy to be called your father, but I will be a faithful brother to you." Thus we parted forever.[192]

---

191. Gobat wrote that Sabagadis caused the Priests to be imprisoned and threatened to cut out their tongues when he returned from the war. It is obvious that Sabagadis was aware of the mischief done by the priests, thus, no wonder he did not have much respect for some of them. Gobat added that Sabagadis respected Girgis more than any other priest. He also noted that there was a great wailing and mourning for Kugler that he had a hard time calming the people down. He used the time to preach and exhort those who came to comfort him and they listened to the message attentively. Extract of a letter from Mr Gobat to Miss Hebler, 25 February 1831, UB SC, CMS/B/OMS/ C M/O28/12; Gobat to his parents, Behate, 25 February 1831, UB SC, CMS/B/OMS/C M/O28/13.

192. Gobat to the Rev E. Bickersteth, Behate, 24 February 1831, UB SC, CMS/B/OMS/ C M/O28/11. Gobat must have been very close to Sabagadis that when he died Sabagadis's son privately informs him. Gobat laments, "What a pity that this excellent prince has been so soon snatched from the mission. He had already promised to give us the first church in his country to instruct his people in." He further noted that Wolde Michael, the heir of Sabagadis shows him friendship and respect but Gobat doubts his motives, which may not be as pious as those of Sabagadis. But after exactly one year in his letter to the Rev E. Bickersteth Gobat praises Wolde Michael as almost the only person in Abyssinia who does not change his word. Gobat to his parents, Behate, 25 February 1831, UB SC, CMS/B/OMS/ C M/O28/13; Gobat to the Rev E. Bickersteth, Adigrate, 27 February 1832, UB SC, CMS/B/OMS/ C M/O73/60.

Gobat and Sabagadis never saw each other again. Sabagadis was killed in the battle.[193] Gobat learnt that the whole of Amhara was weeping for Sabagadis.[194] Gobat referred to Sabagadis as his best friend, second father[195] and protector.[196] The "Galla" who were against Sabagadis crossed the Tekeze River on Sunday with no resistance simply because Sabagadis was not willing to fight on Sunday.[197] This illustrates the extent of the commitment of the Ethiopians to their faith as they understood it.

4.6. The Aftermath

Suddenly Gobat found himself in a life-threatening situation. The Tigreans were defeated and fled for their lives. Wolde Michael, one of the sons of Sabagadis, came to take Gobat with him to a safer place. Upon the death of Sabagadis he managed a minor victory but the victory was attributed to Gobat. There was a widespread rumour that Gobat, the Englishman had

---

193. Gobat to the Rev E. Bickersteth, Behate, 24 February 1831, UB SC, CMS/B/OMS/ C M/O28/11.

194. Gobat's Journal from 25 February 1830 – 16 February 1833, UB SC, CMS/B/OMS/C M/O28/113, 178.

195. Gobat to his parents, Behate, 25 February 1831, UB SC, CMS/B/OMS/ C M/O28/13.

196. Gobat to the Rev E. Bickersteth, Adigrate, 27 February 1832, UB SC, CMS/B/OMS/ C M/O73/60. Nathaniel Pearce had similar affection for Wolde Sellassie, whom he left with anger because the governor displeased him. While on his way to leave the country, he learned that the "Galla" were about to attack Wolde Sellassie and it was feared that they would overpower him. With visible danger for his life, he returned back to Antalo because he could not bear the idea of the king being overpowered by his enemies. When Wolde Sellassie saw that Mr Pearce came back he was deeply touched and with tears in his eyes asked him to sit down and "ordered a cloth of best quality to be immediately thrown over his shoulder." Mr Pearce went to battle with Wolde Sellassie and fought bravely and advanced into the enemy lines that the king cried out, "Stop, stop that madman!" But Pearce went out of their sight and killed a "Galla" chieftain. His courage won him great admiration. J. J. Halls, ed., *Life and Adventures of Nathaniel Pearce*, 43–48.

197. Sabagadis was killed by the "Galla" on 15 February 1831. Before he died, the "Galla" gave him permission to send his will on one of his prisoner officers as to whom he wanted to take his place. Sabagadis's message to his son Wolde Michael, whom he appointed as his heir was "to do good to his English friends as long as he had it in his power." Upon entering the tent of his execution Sabagadis said to his enemies, "I have only fought in this war to defend the country which you are endeavouring to ruin without cause, and of which I was the father. You may kill my body; but my soul is in the hands of God. Only strike, I do not fear." Gobat's Journal from 25 February 1830 – 16 February 1833, UB SC, CMS/B/OMS/C M/O28/113, 167; Gobat to his parents, Behate, 25 February 1831, UB SC, CMS/B/OMS/ C M/O28/13.

given Wolde Michael a medicine which made him victorious.[198] There was no neutral ground and little natural explanation for events. As far as the Ethiopians were concerned there were powers always at work and members of clergy were good in manipulating the powers. Perhaps Gobat was thought to have had the white man's power at his disposal.

Upon the death of Kugler and Sabagadis, Gobat was discouraged. The country was plunged into civil war and Gobat seems to have lost all hope. He described the country, as a "miserable country" and "dark land."[199] To make matters worse, Aichinger was seriously ill. But Gobat wrote that he was strengthened by the grace of God.[200] Here are his words:

> Now that everything is changed around me, I am come to hang my harp on the thorns of the desert, inhabited by the wild shohos.[201] My brother Kugler is no more: my best friend and second father, Sebegadis, is no more.[202] Aichinger is the only friend who shares with me the grief of seeing Abyssinia plunged in every kind of misery. There is not even one around us who desires to hear us sing the songs of Zion. Nevertheless, the Eternal, Our Father, reigns; it is He who inflicts the wound and who binds it up; He wounds, and his hands heal, Can evil happen to a country, which He has not decreed? – And if the

---

198. Gobat's Journal from 25 February 1830 – 16 February 1833, UB SC, CMS/B/OMS/C M/O28/113, 176. Krapf related a similar story of Sahle Sellassie, the king of Shewa, asking him for a medicine which would protect him in war. Isenberg and Krapf, *Journals*, 73. The belief in medicine to protect against harm was also mentioned in the fifteenth-century hagiography of Aba Estifanos. When Aba Estifanos and his followers would not relent to King Zer'a Ya'iqob's order to bow down for him, he had his men search the monks thoroughly suspecting that they had medicine which protected them against the torture. Getatchew Haile, *Dekike Estifanos: Behig Amlak* (Addis Ababa: Addis Ababa University Press, 2010), 109. Pupils of traditional school of EOC were given "medicine" in order to help them remember their lessons. Pankhurst, "The Foundations of Education," 241–290, 242.

199. Gobat to the Rev E. Bickersteth, Behate, 24 February 1831, UB SC, CMS/B/OMS/ C M/O28/11; Gobat to his parents, Behate, 25 February 1831, UB SC, CMS/B/OMS/ C M/O28/13.

200. Extract of a letter from Mr Gobat to Miss Hebler, 25 February 1831, UB SC, CMS/B/OMS/ C M/O28/12.

201. In closing his letter to his parents Gobat says, ". . . remember me in my exile." Gobat to his parents, Behate, 25 February 1831, UB SC, CMS/B/OMS/C M/O28/13.

202. When Gobat learned the death of Sabagadis privately, he says he nearly fainted, but Sabagadis's son would not let him weep, fearing that people would be suspicious. Gobat to his parents, Behate, 25 February 1831, UB SC, CMS/B/OMS/ C M/O28/13.

misery which hangs over this country comes from the Lord, it is, perhaps only a fatherly chastisement, which shall hereafter prove an occasion of joy to His children.[203]

Gobat further remarked that he was happier when he was in Gondar than in any of the places he had been in Abyssinia, because from dawn to dusk people came to hear the word of God. He noted that some wanted to hear and pass judgment, but others to obtain knowledge of the way of salvation.[204] "There were some priests at Gondar who were opposed to me; but because the better instructed came, as they said, to take lessons of me, they dared not speak too loud. The priests, in general are very ignorant,[205] and for the last thirty years, since the Galla have governed the interior, they have lost much of the esteem and awe which the public had for them."[206]

Worse still, the greatest fears of Ali were actualized. From the beginning he had warned Kugler and Gobat to stop arguing with the clergy about fasting and the position of Mary, lest they consider them Muslims. Gobat wrote, "The greater part of the monks have become my enemies and call me a Mussulman; because I condemn the adoration of the Virgin Mary, and have no confidence in her intercession; but the better informed, and consequently the most influential, always testify friendship for me; . . ."[207]

Gobat fled for his life along with Aichinger. He reported that there was lawlessness and disorder everywhere – robbery and looting were common.[208] However, Gobat decided to stay when he could have left the country for Egypt before the way to Massawa was closed. Because of the instability of the country, he was not able to do anything and very distressed at the fact.

---

203. Gobat to his parents, Behate, 25 February 1831, UB SC, CMS/B/OMS/ C M/ O28/13.

204. Gobat to his parents, Behate, 25 February 1831, UB SC, CMS/B/OMS/ C M/ O28/13.

205. In 1842 Krapf noted that the Abuna who resided in Gondar daily ordained about a thousand people. All that was required of them was an ability to read the Ethiopic Gospel, sing from the book of Yared, and have beard so as to determine their age. The Abuna then lays hands on them for a cost of one or two pieces of salt. Isenberg and Krapf, *Journals*, 308–309.

206. Gobat to his parents, Behate, 25 February 1831, UB SC, CMS/B/OMS/ C M/ O28/13.

207. Gobat's Journal from 25 February 1830 – 16 February 1833, UB SC, CMS/B/OMS/C M/O28/113, 197.

208. Gobat to his parents, Behate, 25 February 1831, UB SC, CMS/B/OMS/ C M/ O28/13.

He wrote to his parents that he felt "shut out from the assembly of those who praise the Eternal for the great salvation which he has given us in Jesus." He also was discouraged because he found Tigrigna difficult to master and people there were not interested in listening to "the Word of Life."[209]

The country was ruined with constant war among the rival chiefs and the raids of the Galla against them all. In revenge for the death of Marie, the Galla ravaged the country burning and plundering villages. Gobat wrote that the people of Gondar were hoping to be delivered from the "tyranny of the Galla."[210]

After a year of uncertainty, Gobat decided to leave the country and Wolde Michael who initially was not willing to let him go finally consented. Gobat noted that all the most respectable monks accompanied him some distance and he exhorted them "with witness to give their hearts unreservedly to Jesus, and to expect everything from His grace." Just before Gobat departed, he had an unexpected "parting gift." Gobat recounted the story,

> A learned man, Alaca Wolda Selassé of Shua, who came every day to see me with a number of dogmatic questions; but for whom I had no particular attachment, because he always opposed in a very dry manner everything I said, suddenly burst into tears and told me in the presence of all the monks: "Now that you are leaving I ask your pardon for all the trouble that I have caused you, I had heard speak of you at Gondar, & your doctrine had excited in me doubts on several points. My chief end in coming here was to see you and to hear the proofs that you had of your doctrine in opposition to ours. I resisted you as much as I could, being already several times convinced of the truth of your words; but it was in order to have more proofs.

---

209. Gobat to his parents, Adigrate, 26 February 1832, UB SC, CMS/B/OMS/ C M/O28/14A.

210. Gobat's servant was imprisoned while in Adwa to check on the security of the place for Gobat. The chiefs there demanded of the servant to give them the treasures of Gobat which is hidden there. Gobat to the Rev E. Bickersteth, Adigrate, 27 February 1832, UB SC, CMS/B/OMS/ C M/O73/60. Gobat himself slightly escapes plundering several times because it was believed that he has treasures which he has brought from Europe and collected in Abyssinia. Gobat to his parents, Adigrate, 26 February 1832, UB SC, CMS/B/OMS/ C M/O28/14A.

> Now that we are parting, perhaps for life, I ought to open my heart to you. It is you who have opened my eyes. I will let your instructions dwell in my heart, and I will publicly call myself your disciple. You are my father."[211]

The Aleqa wept as he saw Gobat off. The words of the Aleqa must have encouraged Gobat that his toil was not futile and that he communicated even to those who appeared to oppose his message. On his way to Egypt he met Wubie and his army. Wubie received him well. Because of the continuous fight between Wubie and Sabagadis's sons, Gobat was trapped in the middle and stayed with Wubie and his army. While staying there he shared the Gospel with as many people as he could in Wubie's tent. "I thought it my duty to avoid wounding their feelings, and I endeavoured to tell them what there was positive in religion, rather than contradict them when it was not absolutely necessary."[212]

Little did he know that he would be cornered to speak his mind on Mariology, a sensitive issue which he had hoped to avoid all along. There he was surrounded by Abyssinian soldiers who for the most part were devoutly Orthodox Christians, and Gobat was on his way back home. It is hard to imagine how they would have reacted if he were not tactful in his reply. He recounted the story:

> But once, when Oubea's tent was full of people, a priest suddenly asked me why I did not wish them to call Mary "Mother of God" to which I simply replied that Jesus Christ being truly God and truly man I did not in one sense object to their calling Mary "Mother of God," if they did not thence draw the conclusion that they ought to invoke and worship her, as if a feeble creature could be placed by the side of the only God and saviour of the world in the work of our redemption; besides that the reason which God has given us, always finds a contradiction in the title "Mother of God"; it is as if we said that the Eternal, the creator of the universe, took his origin from a creature of

---

211. Gobat's Journal from 25 February 1830 – 16 February 1833, UB SC, CMS/B/OMS/C M/O28/113, 200.

212. Gobat's Journal from 25 February 1830 – 16 February 1833, UB SC, CMS/B/OMS/C M/O28/113, 201.

a day. "It would be much better to call her simply 'Mother of Jesus' as the Apostles called her, and to believe as the Gospel says, that if we imitate Mary in her faith, her humility, her love, and her obedience, Jesus Christ will be as nearly united to us as to Mary." Oubie interrupted me, saying – "It must be confessed that we are much too presumptuous in calling Mary 'Mother of God,' without being authorized to do so by the Gospel; I am also of opinion that it would be much better to call her 'Mother of Jesus.'"[213]

It is not difficult to imagine how relieved Gobat must have felt with Wubie's agreement to his reply. In addition to that, Gobat had a good reputation over the years of his stay in Abyssinia, so that his remarks were well taken. Even Wubie, who knew Gobat's closest association with his opponents (Sabagadis and his sons), maintained a high opinion about him. In fact, he sent off Gobat with a gift of thirty talaris.[214] The gift came in useful, as he was nearly out of money.[215] In addition to that Wubie arranged for Gobat to have a good recommendation to the custom house officer and chief of the district of Halai to render him safely to Massawa. Gobat was deeply moved and remarked, "Thus all the great people of Abyssinia who know me consider themselves as my friends."[216]

Before he departed Gobat gave the copies of Amharic and Ethiopic Gospels to the secretary of Wubie to distribute them. As a final word of encouragement after his years of hard work Gobat learnt that Wolde Sellassie, the governor of Wolcait, had received a copy of the Gospels in Amharic and he read it day and night. He even wanted to know when they could have the rest of the New Testament in Amharic.[217]

The missionaries had been correct in stressing the role of vernacular scriptures in reforming the church and their sacrificial service, which appeared to bear no visible fruit, had the potential to bring gradual change. Gobat left the country with mixed feelings,

---

213. Gobat's Journal from 25 February 1830 – 16 February 1833, 201.
214. Gobat's Journal from 25 February 1830 – 16 February 1833, 202.
215. Gobat's Journal from 25 February 1830 – 16 February 1833, 197.
216. Gobat's Journal from 25 February 1830 – 16 February 1833, 202.
217. Gobat's Journal from 25 February 1830 – 16 February 1833, 202.

I quitted Halai with a heavy heart, on casting the last glance towards a country where I have just passed three years. On passing to Halai three years ago, I said to myself that if I could contribute in any way to the salvation of a single sinner, I should rejoice at having come into this country; and now it seems to me that if there only remained a single man in Abyssinia who did not know Jesus, I should esteem myself happy to consecrate my life to bring him to the good shepherd. Walking along, I returned thanks to God for all the good that he has done for me in this country; but there was a voice within which could only say Grace! Grace![218]

Gobat's observation towards the end of his ministry in Ethiopia summed up his perception of the state of Christians in Ethiopia. As noted earlier, he had encountered serious opposition because of his teaching regarding Mary and he wrote of the response of people towards his teaching, ". . . there are even some who condemn the worship of creatures and who begin to doubt if the invocation of the Virgin is permitted; but I know none who sincerely seek the Saviour."[219] He made similar remarks in the letter to his parents,

I knew no one there who had a vital acquaintance with the Saviour, but I have known many who are sensible of their spiritual misery and who can find no rest in the doctrines of men, or in the merit of their own works. With many the fear of doing wrong in acting against the torrent of superstition hinders them from beginning their conversion by an entire surrender of themselves, and a full assurance of faith in the Saviour.[220]

Gobat had spent his last year in Ethiopia running for his life so he was not able to have any meaningful dialogue with people. So, the above quotation from a letter to his parents might as well be taken as his last remark about his first missionary service to them. He left Massawa on 12 December 1832 with two young students Hadera and Kidane Mariam who were related to Sabagadis, and arrived in Cairo after two months. In April 1833, he proceeded to Europe leaving the boys in the care of Rev Carl Wilhelm Isenberg, a German Lutheran trained at Basel Missionary Seminary who had been

---

218. Gobat's Journal from 25 February 1830 – 16 February 1833, 203–204.
219. Gobat's Journal from 25 February 1830 – 16 February 1833, 197.
220. Gobat to his parents, Behate, 25 February 1831, UB SC, CMS/B/OMS/ C M/ O28/13.

recruited by CMS to replace Kugler. Gobat intended to report and discuss with CMS how to renew the mission's undertakings in Ethiopia.

4.7. Conclusion of the First Attempt to Revitalize the Church of Ethiopia

The efforts of the first CMS missionaries were not as fruitful as they had expected them to be. However, they enjoyed a degree of success in their ministry. Especially, distributing the Scriptures proved to be a yeast of reformation as will be shown later on. Besides having a meaningful theological dialogue with prominent people, some of their servants showed signs of genuine change of heart. Girgis was one of the disciples of the CMS missionaries and in a letter to the Church in England showed his love for the missionaries. ". . . Your love has much been heard of in our country. Your sons have arrived and have made us understand it. Do not forget us for the Lord's sake. We are attracted by your love, having heard your statutes & having seen your doings in your sons Mr^{ss} Gobat and Kugler. Your liberality is attested by your sons."[221]

The peaceful theological dialogue was quite encouraging to the missionaries, but the outcome was based on the position of the church of Alexandria as related by Girgis. The missionaries had great hopes for Girgis's future service in the church. In fact, the change of life of individuals was what the missionaries could count as showing the success of their ministry. Gobat remarked:

> I cannot say that I know of any one truly converted, but I have some friends among the young scholars of whom I have much hope. There is, especially a young Hailasihlasse of Sohoa whom sees likely to be very useful. When I shall return to Gondar with a great number of copies of the Gospel, he will conduct me to Sohoa, introduce me to the King, his friend, & then go with me to establish a Mission among the Galla.[222]

---

221. Wolda Girgis to the Christian Society which is in England, 1 October 1830, UB SC, CMS/B/OMS/ C M/O46/23B.

222. Gobat to his sisters, Gondar, 24 June 1830, UB SC, CMS/B/OMS/ C M/O28/9.

Thus we can see that the missionaries had both encouraging and disheartening experiences in their stay in Ethiopia. However, neither the head on confrontations of Kugler nor the tactful discussions of Gobat or the Scripture distribution brought the kind of change the missionaries had in mind. One factor was the approach of Kugler which condemned nearly all of the practices of the people and naturally made the people defensive. Second, the tradition of the church which interacted with the culture for centuries was very difficult to uproot with a handful of foreign agents. Third, the church of Ethiopia was under the church of Alexandria and did not have the kind of centralized administration we now see, and fourthly; in spite of Scripture distribution, people were illiterate so they still depended on the semi-literate and inadequately trained clergy to instruct them.

The kind of Christianity the missionaries found in Ethiopia was quite different from what they had in mind. Many of the practices including compulsory fasting and "pilgrimages as good works designed to earn forgiveness" were rejected by the Reformers in Europe.[223] The missionaries' passion for the reformation of the church and concern for the wellbeing of Abyssinia were often expressed.[224] No matter how superstitious their faith might have appeared to the missionaries, they recognized that Ethiopian Christians were ready to die for their faith.[225] The Orthodox faith had become part of their identity and the ingredients which gave it the kind of form it assumed over

---

223. Spitz, *Rise of Modern Europe*, 155–156.

224. In a letter to the CMS committee, Kugler reported about the conquest of some villages by the Turks, and that they burned down churches and set out to convert the people to Islam by instruction or force. The people of Tigray were not afraid of the Turks. They were ready to fight for their faith, but Kugler commented that they were ignorant of the power of the Pasha. "A Christian nation, which has been preserved by divine providence for so many hundred years is now threatened to be forced into Mohammedanism. I cannot describe to you how quickly my blood rolls and how it boils when I reflect a little on this gloom, which has now encompassed us." Kugler to D. Coates, 6 August 1830, Quila, UB SC, CMS/B/OMS/ C M/O46/22.

225. Kugler reports about the conquest of some villages by the Turks. They have burned down churches and set out to convert the people to Islam by instruction or force. Kugler says that the people in Tigrai were not afraid of the Pasha because he says, they are ignorant of his force. "A Christian nation, which has been preserved by divine providence for so many hundred years is now threatened to be forced into Mohammedanism. I can not describe to you how quickly my blood rolls and how it boils when I reflect a little on this gloom, which has now encompassed us." Kugler to D. Coates, 6 August 1830, Quila, UB SC, CMS/B/OMS/ C M/O46/22.

the centuries were highly intermingled with that one identity, and, naturally, were very difficult to give up.

4.8. New Recruits, Greater Challenges

The CMS agreed to renew its efforts of reformation in the church of Ethiopia and sent out Gobat and Isenberg, along with their wives and two German craftsmen, one of whom was Sabagadis's favourite, Aichinger. Isenberg spent some time in Jerusalem to study more Amharic and attain a status among the Orthodox as a pilgrim to the Holy Sepulchre. In October 1834 Gobat and Isenberg along with their wives, the craftsmen and the two Ethiopian students proceded to Ethiopia. On their way, while they were in Jeddah, Gobat fell ill with symptoms of dysentery and his condition grew worse while in Massawa, but he was determined to proceed. They arrived in Adwa in 1835 after Easter but Gobat, who was anxious to settle in Gondar, collapsed. Isenberg, however, insisted that they should settle in Adwa. Gobat yielded with misgivings, and travelled to secure permission from Wubie, whose camp was outside of Adwa. The journey sapped his energy and confined him to bed for more than a year. On the top of that, the conflict between him and Isenberg was increasing each day.[226]

From his previous stay in Ethiopia Gobat was wont to dress, eat and live like an Ethiopian. Identification, he believed, was the practice of the Lord when on earth and should be made a principle of approach in order to "get access into the heart of the Abyssinians and influence them." Isenberg was of a different opinion, believing that he would exert more influence by keeping aloof. Already while in Egypt Gobat had noted that they represented views fundamentally at variance but he hoped that it would never cause any discord.[227]

The hardliner Isenberg concluded that the mind of Abyssinians was "closely attached to superstition and ignorance" – so he did not desire to identify himself with and engage them.[228] His judgment of the spiritual status of the clergy was not different from that of Gobat and Kugler, but

---

226. Aren, *Evangelical Pioneers*, 60–62.
227. Aren, 62.
228. Donald Crummey, *Priests and Politicians* (Oxford: Clarendon Press, 1972), 41.

his aloofness was quite the opposite of Kugler's and Gobat's attitude towards the church of Ethiopia. Against the will of Gobat he established a house congregation with the two young men Hadera and Kidane Mariam (whom he confirmed while in Egypt) as members. He administered Holy Communion and exercised control over the members. He even took the willingness of Aichinger to work for Medhane Alem Church as apostasy and deprived him of his tools. Isenberg's actions were quite contrary to the original intentions of the CMS, and heavy consequences were welling up. Gobat was worried about the ramifications of the actions of Isenberg, but there was little he could do about it, because of his prolonged illness. After watching helplessly the destruction that Isenberg's radical actions were building up, Gobat decided to return home, along with his wife. Hadera helped to carry him on a litter to the coast.[229]

Isenberg focused on studying the language and translating the New Testament into Tigrigna "turning a blind eye to clerical opposition."[230] Aleqa Kidane Mariam of the Medhane Alem Church in Adwa, kept asking Isenberg to be and live like Gobat, to which Isenberg replied that his belief was similar to that of Gobat but Gobat was bedridden and he was not. This makes it clear that Isenberg did not wish to follow in the footsteps of Gobat. According to him, identifying with the people would send the wrong message.

---

229. Aren, *Evangelical Pioneers*, 62–63. Perhaps unable to cope with the sternness of Isenberg, the two German artisans left the mission. Aren, *Evangelical Pioneers*, 64. Gobat spoke highly of Hadera. From all of the people he mentioned in his letter, it was Hadera who persevered to the end. Hadera assumed the difficult responsibility of caring for Gobat, his wife and their fifteen months old baby girl on their way to the port. Unfortunately, all three of them were very sick and needed special attention which Hadera sought to offer cheerfully. In addition to that Hadera was in charge of the nineteen people who were with them to help in one way or another. Gobat and his wife were so grateful to Hadera's service that they decided to take him with them to Bruggen. There he was placed in a school and studied German. Unfortunately, he was not able to survive the harsh climate of Switzerland and died. His hope of returning home and educating his people did not materialize. Samuel Gobat, "A Short Biography of the Abyssinian Hadera," UB SC, CMS/B/OMS/C M 028/34B, 9ff. Earlier in 1799, twenty-five children were taken to England from Sierra Leone with a hope of training them to become missionaries to their own people. Unfortunately all but six died because they "failed to accustom themselves to the rigours of the English climate" and the survivors were shipped back to Sierra Leone. Hennel, *John Venn*, 241–242.

230. Aren, *Evangelical Pioneers*, 64.

In spite of the attitude of Isenberg, there was recognition of CMS by the authorities. The mission was permitted to buy a piece of land on which buildings were erected. This implies that there was a degree of tolerance. Rev Carl Heinrich Blumhardt arrived in Adwa in January 1837. There is no doubt that the aloof attitude of Isenberg, which easily could be taken as contempt, must have displeased the clergy of the church. Such displeasure was evident during Blumhardt's second visit to Wubie, and the missionaries blamed it "on clerical intrigue."[231] In the meantime the missionaries received a letter from the king of Shewa asking for skilled men and medicine and also for the distribution of the Scripture in his kingdom.[232] We shall discuss the reply later.

In Adwa, however, there was a growing tension and opposition to their work led by Aleqa Kidane Mariam, who had formerly voiced his disapproval of the missionaries by refusing to have Kugler buried in the church built by Sabagadis. Aren notes that Aleqa Kidane Mariam considered the return of the missionaries a serious threat to the indigenous Ethiopian tradition. He had a bitter dispute with Isenberg, whom he accused of blaspheming God and the saints and introducing a strange faith which disturbed the country. Apparently, Isenberg's holding services in his house and administering Holy Communion displeased the clergy because it was strange to the Ethiopian concept of a church.[233]

The arrival of Johann Ludwig Krapf in 1837 further irritated the clergy. Krapf, a twenty-seven year old German Lutheran had been trained in Basel. He studied Greek, Hebrew, Italian, French, Latin and Amharic.[234] His arrival gave the clergy the impression that with the growing number of missionaries would increase their influence. While Wubie was in Aksum to collect his annual revenues the missionaries went there to pay their respect to him. Krapf presented gifts to the prince and was promised protection. Aleqa Kidane Mariam, however, was so determined to limit the influence of the missionaries that he banned any association with them. This ban affected two prominent priests of Wubie's court: Tekle-Giorgis and Habte-Sellassie who

---

231. Aren, 66.
232. Aren, 64.
233. Aren, 66.
234. Krapf, *Travels, Researches*, 1–12.

also were charged with "Protestant leanings." Wubie was angry at Kidane Mariam but left for a war without dealing with the matter.[235]

When Habte Sellassie reprimanded him, Aleqa Kidane Mariam invited the missionaries to celebrate Holy Communion in his church according to the rite of the Church of England. But he quickly changed his mind and offered toleration on condition that they attend the Ethiopian Epiphany and declare the Ethiopians as Christian brothers. The missionaries found themselves in a difficult position. According to Blumhardt they feared that participation in the ceremony might be interpreted as acknowledgement of the errors of the church. According to Isenberg, however, they offered to accept the proposal on the condition that they would be allowed to exercise their faith at their church using vernaculars. Tekle Giorgis, who was trying to mediate, decided not to deliver Isenberg's request. "With cooperation and mutual recognition rejected, a total breakdown of relations quickly ensued."[236] Though there had been tensions mounting from time to time, the orders of Wubie for their expulsion from Adwa on 9 March 1838 which they obeyed after three days appeared to be caused for the most part by the tactless and provocative actions of Isenberg.[237]

4.9. CMS in Shewa

After more than seven years from the end of the first missionary service of Gobat in Ethiopia, Isenberg wrote to him from Adwa that he and his partner Blumhardt had received an invitation from the king of Shewa "to go and preach the Gospel in his kingdom." Blumhardt was willing to go and started

---

235. Aren, *Evangelical Pioneers*, 67.

236. Aren, 67.

237. He believed in keeping the Abyssinians at bay and wanted them to recognize him as their missionary and considered any actions of tolerance on their part as an indication of the missionaries being perceived as the Ethiopians' proselytes. Aren, *Evangelical Pioneers*, fn. 114, 67. He also made a wrong move in taking two newcomers (Italian and French) into his protection and refusing the customs request to examine their bags. When asked by Wubie to explain his actions he complained that the authorities did not show due respect for Europeans and warned that "their folly in believing every tale that was spread about ourselves in particular and the English and Franks in general, would be attended with the worst consequences." Interestingly, the gentlemen he tried to protect were given permission to stay when the missionaries were expelled and Isenberg and Krapf were quick to blame Catholic intrigue for the failure of their mission. Krapf, *Travels, Researches*, 110; Aren, *Evangelical Pioneers*, 69.

to work hard to acquire sufficient knowledge of the language to preach in it. In the meantime, Isenberg set out to explain their work and ended with a rather lengthy commentary on the Bible and the history of the kingdom of God reaching to their own time, along with exhortations. Isenberg noted, "I made the proposition to the King that in case he should wish for us with such a doctrine in our mouth and such a work in our hands we would be ready to come to him." Neither Isenberg nor Blumhardt had any intention of removing the mission station from Adwa.[238]

Isenberg noted, "Adowa must remain a missionary station if it was only to keep up communicating with the read (sic) Sea and Europe, though circumstances may be more promising elsewhere, as Shewa and Gondar."[239] They received a reply from the king of Shewa in September 1837, and Isenberg reported to London that they were invited to teach the gospel in Shewa. It appeared that they had read into the letter of the king the things they had in mind. They became painfully aware of the intentions of the king after they arrived to Shewa.[240]

After a short interval in Egypt they travelled to Shewa and arrived on 31 May, 1839, informed the king of their arrival and waited until they were invited to proceed. They received the message of the king inviting them to his country but asking for "medicine, a gun, masons, etc" without mentioning their mission work.[241]

When they arrived at the court of the king, they were warmly received. Unlike the first group of missionaries, Isenberg and his group were upfront about their intentions in coming to Shewa. They explained to the king that they had various skills which they were willing to teach and make use of, but their primary mission of coming to Abyssinia was to preach the gospel. They

---

238. Extract of a letter from Isenberg to Rev Samuel Gobat, 28 September 1837, UB SC, CMS/B/OMS/C M/O28/31B.

239. Extract of a letter from Isenberg to Rev Samuel Gobat, 28 September 1837, UB SC, CMS/B/OMS/C M/O28/31B.

240. Aren remarked, "Apparently Isenberg was blind to the real purport of the royal invitation, but he was by no means the only one. He read into the message what he hoped to find. Many others were to do the same after him. For almost half a century similar overtures were made now and then, missions indulging in wishful hopes of gospel outreach, princes easer to profit from Western technique and ingenious inventions, both factors together causing much suffering and many disappointments." Aren, *Evangelical Pioneers*, 65.

241. Aren, 70–71.

asked the king to give them young men to instruct. Sahle Sellassie received their gifts graciously and said that he would have preferred the Ethiopic New Testament to the Amharic one. He also asked them to give him medication, but permission for mission work had to wait. "He then observed that with regards to our principal object, he would have further conversation with us in future, as there were a great many things to be considered relative to this subject. . ."[242] Most probably the king was aware of their expulsion from Adwa for religious reasons, and wanted to keep a closer eye on them even regarding the use of their skills.

Therefore he ordered them not to give any medicine to people, and would not give them young boys to instruct as they requested.[243] Instead, he sent Aleqa Wolde Ser'at, the head of the Medhane Alem Church in Ankober, to study their language. Ironically, in Shewa the first scholar of the missionaries turned out to be the Aleqa of the Medhane Alem Church in Ankober. It may be recalled that the Aleqa of the Medhane Alem Church in Tigray had expelled them, but the Aleqa of the Medhane Alem Church in Ankober received instruction from them. But the missionaries did not get to decide the subject, he did. He told them that he desired to study geography. As for the Bible he said that he had enough knowledge and wanted to learn something he did not know.[244]

The missionaries perceived the king as too narrow-minded.[245] They were well provided for by the king, but their request for permission to teach the gospel was ignored since like Sabagadis, the king was more interested in learning their skills. Whatever he saw and heard which appeared to be new,

---

242. Isenberg and Krapf, *Journals*, 59.

243. The king wanted to keep an eye on them that they were not allowed to use their mules apart from his permission. Isenberg and Krapf, *Journals*, 68.

244. He was initially sent by the king to study their language and when Krapf wanted to read the Bible with him Aleqa Serat tells him he knew the Bible and desired to learn something which he did not know. Isenberg and Krapf, *Journals*, 63, 76.

245. They refer to two of his actions as examples of his narrow mindedness: "There was a small bridge built over the river Beresa by an Albanese man but nobody was allowed to pass over it except the king. A Greek man built a mill but nobody was allowed to use it, nobody except the king was allowed to prepare the Abyssinian hydromel . . ." Isenberg and Krapf, *Journals*, 64–65. Pankhurst, however, noted that the water mill was not put to use because of opposition from the priests. Richard Pankhurst, "The Role of Foreigners in Nineteenth Century Ethiopia, Prior to the Rise of Menelik," *Boston University Papers on Africa* 2 (1966): 181–214.

he wanted his servants to learn, but he would not give young men to the missionaries to be taught the gospel. The missionaries were aware of the king's desires. They noted, "The king is anxious to get from Europeans all that he sees and hears."[246]

However, they were not forbidden to distribute Scriptures. Thus, Krapf and Isenberg were able to distribute the Gospels and the New Testament to as many people as they could. Priests and lay people always came asking for the Scriptures. Krapf noted that the people in Shewa preferred the Ethiopic Gospels over the Amharic ones; including a chief priest who refused to accept the Amharic New Testament.[247]

But this seems to have changed later. Two hundred copies of the Amharic Bible which arrived in February 1841 were gone in a day and half. "Riotous scenes were staged by later-comers who refused to believe that there were no more books." The missionaries asked for more copies which they received and distributed right away. By the beginning of 1842 Krapf reported the distribution of one thousand copies.[248]

The missionaries also used different occasions to teach and admonish the people, including the priests, to focus on the Word of God. Most importantly, their attitude towards the Ethiopian Christians changed in Shewa. The priests were favourable to them, too. The priest of St Giorgis's church even invited them to fast with them and partake the Holy Communion "declaring that there was nothing in their doctrine and their lives to prevent it." The missionaries realized that their past attitude in Tigray had hindered the mission work. Thus, they discussed among themselves to consider fasting for three reasons: first, their not fasting had been a continual stumbling block for their mission in Abyssinia. Second, fasting was not sinful and against the principle of the Church of England, and third, they referred to the example of the Apostle Paul. Perhaps worried that their fasting could be taken as legalism they clarified further that their voluntary act of fasting was to consider the weak brethren and had nothing to do with attaining righteousness. The passage they had in mind reads, "But food does not bring us near to God; we are no worse if we do not eat, and no better if we

---

246. Isenberg and Krapf, *Journals*, 64.
247. Isenberg and Krapf, 102.
248. Aren, *Evangelical Pioneers*, 75.

do. Be careful, however, that the exercise of your freedom does not become a stumbling block to the weak." 1 Corinthians 8:8, 9 (NIV). Accordingly Krapf resolved to abstain from meat on Wednesdays and Fridays.[249]

This was by no means an easy decision to make. Even to the modern evangelical mind taking upon oneself Orthodox traditions can be taken as sending the wrong message. Unfortunately, Isenberg did not stay long enough to influence the Shewan Christians with his decision to give way on fasting. In November 1839 he left for Malta to reunite with his family because he had promised to stay in Shewa only for a year.[250] Isenberg's great contribution was his pioneering dictionary of Amharic which was published in 1841.[251]

Krapf enjoyed the care and protection of the king of Shewa and his royal mother's hospitality during his two-year stay.[252] It seemed that the initially hard rulers of the king must have changed. Krapf was able to take in five young boys and instruct them freely. He taught them the Bible, systematic theology, writing, history and geography. He also had some adult scholars learning language and geography.[253]

Upon the departure of Isenberg, Krapf focused on learning Oromo language and diligently collected all the information he could possibly get about the Oromo people. His vivid description of the Oromo as "the Germany of Africa"[254] caught the imagination of his friends back in Europe. "He gave new urgency to the slogan by exclaiming: 'Give us the Gallas and Central Africa is ours.'"[255]

---

249. Isenberg and Krapf, *Journals*, 69, 138–139, 236; Aren, *Evangelical Pioneers*, 74–75. On the top of refraining from being a stumbling block, Krapf also had practical reasons to observe the fast and befriend the priests. He realized that unlike Wubie, the Prince of Tigre, the king of Shewa was more influenced by the priests and that if they were to oppose the mission the king will not protect him. Isenberg and Krapf, *Journals*, 235–236.

250. Aren, *Evangelical Pioneers*, 72.

251. M. Louis Pirouet, "Isenberg, Karl Wilhelm," in *Biographical Dictionary of Christian Missions*, ed. Gerald H. Anderson (Grand Rapids: Eerdmans, 1998), 322.

252. Isenberg and Krapf, *Journals*, 161, 291–294.

253. Isenberg and Krapf, 249–250.

254. Regarding the Oromo he wrote, ". . . I consider them destined by Providence after their conversion to Christianity to attain the importance and fulfil the mission which Heaven has pointed out to the Germans in Europe." Krapf, *Travels, Researches*, 72.

255. Aren, *Evangelical Pioneers*, 72–74.

But he was not able to start a mission among the Oromo because King Sahle Sellassie would not allow him. The king told him that the "Gallas" would kill him and that the Abyssinians had tried different means, including force, to convert them to Christianity but to no avail. Krapf tried to persuade the monarch by arguing that their conversion would enhance his political dominance over the "Galla," but he refused fearing that the British would hold him responsible if anything happened to Krapf while in "Galla" territory. Sahle Sellassie told Krapf that he would fulfil his desires when he conquered their territories.[256] The king issued a decree that the "Galla" in his kingdom were to convert to Christianity.

With mission to the "Galla" in his mind, Krapf did not stop attempting to engage the Abyssinian Christianity. In addition to the emphasis on fasting and almsgiving, he too was concerned with the widespread popularity of charms. Charms for protection, healing and also success were asked from him.[257] Krapf encountered a priest who having acquired a copy of the New Testament from him declared that he wanted to go back to his country and preach the gospel. There was one small problem though. The priest demanded to know if carrying the New Testament on his head would keep him safe from danger on the road. Krapf told him to receive the New Testament into his heart instead.[258] Even when the New Testament was acquired people tended to consider it as a means of protecting them from danger. Krapf lamented:

> The priests, instead of conducting the people to Christ, assume the lordship over them, engrossing their attention with vain fables and stories of saints, to whom they direct them for refuge as their Saviours. Hence, ignorance, superstition, fleshly sins, particularly fornication, have prevailed among the people; so that we may well wonder at the remnant of Christianity which still exists in their country. Who can cure the wounds of Abyssinia, but the Lord by His Spirit and His Word? To give them His Spirit we are unable; but we can serve them by

---

256. Aren, 72–74.
257. Isenberg and Krapf, *Journals*, 132.
258. Isenberg and Krapf, 141–142.

supplying them with the Word of God. The Holy Scriptures must not only be laid down before the people, but they must be explained to them by word and by writing; and the youth must be instructed in the holy truths of the Bible. The Lord be praised that He has enabled us to make a beginning, though a small one.[259]

He observed that religious conversations always reverted to subjects such as worshipping of saints, fasting, ceremonies, etc;[260] the learned men of Abyssinia were lost in vain speculations and caught up with christological disputes.[261] He noted that the Christians "mix all together – Christianity, Judaism, Mahomedanism and Heathenism."[262] Krapf lamented that the Christians partook even in the practices of Pagans.[263] He added:

> We cannot expect a better state of religion among them, inasmuch as a string of silk put around their necks as a sign of their Christianity – mortification of their flesh by much fasting – a strict separation from Mahomedans by not eating with them – their kissing churches – imploring Saints – disputing about the births of Christ – pilgrimages to Jerusalem, or to the grave of Tecla Haimanot – all these things together cannot change their hearts nor secure them against the inroads of Satan.[264]

Unlike Gobat and Kugler, Krapf had the privilege of accompanying King Sahle Sellassie on his annual military expeditions which gave him an opportunity to explore the country of the Oromo ("Galla"). He even visited

---

259. Isenberg and Krapf, 118–119.
260. Isenberg and Krapf, 121.
261. Isenberg and Krapf, 208, 227.
262. Isenberg and Krapf, 118. Just like Gobat, Krapf too allowed his Abyssinian friends to try to cut out the swollen part of his tonsils as they suggested but stopped them after a while when they could not cut it and it was too painful. They told him that the sickness was caused by bad spirits and he would die if he did not follow their instructions. Isenberg and Krapf, *Journals*, 250.
263. He noted that on 9 May 1840 all of the people of Shewa killed a hen in order to prevent sickness or other calamity from coming upon them. "Such is the darkness of this people! It is evident that they have adopted this custom from the 'Gallas.' Such things always lead me to think that there is but little hope of a reformation of this fallen church. However, the Lord can do above what we can understand at present." Isenberg and Krapf, *Journals*, 241.
264. Isenberg and Krapf, *Journals*, 118.

what is now Addis Ababa, which was called Finfine.[265] With the help of his servant, Krapf managed to learn Oromo language and tried to communicate with them. He was impressed by the people's receptivity. His experience further assured him that the mission to the "Galla" would be more productive than to the Abyssinians.[266]

Except for the slow receptivity of Abyssinian Christians to change, Krapf enjoyed the protection and love of the king. The king even honoured him by giving him the Shewan silver sword, a gesture which placed Krapf in the rank of governor.[267] While he was in Shewa, the *Sost Lidet* (Three Births) prevailed against the official Alexandrian *Tewahdo*. When the ban on *Tewahdo* adherents (among whom some of Krapf's best friends were found) was effected, they were banished from Shewa and fled to Gondar and appealed to the Egyptian Abune Selama.[268]

The Abun bade Sahle Sellassie to revoke his decree and reinstate priests who believed in two births "as this was the genuine doctrine of St Mark of Alexandria." But the king refused. This shows that the church of Ethiopia was not centralized at that time and their northern counterparts the Shewan clergy did not feel allegiance to the church of Alexandria. Hence adherents of a given theological position were able to influence the ruler as far as they constituted the majority. Krapf was able to foresee the ramifications of the upper hand of the clergy and feared that the king might not be able to

---

265. Launhardt, *Evangelicals in Addis Ababa*, 9.

266. Isenberg and Krapf, *Journals*, 193. He encountered those who called themselves Christians and observed that the "Galla" were asked to be circumcised, baptized, wear a string of silk around their neck, build churches and make offerings of grain to the priests. This illustrates the kind of commitment that was required of converts who lived in the territories conquered by Orthodox rulers. Such an external requirement was considered as good enough at the time perhaps because of lack of trained clergy to instruct the converts. There were reports of "Galla" converts in Shewa Meda, and Krapf visited them and noted that they were circumcised and built five churches. They begged Krapf to baptize them. Isenberg and Krapf, *Journals*, 242–243. Such experiences made Krapf more anxious to look for ways of crossing over to their territory and preaching the gospel.

267. When Krapf expressed his desire to leave the country the king begged him to remain. When Krapf would not relent he expressed his desire to take hold of Krapf's gun which was at hand. Krapf refused, but when the king insisted, he was so displeased that he indicated how unacceptable such a behaviour would be if heard in Great Britain; to which the king begged Krapf "for Christ's and the Gospel's sake" not to tell this to his countrymen. At this point the messenger of the king hinted that if Krapf had stayed the king had intentions to "invest" him with government. Isenberg and Krapf, *Journals*, 267–269.

268. Isenberg and Krapf, *Journals*, 235–236; Aren, *Evangelical Pioneers*, 78–79.

protect the mission in case of opposition because unlike Wubie (the prince of Tigray) the Shewan king was more influenced by the priests.²⁶⁹

Krapf also acted as a political advisor. Especially in a time when he thought the future of the mission and the king's desire to reform the country were jeopardized, he advised the king to abandon his decision for alliance with France which was mediated by the French traveller Rochet with an attractive offer of European standard military training and firearms in return. Krapf persuaded the king to seek friendship with Britain instead. The king accepted his advice and dispatched official letters to Aden and Bombay.²⁷⁰

A year later, Captain Harris arrived and on 16 November 1841 signed a treaty "which granted protection to British subjects and the right for them to trade and travel on Shewan territory and beyond."²⁷¹ The monks and priests who were so alarmed by Harris's display of wealth and military strength warned their people that "aliens planned to overthrow the ancient faith."²⁷² Such a feeling, suppressed at the time, soon surfaced when the ሦስት ልደት (Three Births) party prevailed over the ተዋህዶ *Tewahdo* in the Church. This party was vehemently against foreign presence in the country, especially missionaries. In addition to its variance with the ተዋህዶ *Tewahdo* position regarding the person of Christ "the new doctrine was coupled with an ardent zeal for the veneration of the Virgin Mary who was said to have died an atoning death for mankind and therefore ought to be worshipped like her Son."²⁷³

Upon the banishment of his priest friends, Krapf did not have support from the Three Births party. After two years in Shewa, he was ready to leave for Egypt with an intention of marrying and returning to Abyssinia, erroneously assuming that the treaty guaranteed continued mission work

---

269. Isenberg and Krapf, 235–236; Aren, 78–79.

270. Aren, 79–80.

271. Aren, 80–81.

272. Aren, 80.

273. Aren, 78–81. The rationale behind such a view appears to be the fact that Christ took flesh from Mary. So when he suffered, he suffered in the flesh which was taken from Mary and the blood he shed was the one he took from Mary. At times there are extreme views which tend to assert that the blood which was shed for us was that of Mary. Hence, she is a co-redeemer. Such view exists to this day and Simret Kifle Egzie contends them. ወቅታዊ ጥያቄዎችና መልሶቻው (Timely questions and answers) Simret Kifle Egzie, *Chora*, no. 29, n.d.: 17–19.

in Shewa. Furthermore, Krapf aspired to cross over to the country of the "Galla" because, like Gobat, he assumed that the country of "Gallas" might offer fewer difficulties for the work of missions "than the people who have more complete systems of idolatry and anti-christian superstitions . . ."[274] Thus, Krapf wanted to return with mission to "Galla" in mind.

King Sahle Sellassie tried to get Krapf to change his mind saying, "You should not leave me, my father, as I shall have no adviser when you are away."[275] But Krapf was determined to leave. On his way, Muslims in Worra Himano[276] showed him a book which was captured during their war with Ras Ali. "It was an Amharic copy of the Gospels printed by the Bible Society, and given by Mr Isenberg to a soldier during his stay at Adwa." Krapf read from Matthew 5 and explained while they listened to him with an attentiveness that amazed him.[277] He remarked, "It is highly gratifying to find, that the seed of eternal life, which has been spread over Abyssinia by our Mission in Tigre, has been carried to the remotest provinces to which a Missionary has scarcely access, and we may confidently trust, that this seed, which we in our short-sightedness consider as lost, will exhibit some rejoicing fruits at the great day of revelation."[278]

Indeed it was a very exciting experience to find the Scriptures in the hands of people but with the widespread illiteracy it was doubtful that the Scripture would have a lasting impact on the common people.[279] The extent of illiteracy makes us wonder why the nineteenth-century Shewan

---

274. Gobat's Journal from 25 February 1830 – 16 February 1833, UB SC, CMS/B/OMS/C M/O28/113, 196.

275. Isenberg and Krapf, *Journals*, 267.

276. Perhaps "Were Yimenu."

277. Isenberg and Krapf, *Journals*, 342.

278. Isenberg and Krapf, 342.

279. Even in the twentieth century the illiteracy of the nobility and the distinguished leaders of the time such as Ras Alula was confirmed by European observers of the time. Some of the observers were stunned at the extent of the illiteracy. For their correspondences the leaders used scribes who were taught how to read and write either in the traditional EOC schools or the missionary schools. In the beginning of the twentieth century the illiteracy was believed to be 99 percent. As for the ministers of the government Dr Merab is reported to have said ". . . only half the council of Ministers could read and write with ease, that three could do neither, and that two others knew no more than how to sign their names. . ." The condition of women was worse. Apart from the princesses it was estimated that only one in one thousand could read and write. Pankhurst, "The Foundations of Education," *Ethiopia Observer* 6, no. 3: 256.

and Tigrean people wanted to have copies of the Scriptures which they were not able to read. Perhaps it was considered as having protective power from evil, as illustrated in Krapf's and Kugler's experiences.[280]

Krapf's stay in Shewa did not turn out to be as satisfying as he expected it to be. He was disappointed to realize that the king was not interested in their mission to reform the church, but wanted skills to train his people. For a prince, having skilled people at his disposal meant power and possible dominance over the other regions. Krapf encountered a similar attitude on his way to Gondar. Rival princes such as the chief of Were Yimenu, desired to find out how many European weapons were given to Sahle Sellassie.[281] The attitude of the general public was the same. Krapf lamented that they were interested in seeking help for their body with no reflection on the salvation of their souls.[282]

Determined to come back to cross over to the "Galla" territory, Krapf left Shewa. Sadly, he was plundered of everything he possessed on the way.[283] He abandoned his desire to visit Gondar and headed for Massawa, eating wild fruits and begging his way along.[284] Just like Gobat, Krapf's criticism of the traditions of the church got him into trouble. He wrote, ". . . they considered me a Mahomedan in secret, because I had spoken against magic, and because I had declared that a man cannot be saved by means of fasting."[285] On the top of that Krapf had no Amharic or Ethiopic New Testament with him, which by then was an identity badge for the missionaries. So on his way to Massawa a priest declared him an impostor under the name of Krapf and the people wanted to imprison him.[286]

Saying the Lord's Prayer with a priest he met on his way proved to be a great encouragement to Krapf.[287] In one instance he was in such bad shape

---

280. Kugler's Journal, 25 February – 24 April 1830, UB SC, CMS/B/OMS/ C M/ O46/24: 14–15; Isenberg and Krapf, *Journals*, 141–142.

281. Isenberg and Krapf, *Journals*, 344.

282. Isenberg and Krapf, 73.

283. Isenberg and Krapf, 326, 376–382.

284. Ironically, the words of a beggar whom Krapf met in Shewa came to pass. When Krapf refused to give him money the beggar told him, "you do not know whether you leave this place a happy man or a beggar like myself." Krapf, *Travels, Researches*, 95.

285. Isenberg and Krapf, *Journals*, 473.

286. Isenberg and Krapf, 473.

287. Isenberg and Krapf, 476.

physically that a monk felt sorry for him and secretly gave him the holy bread which no one who was not in holy orders was allowed to see or taste.[288] While passing through Tigray, the very mention of Gobat's name brought him favour even in the eyes of the people he referred to as "inhospitable Tigreans."[289]

Krapf's general observation about Christianity in Ethiopia was as follows.

> I am firmly convinced that the Abyssinian people would not refuse a reformation, if there were some enlightened teachers among themselves, brought up with a sound knowledge of the Bible, and anointed by the Holy Spirit. But I have a little hope in this respect, though they like to hear a discourse about the Word of God. In all my conversations I endeavour to show them the necessity of relying on the Bible, it being quite sufficient to the knowledge of our salvation. I show them always that there are two seducing ways; either that we add something to the Scriptures, or that we take away from them; explaining the danger of these ways, with the example of Adam and Eve and other instances as well as from the history of the Church.[290]

He seemed to lose hope in the possibility of exerting any change upon Abyssinian Christians and desired to go to the country of Galls instead. Thus, he left the country with a determination to come back, not to renew the church of Abyssinia, but to pass to the "Galla" territory and preach the gospel to them. Krapf felt that perhaps the gospel may go out from the "Galla" to the whole of Abyssinia.[291]

4.10. The End of CMS Mission to Ethiopia

After a few months' stay in Egypt Krapf along with Isenberg and a new missionary, Johannes Muhleisen, attempted to enter Shewa, only to be denied permission by the Sultan. To the shock of the missionaries, the Sultan showed them an official letter from King Sahle Sellassie not to let

---

288. Isenberg and Krapf, 495–496.
289. Isenberg and Krapf, 500, 513–520.
290. Isenberg and Krapf, 200–201.
291. Isenberg and Krapf, 173, 175.

any foreigner proceed to Shewa except Rochet. Such a change of mind on the part of the king must have shocked Krapf in particular, as showing that the French Rochet was able to win the favour of the king. Their pleas to the king proved futile. Aren notes, "The Three Births party, which was now in power, influenced the people to rise in protest against the return of the missionaries." The clergy argued with the monarch: "Their ethos is not like ours and their sacred book is different from that which is accepted in our country. If they are allowed to return, people will fall away from the faith of their fathers."[292]

Harris tried to intervene on their behalf, even resorting to threats which greatly offended the king "who snapped him up with a sharp: "By the death of Wosen-Seged [his father], neither Isenberg nor Krapf shall ever enter my kingdom again!"[293]

By this time the CMS had separated its work in Abyssinia from the Mediterranean Mission and created a new branch with a view of a larger enterprise among the Oromo ("Galla"). Krapf therefore took a different route in order to explore the possibilities of reaching Oromo land.[294] Meanwhile, determined to proceed, Isenberg and Muhleisen attempted to enter Adwa in May 1843 only to encounter a vicious resistance from priests led by Aleqa Kidane Mariam, who took possession of their belongings and house in Adwa. Isenberg appealed to Dejazmach Wubie stating that their ceaseless prayers were that God should forgive him for expelling them. Wubie told them to go to Adwa and await his decision. He strictly ordered them to keep a low profile in the meantime.[295]

The missionaries arrived to Adwa on 21 May 1843 and were met by their opponents at the market place. Kidane Mariam, whom Krapf referred to as "Our old enemy,"[296] came out to meet them with many priests, *debteras* along with the *tabot*,[297] holy books and large silver cross held and bells ringing. A

---

292. Aren, *Evangelical Pioneers*, 81.
293. Aren, 81–82.
294. Aren, 82.
295. Aren, 82.
296. Isenberg and Krapf, *Journals*, 109.
297. "Tabot" is a replica of the ark of the covenant. It provides the EOC adherents with a strong sign of Ethiopian Christian identity.

great crowd of people followed him in a solemn procession. *Aleqa* Kidane Mariam along with his supporters sat on one side, and the missionaries and their supporters on the other side.[298]

Isenberg gives a detailed account of the interrogation:

> After half an hour's consultation, the Alaca sent for us. On our approach, he after a short and un ceremonial sort of salutation, asked me a number of questions at once, Whether I had not changed my faith, whether the faith of the Abyssinians, the faith of Oubie, the faith of Hadji Yohannes and of Demetrios was my faith, whether I worshipped and kissed the cross and the Church; whether I believed in a change of elements in the Lord's Supper and whether I believed in the intercession of St. Mary and the saints for us.[299]

Isenberg refused to answer the questions at first, reasoning that they had no orders from Wubie to investigate their creed, and he appealed to the Coptic priest whom he addressed as *Aba*.[300] Aleqa Kidane Mariam angrily replied, "he is my father, not yours." The Coptic priest talked to Isenberg in Arabic, "Do you not know that you are in Abyssinia and not in Egypt? You must believe here, as the Abyssinians believe."[301]

Isenberg had second thoughts that the occasion provided him with the best and perhaps the last opportunity to testify to "the truth as it is in Jesus." With that in mind he decided to offer his replies to stated questions and began by affirming that they had come in a similar manner to that of Gobat and Kugler with a message of love from a friendly church in England to the church of Abyssinia. He explained that the missionaries did not call upon them to alter the constitution or the usages and the ceremonies of their church; neither should the Abyssinians require them to change theirs. With regard to the elements of the Lord's Supper he said that they did not use the word "change of nature" in reference to the elements, but change

---

298. The Journal of Isenberg, UB SC, CMS/B/OMS/C A5 013/21.
299. The Journal of Isenberg, UB SC, 21 May 1843, Adoa, CMS/B/OMS/C A5 013/21.
300. The EOC followers refer to priests, monks as "Aba" it literally means "Father."
301. The Journal of Isenberg, UB SC, 21 May 1843, Adoa, CMS/B/OMS/C A5 013/21.

of effect.[302] As for the saving power of the cross Isenberg replied that there was a danger in idolizing the cross, but he added that the missionaries were not against kissing the cross.

Regarding Mary, a highly emphasized inquiry, Isenberg replied that she was the greatest of all women and that they had nothing against calling her the Mother of God according to the Council of Ephesus. As for her intercession, Isenberg reasoned that it was not revealed in the Scriptures, although on earth the saints are to intercede for each other through prayer. But putting a creature as a mediator between God and man was against the will of God.[303]

The replies of Isenberg on this occasion were quite tactful. In what appeared to be a desperate measure to mend his badly damaged reputation and the frail relationship of the Mission with the church of Ethiopia, Isenberg went to the extent of acknowledging the Council of Ephesus, and calling Mary the Mother of God unlike Gobat, who insisted on calling her the mother of Jesus as the apostles did.

Aleqa Kidane Mariam appears to have made up his mind long before he heard Isenberg's defence, so the missionary's tactful and sensitive approaches fell on deaf ears. Kidane Mariam rose to his feet and said to the assembly that they had heard for themselves that Isenberg did not know Mary and the saints. Consequently, the head priest called the missionaries incorrigible heretics. Then the priests of the Medhane Alem Church excommunicated the CMS missionaries giving their souls to Satan, their bodies to the hyenas, and their property to thieves. They extended the excommunication to include people who helped the missionaries in any way, but they soon took it back because of a huge cry from the public.

When friends of Isenberg tried to reconcile him with Aleqa Kidane Mariam he repeated his former request that Isenberg should be like Gobat and other white people who did not insist on preaching. To which Isenberg replied that he was like Gobat in his convictions, but Gobat was not able to instruct because of his health problems.

---

302. Even the Reformers Luther and Zwingli were not of one mind regarding how Christ was present during the Holy Communion. Zwingli was strongly opposed to the celebration of the mass as a sacrifice, rather than memorial. Spitz, *Rise of Modern Europe*, 155–156.

303. The Journal of Isenberg, UB SC, 21 May 1843, Adoa, CMS/B/OMS/C A5 013/21.

Isenberg appealed to Wubie but he found that Wubie's attitude towards him was changed because of the allegations he had been hearing. Isenberg was accused of administering Holy Communion, baptizing, marrying and, interring in his compound [304] and blaspheming Mary and the saints. Wubie's judgement was that Isenberg "was just as bad as before. He had again reviled the Virgin Mary and announced his intention of teaching the Scripture."[305] Wubie did not wish to see Isenberg, and sent strict orders that he should go back to his country. Isenberg blamed the Catholic missionary de Jacobis for the attitude of Wubie. It looks as though Protestant and Catholics missionaries were seeking the upper hand with their doctrines. According to Isenberg de Jacobis approached Wubie with guns and many more splendid presents and misinformed the prince that the church of the CMS missionaries in Europe was corrupt and as a result five million people had gone to the Roman Catholics.[306]

Desperate for help, Isenberg appealed to the *Abun* in Gondar, but the Abun was not able to help him. In a lengthy reply he expressed his regret at the fact that Abyssinians did not desire knowledge but material things; and that he had sent a messenger to Kidane Mariam and the clergy of Medhane Alem that they should not show partiality and thus, if they refused to have the CMS missionaries among them, they should expel the Catholic de Jacobis as well.

The missionaries had no choice but to leave. Meanwhile Krapf changed his mind, and along with his expectant wife, and with a large supply of Amharic and Ge'ez Scriptures, attempted to reach his colleagues in Tigray, but he was too late. News of their expulsion awaited him at Massawa. His wife delivered a premature baby girl who died shortly after birth. Krapf named, her "Eneba" which in Amharic means "tear."[307] In spite of their grieving they proceeded to Hamasen and distributed Scriptures. The number of

---

304. This refers to Isenberg's burial of two of his little children and a child of his servant in his garden because he could not get permission to inter them in the churchyard. Extract of a letter from Isenberg to Rev Samuel Gobat, 28 September 1837, UB SC, CMS/B/OMS/C M/O28/31B.

305. Aren, *Evangelical Pioneers*, 83.

306. Krapf also blamed the Catholics for instigating the priests to destroy the Bibles he brought to Adwa. Krapf, *Travels, Researches*, 19.

307. Krapf, *Travels, Researches*, 109.

copies of Scriptures was not enough to meet the demand of lay people and monks. Some books were torn from their hands as several people fought over them.[308] Eventually the Krapfs were joined by their colleagues and they all headed to Massawa. Their departure in May 1843 marked the official closing of CMS mission to revitalize the church of Abyssinia.[309]

Thus, it appeared as though the noble vision of the CMS to revive the church of Abyssinia, which was channelled through missionaries of different calibre and character, came to nothing. At least that was how it appeared at the time, but as noted in chapter 2, there were groups of Bible readers in Tseazega, (the very place where Krapf and his wife distributed the Scriptures for the last time) who traced their roots to the CMS missionaries' distribution of the Scriptures.

4.11. Renewed Efforts of Samuel Gobat

As noted in earlier chapters the coming of Tewodros to power ended the Era of the Princes and restored relative peace in the land in the initial years. His openness to new ideas and the presence of Abune Selama as the head of the church appeared to point to an era of openness for mission work and renovation. Accordingly the initial years of Tewodros's reign were promising. He worked vigorously against slavery, polygamy and injustice by providing a personal example. He impressed his people and foreign visitors as an intelligent man, sensitive to spiritual matters and willing to work with Europeans but he wished to receive no missionaries. Thus, he communicated his intentions to de Jacobis, "We, too, are Christians from the beginning of time. We do not need anybody to teach us Christianity. From now on, your priests should not come to our country . . ." [310] Similar message was conveyed to Gobat, ". . . let not priests who disrupt the faith come to me."[311]

Gobat, who was by then called to the Anglican bishopric of Jerusalem, did not give up. He maintained a close contact with the Ethiopian community

---

308. Aren, *Evangelical Pioneers*, 83.
309. Krapf, *Travels, Researches*, 108, 110.
310. Rubenson, "Consequences of a Colonial Context," 65.
311. Rubenson, 65.

there and devised a new plan to revive the Ethiopian church.[312] To this end he collaborated with C. F. Spittler who was a leader of both the Basel Mission and the Pilgrim Mission. Spittler had a view of sending artisans as lay missionaries, not to preach, but to exert Christian influence, and Gobat supervised the training of six young artisans in Jerusalem in preparation for going to Ethiopia. Krapf, who was about to return to his mission post in Mombasa, after a vacation in Europe, volunteered to investigate the situation of Ethiopia and introduce the missionaries to their new work. Both the missionaries and the senders had great expectations because of the openness of Tewodros towards missionaries. Moreover, they hoped that Abune Selama, an alumnus of CMS school in Egypt, would exert pressure for reformation.[313] Krapf and J. Martin Flad arrived to Tewodros's camp in Debre Tabor on 19 April 1855 and were warmly received by Abune Selama, who praised the devotion of the king to evangelizing the Muslims and the Oromo.[314]

On the following day the Emperor saw the missionaries and expressed his desire for technical assistance. Once again, Tewodros proved that Ethiopian Orthodox monarchs and princes did not look for preachers but artisans. The leaders usually assumed that the white people possessed some kind of skill to pass on to the Ethiopians and acted as agents of the countries they came from. The missionaries on the other hand read into the welcoming messages of the Ethiopian leaders a permission to preach the gospel. Hence great misunderstanding and disappointment arose on both sides.

This time however, it seemed that Gobat and his team had got the message right because they sought to send skilful people who were also able to share the gospel. In May 1856 the four Pilgrim missionaries arrived in Ethiopia. Both Abune Selama and Emperor Tewodros proved to be so much in favour of the distribution of Scriptures in the vernacular that the missionaries were able to distribute the Scriptures freely. The Emperor, however, was

---

312. The unsuccessful approach of the CMS to revive the EOC did not appear to be fully taken up by Pilgrim Mission, or altered to some extent. "The leaders of the Pilgrim Mission promised to recruit new workers for Minilik on condition that they should be permitted to organize independent congregations and administer the sacraments on their own." Aren, *Evangelical Pioneers*, 273, fn. 16.

313. Cf. Zewde, *History of Modern Ethiopia*, 38.

314. Abune Selama must have assumed that the missionaries came to reach the unreached. So he tells them about the enthusiasm of Tewodros to reach the Muslims and Oromo; perhaps explicitly implying that EOC was out of question.

greatly disappointed to find that the missionaries lacked the kind of technical qualifications he was looking for, and left them unemployed for a year.

In the mean time the missionaries started a school in their own homes and their students were mainly Felasha (Ethiopian Jews). Their ministry to Felasha led to the founding of the Felasha Mission in 1859. Eventually the Emperor gave them a piece of land in Gafat and they engaged in handiwork. They were forced to make mortars, because the king wanted to be able to manufacture firearms in Ethiopia instead of begging European countries. The missionaries, who were not trained in such a way, found themselves in a very difficult position. Their hope of using their handiwork skills as a means of teaching the Scriptures was frustrated, because the king put them almost under house arrest until they came up with mortars.

Flad, who on his stay in Gondar developed a special interest in the mission to the Felasha, wanted to continue it and the work proved to be fruitful, but after some time the Felasha converts became an object of attack from both the Orthodox and their own people. The Orthodox accused them of refusing to kiss the cross and venerate the saints, whereas the Felasha priests were upset because the converts attacked their practice of offering sacrifices.

At the end of 1862 Rev Henry Aaron Stern, who himself was a convert from Judaism to Christianity, came for the second time to strengthen the mission work; unfortunately, he did not have a high opinion of Emperor Tewodros whom he referred to as "His Black Majesty." He also had little respect for Ethiopians and their culture. Tewodros on his part disliked Stern for his proud manners. When Stern set out to return home, he stopped by the imperial camp to pay his respects to Tewodros, but to his horror found out that his servants were seriously beaten for bringing him there. Stern's gesture at that moment resulted in him being beaten and detained in heavy chains along with another missionary, Rosenthal,[315] for almost five years.[316]

Such an incident does not necessarily imply that the Ethiopian authorities and the church wanted nothing to do with the missionaries, but indicates that they wished their way of life and identity to be respected. The detained

---

315. Mrs Rosenthal is portrayed as sexually promiscuous in a popular Ethiopian novel written by Birhanu Zerihun entitled "Yetangut Mistir." The book portrays all of the missionaries in Gafat as having a different agenda than preaching the gospel.

316. Aren, *Evangelical Pioneers*, 99, 101–102.

missionaries were rescued by the British army. The renewed efforts of Gobat to revive the church of Ethiopia, therefore, came to nothing.

Conclusion

It is not easy to fully follow up the fruit of the CMS work in Ethiopia. However, it is possible to make general observations on the strengths and weaknesses of the CMS missionaries in Ethiopia. To begin with, most of the missionaries do not appear to have realized the strong influence which the traditions of the church exerted upon the people. By the time the missionaries came, such traditions had taken shape and gained depth over fourteen centuries of interaction with the culture. The tradition of the church of Ethiopia was unique because through the centuries it blended Christianity, Judaism and traditional religion. The prolonged interaction between the faith and culture, and also the bloody battles fought in defence of it, had shaped the experience of the people in such a way that the faith was inseparable from the identity of the people. Thus, attacking the church traditions could as also be taken as attacking the people.

However, this does not mean that there was doctrinal unanimity among all of the Orthodox adherents. There were differences of opinions among the scholars of the church over the years. Some of the conflicts were settled by debate and some at gunpoint. Bloody battles were fought over doctrinal issues and prominent people executed or banished from their regions. Thus, doctrinal differences among the clergy were not new to the Ethiopians. Perhaps for the sake of peace and stability in their kingdom, political leaders of the country tried their best to have different parties debate in the presence of the clergy, the nobility and the Coptic priests or the patriarch. But the party or group which came with a less convincing argument or was not supported by the ruler was expected to renounce its position and join the others under pain of excommunication or banishment from the kingdom. Such exclusions at times resulted in internal conflicts and bloodshed but the Ethiopians resented more the battles initiated by outside forces, especially by missionaries, and there was always a fear of division and disunity when a new approach was presented.

The CMS missionaries, on the other hand, belonged to the tradition of the Reformation and were committed to all of the marks of the Reformation in Europe – passionate to restore the church to its original purity.³¹⁷ Most of all they were committed to the authority of the Scriptures and the saving grace of Jesus Christ. It is evident from the correspondence of Gobat and Kugler that they maintained a high regard for the church of Ethiopia and loved its people dearly.

Over and over in their discussion with the Ethiopians regarding different topics such as fasting, good works and the veneration of the saints, the missionaries had conflict with the Orthodox notions. Thus, they toiled as it were to bring back the church to acknowledge the sole authority of the Bible and the efficiency of the redemptive work of Christ on the cross; thereby pointing out that no human effort was needed to attain acceptance by God, which was already secured by Christ crucified.

However, each missionary approached the church of Ethiopia in a different way. The pioneers did not hesitate to recognize the church as a sister church, but the later ones were uneasy about identifying with it. Gobat cautioned the committee that whoever came to Abyssinia needed "the principals features (sic) of which must be: an active patience."³¹⁸ Gobat was committed to adopting the Ethiopian lifestyle, but for Isenberg that appeared to send a misleading signal. He believed that he would better influence the people by setting himself apart from them, and not by identifying with them as Gobat had done. Gobat wanted to work from within, whereas Isenberg thought separation from the people would serve the purpose. Even then, Isenberg changed his approach after his difficult encounter with the clergy of the church in Tigray and became more tolerant in Shewa. While in Shewa, Krapf and Isenberg went to the church in order to get more acquainted with the people, their clergy and the "manner of their worship."³¹⁹ Thus, there appeared to be a new spirit of openness towards the people. Unfortunately, it was too late to rectify Isenberg's former mistakes.

While in Shewa they had both cultural and doctrinal criticism towards the church. The singing sounded strange to them so they noted, "All that they do in church, is to make a terrible bawling which they call singing."³²⁰

---

317. Spitz, *Rise of Modern Europe*, 155–156.
318. Gobat, General Remarks on Abyssinia, UB SC, CMS/B/OMS/C M/028/114.
319. Isenberg and Krapf, *Journals*, 71.
320. Isenberg and Krapf, 72.

There also were deeper doctrinal differences. The need for a confessor was questioned by Krapf when Aleqa Sekima suggested that Krapf should make him his confessor "yenefs abat."[321] Many of the accounts related by the people appeared to be irrational to Krapf and Isenberg. They did not believe the claim of the people that evil spirits resided in waters, that people possessed by the spirits were able to foretell, etc.[322] And they did not seem to believe in miracles.[323]

Krapf called the baptismal ceremony abominable.[324] The several books which Abyssinians loved and held to as authoritative appeared to be "full of nonsense" to Krapf and Isenberg.[325] Krapf, however, modified his position later, when he told a priest that he did not mean all the books are useless but that they "should examine them to see whether they accord with the Scripture, that being alone the rule of Christian faith and practice."[326] For Krapf and the CMS missionaries, the Scripture alone was the sole authority and they were concerned about the devotion of the Ethiopian Christians to tradition that was supplementary or at times contrary.

The Ethiopian priests seem to have come with answers and explanations for all kinds of questions, some answers were attributed to tradition and others to non-canonical writings. Thus it was believed that there was a cause to every phenomenon, usually a supernatural cause. When the CMS missionaries said that they did not have answers to some of the questions, people were puzzled.[327] The missionaries (perhaps with the exception of Isenberg) did not always look for trouble, or purposely try to show their superiority in doctrine. Gobat observed that in Abyssinia there is always an invitation to take part in what he referred to as "useless reasoning" which he felt cannot always be avoided.[328] Thus, most of the time, their visitors asked them

---

321. Isenberg and Krapf, 173.
322. Isenberg and Krapf, 278, 309–311.
323. Upon hearing the story of the miraculous fountain in Debre Libanos, Isenberg wrote, "When this story was told to us today, we expressed our disbelief; and added, that we wanted neither true nor false miracles, as the miracles of Christ and His Apostles were quite sufficient." Isenberg and Krapf, *Journals*, 121.
324. Isenberg and Krapf, *Journals*, 184.
325. Isenberg and Krapf, 147–148.
326. Isenberg and Krapf, 219.
327. Isenberg and Krapf, 68.
328. Gobat, "General Remarks on Abyssinia," UB SC, CMS/B/OMS/C M/028/114.

questions, and the missionaries tried to speak the truth, as they understood it from their reading of the Bible and the tradition they came from, often sacrificially. They wanted to agree on Scriptural things and were delighted when they found points of agreement.[329]

Gobat testified to the change of life of a number of young men whom he instructed closely. One of them was Girgis, who learned the Gospels by heart and commended as a person who "would not give up a single error unless proven wrong by the Scriptures."[330] Gobat also wrote about his servant Guebrow[331] who testified to the truth he heard in conduct and words. ". . . but what causes me much more joy, is to see that he is much more sensible of his weaknesses & of the corruption of his heart than formerly."[332] In addition to his dedication to read the New Testament until daybreak, Gebru, who was about twenty years of age, was active in sharing his faith with his people. Gobat exclaimed, "He is already acquainted with the historical past, and I may say, better than many European ministers."[333] Another young "Galla" man whose name is not identified visited him twice a day and was determined to preach the gospel to his people once he got the blessing of the Abun.[334]

---

329. Isenberg and Krapf, *Journals*, 154, 220.

330. Journal of Gobat and Kugler, 20 August 1827, UB SC, CMS/ B/ OMS/ C M O73/13.

331. Perhaps, Gebru. Gobat noted that his full name was Guebra Mariam. Gobat to his parents, Behate, 25 February 1831, UB SC, CMS/B/OMS/C M/O28/13.

332. Gobat to his parents, Behate, 25 February 1831, UB SC, CMS/B/OMS/C M/O28/13.

333. Moreover Gebru who was about twenty years of age was not afraid of sharing his views with others, "about the predominant errors of the country" for which he received much criticism and opposition from the priests and others in Adowa. "On that account, for the least fault that he commits, they say to him with a degree of contempt: 'Is that what the Bible, which you read and recommend so much, teaches you?'" Gobat to his parents, Behate, 25 February 1831, UB SC, CMS/B/OMS/C M/O28/13.

334. The boy was sold into slavery at the age of fourteen. His master in Godjam caused him to be baptized and set him free. The lad wished to go back to his country which is not far from Godjam, but desired to know the truths of Christianity. Amazingly, he taught himself to read and write Ethiopic. He then went back to his country and tried to persuade his father to come to the Amhara country and embrace Christianity. His father told him that he had no objection to Christianity "but that having always been free, he could not bear to be regarded as a slave in the Amhara country." "But go" added he, "and bring hither a Christian Priest to instruct us and we will be baptized. We will all submit to his instruction." Unfortunately, the boy was not able to find an intelligent priest who can go with him, so he resolved to be consecrated for ministry. He became a monk in Gondar and proceeded to Tigre "to receive the imposition of hands" from the Abun. On his arrival, the Abun had just died, so he stayed

Krapf also wrote about Demza-Roophael,[335] one of his servants, whom he instructed with the Word of God for two years. He noted that the Word of God was working in his heart and the boy was most attached to him.[336]

However, the missionaries also grieved because of the falling back of some of their disciples. For example, Girgis, who had been close to them since their stay in Egypt, repeatedly indulged in sexual immorality with a prostitute while living with Gobat. When Gobat found out, Girgis repented but was not willing to marry the woman nor stop his involvement with her so Gobat sent him away.[337] Krapf also was betrayed by Demza-Roophael on their way to Massawa. The boy sold off Krapf and his servants to a ruthless prince who plundered all of their belongings.[338]

As for the attitude of the Ethiopians towards the missionaries, the moral uprightness of Kugler and Gobat amazed Sabagadis and Girgis used it to point out that their values were based on their faith. "[H]ere you see true faith in its genuine fruits. We fast, we give alms, they do not fast, but comparing our deeds with theirs what is the result?" The reply was that the CMS missionaries excelled them. Obviously, although they emphasized internal change over external expressions of Christianity, the governor was touched by the depth of their faith.[339] This aspect of their life impressed the people

---

for two years in Tigre waiting for a new Abun to come. Gobat's Journal from 25 February 1830 – 16 February 1833, UB SC, CMS/B/OMS/C M/O28/113, 195–196.

335. Perhaps, Dimtse Rufael.
336. Isenberg and Krapf, *Journals*, 385–386.
337. Girgis eventually left for Egypt along with his concubine and two lads: Hadera and Kidane Mariam, whom he manipulated into serving him freely with a false promise of taking them to Jerusalem. On the way he sold the young men into slavery without their knowledge. Gobat's Journal from 25 February 1830 – 16 February 1833, UB SC, CMS/B/OMS/C M/O28/113, 190–192. Upon hearing their testimony, Gobat remarked, ". . . I ought to say as the last praise to Girgis, that he has enticed in them the desire of knowing the truth." Gobat's Journal from 25 February 1830 – 16 February 1833, UB SC, CMS/B/OMS/C M/O28/113, 190. Together with Gobat, Hadera and Kidane Mariam arrived in Cairo on April 1833. Shortly after that Girgis heard of their coming and visited them. When he saw them he fell to his knees and asked for their forgiveness with tears of remorse. They forgave him and because he was in such destitute state, they supplied for his needs from their salary for several months. Later on he was sent by the Coptic patriarch into a convent in the Syrian desert where he died "in sincere repentance." Gobat, "A Short Biography of the Abyssinian Hadera," 7–8.
338. Isenberg and Krapf, *Journals*, 385–386.
339. Kugler to D. Coates, 2 October 1830, Quila, UB SC, CMS/B/OMS/ C M/O46/23A.

who knew them closely and perhaps led them to tolerate the missionaries for some time.

The missionaries were aware that taking a different approach would most probably win them wider acceptance. Referring to the high degree of acceptance given to a late Armenian priest in Shewa Krapf noted, "It would not be difficult for me to acquire the authority which Muallem had; but as in adhering to the pure Scripture truth, I must oppose the Abyssinians, I cannot therefore expect to obtain such influence."[340] Most of all the place of Mary regularly created conflict. Did the missionaries look at her as ወላዲተ አምላክ (Mother of God)? The Abyssinians demanded to know. The Bible calls her "mother of Jesus" insisted the missionaries from Matthew 1:16 and 25.[341] Isenberg was willing to recognize her as the Mother of God later on, but by then it was too late.

Some of the issues they objected to could have been tolerated. For example, kissing the church,[342] keeping Saturday along with Sunday as Sabbath,[343] wearing a cross and observing fast.[344] But the missionaries were concerned that such practices were evidences of the fact that external adherences to the faith were hailed over internal devotion. Thus, they argued that the cross is to be in our hearts.[345] That is why Krapf advised a priest to take the New Testament into his heart when he asked him about the protective power of carrying the New Testament on his head.

The approach of Isenberg in particular was tactless. Generally speaking, perhaps with the exception of Gobat, the missionaries failed to show a genuine interest in learning the Abyssinian way of doing things. They showed little flexibility to learn but continually pointed out the faults of the Orthodox. They did not appreciate the indigenous Christianity they found on the ground. Their act of correcting the clergy in public was rude because it was disrespectful and most probably disgraced them. They demonstrated

---

340. Isenberg and Krapf, *Journals*, 220.

341. Isenberg and Krapf, 149. Cf. Gobat's Journal from 25 February 1830 – 16 February 1833, UB SC, CMS/B/OMS/C M/O28/113, 201.

342. Isenberg and Krapf, 154.

343. Isenberg and Krapf, 162.

344. The Journal of Isenberg, UB SC, 21 May 1843, Adoa, CMS/B/OMS/C A5 013/21.

345. Isenberg and Krapf, *Journals*, 144.

little tolerance and respect in their attitude, thus, little attention was paid to their message. Moreover, experience and age will not easily be overlooked in Ethiopia; perhaps the fact that the missionaries were not older people had a negative impact on the receptivity to their message.

However, the kings or princes who usually considered themselves as overseers of the church were interested in maintaining friendly relations with Europeans primarily for material and military support. Thus, they desired to keep missionaries on their side, as long as the missionaries did not interfere in church affairs too much. When European nations were asked for such help they usually sent missionaries. The leaders of Ethiopia and the informed people of the land felt that the missionaries served as spies for their countries of origin. These feelings were caused by the actions of some of the missionaries themselves in asking for military intervention when a conflict surfaced. Krapf was open about his dedicating much time "to the cause of the embassy," partly because he was asked to assist by the British envoy and the king of Shewa. Moreover, the king warned Krapf that he would hold him responsible if things went wrong. Krapf also felt that the establishment of the embassy would enhance the spread of the gospel.[346]

The interest of the kings and rulers to learn new skills was not a new development. In fact, all along very few princes and kings of Ethiopia showed interest in the preaching of the missionaries, but sought their skills as physicians, architects, and craftsmen. Thus, when missionaries were sent instead of such specialists they were disappointed. "Since the 16th century, Abyssinia has always asked Europe for the same things: weapons and soldiers during wartime, and *tybabat*, i.e. for arts and skills, technical knowledge in peace-time; and from Europe they are sending missionaries and missionaries. Unwanted guests are not the most pleasant ones."[347]

Some missionaries certainly came with an attitude of superiority and European countries did not take the pleas of Ethiopia too seriously, yet

---

346. Krapf, *Travels, Researches*, 29–33.

347. Bolotov Vasily, "Neskolko stranits iz tserkovnoy istorii Efiopii, I: K voprosu o soedinenii abissin s pravoslavnoi tserkovyu" ("Some Pages from the Ecclesiastic History of Ethiopia I: On the Question of a Union of the Abyssinians with the Orthodox Church"), Hristianskoe chtenie 1884, 450–469 as quoted by Sevir Chernetsov, "Ethiopian Theological Response to European Missionary Proselytizing in the 17th–19th Centuries," in *Ethiopia and the Missions*, Verena Boll et al., eds. (Munster: LIT, 2005), 58.

since its inception in New Testament times the church has sent missionaries, usually uninvited, and worked amid hostile environments. Thus, coming in disguise was not unique to the missionaries who served in Ethiopia. More importantly the Ethiopian Orthodox church itself has a record of imposing (many times on pain of death) its faith on those who practiced traditional religions and Islam. From historical records it is clear that the Protestant missionaries of the nineteenth century acknowledged the Orthodox Church as a national church which needed to be reformed; but had no intention of starting a church of their own, with the exception of Isenberg, who seemed to deviate from the very purpose of the CMS.

Moreover, it is interesting to note that the Orthodox followers and the clergy were open to people like the Roman Catholic Paez and Gobat of the CMS who showed a genuine love and respect for them. But it is also ironic how their successors Mendez and Isenberg failed to follow in the footsteps of their predecessors as they tried to enforce their convictions in their own terms. Perhaps they sought to lay "the proper foundation" from the beginning. Sadly they lacked an open heart, flexibility and respect for the traditions of the people they hoped to reach. These qualities were needed as much as integral proclamation of the gospel. In their interaction with the Orthodox it would be interesting to examine whether the Evangelicals in Ethiopia followed the legacy of Gobat (respectful dialogue) or the legacy of Isenberg (head-on collision).

When we compare the CMS with the later Protestant mission organizations, the difference is visible. The advantages of the successful mission organizations such as the SIM for the most part came from the support and protection of Emperor Haile Sellassie I. In addition to that, the relative stability of the country and the presence of a centralized government and centralized church, the fact that they targeted areas which were not dominated by the Orthodox, or areas where the Orthodox Church failed to have a lasting impact, worked for their advantage. They targeted rural areas and not towns in which the elite of the Amhara group who represented the central government lived, they also preached in the vernaculars, in languages which people understood.

Moreover, the people they reached felt oppressed by both the church and the Amhara, who claimed to have "supernatural" appointment over them, so they looked at Christianity as presented by the missionaries, as a liberating message. They felt freed from bondage of Satan, sin and oppressing people. They felt accepted, appreciated and loved for who they were. Their language was used, they were appointed as heads over their churches. No outside person claimed authority over them. They did not have to learn a foreign language in which to worship the Lord. We should note that many concepts of Christianity were not foreign to the people whom the post CMS mission organizations reached because of the influence of the Orthodox. The still minimal number of Protestant churches in the Northern Ethiopia shows just how difficult it still is to penetrate that stronghold.

The other weakness of the CMS missionaries was their insistence on instructing regularly. Isenberg and Krapf especially showed minimal respect for the long-held traditions of the people. Who likes it when someone from another culture comes and condemns everything you have ever held dear? Even those most respectful of the missionaries, such as Sabagadis, found the criticisms awkward; this was why Sabagadis tried to avoid the discussion about Mary altogether. He did not want to offend the missionaries, neither was he happy with their criticism of nearly all of his religious values, so it was easier for him to avoid the topic.

Gobat's approach for the most part was appreciated by the Ethiopians. He was invited to teach even at the court of the prince and admired for answering every question from the Bible. Gobat claimed that he was offered the position of the Abun;[348] though the genuineness of such an offer is highly questioned given the suspicious attitude of the Orthodox to any teaching which appeared to negate the long held Alexandrian-endorsed position. And Gobat was obviously opposed to a number of the church's teachings, including fasting and the veneration of the saints, but he was careful not to engage in unfruitful debates that would wound their feelings.[349] Like Jowett, whose direction he followed, Gobat was also well aware of the potential of the clergy to incite Christians through unfounded allegations.[350] He did not avoid dialoguing on difficult subjects, but handled them gracefully – in a way which promoted mutual respect and understanding believing that

---

348. Aren, *Evangelical Pioneers*, 58.
349. Aren, 55–58, 62.
350. Crummey, *Priests and Politicians*, 13, 35.

such an approach would bring about the desired reformation in the ancient orthodoxy.[351]

Krapf and Isenberg proved to be more tolerant in Shewa than they had been earlier. At times their failure was caused by the unwillingness of princes to give them opportunity to exert influence on the people. The king of Shewa was more interested in learning their skills. They noted, "The king is anxious to get from Europeans all that he sees and hears."[352] Even the Imam, the chief of Were Yimenu, desired to see the military exercise firsthand from Krapf's people.[353] The missionaries made similar complaints about the people too that they were interested in seeking help for their bodies with no reflection on the salvation of their souls.[354]

If evaluated in their own terms, the CMS missionaries had mixed feelings about the outcome of their stay in Ethiopia. Over and over they lamented that they did not know anyone who was sincere in seeking the Lord.[355] Even some of those whom they praised for their commitment in the beginning did not appear to persevere in the faith.[356] However, there were informed and most influential people who according to Gobat condemned the worship of creatures and "begin to doubt if the invocation of the Virgin is permitted" but Gobat concluded saying, "but I know none who sincerely seek the Saviour."[357]

Such a statement appeared to be offensive to the average Orthodox follower. In fact, it has offended some of the contemporary historians.[358] However, it was not only the CMS missionaries who spoke about the Orthodox Church in such a way, but members of the church itself lamented

---

351. Crummey, 32–33.

352. Isenberg and Krapf, *Journals*, 64.

353. Isenberg and Krapf, 344.

354. Isenberg and Krapf, 72.

355. Gobat's Journal from 25 February 1830 – 16 February 1833, UB SC, CMS/B/OMS/C M/O28/113, 197; Isenberg and Krapf, *Journals*, 118.

356. Gobat's Journal from 25 February 1830 – 16 February 1833, 190–192.

357. Gobat's Journal from 25 February 1830 – 16 February 1833, 197.

358. Taddesse Tamrat quoted the words of Gobat that the Abyssinian Christianity entirely degenerated into superstition, as indicative of his having condescending attitude towards Ethiopian Christianity and that he did not want to allow the clergy to pronounce prayers of absolution on Kugler because he thought of it as a superstitious ceremony. "Evangelizing the Evangelized," 24–25.

over and over about the spiritual waywardness of the clergy and the people. Especially after they read the Bible for themselves and discovered the truth, the usual reaction of informed people, be it members of the clergy or monks, was that of deep desire to see their church reformed. For example, Gobat reports how Hadera and Kidane Mariam, two of the disciples of the CMS missionaries, reflected about their former experience after they studied the New Testament:

> At that time they had a pretty good knowledge of the New Testament . . . they perceived that hitherto they had been Christians only by name. To the conscience, which they had of some former faults and sins, was now added the conviction that their hearts had hitherto been estranged from God, because they had never experienced anything like the forgiveness of sins, the rejoicing in the Lord, and the delight of living in communion with God.[359]

Of course it could be argued that they told Gobat exactly what he wanted to hear simply because he was their master. However, the centrality of the Bible in the worship of the church has been debatable. For the Orthodox the fact that their ancestors fought a continuous battle to protect their tradition and the negative effects of the attempts of outside agents to pervert the Alexandrian faith make them wary of being wounded again. Thus, they are always on guard suspecting the worst and not willing to debate over their tradition, for fear of being led astray. Needless to say the open criticism and attack of the missionaries was less than helpful. In fact, it has made the church more protective and defensive of its strong hold on traditions.

The CMS missionaries on the other hand were surprised to find out that what they considered to be the plain truth of the Scriptures appeared to be new and unheard of by the average Christian.[360] Their impression was that there was intensely misguided religiosity which they attempted to tackle by drawing the attention of the people into the sole authority of the Scriptures. Their diligent distribution of the Scriptures was the greatest

---

359. Gobat, "Short Biography of the Abyssinian Hadera," 6.
360. Part of Rev Christian Kugler's Journal, 25 February – 24 April 1830, UB SC, CMS/B/OMS/ C M/ O46/24, 11, 24, 17; Gobat's Journal from 25 February 1830 – 16 February 1833, UB SC, CMS/B/OMS/C M/O28/113, 189.

of all of their successes. The key to success was indeed to be found within the Ethiopians themselves, as it was initially affirmed by the Society that the Oriental churches possessed "within themselves the principle and the means of reformation."[361]

Unfortunately, the CMS were not always to be remembered as distributors of the Scriptures but as Englishmen who did not fast,[362] and currently, they are portrayed as those who came in the footsteps of the Jesuits.[363] Mahbere Kidusan, one of the contemporary conservative groups within the Orthodox Church, numbers CMS along with the Jesuits as groups which attempted to pervert the Alexandrian faith. The CMS missionaries are called spies who aimed to divide the church, just as the CMS did in India, but it did not succeed in Ethiopia. What the association holds as evidence of the failure of CMS is the absence of any other organization in Ethiopia which calls itself Orthodox apart from the Ethiopian Orthodox church.[364]

The following words of John Venn, one of the founders and the Secretary of CMS, delivered while charging the second group of German missionaries to Sierra Leone in 1806, reveal the source of sustenance of the CMS.

> Though we have not met with immediate success, are we not laying a foundation on which much may be successfully built hereafter? But what have we to do with success? Success belongs to God – duty is our part. Shall we sit still and make no effort for the conversion of our fellow-creatures? Can we acquit ourselves of guilt by waiting longer till we see a more favourable prospect? Our duty, our indispensable duty, is to endeavour; nor are our endeavours at all less acceptable to God, even though they may be unsuccessful.[365]

The CMS looked at the Ethiopians as drawing near the door of the kingdom of heaven, but not inside it.[366] Contemporary Ethiopian Evangelicals seem

---

361. Stock, *History of the Church Missionary Society*, 226–227.
362. Isenberg and Krapf, *Journals*, 516.
363. Malede Wasyihun, *Hamere Tewahdo* (Addis Ababa: Mahbere Kidusan, 2002 Eth. C), 5–6.
364. Malede, *Hamere Tewahdo*, 5–6, 66–70.
365. Hennell, *John Venn*, 244.
366. Isenberg and Krapf, *Journals*, 497.

to reflect similar feelings towards Orthodox adherents as shall be discussed in the next chapter. Obviously parallels are drawn between the Jesuits, the CMS and the Ethiopian reformers in which the Evangelicals are portrayed as the strategic partners of the reformers, carrying forward the conspiracy of missionaries (in this case CMS) to weaken the Orthodox Church as it did in India. Melaku, however, praises Anglicans for not working against the Orthodox Church and taking part in converting EOC members to Protestantism.[367] As will be discussed in the next sections, the legacy of CMS diminished as Evangelicals engaged more and more in sheep-stealing, but in their rejection of images and intercession of the saints, they followed in the footsteps of the CMS. Among several issues, therefore, the Evangelicals' extensive practice of converting Orthodox members and the unwillingness of the Orthodox to acknowledge Evangelicals as authentic Ethiopian Christians continued to divide the two groups.

---

367. Melaku Baweke, ስውር አደጋ (The subtle danger), 32, fn. 21.

CHAPTER 5

Evangelical–Ethiopian Orthodox Church Encounter: A Story of Mutual Antagonism and Misunderstanding

Introduction

The relationship between the Ethiopian Orthodox Church and the Evangelicals for the most part has been characterized by intermittent conflict and laying of blame. Some of the reasons behind the strained relationship were mutual accusations of erroneous teaching and practices, sheep-stealing on the part of Evangelicals and persecution on the part of the EOC.

The EOC's perceptions of Evangelicals have varied over the years. There have been those who disliked everything about Evangelicalism and there have been those who were moderate in their perceptions and open to what they referred to as positive influences from the Evangelicals. Generally speaking, the Orthodox Church has been intolerant towards what it sees as religious or political aggression. However, the ever-growing sharp distinction between the two bodies seems to be a later development simply because Evangelical faith in earlier times was limited to the peripheral people and was not considered a threat to the state church. Former publications of the church thus did not refrain from featuring news of both Protestant and Orthodox churches.[1]

---

1. *Tinsae*, no. 11 (1970 Eth. C), 7–8. A little over a decade ago an official letter was dispatched to all bishops from the Office of the Patriarch with the signature of Aba Qerlos, the General Manager of the EOC. The letter urges each diocese to protect the flock from the destructive campaigns of Evangelicals who are funded by their allies in the Western countries.

Moreover, the Orthodox Church used to send its clergy to both Protestant and Catholic institutions for further studies.[2] However, as Evangelical faith was institutionalized and spread in the urban centres through different means including converting Orthodox members, the Orthodox Church felt threatened and tried to halt these activities by means of force. When exerting force was no longer sanctioned by the government, the Office of the Patriarch admonished bishops to guard the flock from the erroneous teaching of the Evangelicals.[3] But generally speaking, the Synod of the church has been mindful of the constitutional rights of Evangelicals.

This chapter begins by tracing the encounter of the two organizations and then looks at their relationship from each other's point of view. Beginning with the self-perception of each group, it discusses how the Orthodox Church as the pioneer looked at itself and how it related to Evangelical Christianity. It also analyzes how the new communities which came out of the missionary movement in Ethiopia perceived themselves and what factors played a role in the emergence of the identity markers which developed over the years.

5.1. Brief History of the Encounter between Ethiopian Orthodox Church and Evangelicals

As noted in chapter 4, the effort of the nineteenth-century CMS missionaries to draw the attention of the church back to the centrality of the Bible did not succeed; neither did the SEM missionaries' initial attempts to follow in the footsteps of the CMS prosper. The SEM changed course and took up the secondary plan of the CMS: targeting the "pagan" Oromo ("Galla"). The twentieth-century SIM missionaries, however, did not entertain revitalizing the Orthodox Church simply because of their background, which did not

---

Ethiopian Orthodox Tewahedo Church, Patriarchate Head Office, Ref No. 354/8717/91, Date: 28/1/91 Eth. C.

2. "... ለዚዜው [የራሷን የክህነት ማሰልጠኛ] መሥራት ባትችልም እርስዎ ከጠቀሷቸው አብያተ ክርስቲያናት ጋር ተባብራ ካህናቶችን ለማሰልጠን ብትሞክር መልካም ይሆናልታል። ይሁን ለማላት የደፈርነው እክከሁን ልጆቻን ወደ ውጭ ልከ የምታሰለጥነው በ 'ሁላት ባሕርይ' ቦዮች ኦርቶዶክሳውያን፣ በተቀሊካውያንና በፕሮቴስታንቶች ከሊጆች ስለሆን ነው። እንዲህ ከሆነ እዚህ ካሉት ጋር የማትተባበርበት ምክንያት አይገባንም።" The Editor, to Deacon Zelalem Biresaw, Tinsae, no. 27 (1972 Eth. C), 1.

3. Ethiopian Orthodox Tewahedo Church, Patriarchate Head Office, Ref No. 354/8717/91, Date: 28/1/91 Eth. C.

have a place for a national church. They sought individual conversions aiming to reach the so-called "pagan" peoples of Southern Ethiopia.

The southern people's desperation for physical and spiritual freedom prepared their heart for a change and their loose connection to the church was severed. People in the South did not have strong attachment to the EOC to begin with for a number of reasons: the church was associated with the oppressive *Gabar* system, which took the fertile land of the people and turned the people into subjects of the Northern settlers with the help of local chiefs.[4] Second, the Orthodox faith did not offer an adequate solution to suffering caused by traditional religion when the mediums exhausted the people's resources under the pretence of appeasing the supernatural forces.

In other words, the clergy of the EOC did not instruct the people apart from external marks of Christianity and baptism into the faith. The state imposed Orthodox Christianity on the people with an official statement.[5] However, the power of the gospel to set people free from spiritual and physical bondage was not presented well. People who were embittered by both physical and spiritual oppression started to respond to the preaching of the missionaries. However, massive conversion was not seen until indigenous evangelists were involved in the preaching of the gospel. The message was simple. It offered peace with God and freedom from spiritual oppression. The power of the message was not in its mere propositional truth, but the most important aspect was the translation of portions of Scriptures into the mother-tongue and the demonstration, that followed the power encounters. What were these converts to do with their past experiences?

The missionaries did not find a positive category to describe the spiritual experiences of the people, so they categorized most of the practices of traditional religion as demonic and strongly urged the new converts to put it behind them. The missionaries made use of the name of God as it appeared in the traditional religion but the other notions of anthropology,

---

4. Not everyone agrees with the term "conqueror" in reference to the integration of the South into Ethiopia, but it is often used by the people themselves to describe their difficult experience under Northern settlers in which they lost their freedom and land. However it could be argued that people groups were oppressed by their own people, chiefs and religious mediums. Perhaps, the "Amhara" hand felt too heavy because they were not one of their own.

5. Kedamo Mechato, Retired Evangelist of Kale Heywet Church, Interview, 18 January, 2011, Addis Ababa.

environment and the supernatural were not as integrated as they could have been. Because of the pioneering work of the EOC the missionaries did not need to look for categories for spiritual realities and beings such as angels and Satan but they insisted on the need for making a complete break with the past because they believed it was demonic. Eide Øyvind argues that the interaction between Evangelical Christianity and Oromo traditional religion bore evidence of both continuity and conscious dissociation from the traditional religion.[6]

The preaching of the missionaries produced converts and an increase in numbers of converts raised a pragmatic question of what to do with them and how to go about church planting. The need to name these new emerging Christian communities and the difficult task of establishing them as separate entities in a land which had Orthodox faith as a State religion came to the surface. Emperor Haile Sellassie I, who gave permission to foreign missionaries to evangelize those who were outside the influence of the national church, was not happy with the church planting and massive baptisms going on everywhere.[7]

However, the preaching and teaching of the missionaries which was quickly picked up by their first converts produced a steady emergence of a solid body of believers, who identified themselves with the Bible and Christ,[8] and even started to work towards the unity of all Evangelicals in the country.[9] These churches from their inception experienced regular conflict with Orthodox-dominated government authorities and the church as a whole.

At this juncture there are important questions which need to be asked. The first is whether Evangelical Christianity represents continuity or

---

6. Øyvind M. Eide, *Revolution and Religion in Ethiopia* (Addis Ababa: Addis Ababa University Press, 2000), 71–73.

7. Hege, *Beyond Our Prayers*, 38–39, 45–49, 128–131. Cf. Engelsviken, "Pentecostal Revival," 56–57.

8. For example in the Kale Heywet Church after the expulsion of the missionaries who left behind a handful believers, the national evangelists assumed leadership and went on to do massive evangelism and church planting. By the time the missionaries came back they found two hundred churches and about twenty thousand believers in the Kale Heywet churches. Cotterell, *Born at Midnight*, 27ff; 101, 120, 170; Wondiye, Ali, ნመክራ ውስጥ ያበበች ቤት ክርስቲያን *(Church out of tribulation)*, 146–47; Staffan Grenstedt, *Ambaricho and Shonkolla: From Local Independent Church to Evangelical Mainstream in Ethiopia* (Stockholm: Elanders Gotab, 2000), 19.

9. Hege, *Beyond Our Prayers*, 166. Also see appendix 1, 356–360.

discontinuity with Orthodox Christianity. Second, how did the converts view their new identity? Was their conversion an act of rebellion against the EOC? Could the choice of the converts to embrace the new faith be taken as a conscious or unconscious act to avoid EOC's dominance marked by the Amhara political upper hand?

These are not easy questions to answer but a study of the emergence and growth of Evangelicalism in Ethiopia shows that there was a conscious and deliberate departure from the Orthodox Church's long-held traditions.[10] The reasons for such departure vary along ethnic and dogmatic lines, but not all of the values of the ancient church were abandoned, even by the radical Pentecostals.[11] Those who had come from the Orthodox background thus continued to show a lot of respect for the church.[12]

The discontinuity was evident in how the early converts perceived traditional religion and its mediums. As mentioned in chapter 2 those supernatural powers, that formerly were confronted in the ministry of pioneer Orthodox monks, came to be tolerated over the years. In fact, clergy members of the Orthodox Church often played a double role as ministers in the church and also providers of charms and teachers of how to communicate with the spirit world. These realities created a society which appeared to be devoutly Orthodox and yet wished to appease the ancestral and other spirits as well. Therefore, there was a lot of apprehension over the activity of evil spirits. Moreover, magic books and occultism mushroomed, disguised under the names of angels and saints and even the Trinity.[13]

---

10. To prove to the missionaries the authenticity of their conversion candidates used their act of "breaking the fast and, their willingness to eat any type of meat" as a way of proving readiness (which was marked by baptism) to accept the new faith. Fargher, *Origins of the New Churches*, 140.

11. Engelsviken, "Pentecostal Revival," 104.

12. Although the difference seemed to stand out, there are striking similarities between the worldview of Evangelicals and EOC members. If we simply take one example of fulfilling a vow which is common in the EOC and usually an object of criticism from Evangelicals, when the Debre Zeit Mekane Yesus Church which was closed by the Derg was reopened many of the members of the church including its residing priest fulfilled their vows by moving on their knees all the way to the altar of the church from the main gate. *Kale Heywet*, no. 3 (1985 Eth. C), 10.

13. Nigusse Bulcha, Director of Scripture Union, Interview, 30 September 2010, Addis Ababa.

Evangelical converts, however, followed in the footsteps of the ancient monks of the Orthodox Church. They were not afraid of powers who were traditionally believed to be representatives of God. In fact, they made it their task to confront such powers who indwelt individuals. To this end they adapted an indigenous form of preaching which was offensive to the followers of traditional religion. They took to heart the message that Christ, who is the true representative of God, had come to destroy the work of Satan. Consequently, power encounter was a crucial part of such preaching. It was not a mere proclamation of words but was accompanied by deeds – the active confrontation with *Qalichas* proved that the gospel was powerful. Evidence was forthcoming. *Qalichas* who initially threatened the converts with death and tragedy fled the area and people who were afflicted by *Qalichas* and illness came to evangelical centres from near and distant places to seek help and to ask for churches to be established in their villages.[14]

However, the Evangelical faith which was presented mostly as discontinuous to the past traditional experiences and departed from the EOC, affected the identity of Evangelicals. The Evangelicals' self-consciousness, therefore, was shaped by the principles passed on to them by missionaries and also their own ethos of the new faith. Hence, a new kind of Christianity which was significantly different from the Ethiopian Orthodoxy emerged. Needless to say the EOC was not pleased with this development.

In order to understand the attitude of the Orthodox Church towards the Evangelicals, it is helpful to begin with the self-perception of the Orthodox Church. As noted earlier, since Orthodoxy is the oldest religion in the country with its roots in ancient Christianity and was the State religion, its adherents tend to feel superior to the followers of any other faith in Ethiopia. As discussed in chapter 2, the fact that the rulers and monarchs of the country practised Orthodox Christianity enabled it to spread all over the country. As the monarchs expanded their territories, they spread Orthodox Christianity and "Amhara culture" by taking with them clergy and also laity to settle in the new territories. The outcome of such expansion was that the food, language and culture of the northern rulers and settlers spread

---

14. Eide, *Revolution and Religion in Ethiopia*, 71–73.

throughout the country and was promoted as an expression of authentic Ethiopian faith and culture.

Such experience naturally marginalized other languages, faiths and cultures in the minds of the Orthodox, who expected them to adopt the Northern faith and way of life. Orthodox adherents thus felt at home nearly everywhere they went within Ethiopia because their faith was protected. This created a sense of belongingness in the followers of Orthodox and a claim to the whole of Ethiopia for Orthodoxy. The history of the country, which usually is written around the monarchs and rulers and the Orthodox faith, familiarized the history of Northern people in the country. Therefore, the history of Ethiopia is synonymous with the history of its monarchs who usually acted as heads of the church as well. The upper hand that Orthodox Christianity enjoyed for such a long time thus has impacted the adherents in such a way that speaking the language and practising the faith were held high as marks of civilization. The implication towards those who held onto Evangelical Christianity was immense. In the following sections, therefore, we shall discuss the Orthodox perception of themselves and of Evangelicals.

5.1.1. "We Are the Church in Ethiopia"

One of the major obstacles which made it difficult for Evangelicals to have meaningful dialogue with the Orthodox Church over the years was the prime self-perception of the EOC as *the* church in Ethiopia.[15] For a long time the church had been framer of culture and identity and delimiter of Ethiopian Christian tradition. Thus it does not want to lose its historic

---

15. The unique contribution of the church is acknowledged by both Ethiopian and foreign historians and theologians. Sergew Hable Sellassie, a notable Ethiopian historian remarks, "The Church of Ethiopia has been the repository of Ethiopian culture for the last 1,600 years of her existence." Sergew et al., *Church of Ethiopia*, iii. Richard Pankhurst, an expert in the history of Ethiopia describes the Church as "the custodian of the national culture." D. Scanlon, ed., *Ethiopia, Church, State and Education* (New York: Teachers' College Press, 1966), 28. Edward Ullendorff observed, "In its peculiar indigenized form, impregnated with strong Hebraic and archaic Semitic elements as well as pagan residua, Abyssinian Christianity had long become the store-house of the cultural, political, and social life of the people." Ullendorff, *The Ethiopians*, 97. The president of the students' association of Holy Trinity College referred to the Church as "the originator of our faith, the source of our culture and civilization." In the same occasion the Dean of the college called the Church "the vanguard of the cultural life of the Ethiopian nation." He also credited it for shaping every aspect of life in Ethiopia. "Orthodox Church Conference Opens Here," *The Ethiopian Herald*, 12 May 1967, 1.

role. Therefore, the church looked at the development of any other form of Christianity as an intrusion and the groups of Christians as rivals. In the case of the Evangelicals who did not have a strong representation until recently, the church explicitly stated that it had no reason to dialogue with them.[16]

"We are the church in Ethiopia." This is one of the most revealing statements about EOC's perception of itself. There is a strong sense of self-assertion, confidence and even a feeling of superiority in relation to nearly all other forms of Christianity. Such a feeling stems from the historic precedence of Orthodoxy to all other churches or expressions of Christianity in Ethiopia and its roots in early Christianity. Second, the prominent role of the church in defending the sovereignty of the country, and third, the long-lived interaction of the faith with the culture which made the church Ethiopian, a parcel of one's own identity. In other words, from EOC's point of view, it can take the sole credit for the preservation of the culture, national identity and Christianization of every facet of the life of Ethiopians.[17]

The self-perception of the church was not always expressed in an arrogant manner but also through apologetics. For instance, the seventeenth-century fathers of the church, who were not threatened by the "Lutherans," still felt that they had to address the doctrinal differences between what they referred to as the "German Protestans" (sic) and the Ethiopian Orthodox. The differences included Mariology, Ecclesiology, Sacraments, Eschatology, faith and prayer.[18]

A similar statement is found in the apologia of ancient EOC fathers, which gives a detailed account, but with no spirit of animosity, although it clearly indicates that the doctrine of both Roman Catholicism and Protestantism was apostate. The statements, which were meant to show the difference of EOC faith from "the religion of Germany," further indicated two major apostasies: rejection of reverence for the Mother of God and apostolic succession.[19] These two examples from the seventeenth century imply

---

16. Hege, *Beyond Our Prayers*, 243.

17. Daniel Seife Michael, Teacher at Holy Trinity Theological College, Interview, 8 September 2010, Addis Ababa.

18. Editorial, *Hamer*, no. 1, (Tahsas/Tir, 1990 Eth. C), 13.

19. የጀርመን ሃይማኖት ከኛ የሚለይበት ብዙን ነው፡፡ መጀመሪያ ክህደቱ ለእግዝእትን ማርያም ሰጊድ አይገባትም ይላል፡፡ እኛ ግን ንስግድላታለን፡፡ የፈጠሪ እናት ብለን ቅዱስ ዮሴፍ ሰገደላት ብሎ እንደመሰከረ፡፡ መጽሐፍ ጠይተን ደግሞም እግዚትን መላክት ወለብሳ መንግሥተ ሰማያት ወምድር እንደሆነች አምነን፡፡ Amsalu Aklilu, The Amharic Text

that EOC considered Protestantism/Lutheranism as "የክህደት ትምህርት" (a teaching of apostasy, a teaching which was not in accordance to the gospel).

With such a perspective of Protestantism in view, the coming of missionaries in the nineteenth centuary did not please the church. The missionaries on the other hand were not always wise in their relationships with the ancient church. Their indiscriminate criticism of the Orthodox, which was successfully taken up by their Ethiopian counterparts, strengthened the dividing walls. Naturally the EOC looked at the Ethiopian Protestants as extensions of the foreign missions, never willing to acknowledge them officially as authentic Ethiopian Christians.[20] A case in point was the patriarchs' unwillingness to call the pioneer Evangelical church, Mekane Yesus, by its name but as "Ato Amanuel's association" after the name of its prominent leader and the Minster of Education at the time.[21] The motive behind such thinking was illustrated in the words of Merqorios Arega, the late administrator of the Addis Ababa Diocese.

> But according to the custom of Ethiopia, Ethiopia meant Orthodox *tewahdo* and Orthodox *tewahdo* meant Ethiopia. But nowadays while Luther's kingdom and the leader[s] of his religion are Germany and Engliz,[22] it is referred to as Ethiopian Evangelical. Also while the Catholic leader and head is Batican (sic) Roma, it is referred to as the Ethiopian Catholic; the followers of Mohammed are called Ethiopian Muslims regardless of receiving orders from Mecca. We should realize that all of this

---

book, Addis Ababa University, 1974. Cited by Nigusse Bulcha, "በሥላሴ አማኞች መካከል ስላሚደረግ ትብብር," (Unpublished paper presented at Trinitarians' workshop, Mekane Yesus Seminary, Addis Ababa, 2010).

20. Daniel Seife Michael, Interview, 8 September, 2010; Giday Beyene, "The Impact of Protestantism on the Ethiopian Orthodox Church: Evangelization and Proselytization," BTh thesis (Addis Ababa: Holy Trinity Theological College, 1999), 27.

21. Engelsviken notes the difficulty encountered by the Mekane Yesus Church when they applied for registration. The main opponent was the EOC. They were eventually given permission to function but not to include the adjective "Ethiopian" but "in Ethiopia" into their name. In front of the emperor, the EOC patriarch repeatedly referred to the Mekane Yesus Church as "Ato Amanuel's association" after the name of Amanuel Abraham. Ato Amanuel protested strongly. The Emperor said to the patriarch, "Now, listen; it has been granted to the people to worship their Creator as they see fit, and We have declared that religion is the affair of the individual and the nations (sic) the affair of all the people." Engelsviken, "Pentecostal Revival," 154, fn. 5.

22. Ethiopians call Britain "Engliz."

is historical error. It is only the Ethiopian Orthodox church that has the right to be called by the name of Ethiopia ... we are not saying that [other faiths] should not exist but they should not be untruthful, they should not call their religion Ethiopian. Why overlook that the Ethiopian faith is Orthodox *tewahdo*.[23]

Such convictions have multifaceted ramifications. Even the political leaders of the country either believed the notion that the legitimate form of Christianity in Ethiopia was Orthodox Christianity or used it to stay in power, as illustrated in the action of King Fasiledes (1632–1667). After the bloody civil war between Ethiopian Catholics and Orthodox followers was halted, the king decreed, ሃይማኖት ይመለስ "Haymanot yimeles" (Let *the faith* be reinstituted). The faith, which traced its roots all the way back to the apostles; established on the foundations which were laid down by St Mark via the church of Alexandria – hence, the firm conviction of the Orthodox Church that it is *the* church in Ethiopia. The conviction provided the Orthodox (especially in the North) with a strong sense of identity and enabled them to retain the faith. Getatchew Haile, a notable cataloguer of Ethiopian studies and a devout EOC follower, echoes similar feelings about the inseparability of Ethiopian identity and Orthodox faith.

> I used to believe that I love the *tewahido* Christianity because it is the Orthodox or the right faith. I do not believe that any more. I believe that I love my church – which happens to be the true church of Christ – because it is mine, like my mother, like my father, my wife, my children and like my country. I also believe that if I had been born into another faith – e.g. as a Swede in the Swedish church – I would have been a faithful and loyal adherent of that faith. The truth therefore, lies not

---

23. "እንደ ኢትዮጵያ ሥርዓት ግን ኢትዮጵያ ማለት ኦርቶዶክስ ተዋሕዶ ኦርቶዶክስ ተዋሕዶ ማለት ኢትዮጵያ ማለት ነበር ዛሬ ግን የሉተርም መንግሥቴና የሃይማኖት መሪው ጀርመንና እንግሊዝ ሆኖ ሳለ የኢትዮጵያ ወንጌላዊት ተብሎ ይጠራል የካቶሊክም መሪው አዛዣ ባቲካን ሮማ ሆኖ ሳለ የኢትዮጵያ ካቶሊክ ተብሎ ይጠራል፤ የመሐመድም ተከታዮች ከመካ ሲተላለፍላቸው ኢትዮጵያውያን እስላሞች ተብለው ይጠራሉ። ይህ ሁሉ የታሪክ ስሕተት መሆኑን ልንገነዘብ ይገባናል በኢትዮጵያ ስም መጠራት ያለባት የኢትዮጵያ ኦርቶዶክስ ተዋሕዶ ቤተ ክርስቲያን ብቻ ናት . . . አይኑሩ ማለታችን ሳይሆን አይዋሹ የኢትዮጵያ ሃይማኖት አይበሉ የኢትዮጵያ ሃይማኖት ኦርቶዶክስ ተዋሕዶ መሆኑን ለምን ይዘነጋል።" Merqorios Arega, ታሪህን ዕወቅ እንዳትሆን መናፍቅ (Be informed of your history so that you might not become *menafiq*) (Addis Ababa: Tinsae Zegubae Printing Press, 1991 Eth. C), 3.

in who is in the right and who is in the wrong, but in who is born where.[24]

Getatchew reflects a common belief held among lay EOC adherents that people should retain the faith of their ancestors. Some even believe that failing to do so will result in a curse or unsuccessfulness in life. This shows how the faith was interwoven with the culture providing the people with a strong sense of identity. Paradoxically, however, at least from the perspective of the church, the argument that the truth is to be found "in who is born where and not in who is right" did not stop it from converting followers of primal religions who also had an identity of their own. Taddesse Tamrat writes, ". . . the Christian kingdom did not at all respect the religious institutions of its pagan subjects, who were automatically presumed to be a preserve of the church, as soon as they were conquered militarily. Their land with all its people and other resources, was divided and distributed as fiefs among the Christian political and military officials, thus constituting a number of administrative units."[25]

This "We are the church" sentiment was communicated to the Catholics also. In fact, EOC's attitude towards them was much more suspicious. The scar caused by the bloody civil war attributed to the Jesuits, and the Italian aggression in 1895 and conquest in the 1930s was not forgotten, so that minor or major acts which appeared to downplay the historic position of the EOC reminded them of the civil war caused by Jesuits.

For example, when the Catholic Church in Ethiopia celebrated the appointment of its first cardinal about twenty-five years ago, it allegedly referred to the occasion as "an unprecedented honour for Ethiopia since the coming of Christianity in the fourth century." These statements angered the EOC and its Synod officially described the statement of the Catholic Church in Ethiopia as "denying the existence of the Ethiopian Orthodox Church," "defiling the glory of the country," "dishonouring statement" and "Catholic intrusion." The Orthodox statement added, "in vain does the Catholic church attach the name of the country with an appointment which

---

24. Getatchew Haile, "Missionary Dream," 3.
25. Taddesse Tamrat, *Church and State*, 231.

does not represent the country at all."[26] For the onlooker it might appear that the Catholics were simply celebrating their big day, but the Orthodox Church felt provoked by the statement which appeared to undermine it.

We find similar sentiments expressed during the coming of the Derg which the Orthodox described as an "atheistic internal menace."[27] The Derg confiscated the church's countless properties including massive amounts of land.[28] The church was criticized as accomplice of the imperial regime by teaching that the emperors were appointed by God.[29] Abune Theophilos,[30] the patriarch at the time, tried his best to persuade the communist cadres to include in the new "constitution some articles which guarantee the rights of th (sic) church to be respected."[31]

The church enjoyed such a prestigious position for so long a time that it was not easy to number it with other churches which as far as EOC was concerned were not connected to historic Christianity, apparently had not done much for the country, worse still, whose development was considered as a threat to the church. Thus, the authorities of the church attempted to restrain the growth of these churches. When unable to do so, or when they

---

26. EOC was upfront about its longstanding resistance to the establishment of a Roman Catholic bishopric in Ethiopia because there already was an established EOC headed by an apostolic patriarch. The Synod stated that it did not appreciate the Catholic Church's copying of the EOC calendar, indigenous singing inaugurated by St Yared, and the naming of its diocese "Hagere Sibket." These appeared to be a deliberate attempts to confuse EOC members and compete with instead of respect the EOC. The Synod stated that it did not wish to remind its members of the past provocative actions of the Catholics but warn the Catholic Church not to repeat offensive acts which are not helpful for peaceful co-existence. Editor, "ጭፍን የታሪክ ቅስጣ" (Deliberate perversion of history), Zena Bete Kristian, no. 96 (30 Yekatit 1978 Eth. C), 1–2, 4, 7.

27. Sergew et al., *Church of Ethiopia Past and Present*, 17.

28. There was resentment towards the wealth of the church and its demand for government support. A writer noted that the financial wealth of the church was acquired from the poor people of the nation and must be put to the use of the people. The Church has no reason to ask for federal support. Belay Woldeyes, "ሃይማኖት በኢትዮጵያ ላይ ላይን" (An overview of religion in Ethiopia), Yezareyitu Ethiopia (Tir 10, 1967 Eth. C), 5.

29. Belay Woldeyes, "ሃይማኖት በኢትዮጵያ" Yezareyitu Ethiopia, 2.

30. He was so hostile to Evangelicals that he is said to have remarked that he would rather see Ethiopia taken over by Muslims than Protestants. Tormod Engelsvikan, Molo Wongel, 1975, 38. Gorgorios writes in the same vein attributing the divisions in the church and attempts to conquer Ethiopia to the work of the missionaries. Gorgorios, የኢትዮጵያ ኦርቶዶክስ ተዋህዶ ቤተ ክርስቲያን ታሪክ, 78ff.

31. Paulos, *Brief Life History of His Holiness*, 198.

failed to understand them, they called them names, and some of the names as will be discussed below, had serious repercussions.

5.1.2. The *Tsere-Mariam* Accusation against the Evangelicals through the Centuries

The depiction of Evangelicals as "Anti-Mary" was adopted from the fifteenth-century controversy between the Tigrean Estifanosites and the Orthodox clergy subsequent to the decrees of Emperor Zer'a Ya'iqob that Mary and the Cross were to be venerated.[32] Estifanosites rose during the reign of King Yishak (1406–1421) but when Aba Estifanos appeared before the king's court accused of apostasy, he defended his position in the presence of the king and the bishop. Upon hearing him, the king declared that Estifanos's teaching was Orthodox and allowed him to continue to teach.[33]

Initially, however, to the astonishment of the clergy, Emperor Zer'a Ya'iqob also granted the movement freedom to worship and teach. He summoned Estifanos before the council of clergy and inquired about his views. Estifanos replied, "I worship the Father, the Son and the Holy Ghost, and I prostrate before this. I shall not add to this . . . for the love of the rulers of this world."[34]

The king was incited by jealous monks to persecute Estifanos and his followers. Estifanosites followed a strict monastic order which got them in trouble with the other monks who were lenient to the extent of acquiring land and dwelling in well-built houses. The accusations of such monks resulted in the persecution of Estifanos and his disciples. The king attempted

---

32. Refusal to venerate the cross and Mary was not new. According to Getatchew, during the reign of Yagbea Tsion (1278 – 1286) about hundred and fifty years prior to the rise of Estifanosites, a group of people refused to bow down for Mary's picture and the cross. But the king claimed that he saw a vision in which Mary appeared to him and told him that bowing down/reverence is due to her picture and the cross of her Son. Subsequently the king decreed that he will hung those who refuse to venerate Mary and the cross and confiscate their property and burn their houses. Then the people relented to abide by his laws and their lives were spared. But there is no evidence as to whether the Estifanosites were aware of this history. Getatchew Haile, ደቂ እስጢፋኖስ፣ በሕግ አምላክ (The disciples of Estifanos: An appeal) 2nd edition (Addis Ababa: Addis Ababa University Press, 2010), 24.

33. Getatchew Haile, ደቂ እስጢፋኖስ፣ 82–90.

34. Taddesse Tamrat, "Some Notes on the Fifteenth Century Stephanite 'Heresy' in the Ethiopian Church," *Rassegna di Studi Etiopici* 22 (1966), as quoted by Fekadu Gurmessa, *Evangelical Faith Movement in Ethiopia* (Minneapolis, MN: Lutheran University Press, 2009), 48.

to debate with Aba Estifanos and his followers but when they refused to relent, he had them flogged and sent them back. Although he initially showed favour towards Estifanos, Zer'a Ya'iqob gave in to the accusations that his teaching in opposition to prostrating before any creature but God would eventually turn all of the king's subjects against him.[35]

When he realized that they were vehemently opposed to bowing down for him, pictures of Mary and the cross, the king's patience grew thin. Moreover, the theological controversy between the Estifanosites and their opponents was dividing the church because Aba Estifanos had a large following. Therefore, Zer'a Ya'iqob wanted to eliminate him and his disciples. The refusal of Aba Estifanos and his followers to honour the decree of the king subjected them to unspeakable atrocities and many of them were tortured to death. Estifanos himself was tortured beyond measure before being exiled to a land of Muslims in which he died after six months with the name of Christ on his lips.[36]

The refusal of Aba Estifanos and his followers to bow down to images of Mary, however, earned them a new name *tsere Mariam* (enemies of Mary) which also was used as a badge for Evangelicals.[37] Evangelicals have honoured the memory of Aba Estifanos and identified themselves with him, but not all Orthodox theologians agree that Evangelicals indeed follow in the footsteps of Aba Estifanos.

Daniel Seife Michael, a teacher of theology at Holy Trinity Theological College, argues that the accusations against Aba Estifanos were more political than dogmatic. According to Daniel, Aba Estifanos was not "anti-Mary" in the sense of the term which Evangelicals identify themselves with, neither was he against the use of the cross. In fact, he established a church in honour of St Mary and beginning from his time for two hundred years the best known kinds of crosses in the church were made by monks from the monastery established by Aba Estifanos.[38]

---

35. Getatchew Haile, ደቂቀ እስጢፋኖስ, 90ff.

36. Getatchew Haile, 111–112.

37. Merid notes that it was also used against the Jesuits and their followers who were accused of denying the status of Mary as "theotokos." Aregay, "Legacy of Jesuit Missionary," 51–52.

38. Daniel Seife Michael, Interview, 8 September 2010.

The written evidence of Estifanosites seems to validate the argument of Daniel. According to their writings they had such a great affection for Mary that in all of their books they drew her holding the baby Jesus. They chanted the praises of Aba Ephrem and beseeched Mary to intercede on their behalf. But they refused to obey the decree of the king that people were to bow down to Mary's picture. Estifanosites believed that it was contrary to God's commandment that his people should not bow down to any image.[39] Thus, they refused to bow down for the king either, and the king wanted to eliminate them particularly for this reason, although he used Mary and the cross as a pretext.[40]

The controversy with Estifanosites resulted in the production of strong assertions regarding Mary and the cross which were incorporated into the daily readings of the church. Part of the reading in honour of Mary and the cross asserted, ". . . our Lady Mary is the saviour of all . . . worship and prostration to her together with her son . . . O, Cross, the king of woods, you are honourable, wooden cross, you are honourable, you are sanctified through the word and blood of Christ . . . these two creatures deserve the adoration due to the creator, for in their glory they are equal [to the creator]."[41]

On the other hand, the EOC did not canonize Aba Estifanos, neither were his followers anathematized by the bishops of the church. It was Zer'a Ya'iqob who excommunicated them.[42] However, the Council of Scholars of the church remarked that "Estifa" has not fully accepted the Orthodox faith and teaching.[43] The church does not honour Aba Estifanos in the same

---

39. Exodus 20:1–6.

40. The hagiography of Aba Estifanos as translated by Getatchew Haile narrates the encounter of Aba Estifanos and emperor Zer'a Ya'iqob, but there is not a single reference in the interrogation of Zer'a Ya'iqob about the position of Aba Estifanos regarding the veneration of Mary. Although there is a reference to the accusation of his opponents that Aba Estifanos taught against the praythe researcherer of Mary as described in Bartos claiming that Mary's prayer was "my soul glorifies the Lord." Getatchew, ደቂቀ እስጢፋኖስ፣ 94, cf. 92–115.

41. ". . . ሁሉን የምታድን እመቤታችን ማርያም ነች፡፡ . . . ለሷ ክብርና ስብሐት ይገባታል፤ ከልጇም ጋራ አምልኮና ስግደት . . . የእንጨቶች ንጉሥ መስቀል ሆይ፤ ክቡር ነህ፤ የመስቀል እንጨት ሆይ፤ ክቡር ነህ፤ በክርስቶስ በቃል ደም የተቀደስክ ክቡር ነህ . . . ለዚሁ ሁለት ፍጡሮች የፈጣሪ ስብሐት ይገባቸዋል፤ በክብራቸው ተካካሎዋናና፡፡"Getatchew Haile, ደቂቀ እስጢፋኖስ፣ 38–41. Translation by the researcher.

42. Getatchew Haile, ደቂቀ እስጢፋኖስ፣ 15–16 (forward); 23–28.

43. "ደቂቀ እዝራ ለመስቀልና ለማርያም ስግደዋል በማርያም ስም የጉንዳ ጉንዲ ማርያም ገዳምን መስርተዋል፡፡ ሆኖም ይህ የምሥክርነት ቃል እስጢፋን አይጨምርም፡፡ ይኸውም እርሱ . . . የቤተክርስቲያኑን ኦርቶዶክሳዊ እምነትና ትምህርት በሙሉ ስላልተቀበለ ነው፡" ዑቆ ኢያስቴክሙ፡ እንዳያስቴሁ ተጠንቀ, መናፍቃ ጌታቸው "ገደል ወይስ ገደል" በማለት ለጸፈው የሀይደት ትምህርት ካኢትዮጵያ ኦርዶክስ ተዋሕዶ ቤተ ክርስቲያን ሊቃውንት ጉባኤ የተሰጠ መልስ

way as they honour other Ethiopian church fathers. A book attributed to Aba Giorgis of Gascha,[44] one of the most respected scholars of the church who produced a lot of literature prior to the reign of Zer'a Ya'iqob, reads:

> These apostates whom we call *tsere Mariam* say that [Mary] had intercourse with Joseph after she gave birth to our Saviour Jesus Christ. What kind of heart conceived such abomination, what kind of mouth dared to speak it. Such a despicable insult is more wretched than filthy rags[45] . . . these apostates who mock the virginity of our Lady, the Mother of Divine have no righteousness in this world or beyond. Their sins will not be forgiven whether they repent, fast or pray in upright position. If anyone comes back from their faith to our faith, let [them] re-baptize him because their baptism is not like that of Christ; for they have disrespected the mother of Christ. The power of God will not rest on their sacrifices for they have spoken words of apostasy against the mother of God, the one overshadowed by the power of God. The grace of God shall not come upon those who have defiled the account of the virgin, the chosen one of the Holy Spirit."[46]

It is not clear whom the writer has in mind since this text must have been written prior to the rise of Protestantism. The suggestion that the *Tsere-Mariam* should be re-baptized if they desired to join the church, also

---

(Beware not to be deceived, a reply from the Council of Scholars of the Ethiopian Orthodox Tewahdo Church to the apostasy writing of the *menafiq*) Getachew, "Gedil Weys Gedel" (Addis Ababa: Tinsae Zegubae Printing Press, 1996 Eth. C), 19.

44. He was the teacher of the children of king Dawit at the royal court. Tadesse Tamrat, *Church and State*, 277.

45. Most likely an allusion to Isaiah 64:6.

46. "እነሀ ዐረ ማርያም የምንላቸው ከሃዲያን መድኃኒታችን ኢየሱስ ክርስቶስን ከወለደች በኋላ ከዮሴፍ ጋር ተገናኙች ይላሉ እንዲህ ያለውን ነቀፋ ያሰበ ምን ልብ ነው ይህንስ ለመናገር የደፈረ ምን አንደበት ነው ይህ የድፍረት ስድብ ከሊቆች የደም ጨርቅ . . . የረከስ ነው . . . እነዚህ የመለኮት እናት በሆነች በእመቤታችን ድንግልና ላይ የተዘባቱ ከሃዲዎች ጎን በዚህም ዓለም በሚመጣውም ዓለም ንጽህና የላቸውም በንስሓ በጾም ቁሞ በመጸለይም ቢሆን ኃጢአታቸውን አይፋቅላቸውም ከእርሶቹም እምነት ወደ እኛ ሃይማኖት የተመለሰ ቢኖር እንደገና ያጥምቁት ጥምቀታቸው እንደ ክርስቶስ ጥምቀት አይደለምና በክርስቶስም እናት ላይ የድፍረት ቃል ተናግረዋልና ኃይለ ልዑልም በመሥዋዕታቸው ላይ አያርፍም ኃይለ ልዑል በጋረዳት በድንግል ማርያም ላይ የክህደት ቃል ተናግረዋልና መንፈስ ቅዱስ የመረጣት የድንግልን ዜና በአርከሱ ሰዎች የመንፈስ ቅዱስ ረድኤት አያርፍባቸውም፡፡" Hawaze Birhan Wolde Michael et al., መጽሐፈ ሚስጢር ዘንብለ ጊዮርጊስ ዘጋሰጫ፣ (Aba Giorgis of Gascha's Book of Mysteries) (Addis Ababa: Ethiopian National Archives and Library, 2001 Eth. C), 150–151.

raises questions because in the fourteenth century, there was no organized separate Christian body in the country. Perhaps, this is a scribal addition to the original words of Giorgis of Gascha. At any rate, it shows that any group whose teaching appeared to disgrace Mary was labelled as *Tsere-Mariam*. The Evangelicals' repeated attack on EOC's devotion to Mary in a way which sounded devoid of reverence to her was abominable to the EOC followers.[47] The missionaries had similar views regarding Mary. Nathan B. Hege notes, "It did not occur to Protestant missionaries that, within the bounds of Scripture, they could have smoothed their relationships with Orthodox people more often by speaking positively of Mary's unique place in salvation history. Instead, they tended to argue about whether Mary had influence with her son."[48]

The Evangelicals' controversy over Mary arises from determination to retain the centrality of Christ as attested in the Bible, but it lacks knowledge of the history of the Orthodox Church and the ramifications of "dishonouring" Mary. The place of Mary in salvation is crucial in Orthodox theology; at least from the point of view of its scholars, attacking Mary is understood as attacking her Son. Therefore, the one who argues that Mary had original sin and that she was not perpetually a virgin is not considered as heretical, but apostate; (not just *menafiq* "መናፍቅ" but *kehadi* "ከሃዲ').[49]

The following quotation from Aba Giorgis sheds further light on what is at stake in the discussion. ". . . if the Holy Spirit did not allow [Joseph] to come near her until she conceived the Son of God and after she gave birth to Him, how can they say that she had intercourse with Joseph . . . what fleshly body can come near to the dwelling place of Divine? What person can get

---

47. Taddesse Tamrat, "Evangelizing the Evangelized," 22.
48. Hege, *Beyond Our Prayers*, 55.
49. Aba Giorgis Zegascha calls her "የእሳት እናት" (the Mother of fire) to imply the holiness of Christ her Son. Hawaz Birhan, *Metsehafe Mistir*, 149. This provides us with one of the profound expressions of Ethiopian scholars in reference to the incarnation. Daniel noted, "Whatever we use to describe Christ with, she too is to be affirmed. Christ is light: she is the mother of light, Christ is salvation: she is mother of salvation. With our salvation and all of the blessings we have gained from Christ, she is the mother of all those blessings and gifts of God. Christ is life, she is mother of life, Christ is Saviour, she is mother of Saviour." O.i, Daniel, 8 September 2010; Birhanu Gobena argued that asserting the intercession of Christ is denying his deity. Birhanu Gobena, "ትምህርተ ሃይማኖት," *Hamer*, no. 1 (Megabit, 1986 Eth. C), 4–6.

into the quarters of the Divine."⁵⁰ This argument clearly showed what the EOC is trying to protect by vehemently refusing to accept the motherhood of Mary to other children but Jesus. In other words, it is the divinity of Jesus; "because God used the womb of Mary as his dwelling place, no human being, no flesh, ever stayed in the dwelling place of God."⁵¹

The other point of departure from Evangelicals has to do with the intercessory role of the saints, Mary being the prime one. As for the legitimacy of addressing prayers to the saints, the EOC strongly believes that the intercession of the saints and almsgiving in their remembrance are attested in the Bible: "He who receives you receives me, and . . . anyone who receives a prophet because he is a prophet will receive a prophet's reward, . . ." (Matt 10:40–42) The Amharic translation shows the idea behind it. It reads, "Anyone who receives a prophet in the name of a prophet . . ." ⁵² "I tell you the truth, whatever you bind on earth will be bound in heaven, and whatever you loose on earth will be loosed in heaven" (Matt 18:18). By citing the above passages, Mekonnen Workneh, a history instructor at the Holy Trinity Theological College, argues that the dead Saints are living with Christ, so we may ask them to intercede on our behalf. He further reasons,

> It is customary in the Protestant tradition to ask their friends or even neighbours to pray for them when there is a need. If a neighbour or a friend whose work is not yet attested by God is fit to intercede on their friend's behalf, how much more would the saints whom Christ has glorified intercede for us from their perfect state? Besides, God does not disrobe them of his grace because his gifts are irrevocable and his impartation of grace is eternal. The saints are given authority while living on earth,

---

50. "የእግዚአብሔርንም ልጅ እስከ ፀነሰችበት ጊዜ ድረስና እሱንም ከወለደችው በኋላ መንፈስ ቅዱስ ወደ እሷ ለመምረብ ካልፈቀደላት . . . ከወለደችውስ በኋላ መንፈስ ቅዱስ ወደ እሷ ለመምረብ እንዴት ይፈቅድላታል የመለኮትንስ አጸራኽ ምን ሥጋዊ አካል ሊቀርባት ይችላል ወደ መላኮት እልፍኝስ ምን ስው መግባት ይችላል፡፡" Hawaze Birhan, መጽሐፈ ምሥጢር, 150–151.

51. Hawaze Birhan, *Metsehafe Mistir*, 151–152. The allusion is to Ezekiel 44:1–2 "This gate is to remain shut. It must not be opened; no-one may enter through it. It is to remain shut because the Lord, the God of Israel, has entered through it." Cf. Song of Songs 4:12.

52. The believers in Hadiya took these words literally and would not let anybody pass by without having something to eat and drink, then they used to tell the person about Jesus. Temesgen Sahle, የአባባ ጻሏም እና የአባባ ደዴቦ ምሥክርነት (The testimony of Ababa Daemo and Ababa Dedebo), *Kale Heywet*, no. 25 (1994 Eth. C), 5.

and God does not take it away from them while living with him in glory.[53]

There is more to Mariology and its ramifications with regard to the authority of the Bible and also the relationship between Orthodox Church and the Evangelicals; it will be discussed in more detail later on.

5.1.3. The Depiction of Evangelicals as *Mete* (Foreign)

Prior to the coming of the Derg the term "mission" was used as one of the badges of Evangelical Christians. This implies that Evangelicals were identified with foreign missions and their faith was not considered as an authentic Ethiopian expression of Christianity. Consequently, the Orthodox Church was not happy with the development of the first organized Evangelical church Mekane Yesus and used their influence in the government to hinder the appropriation of the Ethiopian identity of the Mekane Yesus Church.[54]

The period that followed the fall of Haile Sellassie posed a serious threat for all expressions of faith, especially Christianity. More damagingly still, the Derg took time to systematically condemn Evangelicals through the state-owned media and introduced the deadliest categorization of Evangelicals. There was deliberate association of the faith with foreign involvement.[55] We have seen that the EOC identified Evangelicals with foreign missionaries and the Derg associated them with Western countries which were not supportive of its ideology. The propaganda against Evangelicals was steadily released in state papers:

> In recent years Christian religions with different names have come to our country. . . . Out of these foreign faiths (*metewoch*)[56] the teaching and practice of some of them perhaps imply that they are directly related to Imperialism. They have caused the citizens to foster "this world is not my home" mentality affecting the self-esteem of citizens and promoting laziness. Indirectly

---

53. Mekonnen, Workneh, Teacher at Holy Trinity Theological College, Interview, 5 November, 2010, Addis Ababa.

54. Bakke, "Models of Leadership," 156.

55. Bezabih Workneh, Minister at Mulu Wongel Church, 25 February, 2011, Addis Ababa.

56. This is the plural form of the Amharic adjective *mete*.

they have discouraged students from learning.... When students were fighting to overthrow the former regime most of the youth belonging to these religions did not participate. Instead they replied, "We will pray to God because the instability is caused by worldliness. You too stop talking about the sin of others, rather, receive Jesus and you will find peace and be able to stop worrying about the others . . ."[57]

Eshete notes that unlike the other references to Evangelical Christians such as *Tsere-Mariam* and *Pente*, which "signified cultural or theological orientation, the term '*mete*'[58] was a politically loaded concept, purposely chosen . . . [it] was used deliberately as an exclusionary tool targeting the Evangelicals for the perpetration of isolated attacks."[59] By calling the Evangelicals *mete* the state media identified them with outside forces which they regarded as their ideological enemies. The other state-owned newspaper declared,

We cannot tolerate those who are conspiring against our revolution in different ways; those who work to reverse the revolution, the fruits of the monopoly capitalism and the protectors of the interests of worldwide imperialists. They work to incapacitate the mind of the society. Among the provinces of Ethiopia we presume that Sidamo might be their centre for such manipulation and conspiracy under the pretence of religion.[60]

---

57. "ከጥቂት ዓመታት ወዲህ በልዩ ልዩ ስሞች የሚጠሩ የክርስትና ሃይማኖቶች ወደ ሀገራችን በብዛት ገብተዋል፡ ፡ . . . ከእነዚህ መጤዎች ውስጥ አንዳንዶቹ የሚያስተምሩትና የሚፈጽሙት ድርጊት ከአምፔሪያሊዝም ጋር በቀጥታ ግንኙነት ያላቸው መስሎ ያስገምታቸዋል፡፡ ዜጋውን ስንፍናና ብርስ አለመተማመንን አዘናግቶ "ይህ ዓለም ቤቴ አይደለም" ብሎ እንዲቀመጥ ገፋፍተዋል፡፡ ተማሪው እንዳይማር በተዘዋዋሪ መንገድ ከልክለዋል፡፡ . . . ተማሪዎች ያፈረሱን መንግሥት ለመጣል በሚታገሉበት ጊዜ እነዚህን ሃይማኖቶች የሚያምልኩ ወጣቶች አብዛኞቹ አልተሰለፉም፡፡ "እኛ ወደ እግዚአብሔር በጸሎት እንላምናለን ብጥብጥ የመጣው ዓለማዊ ስለበዛ ነው፡፡ ይልቅስ ስለ ሰው ኃጢአት ከምታወራ ኢየሱስን ተቀበል ከዚያ ወዲያ ስለሰው አትጨነቅም ሰላም ታገኛለህ . . . ብላው ነው የሚመልሱት፡" Belay Woldeyes, "ሃይማኖት በኢትዮጵያ ላይ ላዩን," 5.

58. *Mete* is an adjective which literally means, new comer, something which was not there originally.

59. Eshete, *Evangelical Movement*, 217.

60. "ከፐታሊዝም ውልደ የሆኑ የዓላም አቀፍ ኢምፔሪያሊስቶች ጥቅም አስከባሪዎች የጉብረተሰብ አእምሮ አከላሾች፡ የአብዮቱ ቀለበሾች የሆኑትን ዛሬ በልዩ ልዩ ዘዴ በአብዮታችን ደገ ሲሰሩ በቸልታ ልናልፋቸው አንችልም . . . በሃይማኖት ስም በኢትዮጵያ ውስጥ . . . ተንከል ከሚሠራበቱው የኢትዮጵያ ክፍላተ ሀገሮች ውስጥ ሲዳም ክፍለ ሀገር ዋነኛ ሳትሆን እንደማትቀር እንገምታለን፡ Yirga Haile Mariam, "በሃይማኖት ስም ወጣቱን ከትግል መድረክ ለማዘናጋት በፀረ አብዮተኞች የሚደረግ ደባ" (The conspiracy of anti-revolutionary people), Addis Zemen (12 Ginbot 1971 Eth. C), 3.

The new name was quickly taken up by the Orthodox. However, the word *mete*, is a later development, although the concept of foreignness in reference to Evangelicalism was not new.[61] The informed Orthodox used the term *mete* to imply that Protestantism was not in the tradition of historic Christianity.[62] The general public, however, used the notion to attack Evangelicals.[63] Evangelicals were not considered enemies of society or threats to the nation prior to the Derg. It was the Derg that popularized such a notion.[64] With it came massive organized persecution led by Derg authorities, who diligently used Orthodox people. The title "foreign" gave EOC followers ground to uproot what was rated as dangerous faith before it spread and divided the nation. The Evangelicals were easy prey because their faith was relatively new and did not have as many adherents as the historic church. In addition to that, they maintained an other-worldly orientation by stressing "piety, holiness and purity of faith."[65] Persecution continued even after the fall of the Derg, in some instances with association of the faith with Satan.[66]

---

61. The early opposition against Evangelicals was theological and doctrinal. The argument against them was not that they were not upright morally, but that their teaching was not correct. So the effort was to refute their doctrine and not to attack them personally. Nigusse Bulcha, Director of Scripture Union, Interview, 30 September 2010, Addis Ababa.

62. Cf. "Protestants originated with Luther, so they are dissenters." Daniel, Interview, 8 September, 2010.

63. "መጤ የመጠቃቃት ቃል ነው።" Mekonnen, Interview, 15 November, 2010. Cf. "The term '*mete*' has negative connotation and I think it should not be used at all." Informant G, February, 2011, Addis Ababa.

64. Bezabih, Interview, 25 February 2011.

65. Eshete, *Evangelical Movement*, 216, 218. Some of the requirements for membership in the Evangelical churches in the early 1970s included not smoking, not drinking coffee, both husband and wife joining the church together, and marrying a virgin girl. Solomon Bizuwork, የማን ቤት ክርስቲያን አባል ነህ? (Where is your church membership?), *Birhan*, no. 9 (1967 Eth. C), 14. Evangelicals were accused of encouraging laziness in the name of the help of Jesus. The writer notes that hard working students stopped studying believing that Jesus will help them pass the exam. A story of one entertainer who left his work after he changed his religion was cited. He claimed, "I have received Jesus and my religion does not allow that I continue in my work." "የሱስን ተቀብዬሁ። ሃይማኖቴ አይፈቅድልኝም ለማስተዋቅ" Belay Woldeyes, "ሃይማኖት በኢትዮጵያ ላይ ላዩን," 5.

66. In Gojjam (northern Ethiopia) Yismala town there was a wave of terrible persecution. In one instance the whole town came to a house where a handful of believers were sitting. After beating them up so badly, they took them around the town hitting and kicking them while singing and dancing, literally: "What do you have to eat now Satan?! Pente ate dust" (Eating dust is an expression of complete destruction) "እንግዲህ ሰይጣን ምን ትበላ፤ ጴንጤ አፈር በላ" and the believers were thrown out of town. Editor, "በኢትዮጵያ ስደት እንደ ሰደድ እሳት" (Persecution in Ethiopia spread like a wildfire), *Hiwot*, no. 12, (Meskerem 1986

As stated above, Evangelical Christians were usually identified with their founding mission organizations. Even churches such as Mulu Wongel, which were indigenous with no outside support of any kind, were usually numbered among the other Evangelical churches. Among other things such identification took place because of the continued communication with or dependence on mission organizations, alleged non-authenticity of the Evangelical expression of Christianity and the accusation that Evangelicals were unpatriotic.[67]

There are numerous Evangelical practices which are not customary among the Orthodox especially in the church. The dress code of the Evangelicals, the title of the ministers, the time and manner of worship, and the shouting

---

Eth. C), 28. When similar kind of persecution against Evangelicals spread throughout the country, an editor of the Kale Heywet magazine lamented that the clergy of the EOC were inciting their people against Evangelicals and leading to the shedding of blood. He appealed, "የወንጌልን ቃል ካወቁ በወንጌል አምላክ! ሕግን ከፈሩ በሕግ አምላክ! ብርታታቸውን ተማምነው ከሆነ በጉልበት አምላክ!" (If they know the word of the gospel, I appeal to them in the name of the God of the gospel; if they fear the law, I appeal to them in the name of the God of the law; if they rely on their strength, I appeal to them in the name of the God of power). Editor's Appeal, *Kale Heywet*, no. 15 (1990 Eth. C), 17.

67. There was a widely held view that Evangelicals were not committed to their country. Such a perception largely affected those who were members of the defence force. An air force pilot, Endegena Taddesse who was an Evangelical Christian noted that Evangelicals were not considered fit to be soldiers being portrayed as having no purpose in life and as a burden on the country. Endegena said that their commanders were concerned about the rumour and did not know how to go about it. When he was asked whether his Christianity did not conflict with his military mission which involved killing people. He replied, "Not at all. The Bible says give Caesar's what is due to him and God what is due to him. I am a citizen of the country and am a soldier who is to defend the country's sovereignty. Besides, Moses, who gave the command "Do not kill" was the one who led the people into a war." Endegena Tadesse, Interview, *Kale Heywet*, no. 19 (1991 Eth. C), 16–18. Part of the reason was that during the Derg time all Evangelicals were mistakenly identified with Jehovah's witnesses who refused to fight for their countries, but even at that time some Evangelical commanders of the army impressed the top officials including the president Mengistu Haile Mariam. General Taye Tilahun was one of a kind. His famous saying was, "በሀገሬ ጉዳይ ላይ አልደራደርም፤ ለሀገሬ ክብርና ነፃነት እስከመጨረሻው ቆሜ እዋደቃለሁ::" (I do not negotiate in matters that have to do with my country. I will fight for the honour and freedom of my country until the end). President Mengistu testified about General Taye, "ታዬ ጥላሁን ለሥራቸው ካላቸው ብቃት ሌላ ሃይማኖተኛ ሰው ናቸው:: እኔ ደግሞ ሠላሳውን ከሚቀባጥር ወይከሬ ከሚኒስት ነኝ ባይ በሃይማኖታዊ እምነት ድርቅ ያለ እውነተኛ ሰው በጣም አከብራለሁ:: የሚያምንበትን ነገር ሳይዋሽ ፊት ለፊት እውጥቶ የሚናገር ሰው ለሌላውም ነገር እምነት ሊጣልበት ይችላል:" (General Taye is an efficient, trustworthy religious person. As for me I highly respect someone who is truthful with unwavering commitment to his religion than someone who calls himself Communist but is full of lies and deception because the one who openly stands for what he believes in is dependable to assume other responsibilities too). Taye Tilahun, "የጄነራሉ ወዳጆች ምሥክርነት" (The testimony of friends of the General), *Kale Heywet*, no. 30 (1997 Eth. C), 15, 17.

and free movement during worship are abhorred by the Orthodox Church. Furthermore public speaking in tongues and the role of women in ministry perplex EOC adherents and they ask, "What is this? Where did they get it from?"[68]

As will be discussed below, with the coming of Pentecostalism what was started with the missionaries was further strengthened and more and more boundaries were marked which further isolated the Evangelicals from the community around them.[69] In a sense Evangelicals developed a lifestyle and expressions peculiar to them, which for the most part were seen as resembling the West and direct translations or adoptions from the English language.[70] The Orthodox Church retained her accusation that Ethiopian Evangelicals were not only opposed to culture and society, but were also "culture-less, tradition-less." A disturbing accusation was that of encouraging amnesia with respect to the experience of the EOC's adherents prior to their conversion to Protestantism, thereby deliberately detaching them from reality and their identity.[71]

More scandalous still was the continual tendency among Protestants to split and form new churches at times, giving the new churches strange

---

68. Daniel, Interview, 8 September 2010. የገሃነም ደጆች, *Sem'ea Tsidq* 10, no. 77 (Yekatit 1995 Eth. C), 16; Eshete, *Evangelical Movement*, 176. Regarding the manifestations in the Evangelical churches, the EOC minister Aba W/Tinsae Ayalneh remarks, "The shaking and yelling that is going on in the name of the Holy Spirit has concerned us greatly. The grace of the Holy Spirit gives joy and peace, but it does not trouble or cause disorder . . . such actions are leaning towards the evil spirit." Aba W/Tinsae, "ልሳን" (Tongues), *Hamer*, no. 3 (Miazia, 1985 Eth. C), 11.

69. Eshete, *Evangelical Movement*, 85–86.

70. For instance, Evangelicals call their meetings "conference," their halls "Church" (although the sign board reads "Bete Kristian" people refer to it as church), their group of singers "choir," their activities "program," the ministers "pastors," architecture of their church buildings does not resemble that of the EOC, and so on. (But there are at least two Evangelical churches in Addis that adopted EOC's kind of architecture: Misrak Meserete Kristos even has the cross at the top and at times EOC members mistake it for their church, and Bethel Mekane Yesus Church resembles the rock hewn EOC Church in Lalibela. *Kale Heywet*, no. 2 (1985 Eth. C), 25. Moreover they go for worship from 9:00–12:00 whereas the EOC members worship early in the morning with an empty stomach. Evangelicals do not pay attention to their dress code while going to church but EOC followers put on "Netela" (traditional cloth) while going to church. Now there is a growing complaint that the Evangelical influence is changing the EOC youth who are daring to go into the compound of the church with t-shirts on! Bezabeh, Interview, 25 February 2011.

71. Esubalew Belete, የገሃነም ደጆች (Gates of hell) (Addis Ababa: n.p., 2004), 334.

names usually identifying them as international instead of Ethiopian.[72] For the Orthodox who strongly believe in the national church and who tend to group all Protestants together as one big category, the ever-increasing number of Protestant factions creates serious questions about the credibility of the camp.[73] A writer of Mahbere Kidusan, a conservative association within the structure of the Orthodox Church, remarks that opening a church among Protestants is as easy as beginning a small shop. "አንዱ አንዱን ይነጥቃል፣ ይክንናል፣ ይገነጥላል። ምክንያቱም በፕሮቴስታንቶች ዘንድ "ቸርች" መመሥረት ቀላል ነው . . . ቸርች እንደ ሱቅ ነው የሚቆቆመው።"[74]

Moreover, Evangelicals were considered as having a secret agenda of undermining the Orthodox faith, thereby causing the country as a whole to disintegrate.[75] However, more than the Ethiopian Evangelicals, EOC theologians blamed the missionaries for sowing a seed which resulted in the negative attitude of Evangelicals towards it which resulted in the Evangelicals distancing themselves from the church.[76]

---

72. For example: Faith Bible International Church which is usually called (FBI), the Seven thousand Elect Church. The FBI church has a big banner in English at its junction with no Amharic translation which reads, "Jesus is our Saviour." Another popular church with the youth is called "You–Go City Church" because the hall they use belongs to Yugoslavian community and was known as Yugo Club. The leaders of the church have adopted the name but the English banner of the church reads "I belong to Jesus." This is perhaps to reach the modern generation which tends to exalt English over the vernacular. In addition to that some who split from existing churches would take names which resonate their former church. For example those who split from Kale Heywet called their church Yehiwot Qal, those who split from Mulu Wongel called it Yeselam Wongel, etc. The claims of some ministers about their unique appointment by Christ to have authority over the church at times come close to that of the Pope of Rome.

73. "ዛሬ ስለ ፕሮቴስታንት መናገር እጅግ አስቸጋሪ ነው። አስቸጋሪቱም የሚመነጨው አንድ የእምነት ተቋም ለአንድ ፕሮቴስታንት ሊደርሰው እስከሚችል ድረስ እርስ በርሱ በመከፋፈሉና በመጣላቱ የተነሳ ነው፡" Nowadays, it is difficult to talk about Protestantism because it is utterly divided almost in the number of its members and they are animus to each other. የገናነም ደጆች፣ *Sem'ea Tsidq* 10, no.77 (Yekatit 1995 Eth. C), 13.

74. የገናነም ደጆች, *Sem'ea Tsidq* 10, no. 77 (Yekatit 1995 Eth. C), 14.

75. Melese Atnafu, "The Conversion of Addis Ababa Population from Orthodox Tewahedo Church to Protestant Denominations," BTh thesis (Addis Ababa: Holy Trinity College, 1999), 20.

76. Daniel, Interview, 8 September 2010; Giday Beyene, "The Impact of Protestantism on the Ethiopian Orthodox Church," 26, 33; Melese Atnafu, "Conversion of Addis Ababa Population," 7–8, 18, 20; Gerimame Yohannes, "The Problem of Proselytism from EOTC to Other Denominations," BTh thesis (Addis Ababa: Holy Trinity Theological College, 2007), 12, 31; Melaku Baweke, ስውሩ አደጋ (The subtle danger), 29.

The EOC appears to resent the spread of Evangelical churches in Southern Ethiopia. Although the area is highly populated by Evangelicals EOC continues to seek to "bring them back." In fact, there is a renewed and strong campaign by Mahbere Kidusan towards the conversion of peripheral people of Southern and Western Ethiopia to the Orthodox Church and there are claims of the conversion of many, even among the *Hamer* people group, which is known for its fierce resistance to Christianity.[77] Renewed effort to "restore" those who have joined Evangelical churches is yet another evidence of EOC's perception that Ethiopia has been for EOC since the beginning of time. The memory of Christianity's coming from outside has nearly faded away. Because it is quite intertwined with the Ethiopian culture it is merely impossible to separate the two. Ayele correctly observes,

> The long-lasting coexistence in contact and inter-action between the Christian faith and the Ethiopian culture gave rise to the characteristc (sic) Christian tradition of the country. Christianity is so incarnated in the Ethiopian culture that it has become one of the constituent elements of it. This is why the pride of the Ethiopian peoples in their own Christian tradition does not admit of foreign language and expression of faith. In fact, the European tradition imported by the missionaries has always been considered foreign by the Ethiopians.[78]

Even though all missionaries did not come with superior feelings or disregard for the EOC, the distant attitude of Evangelicals sounded unpatriotic.[79]

---

77. www.eotc-mkidusan.org, Enkuan_Lelidet_Aderesachihu_2002, pdf. Describing its evangelistic campaign Mahbere Kidusan remarked, "In addition to creating an opportunity for many believers to hear the Word of God, followers of other faiths were also baptized and found sonship of the Trinity." "በርካታ ምእመናን ቃለ እግዚአብሔርን ከማግኘታቸው በተጨማሪ የሌላ እምነት ተከታዮችም በመጠመቃቸው የሥላሴን ልጅነት አግኝተዋል፡" Dereje Te'ezazu, ክህስት ሺ በላይ ኢ-አማንያን ዳግመኛ ተወላዱ. (More than three thousand unbelievers were born again), www.eotc-mkidusan.org, accessed 1 May 2011.

78. Ayele Tekelehaymanot, "The Struggle for the 'Ethiopianization' of the Roman Catholic Tradition," in *The Missionary Factor in Ethiopia* (Frankfurt: Peter Lang, 1998), 143.

79. Melese argues that the Protestant approach aims at demolishing the EOC heritage and their teaching "creates loss of patriotism, national spirit, . . . and love which is the detrimental of internal conflict and divisiveness among the members of the Orthodox Church." Melese, "Conversion of Addis Ababa Population," 12, 20. Such an accusation is believed to have originated with the Derg regime which in its formative years studied the religious institutions and their potential to pose a threat to its atheist ideology. The regime

Again conflicting messages were sent to Evangelicals. On the one hand they were regarded as unpatriotic because they tended to retreat into prayer and deferred active participation on national matters. For the Orthodox, which knew no dichotomy between national affairs and church affairs, such an approach could only be interpreted as unpatriotic.[80]

On the other hand, the involvement of the few Evangelicals in state matters was resented and presented as though they were objects of intrusion by foreign forces. Such resentment went to the extent of blaming the constitution which secured religious freedom.[81] Even the adoption by Evangelicals of EOC's clerical titles was criticized.[82] This refers to a number of Orthodox priests who became leaders of the Mekane Yesus Church and retained their titles. In fact, because of them Mekane Yesus adopted the Orthodox title ቄስ "Qes" to refer to all her ordained ministers. However, the depiction *mete* or "mission" to imply the non-authenticity of Ethiopian Evangelicals was not appreciated. Bakke, one of the Lutheran missionaries, argues,

---

rated EOC as most patriotic, Islam and Evangelicals as non-patriotic. Hence, it devised a way of keeping Islam in check. As for the Evangelicals which were minority, the regime thought it could wipe them out from the face of the country. Solomon Abebe, Pastor of YeEgziabher Birhan Church (EOC Reformed), Assela, Interview, 25 February, 2011, Addis Ababa.

80. "The EOC teaches peace and preaches love. But if any aggressor comes he will be dealt with severely. Accordingly, in the rural parts of Ethiopia, clergy members usually carry an iron staff which has the cross at its top and a sharp bottom. This is to bless with the cross the one who comes in peace and stub the one who comes with hatred." "የኢትዮጵያ ኦርቶዶክስ ተዋህዶ ቤተ ክርስቲያን ሰላምን ታስተምራለች ፍቅርን ትሰብካለች፡፡ ብኛፍ ለሚመጣውም ዋጋውን ትሰጣለች፡ ፡ በዚህ መሠረት በገጠሩ ኢትዮጵያ ያሉት ካህናት ከላይ መስቀል ከታች ሹል ያለው የብረት ዘንግ ከእጃቸው አይለዪም፡ ፡ በሰላም የመጣውን በመስቀሉ ለመባረክ በዕብዕ የመጣውን በሹሉ ለመዘርዘሩ ነው፡፡ *Tinsae*, no. 8 (1970 Eth. C), 7. This is the official publication of the church. There it is, with no apology EOC states dual role of its clergy: that of blessing with the cross and that of attacking with the blade. It seems that the cross and the blade were inseparable.

81. Tewodros Tesfaye, የማስጠንቀቂያው ደወል፤ ማርክሲዝም ዘ ከምይኒዝም የሱሳዊ ፋሺዝም ዘ ዲሞክራሲ ጥፋት በገረ እግዚአብሔር ኢትዮጵያ (The wake up call) (Addis Ababa: n.p., 2002 Eth. C), 16ff. Some Evangelicals too implied that the religious freedom (the constitution) was to blame for strange, reckless and unbiblical practices in the Evangelical stream arguing that the freedom opened the way for unrestrained actions. Paulos Fekadu, የነጻነት መዘዝ (Consequence of freedom), October 2009. The foreknown gospel singer Dereje Kebede seems to share similar convictions that the religious freedom enlarged the "narrow gate" of the church and wolves got in. Dereje Kebede, የአድናቆት ቀን ለእግዚአብሔር, vol. 9, Audio Songs, 2009.

82. Writing about the conversion of EOC priests and the establishment of Evangelical churches Merqorios resented, "የእኛን ካህናትና የእኛን ስም እንኪን ሲይዙ ለምን ያለ የለም፡" (No one questioned them when they took our priests and adopted our titles). Merqorios Arega, ታሪክህን ዕወቅ እንዳትሆን መናፍቅ (Be informed of your history so that you might not become *menafiq*) (Addis Ababa: Tinsae Zegubae Printing, 1991 Eth. C), 64.

To classify the Evangelical churches in Ethiopia today as "missions" is thus an insult, and simply not true. The removal of missionaries from the country will not result in a return to a previous stage or to the disappearance of the churches not belonging to the Orthodox fold. Whether we approve of this or not, the result is there to see. It is exemplified by persons who, combining the best from many traditions, stand on their feet, independent in relation to missionary fathers or others who might claim parental rights. The missions and missionaries have, together with others, contributed to the fostering of leaders who have found their own Ethiopian identity based on a foundation independent of the old traditional centre, the Amhara political power and the Ethiopian Orthodox Church.[83]

Therefore, neither Evangelicals nor their founding missions agree with the depiction of Evangelicals as "mission" churches or መጤ (foreign), because Evangelical Christianity which was preached by the missionaries spread, developed and took shape under the ministry of Ethiopian agents.

5.1.4. Longstanding Doctrinal Differences between EOC and Evangelicals: The Depiction of Evangelicals as *Menafiq* and "Thieves"

Before we discuss different doctrines and practices which are used to justify the *menafiq* assertion of the Orthodox Church, we shall discuss the meaning of the word *menafiq* and its general usage by Orthodox people. The root word for *menafiq* መናፍቅ is *nefeqe* "ነፈቀ" which means to waver. It is used in the context of a given religion to describe someone who does not adhere to some of the foundational beliefs. "በአንድ ሃይማኖት ውስጥ አጠቃላይ ከሆነው ከእምነቱ ድንጋጌ ውጭ ለዮት ያለ መንገድ ይዞ የሚከተልና በእምነቱ ውስጥ ያሉትን አንዳንድ መሠረታዊ ነገሮች የማይቀበል፣ ተጠራጣሪ።"[84] "ወላዋይ በያዘው የማይረጋ"[85] Its growing connotation, however, is "heretic." Historically, the term was not applied

---

83. Bakke, *Christian Ministry*, 167.
84. Amharic Dictionary, Addis Ababa, Institute of Ethiopian Languages Studies, 2001 Eth. C, 57.
85. Dereje and Beza, መቅደስ የገቡ መናፍቃን *(Menafiqan who entered the temple)* (Bahir Dar: n.p., 2008), 1.

in reference to an innocent inquirer but to someone who tended to reject or pervert the dogmas of the church or even the Bible.[86]

For example the term was used in reference to Christians who supported apartheid in South Africa. The church called them *menafiq* who in denying the brotherhood of their fellow human beings denied the fatherhood of God and were to be anathematized.[87] In the same vein the term *menafiq* is used in parallelism with the words, sinner, liar, brutal, pagan, thief and satanic.[88] The term *menafiq* is also associated with erroneous teaching.[89] People like Gragn Mohammed and Yodit who attempted to exterminate Ethiopian Christianity were also referred to as *menafiqan*.[90] In contemporary times *menafiq* is usually interchangeably used with "Protestant" in the writings of Mahbere Kidusan, but sometimes the society appears to make distinction between pagans and *menafiqan*.[91] Some writers even equate the term *menafiq* with the English word "cult."[92]

---

86. Gorgorios clearly stated, "The EOC has no dogmatic or canonical relationship with the Western Churches." Gorgorios, የኢትዮጵያ ኦርቶዶክስ ተዋህዶ ቤተ ክርስቲያን, 156. When Evangelicals are called *menafiq* they understand the connotation to be "heretic." Hailu Letta, General Manager of Agar Microfinance Sc. Co., Elder of Ketta Genet Church, Interview, 18 February 2011, Addis Ababa; Alemu Shetta (Rev), Secretary of the Evangelical Churches Fellowship of Ethiopia, Interview, 4 February 2011, Addis Ababa.

87. በኖርዌይ የተደረገው የአምነትና የሥርዓት ጉባኤ የዘር መድልዎን አወገዘ (The assembly of faith and order that was held in Norway denounced racism), *Zena Bete Kristian*, no. 96 (Pagume 5, 1977 Eth. C), 1, 4–5.

88. The writer noted that it would be better to be a believer and not a doubter, Christian and not pagan, and not doubting is better than doubting. He further wrote the "dreadfulness of being labelled as *menafiq* and pagan . . . sinner and satanic." He regards these labels as terrible damages to a person's reputation and a good name (standing), Nebiye-Leul Mengistu, ከመልካም ሽቱ መልካም ስም ይሻላል (A good name is more desirable than a good perfume), *Zena Bete Kristian*, no. 37 (Hidar 30, 1941 Eth. C), 312.

89. Here *menafiq* is attributed to people who divide the person of Christ and argue that He was omniscient in his deity but ignorant in his humanity. *Zena Bete Kristian*, no. 32 (Sene 30, 1940), 266. During the reign of Yohannes IV the three births/nativities Christology was referred to as *Nufaqe*. Paulos Gnogno, *Ate Menelik*, 3rd edition (Addis Ababa: n.p., 1999 Eth. C), 59.

90. Efrem Beyene, በኦርቶዶክስ ስም የሚነግዱ መናፍቃን በራሳቸው አንደበት ተጋለጡ (*Menafiqan* under the pretence of Orthodox disclosed themselves), *Lisane Tewahdo ZeOrtodox*, no. 9 (1987 Eth. C), 46.

91. Niqu (Beware), *Sime'a Tsidq ZeOrtodox Tewahdo* 18, no. 209 (Meskerem 16–30, 2003 Eth. C), 10ff; Fetlework Desta, ከተለያዩ ሀገረ ስብከቶች የተውጣጡ ሠልጣኞች ተመረቁ (Trainees from several dioceses graduated), www.eotc-mkidusan.org, accessed 7 March 2011.

92. Esubalew, የግላጭ ይጆች, 237–238. At times Evangelicals too use the word in reference to faith teachers, Jehovah's Witnesses and Jesus Only (Oneness Pentecostalism) adherents. *Kale Heywet*, no. 26 (1995 Eth. C), 23.

The common rationale behind the usage of the term in reference to Evangelicals has to do with their faith and practices; thus the association of Evangelicals with heretics is not a new development. Rather, all of the charges brought against Isenberg, the eighteenth-century CMS missionary, were echoed in one way or another against Evangelicals. Isenberg was accused of blasphemy against God and the saints, disturbing the country by false doctrine and strange religious practices, and turning private houses into churches. All of these accusations were held against Evangelicals over the years.[93]

Most of the arguments used to question the unorthodoxy of Evangelicals have to do with Christology, bibliology, ecclesiology and Mariology. Out of these the doctrine of the Bible and Mary are the chief ones and will be discussed in detail later on. In a book prepared by the Council of Scholars of the church three things are mentioned to validate the label *menafiqan* towards Evangelicals: first the Bible they have is incomplete because it has only sixty-six books. Second, Evangelicals do not know books designated by the apostles such as the Synod. Third, they have no books of canon law which were set apart by the scholars of the church under the guidance of the Holy Spirit.[94]

Now we shall discuss the doctrinal differences which are used to refer to Evangelicals as *menafiq*. One of the most attacked doctrines of Evangelicals is *sola fide* which Orthodox followers consider to be devoid of good works. Theologians of the church fear that the emphasis laid on faith alone for salvation would lead the nation into lawlessness.[95] In other words, they accuse

---

93. "A thief in stealing the faith" was one of the accusations made against Isenberg in the 19th century. Aren, *Evangelical Pioneers to Ethiopia*, 66.

94. The scholars did not use the word "Evangelical" to qualify who exactly they had in mind when writing about *menafiqan* but from the context of the book, it is clear that they are referring to Evangelicals. መጽሐፍቱ ጎደሎ ነው፤ በሐዋርያት የተወሰኑ እንደ ሲኖዶስ ያሉ መጻሕፍትን አታውቁትም፤ በመንፈስ ቅዱስ ተመርተው የቤተ ክርስቲያን ሊቃውንት የወሰኗቸው የቀኖና መጻሕፍት የሉአችሁም። ዑቅ ኢያስሕትክሙ፤ እንዳያስትችሁ ተጠንቀቁ, መናፍቁ ጌታቸው "ጌድል ወይስ ጌደል" በማለት ለጻፈው የሀይደት ትምህርት ከኢትዮጵያ ኦርቶዶክስ ተዋሕዶ ቤተ ክርስቲያን ሊቃውንት ጉባኤ የተሰጠ መልስ (Beware not to be deceived, a reply from the Council of Scholars of the Ethiopian Orthodox Tewahdo Church to the apostasy writing of the *menafiq*. Getachew, "Gedil Weys Gedel," (Addis Ababa: Tinsae Zegubae Printing, 1996 Eth. C), 10, 20.

95. ንቁ (Beware), *Sime'a Tsidq ZeOrthodox Tewahdo* 18, no. 209 (Meskerem 16–30, 2003 Eth. C), 13; Esubalew Belete, የገሃነም ደጆች (Gates of hell), 390. But Misikire Birhan presented balanced teaching. In fact, it featured a painting of a person riding a chariot with inscriptions

Evangelicals of teaching that regardless of how a person leads his life, "as long as he comes to the hall of Evangelicals at the end of the week and shouts, he is saved, but such a teaching does not produce good citizens."[96] In other words, the justification of the usage of *menafiq* extends to the Evangelicals' supposed lesser place for fasting and almsgiving.

Another doctrinal basis of difference is the priesthood of all believers and the administration of gifts of the Holy Spirit. A writer on Mahbere Kidusan's publication notes, "Everyone claims to have been anointed, everyone wants to lay hands on, and everyone who feels warmed up is a healer and anyone who feels like it speaks in tongues and everyone who wishes to be a pastor would become one and the end result is splitting."[97] The argument here has to do with the Evangelical doctrine of the church, which gives room for all believers to claim to have gifts and that some use this as a means to split the church.

In addition to the weak structures of Evangelical churches, the doctrine of Christ is used to accuse them as *menafiqan*. Evangelicals accept the Council of Chalcedon's declaration about the natures of Christ. Therefore, at times, they are accused of believing that the two natures existed in separation without unity.[98] Moreover, the intercessory role of Christ poses a serious problem to the Orthodox because it nullifies the need for human or angelic intercessors, most importantly, Mary. At times the question is framed around the divine nature of Christ. The Orthodox Church asserts that Christ is the one who accepts intercession and not the one who offers it.

"Work" on one of the wheels and "Faith" on the other, thus, it showed the inseparability of both. Misikire Birhan (Megabit and Miazia, 1958 Eth. C), 7.

96. Daniel, Interview, 8 September, 2010. One of the publications of Mahbere Kidusan, attempts to unpack the implications behind salvation by grace. "There is no use in claiming that one is saved by grace while having empty life; instead, there must be obedience to the law and commandments of the gospels. How is Salvation in Christ Alone?" Deacon Dejene, "በፀጋው መዳን እንዴት ነው?" (What does salvation by grace mean?), *Hamer*, no. 4 (Hidar 1988 Eth. C), 23, 25.

97. "ሁሉ ባላቀባት፣ ሁሉ እጁ ጨኻ፣ የሞቀው ሁሉ ፈዋሽ፣ ያማረው ሁሉ ልሳን ተናጋሪ፣ የወደደ ሁሉ ፓስተር እየሆነ መባተተን ነው።"የገሃገም ደጆች፣ *Sem'ea Tsidq* 10, no. 77 (Yekatit 1995 Eth. C), 14.

98. Daniel Kibret, ኦርቶዶክስ መልስ አላት፣ ከፕሮቴስታንቶች ለሚነሱ እንዳንድ ጥያቄዎች የተሰጡ መልሶች (Orthodox replies: Answers given for some of the questions raised by Protestants) (Addis Ababa: n.p., 2000 Eth. C), 2.

To this end it has gone as far as altering New Testament passages such as Romans 8:34[99] which speak about the intercession of Christ. The new EOC version of the Bible reads, "the one who judges (የሚፈርድው) on our behalf." Also the new translation has dropped "God" from 2 Corinthians 1:3; Ephesians 1:3 and 1 Peter 1:3 and reads, "the Father of our Lord Jesus Christ."[100] This has alarmed some Evangelicals and Orthodox alike as a clear deviation from the assertions of the Bible, and as a grave precedent which opens the door for endless alterations based on human reason and institutional preference.[101]

Yilma Getahun, Secretary of the Bible Society of Ethiopia, notes that the EOC version of the Bible was not produced in order to make some alterations, as it is widely assumed by Evangelicals. According to him, since the fall of Communism the Orthodox churches including those in Eastern Europe have been asking the United Bible Societies for revised editions of the Bible for Orthodox churches based on the Septuagint and the former translations in their respective ancient languages. The Ethiopian Orthodox version therefore, is to be seen against this background.[102]

---

99. In his book entitled Milja Erqe Ena Selam, Aleqa Ayalew Tamiru who was the head of the Council of Scholars of the Orthodox Church, argued that the phrase in the Amharic Bible which says "the one who intercedes on our behalf" is wrong (ጥፋት ነው). He based his arguments against the passage on the words of Jesus in John 17:4 that he brought the Father glory by completing the work the Father gave him to do. According to Aleqa Ayalew, the passage in John implies that Jesus has finished his work. Once he has finished his work, there is no new ministry of intercession. ". . . ክረገ በአብ ቀኝ ከተቀመጠ በኋላ አዲስ አገልግሎት የሆነ ተቀምጦ ምልጃ የለምና . . ." Ayalew Tamiru, Milja Ena Erqe Selam, 1992 Eth. C, 28. (Quoted by Dereje and Beza, *Meqdes Yegebu Menafiqan*, 93.)

100. The variance in Rom 8:34 is indicated in the footnote that the Septuagint says "intercedes." Similar alteration of the word "intercedes" is applied in reference to the Holy Spirit in Rom 8:26 followed by a footnote that states that there is a wide difference between the Ge'ez version and that of the Septuagint but it does not say what the difference is. However, no footnote explanation is offered for the variance created in dropping "God" from Pauline and Peter's epistles. The Amharic Bible with the Old Testament based on Septuagint published by the Ethiopian Bible Society for the Ethiopian Orthodox Church, 2007. Mahbere Bekur voiced its strong opposition to the alteration. Editor, "አቤት!. . . አቤት! የ. . . . ያሁ!" *(Appeal), Chora*, no. 36 (n.d.).

101. Agizachew Tefera (Deacon), Editor-in-Chief of *Chora*, the Publication of Mahbere Bekur, Interview, 13 June 2011.

102. According to Yilma, scholars of the Orthodox Church with assistance of experts from United Bible Society worked on the translation for fourteen years. Dr Mikre Sellassie and foreign consultants examined the translation before its printing. Yilma Getahun, Secretary of the Bible Society of Ethiopia, Interview, 5 October 2010, Addis Ababa.

Yilma expresses his perplexity on the numerous non-constructive criticisms and asks, "Do not Protestants have more than thirty versions of the Bible? Why is it suddenly a problem when the Orthodox Church wished to have its own?" However, the Orthodox scholars have not disregarded the feedback they got from Orthodox and Evangelicals alike. Yilma notes that currently, the team is doing a revision and expressed his confidence that the revised version will address the concerns on a number of passages including Romans 8:34.[103]

In addition to accusing Evangelicals of heresy, the Orthodox Church also resents its members' flocking into the Protestant churches,[104] calling Protestants "thieves."[105] Such developments worry the Orthodox Church because numbers are power; the more members the Protestants acquire, the more important they will be, overshadowing the ancient church.[106] Regarding the recent statistical growth of the Evangelicals Daniel comments, "It is acquired through sheep-stealing. Some members of the Orthodox Church have found registration in the Evangelical churches and that is all there is to it. The Bible says, "'you will know them by their fruits' and it would be silly to expect an orange from a thorn bush. They are thieves."[107]

---

103. Yilma, Interview, 19 April, 2011, Addis Ababa.

104. Usually the term "proselytism" is used to describe the act. Historically, however, a proselyte was a Gentile who became a Jew, and those accepted the obligations of Torah and circumcision. To the knowledge of the writer, with the exception of the Mekane Yesus Church, the other Evangelical churches re-baptize people who come from the EOC. Perhaps this is one of the main reasons why EOC theologians refer to the conversion of Orthodox to Evangelical faith as an act of "proselytism."

105. The EOC accuses Evangelicals of breaking the policy of WCC against sheep-stealing among its members. Ethiopian Orthodox Church's Council of Scholars, ሃይማኖት ያለያን መቃብር አንድ አያደርግንም (What a religion has separated a burial site will not unite) (Addis Ababa: EOC, 1987 Eth. C), 46. Both Daniel and Mekonnen also assume that all Evangelical churches are members of the WCC and wonder why as forerunners in establishing World Council of Churches, do not abide by its regulations against sheep-stealing. Daniel, Interview, 8 September, 2010; Mekonnen, Interview, 15 November, 2010. The fact of the matter is except for Mekane Yesus, none of the Evangelical churches is a member of WCC because it is considered liberal. Even Mekane Yesus's membership is through the Lutheran World Federation.

106. Melese, "Conversion of Addis Ababa Population," 18.

107. Daniel, Interview, 8 September 2010.

Evangelicals' door-to-door and street evangelism in towns and even rural places angered the EOC.[108] The Orthodox Church considered their action as invading people's privacy and provoking the church to defend itself. In fact, door-to-door evangelism was regarded as inviting trouble, and an expression of the highest disrespect for the EOC. From the EOC's point of view Evangelicals initiated trouble by verbally attacking it and proselytizing its members. Unfortunately, the EOC's attempts to defend itself at times got out of hand.[109]

Some Orthodox theologians believe that Evangelicals have an agenda to weaken the ancient church and wonder why.[110] The Council of Scholars noted, "*menafiqan* are envious of the vibrancy of our church, thus, endeavour to make it as empty as theirs."[111] The public expresses its disapproval of "proselytism" by declaring, "ማተቤን አልበጥስም" (I will not remove my cord).[112] Regarding the "sheep stealing" of Evangelicals, Aba Gorgorios, the late Archbishop of Shewa, remarked:

> Since the sixteenth century, they have been spying the country coming with different forms. Currently they are taking many believers out of their church. This is not gospel preaching, but an open invasion. Detaching a person from his history and tradition by means of huge sum of money is not the will of

---

108. Sorsa Sumamo, *Bivocational Missionary-Evangelist: The Story of an Itinerant Preacher in Northern Sidama* (Canada: Enterprise Publications, 2002), 65.

109. Daniel, Interview, 8 September, 2010. But not all preachers forced their message on people. W/ro Roman H/Mariam, the pioneer woman evangelist of Kale Heywet Church in Addis speaks of sharing the gospel with those who were willing to listen. She would go from house to house and ask people if they would like to hear the Word of God. Roman H/Mariam, Interview, Kale Heywet, no. 2 (1985 Eth. C), 16.

110. Daniel, Interview, 8 September 2010; Mekonnen, Interview, 15 November, 2010; Asrat Kebede, Editor-in-Chief of Sem'ea Tsidq, one of the publications of Mahbere Kidusan, Interview, 30 December 2010, Addis Ababa; Informant G, Interview, February 2011.

111. "መናፍቃን ምቀኞች ስለሆኑ ምን ጊዜም በቤተ ክርስቲያናችን ላይ የወረራ ዘመቻ የሚያካሄዱትም፣ የእኛን ቤተ ክርስቲያን እንደ እነሱ ሰው አልባ አድርገው ለማስቀረት ነው።" The EOTC Council of Scholars, እንዳያስቱችሁ ተጠንቀቁ, 5.

112. Posted on taxi, 12 November 2010. The baptismal cord (a black thread tied around a throat) is important in the EOC because it signifies belongingness to the Orthodox Church. The removal of it connotes apostasy. If it is said, "so and so has removed (cut) his cord" it means the person has left the faith. It even implied converting to Islam. Paulos Gnogno, *Ate Menelik*, 3rd edition (Addis Ababa: n.p., 1999 Eth. C), 66.

the Holy Spirit but Satan. Believers should be alert not to be like Esau who sold his birthright in exchange for lentil stew.[113]

Here we recall the account of a dream of a former Orthodox adherent in which he saw himself pulling down the old church in order to build a new one. The convert whom Aren refers to as Haile-Ab understood his dream as a call of the Lord to ministry and it is not clear whether the missionaries tried to correct his views on pulling down the old church. Rather his dream seems to be understood as an impact of his access to the Scriptures in Amharic. According to Aren his devoted study of the Bible gave birth to a concern for church reform and proclamation of the gospel.[114]

The Orthodox have a major problem with such notions, and wonder, "Why dismantle the old church?"[115] Mahbere Kidusan does not seem to wonder whether Evangelicals were intent on dismantling the old church, rather it asserts with certainty that the whole plan is to destroy the church and in so doing, the country. According to the association, all the conferences and campaigns of m*enafiqan* aim to weaken the nation's love for its country and nothing else. The association accuses not only the Ethiopian *menafiqan*, but others all over the world.

A case in point is the sermon of a pastor of Rhema church in which he reportedly said that there was no blessing in being poor; if that were the case Ethiopia would have been the most blessed country in the world. His sermon is presented as evidence that *menafiqan* have not only done no good for this country, but nothing good comes out of their mouth concerning Ethiopia.[116] It is possible that the pastor was propagating prosperity gospel, because that was the distinguishing mark of the Rhema church in the mid 1990s.

Getatchew expresses similar feelings towards the planting of new churches by the missionaries. He states his respect towards those who converted to Evangelical Christianity from traditional religions, but feels outrage towards

---

113. Gorgorios, የኢትዮጵያ ኦርቶዶክስ ተዋህዶ ቤተ ክርስቲያን ታሪክ፣, 156.

114. Aren, *Evangelical Pioneers*, 187.

115. Getatchew Haile, "Missionary Dream," 7. Giday explicitly argues that Protestant missionaries aimed to "eradicate" EOC's culture, religion and tradition and "to plant the new religion – Protestantism." Giday, "The Impact of Protestantism on the Ethiopian Orthodox Church," 33.

116. Editorial, *Hamer*, no. 5 (Tahsas/Tir, 1993 Eth. C), 4.

those who converted from the Orthodox.[117] For the most part Evangelicals refrain from public criticism of the Orthodox Church, but when some prominent preachers started to speak of their resentment towards the Orthodox Church, their criticisms were considered provocative.

For example, the remarks of Dr Tolossa, well-known Evangelical preacher, echoing the conclusion of the Derg that the Orthodox Church is to blame for the backwardness of the nation, provoked a lot of anger from the Orthodox.[118] Although he was not the first one to blame the church of the backwardness of the nation,[119] his statements have ever since been used to build arguments against Evangelicals.[120]

In a sense, Dr Tolossa's remarks sound as though they come out of utter frustration over the poverty of the nation, which has not changed despite the presence of Christianity for seventeen centuries. However, the Christianity in view has a different theology of poverty and suffering. Its understanding of the signs of righteousness is far from that of the popular prosperity gospel. Poverty is not a sign of divine displeasure, neither is self-denial foolishness. On the contrary, the ascetic life is sought for. Thus, the more people are committed to God the more they ought to despise this world and this means

---

117. Getatchew Haile, "Missionary Dream," 7.

118. "Lord Jesus is forgotten. Be mindful, go to monasteries and visit them to see what they read. They do not even know the Bible! How can one become a monk without the knowledge of the Bible? This shows the depth of the nation's failure; the extent of our misleading . . . because of this Ethiopians have grasped neither the earthly things nor the heavenly ones. The only way for Ethiopia to be free from this destituteness is to eradicate this fruitless faith, which has held her soul captive for so long." Quoted by Melaku Baweke, ስውሩ አደጋ (The subtle danger), 28. (Translation by the researcher).

119. During the rise of the Derg, such sentiment was common. Religious organizations, EOC being the prime one, were accused of misleading the nation. The Orthodox Church was accused of assigning most of the days of the month as sacred days in which working on the farm was not allowed. Belay Woldeyes, "ሃይማኖት በኢትዮጵያ ላይ ለይን," 5.

120. In his book written in response to Dr Tolosa's remarks about the Orthodox, Melaku indiscriminately criticizes Protestants and refers to them as "Enemies of this [Orthodox] Church who are born of the missionaries, but not God." "ከእግዚአብሔር ሳይሆን ከሚስዮናውያን የተወለዱ የሀገሪቱ ቤተ ክርስቲያን ጠላቶች" and admonishes fellow Orthodox adherents to ask the fathers of the church when they have questions, instead of going to these enemies of the church who are blinded in the spirit of business and denominationalism. "ጥያቄ ሲያጋጥም በድርጅት እና በንግድ መንፈስ ወደ ታወሩትና የሀገሪቱ ቤተ ክርስቲያን ጠላቶች ወደ ሆኑት ሳይሆን ወደ ቤተ ክርስቲያን አባው ሂንደ ሃይሀ ጥይቅ" Melaku, ስውሩ አደጋ, 9, 88–89. In demonizing Protestants with whom he worked together once, he seems to be trying to make it up to his church and build confidence among the Orthodox followers about his recommitment to his church and severance of his relationship with the Protestants.

detaching themselves from the world and all that it has to offer. However, it can be argued that the numerous holidays of the church in which working is not allowed, and the legendary lifestyle of the wandering student who supports himself through begging while studying, may have affected the work ethic of the nation.[121]

The clergy, however, believe that such remarks indicate of the disregard of the Evangelicals for the EOC's contribution towards the preservation of Christianity and the existence of the nation as a whole. In fact, they wonder why Evangelicals continue to attack the EOC without taking into consideration what has happened to Christianity in Europe, the land of their "spiritual ancestors." An EOC priest remarked, "The churches in Europe are turning into night clubs. This shows that the foundation of the faith was not truthful. What I do not understand is why Evangelicals insist on converting the ancient Orthodox Church into Lutheranism instead of maintaining it. I just do not get it. What good has Lutheranism done on its soil? This makes me wonder what the agenda of Evangelicals is."[122]

However, the Bible readers within the EOC claim to have been persecuted because of their desire to study and teach the Bible and portions of it in the vernaculars; concluding that, among other things, the EOC's active persecution of Bible readers has led to the establishment of other churches.

---

121. A writer for Mahbere Kidusan argues that the lifestyle of "yeqolo temari" is to be looked upon as cost sharing and, not begging. www.eotc-mkidusan.org, T/Selassie Tsega Kiros, አብነት ትምህርት ቤቱ "በእንት ስማ ለማርያም" ይዘከራል፣ accessed 5 May 2011. The begging can be compared to the modern fund raising, which is also a kind of begging, but it opens the way for students to cover their expenses. Thus, it may not be fair to question the work ethics of the Wandering Students who live out "give us today our daily bread" in order to focus on their painstaking studies.

122. Informant G, Interview, February 2011. Moreover, what is currently going on in Protestant churches in Europe is considered as representative of Evangelicalism in general. Churches are being sold, homosexuals are married in the church; consequently the pews of Protestant churches in Europe are empty. EOTC Council of Scholars, እንዳያቴችሁ ተጠንቀቁ፣ 7. Mahbere Kidusan presents such facts as evidence that it was not of God to begin with. It quotes the words of Evangelist Tariku that Protestantism is diminishing in its origin "የፕሮቴስታንቱ ዓለም ምንጭ በይ እየሆነ ነው።" Mahbere Kidusan added, first the Spirit of God and subsequently the people abandoned Protestantism. "መጀመሪያ መንፈስ እግዚአብሔር ተለየው በኋላም ሕዝቡ ተለየው።" የገሃገም ይጆች, Sem'ea Tsidq 10, no. 77 (Yekatit 1995 Eth. C), 14. "It is not in Ethiopia, but in the countries which the people of the 'menafiq' spread immensely, Christianity has lost its fervour and churches are being empty." "በአሁኑ ጊዜ የክርስትና ትምህርት እየዘዘነና የአባያት ክርስቲያን ሕንጻዎችም ሰው አልባ ሆነው እየቀሩ በመዘጋት ላይ የሚገኙት የመናፍቁ ወገኖች በስፋት በተቀሳቀሱበቸው ሀገሮች እንጂ፣ በኢትዮጵያ አይደለም።, EOTC Council of Scholars, እንዳያቴችሁ ተጠንቀቁ፣ 4–5.

Solomon Tilahun, the former dean of Pentecostal Theological College, observed that the church structures are also to share the blame for the flocking of its members to Evangelical churches. According to him the overemphasis on traditional approach with little attention paid to its relevance is among the reasons why people leave the church. He added, "The Evangelical claim for experiential relationship with the Lord and deliverance from different addictions such as drug use, tobacco, sexual immorality and so on provides a powerful testimony and attracts people to Evangelical churches."[123]

In a dramatic turn of events the Mahbere Kidusan's media claimed the conversion of multitudes to Orthodox Christianity because of an angelic visitation inside a cave in Gamo, Southern Ethiopia. Evangelicals in the area were accused of denouncing the noise heard coming out of the cave as satanic, but the alleged supernatural occurrences persisted, causing both the Orthodox and government authorities to examine the claims. According to *Hamer*,[124] the end result was conversion of multitudes because of the revelation of angels who told them that there was only one true faith, which is Orthodox Christianity. "As for the other faiths," the angels told them, "they will vanish."[125]

It appeared as though the Orthodox Church was vindicated by the alleged decision of some Evangelical Christians to join it; just as Aba Gorgorios urged them to do nearly forty-three years ago, "To our brothers who are wandering in other Western churches, we urge them your country is the one and only Ethiopia, your identity is based on your faith as expressed in one Orthodox Tewahdo church, so think about it right now."[126]

---

123. Solomon Tilahun, Former Dean of Pentecostal Theological College, Interview, 2 September 2010.

124. *Hamer* is the magazine of Mahbere Kidusan which is issued every other month.

125. According to *Hamer*, a government official who supposedly went into the cave said that he saw holy objects dedicated to the Trinity, Mary, etc and also a writing which read, "Jesus is Lord." The alleged converts included former Kale Heywet Church members who presumably joined the EOC. "የቦረዳው ድንቅ ዋሻ "(The marvellous cave of Boreda), *Hamer*, no. 1 (Tir 1985 Eth. C), 15–16, 24. An Orthodox priest remarked, "Those who convert to Protestantism do it for material benefit and at times because of administerial problems in the Orthodox Church, but those who come back to the Orthodox Church surely come back out of conviction that indeed the Orthodox Church is the true Church of Christ." Informant G, Interview, February, 2011.

126. Gorgorios, የኢትዮጵያ ኦርቶዶክስ ተዋህዶ ቤተ ክርስቲያን ታሪክ, 156. Mahbere Kidusan reported that more than 400 people were baptized into the EOC from Gumuz people group

However Ato Desta Anjejo, the Secretary of Gamo Kale Heywet Church, who is originally from Boreda area, says that the story was fabricated and there never was any angelic appearance. According to him, the man who claimed all this was a spiritually troubled man, and the family has been under the influence of ancestral spirits for a long time.[127]

As for the Evangelicals' reaction to the *menafiq* label, they do not accept it because they do not deny the Trinity, nor the deity of Christ. Some get annoyed because they feel that those who call them *menafiq* do not have adequate knowledge of the Bible.[128] In their book entitled *Meqdes Yegebu Menafiqan*, the authors, who refer to themselves as deacons of the Orthodox Church, use the term *menafiq* differently. They used it in reference to Orthodox adherents who fabricate anti-scriptural hagiographies in the name of saints and those who accept such traditions and writings as authoritative.[129]

5.1.5. The Ethiopian Orthodox Church's Perception of Pentecostals

Pentecostals are treated here separately because of the unprecedented way in which their spread impacted the relationship between Evangelicals and the Orthodox Church. Generally speaking, the so-called mainline Evangelical churches such as Mekane Yesus and Kale Heywet, tried to avoid a direct clash with the EOC over the years. As a result of painful intermittent conflict, they learnt to find ways of co-existing with the Orthodox. In particular, their

---

in Western Ethiopia. Berihun Tefera, for Mahbere Kidusan, http://www.eotc-mkidusan.org, accessed 12 March 2011.

127. He said that there is a small spring that flows out of the cave and the area is surrounded by forest. Desta said that he went inside the cave and examined it for himself after the claim of supernatural occurrences. Desta also denied any conversion of Kale Heywet members and asserted that the alleged converts are members of Kale Heywet Church and still living in that area. He confirmed that many EOC members come into the area hoping for healing, they drink from the water, apply the clay on their skin, etc., but there is no tangible healing or deliverance. According to him the whole thing is demonic. Desta Birhanu, the Secretary of Gamo Kale Heywet Church, Interview via telephone, 12 April 2011. Cf. Memhir Getachew, ገድለ ወይስ ገደል, (Addis Ababa: n.p., 1995 Eth. C), 72.

128. Bezuayehu Abera, Former devout Orthodox follower currently member of Gospel Light Church, Interview, 14 February 2011, Addis Ababa; Engidash Markos, Secretary of Publication Department at the Evangelical Theological College, Interview, 18 February 2011, Addis Ababa.

129. Dereje and Beza, *Meqdes Yegebu Menafiqan*, 6–9; Getachew, ገድለ ወይስ ገደል, 119.

numerical growth in the rural areas of southern and south-western Ethiopia which were not strong territory for the EOC was not considered a strong threat to the existence of the Orthodox Church.

The coming of the Pentecostal/Charismatic movement, however, changed both the face of Evangelical Christianity and opened a new chapter of severe persecution upon Evangelicals. Pentecostalism "invaded" the cities and the towns which were the territory of the Orthodox and infuriated both the government and the church. Eshete notes, "By and large, Evangelical Christianity had been a southern phenomenon and was viewed as the religion of the peripheral people. The Pentecostal movement introduced a new shift as its presence was felt in the central and northern regions of Ethiopia . . . the young Pentecostals targeted their Orthodox peers and broke into areas that had been closed to Western missionaries. In so doing they posed challenges to the national church in ways missionaries had not done before."[130]

The phenomenal Pentecostal movement brought to the centre of attention what had been safely labelled as *tsere Mariam* and more or less confined to the peripheral people.[131] Consequently, Evangelicals who were formerly referred to as "Mission" (to imply their association with the foreign missionaries), were collectively given a new name. With the rise and subsequent spread of the formidable Pentecostal movement, the public halted the name "Mission" and took up *Pente*[132] as the badge of identity for all Evangelicals.

The movement among the youth was not tolerated by the ancient church, nor by the Ministry of the Interior. The chief of public security issued a letter on 9 November 1971 in an attempt to halt the spread of Pentecostalism.

---

130. Eshete, *Evangelical Movement*, 182.

131. Bezabih, Interview, 25 February 2011; Bekele, Wolde Kidan, Senior Pastor of Mulu Wongel Church, 25 August 2010, Addis Ababa.

132. Most likely the dwellers of Addis took the prefix "Pente" from the adjective "Pentecosteawi" in Amharic and ever since the name was used to refer to all Evangelicals. As the time of its first usage, some sources say that it was started in the late 1950s in the Haile Sellassie University. Getachew Belete, *Agony and Hallelujah*, 53. Eshete writes that the mob attack on Pentecostals in smaller towns and later on in Addis was widely covered by the media which referred to the group as followers of unknown religion. Because of these incidents "the term 'Pente' entered into the public usage." Eshete, *Evangelical Movement*, 178. There was wide propaganda against youth movement in the schools after the fall of the imperial regime. Addis Zemen gazette accuses the followers of "Pentecoste" as attempting to hinder the revolution. Yirga Haile Mariam, በሃይማኖት ስም የሚነግዱ ወጣቶን ከትግል መድረክ ለማዘናጋት በጀር አብዮተኞች የሚደርግ ደባ፣ Addis Zemen (Ginbot 12, 1971 Eth. C), 9.

The letter was sent to all government and military officials, the Orthodox parishes and school directors. It "accused Pentecostals of engaging in antisocial and immoral activities such as promiscuous sexual engagements and duping of young men and women to make them believe in miracles through concocted stories of miraculous healing. The letter . . . alleged that the Pentecostal movement was not only illegal but dangerous to the unity of the nation and had to be suppressed by all means."[133]

Such an official letter validated the harassment of Pentecostals and they appealed to the emperor, who gave them audience in the presence of the Minister of Justice on 26 April 1972. He listened to their pleas and advised them to work out their problems with the EOC. They tried to talk to the Patriarch but to no avail. He mocked, "why do you want to open a kiosk when there is already a large mall?" What followed was open arrest of Pentecostals throughout the country. They were thrown into prison without being tried in court. They were tortured and their hair was shaved. The EOC was a main collaborator in their persecution.[134] Eshete observes that greater forces apart from mere religious motifs were behind the conflict. "The issue is not religion per se; it has a great deal to do with that of national identity, and for that matter, an identity that apparently seems to have been misconstrued as immutable and fixed. Any innovation or reform attempt that falls outside the doctrine of the Orthodox Church is considered a transgression or sin and is therefore condemned."[135]

The Pentecostals on the other hand were passionate to challenge such a fixed identity by redefining spirituality along ethical lines. The need for personal conversion which was emphasized by the missionaries was furthered by Pentecostals. They vehemently rejected the soteriology of the Orthodox members, in which salvation came was by virtue of belonging to the national church. They boldly preached on streets, in their work places and to their neighbours. The aggressive evangelism accompanied with miracles resulted in Orthodox people flocking into their churches. They drew clear boundaries

---

133. Eshete, *Evangelical Movement*, 178.
134. Eshete, 180–181.
135. Eshete, 182.

between sacred and secular which meant that any activity which did not explicitly promote the preaching of the gospel was considered as secular.¹³⁶

The Orthodox were provoked by the unprecedented sheep-stealing by Pentecostals and was annoyed with their worship services which made room for emotions to surface in the church. To the Orthodox who are used to maintaining solemness in the church and who stand still in the presence of God, the loud services of Pentecostals in which people freely moved from place to place were abominable.¹³⁷ In addition to the active preaching, the great emphasis on manifestations of the gifts of the Holy Spirit attracted onlookers who for the most part were Orthodox adherents and ended up joining Pentecostals.

Some of the actions of Pentecostals constituted a conscious departure from the traditional expressions of Christianity. Generally speaking, the term "tradition" connoted something which is passed on and adopted with little or no reflection. Thus, they do not want to say "the faith of my ancestors" but "my faith." Such isolation of oneself from the community was detestable to the Orthodox. Pentecostals, however, did not show high regard for the Orthodox or for the older Evangelical churches.¹³⁸ The way Pentecostalism changed the expression of Ethiopian Evangelical Christianity and the opposition its radical actions generated, were at times resented even by other Evangelicals.¹³⁹

---

136. They were accused of promoting "This world is not my home" mentality. Belay Woldeyes, ሃይማኖት በኢትዮጵያ ላይ ላይን (An overview of religion in Ethiopia), Yezareyitu Ethiopia (Tir 10, 1967 Eth. C), 5.

137. Nigusse remarked that such a noise is not always justifiable, but should also be looked in view of practical problem of not having their own place of worship. Many churches rent residences and worship in canopies. Not having their own place is a major problem. Nigusse Bulcha, Interview, 30 September 2010, Addis Ababa.

138. During Christmas in 1993 the Asosa Mulu Wongel Church dispatched a letter of invitation to a conference to numerous bodies including the Orthodox Church in the area. The reply from the EOC administrator of the region was full of rage. He called them "children of Luther" and considered the invitation as provocative and satanic. "How dare you invite the ancient Church to teach the Word of God. They were warned to refrain from such satanic act. The letter also stated that since they are children of the Devil and Arius, they are not called to preach the gospel and noted, "do not forget who you are and the extent of your power." "ምንታችሁንና አቅማችሁን ከውጣሁ እንድትመጥኑ እናሳስባለን፡," Girma Zewde, *Ethiopis*, vol. 2 (Addis Ababa: n.p., 1992 Eth. C), 100–101.

139. Solomon Tilahun, a teacher and Christian writer remarks, "As for the Pentecostal movement, I think it has played a major role for the expansion of Evangelical faith. If it were not for the coming of Pentecostal movement I presume we would have been less

As far as the Orthodox Church was concerned, there was little distinction between the decades old Evangelical churches and the new emerging Pentecostal movement; for they all had their origin in Luther. All were Lutherans who day and night dreamt about ways of stealing the flock of EOC. Thus, the "provocation" by the Pentecostals resulted in the persecution of all Evangelicals.

5.1.6. Concluding Remarks

The ever-growing negative descriptions of Evangelical Christians appear to include more and more unfounded accusations and slanders. Evangelicals who for a long time were a small minority, but now have shown a substantial growth, are no longer simply remaining on the receiving end of the attack; but some are lashing out through other media by openly attacking the Orthodox's devotion to Mary and the saints.

Some EOC followers on the other hand attack Luther as the founder of Evangelicalism.[140] The inference is that Lutherans[141] promote division, selfishness, and ethno-centrisism just like their founder.[142] However ridiculous for informed persons, the general public believes such stories. In a society which makes little distinction between a person and his or her thoughts, such slander can be effective.[143]

---

in number but stronger in doctrine and sober in practice. Pentecostalism has given birth to people who are countless in number but non Evangelical in their doctrine." Solomon Tilahun, Interview 2 September 2010, Addis Ababa. "The loud prayer which was not common before Pentecostalism has made us very unpopular. More and more provocative teaching and sermons also developed with the coming of Pentecostalism." Getachew Belete, Interview, 18 August 2010.

140. *Hamere* Tewahdo (Nehasse 2002 Eth. C), 35–60.

141. The researcher uses this term to represent all Protestants.

142. Esubalew, ፖ'ሃ፣ም ይጀቸ, 83–92, 412. The EOC is credited with doing similar things (e.g. defending the country against foreign intrusion) which Esubalew accuses Luther with, and also EOC is accused of some of the alleged wrongs which Luther is charged with, e.g. promoting the dominance of Northern rulers, refusing to recognize people of other faiths as Ethiopians and labelling them as unauthentic, holding on to the ancient Ge'ez and Amharic as proper languages of the church and refusing to translate the liturgy into other Ethiopian mother-tongues. Moreover, Evangelicals are openly accused by EOC members as failing to appreciate indigenous expressions of Christianity. Thus, accusing Luther of patriotism which Evangelicals are accused of not showing appears to contradict each other.

143. Esubalew, who claims to have had converted to Protestantism in his disillusionment, but now restored to the true church, lashes back with the darkest images possible: black Protestants (perhaps to imply that Protestantism is the faith of the white people), jihadists, murderers, propagandists, gates of hell, white-man worshippers, witnesses of falsehood,

Some of the statements against Evangelicals arise out of resentment of their indiscriminate criticism of Orthodoxy and their having numerous factions as opposed to the unified EOC. Moreover, Menelik's popular word of caution about foreigners' strategy to take over Ethiopia is not forgotten: "First the missionary, then the consul, then the soldier." Hence, even "pagans" joining Evangelicals was not considered with favour; worse still was converting from EOC to Protestantism. Such an action was considered as betraying the national colours and all that they stood for.

However, even though they may not be aware of it, Evangelicals have developed a tradition of their own, and usually do things in a given pattern, paying great attention to the views of their founders. In the case of the relatively new churches, the pastors assume great authority over the believers.[144] Unfortunately, the backbiting among Evangelicals and their taking their cases to court was a stumbling block for the Orthodox; the admiration which Evangelicals' once enjoyed due to their upright life style, is now being eroded.[145]

There is enough evidence to show that some of the persecution by and conflict with the Orthodox followers was caused by the insensitivity of Evangelicals and their display of unfamiliar features of Evangelical Christianity which were not vital to the faith and could have been avoided. However, there is also enough evidence of negative attitudes of the Orthodox Church towards Evangelical Christians since the inception of the faith. In

---

extremists, anti-citizenship, anti-family, anti-Ethiopia, anti-unity, Bible worshippers, agents of Western countries, parasites, brain washers, money launderers, mad people, corrupt, anti-tewahdo, ethno-centric. Esubalew, የጥናት ዳጆች, 113–114, 234–294, 295–356, 359.

144. The founders are referred to as "ባለራዕይና መስራች" (visionary and founder), many times claiming absolute authority over the church. At times the unquestionable authority reminds one of the Pope of Roman Catholic Church. It is not unusual to meet members who passionately defend their pastor and look up to him nearly as infallible. A year and half ago the Gospel Light Church appointed its founding pastor Daniel Mekonnen as Apostle, a title which was the first one to be given to an Evangelical pastor in Ethiopia, ever. The occasion naturally raised a lot of questions among Evangelicals. Some boycotted the ceremony and others chose to remain silent. Some openly wrote against what they described as "abominable" act. Paulos Fekadu, የነጻነት መዘዝ (The consequence of freedom), October 2009. What interested me (the researcher) was the reflection of one of the members of this particular church. While discussing issues that concerned his pastor, the young man told us that we were in no position to question anything the pastor did. According to him, we needed an anointing equal to that of an apostle in order to challenge the apostle. ETC, Private Conversation, January 2010.

145. *Gesame* 5, no. 6 (Sene 1999 Eth. C), 1, 3–5, 9–11; *Gesame* 5, no. 4 (Megabit, 1999 Eth. C), 1, 9.

fact, in contrast to the attitude towards Evangelicals, the attitude towards Ethiopian Muslims was not so negative. Although EOC members did not wish to have table fellowship with Muslims and tried to hinder the expansion of Islam, Muslim Ethiopians were not objects of ridicule and insult.[146]

5.2. The Evangelicals' Perceptions of the EOC

As discussed in the previous section, Orthodox Christianity spread as the faith of the ruling class who imposed it on the people they conquered. The pressure to accept Orthodox Christianity produced two kinds of sentiment; first, acceptance, shown in the desire to speak the language and belong to the church for the sake of prestige and power. Second, resentment, shown in the labelling of Orthodox Christianity as a means of oppression. The second sentiment contributed to the growth of Evangelical churches among peripheral peoples.

After the establishment of Evangelical churches as separate entities, one of the prime reasons for conflict between Evangelicals and the Orthodox Church was the Evangelicals' act of converting Orthodox members. The Orthodox believe that the "expansion of Protestantism" or the "sheep-stealing" was facilitated through different methods, one of which was making visitors feel welcome in Protestant churches. The personal care which is extended to newcomers wins their heart.[147] In addition, the attraction of modernization, the pretext of education, the offer of health care and poverty alleviation are also listed as reasons for Orthodox people joining the Evangelicals.

---

146. Orthodox Christians also have reservations about eating the meat of an animal killed by Evangelicals because they do not consider the faith legitimate and eating such meat would defile them. Usually Evangelicals have the animal killed by an EOC person who has the baptismal cord around his neck. In some places EOC members will not use the blade or knife of Evangelicals. An annoyed Evangelical noted, "ጾመኛው ኦርቶዶክስ እኔን ከናቀኝና ከጣላኝ፣ እምነቴን እንደ እርኩስ ነገር በመቁጠር በቤቴ ያለውን ቢላዋና የመሳሰሉትን እንደ እርኩስ ነገር ከጠራቸው፣ እኔ ለምን እርሱን በመለማመጥ ሃይማኖቴን ንቄ የእርሱን ሃይማኖት እንደማክብረው ብዙም አይገባኝም።" (If the Orthodox who is observing fast dislikes me and despises my faith and is disgusted of using objects in my house, I do not see why I should show any respect to his faith.) Birhanu Wolde, መጽሐፍ ቅዱስ ወይስ ባህል? ይታሰብበት፣ (Priority to the Bible or tradition?) *Kale Heywet*, no. 25 (1994 Eth. C), 22.

147. Esubalew, የገጠም ደጆች, 336–337. Esubalew refers to such atmosphere as false love and a snare to lure EOC adherents who usually do not find such kind of acceptance and love in their church.

However, Orthodox theologians also recognized areas needing improvement within their own church which gave members legitimate reasons for leaving. The use of unintelligible language in the church, the ignorance and wayward life style of its clergy, the prevalence of corruption, witchcraft and backbiting among the clergy are some of the reasons why EOC members turned to Protestantism.[148]

This shows acknowledgement on the part of the clergy of the Orthodox Church that Evangelical Christianity offered something which was not available in the Orthodox Church. There is a level of openness on the part of the Orthodox people to pay attention to the issues which cause the flocking of Orthodox to Evangelical churches. The Evangelicals, however, adamantly identify themselves with the Bible and reject core teachings of the Orthodox; the main ones being the status of the saints and deutreo-canonical books. In the following section, we shall examine how Evangelicals view themselves and why.

5.2.1. The Evangelicals' Perception of Themselves as Believers "አማኞች"

The critical attitude and superior feelings of Evangelicals towards the EOC reflect their self-depiction as true believers. Moreover, the term "believer" is used for two reasons: first, in many places missionary converts were given a new name by the community around them and this new name usually associated them with Jesus and or with their new code of conduct. Hence, the mockery towards them usually involved the name of Jesus, whose name they invoked in the face of difficulties, apprehension, or danger of any kind, and also to offer praises.[149]

---

148. Merqorios, ታሪክህን ዕወቅ፣, 65; Giday, "Impact of Protestantism," 5; Melese Atnafu, *Conversion of Addis Ababa Population, Essay*, 12–15; Gerimame Yohannes, "Problem of Proselytism," 34, 43–45.

149. Crying out "Be Eyesus Sim!" (in the name of Jesus!) is common in the face of any kind of accident and on hearing horrific news. A case in point is the story of a mother whose daughter became an Evangelical and the mother was not happy about it but heard the name of Jesus uttered by her daughter all the time. While the mother went to consult diviner ጠንቋይ *tenquway* about something, he tells her that it would be done but she had to sacrifice one of her children. The woman was so shocked that she uttered "Beyesus Sim!" and while the name was on her lips the *tenquway* fell to the ground so violently and started groaning. The woman fled the house as fast as she could. Wubshet Sahilu, ምህረቱን እናገረው (I proclaim his mercy), *Gesame* 2, no. 13 (Tir 2002 Eth. C), 20. It seems that the name of Jesus is used as a magical name even by those who mock the Evangelicals for calling Jesus

Secondly, there was a practical problem in differentiating their members from those of the Orthodox because the EOC, which used the term "Christian" officially, was not eager to recognize Evangelicals as fellow Christians.[150] The term "Christian" also served to differentiate the Orthodox from Muslims. There is a boundary drawn between Orthodox and Muslims in Ethiopia in which table fellowship among the two is restricted.[151] But, the depiction of oneself as a "believer" made it evident that the Orthodox followers were by implication unbelievers. "Traditionally Orthodox Christians knew of only two religions: Islam and Christianity. If a person wasn't a baptized Christian or a Muslim then he had "no religion."' And those who had no religion were potential members of the Orthodox Church.[152]

Evangelicals did not fight for the title "Christian" although sometimes they tried to reason based on the origin of the name "Christian" that they were entitled to be called by it. Most of the time, however, they opted for

---

all the time. Thus, invoking the name of Jesus is becoming common at a sudden probability of a road accident or when any kind of calamity is caused. One will be heard crying out "Be Eyesus sim" only to continue their conversation with the customary EOC affirmation "Emebeten." The Orthodox swear by the names of the saints, angels and more frequently by the name of Mary, እምቤትን "Emebeten" (as my Lady lives), እም ብርሃንን "Eme Birhanin" (as the mother of light lives), etc.

150. Mekane Yesus use the term ምዕመናን "Me'emenan" to refer to a community of believers. This is a common name used by the clergy of the EOC to address their audience while teaching or preaching. Also "የተወደዳችሁ የእግዚአብሔር/የክርስቶስ ቤተሰቦች" (Beloved household of God/Christ) is another common way in EOC to address the assembly.

151. People are expected to be committed either to Islam or the Orthodox Christianity. Ministering in the context of both Islam and Orthodox Christians is difficult when it comes to eating meat. Trying to communicate freedom from legalism by eating meat without distinction backfires as illustrated in the following experience of a Mennonite missionary. "The missionary homemaker was expecting guests and asked her cook to buy meat in the local market. The cook reminded her that Wednesday is a fast day, so no 'Christian' meat available . . . 'Well, then buy meat from the Muslim shop today,' the homemaker told her cook. The cook, a devout Orthodox Christian, acted as though he was asked to do an impossible task. 'Muslims meat?' he exclaimed. 'I can not touch it; it has not been blessed by the priest or slaughtered in the name of the Trinity. Muslims slaughter their animals in the name of Allah.' In desperation, the woman was ready to go to the market and buy the meat herself. However, her cook said he could not in good conscience prepare the dinner, for he would be working in a 'defiled' kitchen . . . The homemaker could have solved her problem by serving only vegetables on Wednesdays and Fridays. Yet she remembered that missionaries were there to bring Muslims also to Christ. By eating their meat sometimes, she could show that true faith does not depend on habits of diet. Meanwhile, both Orthodox Christians and Muslims were watching, amazed that the missionary did not seem to have any scruples at all." Hege, *Beyond Our Prayers*, 52–53.

152. Sorsa Sumamo, *Bivocational Missionary-Evangelist*, 15–16.

"አማኞች/በጌታ የሆኑ" "believers/in the Lord." In the case of the Pentecostal movement, the term "in the Lord" appears to have emerged out of a conscious departure from the traditional Orthodox notion of the term "Christian" which was believed to be devoid of its proper meaning. Hence, they desired to distance themselves from it.[153] Even those who have left the Orthodox Church and joined Evangelical churches describe their new identity as being "in the Lord," or speaking of their conversion experience, they say, ጌታን አገኘሁ "I found the Lord" or, even ጌታ አገኘኝ "the Lord found me." There is clear sense of a new beginning; they were lost and now they are found. Regarding his new experience Nigusse remarks, "It was not a matter of changing a church for me, rather, from treasuring the Bible as an object which imparts power through physical contact to understanding the words of it and turning to Christ as my Lord."[154]

There was continuity with the Orthodox Church in matters which had to do with biblical doctrines, but there also was sharp discontinuity with the tradition of the church which exalted the saints, angels and traditional writings. The discontinuity is illustrated in the depiction of the experience of former Orthodox followers as "የበራላቸው" "enlightened." The implication which an average Orthodox adherent will read behind such words is that the Orthodox are in darkness.[155]

In fact, evangelists are not afraid of using the darkness/light contrast while they preach in the church, at bus stops, inside public transportation or anywhere else. They will raise their voice and cry out, ወንድሜ ሆይ ከጨለማ ውጣ "My brother, come out of darkness." Such an approach infuriates the Orthodox.[156] Daniel retorts, "Do you not know that it is the Orthodox fathers who gave you the Bible to begin with? Look who is asking whom to come out of the darkness!"[157]

---

153. Tamiru Zeleke, "The Mission Strategy of the Mulu Wongel Church," (MTh diss., Ghana, Akropong, Akrofi-Christaller Institute, 2008), 47–49.

154. Nigusse Bulcha, Director of Scripture Union, Interview, 30 September 2010, Addis Abab.

155. *Gesame*, ምሥክርነት፣ መንፈሱ በሰው ተመስሎ ይገለጥልኛል (Testimony: The spirit appears to me in human form) 2, no. 3 (Tir, 2000 Eth. C), 21–24; Daniel, Interview, 8 September, 2010.

156. Daniel, Interview, 8 September, 2010; Mekonnen, Interview, 15 November, 2010.

157. Daniel, Interview, 8 September, 2010. He seems to be under the impression that Nicaea settled the Canon.

Similar remarks were made in *Hamer* magazine, the publication of Mahbere Kidusan, in response to a letter of *yeqolo temari* (traditional school pupil) who wrote that in his area *menafiqan* were bombarding them saying, ጌታን ተቀበል "receive the Lord" The editor's reply depicted Evangelicals as ignorant, incompetent, foreign (*mete*), not fit to teach and preach, and indwelt by a spirit who twists the truth. He urged the writer to stand up to these intruders.[158]

In addition to rarely using the name "Christian" which is associated with the Orthodox, Evangelicals call their meeting place "የጸሎት ቤት" (*yetselot bet*) literally, house of prayer in Amharic, and names which had the same meaning were given in other languages.[159] This does not mean that the name "House/Assembly of Christians" "ቤተ ክርስቲያን" (Bete Kristian) which usually refers to the Orthodox Church, is not used at all, but its usage in the urban areas was limited. "Bete Kristian" is used for official correspondence and on the letterhead of Evangelical churches. But unofficially, the English term "church" is common in townships and cities around Ethiopia in reference to the building. However, as far as the Orthodox are concerned, the term "church" signifies the foreignness of the Protestant faith. Some even get confused when they hear Evangelicals refer to their assembly as "Bete Kristian." Similar remarks are made about the name of Jesus as illustrated in the following remark of the mother of one of my informants, "Eyesus is yours, but ours is Medhane Alem."[160]

5.2.2. The Evangelical View of the Ethiopian Orthodox Church as Authoritarian and Discriminatory

As we have seen, prior to the coming of Protestant missionaries the church as state religion attempted to Christianize the followers of primal religion in Southern Ethiopia, which was reabsorbed into the greater Ethiopia during

---

158. "ማን ማንን ይሰብካል? እንኪን ቅነ ሊቀኛ አንድ ቃል እንኪን እስከ ግማሽ ዘር ማርባት የማይችል ጥራ ጬዋ ሁሉ . . . እንዴት ሊሰብክና ሊያስተምር ይችላል? ይህን የሚናገረውን የማያውቅ መጤ ሁሉ የሚገባውን መልስ ለመስጠት . . . የቀናውን አጣሞ የሚያሳያቸው መንፈስ ከሳያቸው እንዲርቅ . . ." *Hamer*, no. 2 (Ginbot/Sene, 1998 Eth. C), 6.

159. Sorsa, *Bivocational Missionary-Evangelist*, 125.

160. Getachew Belete, Interview, 18 August 2010, Addis Ababa. Usually, Orthodox adherents call Jesus Christ "Medhane Alem " which means Saviour of the world. When they call him by his name, they include his titles: "Our Lord and Saviour Jesus Christ." The Evangelicals' tendency to call him "Jesus," therefore, is not well taken by the Orthodox.

emperor Menelik's expansion.[161] The natives who felt dominated both politically and religiously looked at the Orthodox faith as the religion of the Amhara settlers, who under the pretence of expanding civilization were present in the area to ensure political and religious control. There was a significant religious influence exerted by the Orthodox upon the peripheral people of Southern Ethiopia, especially by Tekle Haymanot.

However, the people resented the Orthodox Church because it accompanied the ruling class. Orthodox monks tended to move independently and preach the gospel extensively. However, the state protection they enjoyed once a given emperor reached the area gave the impression that the faith was inseparable from political domination. As soon as a given king from the North conquered more areas, usually by humiliating the traditional leadership, priests of the Orthodox Church were sent to build churches, primarily for northern settlers and their families. Bakke notes that the Amhara imposed heavy taxes and ruled the people in nearly slave-like conditions.[162] The local people felt that the church did not speak against such harsh treatment of them; on the contrary, attempting to rebel against the king resulted in excommunication from the church. Moreover, the church demanded taxes for itself and forced people to build churches. From the point of view of the local people there seemed to be no difference between the church and the state – both were oppressive and worked interdependently to bring people into the church and the political kingdom.[163] Consequently, conversion to Orthodox Christianity in the South did not always come out of conviction but fear, and the necessity of finding a job or gaining access to education.[164] However, some groups in the south do not seem to exhibit any resentment towards the Amhara and the presence of the EOC. Such fact implies that the negative perceptions of the Orthodox and the Amhara were not always shared by all.

---

161. Emperor Menelik was determined to extend his kingdom to the "ancient territories of Ethiopia." Paulos Ggnogno, *Ate Menelik*, 3rd edition (Addis Ababa: 1999 Eth. C), 106–107.

162. Bakke, "Models of Leadership," 161; Petersen, ed., *Stories of Bale*, 37–38.

163. Ermias Guisha Mamo, "Knowing God in Ritual Context in Special Reference to the Hamar People of Southwest Ethiopia," (PhD thesis, Fuller Theological Seminary, 2008), 104–105.

164. Bakke, "Models of Leadership," 161; Petersen, ed., *Stories of Bale*, 37–38.

Eventually the church halted forced conversions, and instead tried to attract people with the offer of power, position and prestige. In southern Omo the converts were given new names and with it their status was raised because being "an Amhara" was considered a higher social status. More importantly, the church condemned the enslavement of Christians. This gave incentive for Southern peoples to wish to be converted, even beg the Orthodox to make them Christian in order "to escape from the worst aspects of Abyssinian domination."[165] However, there was very little assimilation of the indigenous converts.[166] It did not go beyond inviting them for feasts, but they were treated a little better than the others in their relationship with the landlords, who were Christians.[167] But for the people at large, conversion sounded like trading their identity in exchange for that of the Amhara. Becoming Christian was considered as becoming Amhara.[168]

After the coming of Evangelical Christianity, the EOC continued to require members of Evangelical churches to pay an annual tax. Evangelicals in Kembatta and Hadiya area refused to pay and this resulted in confrontation between the people and the police. In the havoc that followed the police shot to maintain order and one man was killed. Leaders of Evangelicals were charged with murder and imprisoned in Addis Ababa. They appealed to Haile Sellassie and he sent Asrate Kassa[169] to Hosana to investigate the

---

165. Donald L. Donham, "The Making of an Imperial State," in *The Southern Marches of Imperial Ethiopia*, ed. Donald L. Donham and Wendy James (Addis Ababa: Addis Ababa University Press, 2002), 11. Cf. Mekuria Bulcha, *The Making of the Oromo Diaspora: A Historical Sociology of Forced Migration* (Minneapolis, MN: Kirk House, 2002), 44.

166. Some people groups in the South had little attachment to Ethiopia as a nation. During the Derg regime, Hamar people were asked to send some of their young people for national service. A Hamar elder asked the cadre, "What is Ethiopia?" The cadre told him that it was his country. The man replied, "My country is right here and I will take care of it and protect it. Let those who live out there fight for their own land. Why should I ask our youth to go and fight for somebody else?" Ermias Mamo, Dean of Students, Ethiopian Graduate School of Theology, Interview, 1 October 2010, Addis Ababa.

167. Ermias, Interview, 1 October 2010.

168. Mehari Choramo, *Ethiopian Pioneer Missionary: Autobiography of Evangelist Mehari Choramo* (Edmonton: Enterprise, 1997), 45. The experience of some people groups in South Omo was different. Any form of Christianity was considered as the religion of the Amhara and Amhara for them was any fair-skinned person. So converting to Christianity (Orthodox and Evangelical alike) was despised as becoming Amhara; as trading one's identity to somebody else's. Ermias, Interview, 1 October 2010.

169. He was the one who gave permission to Aleqa Meseret Sibhat Leab (who later was expelled from EOC because of his Evangelical convictions) to use the massive EOC

matter and he stayed in the district town Hosana from 21 to 27 December 1950. His intervention led to the agreement that Evangelicals should not pay tax to the church and were not required to assist when Orthodox churches were built, and should not preach to Orthodox congregations.[170]

Even though the converts tried to stay out of the way of the Orthodox Church, their evangelistic activities in the country brought opposition from the clergy of the church. Sorsa, who used to preach in the rural areas of Sidama, notes that their ministry was considered provocative.

> Muslims had no problem understanding the difference between their message and ours. The same could not be said of members of the Ethiopian Orthodox church. It was difficult for them not to interpret what we were preaching as anything but competitive, and many of the priests and deacons were provoked by our use of the Amharic Bible . . . Often the people who lived in the urban centres considered themselves religiously superior to those of us who lived in the country.[171]

The government officials established towns as centres of their rule and usually a considerable number of northern people lived in these centres, and churches were erected, leading to the conclusion that the urban areas belonged to them. The evangelists also initially avoided urban centres because they felt that they belonged to the Orthodox Church. Sorsa notes, "Priests and deacons of the Ethiopian Orthodox church considered the town inviolable. Urban centres were at least one geographical area that they could

---

literature for research which eventually was published as a book "Seme'a Tsidq Biherawi." The literature was on display in Gondar on the occasion of the silver jubilee of the reign of Haile Sellassie in 1940. Interview, "ከአለቃ መሠረት ስብሐት ለአብ ጋር በየጊዜው ተደርጎ ከነበረው ቃለ ምልልስ የተወሰደ" (Taken from interview held with Aleqa Meseret Sibhat Leab over a period of time), *Chora*, no. 14 (n.d.), 15.

170. Asrate Kassa discussed the matter with Dr R. N. Thompson, the missionary in charge and came to the following agreement in addition to the above-mentioned ones. "The mission schools were to be open to all and not to believers only, secondly pastors and elders were to refrain from taking part in politics. Thirdly he guaranteed freedom for preaching in Kembattaarea, 'except in the immediate vicinity of Orthodox churches or preaching directly to Orthodox Church congregation.' Fourth, permission to build church on any privately owned land was granted and there was assurance that 'believers might not be arrested on merely religious charges.'" Cotterell, *Born at Midnight*, 148–149.

171. Sorsa Sumamo, *Bivocational Missionary-Evangelist*, 15.

protect and fight for."¹⁷² Although southern Ethiopia is believed to be the stronghold of Evangelicals, the towns are still highly populated by members of the Orthodox Church, who are accused of looking down on the indigenous people around them.¹⁷³

There was evidence of an ethnic undertone at work in southern Ethiopia. In Sidama it was noted that the church made little effort to reach local people but sought to protect the rights of the Amhara rulers. Those who were converted from the local population were discriminated against. Some resented the fact that they were not allowed to enter the Orthodox churches which they had helped build in their own villages.¹⁷⁴

The undesirable effect of such discrimination created a sense that Orthodoxy was a tribal religion.¹⁷⁵ The EOC was granted a large amount of land in the south and priests were given land as private property and grew wealthier thereby, becoming the nobility and the upper class. In some districts in the south local inhabitants were displaced because of such land grants to the church and its clergy.¹⁷⁶ The displacement, ethnic undertones and the use of unintelligible language created a rift between the clergy and the local people they were trying to Christianize.

---

172. Sorsa, 16.

173. Ermias Mamo, Interview, 1 October 2010; Alemu Shetta, Interview, 4 February 2011. In Kembatta area, there are many northern Orthodox settlers who took Kembata wives so there is integration with the society. But the Northern settlers and their families for the most part are still staunch Orthodox followers despite strong Evangelical presence all around them. They walk a distance (about 3–5 kms) to go to Orthodox Church which usually is far from their villages.

174. Arne Tolo, *Sidama and Ethiopian: The Emergence of the Mekane Yesus Church in Sidama* (Uppsala: Uppsala University, 1998), 85–89. There were some missionaries who reflected similar sentiments. They insisted on being addressed as "እመቤቴ" (my lady) and "ጌቶች" (my lord). When local people went to their house they would not let them in but talk to them on the doorstep and send them away. Alemu Shetta, Interview, 4 February 2011; Ermias Mamo, Interview, 1 October 2010.

175. The Church of Ethiopia was not alone in behaving in such a way to lead to the above conclusion. Andrew Walls notes, "In its essence, Western Christianity is a tribal religion; and tribal religion is fundamentally more about acknowledged symbols, and customs and recognized practice, than about faith. At the same time, it can be a powerful constituent of identity ('Remember that we are English, that we are Christians')." Thus, at this particular time in history Christianity seems inseparable from "the categories of European life and thought." Andrew Walls, *The Cross-Cultural Process in Christian History* (Maryknoll, NY: Orbis Books, 2002), 220.

176. Bakke, *Christian Ministry*, 109–110.

The church could have done better in reaching more people with the message of the gospel. However, factors such as the inadequate training of its clergy,[177] the inaccessibility of the Bible in the vernaculars, and preaching what Ermias Mamo calls, "an ethnocentric gospel" hindered the advancement of the gospel in parts of Ethiopia.[178]

Moreover, in most cases the church did not recruit indigenous people to assume ministry in the church; perhaps because of the language factor, but also for ethnic reasons.[179] More offensive still was that the church did not allow indigenous converts to be buried in the vicinity of the church. Converts were buried at the outskirts of the church's massive, but the settlers were buried inside the main compound.[180] Referring to the experience of Orthodox converts in South Omo, Ermias notes,

> Embracing the new religion, Orthodox Christianity, might give one new status before the Amhara but from the perspective of the local people the person is betraying his/her culture. In the other words, the convert is neither accepted as a full member by the Orthodox Church nor appreciated by his own people since he abandoned his own tradition.[181]

Furthermore the degrading portrayal of the local people aggravated the enmity and widened the gap between the Orthodox and local people.[182] The

---

177. The Orthodox Church is not the only church accused of sending out clergy without adequately training them. Ermias notes that in its haste to send workers into the plentiful harvest Kale Heywet Church, the largest Evangelical church in Ethiopia, also sent out non-trained evangelists in its formative years and the end result was "the multiplication of nominal Christians who are not discipled." Ermias Guisha Mamo, "Knowing God in Ritual Context," 124.

178. Ermias, "Knowing God in Ritual Context," 99.

179. Taddesse Tamrat, *Church and State*, 232–233. But Evangelist Kedamo Mechato notes that there were Hadiya priests of the EOC. In fact, it was a Hadiya priest who converted him to Orthodoxy. Kedamo, Mechato, O.i, 18 January 2011, Addis Ababa.

180. Ermias, Interview, 1 October 2010; Tesfahun Hatia, Dean of Student at Pentecostal Theological College, Interview, 5 October 2010, Addis Ababa; Alemu Shetta, Interview, 4 February 2011.

181. Ermias, "Knowing God in Ritual Context," 100.

182. There was social ostratization based on skin colour, lifestyle and religion and urban dwellers and settlers in the country were no exception. They considered themselves civilized and tended to look down on the local people and abused them verbally by calling them "shanqilla, bariya, tinb." These names usually refer to dark skinned Ethiopians and their way of life and also country people who were not Orthodox and could not speak Amharic well.

refusal of the Orthodox Church to acknowledge the Evangelicals as fellow Christians led to the portrayal of the church as bigoted, rigid, and with discriminating structures.

5.2.3. The Evangelical Depiction of the Orthodox as *Ahzab*/without Christ

The massiveness of the church made it difficult to follow up its members strictly. People with all kinds of lifestyles claimed to be of the church which in turn resulted in infiltration of numerous non-Christian practices into the main stream of the church. The result was a growing number of Christians who had the thread around their necks but in practice did not live any differently from those who did not call themselves Christians. In other words, the common Orthodox followers tend to unquestioningly go by ordinances and normative values as handed down to them by their ancestors. The name "Christian" thus was reduced to an external description rather than signifying internal change and commitment.[183] Thus, the Orthodox were criticized as *ahzab*[184] a term which connoted people who do not know God.[185]

"Amhara were, first of all, Orthodox Christians. Second, they spoke Amharic. And, . . . they were not markedly negroid in racial features." Donham, "Making of an Imperial State," 12.

183. Such a tendency of defining Christian faith against external manifestations such as refraining from drinking alcohol, chewing chat, or listening to secular music, etc., is common in the south where Evangelical Christianity is passed on to three or four generations. In such situations, drinking alcohol or listening to secular music is usually taken as an indication that the person has regressed from the faith. Thus some Evangelical Christians practise the above things secretly for fear of rejection as opposed to the Orthodox Christians who do them openly and still claim to be Orthodox Christians.

184. This is the term which is used in the Amharic Bible to refer to "nations" or "gentiles." The usage of it in reference to EOC depicted the absence of transformation. "I have mixed feelings for the term 'ahzab.' On one hand there is a little bit of biblical element to the usage of it because Paul himself uses it in reference to those who are far from Christ and not only those who are not children of Israel. The concept of heathen is behind there. On the other hand the usage in reference to a Christian body sounds inappropriate. When Paul warns his audience not to become like 'gentiles' he has moral uprightness in mind. From this point of view regardless of one's race and denomination, a person might have gentile tendencies. So we could say that such a usage has some justifications." Nigusse Bulcha, Director of Scripture Union, Interview, 30 September 2010.

185. The adjective "ዓለማውያን" (worldly) was also used to show the lifestyle of EOC followers. Evangelicals did not deny that EOC followers have knowledge about Christ. The criticism is that they did not have adequate knowledge and what they know they do not practise and this can only mean they have not understood the gospel, which leads to the conclusion that they are not "born again."

Evangelicals were aghast at the multitude of testimonies[186] printed in magazines which recounted how some of the clergy of the Orthodox Church practiced occultism and actually taught people how to go about it.[187] The way former divination or occult practitioners told their story at times made this appear to be a normative practise in the Orthodox Church. The apprehension about discarding objects dedicated to ancestral spirits was contrary to the experience of Evangelicals who boldly confronted evil spirits in the name of Jesus.[188] Concerning the spiritual realm Ethiopian Evangelicalism conveniently have two categories: the Holy Spirit and demons. Sometimes the soul is referred to as the "spirit" of the person. Ancestral spirits are thus categorized as demonic because Evangelical theology has no place for human "spirits" to roam about after death.[189]

The steady lingering of ancestral worship and consultation of diviners well into seventeen-centuries-long Christianity, therefore, served as evidence of the EOC's evangelistic and pastoral strategies which tolerated

---

186. Some of the stories were exaggerated just like hagiographies of saints in the Orthodox Church. Cf. Mihretu Petros, የንባብ ባህልና ቤተክርስቲያን General Analysis on the Reading Habit of Ethiopian Evangelical Christians (Addis Ababa: SIM Publications, 2007): 105–106.

187. Misikire Birhan, no. 74 (Hidar-Tahsas, 1959 Eth. C); Fantu, "የጎዴ አምልኮና አሠራር" (Divination), *Hiwot*, no. 4 (Tir/Yekatit, 1986 Eth. C), 19–21; Tigist Tafesse, "ምሥክርነት፣ ተራው የኔ ነው" (Testimony, it is my turn), *Gesame* 2, no. 12 (Miyazia 2002 Eth. C, 13–15, 23; Wubshet Sahilu, ምሕረቱን አናገረው (I proclaim his mercy), 20; Tesfaye Gebre, ቤተ መንግሥቱ የተአለለበት ጥንቆላ" (Occultism that deceived the State House), *Gesame* 2, no. 5 (Ginbot, 2000 Eth. C), 15–17; Bethlehem Abebe, "አጅነቱን ሳለውቀው አደግሁ" (I never enjoyed my childhood), *Gesame* 2, no. 4 (Megabit, 2000), 21–25.

188. Bekele W/Kidan, Interview, 25 August 2010, Addis Ababa. Mekonnen admired the boldness of Evangelicals in confronting *tenquwayoch* (mediums of evil spirits) and remarked that generally speaking there is a hesitance on the part of the EOC regarding confronting *tenquwayoch* and admonishing clergy members who practise witchcraft. Mekonnen, Interview, 14 November, 2010. The ongoing practice of witchcraft alongside religious instruction and the apparent tolerance of the church is deeply regretted by some EOC clergy members. Dereje and Beza, መቅደስ የገቡ መናፍቃን (Menafiqan in the temple) (Bahir Dar: 2008), 7–8.

189. Stories of protection provided by ancestral spirits are not common, rather destructive forces in the name of ancestral spirits is quite common. There is the story of a young boy Jarsa Utta who was forced to eat cow's dung for fourteen days each morning by the ancestral spirit who possessed his maternal uncle. The spirit killed his father and three nieces and when Jarsa got married and had children, he killed all of his children and even his wife. Then when he threatened to kill him Jarsa remembered the story he heard about a man who was spared from death by believing in Jesus and he went to Christians and accepted Jesus. Then he started to sleep peacefully and bore four children from his third wife and now is an evangelist. አሥራ አራት ቀን የከብት እስት የበላው ሰው ወንጌላዊ ሆነ (The man who was made to feed on animal dung for fourteen days became an evangelist), *Kale Heywet*, no. 26 (1995 Eth. C), 5–6, 22.

these practices.¹⁹⁰ It seemed to imply that the church did not adequately cater for the spiritual needs of the people; hence, as discussed in chapter 2, they still held on to their traditional avenues for the times when healing did not materialize at the sacred fountains of the church.¹⁹¹

For the most part, Evangelicals who have discovered the gifts of the Holy Spirit as safe channels for such spiritual quests tend to look down on Orthodox members' involvement in what is regarded both by missionaries and Evangelicals as "demonic worship." In addition to the lingering of the traditional practices, the forceful imposition of Christianity with mass baptism accompanied with little instruction from the Bible has affected the credibility of the church.¹⁹² The Oromo people in northern Ethiopia were also forcefully converted from Islam to EOC.¹⁹³ They were instructed to fast, to make confession and to observe the holidays. Apart from that they

---

190. Stories of people tormented by ancestral spirit regardless of their membership at the EOC did not make sense for Evangelicals. Thus, those who torment and demand for sacrifices were evil spirits and they were to come out in the name of Jesus, period! They are not to be prayed to, or appeased through sacrifice to have mercy on the people they possessed. The deliverance of those coming to Evangelical churches made Evangelical question whether there was real deliverance at EOC. Woineshet Assefa, "ቀዳሚዋ ዘሪ - የዘሪዋ ዘማሪ" (the singer), *Kale Heywet*, no. 29 (1996 Eth. C), 23–24. One of the most romanticized stories of the EOC in which Saint Gerima was believed to have been pulled up the rocky Church by a huge serpent does not seem to fit the theology of some Evangelical preachers. "How can a serpent pull a saint up the Church? The Bible says that you crush the head of the serpent, so we will crush its head for you!" Dawit Molalegn, ቀሉ ስለሞጥ አይቅልስባችሁ፣ (Do not take [the humble gospel] for granted), (Audiovisual sermon), n.d.

191. These are referred to as "tsebel" and people visit them for physical healing and deliverance from evil spirits. Evangelicals tend to be critical of the authenticity of the healing claimed at these places but some turn to the "sacred water" packed by T. B. Joshua of Nigerian Synagogue of All Nations for healing. Rahel Abayneh, በአተዛም ችግር ዙሪያ እስካሁን ድረስ በኢትዮጵያ ውስጥ የተደረገ ጥናት የለም (No study has been made regarding autism in Ethiopia) *Milja*, no. 15 (Tir 1- Miazia 30, 2003 Eth. C), 8; Paulos Fekadu, Brothers, http://www.ethiocross.com, accessed 16 April 2011.

192. Sorsa Sumamo, *Bivocational Missionary-Evangelist*, 64; Staffan Grenstedt, *Ambaricho and Shonkolla: From Local Independent Church to Evangelical Mainstream in Ethiopia* (Stockholm: Elanders Gotab, 2000), 5.

193. A turn of events took place during the five-year Italian conquest. The Fascists favoured Islam in order to weaken the strong Orthodox influence. Accordingly they demolished churches and built about fifty brand new mosques with stones and renovated about sixteen mosques. They also sought to win the favour of Ethiopian Muslims by paving the way for them to visit Medina. Fascists believed that the Amhara people, who were politically and economically dominant and the Orthodox Church were their chief enemies. Thus, in order to further weaken the Orthodox Church they evicted 600,000–800,000 Amharic speakers from Harar and Sidama provinces. Wondiye, በመከራ ውስጥ ያበበች ቤተ ክርስቲያን *(Church out of tribulation)*, 147–150.

were not forced to stop their pagan rituals. In fact, Christians who lived among them took part in the rituals.[194]

The forceful conversions, mass baptisms, and the enforcement of "Amhara" culture had both religious and political motives.[195] As for the lack of biblical instruction for the converts, the clergy themselves did not have adequate knowledge of the Scriptures.[196] The centrality of traditions rather than the Bible in the lives of the people and the ignorance of many, including some priests, about the Bible gave rise to the categorization "without Christ." The boldness of Orthodox monks such as St Antony who confronted evil spirits by going to tombs, which were believed to be their abode, were taken up by the monks of the church such as Estifanos. However, the adoption of traditional worldviews about spirits along with Christianity and the apprehension regarding evil spirits among the contemporary Orthodox adherents seem to Evangelicals to be placating rather than challenging the spirits.[197] Speaking of the difference Evangelical faith makes, a former Orthodox member remarks,

> In Orthodox Church the lay people used to be spectators, (now it is changing) but in those days, we would hear priests pray, preach, chant, and sing. Some people who have knowledge join in the mass, but most people would just listen to the priests. We joined in for the apostles' prayer and that was about it. I did not read the Bible for myself. Evangelicals gave me the Bible to read for myself. I was even asked to share my insights and pray in the presence of others. I was uncomfortable in the beginning because I did not know how to go about it. A lay man was to share insights from the Bible and pray for others?!

---

194. Hastings, *Church in Africa*, 238–239.

195. Bo Ericksson, Mirjam Eriksson, Erik Johansson, *The Gospel of Restoration: Experiences from a Field Study in Ethiopia* (Sweden: Swedish Institute of Missionary Research, 1999), 27.

196. Birhanu Dido, "Achievements of the First Evangelical Missionaries in Bale," in *Stories of Bale* (Addis Ababa: n.p., 2005), 47.

197. But beside the bold confrontation of demons and their human counterparts, it can also be argued that the Evangelicals' worship services and prayer meetings which begin with an extended time of rebuking the involvement of demons with a loud voice and with a lot of passion might imply a hint of apprehension at the face of evil spirits. Moreover, there is a tendency of suspecting the involvement of demons behind almost all tragedy or misfortune.

It was a new experience. I was no more a spectator but an active participant in the worship, singing, sharing of the Bible. That was the breakthrough.[198]

Another reason behind depicting the Orthodox as "without Christ" is its persecution of Evangelical believers. With the coming of the Derg to power in 1974, the life of Evangelicals in rural areas and small towns throughout the country became increasingly difficult because they were isolated from their communities. Such isolation was intensified by Orthodox priests who forbade any association with Evangelicals on pain of excommunication.

Those who had borne the name but never understood the truth of Christianity, and new converts from traditional religion were alike puzzled by the antagonism of the Orthodox clergy who had formerly shown little concern for their spiritual growth, nor instructed them in the teaching of the Bible. To say the least, it led them to question the authenticity of the faith of those who had ventured out to the South and West under the pretence of Christianizing pagans.[199]

In Southern Ethiopia, imprisoned believers were forced to hard labour by government officials. The officials forced them to work like slaves. They told them, "If you had been baptized into the Orthodox Church this would not have happened to you. Even now, all you need to do is to be baptized by a priest and you can go home today." Those embittered by the hard labour opted for an easy way out of prison, abandoning Evangelical faith and converting to the EOC.[200]

There is no recorded physical retaliation from the Evangelicals.[201] The usual Evangelical response to such persecution was non-violence, based on

---

198. Bezabeh, Interview, 25 February 2011.

199. Bakke remarks, "It is obvious that the call to serve the church in the south was often accepted more from a craving after land than out of a concern for the pagans. The conversion of the incorporated peoples was not really in the best interest of the Amhara. They were stronger as long as they could monopolize Christianity without making this an instrument for the others to gain equal status." Bakke, *Christian Ministry*, 109.

200. Mehari, *Ethiopian Pioneer Missionary*, 45.

201. In one of southern Ethiopia's towns, Arba Minch, located in a province which had a massive Evangelical presence, the persecution was intense during a conference prepared by Evangelical Churches Fellowship in Arba Minch from Ginbot 8–10, 1989 Eth. C. The EOC was accused of coaching killing, raping of women on the streets and confiscation of property. The Archbishop of the EOC allegedly was parading in a car decorated with the national colours, inciting violence. Addise Amado, *Persecution in Ethiopia* (Addis Ababa:

the teachings of the New Testament that Christ's followers would suffer for his name. There also was a tremendous joy over suffering for the sake of Christ.[202] This appears to be similar to the experience of the apostles who rejoiced when they suffered for the sake of Christ. Their perception of the perpetuators of the persecution, however, was affected; leading them to question the legitimacy of their claim to be Christians.

Perhaps the most serious of all accusations against EOC is in regard to the status of the Bible. By contrast with the Evangelicals' practice it is not customary for EOC priests to carry the Bible with them. In fact, many of them do not have a copy of the Bible.[203] Persons who are familiar with the Bible and primarily base their arguments on it will be called *menafiq* or at least be suspected of being under the influence of Evangelicals.

5.3. The Two Great Battle Grounds and One of the Consequences

Thus far, different issues which create conflict and intolerance between the Orthodox and Evangelicals have been discussed. Of all the issues, the status of Mary and of the Bible are the main ones which drive the two bodies apart. All other issues relate to these two in one way or the other. Thus, we shall attempt to discuss the status of Mary and that of the Bible in some detail below and look at one of the appalling consequences of the rejection of Evangelicals.

5.3.1. The Mother of God, the Mother of Jesus

Evangelicals seem to always have problem with some of the doctrines of the Orthodox Church which uniquely mix elements of primal religion, with the Old Testament Jewish traditions and Christianity. The concern

---

Voice of Martyrs (VOM) Ethiopia, 2003): 50ff. Cf. Adane Dechasa, ስደት ለመልካችን ሁነልን (The persecution worked for our good) *Birhan*, no. 29 (1989 Eth. C), 28.

202. There is a story of a believer during the Derg regime who did not participate in a former meeting in which many believers were beaten up but when he had his share of the assault later on joyfully remarked, "This time I was fortunate enough to share the beatings." It is not that the Evangelicals were going out of their way looking for trouble but when persecuted for their faith, they rejoiced. Engelsviken, "Pentecostal Revival," 163–164. Cf. Hege, *Beyond Our Prayer*, 23; Sorsa, *Bivocational Missionary-Evangelist*, 65.

203. Liqe Hiruyan, Former Head of the Northern Orthodox churches, discussion held in February, 2008.

of Evangelicals is that the Orthodox Church has its priorities mixed up. It gives primacy to the intercessory role of the Saints, praying for the dead, fasting and rituals and in so doing undermine the authority of the Bible. This greatly affects the centrality of Christ and his redemptive work. In addition to that, the elevation of Mary has always been an issue of great conflict and misunderstanding between the Ethiopian Orthodox Church and Evangelicals.

Scholars of the Orthodox church quote Romans 8:16–17 and 2 Timothy 2:10–12 and explain Mariology as upheld by the EOC, as a fulfilment of God's promise that his children share in his glory. They add, "We glorify God because he is glorious in his nature. We glorify our Lady because she is the mother of God, our mother in covenant, and our intercessor" አማላጅ (Amalaj). (John 19:26–27; Luke 1:48).[204] In the same vein Daniel defends EOC's Mariology as implying the relevance of God's power, the closeness of his acts, and the token of the glory of Christ; "after all, it is Him who said that those who believe in Him will share in His glory."[205]

As discussed earlier, "*tsere Mariam*" "ፀረ-ማርያም" is one of the depictions of Evangelicals not only because they deny her intercession but also her perpetual virginity and purity from original sin. Together with the church of Alexandria the Ethiopian Orthodox Church believes that Mary's flesh was earthly and not divine, but unlike the church of Alexandria, the EOC believes that she was free from original sin. Such a claim of her highest sanctity sets her apart from her fellow human beings. The Evangelicals' denial of the above claims, therefore, are not tolerated by the Orthodox Church.

At this juncture discussion of the origin of the Cult of Mary is important to understand the current ever-growing trends of exalting Mary as "Coredeemer." There is an inquiry as to the sources of Ethiopian Orthodox church's strong attachment to Mary, (often in a manner which seems to exceed its attachment to the Son).

As discussed in chapter 2 there are affirmations adopted from the teaching of the church fathers.[206] Aba Ephrem of Syria is credited with inaugurat-

---

204. The EOTC Council of Scholars, እንደየስታችሁ ተጠንቀቁ, 46.

205. Daniel, Interview, 8 September, 2010.

206. John R. Willis, ed., *The Teachings of the Church Fathers* (San Francisco: Ignatius Press, 1966), 358–361, 134. St Ephrem wrote, "Truly you, Lord, and your mother are the

ing a new era of praising the Son and the Mother in one breath which has influenced the Ethiopian Orthodox Church's Mariology to a great extent. Some of the teachings about Mary therefore, were handed down to the EOC from the church fathers and did not originate in the Orthodox monasteries. Neither did *Wudasse Mariam* (Praise of Mary), one of the principal writings which promotes devotion to Mary. It was composed by the Syrian St Ephrem, although there are claims that it has been substantially revised by Ethiopians to serve the purpose of exalting Mary.[207] However, the doctrine of Mary was contested in the early church.[208]

Afework observes that with the Syrian Frumentius "ፍሬምናጦስ" as its first bishop, Ethiopian Christianity was introduced to Mariology from its inception. Frumentius honoured Mary by naming after her the first church building erected by the king, Aksum Tsion (St Mary of Zion) and the first Christian fellowship "Mahbere Mariam Tsion" (Society of Mary Zion).[209] However, Ethiopians continued to develop Mariology by adding a flavour of their own such as the famous God's covenant with Mary regarding Ethiopia which we shall discuss in due time.

In the EOC's official tradition, Mary was not exalted by her own merit but in relation to Christ and his work of salvation. However, the era that followed the reigns of King Dawit who is credited with a selection of translation of *Miracles of Mary* into Ge'ez, and his heir Zer'a Ya'iqob, inaugurated a new era of unprecedented devotion to Mary. Born as a result of his mother's vows to Mary, Zer'a Ya'iqob was dedicated to her as a baby. He did not introduce devotion to Mary, but developed it further by attributing to her the image of "co-redeemer" in a way which deviated from the Orthodox Mariology

---

only ones who are beautiful, completely so in every respect; for, Lord, there is no spot in you, nor any spot at all in your mother." Willis, ed., *Teachings of the Church Fathers*, 361.

207. Solomon Abebe, Interview, 25 February, 2011, Addis Ababa.

208. St Jerome affirmed, "We believe that God was born of the Virgin, because we read it. That Mary was married after she brought forth, we do not believe, because we do not read it. Nor we say this to condemn marriage . . . for virginity itself is the fruit of marriage. . . . You say that Mary did not continue a virgin: I claim still more, that Joseph himself on account of Mary was a virgin, so that from a virgin wedlock a virgin son was born." Willis, ed., *Teachings of the Church Fathers*, 358.

209. Afework Hailu, "Survey of the Ethiopian," 60–62.

elsewhere.[210] These distinct developments on the doctrine of Mary were based on the numerous writings produced by Zer'a Ya'iqob himself and priests at his court whom he highly encouraged to write.

Perhaps the most notable decree made by Zer'a Ya'iqob was the veneration of Mary and the Cross. "Jesus in Zara Ya'iqob's writing is in fact called 'her Son' (*Walda*) or 'the Son of Mary' (*Walda Maryam*), more than 'Jesus' or 'the Son of God.' And 'the body of Mary is . . . the body of God,' rather than 'the body of Christ is the body of Mary.'"[211] This shows that the theology of Zer'a Ya'iqob was not christo-centric.

The translation of her miracles from foreign sources, which was started by his father Dawit (1382–1413), increased significantly during his reign with further translations and the composition of local miracles at his palace. Among these were miracles intended as attacks upon the scholars and spiritual leaders (heads of monasteries) who objected to the extreme and undue reverence of Mary and to the unreasonable quantity and quality of her miracles. These miracle stories were designed to be read in the churches and monasteries of the empire, as they indeed still are, during daily church services along with the gospels.[212]

As illustrated in the meaning given to her name "guide to the kingdom of heaven," the texts written by Zer'a Ya'iqob and his scribes attributed to Mary the titles of Jesus Christ. Mary is presented as if the whole world was created for her. She is referred to as a redeemer of sinners and the giver of grace to those who serve her. The following is taken from Getatchew Haile's translation of the collection of her miracles that are read along with the gospels daily in the Orthodox Church and its monasteries.

> O my Son, my beloved, and my salvation, (you are) my hope and my refuge; and my trust is in you. . . . And now listen to my prayer and petition and give ear to the word of my mouth which I, your mother, and I, your handmaid, tell you. (It is)

---

210. ". . . our Lady Mary is the saviour of all . . . worship and prostration to her together with her son . . ." ". . . ሁሉን የምታድን እምቤታችን ማርያም ነች።. . . ለጊ ክብርና ስብሐት ይገባታል፤ ክል፳ም ጋራ አምልኮና ስግደት . . ." Getatchew Haile, ደቂቀ እስጢፋኖስ፣ 38–41. Translation by the researcher.

211. Getatchew Haile, *The Mariology of Emperor Zara Ya'eqob of Ethiopia* (Rome: Pontificium Institutum Studiorum Orientalium, 1992), 2.

212. Getatchew Haile, *Mariology of Emperor Zara Ya'eqob*, 2.

concerning him who makes my memorial, builds a church in my name, clothes the naked in my name, visits the sick, feeds the hungry, gives water to the thirsty or comforts the grief-stricken, gives joy to the distressed, or copies praises, names his son(s) and daughter(s) in my name,[213] or chants hymns in my name and on my name and on my holy days(s): Reward him, O Lord, with a good reward which the eyes have not seen, the ear has not heard, and has not been conceived in the heart of man. I petition you, O Lord, and supplicate to you for everyone who believes in me: Make him free from Hades, remembering the hunger and thirst and all temptations which befell me while with you." Our Lord Jesus Christ answered; he said to her, "Let it be as you said. I shall fulfil all your wishes. Was I not incarnated for this? I swear to you by myself lest I deny my covenant."[214]

The Orthodox Church over the years has made use of notions of Mary from the Bible and heavily depended on the writings of the church fathers and indigenous traditions regarding the status of Mary. A number of New Testament pseudonymous books are credited with the information about Mary of which Protoevangelium of James is most notable. These writings speak of her miraculous birth, the dedication of her parents and her extraordinary upbringing in the temple eating heavenly food, her leading a blameless life and finally God stretching out his undefiled hands to receive her blameless soul while nearly all the apostles witnessed; and the numerous miracles attributed to her body before it was laid to rest.[215]

Moreover, one of the books "Sene Golgotha" which is believed to have been written in the era of Zer'a Ya'iqob, claims that as a response to the

---

213. The Council of Scholars remarked, that giving the name of a saint to a child is meant to encourage the child to imitate the saint. However "The Ethiopian Orthodox Tewahdo Church does not teach that a person will be saved without faith and good works simply because he was given a name of a saint." የኢትዮጵያ ኦርቶዶክስ ቤተ ክርስቲያን ያለ ምግባርና ያለ ሃይማኖት ሰው በስም ብቻ ይድናል ብላ አታስተምርም, The EOTC Council of Scholars, እንዳያስታችሁ ተጠንቀቁ, 44.

214. Getatchew Haile, *Mariology of Emperor Zara Ya'eqob*, 6.

215. Protoevangelium of James, www.earlychurchtexts.com, accessed on 12 May 2011.

request of his mother, Christ entered into a covenant with her.[216] The claim that Christ entered into a covenant of mercy with Mary ኪዳነ ምሕረት (Kidane Mihret) is powerfully illustrated with the story of a cannibal who ate seventy-eight people and was about to devour one more man but found out that the poor man was covered with sores. When the poor man begged the cannibal for a handful of water in the name of the Trinity, he did not mind him, but when the beggar mentioned the name of Mary, the cannibal was touched and gave him a drop of water, and behold, on the day of judgment Mary intervened and had the angels stopped by Jesus from throwing this cannibal into the lake of fire. She reminded Jesus of his covenant with her, and Jesus had mercy on the cannibal.[217] The story is further implanted into the heart of the people through its incorporation into assigned readings during worship in the church and Mary is affectionately called "የበላዒ ሰብ እመቤት" (the Lady of the cannibal).[218]

> We supplicate the holy tabernacle, the fountain of life
> who bore and contained the prosphora.
> The greatness of her honour is admired
> When her miracle is read:

---

216. Tesfa G. Sellassie, ed., ስነ ገለጋታ (Addis Ababa: Tesfa Printing Press, 1984 Eth. C), 1–3.

217. When the poor man covered with sores asked the cannibal for water "for the sake of Our Lady Mary, the God-bearer." The cannibal said to the poor man, "Truly, I, too have heard since my youth that she is good and that she saves (one) by her prayer and delivers from Hades. I, too, take refuge now with her." Then he said to the poor (man), "Take; drink for the sake of the name of the holy Virgin Mary, the God-bearer!" When the cannibal died and he was about to be sent to hell by Christ but Mary said to Jesus, "He has given water to drink to a poor (man) for the sake of my name. And you have said to me, "He who has made you memorial and invoked your name will live an everlasting life." The Lord said to her, "I shall not deny my oath." And he had his angels put on a scale the seventy eight souls and the handful of water given in the name of Mary. The Virgin came closer so as to let her shadow fall onto the handful of water, and behold the water outweighed the seventy eight souls. The cannibal entered eternal life. Getatchew Haile, *Mariology of Emperor Zara Ya'eqob*, 8–9.

218. But when Zer'a Ya'iqob sent a copy of *Miracles of Mary* to all monasteries and churches and prescribed portions of it to be read in the church, there was a lot of opposition. One of the heads of churches who was determined not to make the *Miracles of Mary* part of the reading in his Church reasoned, "I teach my children the strict discipline as stated in the monastic tradition and some of them live in caves and some of them lead a disciplined life. If sinners hear this miracle [the justification of the cannibal] of the perpetual Virgin Mary, the Mother of God, they will give up their life of fasting and struggle and become lazy." Getatchew Haile, ደቂቀ እስጢፋኖስ "በሕግ አምላክ" (Disciples of Estifanos, an appeal) (Addis Ababa: AAU Press, 2010), 26. Translation by the researcher.

The man with a corrupted heart, who ate the body of his
>fellow (man),
by invoking the name of Mary,
entered the kingdom of heaven for a handful of cold water.
Listen and admire!
Love the history that recalls her!
Remember her reign!
The one who saves all[219] is Our Lady Mary.

Come, let us prostrate ourselves and sing for her reign,
she who carried and contained in her womb
the Lord of heaven and earth, the forgiver of sin and
>transgression.
Without exalting the rich
Nor despising the poor,
Mary loves everyone who performs good deeds,
she who is the sister of the vigilant Angels,
The daughter of the virtuous Prophets,
Honor and glory are meet for her,
with worship and prostration to her together with her Son,
on earth and in heaven,
in the sea(s) and in the abysses, forever. Amen.[220]

The implications of this story are beyond measure, because it gives unique assurance to Ethiopian Christians that as long as they give alms and do good works in Mary's name they are covered for eternity through the covenant of Christ to his mother. According to *Tamre Maryam* (*Miracles of Mary*) there is salvation by invoking her name regardless of the extent of sin one may have committed in his/her lifetime.[221]

---

219. Emphasis by the researcher.

220. Getatchew Haile, trans., *A Third Supplication for the Reading of the Miracles of Mary, The Cause of Estifanosites: A Fundamental Sect in the Church of Ethiopia*, Appendix V, in Religion Miscellanea 3, Addis Ababa, Institute of Ethiopian Studies, n.d., 132.

221. Similar hagiographies of the saints who are able to save people from hell are numerous. There is even a story of Kristos Semra who attempted to reconcile God and Satan. She asked God for permission to try to reconcile him with Satan and God replied that she could try but warned her that Satan would not agree. While gone to call Satan, he overpowers her and throws her deep into hell. Michael was sent to rescue her who in his

Zer'a Ya'iqob wished to extend to Mary the worship which was due to Christ because he believed that perfect purity and virginity [which characterized Mary] were divine.[222] His excessive veneration of Mary and claim that almsgiving in her name would equal righteousness was questioned by his contemporaries. Getatchew notes that there seem to have been church scholars who rejected the teaching of the excessive veneration of the Blessed Virgin on the ground that Mary had not been the concern or subject of the writers of the Scriptures; she is not conspicuous in the writings of the prophets and the apostles, at least not at the level of intensity presented by Zer'a Ya'iqob.[223]

Admasu Jembere, one of the theologians of the Orthodox Church, attempted to clarify the doctrine of righteousness through alms-giving in the name of Mary. "We do not believe, nor teach others that a prayer offered on behalf of a person who does not turn away from sin in repentance and ask for a prayer and intercession, but continues to swim in the sea of sin, will save him."[224] In the same vein, Seife Sellassie Yohannes, an instructor in theology at St Paul Theological College asserts in an article published in mid 1960s,

> On the merit of her motherhood to Christ who is fully God and fully man, St. Mary will pray for mercy to all those who beseech her according to the covenant . . . however, all of the books which are written in honour of St Mary do not imply that a person who does not believe in Christ her Son and demonstrate the evidence of his faith in good works, be saved simply by calling the name of Mary or taking her name. For Virgin Mary is the favour to the righteous and support for the holy, but not a hope for the rebellious and unbelievers . . . when we

---

attempt of searching for her soul ended up pulling out of hell numerous souls. Kristos Samra is believed to have received a covenant from God which enables her to save three thousand souls each day. Getachew, ገድል ወይስ ገድል (Addis Ababa: 1995 Eth. C), 74–75.

222. Getatchew Haile, *Mariology of Emperor Zara Ya'eqob*, 63.

223. Getatchew Haile, 65.

224. "ማንም ሰው ቢኽን ከኃጢአቱ ተመልሶ ንስሃ ገብቶ ጸልይልኝ አማልዱኝ ሳይል እርሱ በኃጢአት ባሕር እየዋኘ ሌላው ቢጸልይለት ይድናል ብለን እናምንም ሌላውም እናስተምርም።" Admasu Jembere, ከኩሃ ሃይማኖት (*The foundation of faith*) (Addis Ababa: Tinsae Zegubae Printing, 1949 Eth. C), 169. (Translation by the researcher).

attest that St Virgin Mary intercedes on our behalf according to the covenant we are not setting aside the mercifulness of her Son our savior Jesus Christ because she gained this grace because of her motherhood to him, so primarily we have to believe in his mercifulness and that he is the saviour.[225]

But the statement of Seife Sellassie falls short of reflecting the situation because "salvation by solely calling Mary's name" is exactly what Tamre Mariam clearly assures people of. Perhaps because of intense pressure from the reformed groups as a result of embarrassment over Zer'a Ya'iqob's formula which exalts Mary and the Cross as equal to creator, the explanation offered by the Council of Scholars of the Orthodox Church denies the deifying implications of the text.

According to them the phrase, "for in their glory they are equal [to the creator]" compares Mary and the Cross with each other, and implies that when God assumed humanity from the Virgin Mary to save the world, his glory was revealed in Mary and the Cross. This is not meant to compare Mary and the Cross with the creator. The implication behind the assertion that Mary and the Cross deserve glory refers to the glory which God ordained for them. Perhaps unable to offer satisfactory explanation for the apparent contradiction of the text with the Bible, the scholars added that these readings have deeper meaning which will not be easily grasped.[226] The

---

225. "ድንግል ማርያም በአንድ ጊዜ ፍዳም ሰው ፍዳም አምላክ ብላን ላምናምነው ኢየሱስ ክርስቶስ እናት ስለሆነች በቃል ኪዳንዋ ለተማፅኑ ሁሉ ምሕረትን ክልጅዋ ዘንድ ትለምንላቸዋለች . . . ነገር ግን ማንም ሰው ክርስቶ በተወላደው በክርስቶስ ሳያምኑ ለአምነቱ መግለጫና ፍሬ የሚሆነውም መልካም ምግባር ሳያሰይ የድንግል ማርያምን ስም በመጥራትና በስምዋ በመሰየም ብቻ እንደሚድን ስለ እምቤታችን ቅድስት ድንግል ማርያም የተጻፉ መጻሕፍት ሁሉ አያስረዳም፡፡ ምክንያቱም ቅድስት ድንግል ማርያም የደረቃን ምገስ የቀዲሳን መመኪያ ናት እንጂ የዓለሞችና የአካማንያን ተስፋ አይደለችምና . . . ቅድስት ድንግል ማርያም በተሰዎት ቃል ኪዳን መሠረት ታማልደናለች በምልበት ጊዜ የልጅዋ የመድኃኒታችን የኢየሱስ ክርስቶስን መሐሪነት በመዘንጋት አይደለም፡፡ እርሶ ይህን ፀጋና ምገስ ለማግኘት የቻለቹው ንታችን ክርስቶስን በመውለደ ነውና በቅድሚያ የእርሱን አዳኝነት እንድንምን ያለልገል፡," Seife Sellassie Yohannes, የምሕረት ቃል ኪዳን (The Covenant of Mercy), Tinsae, no. 29 (Yekatit 1972 Eth. C), 3–4. (Translation by the researcher).

226. "በክብር ተካካዋል የሚለው ሁለቱን እምቤታችንን ቅድስት ድንግል ማርያምንና መስቀልን እንጂ፤ አነሱ ክፈጣሪ ጋር ተካካዋል የማል ትርጉም የለውም፤ የትርጓሜ ስልቱ፤ እግ የረቀቀና የመጠቀ ስለሆነ እንደ አነት ያላ የማይደውስ ድውይ፤ የማይመለስ ጉጉይ፤ ሊደርስበት ሊረዳው አይችልም፡፡ በሌላም በኩል ክቡር ይገለጣዋል ሲባል፤ ሊፈጣሪ ያለው ክብር፤ ለድንግል ማርያምና ለመስቀል ይገለጣዋል ማለት ሳይሆን፤ ፈጣሪ የሰጣቸው ወይም ፈጣሪ እነርሱን ያክበረብት ክብር ይገለጣዋል ማለት ነው፤ በክብር ተካካዋል ማለትም፤ ቅድስት ድንግል ማርያምና መስቀል ክአምላክ ጋር በክብር ተካካዋል ማለት አይደለም፡፡ ነገር ግን ዓለም ለማዳን ክድንግል ማርያም ክአጋባ ሥጋ፤ ክነስክፍ ነፍስ ነስቶ፤ የተወላደው አምላክ በመስቀል ሳለምን በዳነ ጊዜ፤ በቅድስት ማርያምና በቅስ መስቀል የእርሱ ክብር ተገለጠ ማለት ነው፡," The EOTC Council of Scholars, እንዳያታችሁ ተጠንቀቁ፤ 48–49.

consistent objection of the Orthodox Church to the accusation that they worship Mary also serves as indication that Zer'a Ya'iqob's Mariology is not boldly acclaimed, at least not her equality to the Son.

In addition to the reaction of some theologians, what goes on in the feast days which are meant to commemorate Mary raises serious questions even among the youth of the church. In the late seventies, the youth in the EOC used the official media of the church to openly speak against what they considered as demonic worship in disguise on official feast days in commemoration to the saints. The chief of such holidays was "ግንቦት ማርያም" (Ginbot Mariam) which is believed to be the birthday of Mary.[227]

Evangelicals rejoice in such a reaction from the Orthodox in opposition to the exaltation of creatures as high as the Creator, or at times, even higher than the Creator. However, they do not always realize that most of the time, the mother and Son are inseparable in the minds of Orthodox followers. The Orthodox do not see how exalting the mother affects the glory of the Son. Evangelicals at times show little understanding of the dynamics at work while disregarding Mary. In order to exalt the Saviour, they diminish the role of Mary in God's plan of salvation.

Such a radical approach is rejected by Afework Hailu, a former Orthodox member. In an article entitled "Protestants should give Due Respect to Mary" Afework expresses his concern over the implications of unwarranted claims made against Mary's part in God's plan of salvation. He argues, "In order to

---

227. The youth broke evil worship objects and instructed the people against these evil practices. The people responded by bringing their worship objects and animals dedicated for evil spirits to the Church and the clergy did not stop them. The priests supported the youth and discarded the objects and sprinkled those to be kept with holy water. The youth urged, "The pure worship of God is to be restoredeverywhere." "ጠንቋዮች ተጋለጡ" (Diviners exposed), *Tinsae*, no. 15 (1971 Eth. C), 19–23, there is a report which refers to the campaigning of Kibre Tewahdo Ortodoxawit Haymanot Yewotatoch Menfesawi Mahber, specifically referred also to the commemoration of Mary on Ginbot 1st (May 8/9) as serving demonic purposes. The person who reported wrote, "Satan uses this annual big holiday to deceive people under the pretext of commemorating our lady and her name. The fact that he expanded human traditional rituals and unwholesome worship and has enslaved people with the means of it is to crate animosity between God and humanity." "በተለይ ትልቁ በዓል በየዓመቱ በግንቦት ማርያም ዕለት ነው። በዚህ አንጻረ ሰይጣን በተንኮሉና በጥበቡ ማርያምን ያስከበረ በማስመሰል በአመቤታችን በማርያም ዕለት ክብርና በስሟ በመሰየም የሰውን ልማዳዊ ሥርዓትና አምልክ ባዕድን ማሠራጨቱ ሰውን ከዚህ ልማዶች ጋር ማቆራኘቱ ከአምላክ ጋር ለማጣላት መሆኑ ግልጽ ነው።" In a similar vein pagan worship and preparing feast in remembrance of the dead were renounced by a writer who claimed that the Church is opposed to pagan worshi Esayiyas Wondimagegnehu, "የባህል አስረኛ" (Prisoner of culture), *Tinsae*, no. 22 (1971 Eth. C), 4.

avoid talking about Mary, in order to exclude Mary, we should not mix the gospel with falsehood, we should be careful not to teach erroneous teaching about Christ." Afework challenges the view that where Christ assumed flesh from is irrelevant for the salvation of humanity. He painstakingly shows how such an argument shakes the basic tenets of the Christian doctrine, the incarnation and the substitutionary death of Christ.[228]

In addition to the exaltation of Mary which was ordained by emperor Zer'a Ya'iqob, it seems that the Evangelicals' disregard for Mary is causing the Orthodox to specifically stress their devotion to her in unprecedented ways. The ever-growing popular sayings and slogans reflect a greater devotion to the Mother of God "ወላዲተ አምላክ." These slogans are usually found on taxis, private cars and even government-owned public transportation. This work has paid particular attention to popular theologies reflected with sayings and poems posted on taxis in Addis. At times the taxi drivers seem to have strong opinion about a particular theology but the posters are produced for commercial purposes.[229]

Some of the slogans clearly have an Evangelical audience in mind; a case in point is, "whether you like it or not our Lady is an intercessor."[230] The role of Mary in the salvation of humanity is highlighted in different ways, even to the extent of bringing her to the centre of God's plan of salvation. One of the most popular slogans which has the potential to shock when read for the first time asserts, "Without the intercession of the Mother of God the world will not be saved."[231] In the same vein another slogan reads, "There is no Christianity apart from Mary."[232] These two slogans clearly present Mary as the focal point of redemption with no mention of the name of Jesus. Needless to say they force onlookers to wonder what the writers were thinking when they attribute to Mary the fruits of the sacrificial death of Christ. But they provide us with yet another example that in the mind of the Orthodox Mary and Christ are inseparable. The following slogan

---

228. Afework Hailu, "ፕሮቴስታንቶች ለማርያም ተገቢውን ሥፍራ ሊሰጡ ይገባል" (Protestants should give Mary due respect), *Gesame* 3, no. 9 (Nehasse, 1997 Eth. C), 15; 13.

229. Fire Hiwot, Trader of banners, posters and car decorations, Interview, January 2011, Addis Ababa. Cf. Tamrat, Taxi driver, December 2010, Addis Ababa.

230. "ወደድከም ጠላህም እመቤታችን አማላጅ ናት," posted on a taxi, 3 June 2010.

231. "ያለ ወላዲተ አምላክ አማላጅነት ዓለም አይድንም," posted on a taxi, 14 May 2010.

232. "ያለ ማርያም ክርስትና የለም," posted on a taxi, 18 July 2010.

reflects similar belief. "If one has the Mother and the Son, what can he possibly lack?"[233]

Some of the writings attempt to capture the full humanity of Christ profoundly. In one of such poems, the writer beseeches Mary, "for you are the one who breastfed him and tearfully fled to Egypt to keep him safe, intercede on my behalf with your Son O mother of my Lord."[234] The eyes of the Evangelical might focus on the intercession of Mary, but the poem portrays the humanity of Jesus by highlighting the motherhood of Mary, how she carried baby Jesus in her arms. This powerfully reflects the mystery of the incarnation: God with us.

Some slogans address the mother and Son together: "The world is saved by you and in your Son it found peace."[235] This one sounds like a reaction against Evangelicals' disregard for Mary. And another read: "The Virgin gave birth to her creator, and He created her."[236] Perhaps Evangelicals would have preferred to read the passive voice, "The creator was born from the virgin" instead of "the virgin gave birth to her creator." This way it shows that the Virgin did not give birth to the creator out of her own free will, but that she was chosen by Him to bear him in her womb. But the birth of Christ is prophesied in active voice in the Scriptures as well.

The slogan theology is used both by Orthodox and Evangelical taxi drivers. For example, it is not unusual to find oneself in the front seat of a taxi which has "Without the intercession of the Mother of God, the world will not be saved" and see another Taxi right in front of it which in its rear window has the passage from Acts 16:31: "believe in the Lord Jesus, and you will be saved – you and your household."[237]

Some slogans which have Scripture passages taken out of their context appear to have been meant to assert the position of the Orthodox Church on the intercessory role of the saints; "Do you not know that the saints will

---

233. "እናትና ልጅን የያዘ ምን ይሆናል," posted on a taxi, 19 August 2010.

234. "በጡባሽው ጡትሽ በዚያ በወተቴ፣ በፈሰስሽው እንባ በግብጽ በስደቴ፣ ከልጅሽ አማልጂኝ የጌታዬ እናቴ," posted on a taxi, 15 December 2010.

235. "ዓለም ባንቺ ዳነ በልጅሽም ሰላም ሆነ," posted on a taxi, 19 December 2010.

236. "ድንግል ፈጣሪዋን ወለደችው እርሱም እርሷን ፈጠራት," posted on a taxi, 7 May 2010.

237. Both Taxies were spotted on 18 February 2011. Interestingly the writings on private cars which reflect Evangelical convictions were in English: "I belong to Jesus," 26 May 2010; "Jesus is the answer," 14 June 2010.

judge the world?" (1 Cor 6:2). Of course there are some who have posted on their front mirror: "Jesus is Lord"[238] (which usually is the slogan of Protestants) and yet on the inner side of the ceiling of the taxi a huge banner is hung which reads, "St [Mary], intercede on our behalf."[239] It seems that there is a concern to secure maximum protection with a prayer to Mary and an affirmation of Jesus's lordship.

Some of the printed messages are at times used to hold together a broken window or just as decorations for the interior of the vehicle. There also are Scripture passages posted which refer to Mary. For example there are the words of Elizabeth while greeting Mary: "But why am I so favoured, that the mother of my Lord should come to me?"[240] And Mary's words, "Generations will call me blessed."[241] Such writings seem to be an attempt to validate the veneration of Mary.

Mekonnen looks at most of these slogans as belonging to one package of defending faith. He remarks, "These sayings are triggered by the Protestants' disregard for Mary and also Muslims' growing habit of posting Quranic quotations on their vehicle which read: "Say it, Allah is one God, he does not give birth, neither is he born."[242] Mekonnen says that these slogans do not necessarily represent the official position of the church. They are just the public's way of expressing its beliefs.[243]

Regarding the slogans which magnify Mary's role in salvation, a priest of the EOC remarked that they are simply reflections of Christ and his work of salvation. "No doubt they raise eye brows when you see them for the first time, but the emphasis on Mary shows the centrality of the incarnation in God's plan of salvation and that is how I look at them."[244]

---

238. This is a typical slogan of Ethiopian Evangelicals and it tends to annoy EOC members for a number of reasons. For one thing the EOC adherents do not use the name Jesus without Christ. The usual title they use in reference to Jesus is Medhane Alem (Saviour of the world) or our Lord and saviour Jesus Christ. So using the name "Jesus" appears to annoy them. More so the slogan that "Jesus is Lord." Some sarcastically comment, "who said that he is a servant to cause you to shout that he is Lord?!

239. ቅድስት ሆይ አማልጂኝ Posted on a taxi, 21 February 2011.

240. Posted on a taxi, 16 February 2011.

241. Posted on a taxi, 16 February 2011.

242. Posted on a taxi, May, 2010.

243. Mekonnen, Interview 15 November 2010, Addis Ababa.

244. Informant G, Interview, February 2011, Addis Ababa.

There is no question that many of the slogans are formulated to refute the Evangelicals' stand about Mary's status. The message to Evangelicals seems to be that they cannot talk about Christ and his salvation apart from Mary and the incarnation (the humanity he assumed from her). But there is a concern that such radical slogans may eventually become adopted into the dogmas of the church, especially in view of the antagonistic beliefs of Evangelicals regarding Mary.[245] It may also be noted that they are the reflections of the "hidden dogma" which is at work in the church. In other words, some of the unwarranted writings and hagiographies which are read in the church during worship elevate Mary into the same status to that of Christ. Although the church does not officially endorse such an exaltation of Mary and denies worshipping her, its tolerance of such readings shows that a more powerful "hidden dogma" has the upper hand in the church.

On the other hand, there are clear examples of utter deviation from the Bible by the clergy of the Orthodox Church. Such shocking teachings and actions might be blamed on the Evangelicals' tendency to disregard Mary in order to exalt Christ and the Bible. However, the Orthodox's reaction of downplaying Jesus Christ in order to exalt Mary clearly calls for a decisive measure by the church's Council of Scholars.

A case in point is a video entitled "የተኩላዎቹ ምስጢር ሲጋለጥ" (The Scheme of the Wolves Revealed), which showed the "exorcism" of young people who were "possessed" by evil spirits. When confronted by the priest, the "demons" identified themselves as the spirits of "Jesus of darkness," "Jesus of the abyss," "Jesus of Nazareth," "*menafiqan*." The saga comes to a climax with the "exorcist" sending the "possessed" men and women to beat up Evangelicals seated in front of the assembly. The crowd cheers, applauds, ululates and appears to be amused at watching Evangelicals beaten up, despite repeatedly calling the name of Jesus to command the "spirits" to let go off them. The "spirits" were allegedly "exorcised" in the name of Mary[246] and the crowd goes wild

---

245. Informant D, Interview, 18 August 2010, Addis Ababa.

246. The twist of "exorcising" the "spirit of Jesus" in the name of Mary seemed self evident that the scene was a rehearsed drama.

and the Evangelicals shout at the top of their voice, "We are not commanded to exorcise spirits in the name of Mary, but Jesus Christ."[247]

The producers of the video appear to have aimed at damaging the credibility of the Evangelicals' claim that they perform miracles in the name of Jesus, while they were not able to protect themselves from a physical attack by "demoniacs" though repeatedly invoking the name of Jesus, whom they loved dearly and preached about so passionately.[248]

In the face of such controversies, Orthodox writers and theologians do not deny the inadequacy of the knowledge of the Scriptures among their members and even some of the clergy. However, they highly resent the Evangelicals' consideration of their regard for the saints and angels as idolatry and a practice of *Ahzab* (pagans).[249] The argument behind the elevation

---

247. A video footage entitled የተኩላዎቹ ምስጢር ሲጋለጥ (The scheme of the wolves revealed). The video shooting shows the "possessed" people being interrogated one by one and the "evil spirits" in them affirm that they are related to Jesus. One says, he was possessed while singing and the boy sings one of the Evangelical songs which says "Jesus is my peace." All of the "possessed" people cry "Hallelujah!" with a loud voice. There are five people presented as Evangelicals (four men and one woman) seated at the front row while everybody else is seated on the ground and the Evangelicals try to speak up each time the teacher talks to those who were "possessed" by the evil spirit. When the preacher commands the spirits to come out in the name of Mary and touches the forehead of one of the "possessed" with the picture of Mary the boy cries out in agony that he is set on fire. The Evangelical man cries out, "We are commanded not to worship any images! We are not commanded to exorcise in the name of Mary, but Jesus." Then the teacher turns to the "possessed" people and tells them to go get the pastors and ridicules, "Here it is, you command it out in the name of Jesus." The pastors are beaten up by the "possessed" people despite calling the name of Jesus. Then the preacher places Mary's picture on each "possessed" person's forehead commanding the spirit to come out. He commands the spirit to come out in the name of the Holy Trinity, Abune Gebre Menfes Qidus, and Mary, but not even once did he mention the name of Jesus in commanding the "spirit" out. He asks the crowd "is it possible to let loose in the name of Jesus the spirit who is bound in the name of Mary?" and the crowd shouts back, "No!" He turns towards the Evangelicals and mocks them, "they cannot defend themselves from Satan's attack. Satan is not able to defend himself against himself." The "delivered" men and women stand up covered with traditional clothe, take up the tambourine singing praises and dancing to the Lord along with the preachers. In his reply to the above video an Evangelical person came up with a title, "ተኩላው ማነው?" (Who is the wolf?) and argued that the "spirit-possessed" people's saga appeared to be fabricated and that the whole scenario is against the respected tradition of the Orthodox Church.

The presented avoided generalization and expressed deep respect for the EOC Clips of the VCD used by Teshome Shiferaw, ተኩላው ማነው? (Who is the wolf?), (Audiovisual presentation), Addis Ababa, Yemelekot Dimts Agelgelot, 2003 Eth. C.

248. The preacher mocked Evangelicals for saying "I love you, Jesus" and remarked that this is not the correct way of addressing God.

249. Esubalew, Belete, የገሃነም ደጆች (Gates of hell), 113; Daniel, Interview, 8 September 2010; Mekonnen, Interview, 15 November 2010.

of the saints is that they are fellow human beings who reflect the glory of Christ. "The saints display his glory and again, it is because of Christ that they are venerated. Thus, their veneration comes as a result of Christ's glory displayed on them. These are his followers, his martyrs, they reflect his glory. Successful soldiers bring glory to their commander. Likewise Jesus as the commander is exalted in what he has done through the saints."[250]

Daniel argues that pictures signify more than words could ever communicate.[251] He asks, "Do we not partake the grace of God and be edified by reading the story of the saints in the Bible? The same principle applies to the icons and pictures of the saints. If reading letters imparts grace, how much more would looking at their picture and touching it impart the grace? After all letters come with various shapes and they are like pictures which we make sense out of by reading."[252]

As for the concern of Evangelicals that the kissing and veneration of images is contrary to the commandment of God against image worship, Daniel notes that the iconographic tradition of the Orthodox Church makes a distinction between images and pictures. The church does not teach her members to worship the saints or their pictures, but to give due honour to those who deserve it. There are three kinds of *sigdet*,[253] "prostration" in the Dogma of the church: prostration of honour (which is due to respectable people), prostration of grace (which is due to the saints), and prostration of worship (which is due only to God). Daniel acknowledged that it is possible for people to unknowingly mix these up and prostrate and pray in a manner which appears to the onlooker to be worship. "But we are talking about God here. To begin with there is no perfect way of worshipping God

---

250. Daniel, Interview, 8 September 2010.

251. In the EOC tradition images are considered to be representations of the portrayed person. For example they believe that miracles can be performed through the use of the image of Mary. There is a concern about the inappropriate use of images of the Saints which are supposed to be venerated. Wearing T-shirts and hats with imprinted images of the saints and selling the images of the saints along with the pictures of Holy Wood celebrities upsets some Orthodox people. Hiwot Zefre Kidusan, "ቅዱሳት ሥዕላት በነጋ ገበያ" (Holy pictures on sale), *Hamer* 8 (Yekatit 2002 Eth. C), 40.

252. Daniel, Interview, 8 September 2010.

253. This Amharic noun is used in reference to worship of God, as much as just courteous bowing down.

for humans. We all fall short of God's glory. So God, who searches people's heart, will take the worship that is due to Him."[254]

In response to the accusation that EOC followers worship Mary, Mihretab, one of the Orthodox teachers asks, "Have we ever said that Mary is our creator? Did we ever say that Mary was crucified on our behalf? We do not worship her but give her the honour that is due to her."[255]

In practice, however, the above things seem to be widely affirmed. The presence of exceptional love for Mary, which perhaps has its roots in the claim that Mary is the divinely appointed guardian of Ethiopia, at times is expressed in ways which equate her with the Creator.[256] There also is a tradition which claims that Mary and her family came to Ethiopia from Egypt in their flight from Herod. The Ethiopians were so kind to the family that Mary blessed them, their land and their generations. Jesus then promised Mary Ethiopia to be hers forever as a tithe.[257]

Besides the taxi slogans, the use of audio and visual media in propaganda against each other is growing at an alarming rate. Evangelical preachers and teachers appear to have shaken off their fear of the Orthodox; hence, an open and direct attack of the structures of the church has been launched. A strong response of Orthodox followers which addresses the whole Evangelical community is indiscriminate.

---

254. Daniel, Interview, 8 September 2010.

255. Mihretab Assefa፣ ፕሮቴስታንታዊ ጂሃድ በተዋህዶ ላይ ሲፋፋም (Protestant jihad against Tewahdo), (Audiovisual presentation), Addis Ababa, Ab Spiritual Songs House, n.d.

256. It is not uncommon to hear scriptures in songs which attribute to Mary what is ascribed to God. For example Engidawork Bekele takes the words of Psalm 116:12, "How can I repay the Lord for all his goodness to me?" and replaces them with "How can I repay my Lady for all her goodness to me." Psalm 40:1 says, "I waited patiently for the Lord; he turned to me and heard my cry." The singer says, "I waited patiently for Covenant of Mercy (Kidane Mihret)" ". . . I passed through the time of trial by drawing near to you O redeemer of the world . . ." In the same song Engidawork takes the prayer of Hannah from 1 Samuel 2 and sings them to Mary and Jesus, "My heart rejoices in you [Mary], your servant delights in your deliverance [Mary], your Son has broken the bows of the worriers." The passage in Romans 8:35 which reads, "Who shall separate us from the love of Christ . . ." provides us with another example. The singer says, "Who shall separate me from the love of My Lady?" Deacon Engidawork Bekele, ዕጅ ጠናሁ (I waited patiently) 9, (Audiovisual songs), Addis Ababa, Agape Spiritual Songs Shop, n.d. Cf. Agizachew Tefera, የለውጥ ያሀ (The need for change) (Addis Ababa: n.p., 2001 Eth. C): 207–210.

257. Budge, *Legends of Our Lady*, LXIV; Tamre Mariyam Geez and Amharic (Addis Ababa: Tinsae Zegubae Printing Press, 1989 Eth. C): 38, 132–133; Ayalew, Tamiru, መጽ ተአምደና ከተኩላ ዝምደና፣ (Addis Ababa: n.p., 1953 Eth. C), 231, 233.

One of such VCDs[258] was released by Ephrem Ketema entitled ተቐል "Tekel," based on Dan 5:27.[259] The cover of the VCD which has a picture of a beast with seven heads, and ten horns seems to allude to Revelation 16–19. The speaker negates the claims of "Tamre Mariam" (*Miracles of Mary*), one of the most treasured books of the EOC, with a stern and commanding voice. The preacher uses the strongest terms possible claiming that the "Mary" of Tamre Mariam does not represent Mary the mother of Jesus. Ephrem argues that Tamre Mariam and the other traditional books of the church which are far from the Bible have only created a generation which does not know God, is ignorant of the Bible, follows fables instead of the Bible, and has gone into prostitution, adultery, and drunkenness. He concludes that Tamre Mariam has not contributed any good to the church and is of the Devil.[260]

A selective response from one of the Orthodox teachers, Tariku Abebe, came with a VCD entitled, "Give honour to whom it is due."[261] On the reverse side of the VCD Ephrem's words (which he used to describe the Mary of Tamre Mariam), are taken out of their context and applied to the Mother of Jesus. One such quotation reads, "Mary is an adulterous, merciless, blood-thirsty, evil woman who was possessed by an evil spirit of the desert." Just above Ephrem's saying, Tariku's reply is quoted: "Our Lady Saint Virgin Mary is the queen of heaven and earth, tender hearted, compassionate to the distressed and intercessor of the world."[262]

At any rate, Ephrem's VCD shows his strong feeling against Mariology and unwillingness to even try to cite any verse which exalted Christ. To some extent this reflects the tendency to avoid Mariology altogether resenting that in the name of Mary the centrality of Christ is undermined.[263] On

---

258. VCD is a video recording device similar to DVD.

259. Ephrem Ketema, ተቐል (Tekel), (Audiovisual presentation), Addis Ababa, Abrsh Video Production and Photo, n.d. Daniel 5:27 gives the meaning of "Tekel" as, "You have been weighed on the scales and found wanting."

260. Ephrem Ketema, ተቐል (Tekel), (Audiovisual presentation), Addis Ababa, Abrsh Video Production and Photo, n.d.

261. Tariku uses the Amharic word "ክብር" and it is here translated to mean "honour." The term is also used to refer to "glory." Hence, the confusion in using it for God and humans.

262. Tariku Abera, ክብር ለሚገባው ክብርን ስጡ (Give glory to whom it is due) (Audiovisual presentation), Addis Ababa, Antsokiya Spiritual Songs House, n.d.

263. Ephrem's approach is mostly disrespectful with obvious contempt for what people hold as dear.

the other hand Tariku painstakingly attempts to justify Tamre Mariam's claims, even the one that says, "know very well that He created our Lady [made her] the saviour of the world."²⁶⁴ His presentation implies that there is little preparation on the part of some Orthodox theologians to challenge unbiblical assertions with the truth of the Scriptures. Perhaps because of the wide acceptance of the book, there appears to be fear of contradicting it, lest they will be labelled *tehadiso*.²⁶⁵

However, as shown above, there were Orthodox voices of the clergy and laity against non-Christian practices. Thus, the attitude of Ephrem (which is aggressive) was detestable to the EOC respondent. If Ephrem were to communicate his message with a spirit of humility, love and without generalization, the reception of his message might have been different.

The approach of Ephrem and the EOC priests in the video, "የተኩላዎች ሚስጢር ሲጋለጥ," appear to be less than helpful for the cause of the gospel. The back and forth accusation between the Orthodox Church and Evangelicals makes one wonder whether the whole idea behind the production of audio and visual messages which are full of demonizing one another, is making money out of their sale. There are some that are wholesome, but many of them appear to add fuel to the already aggravated situation. Needless to say they have the potential to lead the Orthodox to the conclusion that Evangelicals indeed are enemies of Mary. On the other hand it strengthens the already formulated conclusion of Evangelicals that the Orthodox Church is more interested in traditions apart from the Bible and that it does not give prominence to the Bible and all it asserts about Christ.

As for the growing tendency in the Ethiopian Orthodox church to use the Scriptures to assert a given doctrine, some Evangelicals believe that it was

---

264. Tamre Mariyam, 48.

265. A written critique was produced by Yabsira Girum. He criticizes Tariku about quoting Tamre Mariam as authoritative source. The writer calls Tamre Mariam የተረት መጽሐፍ (Book of tales). He remarked that Tariku spoke what he did not because he does not know the truth, but just for the marketability of his VCD "እንዲህ የሚያደርጉትም የሚሰብኩት ነገር ስህተት መሆኑ ሳይገባቸው ቀርቶ ነው ማለት አይቻልም፡፡ ነገር ግን የወንጌሉ ብርሃን ባለገላቸው ወገኖች ዘንድ ተቀባይነትን ለማትረፍ ነው ተብሎ ይታሰባል፡፡ ምናልባትም በዚህ ክንቱ ስብከት በጨለማ ያለውን ሕዝብ ዐይን ይበልጥ አሳውሮ የሀሴት ገበያውን ለማድራትም ሊሆን ይችላል፡" Yabsira Girum, ለታምረ ማርያም አትከራከር፤ ክብር ለሚገባው ክብርን ስጡ ለሚለው የመምህር ታሪኩ አበራ ስብከት የተሰጠ ምላሽ (Do not defend Tamre Mariam, a response to Tariku Abera's sermon on the topic, "Give glory to whome it is due") (Addis Ababa: n.p., 2003 Eth. C), 42.

the result of the Evangelicals' presence,[266] but some of the EOC teachers differ, denying any kind of influence from the Evangelicals.[267] Some admit that the Evangelicals have influenced Orthodox both for the better and for the worse.[268] The high place reserved for Mary is one of the doctrines that appear to be unbridgeable between Evangelicals and the Orthodox Church. The claims of the church that its devotion to Mary is meant to exalt Christ has not convinced Evangelicals.

The numerous stories told about Mary immensely concern the Evangelicals. In fact, they accuse the church of equating Mary with the Son, but this is vehemently denied by the Orthodox. The basis for hailing Mary, according to Orthodox theologians, rests solely on the work of God that set her apart from all women; as it is attested in the Scriptures. By hailing her, they hail Christ whom she bore. Daniel argues:

> The honour and adoration attributed to Mary is not by her own merit. If not for God's glorious plan of choosing her to bear the saviour she would have remained an ordinary girl from Galilee and no one would have put an eye on her. Then how can you accuse us of worshipping Mary? Can't you see it is the Son she carried we are worshipping? Do you understand the glory of God? Then think for a moment the mind-boggling concept of the young Mary carrying the creator in her womb. Does this not call for awe, and praise. She represented humanity in giving God her flesh by which Christ assumed humanity. It is Christ we are honoring and not Mary apart from him.[269]

The EOC reformation movements, however, bring forth strong arguments in support of the misplaced status of Mary. In fact, they argue that

---

266. Nigusse, Interview, 30 September 2010; Bekele W/Kidan, Interview, 25 August 2010.

267. Daniel, 8 September 2010.

268. Mekonnen, Interview, 15 November 2010.

269. Daniel, Interview, 8 September 2010. Daniel believes that dictating people as to how to worship God reflects the mentality of missionaries; the way in which they try to show superiority. "They want to show that they know what is best for others. There is no spirit of teachability and humility. They always feel that they know it all and feel that those who do not do things their way are doomed. We do not do that. We respect people's expressions of worship to God. We never assume lordship over them." Daniel, Interview, 30 December 2010, Addis Ababa.

Mary has so overshadowed Christ that the whole worship of the church revolves around her and not Christ. A simple example they say is the teaching of the EOC that listening to Mary's miracles read would impart equal grace to partaking in the Eucharist.[270]

Mekonnen, the teacher of history in Holy Trinity Theological College, however, looks at these words as an Alexandrian conspiracy to ensure the continual dependence of the church of Ethiopia on the church of Alexandria. According to him, the church of Alexandria is open all the time for its members to partake in the Eucharist, but the Egyptian bishops wanted the Ethiopians to remain ignorant about the teaching of the Bible.[271] Daniel responds that the reading that equates listening to Mary's miracle to partaking in the Eucharist is not commonly used and when it is used the motive behind it is not to exalt Mary, but to help those who for one reason or another are unable to partake in the Eucharist to reflect on the miraculous conception of Christ.[272]

The natural Evangelical tendency of avoiding talking about Mary at all costs is apparently a reaction against the Orthodox Church's utter devotion to the Mother of God. As far as the church is concerned, each statement Evangelicals make against Mary only signifies their rejection of her stand, thereby showing their true colours. But when Evangelicals speak about her, that is looked at suspiciously, as a strategy to attract the attention of Orthodox people and "mislead" them into turning to Protestantism.

Such a conclusion is not groundless, but based on printed practical guides on how to share the gospel with EOC followers. Some guidelines advise Evangelicals to avoid head on clashes on matters concerning Mary, but to show respect for her. Such guidelines suggest that the best approach is to avoid bringing up issues which are vital for the Orthodox such as Mary and the angels. Mahbere Kidusan asks, "What is the need for evangelizing Christians in the first place?" They warn their audience that *menafiqan* are using the pictures of Mary and angels which they used to detest, and the strategy is to appear as Orthodox adherents.[273] For an Orthodox person

---

270. Solomon Abebe Interview, 25 February 2011.
271. Mekonnen, Interview, 15 November 2010.
272. Daniel, Interview, 8 September 2010.
273. *Hamer*, no. 5 (Tahsas/Tir, 1993 Eth. C), 2.

who reads such guidelines, the mention of Mary in their conversation with Evangelicals should put them on their guard because they would look at it as a strategy to get their attention.

It is explicitly stated in the writings of the Orthodox that the church does not worship Mary, but honours her.[274] However, the various allusions to her glorified role in salvation, the readings which equate her with Christ and the claims which give her authority to pronounce forgiveness are not adequately explained. In other words, while the writings and allusions attribute to Mary more than honour the theologians of the church are at pains to justify them. Thus, the theologians of the church are yet to engage texts prominent in the tradition which are clearly in opposition to the Bible. They also need to pay attention to the concern that people are being led astray because of unwarranted writings which boldly attribute the position of Christ to Mary. In such discussions what is at stake is not the honour of Evangelicals, but the glory of Christ himself, who is the head of the church.

5.3.2. Sola Scriptura and the Mother-Tongue Translations of the Bible

Both the Ethiopian Orthodox church and Evangelicals claim that the Bible is their foundation. However the insistence of Evangelicals that the Bible is the sole authority and consequent disinterest in the tradition of the church, continues to divide the two groups. In fact, most of the differences between Evangelicals and the Orthodox Church rest on the authority and status of the Bible, because Evangelicals limit themselves to the sixty-six books while the Orthodox Church acknowledges other extra traditions.[275]

The Evangelicals' concerns about the status of the Bible in the Orthodox Church upsets Orthodox theologians. Daniel argues that it is the 318 Orthodox fathers who canonized the Bible and gave it to the world to begin with.[276] Such respectable fathers have left behind numerous written

---

274. Ayalew notes that the EOC does not worship Mary. The Church does not give Mary what is due to God. Ayalew, 1953 Eth. C, 231, 233. Similarly Getatchew writes, "The Church venerates the Saint Virgin Mother of God, but she does not worship [her]." "ቤተ ክርስቲያኒ ቅድስት ድንግል ወላዲተ አምላክን ታከብራለች እንጃ አታመልካትም፤" Getatchew Haile, ደቀ እስጢፋኖስ, 25.

275. The Bible is the tradition with capital "T" and other traditions are with small "t." Daniel, Interview, 8 September 2010.

276. Daniel, Interview, 8 September 2010.

traditions which are revered by the church. EOC theologians argue that the Bible comprises selected stories and messages out of the huge amount of tradition which the church uses to explain difficult passages and also study the background of heroes of the Bible. In other words, the EOC does not limit itself to the canonical books of the Bible.[277] The average Ethiopian Evangelical might not be familiar with the writings of church fathers and the details about how the Bible came into existence, but the Bible's assertions are not questioned and it is accepted as the final authority in matters of faith and practice.

However, the Bible became available with modernity, literacy and printing, but it was not so in the ancient times. The high rate of illiteracy and the scarcity of the Bible made people dependent on the interpretation of the clergy and the traditional books which were available. Even after its availability, the Evangelicals' distance from the Orthodox tradition and their strong identification with the Bible perhaps made the Orthodox suspicious of reading it independently. It seems that the strong tendency of relying on traditional books and the interpretation of the clergy stems from fear of falling into what is considered as "the Evangelical understanding of the Bible."[278]

The Bible was not an open book in the history of the church of Ethiopia for a number of reasons, one of which was the medium of worship being the ancient sacred (but once a vernacular) language Ge'ez, and another, because of its scarcity. Thus, the people were used to hearing priests read portions of the Scriptures but individuals did not own a copy for themselves. As discussed in chapter 4 in the account of the CMS missionaries' ministry in Ethiopia, there was a great scarcity of the Scriptures and the few people who owned it tended to use it as an object of protection from evil.

The CMS missionaries' effort to have Christians read the Bible for themselves was not successful, but as discussed earlier, they noted that the tremendous hunger for the Amharic and even Ge'ez Scriptures was never satisfied. The missionaries were able to see that even the priests had inadequate

---

277. Mekonnen, Interview, 15 November 2010.

278. The mistrust is so great that people prefer Wudasse Mariam to the Bible. In the Orthodox strong holds, when people are presented with a copy of the Bible which does not have the Lalibela cross on its cover page, they would reject it as the Bible of Evangelicals. Yilma Getahun, Interview, 19 April 2011.

knowledge of the Scriptures and based their arguments more on traditional writings than on the Bible. Thus, the status of the Bible in the history of the church of Ethiopia was not as strong as it is at times claimed. Wondiye notes that in addition to the limited distribution of the Bible, "many people did not have access to it or worse; those who had access were not in a position to tell its difference from the other holy writings hailed by the Orthodox Church."[279]

Emperor Haile Sellassie, however, saw the need for the people to have an informed basis for their faith and also sought to change the negative attitude of the clergy towards the former version of the Amharic Bible which was translated by foreigners. Towards this end he brought together a team of eighteen scholars, twelve Ethiopians and six expatriates, to translate the Bible into Amharic. The work of translation which was interrupted during the Italian conquest was completed in 1962. The Bible was sold at a cheap price and even given freely to ensure its wide distribution.[280]

Bible translation, literacy and the use of Amharic played a major role in the expansion of Evangelical Christianity. With the translation of the Bible into Amharic, concealing the truth of the Scripture from the public because of fear of corruption, or fear of jeopardizing the clergy's prestigious position in the society, was challenged.

The Bible became an open book and missionaries played a major part in the translation of portions of the Bible into the mother-tongues of peripheral people. The coming of two major mission organizations: Swedish Evangelical Mission (SEM) and Sudan Interior Mission (SIM) which gave birth to two large Evangelical churches in Ethiopia: Ethiopian Evangelical Church Mekane Yesus (EECMY) and Ethiopian Kale Heywet Church (EKHC) consecutively played major roles in delivering peripheral people from physical, spiritual and economic bondage through literacy and the translation of the Bible into the mother-tongue. The Meserete Kristos Church which emerged out of the ministry of Mennonite missionaries in Ethiopia also played its part by spreading the gospel through medical work and education especially in the eastern part of Ethiopia.

---

279. Wondiye, *Church Out of Tribulation*, 128, 130.
280. Eshete, *Evangelical Movement*, 125–127.

Lamin Sanneh discussed how the translation of the Scriptures into mother-tongues limited the transmission of "Western cultural presuppositions" and enabled indigenous Christianity to thrive.[281] The Ethiopian situation, however, is a bit different from other African countries which prior to the availability of mother-tongue Scriptures read the Bible in foreign languages. Unlike many African countries, Ethiopia already had the Bible in the vernacular Ge'ez since the fourth century. When Amharic emerged as the vernacular and the Bible was translated into the national language, Amharic, in the nineteenth century, it was greatly utilized by people groups whose mother-tongue was not Amharic. Moreover the Amharic Bible continued to be used as supplementary where portions of the Bible or only the New Testament was translated into the mother-tongue. Thus in the Ethiopian context it is the use of mother-tongues while preaching from Amharic Bible, which had significant effect upon the listeners. As will be discussed below, knowledge of Amharic and the possession of the Amharic Bible enabled evangelists to cross ethnic boundaries and use interpreters to preach.

The Orthodox Church pioneered traditional education in Ethiopia, and the mission organizations beginning with the CMS promoted modern education.[282] Thus, translation, literacy and Evangelical Christianity were inseparable. Mission organizations spread modern education both formally in classroom settings and also informally by using every opportunity to teach people.[283] According to Bakke, the mission schools throughout the country impacted not only the converts of Evangelical Christianity, but also the secular leaders of Ethiopia.[284]

---

281. Sanneh, *Translating the Message*, 200–203.

282. In the 1830s Isenberg and Krapf of Church Missionary Society (CMS) ran a school for thirty to forty boys in Shewa. Young men educated by missionaries were also active in the field of education and missions. It is reported that there were thirty to fifty boys in each of the schools at Jenda and Assoso in 1881. The activity of the Ethiopians and missionaries impressed the regional king Tekle Haymanot that he requested for another school to be opened in Guduru. Moreover, there was a boys' school established in 1897 at Zazega and a girls' school in Monkullu. Besides other lessons, the boys' school offered instruction in typography, bookbinding and carpentry whereas the girls' school taught spinning, weaving and housework. Pankhurst, "Foundations of Education," 254–255.

283. Pankhurst, "Foundations of Education," 255.

284. Bakke, "Models of Leadership," 164.

However, introducing modern education, which was channelled by Western agents, was not easy. The illiteracy of the nobility and the distinguished leaders of the time such as Ras Alula, was confirmed by European observers of the time. Some of the observers were stunned at the extent of the illiteracy which was believed to be 99 percent at the beginning of the twentieth century. For their correspondence the leaders used scribes who were taught how to read and write either in the traditional EOC schools or the missionary schools.[285]

The rampancy of illiteracy may have limited the influence that the Bible distributed by the CMS missionaries might have exerted on the people. Even those who passed through the Orthodox traditional schools and were able to read had poor writing skills simply because they did not practice writing. As well as the low regard of people for modern education, there was also the fear that modern education and Bible reading would destabilize the country. For example during the reign of Yohannes the reading of the vernacular Scriptures and any attempt at ecclesiastical reform was denounced as a "Western heresy." The close relationship between the missionaries and the "Bible readers" in Tigray made the allegation appear even more plausible.[286]

However, mission agencies were deeply involved in education work and seized the opportunity to offer Bible classes alongside it.[287] The preaching of the gospel in mother-tongues played a major role in promoting Evangelical

---

285. As for the ministers of the government Dr Merab is reported to have said ". . . only half the council of Ministers could read and write with ease, that three could do neither, and that two others knew no more than how to sign their names . . ." The condition of women was worse. Apart from the princesses it was estimated that one in one thousand could read and write. Pankhurst, "Foundations of Education," 256.

286. Aren, *Evangelical Pioneers*, 183. The allegations against Bible readers were made by some of the clergy of the Church and Abune Atnateos sent Lij Markos as his personal envoy, to look into the matter. The Abun ordered Markos to cause the reformers no harm, but only prevent them from officiating in the church, but if they refuse to obey the Abun's orders, they were to be excommunicated. Markos reported that he did not find anything wrong with their faith, but the clergy appealed to emperor Yohannes accusing Markos of taking bribe from the missionaries in order to deliver a positive report about the Bible readers. Yohannes refused to listen to them and pointed out that he could not see any deviation from the truth in the statement of faith the Bible readers submitted. After some time, however, he relented to the wishes of some of the clergy. Aren, *Evangelical Pioneers*, 179.

287. Hege, *Beyond Our Prayers*, 67ff.

Christianity.²⁸⁸ In some of the Kale Heywet churches the phrase "he heard the gospel" was synonymous with "he learnt the letters and read the book" because the gospel and literacy were inseparable.²⁸⁹ The implications were immense. A sense of excitement was created over the newly asserted religious identity. People were able to accept Christianity without having to learn another language. For people whose language and culture were seldom taken into consideration the act of the missionaries in learning and using their language for preaching served as a proof that the God of the Bible spoke the people's language.

In Western Ethiopia among the Oromo people group, the Bible was translated into Oromiffa by Onesimus Nesib and Aster Genno. Eide notes that the translation of the Bible played a major role in helping people establish an Oromo consciousness and this gave rise to indigenous Evangelical Christianity.²⁹⁰

Among people groups of the south, portions of the New Testament were translated. For instance the Gospel of Mark was the first to be translated into Gofa language and the Gospel of Matthew into the Hadiya language.²⁹¹ A number of preachers (Ethiopian converts) had a knowledge of Amharic so they made use of the Amharic Bible. "This ability to use the Amharic Bible meant that they had their own source of authority when the expatriates left."²⁹² The missionaries also sought to print small pamphlets with a simple message of the gospel.²⁹³

---

288. Wondiye Ali, *Church Out of Tribulation*, 128–131. In the footsteps of the CMS missionaries, the Swedish missionaries in Eritrea were determined to distribute the New Testament in Amharic. When Qes Gebre-Ewostateos, an Orthodox priest, got hold of the New Testament, he came to "an Evangelical understanding of salvation " and eventually travelled to Wollega, Western Ethiopia to reach the Oromo. Although he was accused of being an enemy of Mary in his home he joined the EOC at Bodji, Wollega and introduced many reforms such as vernacular Scripture reading, a sermon in the church service, educating ordinary people and then admitting them to the Holy Communion, etc. Bakke, *Christian Ministry*, 110–111.

289. Wondiye, *Church Out of Tribulation*, 106.

290. Øyvind M. Eide, *Revolution and Religion in Ethiopia* (Addis Ababa: Addis Ababa University Press, 2000), 71–73.

291. Wondiye, *Church Out of Tribulation*, 128, 130.

292. Fargher, *Origins of New Churches*, 168.

293. Alemu notes that there was an Amharic pamphlet entitled *yedehnenet mesekal* (The ladder of salvation) which outlined the way of salvation which had a cover beautified with the national colours. Alemu Himbaru, ወንጌል ነጻ ያወጣል (The gospel sets free), n.d., 13.

However, enforcing the use of other national languages instead of the vernacular Amharic or even encouraging the use of both concurrently was unacceptable to the state authorities because such measures were feared to jeopardize the unity of the nation. In fact, people who did not speak these languages were not accepted into the ministry of the church, primarily for practical reasons, but also with some ethnic undertones.[294]

The emperors promoted the use of Amharic for political reasons. Menelik tried to spread the use of Amharic in order to unite the country. To this end he forbade the public use of all national languages except for Amharic. French and English, however, were used as media of instruction in schools.[295] During Haile Sellassie's regime similar measures were taken. The Minister of Education proposed an even more fundamental measure.

> The strength of a country lies in its unity, and unity is born of [common] language, customs, and religion. Thus, to safeguard the ancient sovereignty of Ethiopia and to reinforce its unity, our language and our religion should be proclaimed over the whole of Ethiopia. Otherwise, unity will never be attained . . . Amharic and Ge'ez should be decreed official languages for secular as well as religious affairs and all pagan languages should be banned.[296]

Clearly, the development of other national languages and religions was perceived as a threat to national unity.

During its conquest of Ethiopia, Italy was threatened by the development of Amharic as the national language and the influence of Orthodox faith and it was determined to undermine them both. Eriksson notes that in order to defeat nationalists and to lower the status of Amharic, the Italians divided the country along ethnic lines and made some local languages the media of instruction in schools; but upon his restoration to the throne Haile

---

294. Taddesse Tamrat, *Church and State*, 232–233.
295. Ericksson, et al., *The Gospel of Restoration*, 27.
296. "ያገር ጉልበት አንድነት ነው፤ አንድነትንም የሚወልደው ቋንቋ ልማድና ሃይማኖት ነው፡፡ ስለዚህ ኢትዮጵያ ቀዳማዊ መሆኗን ለማስከበርና አንድነቷንም ለማጽናት እስካሁን በቆየው ልማዳችን ተማሪ ቤቶቻችን አስፋተን ቋንቋችንና ሃይማኖታችንን በመላው በኢትዮጵያ ግዛት በአዋጅ እንዘርጋው ይህ ካልሆነ እስከ መቼውም ድረስ አንድነት አይገኝም፡ ፡ . . . በመላ በኢትዮጵያ ግዛት ለሥጋዊና ለመንፈሳዊ ሥራ ያማሪኛና የግዕዝ ቋንቋ ብቻ ብቻ በሕግ ጸንተው እንዲፀኑ ሌላው ማናቸውም የአረማውያን ቋንቋ ሁሉ እንዲደመስስ ያስፈልጋል።" Quoted by Bahru Zewde, *Pioneers of Change in Ethiopia* (Addis Ababa: Addis Ababa University, 2002), 140.

Sellassie made English the medium of instruction and in 1958/59 Amharic replaced English, as the medium in schools and books in Amharic became available. All foreign missionaries were expected to learn Amharic and use it in their endeavours to preach the gospel and no other national language was permitted. Haile Sellassie desired to promote oneness by suppressing all other Ethiopian languages.[297]

The restriction was applicable throughout the country. Sorsa notes that government officials strictly forbade SIM to allow anyone to use preaching records in Sidamo language, but only in Amharic.[298] Children were disciplined when found using their mother-tongue in a school compound. Unfortunately, such acts made people ashamed of their mother-tongue so that many went to the extent of changing their local names to Amharic in order to hide their ethnic identity.[299] It could be argued that the strict measures on the part of the government were connected to their little regard for other languages. However, the political incentive for keeping the other languages at bay, was perhaps equally strong with the desire to hold together a vast multi-ethnic country like Ethiopia.

There also was a practical problem at hand. The missionaries, who were instructed by their mission to learn the local languages and not Amharic, were at times unable to interact with the district authorities, nor with the Orthodox priests who usually spoke Amharic. For instance in Wolaitta the missionaries learned the Wolaitta language but SIM prohibited them from learning Amharic and "this effectively segregated them from the Amharas and thus from any significant interaction with the Orthodox Church."[300] But this was exactly what both the Orthodox Church and the state wanted, restricting the missionaries from interacting with the Orthodox followers.

Fargher makes the observation that even the emperor could not have come up with a better policy than prohibiting the study of Amharic in his desire to limit their contact with the church. Moreover the policy of the

---

297. Bo Ericksson et al., *The Gospel of Restoration: Experiences from a Field Study in Ethiopia* (Sweden: Swedish Institute of Missionary Research, 1999), 28.

298. Sorsa, *Bivocational Missionary-Evangelist*, 155.

299. Mekuria Bulcha, "The Language Policies of Ethiopian Regimes and the History of Written Afaan Oromo, 1844–1994," in *Journal of Oromo Studies* 1, no. 2, (Winter 1994): 91–115, as cited by Eriksson et al., 29.

300. Mehari, *Ethiopian Pioneer Missionary*, 45.

mission was quite helpful to protect the missionaries if any accusation was to arise as to their involvement with the Orthodox Church.[301] Ironically the very thing the state prohibited (using local languages) successfully isolated the missionaries and protected them from breaking the imperial regulation of having any contact with the Orthodox Church.

But the missionaries at times found themselves torn between the policy of the mission and that of the state. They were not allowed by the Director of SIM in Ethiopia to learn Amharic and on the other hand the government threatened them with deportation if they used the vernaculars in the schools they operated.[302] In spite of the fact that none of the older people spoke Amharic, the Ministry of Education strictly prohibited the use of the vernaculars in schools.[303] Missions such as the Mennonites did not require their missionaries to study indigenous language before starting mission work, but the missionaries insisted on learning the government sanctioned Amharic.[304] But when reaching Oromo-speaking Muslims was considered, the missionaries wondered, "how could one expect a people to turn to Christ if their teacher did not even think it important enough to communicate in their native Oromo tongue?"[305]

The policy of SIM on the other hand had implications on the ground, as illustrated by Sorsa, one of the pioneer missionaries in Wolaitta.[306] "Mr Ohman was the only teacher who taught using the Walayta language. He didn't read or speak Amharic so he couldn't use the Amharic Bible. He used his English Bible, taught in the Walayta language and we had our Amharic Bibles. But somehow or other, between the mix of the three languages we did learn something."[307]

---

301. Mehari, 91–92.

302. The missionaries in the "open areas" were allowed to use local languages on the lowest level of instruction. Negarit Gazeta, 12, Decree No. 3, Articles 13 and 14, 27 August 1944. Cf. Tolo, *Sidama and Ethiopia*, 124–131.

303. Fargher, *Origins of New Churches*, 295, 297.

304. Hege, *Beyond Our Prayers*, 59–62.

305. Hege, 63.

306. The name Wolaitta is spelled differently by different authors. I will use "Wolaitta" consistently unless quoting others.

307. Sumamo, *Bivocational Missionary-Evangelist*, 40.

Literacy and Bible translation, therefore, promoted both religious and national identity. The fact that people were taught to read and write enabled them to read the law of Ethiopia for themselves on different matters, especially land ownership. Because of their ignorance representatives of the landowners took advantage of them but when believers started to submit legitimate grievances to government officials they won cases and this made the local authorities angry. "Over a period of decades people were set free from their economic slavery."[308] Literacy and Bible learning went hand-in-hand in empowering the people both spiritually and socially.

The Bible was one of the provocative symbols of the new freedom which the believers had discovered. It was a highly visible indicator that we had gained a new freedom. A fascinating complication was that the Bible we used was in the Amharic language, not our own! Orthodox Christians claimed that their Bible in Ge'ez, the ancient language of the Ethiopian Orthodox Church, was more accurate. But they also knew that the Amharic translation, authorized by Emperor Haile Sellassie, was substantially the same as theirs.[309]

In the same line Bakke comments, "Initially education was promoted in order to strengthen the Christian life of the individual and to produce teachers for others, but it often furthered a social and political consciousness and critical attitude towards political structures and conditions. The educational activities, therefore, contributed towards developing an elite conscious of their ethnic identity."[310]

Literacy also served as effective means of preaching the gospel. The evangelists would offer to teach the Amharic alphabets to their neighbours and in so doing shared the gospel with them.[311] Thus the new converts were heavily involved in learning to read and write. Those who mastered the Amharic alphabets would teach children and adults. Being able to read the Bible was a powerful incentive for diligent learning which enhanced the spread of the gospel.[312]

---

308. Sorsa, 152.
309. Sorsa, 101.
310. Bakke, "Models of Leadership," 162–163.
311. Mehari, *Ethiopian Pioneer Missionary*, 49.
312. Alemu, ወንጌል ነጋ ያወጣል፣, 25–26.

The the Amharic language was not resented by all, because initially the new believers used the Amharic Bible for their Bible study and also Amharic to communicate with people of other ethnic groups. Sorsa notes that in the urban setting using Amharic was a means of social mobility because a move into the cash economy required the comprehension of Amharic.[313] The most powerful incentive to read and speak Amharic was the access to the Bible which it allowed. "The only Bible we had was in Amharic, a second language to all of us."[314] He shares his own experience as an example.

> From the moment I saw the book in the hands of the preachers I wanted one. I knew I had to have one. I wanted to learn the Amharic letters in order to read the Bible. Later teaching people to read Amharic would become an important part of my work. I wanted people to have access to God's Word and at that time there was only one way: the Amharic Bible. "I absolutely must have one," was the thought that grabbed my heart the very first time I saw Ato Tadessa preaching from a huge Bible. But I had to wait more than a year before I could find money to buy one. . . . When one of our cows had a calf [my father] gave the calf to me. It was the only thing in the world I had at that time that I could sell. . . . I sold my heifer for five birr and bought a Bible. . . . My father was very proud of me when I could carry this big book around with me.[315]

Paul Balisky appropriately observes that the Bible for the Evangelical Christians was "the external sign of their belief system."[316] The believers in Wolaitta began to read the Amharic Bible and shared what they learned. Fortunately for them there were fluent Amharic speakers close by who could help when they came across expressions and words which they did not understand.[317] Portions of the New Testament were available in vernaculars in areas where missionaries worked and at times it took a long time for

---

313. Sorsa, *Bivocational Missionary-Evangelist*, 14.
314. Sorsa, 30.
315. Sorsa, 32–33.
316. As cited by Sorsa, 33.
317. Sorsa, 34, 40, 101.

the whole of the New Testament to appear. For instance in the case of the Kembatta people, the New Testament became available after thirteen years of hard work (1978–1991) and translation of the Old Testament was started in 2001 and is still in progress.[318] Thus the Amharic Bible continues to play an important part in the churches in Kembatta.[319]

Amharic was used as a medium of preaching in Sidamo province as well. Initially the evangelists from Wolaitta were not able to speak Sidama and they looked for people who spoke Amharic even among the listeners and preached with an interpreter. The Amharic Bible and their knowledge of Amharic were assets that helped them to communicate with the Sidamo until they learnt their language.[320]

Thus, Amharic served to enhance communication. In other words, it served as a powerful vehicle of literacy, civilization and Christian learning. When it emerged as the national language it became both practical and prestigious.[321] What English is to the modern generation, Amharic was to the people from the minority ethnic groups. More importantly Amharic as the national language and the vehicle of modernity made communication easier between people of different ethnic groups thereby addressing the practical concern of being cut off from the rest of Ethiopia.

The contribution of the missionaries in translation and promoting literacy is immeasurable. Especially their endeavour to help people read the Bible for themselves was a great source of empowerment. Eshete remarks, ". . . the missionaries in Ethiopia did more service to the expansion of the Evangelical faith by their contribution in the production of scriptural literature, mainly

---

318. Tamiru Abamo (One of the Wycliffe translators of the Bible in Kembatigna) to Seblewengel Daniel, 23 Nehasse 1997 Eth. C.

319. When a translation was not available someone (usually from the audience) was asked to read in Amharic and the preacher would translate into Kembatigna sentence by sentence and then continue to preach in Kembatigna. But with the coming of the current government in 1990 another practical problem has surfaced. The education policy was changed so that each people group was to use its own language in the government schools. This inaugurated a shift from Ge'ez scripts to Latin scripts but the vernacular translations of the Bible are in Ge'ez scripts. Thus those who have gone to school within the period of the last twenty years are to make extra efforts to take the Amharic lessons seriously, lest they will not be able to read their Bible.

320. Sorsa, *Bivocational Missionary-Evangelist*, 64.

321. Fargher, *Origins of the New Churches*, 169.

the translation of the Bible and its dissemination, than by their mere physical presence (and their accompanying programs) in various sites."[322]

The Ethiopian Evangelical Christian story provides evidence of empowerment and self assertion which came as a result of the translation of the Bible into the vernaculars and the literacy which enabled people to read the Bible. Eshete observes, "Since carrying the Bible has been an important feature of Evangelical Christianity, even in today's Ethiopia a person carrying the Bible will automatically be considered a *Pente* . . ."[323] Thus, the act of carrying the Bible, rare among Orthodox believers has become the norm in Evangelical Christianity providing a powerful identity mark and displaying the role of the Bible as a vehicle of Evangelical Christianity.

However, it is not only carrying and studying the Bible that set Evangelicals apart from the EOC's tradition, but also the method of interpretation. The tradition of Evangelical Christianity which encourages everyone to read the Bible for themselves and share the insights with each other gave a platform for believers to illustrate the truth of the Scriptures with their firsthand experiences. Thus, the truth as revealed in the Scriptures was not merely a past history; instead the experiences provided evidence that the living God was at work in their lives here and now. Such experiences rooted the message deep into the hearts of the adherents and asserted their Evangelical identity.

The Evangelical "Sola Scriptura" which implies no additional revelation apart from the Bible, was modified with the coming of the Pentecostal movement which brought the so-called charismatic gifts of the Spirit to the centre of the life of the church, though with the understanding that everything should still to be weighed against the Bible. Generally speaking, however, the memory of the Scripture being canonized by the church fathers is not strong among the Evangelicals, who do not show much attachment to the fathers of the church.

The Ethiopian Orthodox church, therefore, accuses Evangelicals of adopting a dynamic interpretation method. Daniel notes, "The reformists [i.e. Evangelicals] want to reform the Scripture according to any kind of culture

---

322. Eshete, *Evangelical Movement*, 130.
323. Eshete, 127.

or social structure in a way which is compatible to a given society, in a way which fits people's interest. Thus, there would be an inevitable conflict between those who want to preserve Christianity as it is and those who want to modify it to fit a certain pattern of life."[324]

Thus, there is mistrust of the Evangelical interpretation of the Scriptures, which is dynamic, as opposed to the EOC's approach of limiting itself to the *Andemta*, the sole authoritative interpretation which according to tradition was compiled by itinerant Orthodox scholars in the ninth century. Scholars of the church are allowed to interpret the Scriptures within the bounds of the *Andemta* commentary, but if their interpretation appears to contradict the existing tradition, it will not be acceptable.

The centrality of the Bible as the only authoritative tradition indeed has been one of the marks of Evangelicalism in Ethiopia so much so that Evangelicals have been accused of bibliolatry.[325] In the footsteps of the Reformers, Evangelicals look at themselves as those who have understood and accepted the only way of salvation, which is faith in Christ Jesus as attested by the Scriptures. Such a perception at times causes some Evangelicals to speak of the Orthodox tradition in disrespectful terms.[326] Others high-

---

324. Daniel, Interview, 8 September 2010.

325. However, there is a growing interest in hagiographic type of testimonies and running after people who claim to have received revelation from God. The tendency of leaning on the "charismatic" gifts of the Spirit with little desire to a disciplined reading of the Bible is a growing concern of leaders of the church. Bekele Wolde Kidan, Interview, 25 August 2010; Nigusse Bulcha, Interview, 30 September 2010; Cf. Mihretu Petros, የንባብ ባህልና ቤተክርስቲያን *General Analysis on the Reading Habit of Ethiopian Evangelical Christians* (Addis Ababa: SIM Publications, 2007), 105–106.

326. The conflict between the Evangelical conviction about the sufficiency of faith and the Orthodox emphasis on the necessity of work for salvation at times results with radical criticism. Pastor Dawit's sermon is a case in point. After narrating how helpless he felt when making vows to angels and trying so hard as an Orthodox adherent did not free him from alcoholism and addiction to cigarette and chat (narcotic leaves), Dawit notes, "It is Jesus the Nazarene who changed our lives. Let me tell you something, the burden which is laid on the saints and the land of Ethiopia will be lifted in the name of Jesus. We are tired of it. We do not want to bear burden because Jesus has bore it all. He has carried it on our behalf. Why should I now suffer? No way! We do not have a Scripture that says, 'You will not go to heaven unless you walk bare-footed, eat wild leaves and hide in a cave until your face becomes pale.' I tell you, woe to those who walk bare-footed, who eat wild leaves while there is fine food. The Scripture says, 'I thank you for you have made me fearfully and wonderfully.' You will be held responsible for torturing yourself because the body is made for the Lord. And now you would say, 'How is it possible that those who eat wild leaves will not enter heaven?' I tell you, they will not enter. I call God as my witness when I say that they will not enter heaven. I am not speaking from myself. It is the Scripture that affirms

light that it is the reading of the Bible that constitutes the main difference between the tradition of the Orthodox and Evangelicals.

The Orthodox Church teaches people the fear of God but the reading of the Bible is not central to the life of the church. There is little encouragement for people to read the Bible. I felt vacancy in my life, regardless of leading upright life, visiting well-known monasteries and doing good work. I did not have peace, nor assurance of my eternal destiny. I was led to Christ through my reading of the Bible which eventually took me to the Evangelical church and they helped me understand the gospel. Once I came to understand that God saved me by his grace through Christ, my heart was filled with peace and assurance of eternal life.[327]

The other concern is the variance in the number of books incorporated in the EOC canon. Both the number of the additional books, and the individual books included seem to vary.[328] There appears to be a renewed interest in maintaining eighty-one as the standard number, but even then, the individual books which are included are not the same. At times the table of contents states that the books are eighty-one but the books do not add up to the "standard number."[329] However, the apocryphal books seem to pose little problem compared to the other writings which are not canonized by the church, but widely read among the people.

With regard to the hagiographies of saints and other collections of literature that form part of the libraries of Orthodox churches, the Orthodox church does not guarantee their official acceptability as authoritative. Neither

---

it. [He] said I am the way, but he did not say, 'The cave is the way.'" " . . . በቀላል መንገድ ነው እንጂ የናዝራቴ ኢየሱስ በመንገዱ ለቅም እዚህ ያደረሰን . . አንድ ታሪክ ለለያሁ ኢትዮጵያ ውስጥ ያለ ከባድ ነገር ሁሉ ከቅዱሳንም በጠቃላይ ከምድራችን በኢየሱስ ስም ይወገዳል። እንፈልግም በቃ ይከመን የሚያደየም ነገር እንፈልግም፤ ከባዱን ነገር ኢየሱስ ወስዶልናል፤ ጠቅልሎ ተሸምልናል፤ እኔ ምን ብዬ ነው ዛሬ መከራ የምበላው፤ እንዴ!! አይሰራም፤ : ተረክዘህ ካለተሰጠቀ፤ ቅጠል ካለሀለሁ፤ ዋሻ ውስጥ ተደብቀህ ሩቱብ ቤጭ ካለሆነ መንግስተ ሰማያት አትገባም የሚል መጽሐፍ የለንም። እንደውም እግራችውን የሚሰነጥቁ ምን የመሰለ ነጭ ጫፍ እያለ ቅጠል ለሚበላ ወዮላችው፤ መጽሐፍ ነው "ውብና ድንቅ ሆኜ ተፈጥሬአለሁና እግዚአብሔርን አመሰግናለሁ" ያለው. . . . ትጠቅብታለሁ ለስነጠቅለው ተረክዝ፤ ሥጋም ለጌታ ነው . . . "ምንድነው ታዲያ እንርሱ ቅጠል በለተው ለይገቡ ነው እንዴ ወይ እግዚአብሔር መንግስት ትላላችሁ . . . አይገቡም፤ እግዚአብሔር ምስከሩ አይገቡም፤ እኔ አይደለሁም መጽሐፉ ነው ያለው፤ ብሩ እኔ ነኝ ነው ያለው ዋሻ ነው አላለም።" Dawit Molalegn, ቀሉ ስለመጣ አይቀላበችሁ፤ (Do not take [the humble gospel] for granted), (Audiovisual sermon), n.d.

327. Bezuayehu Abera, O.i, February 2011, Addis Ababa.

328. Cf. Dibekulu Zewde, ቅዱሳት መጻሕፍትና ምንጮች-ቀኖናት በኢትዮጵያ ኦርቶዶክስ ቤተ ክርስቲያን (Scriptures and the sources of the Ethiopian Orthodox Church's canon), (Addis Ababa, The Author, 1987 Eth. C), 81, 96–146.

329. Agizachew Tefera, 13 June 2011.

does it assure that they are used for teaching and prayer by the church.³³⁰ However, the Orthodox Church is yet to sift through the massive literature collection accessed by its members and educate its people as to which ones are useful for instruction.

However, the accusation of some former members of EOC that the church forbids the reading of the Bible and expelled them because of it, is absolutely unacceptable to the EOC. Daniel responds that Orthodox Church holds the gospels so high that its daily readings are mostly from the gospels. Another priest says that it is not because of their reading of the Bible that they are expelled, it is when they attempt to alter the pillars of EOC's faith.³³¹

Another priest added, "No one is forced to adhere by the Dogmas of the church without his/her will, but they are not allowed to stay and try to dismantle the church. If they do not agree with the church's dogma, they can go their separate way. But they are not allowed to stay and cause trouble."³³² Even such expulsion does not come right away, but after a long period of trying to restore them to Orthodoxy and this process begins with the father confessor of the dissenter and eventually involves the scholars of the local church. None of them accept the claim of many that they were expelled because they insisted on reading the Bible.³³³

Thus, according to its theologians, the Protestant questioning of the status of the Bible in the EOC is not well grounded for the most part. However, numerous stories of scholars of the church tell that they were tried and warned not to teach or write in a certain way, anathematized, imprisoned and publicly stoned. It appears that preaching exclusively from the Bible got the teachers in trouble.³³⁴ Aleqa Meseret writes that he was expelled from

---

330. "በቤተ ክርስቲያን ቤተ መዘክር እንደ መዘክርነቱ ብዙ መጻሕፍት ሊገኙ ይችላሉ። በቤተ ክርስቲያን ቤተ መዘክር የሚገኙ መጻሕፍት ሁሉ የተምህርትና የጸሎት መጻሕፍት ናቸው ማለትም አይደለም፤" The EOTC Council of Scholars, እንዳየታችሁ ተጠቅቁ፣ 52.

331. Daniel, Interview, 8 September 2010.

332. Informant G, Interview, February 2011.

333. Asrat Kebede, Editor in-chief of *Seme'a Tsidq* gazette, the publication of Mahbere Kidusan, Interview, 30 December 2010, Addis Ababa.

334. A case in point is the story of Aleqa Beyene Damtew, who according to Aleqa Meseret's account preached and taught only from the Bible. He was dragged out of the church and stoned on Good Friday by chief priests, deacons and the public as well. Similarly, Abune Filipos who insisted on exclusive preaching from the Bible was imprisoned. Aleqa Taye too lost his property and was imprisoned for similar reasons. *Chora*, no. 14, n.d.: 8–9; *Chora*, no. 39 (2002 Eth. C): 12–18; Editor, "የሐመን ምሥክር፣ አላቃ ታዬ ገብረ ማርያም (1888–1974 sic) (Witness

Siwasew Birhane Kidus Paulos School in 1954,[335] accused of teaching the Bible to students.[336] The question remains why clergy members who preach quoting traditions which are contrary to the Bible seem to have no opposition, but those who focus only on the Bible seem to be labelled as *menafiq*.[337]

Thus, the sole authority of the Bible remains the main point of difference between Evangelicals and the Orthodox. Even the elevation of Mary is rejected by Evangelicals simply because of the status of the Bible which is to govern all convictions. The unwillingness of both Evangelicals and Orthodox to tolerate one another and learn from each other had grave repercussions over the years. One of which, as we will discuss below, was the issue of burial place.

5.3.3. The Issue of Burial

The question of the ground for burial of the dead has been a source of great conflict and bitterness between Evangelicals and the Orthodox Church for a long time. Taddesse Tamrat traces the inauguration of the issue to the controversy between Gobat and priests of St Giorgis church in Tigray regarding the absolution and burial of the body of Kugler.[338] Ever since then, denying burial ground became a powerful symbol of rejection. Isenberg suffered a similar fate when two of his babies died. It was not only Isenberg's children; but his servant's child, who died soon after, was not allowed to be buried in the vicinity of the church. Thus, Isenberg was forced to bury the bodies of the children in his garden one after the other.[339]

---

through time, Aleqa Taye Gebre Mariam), no. 40 (Tahsas 2003 Eth. C), 10–15. Similar stories of expulsion, and harassment upon EOC members who questioned the legitimacy of traditions which appeared to contradict the Scriptures is echoed by Evangelical publications too. *Gesame* 2, no. 12 (Tir 2002 Eth. C), 9–11, 24; *Gesame* 2, no. 2 (November 2000), 3–6.

335. The date of his expulsion was gathered from Staffan Grenstedt to the researcher via email.

336. *Chora*, no. 14, n.d., 15.

337. There is a feeling that the general public seem to show more openness to the exclusive preaching of the Bible than clergy members. At times, when preachers opt to repeatedly referring to tradition and slandering Evangelicals audiences grow impatient. Yilma Getahun, Interview, 19 April 2011, Addis Ababa.

338. Taddesse Tamrat, "Evangelizing the Evangelized," 25.

339. On the burial of his little girl, Isenberg preached from 1 Cor 15. As he was in the middle of reading the argument of Paul in the passage some people left the scene to report that Isenberg did not believe in the resurrection of Jesus. Consequently his servant's child who died soon after was refused a burial place and was buried next to Isenberg's girl. After a year

The denial of burial ground to people who were accused of being *tsere Mariam* continued. Aleqa Taye (1898–1924) was one such person. In his lifetime enjoyed protection from emperor Menelik, but after the illness and death of Menelik, he suffered because of his convictions. When he died, his family was not allowed to bury him in the compound of the church and they laid his body to rest in a place allocated by Menelik for foreigners.[340] Members of the Orthodox Church in Wollega who wished to reform the church suffered a similar fate after a growing intolerance and denial of the sacraments. The hostility of the Orthodox Church towards them came to a climax in its refusal to allow them to bury their dead in the compound of the church.[341]

During Haile Sellassie's reign, Evangelicals in the countryside were able to inter their dead in their own land, but for those who lived in areas with strong Orthodox presence the issue of burial created a serious problem. It became acute with the numerical growth of believers all over the country, especially in the urban centres. During the era of the Derg, Evangelical Christians suffered unspeakable atrocities. What was rated as the worst form of punishment of all was that of denying them burial grounds. Many were beaten to death simply because of their religious convictions. Mourners carried the body of their loved ones in search of a place to lay them to rest. Bodies were dug out of graves and thrown to wild beasts. The family of the dead was not allowed to attend the burial of their loved ones on pain of excommunication.[342]

Because of the severity of the problem, some Evangelicals at times opted to offer unusual prayers. A prayer of W/ro Yeshi, a widow in Bale, was a case in point. In 1969 (Eth. C), Evangelicals in that area were accused of teaching against military service of citizens. They denied the accusation, but the cadres had already made up their mind to send to the war front W/

---

the new born baby boy of Isenberg died and he too was buried in the garden. Isenberg was later accused of turning his house into a church by administering the sacraments, interring bodies in his compound, and teaching strange things. Extract of a letter from Isenberg to Rev Gobat, Samuel, 28 September 1837, UB SC, CMS/B/OMS/ C M/O28/31B.

340. የሕመን ምሥክር (Witness through time), *Chora*, no. 40 (Tahsas 2003 Eth. C), 15.

341. Bakke, *Christian Ministry*, 112.

342. Addise Amado, *Persecution in Ethiopia* (Addis Ababa: Voice of Martyrs (VOM) Ethiopia, 2003), 57ff.

ro Yeshi's husband, a devout believer and a father of five children with the sixth one on its way. He was the only bread winner of the family but was sent along with seven other men from the area. When the news of his death arrived home, his widow prayed that his body would not be recovered. She knew the Orthodox Church would not let her bury him at home and even heard people conspiring not to have her bury him. All of the bodies of the soldiers who died along with him were sent home, except his.[343]

As Evangelical faith was more and more institutionalized, the need for a separate burial site became clear, but securing a cemetery was not easy with the opposition from the Orthodox Church. Evangelicals in the neighbourhood of small towns and communities were forced to carry bodies to big cities like Addis Ababa. Many were forced to bury their dead in their gardens and were tormented by the consciousness of having a dead body in their yard.[344] An example of the suffering caused by this policy is the case of some family members who were unable to inter their dead in Holeta town (40 kms away from Addis) carried the body and buried it in Qechene Medhane Alem church in Addis Ababa, but were beaten up by a mob and made to dig out and take the body away.[345] Needless to say, serious illness created anxiety among family members about the fate of the body if the person were to die.

But why refuse dead Evangelicals a place of rest? Out of the remarks of Gobat in 1830, one of the reasons why the priests refused to inter the body of Kugler, provides us with a window to understand the root causes for what reads like inhuman treatment of Evangelicals. According to Gobat, a major reason why the priests refused to bury Kugler's body was because he would not allow them to perform the absolution. In Orthodox theology of death and afterlife, burial is not a single event. There is a package of ceremonies which come with it. There is a strong belief in the mercy of God upon the dead as prayers are offered and alms are given on their behalf. Thus, great importance is attached to being buried in the vicinity of the church, where the clergy continuously offer prayer and praises to God.

---

343. Getachew Belete, እንባና ሃሌሉያ (*Agonies and Hallelujah*), 263–266.
344. Addise, *Persecution in Ethiopia*, 55.
345. Addise, 55–56.

When an Orthodox follower dies, there will be a performance of rituals on the third, seventh, twelfth or fourteenth, thirtieth, fortieth, and eightieth days. Then the rituals will be done in the sixth month and after a year as well. These ceremonies are done in remembrance of the dead and prayers are offered on their behalf so that God will have mercy on their souls. Unlike Evangelical theology which has no room for salvation of souls after death, Orthodox theology integrates the rites performed over the body as vital for the fate of the departed. Thus, the family of the dead sees to it that all of the needed rites are performed over the body of their loved ones. Such a theology of death and afterlife creates a problem when Evangelicals who do not believe in any of the rites and are unwilling to participate in them want to be buried along with Orthodox adherents.

The issue of burial is not limited to the absence of constitutional freedom of worship. Upon the fall of the Derg, the transitional government issued freedom of worship to all, and addressed the practical problem of burial place specifically.[346] The letter was dispatched to the Office of the Ethiopian Orthodox church, the Council of Islamic Affairs, Catholic Church of Ethiopia, and the Office of the Evangelical church (most probably Mekane Yesus). The letter stated the right of citizens to express their worship and that it is a federal offence to deny them place of gathering and burial ground. In communities which were dominated by Orthodox members, how were such matters to be handled in view of the newly acquired religious freedom? It is obvious that Evangelicals would not be taken to the burial ground of Muslims. So how was this religious freedom and the law of the government against denying burial ground to be approached? The gravity of the problem is illustrated by the initiative of the Patriarch to have a book published in 1987 Year of Mercy in order to address the controversy.

The title of the book makes the content clear, "ሃይማኖት የለየንን መቃብር አንድ አያደርገንም" (What Religion has Separated, a Burial site would not Unite). The purpose of the book is spelled out in the introduction, "This book is published mainly to state the position of our church regarding matters of burial ground between the Ethiopian Orthodox Tewahdo Church and several

---

346. The Transitional Government of Ethiopia Office of the Prime Minister, Ginbot 14, 1984 Eth. C, no. ፪10/55. The copy of the letter is retained in Getachew Belete, *Agonies*, 317–318.

followers of *mete* religion."³⁴⁷ The book begins with stating the doctrinal differences between the Orthodox and Evangelicals and gives two main reasons why Evangelicals are not to be buried along with the Orthodox.

The reasons are that followers of *mete* religion have abandoned the Orthodox Church and their doctrine is different. "Those who do not accept what God has spoken, do not obey his commands, have gone astray from the correct faith and teaching and followed false prophets in the way of destruction; those who have disrespected the faith and teaching, culture, tradition, custom and guidelines of their fathers and followed the ways of foreigners; the teachers of error who spread *nufaqe*, the *menafiqan*; they will not be able to share the inheritance of the remains of the fathers in the holy church."³⁴⁸ The writers cite the Old Testament and the writings of the fathers to argue that believers have no fellowship with *menafiqan*, just as light has no fellowship with darkness, and the circumcised with pagans.³⁴⁹

The main reason which is related to abandoning the church is the doctrinal difference between the two groups.

> While it is obvious that there is a difference between us the trouble that the foreign (*mete*) religion followers cause by claiming to have a burial site in the vicinity of the EOC is meant to disrupt the long-lived peace and unity of the society. Supported by local authorities who sympathize with them the conspiracy of these opportunist individuals and groups concerning burial site is disrupting the peaceful life of Christians throughout the country.³⁵⁰

---

347. "መጽሐፉ የተተመበት ዋና ምክንያትም በኢትዮጵያ ኦርቶዶክስ ተዋህዶ ቤተ ክርስቲያንና በተለያዩ የመጤ እምነት ተከታዮች መካከል ያለውን የመካን መቃብር ልዩነት አስመልክቶ የቤተ ክርስቲያናችን አቋም ለመግለፅ ነው።" Translation by the researcher. ሃይማኖት የለየን መቃብር አንድ አያደርገንም (What religion has separated a burial site will not unite) (Addis Ababa: Tinsae Zegubae Printing, 1987 Eth. C), Introduction.

348. "ከእግዚአብሔር የተነገሩን የማይቀበሉ የታዘዘውን የማይፈጽሙ ከትክክለኛው እምነትና ትምህርት ወጥተው ሐሳውያን ነቢያት በሚያመለክትዋቸው የጥፋት መንገድ የሚሄዱ፣ . . . የአባቶቻቸውን እምነትና ትምህርት፣ ባህልና ትውፊት፣ ልማድና ሥርዓት አያለው የዐዐዳን መንገድ የተከተሉ ሐሰትን የሚያስተምሩ ሐሳውያን፣ ኑፋቄን የሚዘሩ መናፍቃንም በአባቶች አፅመ ርስት በቅድስት ቤተ ክርስቲያን የመቃብር ውርስ ሊካፈሉ አይችሉም። ድርሻም የላቸውም።" (Translation by the researcher.) ሃይማኖት የለየን መቃብር አንድ አያደርገንም, 40

349. ሃይማኖት የለየን መቃብር አንድ አያደርገንም, 39.

350. ሃይማኖት የለየን መቃብር አንድ አያደርገንም, 46–47. (Translation by the researcher.)

The writers of the book argue that Evangelicals are of a different tradition, which is not only different but also contrary to that of the Orthodox Church, and accuse them of aiming to purposely incite trouble by asking to be buried along with Orthodox adherents. The writers remark, "This is the church which they have hated, criticized and left and now they want to be united with us in burial . . ." "በሕይወት እያሉ ጠልተው በማስጠላት ነቅፈው በማስነቅፉ በተለየአት ቤተ ክርስቲያን የመቃብር ደልነት መጠየቃቸው . . ."[351] The writers assert that those who wish to share burial ground do not honour the cross, absolution, incense and offering for the dead – they consider the body and blood as a remembrance of Christ while the Orthodox Church believes in the presence of the Lord in the elements.[352] The writers underlined that there is an unbridgeable doctrinal gap between the Orthodox and the *mete* religion followers.

The reply of an Orthodox priest to a bereaved Evangelical mother explains it, "The child does not even have a 'Soul father' (Godfather) so how could we possibly allow you to put this unsanctified body in holy ground?"[353] The church thus believed that it has no obligation to receive in its sacred grounds the remains of followers of *mete* religion, who have abandoned the Orthodox faith.

In addition, the control of access to burial grounds was also addressing the problem of the flocking of its members into Evangelical churches. The fear of not having a proper burial has made many remain in the Orthodox Church, especially older people. Thus, if the church allows Evangelicals to share its burial sites, the leaders fear that the Orthodox Church will lose its members.[354] When unable to monitor the spread of *tehadiso* movement as will be discussed in the next chapter, the clergy threatened parents of young

---

351. ሃይማኖት የለየን መቃብር አንድ አያደርገንም, 46–47. (Translation by the researcher.)

352. "አማናዊ ሥጋ ወልድ፤ አማናዊ ደም ወልደ እግዚአብሔር ብላነ ነው።. . . ባጠቃላይ በምሥጢራት ቤተ ክርስቲያን አንገናኝም፡፡ ስለዚህ በትምህርት ሃይማኖትና በቆና ቤተ ክርስቲያን የመይመስለንን በምሥጢራት ቤተ ክርስቲያን ከጃ ጋር አንድነት የለላቸውን በመካነ መቃብር እንበዕለም፡፡" ሃይማኖት የለየን መቃብር አንድ አያደርገንም, 46.

353. John Cumbers, *Count It All Joy: Testimonies from a Persecuted Church* (Kearney, NE: Morris Publishing, 1995), 141. Similarly, Meserete Kristos Church members in Wonji, were not allowed to bury their dead. Hege, *Beyond Our Prayers*, 134.

354. Informant D, 18 August 2010, Addis Ababa.

people with denial of burial place unless they expelled their children from the house, and parents relented.³⁵⁵

We see from the arguments of the Orthodox church outlined above that the church felt justified in refusing to inter bodies of *mete* religion followers in its compound. However, the problem is deeper than the Evangelicals' alleged desire to be buried in the Orthodox vicinity. There were Orthodox followers who were determined to make Evangelicals feel like strangers in their own country of birth.³⁵⁶ A case in point is the experience of Evangelicals in Gurage, Southern Ethiopia in 1995. There was a lot of conflict in matters of burial ground so the government gave a plot of land to be used by Evangelicals as a cemetery. While they were about to bury a body the clergy incited the Orthodox followers who came and disrupted the burial and the believers were forced to inter the body in their own land. In the same area another Evangelical person's body was buried forty kilometres away in Hosana town, because of the Orthodox clergy's refusal to let Evangelicals use the burial ground allocated to them by the government.³⁵⁷ The severity of the problem led an Evangelical believer to allocate a place from his own land as burial ground for members of his church.³⁵⁸ It was as though Evangelicals were not allowed to live let alone to be buried in their motherland.

---

355. Mezgebu Tsemru, pastor of Amanuel United Church, Interview, 23 August 2010.

356. In 1994 Eth. C in the town of Addis Alem, there was a decision made by Orthodox followers which had three points: first, no one was to talk to them or share in their joy or sorrow, no one was to use their car or sit next to them in the car. Second, they were to be beaten up wherever and whenever possible. Third, when one of them dies, they are not to bury in the Church there or anywhere. "let the body rote in their house." "በቤታቸው ይበስብስ" Girma Zewde, *Ethiopis*, vol. 2 (Addis Ababa: n.p., 1992 Eth. C), 97.

357. Getachew, *Agonies*, 319–320. There also was a report of a young "Pente" in Chefe Donsa (around Debre Zeit town) who was killed by a mob incited by the clergy of the church. After they killed him, they hanged his body on a tree. After six days they dug out his body and burned it. These horrendous actions of the clergy had wide coverage at the time. Girma Zewde, *Ethiopis*, vol. 2, 1992, 65–67. Similarly a body of a young girl which was buried in the place allocated for Evangelicals was dug out and thrown away in September 1998 and was reburied. But again because of further threat to dig out the body once more, her family took the body out and entered it 85 kilometres away from their home town. Girma, *Ethiopis*, vol. 2: 102–103.

358. Getachew, *Agonies*, 321. Ato Mulate Taye, the first Secretary of Evangelical Churches Fellowship of Ethiopia (ECFE) complained that the place of burial engaged his time more than other issues. According to him, Evangelicals were treated as second class citizen in their own country. He cited one example that the place allocated to Evangelicals as burial site by the government in Addis Ababa was taken away and handed over to an investor who claimed that the place was given to him. Even though ECFE provided all the

However, as will be seen below, the issue of burial is not exclusive to the Orthodox. Symbols of unity such as having table fellowship and sharing a graveyard are so powerful and important that even Kale Heywet members denied a burial ground to a group of people who had left them in order to establish their own independent church.[359]

The controversy over burial grounds shows a deep problem of intolerance and hatred towards Evangelicals. The rift between Orthodox and Evangelicals widened over the years primarily because of massive conversion of Orthodox members by Evangelicals and persecution and crimes committed by Orthodox followers with little chastisement from the church leadership. The denial of burial ground and disposal of the bodies of honourable human beings only shows the depth of the hatred and resentment of the Orthodox towards Evangelicals.

Conclusion

Evangelical Christianity has been a target of persecution from the established EOC, Islam, the pre-existent traditional religion and also the political authorities.[360] Evangelicals were referred to as anti-Mary, unpatriotic, heretical, and *Pente*. The aggressors from the Orthodox Church regarded their actions as a defence of their interests, religious, political or economic. Thus,

---

documents pertaining to ownership of the place, they did not find hearing at the court. *Kale Heywet* 16 (1990 Eth. C), 8–13.

359. Dawit Bayou, pastor of the Church of God, used to be the Secretary of the Kale Heywet Church (EKHC) in southern Ethiopia Gofa district. He claims that KHC was opposed to his teaching about the unity of the church and miracles and wonders, and he left the church and established "the Church of God." According to him, KHC incited the leaders of government to oppose him and his followers and members of KHC who were in government posts used their position to press the Church of God. Dawit also claimed that there was organized effort to accuse him and members of his church of teaching false teaching and their credibility was purposely undermined. They were excluded from the community and eventually arrested with hard labour. The Evangelicals even denied his members burial ground because they considered them heretic. Pastor Dawit Bayou, በነፃነት ዘመን ስደት (Persecution in an age of freedom), *Gesame*, Special issue (Meskerem, 2000 Eth. C), 5, 14.

360. Right after the fall of the Derg, leaders of Islam and EOC in Dubti town, Northern Ethiopia jointly issued a statement condemning "Pente." They noted that the faith was foreign and is instrumental for outside forces for "indirect colonization" of the country. The leaders admonished those who have joined the "Pente" to turn back to their faiths. Otherwise, they are not to take part in social affairs and buried with the Orthodox or Muslims. Issued in 24/12/84 Eth. C. Girma Zewde, *Ethiopis*, vol. 2, 99.

among the root causes of the persecution are theological, social, political and economic factors.[361]

On the other hand, the EOC also claims to have been the target of attack by Evangelicals. This attack which involves door-to-door evangelism and mass rallies in places where the Orthodox Church is predominant angers the ancient church. The terms used by Evangelicals to refer to the Orthodox followers, include *Ahzab*[362] and "without Christ" which provokes the anger of the church. Even the internal reform movements are regarded as instruments of Evangelicals' subtle agenda of weakening the ancient church. Strong terms have been used to describe the organized effort of Evangelicals to convert Orthodox members. Three of the terms used were "Jihad," "Armageddon" and "Gates of Hell" and they reflect how the Orthodox look at the act of converting Orthodox adherents not only as a rejection of the church of Christ, but as actively siding with enemies (human and the devil) to bring it down.

The attack against the Orthodox came to a climax with the coming of Pentecostals who were "the prime sheep-stealers" from all the Christian churches. They were, therefore, victims of severe persecution by all religious bodies, with minimal sympathy from the mainline Evangelical churches. Ironically, in addition to the external pressure, the expansion of the Pentecostal movement brought together Evangelical churches which joined hands against external pressure and complained to one another about internal "sheep-stealing."

Generally speaking, Evangelicalism ushered in a major change of lifestyle. A cry for independence and a strong sense of self-assertion grounded in their understanding of the Bible affected all areas of the Evangelicals' lives, and dress code and the usage of musical instruments were no exceptions. The EOC has a strong dress code which requires both men and women to wear ነጠላ/ጋቢ, *Netela* or *Gabi* (traditional garments) while in the church compound and around the vicinity of the church. The radical deviation of

---

361. Adise Amado, *Persecution in Ethiopia*, 22. For instance a bar owner in Debre Zeit town was angry because his selling of liquor and providing prostitutes was affected by Pentecostal movement. He along with a moral instructor of EOC (who had religious motivation) incited a huge crowd against believers and brutally beat them up in the fall of 1967 thereby marking the first historical persecution against Pentecostals in Ethiopia. Engelsviken, "Pentecostal Revival," 161.

362. As noted earlier, the connotation of "*Ahzab*" is people who do not know God.

the Evangelicals who dressed as they pleased while in their churches was annoying to the Orthodox.[363] Moreover, the Orthodox avoid the use of modern musical instruments with a controversial exception of the organ. The Evangelicals' usage of nearly all musical instruments thus was not acceptable.

Although the perceptions of the Orthodox towards Evangelicals were not favourable, as shown in this chapter, individual EOC followers admired the moral uprightness of Evangelicals.[364] In fact, it is believed that Evangelicals will not cheat, steal, lie, be adulterous, drink alcohol, be unkind, etc. Even though people do not want to convert to Evangelicalism for many reasons, they still are happy to send their children to Evangelical schools, believing that it will have a positive influence on the moral life of the pupils.

These perceptions most of the time raised very high expectations of Evangelicals, making it difficult for them to go about their daily life. The standard was high, and difficult to achieve all the time. Especially after religious freedom and the subsequent numerical boom of the Evangelical churches, it became more and more difficult to live up to the ideal. The public then appeared to swing to the other extreme of perceiving Evangelicals as untrustworthy.[365]

It appears that the fallibility of Evangelicals has been proven with numerous examples. In fact, some atrocities committed by pastors made the

---

363. Giday Beyene, "The Impact of Protestantism on the Ethiopian Orthodox Church," 37. Although the culture generally expects all to dress modestly, Orthodox adherents do not pay special attention to their dress code unless they are going to the church.

364. Their publications were widely read and even admired. Kale Heywet magazine was liked by even EOC followers. Kale Heywet, no. 4 (1985 Eth. C), 4; Kale Heywet, no. 5 (1985 Eth. C), 2. Some EOC members shared their opinion and offered a piece of advice that the magazine should focus on promoting unity and tolerance among Christians. "የቅጥር አራት ዕትም ይዘት ከሌሎች ዕትሞች ይልቅ የተሻለ ሆኖ በመገኘቱ ይበልጡ ረክቸንታለሁና ቢርቱ። ወደፊትም በእግዚአብሔር ቤተ ክርስቲያን መታነጽ ማበብና ማደግ ላይ አተኩሩ። በቤተክርስቲያናት መካከል ምንም ልዩነት እንዳይፈጥር ተጠንቀቁ። ክርስቲያኖች ቅራኔዎችን ሁሉ አስወግደው ወደ አንድነት እንዲያመሩ ማስተማር ይገባችኋል። አለበዚያ ልዩነትን በልብ ይዞ "ጌታ ኢየሱስ አዳኝ ነው" ብሎ መመስከር ብቻ እውነተኛ መንገድ ላይሆን ይችላል።" ጀምስ ቡፋ ከኢትዮጵያ ኦርቶዶክስ ተዋህዶ ቤተ ክርስቲያን Kale Heywet, No 5 (1985 Eth. C), 1. Similarly Hiwot Megazine which was the publication of Geja Kale Heywet was also widely read. Hiwot, no. 10 (1985 Eth. C), 2. Of all the Evangelical magazines, the oldest and the most widely distributed was Misikire Birhane, which used to be published by "Serawite Kristos (former BCMS), and later taken up by Mekane Yesus. Misikre Birhan used pictures and paintings of EOC and its monasteries. Cf. Misikire Birhan, No 74 (Hidar and Tahsas, 1959 Eth. C).

365. An Orthodox businesswoman said that she admired Evangelicals especially for their speaking softly and their prayerful life. "But, what good is that? They are liars just like everybody else. Even more so, they are not trustworthy at all. You cannot count on them." Fire Hiwot, Trader of banners, posters and car decorations, Interview, January 2011, Addis Ababa.

headlines.³⁶⁶ Some believe that the waywardness was caused by religious freedom which was decreed shortly after the fall of the Derg in 1990.³⁶⁷ These atrocities marred the perceptions of the public further, but the Orthodox Church recognizes that if it does not join hands with Evangelicals, it will not resist the growing movement of Muslim extremists which poses a serious threat for the existence of Christianity altogether.

The doctrinal difference between Evangelicals and EOC can be summed up in the status of the Bible which according to the Evangelicals is to serve as a standard against which to weigh any given doctrine or practice. Thus, the status given to Mary which in the Evangelicals' view is not upheld by the Bible, continues to make it difficult for both parties to see eye to eye. Evangelicals accuse the Orthodox Church of worshipping Mary. The church denies worshiping Mary but in practice its adherents seem to make little distinction between *prostration of worship* (የአምልኮ ስግደት) that is due to God and him alone and *prostration of honour* (የጸጋ ስግደት) that is due to Mary. This implies that the fifteenth-century acclamation of the level of worship which was due to Mary "together with her Son"³⁶⁸ "ከልጇም ጋራ"³⁶⁹ continues to shape the expression of worship in the Orthodox Church. Especially the claim that Jesus gave Mary Ethiopia as her covenant land resulted in much affection for and attachment to Mary as the guardian of Ethiopia.

There seems to be strong evidence to support the Protestant concern that in the structures of the Orthodox Church, Mary is exalted as high as, or even higher than Christ. Although these claims are not accepted by the church's theologians, the fact that Zer'a Ya'iqob's composition, which explicitly exalts her as a saviour, is read as part of the worship in the church appears to prove otherwise. This seems to justify the concern that EOC's unique devotion to draw people to the worship of the one and true God in three persons is substantially affected.

---

366. There was a story of a pastor who raped women who went for a counselling and prayer ministry. Ethiopian TV, Police Program, 2010.

367. Paulos Fekadu, የነጻነት መዘዝ (Consequence of freedom), unpublished article, October 2009.

368. Getatchew Haile, trans., *A Third Supplication for the Reading of the Miracles of Mary, The Cause of Estifanosites: A Fundamental Sect in the Church of Ethiopia*, Appendix V in Religion Miscellanea 3, Addis Ababa, Institute of Ethiopian Studies, n.d., 132.

369. Getatchew Haile, *Dekike Estifanos*, 38.

On the other hand the Evangelicals tie their identity to the Bible but their expression of Christianity lacks indigenization. Perhaps because of their conflict with the Orthodox Church they distance themselves from indigenous Ethiopian expressions of worship and ways of life.[370] Moreover, their indiscriminate criticism of the Orthodox has hurt the feelings of the ancient church, and most of all hindered Evangelicals from admiring the unique Christian heritage which EOC has preserved at an immeasurable cost.[371]

Moreover, the unpredictable nature of Evangelicalism and its dissociation from the EOC has not been helpful. There appears to be a degree of desire to work together for a number of reasons. One of the reasons is internal turmoil. Both Evangelicals and the Ethiopian Orthodox Church have experienced strong storms which in the case of the Orthodox Church came near to splitting it. Evangelicals on the other hand are looking for a more stable and orderly church government. Thus, their admiration for the EOC's indigenous Christian values is growing, and disciplines such as fasting, order in the worship, and spiritual mentorship are being sought after.

The second factor is external, and was exerted by Islam. Just as the persecution from the Derg brought together the Evangelical churches, which resulted in their establishing the Evangelical Churches Fellowship of Ethiopia, so the pressure from Islam is causing the Ethiopian Orthodox Church and Evangelicals to come closer at least at the top level. The Islamic aggression which for a long time was directed at Evangelicals, took a dramatic shift to include the Orthodox in 2006. In Southwestern Ethiopia many Orthodox Christians including priests and monks were massacred and some Orthodox churches burnt down.[372] When Evangelicals were again attacked in March

---

370. Getachew Belete, Former Head of the Publishing Department of Ethiopian Kale Heywet Church, Currently Manager of Aster Nega Publishing Company, Chairman of elders at Kolfe Kale Heywet Church, Interview, 18 August 2010, Addis Ababa.

371. Getachew Belete believes that the negative attitude of Evangelicals towards the EOC has aggravated intolerance and hatred from the EOC. According to him, the EOC is more open than Evangelicals wish to give it credit for and care to admit. Getachew Belete, Former Head of the Publishing Department of Ethiopian Kale Heywet Church, Currently Manager of Aster Nega Publishing, Chairman of elders at Kolfe Kale Heywet Church, Interview, 18 August 2010, Addis Ababa.

372. በጅማና በኢሉባቦር ክርስቲያኖች ሰማእትነት ተቀበሉ (Christians were martyred in Jimma and Illubabor), *Seme'a Tsidq*, 1, no. 21 (Tikimpt 1999 Eth. C); "የሚገድላችሁ ሁሉ እግዚአብሔርን እንደሚያገለግል የሚመስልበት ጊዜ ይመጣል" ዮሐ. 16:2 (Indeed, an hour is coming when those who kill you will think that by doing so they are offering worship to God" John 16:2), *Hohete*

2011 with churches being burned[373] and countless Evangelicals displaced, this angered the Orthodox Church.[374] The church spoke up in defence of Evangelicals calling them "Christian brethren" and warned that they will take matters into their own hands if the government did not intervene to ensure the safety of Christians including Evangelicals in Islam-dominant areas throughout the country.

Finally, the government is playing a role of enforcing peace between religious bodies in the country. Towards this end it allocated burial grounds for Evangelicals and also established "The Directorate of Religion and Faith Affairs" under the federal government with "collaborating with religious organizations in order to promote tolerance" as one of its objectives.

The government also brought together the five religiousorganizations, "the Ethiopian Orthodox Church, Islam, Ethiopian Catholic church, Evangelicals churches Fellowship of Ethiopia (ECFE), and Adventists and formed a council with five members from each organization. The council is known as "የሃይማኖት ተቋማት የሰላምና የጋራ ምክክር ጉባኤ" Inter-Religious Council. The Council's delegates meet twice a month and discuss issues related to tolerance. The Council is also authorized to hold workshops in district towns and create awareness and promote tolerance between adherents of different religions. It was this Council which looked into the matter of Mihretab and Dawit and discussed with the EOC and ECFE respectively what punitive measures were to be taken.[375] Thus, it is considered as a federal offence to

---

Tibeb (Special Issue), Ethiopian Orthodox Tewahdo Church (Addis Ababa Diocess, Tikimpt 1999 Eth. C).

373. A report presented to the Deputy General Secretary of the Ethiopian Kale Heywet Church and the General Secretary of Evangelical Churches Fellowship of Ethiopia indicates that forty-three Kale Heywet, thirteen Mekane Yesus, three Mulu Wongel, seven Adventist and one Oneness Pentecostalism churches were burned down at the time. "The Relief Summary of the Ethiopian Kale Heywet Church," National Task Force, July 2011.

374. Alemu, Interview, 4 February 2011.

375. The Council asked both the EOC and ECFE to summon Mihretab and Dawit respectively and inquire about their VCDs. Both of them were summoned to their respective religious authorities and requested to give a response. Upon hearing their replies, the Council decided that each of them was to write a letter of apology to the organization he offended. Mihretab was chastized for using the term "Jihad" as the title of his VCD and implicating the whole of the Evangelical community as the enemy. Dawit was admonished for ridiculing the EOC in his sermon. Bitew Kassa, Advisor of Religion and Faith Affairs Directorate, Interview, 24 February 2011, Addis Ababa. According to the official report of ECFE to the Religious Council, Dawit regretted his expressions of the Orthodox and took partial responsibility for

write or speak in a manner which incites people of different faiths against one another.

Moreover the Bible Society of Ethiopia has been preparing symposia and workshops with the aim of bringing the Trinitarians (EOC, Catholics and Evangelicals) together.[376] The initiative was inaugurated by Abune Paulos, the Patriarch of the EOC, Abune Birhane Eyesus, the Archbishop of the Catholic Church in Ethiopia, and Rev Alemu Shetta, General Secretary of the Evangelical churches Fellowship of Ethiopia. Delegates of each of the three organizations presented research papers regarding the benefits of cooperation and the dangers of division.[377]

In subsequent meetings which were highly praised as providing venues for unity and cooperation, the three organizations identified four issues of common concern: peace, good governance, environmental issues and unity with diversity.[378] In addition to that they agreed to refrain from taking provocative actions against one another. The Bible Society also organized a workshop for media people of the three faiths and representatives of the three

---

his portrayal of the Church. To Ethiopian Religious Council from ECFE, ኢወአክን/554/2003, Date: 4 Tir 2003 Eth. C. In a subsequent interview, Pastor Dawit expressed his sorrow over the way his words were taken out of context. He noted that the essence of his message, that there is salvationin no one else apart from faith in Jesus Christ is timeless, but if he were to preach the same sermon again he would avoid some of the expressions he used. Mihretab, however, insisted that he was doing apologia of the Orthodox faith so he never apologized. Zerihun Degu to Seblewengel, email, 12 May 2011; Dawit Molalegn, ስለ መምህር ምሕረት አብ ቪሲዲ የምለው አለኝ, (I have something to say about the VCD of Memhir Mihretab), *Trinity* 7 (2003 Eth. C), 2–4. The same magazine has the story of Asfaw Mekonnen, a co-teacher of Mihretab who apparently came to Pastor Dawit's church out of anger to the way Dawit depicted the EOC. During the prayer session, Asfaw started to cry out "When Dawit forgave Mihretab, our work was destroyed." He was taken to the front and stunned to find himself on the pulpit when he gained his consciousness. They explained to him that he was possessed by demons and he was freed through prayer. He said out of his desire for deeper spiritual experience, he befriended a "debtera" (usually are graduates of the higher traditional school of the Church, also accused of involving in occultism) who gave him objects of spell, but leaders of the church warned him, "stay away from this bad man. You will be screwed up" "ከዚህ ሰው እራስኽ፣ ጥፋ ሰው አይደለም ትበላሻለህ." But he did not listen to them and continued his friendship and went into exploring witchcraft book called "Merbebete Solomon." His practices placed him under the power of evil spirits, 5, 8–9.

376. The Bible Society is not trying to eliminate differences between these bodies, but prepare the platform for them to find common grounds and work together on contemporary cultural and religious hurdles of the nation. Yilma Getahun, Interview, 19 April 2011.

377. Mathetes 10 (March 2009), 2–5.

378. Alemu, Interview, 4 February 2011.

faiths made speeches.[379] Delegates of each organization presented papers and another person spoke on the issue from a legal point of view.[380]

More importantly, the fact that the Orthodox are making use of the mother-tongues to preach and teach has great potential to bring the two organizations together. Even Mahbere Kidusan is highly encouraging its members to use mother-tongues while teaching spiritual truths. It also has a plan to teach people in their own tongues. In fact, it reported holding outreaches with Amharic and also Oromiffa.[381]

Clearly, there is a long way to go, but the first steps towards mutual respect and tolerance are taken. Despite a degree of scepticism towards unity among many people on each side, Evangelicals express gratitude for the contribution of the Orthodox Church to the society in general, and there is also desire on the side of the Ethiopian Orthodox Church to put behind them past hurts and work with other churches. Moreover, the contemporary reformation movements within the church have great potential to promote peaceful dialogue between the two bodies. The question is whether they are bringing the two together or tampering with their vital role of promoting mutual understanding.

---

379. Abune Gabriel, the delegate of the EOC stated, "ኦርቶዶክስ፣ ካቶሊክ፣ ፕሮቴስታንት ብንባልም ሁላችንም የምናመልከው ያው አንዱን ክርስቶስን ነው፤ በውስጡ-ደንብ ብንለያይም በክርስቶስ ግን አንለያይም፦" "Even though we are called Orthodox, Catholic, Protestant, all of us worship the one Christ. Although we are divided in constitution, in Christ, however, we are not divided." 4 February 2011, 18–19. Translation done by the researcher.

380. የክርስቲያን ሚድያ ሚና ምን መሆን አለበት (What should be the role of christian media), *Gesame*, no. 13, Meskerem 2003 Eth. C, 18–20. Cf. Mikiyas Belay, "የክርስቲያን ሚዲያውና ችግሮቹ" (The christian media and its problems), Mathetes 16 (July 2010), 2.

381. Fetlework Desta, ከተለያዩ ሀገረ ስብከቶች የተውጣጡ ሰልጣኞች ተመረቁ (The graduation of trainees from different dioceses), www.eotc-mkidusan.org, accessed 13 May 2011.

CHAPTER 6

Contemporary Reformation Impulses in the Ethiopian Orthodox Church

Introduction

In the Ethiopian Orthodox church, historically, the two centres of reformation were the monarchy and monasteries. As discussed in chapter 2, the coming of the nine saints and the *Tsadqan*, who reformed and organized the life of the church provides us with examples of reformation mediated by monks. Monks not only strove to teach the people and evangelize new territories, but also boldly admonished some of the monarchs who led a wayward life. Such actions resulted in their being tortured and banished from their monasteries. On the other hand, the monarchs, who formally were head of the church, were key players of reformation as illustrated in the reign of Zer'a Ya'iqob. The kings sought to promote Christianity in newly conquered territories and took part in doctrinal controversies by way of endorsing or rejecting a given school of thought; such measures shaped Ethiopian Christianity.

However, the kinds of reforms which won favour among the monarchy and among the clergy differed. Many of the attempts to reform doctrines which over the years had assumed foundational status, were frustrated and the individuals who challenged them expelled. Such actions of the church discouraged inquiry and also created in the mind of the public that doctrines such as Mariology were vital for Orthodox identity. The reformation impulses, however, continued to be heard from individuals and groups of people. Especially after the fall of the Derg, the voices of opponents of a number of Orthodox doctrines were heard loudly. Such groups call themselves *tehadiso* (reformers) and there are some differences in how they view and approach the church.

This section, therefore, will examine reformation movements, evaluate the methods they have used over the years and their relationship to one another. Finally it will discuss the interaction of the reformers with Evangelical churches who attempt to support them indirectly and at times directly.

6.1. An Overview of Reformation in the Church

An overview of reformation movements over the centuries demonstrates that the church was not static, but vibrant in its own way. The rise of St Yared, who indigenized the worship style of the church and the integration of the definition of the doctrinal book based on "Qerlos," provide us with evidence of revival in the sixth century. In the seventh century there was a conflict between Muslims and Aksumites. Beginning from the eighth century, Muslims overpowered and took control of the coastal lands thereby cutting off the church of Ethiopia from the rest of the Christian world. During such a trying period, the Ethiopian Christians were forced to practice their religion in isolation and interpret the Scriptures with no interaction with Christians outside of Ethiopia.

Such an experience resulted in the development of questionable doctrines and practices which continued to be matters of great concern.[1] However, in the ninth century, the scholars of the church compiled the *Andemta* commentary, which is the authoritative commentary of the church to this day. The tenth century marked a devastating destruction of many churches and killing of its clergy because of civil war. In the eleventh century the pressure from the Amir in Egypt was felt by the emperors and the church but they did not relent to the desires of the Amir to have them build mosques and protect Muslims. Regardless of the pressure, the Christians in Ethiopia made sure that Islam was restrained.

In the thirteenth century a great number of northern people settled in the pagan Shewa thereby expanding the church's territory and religious upper

---

1. Fekadu Gurmessa, *Evangelical Faith Movement in Ethiopia* (Minneapolis, MN: Lutheran University Press, 2009), 46.

hand. Moreover, the "Solomonic Dynasty" which was restored by Yikunno Amlak further strengthened the Ethiopian Christians and their emperors as the new heirs of the promises of God to Israel, and the divinely appointed kings respectively. Among many factors such a conviction must have contributed to the strengthening of the church regardless of its isolation.

Moreover, as discussed in chapter 2, St Tekle Haymanot, one of the most respected monks in the Ethiopian tradition, came to the scene when he returned to Shewa, his birth place, from his monastic activities in the North. His coming was inspired by the rise of the "Solomonic Dynasty" and a sense of responsibility to preach the gospel to his countrymen who, surrounded by pagans, developed complacency towards Christianity. "He revived the religious consciousness of his fellow Christians and realised the relative degree of Christian learning among them."[2] As noted earlier, Amde Tsion came to power one year after the death of Tekle Haymanot in 1314. During his reign, the revival of monasticism served as an effective vehicle for the expansion of the church in the kingdom.

The extent of the reformation, however, was limited to a number of issues. Major doctrines such as Mariology remained intact because of wider resistance as discussed in chapter 4. Moreover, there was a tendency to retain old traditions with little or no critique. Such an attitude is inbuilt in the ancient traditional school system of the church. The rigorous training the pupils undergo in the traditional school teaches them to duplicate the teachings of the fathers exactly as they were passed on. To some extent there was room for debate, even public debate, which made it possible for views which were first rejected to later make it all the way to the top pillars of faith. The controversy over Sabbath is the case in point.[3] On the other hand it goes without saying that many who dared to differ perished. Thus, monarchs played a big role in setting the agenda regarding which of the doctrines was to be reformed or retained.

As discussed in chapters 1 and 4, the rise of Zer'a Ya'iqob in the fifteenth century who attempted to annihilate pagan worship and produced and translated religious books is crucial in the history of the church. His story

---

2. Taddesse Tamrat, *Church and State*, 168–173.
3. Taddesse Tamrat, 209–231.

is very important not only because he attempted to reform the church in his own way but also because his actions produced a counter-reformation. Nearly all of the reformation attempts after him were aimed at reversing the major religious shift enforced by him. His era thus marks an alteration of the ceremonies and rituals of the ancient church. However, the reformation attempts which aimed to challenge the legacy of Zer'a Ya'iqob did not always have key figures or a major following.

Since the sixteenth century, the church has had intermittent contact with foreign religious forces Islam, Latin Christian and Protestant. These forces affected the church for the better and worse, leaving their mark on it, as discussed in chapter 2. In addition to the intermittent contact with outside forces, the church also was called to reform by her own children. Among the individuals who bravely challenged the priests over unbiblical doctrines including the exalted status of Mary, was Aleqa Taye. He was one of the early people to acquire modern education, and to be influenced by Evangelical Christianity.[4] He went all the way through the church's traditional school acquiring the title "Aleqa" and also was a communicant member of the Bethel congregation in Eritrea. Aleqa Taye's attempts were not appreciated.[5] He was accused of being *tsere Maria* and challenged to prove otherwise by prostrating before the picture of Mary in order to prove his authentic Orthodoxy. Aleqa refused, quoting Exodus 20:1–6. Upon his death, he was denied burial in

---

4. The Lutheran missionaries who were working in the modern Eritrea were the ones who impacted the spiritual understanding of Aleqa Taye. The Bible reading within the Orthodox Church resulted with a movement that eventually produced Mekane Yesus Church. For a brief story of the establishment of Mekane Yesus Church please see pgs 90–96 above.

5. Aleqa was repeatedly accused of propagating foreign teaching. After examining his beliefs Menelik gave him the following official permission to preach and teach. "The Lion of the Tribe of Judah hath conquered. Menelik II, appointed by God, King of Kings in Ethiopia. The man, by name Tayelign Gebra Mariam, who dwelt in Massowah, has visited us. We have tested his belief, and no one on account of his faith may do him any wrong." Gustav Aren, *Envoys of the Gospel in Ethiopia* (Stockholm: EFS Forlaget, 1999), 26. Regardless of the opposition Menelik admired Aleqa Taye and even chose him to go to Germany as professor of Ge'ez for three years and he was able to visit other European countries as well. Based on his experience in Europe Aleqa Taye advised Menelik to act against the bad custom of belittling education and skilful people (such as potters, smiths, tanners). In a letter to Menelik Aleqa implies that the cause of the backwardness of Ethiopia is the people's ignorance and giving low status to work. After four months of Aleqa Taye's letter, Menelik devised a decree which highlighted the needed higher regard for education and work. Solomon Telahun, *Demaqochu* (Addis Ababa: 2000 Eth. C), 66.

the church grounds.⁶ Thus, neither *tehadiso* impulses, nor opposition to it, were foreign to the church.⁷

However, the quest for deeper experiences continued. With the steady spread of education and modernization, the pursuit of "progressive" Ethiopians for a deeper and meaningful spiritual experience came to surface in the 1960s. They critiqued a number of long-held traditions including the exclusive use of Ge'ez in the church, and "the prescribed nature of the religious practices" which did not make space for vibrant expression of faith. The educated people also believed the church was not addressing issues in a way which pertained to the modern lifestyle which their Western education exposed them to. Such concerns gave birth to the establishment of a number of associations which were meant to address relevant issues and prevent the educated from leaving the church altogether.⁸

These associations endeavoured to bring to the attention of the church the need for reformation. "Most of these organizations were sponsored and financed by members of the royal family and the ruling class."⁹ The church and the monarch were not against the associations. In fact, they seem to have encouraged them. A case in point is Haymanote Abew of which the patriarch was the chairman and Haile Sellassie the principal patron.¹⁰

The 1960s quest for reform was not limited to those Ethiopians who were exposed to modern education, but the clergy as well. Some priests trained under the traditional Orthodox order recognized its inadequacy in

---

6. Editor, "የዘመን ምሥክር፤ አለቃ ታዬ ገብረ ማርያም (1888–1974 sic) (Witness through time, Aleqa Taye Gebre Mariam), no. 40 (Tahsas 2003 Eth. C), 10–15.

7. Few examples are the thirteenth-century Yikunno Amlak's flogging Beselota Mikael for opposing his polygamy, Amde Tsion's flogging a monk for having a different opinion about Sabbath in the fourteenth century, and Zer'a Ya'iqob's torturing Estifanosites primarily for their opposition of the veneration of the king in the fifteenth century. Taddesse Tamrat, *Church and State*, 208; Hastings, *Church in Africa*, 27; Getatchew Haile, *Dekike Estifanos: Behig Amlak*, 2nd ed. (Addis Ababa: AAU Press, 2010), 25ff.

8. Eshete lists some of the associations which were formed as follows: Ye Kristianoch Andnet Mahber, Mahbere Hawriyat Fire Haymanot, Yewengel Mele'ektegnoch Ena Ye Ehud Timhirt Mahber, Temro Mastemar, Kesate Birhan, and Haymanote Abew. Eshete, *Evangelical Movement*, 54–57.

9. Eshete, 56.

10. Eshete, 57–58; Melaku Baweke, ስውሩ አደጋ (The subtle danger), 135.

view of the knowledge and modern outlook of the new generation.[11] One area of such concern was the educational system and the recruitment of the clergy.[12] A call for the primacy of Scriptural teaching over other sources has been persistent. After the church became autocephalous in 1959, Abune Filipos, archbishop of the Orthodox Church in Jerusalem, lamented that while under the church of Alexandria, the excuse for not making adequate use of the Bible was the foreignness of the heads of the church, but even after autocephaly the church continues to depend more on tales than the Bible. He even wrote to Haile Sellassie that instead of passing on vain traditional tales to the people, the time was ripe to make use of the vernacular Scripture to teach the gospel by making use of modern knowledge.[13]

The cost of maintaining the inadequate ancient ways of doing theological education was also raised by EOC's clergy members in 1968, and they called for new ways of preaching and teaching.[14] Qes Mekbib Atnaw observed that the clergy monopolized the core part of the traditional education because its content and language were incomprehensible to the laity and that the number of priests who knew the reading along with the interpretation was very few. Thus most priests had been reading, praying, doing the mass and singing in a language they did not understand. He further lamented that the most able of the clergy who knew the interpretation of the Scriptures and *Qene* tended to choose hermit's life and locked themselves up in cemeteries where they chanted their knowledge to themselves so that they would not forget it.[15] This shows the fundamental outlook of some knowledgeable

---

11. Qes Mekbib Atnaw, Tinsae, "የጥንታዊው የሀገር ትምህርት የአማማር አቅድ" (The ancient country education) (Miazia 10, 1960 Eth. C), 31–35. Qes Lesanework Bezabeh, Tinsae, "የኢትዮጵያ ኦርቶዶክስ ተዋህዶ ቤተ ክርስቲያን በተቀዳሚ ማድረግ የሚገባት" *(What the Ethiopian Orthodox Tewahdo Church Needs to Do First)* (30 Nehassie 1963 Eth. C), 27–38.

12. Qes Mekbib, "የጥንታዊው የሀገር ትምህርት የአማማር አቅድ," 31–35; Qes Teshome Zerihun, Tinsae, "የኢትዮጵያ ቤተ ክርስቲያን ዕድገት" *(The growth of the Ethiopian Church)*, 40.

13. "እኔ የምላው በግርማዊነትዎ አስተዋይ መሪነት ተመርጠን ሊቀ ጳጳስ ተብለን የተሾምነው፣ ሶዎች በዘመናቸው የተጠቀሙበትን ተረት እየተረከን ተከናንበን ለመኖር አይደለም:: ግርማዊነትዎ በስተረገሚቸው ቅዱሳት መጻሕፍት ለኢትዮጵያ ሕዝብ ባገሩ ቋንቋ ጌታችን ኢየሱስ ክርስቶስ መሥዋዕት የሆነበትን ሕግ ወንጌልን ልናስተምር ነውና ከንቱ ልማድን ሳይሆን ሐዲስ ኪዳንን እናስተምር:: የቤተክርስቲያናችንንም እርምጃ በሐዲስ ኪዳን በወንጌል ቃል መሠረት ሕዝባችንን ከጊዜው ዕውቀት ጋራ ከመንፈሳዊው ትምህርት በማዘመድ ሥርዓተ ቤተ ክርስቲያናችንን በዘሙኑ ዕውቀት በማሻሻል "እንዲህ አሉ" የሚባለውን ልማድ በቅዱስ ወንጌል ትምህርት ዕይታን ካዲሱ ዘመኑ ዕውቀት ጋር የሐዲስ ኪዳንን ዕውቀት እናስተምረው:" Yezemen Misikir, *Chora*, no. 39 (Hamle 2002 Eth. C), 14.

14. Qes Mekbib Atnaw, "የጥንታዊው የሀገር ትምህርት የአማማር አቅድ," 31–35. Qes Lesanework Bezabeh, "የኢትዮጵያ ኦርቶዶክስ ተዋህዶ ቤተ ክርስቲያን በተቀዳሚ ማድረግ የሚገባት," 27–38.

15. Qes Mekbib, "የጥንታዊው የሀገር ትምህርት የአማማር አቅድ," 31–35.

people in the church who preferred solitude to sharing their knowledge with others. Among other things, such an attitude has hindered the interaction between the learned clergy of the church and the lay people.[16]

Not only the need for but also the scope of renewal was discussed by Qes Mekbib. According to him, apart from the fundamental tenets of Christian faith, the way church education is done, the approach and the methodology needs to be changed in accordance with the time and the needs of the society. He argues that the method of interpretation of scriptures needs to change completely. Otherwise, he warns, the ancient interpretation of Scriptures as it has stood, may well end up in the library and the generation will not benefit from the reading and study of it.[17] Another priest observes that there were men who joined the clergy just for its benefits. He writes that the damage done by such priests is devastating. He suggests that the best way to address such problems is to establish training centres for priests.[18]

In 1969 a similar call for offering relevant modern training for the clergy was echoed. In an article published in the *Ethiopian Herald*, one of the state gazettes, two writers argued that the traditional ecclesiastical training was inadequate to address issues and cope with the new emerging society.[19] The EOC was the main source of education until the beginning of the twentieth century, but this dominance was soon to change with the coming of modern education.[20] In the 1940s, when the modern school system was in its infancy and nearly all educators were foreigners, Karl Pollak, the editor of the *Ethiopian Herald* at the time, expressed his concern that Education should not be

> . . . a mere transplantation of the systems of other countries. It should be a grafting of the old and the new, of the exotic

---

16. In addition, it has opened the way for people with inadequate training and or questionable practices to assume higher positions in the Church. Agizachew Tefera (Deacon), Editor-in-Chief of *Chora*, the Publication of Mahbere Bekur, Interview, 13 June 2011; Informant D, Interview, 18 August 2010, Addis Ababa.

17. Qes Mekbib, "የጥንታዊው የዐገር ትምህርት የአማማር አቅድ," 31–35.

18. Qes Teshome Zerihun, Tinsae, "የኢትዮጵያ ቤተ ክርስቲያን ዕድገት," 40.

19. Negussie Seyoum and Yimenu Yirdaw, *New School Trains Modern Priests for Rural Areas*, The Ethiopian Herald, 27 April 1969, 6.

20. Aymro Wondmagegnehu, ed., *A Short Introduction to the Ethiopian Orthodox Church* (Addis Ababa: Birhanena Selam Printing Press, 1957 Eth. C), 34.

and the indigenous, in a manner to retain and strengthen the many admirable traits and traditions of the people and at the same time to teach them only those newer ways which will bring about a sane constructive and well-grounded Ethiopian citizenry.[21]

Haile Sellassie himself, as noted earlier, was determined to bring reform to the country and the church as well. Thus, he aimed to address the issue of the relevance of ancient church education by establishing modern theological schools which he funded. The Emperor realized that the church needed to have priests and workers "who had not only the traditional training for church work but also a sound general education and special training to relate the Christian faith to the problems of modern life."[22]

Towards this end, the emperor laid the foundation stone for the first modern theological college of the church in 1942 and during the early years of the college covered all of its expenses from his personal fund while the church fully participated in the leadership of the school.[23] In addition to Holy Trinity Theological College, the EOC had one theological school in Aksum and a larger one in Mekele.[24] Haile Sellassie laid the cornerstones for Mekele Theological College in 1968 and donated 31,000 birr for the beginning of the construction. The college aimed to offer Ge'ez, Amharic, Hebrew and Greek in addition to the secular and religious subjects.[25]

It appears that the quest for educational reform was beginning to be satisfied with the opening of modern theological schools. Holy Trinity

---

21. Karl Pollak, "Education and Reform," *The Ethiopian Herald* (12 August 1946), 2.

22. Joseph, "Theological College," 20.

23. Furthermore Trinity Theological College was established and inaugurated in 1960 with H. G. Bishop Trenig Poladian of Armenian Church as Dean. With the inauguration of the Haile Sellassie I University in December 1961 the theological college was incorporated as one of the charter units of the university and the University assumed its administration. Its first graduates were noted as holding important positions and doing valuable work for the country and the Church. Joseph, "Theological College," 20, 30.

24. በትግራይ ጠቅላይ ግዛት ስ *320,000* ብር መንፈሳዊ ትምህርት ቤት ይሰራል (The construction of spiritual school is under way in Tigre Region with 320,000 birr), Addis Zemen (25 Tahsas 1962 Eth. C), 4. Mekele is located in the Northern Ethiopia and is the capital town of Tigray, the home of the current Prime Minister of Ethiopia. Also it is in the same region with Axum, the historic town where the first "Solomonic Dynasty" used to rule from and the ark of the covenant is claimed to be found.

25. "Help Build Mekele Theological College," *The Ethiopian Herald* (28 May 1971), 1.

Theological College in Addis was so popular initially that because of space it turned down many applicants.[26] The students of the theological school were praised for their passion for ministry.[27] The students also organized a platform to discuss the church's concern over foreign missionaries duplicating Christians by re-evangelizing the evangelized.[28] The students sought to provide the society with a platform to discuss relevant issues and the theological school seems to have played an important role in the progress of the church.[29]

Unfortunately, the initial popularity of the theology school faded away after some time. There was a growing sense of dissatisfaction with the achievements of the school as early as 1958. At the time Haile Sellassie expressed his concern to the board members of the Haile Sellassie I University about the slow spiritual growth of the people. He believed that the theological school was not measuring up to its high expectations, and that the spiritual condition of the people had not progressed as much as it should in view of the country's long-lived Christianity. He ordered the board members to study and come up with an effective means of expanding religious education so that the country's spiritual education would not deteriorate.[30]

---

26. የትምህርት ቤቶች ለዕረፍት መዘጋት (Schools on a break), Birhanena Selam, no. 28 (11 Hamle, 1938 Eth. C), 22.

27. The students travelled all over the country to teach the Gospel. The students also formed two associations የዕሁድ ትምህርት ቤት ማህበር (Sunday School Association) and የወንጌል መልዕክተኞች ማህበር (Association of messengers of the gospel). Through these two associations they participated in teaching Bible stories and songs to children throughout the Orthodox churches in Addis Ababa. They visited prisons and hospitals and sought to encourage the prisoners and patients by teaching them spiritual education. They also conducted different programme every Saturday afternoon in churches and sought to have different people participate in discussing burning issues of the time, such as why the youth were far from the Church. በመንሳሳዊ ኮሌጅ የሚካሄደው ማህበር ከፍ ያለ አገልግሎት በመስጠት ላይ ይገኛል (The association which is run by the spiritual college is offering a great service), Ye'Ethiopia Dimts (27 Tahsas 1957 Eth. C), 1, 5.

28. "Orthodox Church Conference Opens Here," *The Ethiopian Herald* (12 May 1967), 1; "Missionaries Refuse to Comment on Criticism by Orthodox Church," *The Ethiopian Herald* (18 May 1967), 1.

29. የመንሳሳዊ ኮሌጅ ተማሪዎች በትያትር ገቢ የድኩማንን ድርጅት ይረዳሉ *(With an income of theatre: Students of the spiritual college help the organization for the disabled)* Ye'Ethiopia Dimts (The Ethiopian Voice) (27 Tahsas 1957 Eth. C), 1, 5.

30. መንሳሳዊ ኮሌጅና መንሳሳዊ ትምህርት በኢትዮጵያ (Spiritual college and spiritual education in Ethiopia), Addis Zemen (13 Miazia 1951 Eth. C), 1.

The students of the theological school on the other hand felt that the benefits of the school were not being recognized. In an article written more than half a century ago, a student lamented that, presumably because of their limited education, the young generation was not paying attention to the priests whom they regarded "as the stain on the white radiance of the day." Among many factors the student believed that such a low opinion had its roots in the failure of the clergy to adequately address the needs of the time. "Hence, the priest who is to be the custodian of this holy vocation should be sufficiently educated to deserve the respect and honour of his position."[31]

Those who were trained at the modern theological school did not feel accepted either. In fact, the student wrote that the general public, including government officials, had a low opinion of them.[32] A decade later, Dr V. C. Samuel, the director of the Holy Trinity Theological College, expressed similar thoughts that the church was not employing the graduates of the theological school and appealed to the church to "help more the endeavour of the institution by recruiting students with a religious interest and by utilizing graduates in the service of the church."[33]

On the other hand the church complained that it had no voice in the recruitment of students and could not afford to hire them. The students were also criticised for a lack of religious devotion and dedication.[34] Qes

---

31. Adugna Amann, "The Theological School at a Glance," *The Ethiopian Herald* (26 July 1960), 2

32. The writer regretted that the unique role the school played in offering both religious and general education was not recognized at all. It was as though the students were accepted neither by the Church nor by the society at large. When they applied for jobs during their vacation, the student wrote, "They usually tell us, 'no room for priests,' an answer that runs counter to the common opinion." Nevertheless, he expresses his concern that materialism was taking over and the priests trained under the traditional order were not equipped to address such issues. Thus, he urged his readers to take the modern theological education seriously. Amann, "Theological School at a Glance," 2.

33. V. C. Samuel, "Theology Graduates Not Employed by Church," *The Ethiopian Herald*, 14 April 1971, 1; See also Dr V. C. Samuel, "Theological College," *The Ethiopian Herald* (16 April 1971), 2.

34. According to Aba Gebre Egziabher Degou, the administrator of the Department of Education at the time, the church leadership did not know who the students were and where they came from and that was the reason for reserve on the church's part in utilizing the graduates. Moreover, the graduates were accused of demanding equal pay with those who had graduated from other fields of study. He added, "Theological College should have been told and agreement should have been secured to the effect that they would not be paid on a College graduate level. Candidates with religious devotion and dedicated to serve the church

Mikre Selassie G/Amanuel, the Assistant Dean of Holy Trinity Theological College at the time, countered the administrator's remarks. He wrote that the church was indeed involved in the recruitment of students because the College required the candidates to come with certification from bishops or distinguished leaders of the church. He further warned that the church was bound to face serious problems if it did not utilize the knowledge and skills of the graduates of higher institutions.[35]

With graduates struggling to find jobs in the church, the intended reform that was hoped to come from the ministry of higher theological institutions did not materialize. Perhaps part of the reason was the apparent tension between the traditional school system and the modern theological school. In 1971 the Director of Holy Trinity noted that the college encountered a twofold problem: that of student enrolment on one hand, and the utilization of the graduates on the other.[36] With the political change in the country in 1974 the school was nationalized and its property confiscated by the Derg regime, but it was reopened in October 1994. The tension between the traditional school system and the modern one is still evident.[37] However, the graduates seem to enjoy wider acceptance at the present time and there is a belief that their ministry has substantially limited the flocking of the Orthodox into the Evangelical churches.[38] The theological institutions of the Orthodox Church seem to have more impact from time to time, thereby realizing Haile Sellassie's old dream of renewing the church in a way which does not alter its foundational doctrines.

Even though a given kind of reformation might be unpopular for one reason or another, *tehadiso*, which has currently assumed a new connotation, was used by the Orthodox Church's media. This contradicts the trend to label reform impulses as *Tsere-Mariam* and caused by foreign agents. The truth

---

forfeiting material needs should have been enrolled in the institution." "Church Wants Voice in Student Recruitment," *The Ethiopian Herald* (15 April 1971), 1.

35. "Assistant Dean Counters Church's Argument," *The Ethiopian Herald* (16 April 1971), 4.

36. Samuel, "Theological College," 2.

37. Informant D, Interview, 18 August 2010.

38. Mekonnen, Interview, 15 November 2010.

is that the call for reform was not simply external as sometimes assumed, but there has been an internal consciousness about the need for reform.[39]

6.2. The Controversy over the Term *Tehadiso*

Currently there is a great deal of difference of opinion regarding the meaning and scope of reformation (*tehadiso*). In fact, the term *tehadiso* is more and more identified with "dissenters" who are accused of joining hands with foreign and indigenous forces who allegedly aim to steal the flock under the pretence of *tehadiso*.[40] The connotation of the term is changing to imply a conspiracy to replace the existing structure of the Orthodox Church with a new content and form. Thus, the term is applied to those who are accused of attempting to shake the foundations of Ethiopian Orthodoxy and dismantle the old church in order to build a new one.[41] Mahbere Kidusan, one of the associations under the church, even argues that *tehadiso* and Protestant are synonymous.[42]

The accusation of *tehadiso* arises for different reasons, the main ones relating to the critique of non-canonical writings and associating with Evangelicals.[43] This new development in the connotation of the term *tehadiso* is making it increasingly difficult to use the term in reference to

---

39. Zena Bete Kristian, the official gazette of the Orthodox Church, had a column which was entitled የተሃድሶ አምድ ለውይይትና ለትምህርት (Column of renewal for discussion and education). The section's purpose was stated. It was to serve as a venue to express opinions regarding the renewal of the church: administerial reforms, increasing the income of the church, elections of the church's leadership, and also ways in which the church would move forward on the way of "tehadiso." The section has a disclaimer that the opinions do not reflect the official position of the church. But it invited discussions on the history of the EOC, the basic doctrines of the Bible, and the philosophy of theological education for the sake of promoting knowledge and sparking discussion. Cf. Zena Bete Kristian, Megabit 30, 1982 Eth. C. The column was more or less regular for about a decade (early 1980s to the early 1990s).

40. Melaku, ስውሩ አደጋ፣, 128–129; Endale Teshi, Interview with Eshetu Alemayehu, Addis Guday 5, no. 92 (Sene 2003 Eth. C), 20.

41. Mahbere Kidusan cited a letter of *tehadiso* propagators whom it referred to as "the thorns of Meseret Sebhat Leab" "የመሠረት ስብሐት ለአብ እሾኾች." The letter was allegedly copied to German mission, Mekane Yesus, Kale Heywet, SIM, and the Evangelical Churches Fellowship of Ethiopia. The alleged aim of the group was to renew the church which in their view has become a haven for witchcraft. የገሃነም ደጆች, *Sem'ea Tsidq* 10, no. 78 (Megabit 1995 Eth. C), 12.

42. የተሃድሶ መናፍቃን ዘመቻ በኢትዮጵያ ቤተ ክርስቲያን ላይ (The campaign of the Tehadiso *menafiqan* against the Ethiopian church), (Addis Ababa, Mahbere Kidusan Documentation Department (2003 Eth. C), 38.

43. የገሃነም ደጆች (Gates of hell), 12–14.

renewal.[44] According to Qesis Melaku Baweke[45] it was the Derg that politicized the term *tehadiso* by naming the group it organized in opposition to Abune Tewoflos "የተሃድሶ ጉባኤ" (Provisional Council for the Renewal of the Church), appointing a new administrator and eventually detaining the patriarch. The Derg spread propaganda against the Patriarch with a slogan, "the Orthodox Church needs *tehadiso*."[46]

The confusion around the term *tehadiso* resulted in growing scepticism within the Orthodox Church towards people identified as reformers, and even to the concept of reform altogether. Although suspicion of people with reformed views, or those who ask too many questions, is not a new development, the printed works of Mahbere Kidusan brought the concept to the centre of discussion in an unprecedented way. Formerly, those who were vocal about their reformed convictions opted to join Evangelical churches.[47] But currently, there are those determined to stay in the church and work towards renewal.

Given the different opinions held on the issue, defining the term, *tehadiso* is vital for the discussion of this chapter. The Amharic word *tehadiso* comes from the verb *adese* which means to renovate an existing structure or thing in order to bring it back to its original form, cleaning something, or beautifying it.[48] Thus, *tehadiso* is a noun which implies the process of renewal, reformation. The meaning does not imply dismantling or creating something new, but restoring the original form by removing the distortion caused by the coming of foreign ingredients. Mahbere Bekur (Association of the Firstborn), which was established by Aleqa Meseret Sebhat Leab, quotes the Amharic dictionary of Aleqa Kidane-Wold Kifle and further elaborates

---

44. Mahbere Kidusan is the champion of the new connotation by exclusively applying the term to groups which have left or are expelled from the EOC because of their alleged desire or attempt to obliterate the structure of the ancient church.

45. He joined a *tehadiso* group during the havoc caused by the decimation of Haymanote Abew and was restored to the clerical office of the Orthodox Church under the "exiled" Patriarch and Synod in North America. Mahbere Kidusan refers to him as opportunist. "የገሃነም ደጃች" (Gates of hell), 12.

46. Melaku refers to Mahbere Kidusan as walking in the footsteps of this atheist grou Melaku, ስውሩ አደጋ, 123–25. Cf. Paulos, *Brief Life History of His Holiness*, 85–86.

47. Eshete, *Evangelical Movement*, 59–60.

48. አደሰ 1. ጠገነ፡አርጌውን አዲስ እንዲሆን ወይም እንዳመስል አድርጎ ሰራ, 2. አፀዳ፡ አሳመረ, Amharic Dictionary (2001 Eth. C), 338.

tehadiso as "protecting something to maintain its original form, correcting the spoiled, mending the broken and enabling it to perform its duty."[49]

We have noted that the Orthodox Church was not troubled by foreign missions as much as by the spread of Ethiopian Pentecostals.[50] Now it appears that much more troubling developments are underway, and on an unprecedented scale, that is, a reformation movement from within the structures of the church. Evidence of their potential to bring change in the church is the continual propaganda of Mahbere Kidusan against them in most of its monthly issues. The *tehadiso* propagators are aware of the opposition from some of the clergy members and strive to affirm that *tehadiso* does not mean introducing something new, but reviving the foundational teaching by removing the "dirt" which has accumulated over the years.[51]

As for the understanding of the meaning of the term *tehadiso* in terms of its practical outworking, again there are different views. The inadequate knowledge on the part of the propagators of *tehadiso* about the universality of doctrines such as the intercessory role of Mary throughout the Orthodox churches is a handicap to their efforts to bring renewal.

Contemporary writers are employing a new Amharic term, "ለውጥ" *lewut*[52] which means "change." The implications behind the term still stand although the word *tehadiso* may not be used now.[53] However, the argument for the

---

49. ". . . ተሐድሶ ማለት የነበረውንና ያለውን ነገር የተበላሸውን በማስተካከል፣ የተሰበረውን በመጠገን፣ ሊሰጥ የሚገባውን አገልግሎት መስጠቱን የሚታይበት . . ." *Chora*, no. 29, n.d., 6–7. (Translation by the researcher.)

50. Eshete, *Evangelical Movement*, 182.

51. *Chora*, no. 29, n.d., 7.

52. አዲስ ሁኔታ፣ የተለየ ነገር፣ ልዩነት፡. This term connotes the change of something in exchange for something else, thus, it might imply the loss of its former nature, colour or condition in exchange for a new form. Amharic Dictionary, Addis Ababa, Institute of Ethiopian Languages Studies (Addis Ababa University Press, 2001 Eth. C), 21.

53. Agizachew Tefera, የለውጥ ያሁ (The need for change) (Addis Ababa, 2001 Eth. C). Mahbere Kidusan also used the term *lewut*. It asserted that the Church needs administerial *lewut* and then explained the scope of the "change" it has in mind. "The Church needs change which does not defy her canonical authority, which does not affect her values, which is based on research/study, and which is practical . . .the synod should be the one to lead the process of change and no change should be attempted without the permissionof the Holy Synod and to protect the process of change the government's protection is vital." "ቀኖናዊ ሥልጣኑን የማያዳፍር፣ እሴቶቹን የማይነካ፣ በጥናት ላይ የተመሠረተ በሥርዓት የሚተገበር ለውጥ፣ ለቤተክርስቲያን፡" ለውጡን በባለቤትነት መምራት ያለበት የቤተ ክርስቲያኒቱ የበላይ አካል ቅዱስ ሲኖዶስ ሙሆን ይገባዋል፡:. . . . በቤተክርስቲያኒቱ የሚካሄድ ማንኛውም ለውጥ ግን ያለ ሲኖዶስ ዕውቅና እና ፈቃድ በሌሎች አካላት ተጽእኖም እንዳይወድቅ የመንግሥት የጥብቃ እገዛ ያስፈልገዋል፡፡ ለውጥ(sic) ለቤተክርስቲያን, www.eotc-mkidusan.org, accessed 2 May 2011.

Contemporary Reformation Impulses in the Ethiopian Orthodox Church

need for *tehadiso* remains, with citations of the explicit teaching of the Bible about reformation, and the ministry of agents of reformation in the Bible such as Ezra and Nehemiah. This approach is exemplified by the writings of Mahbere Bekur. The association continues to argue that according to the Bible, renewal is to be part and parcel of the church.[54]

The cry for reform also includes administrative changes. As for the meaning of reformation in the church there is high emphasis by the theologians of the church and also Mahbere Kidusan that the church does not need dogmatic and canonical, but administrative reforms. This point is stressed again and again, because of numerous groups which claim that the church needs reformation. Christine Chaillot writes that reformation for the Orthodox Church includes, "Restoration and renewal of individual people, the church, church movements, the monarch, doctrinal positions, the building of the church, evangelization of pagans, revival of spiritual life, monastic revival, and the like."[55] Chaillot's definition includes the restoration and renewal of "doctrinal positions" but the church has been vehement about the perfect status of its doctrinal position.[56] However, at times Orthodox writers who are strongly against *tehadiso* admit that there are erroneous teachings which infiltrated the structures of the church.[57]

---

54. ዕዝራና የተሃድሶ አገልግሎቱ (Ezra and his ministry of reformation), *Chora*, 18, n.d: 13–15; ዘሩባቤልና የተሃድሶ አገልግሎቱ (Zerubbabel and his ministry of reformation), *Chora*, no. 16, n.d.: 22–23; *Chora*, no. 17, n.d.: 21–23; *Chora* 19, n.d., ነህምያና የተሃድሶ አገልግሎቱ (Nehemiah and his ministry of reformation), 25–26, 20; *Chora* 33, n.d.: 14–20.

55. Chaillot Christine, *The Ethiopian Orthodox Church: A Brief Introduction to Its Life and Spirituality* (Paris: Inter Orthodox Dialogue, 2002), 31–34. Cf. Taddesse Tamrat, *Church and State*, 114.

56. The scholars of the church at times go a great length to explain apparent contradictions in the tradition. Burial ceremony is a case in point. Perhaps because of the ignorance of the majority to Ge'ez, the passages the clergy use to perform absolution over the body of the dead include the Psalms in which the author curses his enemies or refers to the curses of his enemies upon him. These Psalms, which traditionally are referred to as "imprecatory," are in view with Psalm 109 being the chief one. Getachew, the writer of Gedil Weys Gedil, pointed this out and the Council of Scholars replied as to why they chant such passages over the dead. According to them several Psalms which speak of the mercy of the Lord are used for prayer, as for this particular passage, "You will not be able to understand that our inclusion of words of curse in the chanting has deeper meaning and approach." ". . . አንተ የጠቀስከውን የመርገም ቃል ጨምረን መድገማችን በጥልቅ አስተያያት ሲመረምሩት ላይ ትርጉምና ስልት ያለው መሆኑን አንተ ልታውቀውና ልትረዳው አትችልም፡" The EOTC Council of Scholars, እንዳያስታችሁ ተጠቀቁ፣ 43.

57. ". . . it is obvious that there are weeds sown by the enemy. Our Church needs to remove such weeds which are mixed with her pure teaching." ". . .እንደዚሁ ደግሞ ጠላት የዘራቸው እንክርዳዶች እንዳሉም ይታወቃል . . . ቤተ ክርስቲያናችን በንጹህ ትምህርቷ ውስጥ የገቡ ጥቂት እንክርዳዶችን ማስወገድ

6.3. An Overview of Reformation Movements

The impulse for change has always been part of the church. Some cries for change were accepted after some bloodshed, some were suppressed with the use of force. The role of the emperors, especially Zer'a Ya'iqob, enabled some doctrines to be accepted as part of Orthodoxy. Thus, explicit calls for renewal continue to be voiced by pointing out erroneous teachings as Zer'a Ya'iqob did, and even stating that such teachings are of demonic origin. In reference to the departure of the Orthodox Church from its original foundation as laid down by Frumentius, Mahbere Bekur laments: "Our Association of Zion has lost its faith, but retained the name. The fundamental faith fell apart and the structures demolished. On the wreckage, different writings which provided a haven for evil spirits and shelter for demons and witchcraft emerged. As a result of such developments over the centuries, the people were led into Babylon-like foreign worship and spiritual bondage."[58]

The establishment of Evangelical Christianity, which comprised former members of the EOC and pagans, contributed to the continued questioning of some of the long-held traditions of the EOC. The conflict with the clergy of the established church led some to wish to convert the church to the Protestant tradition, especially Lutheran.[59] Those who were influenced by the Pentecostal movement or had the experience of the so-called charismatic gifts of the Spirit judged the church against Pentecostal tradition.

Thus, both the scope of and approach to reform varies from group to group. Some long to see structural change, others work towards administrative change. Some groups were expelled from the church because they insisted on making use of modern musical instruments in the church. There are preachers and singers who do not seem to have a clear goal in mind but

---

አለባት" Aemere Awoke, *Mikurabe Tsidq* (Synagogue of righteousness) (Addis Ababa, 2001 Eth. C), 72.

58. "የእኛቱ ማህበረ ጽዮን ሰማያዊት ከማቅረዚ ስያሜ መኖር በቀር የእምነት አስተምህሮዊ ወድሞና የፍርስራሽ ክምር ተጭኖት ላዓመታት ኖረ፡ ... ለመናፍስት መደበቂያ የሚያገለግሉ የአስማትና የክፉ መናፍስት መፈልፈያ የኾኑ አዋልድ መጻሕፍት በቀሉበት። ሕዝባችንም ባቢሉንን በምትመስል የባዕድ አምልኮ መነክሪያ በኸነት፤ የመንፈሳዊ ባርነት ግዛት ውስጥ ከወደቀ በመቶ የሚቆጠሩ ዓመታት አለፉ።" *Chora* 33 (n.d.), 16.

59. Aleqa Meseret Sebhat Leab was criticized for reflecting such a tendency. Solomon Abebe, Interview, 25 February 2011. Perhaps such criticism was based on his joining the Mekane Yesus Church which had a somewhat closer resemblance to the EOC than the other Evangelical churches.

are counted among *tehadiso*. There are even organized groups of people who do not deserve to be called Orthodox reformers to begin with because they are basically run by Evangelicals who have called themselves reformers.[60]

There is no systematic and clear articulation of what reformation entails. However, many acknowledge unifying factors in the vital Christian doctrines such as the Trinity, but desire to see the authority of the Bible exercised over all tradition so that practices contrary to the teaching of the Bible will cease.[61] When they say the Bible, they have the sixty-six books in mind because like Evangelicals, reformers (except for Mahbere Kidusan) reject the authoritative use of apocryphal books.[62]

Two questions remain most controversial in discussion of reformation in the EOC. First, what is the kind of reformation that the church needs? And second, what are the guidelines that need to be used to bring about reform? Although there is difference of opinion on the meaning and extent of reformation, all groups agree on this one thing: that the church needs administrative *tehadiso* (renewal).[63]

6.3.1. Aba Estifanos, the "Ancestor" of Modern Reformers

The story of Aba Estifanos is briefly discussed in the earlier part of this work, and he is very important for the discussion of reformation, because nearly all reformation groups look upon him as their spiritual ancestor. Some even trace their movements to the life and works of the fifteenth-century Estifanosites. Two of the things he stood against were prostrating before the

---

60. Solomon Abebe, Interview, 25 February 2011.

61. Mezgebu, Tsemru, Pastor of Amanuel United Church, and Secretary of Amanuel United Denomination, Interview, 23 August 2010, Addis Ababa. Solomon has similar idea. Solomon Abebe, Interview, 25 February 2011.

62. Mezgebu Tsemru argues that stressing on the eighty-one books is a new trend. As far as he knows, EOC used the Amharic Bible with the sixty-six books. Mezgebu Tsemru, Phone Interview, 18 February 2011. Agizachew has similar arguments. He remarked that the EOC says that its Bible comprises eighty-one books, but the additional books and their number as published in one version is different from the other one. At times there appears to be conscious effort to make them eighty-one. Agizachew Tefera, Interview, 13 June 2011. Cf. Dibekulu Zewde, ቅዱሳት መጻሕፍትና ምንጮች-ቀኖናት በኢትዮጵያ ኦርቶዶክስ ቤተ ክርስቲያን (Scriptures and the sources of the Ethiopian Orthodox Church's canon), 99–146, 81.

63. Daniel, Interview, 8 September 2010; Mezgebu, Interview, 23 August 2010; Agizachew, Interview, 19 February 2011; Informant G, Interview, February 2011; Begashaw Desalegn, የመስቀሉ ሥር ቁማርተኞች (Gamblers under the cross) 1, (Addis Ababa: n.p., 1998 Eth. C); Mekonnen, Interview, 15 November 2010.

picture of Mary and before the Cross. In these two aspects both reformers and Evangelicals identify themselves with Aba Estifanos and many regret the suppression of the movement which could have brought reformation to the church long before the sixteenth-century reformation of Luther.[64] Such views are based on the conviction that Aba Estifanos was against the veneration of Mary and the cross, which are seen as having affected the status of the Bible as the authoritative tradition and the centrality of Christ for salvation.

As mentioned in chapter 5 Aba Estifanos came to prominence during the reign of Emperor Yishaq (1406–1421) who decided to tolerate Aba Estifanos and his disciples after a thorough inquiry into their doctrine and practices.[65] Getatchew Haile's work on Aba Estifanos does not imply that Aba Estifanos was "anti Mary" in the "Evangelical" sense; rather his opposition to the monastic order of the time and veneration of the king made him a target of persecution both from the heads of the established monastic order and king Zer'a Ya'iqob. The "anti Mary" accusation, therefore, was an excuse to banish Estifanosites.[66] The convictions of Aba Estifanos about the veneration of the king, and his refusal to venerate the picture of Mary and the wooden cross resulted in a major movement against Zer'a Ya'iqob's decrees to exalt Mary. However, it is not clear whether Aba Estifanos and his followers attempted to alter the high regard for Mary which was already held by the church. In fact, his hagiography as cited by Getatchew noted that the climax of Aba Estifanos' ascetic life was the revelation of heavenly mysteries and that one of such experiences was his encounter with Mary.[67]

However, there is similarity in the accusation brought against Aba Estifanos and Evangelicals; that they introduced new teaching. Aba Estifanos wrote, "They rose against me in animosity and said 'You are teaching a foreign teaching which is not of this country.' What is the education of this country? How is it different? I know none but all that is in Christ and the one church."[68] Perhaps such accusation referred to his extreme ascetic life

---

64. Bekele W/Kidan, Interview, 25 August 2010; *Kale Heywet* 13 (1998 Eth. C), 14–15.
65. Getatchew, ደቂቀ እስጢፋኖስ፣ 82–90.
66. Getatchew, 23ff.
67. Getatchew, 69.
68. "የሀገራችን ትምህርት ያልሆነ ታስተምራለህ" ሲሉ በጥል ተነሡብኝ። የዚች ሀገር ትምህርት ምንድነው? እንዴትስ የሌላ ነው? በክርስቶስና በአንዲት ቤተ ክርስቲያን ከሆነው ሁሉ በቀር ሌላ አላውቅም," Getatchew, ደቂቀ እስጢፋኖስ፣ 55; cf. 80, 87. The hagiographer added that Aba Estifanos was enlightened by

because the monks accused him of establishing a trend which was different from what they were used to and in doing so he was attracting others into the kind of solitude and ascetic life he practised.

As for the legacy of Estifanos, who was accused of being *Tsere-Mariam*, Tibebe Eshete notes that Mahbere Bekur (Society of the first born) directly traces its roots to him. In fact, Eshete regards its founder Aleqa Meseret as "the modern-day incarnation of the voice of Estifanos after four hundred years of silence."[69] Mahbere Bekur "considers the church to have strayed under the influence of Zer'a Ya'iqob and seeks to restore it by reviving its 'pre-Zer'a Ya'iqob essence and purity.'" The association believes that Aba Estifanos was sent by God to uproot traditional beliefs and practices and serve as an instrument of healing in the Orthodox Church.[70] Zer'a Ya'iqob on the other hand is referred to as a preacher of a "different gospel." He is even likened to the Neros of the Roman Empire because he demanded worship which was due only to God and committed despicable atrocities against Estifanosites, who refused to worship him. In addition to that, under the pretence of honouring Mary, he attributed Christ's glory to her, thereby leading the people away from the worship of the triune God.[71]

The strong feelings of *tehadiso* people against Zer'a Ya'iqob are evident and understandable given the way he significantly altered the track of the Orthodox Church away from the Bible and even from the tradition of the

---

the treasures of the Lord, the Old and New Testaments in order to serve the mysteries of the Holy Spirit who revealed to him everything as he stood at the shore along with the holy ones. He used to hear a voice asking him to hasten and help so and so who was being tempted by the enemy's force. Getatchew, 70.

69. Eshete, *Evangelical Movement*, 47. It is debatable whether there was a "silence" for four hundred years; rather a repeated effort to silence reformers. For example there were EOC reformers in Hamasen in the nineteenth century and among them Aleqa Taye is noteworthy for his relentless efforts to reform the EOC. Perhaps Eshete is referring to an organized effort to reform the church. Nevertheless, Aleqa Taye who was renowned for his evangelical convictions openly shared them in EOC. He had access to the emperor and also the authorities of the church because of his scholarly background in the EOC.

70. Moreover, Nahu Adam draws the attention of his readers to the accountability of EOC for how its head Zer'a Ya'iqob shed the blood of Aba Estifanos and his followers. The writer strongly asserted that the church and its members are to repent with fasting and prayer in order to receive forgiveness from the Lord because the blood of Estifanosites still "cries out to the Lord from the ground." Nahu Adam, ክርስትና በኢትዮጵያ፡ የእግዚአብሔር መንግሥት ታሪክ (*Christianity in Ethiopia: The history of the kingdom of God*) *Chora*, no. 18, n.d., 18–19.

71. Nahu Adam, 25, 17.

rest of the Orthodox churches.[72] Although Aba Estifanos's position regarding Mary appears to be rather different from that of the modern *tehadiso* people and Evangelicals, the church does not consider his position as fully Orthodox. In a book prepared by the Council of Scholars of the church, there is a remark that "Estifa[73] has not fully accepted the Orthodox teaching and faith of the church."[74]

This statement, therefore, serves as evidence that Aba Estifanos is not numbered among the fathers of the church. Moreover, the fact that the accusations made against him were echoed throughout the years against numerous reformers seem to give enough ground for the contemporary reformers to look upon him as their "spiritual ancestor" who was the forerunner of reformation in the Orthodox Church.

Solomon Abebe believes that Aba Estifanos and his disciples followed the correct approach for reformation. They were devoutly Orthodox in every way, but when Zer'a Ya'iqob introduced new unbiblical trends, they resisted him. Apart from that they had no agenda of altering Orthodoxy.[75] Their approach thus provides us with authentic reformation impulses, which were not influenced by any external body. Unlike Aba Estifanos and his disciples, the contemporary reformers are surrounded with numerous Christian bodies. Therefore, they face strong temptation to copy the Evangelical tradition or leave the Orthodox Church when opposition gets stronger.

---

72. "ራሰዋን ኦርቶዶክስ ተዋሕዶ በሚል ስያሜ የለየበት ትልቁና ብቸኛው ምክንያት ምሥጢረ ሥላሴንና ምሥጢረ ሥጋዎን ለመግለጽ አስቀድሞ የቀረጸቸው፣ የምትገለገልበትና የምታገለግልበት የነገረ መለከት አስተምህሮዋ ነው እንጂ ከዘርዐ ያዕቆብ የተላለፈባት ግዑዝናና መናፍስትን የማምላክ ውርደት አልነበረም፡፡ ስለሆነም ቢያንስ "ኦርቶዶክስ ተሕዶ የተሰኘችበት አስተምህሮዋ በጥራት ሊጠበቅላት ይገባል፡" (The Church named herself Orthodox Tewahdo because of her theology which described the mystery of the Trinity and the mystery of incarnation, but not the lowly practise of worshipping creatures and spirits as handed down to her from Zer'a Ya'iqob. Therefore at least her doctrine from which she derived the name "Orthodox" should be maintained) *Chora* 16, n.d., 1.

73. Emperor Zer'a Ya'iqob referred to Aba Estifanos as "Estifa" and his followers as Deqiqe Estifa. The disciples of Estifanos understood "Estifa" to imply the Egyptian rendering of Satan. They referred to the king as "Dib Tser" (Hyena), and Zeragon (Dragon). Getatchew, ደቂቀ እስጢፋኖስ፣ 28. Perhaps the contemporary church scholars' usage of "Estifa" instead of "Aba Estifanos" implies a rejection of his legacy.

74. ዑቁ ኢያስሕቴክም፣ መናፍቁ ጌታቸው "ገድል ወይስ ገደል" በማላት ለጻፈው የሀይደት ትምህርት ከኢትዮጵያ ኦርቶዶክስ ተዋሕዶ ቤተ ክርስቲያን ሊቃውንት ጉባኤ የተሰጠ መልስ, (A reply from the Council of Scholars of the Ethiopian Orthodox Tewahdo Church to apostasy writing of the *menafiq* Getatchew entitled "Gedil Weys Gedel" (Addis Ababa: Tinsae Zegubae Printing Press, 1996 Eth. C), 19.

75. Solomon Abebe, Interview, 25 February 2011.

6.3.2. Expelled Insiders

As noted earlier, there have always been voices of reformation in the church, heard at times very loudly, and at times faintly, but which ended up mostly silenced. But from time to time the cry for renewal would resurface in a sustained way. One of the organized venues for renewal was Haymanote Abew, which enjoyed the support of both Haile Sellassie and Abune Basilios in its efforts to retain the Orthodox faith among the youth and the educated men of the country. Through the establishment of Haymanote Abew, Haile Sellassie and the church hoped to keep kindled the light of Orthodox faith amid the heavy presence of Jesuit teachers, headmasters and professors.[76]

In addition, the association seems to have wanted to minimize the influence exerted by the Western academy, which was saturated with Enlightenment thinking acquired by young people from European and American universities. The association prepared Bible study materials in Amharic, took part in charitable works and was committed to the maintenance of Ethiopian identity by withstanding the influence of Western thinking.[77]

Most importantly, the members sought to examine the teaching of the church, the missionaries and the church fathers in the light of the Bible. Their investigation led them to see two things: first, that the teaching of the Evangelicals and the missionaries was biblical and similar to the teaching of the church fathers, and second, that their call for the reformation of the EOC was legitimate in light of the Scriptures. The discovery encouraged them to seek to join hands with Evangelicals in order to renew the EOC but also got them in trouble with the clergy of the church.[78]

Haymanote Abew provided the youth with a platform to express their opinions based on the study of the Scriptures and sing gospel songs, even with the use of an organ, which is now considered as a worldly instrument. One of the accusations against Haymanote Abew was that the preaching

---

76. Melaku, ስውፍ አይጋኑ, 135.

77. Eshete, *Evangelical Movement*, 58–59.

78. Melaku, ስውፍ አይጋኑ, 129–140; Daniel Teshome, "The Current Reformation Movement within the Ethiopian Orthodox Tewahedo Church (1987–2007)" (MTh diss., Addis Ababa, Ethiopian Graduate School of Theology, 2007), 118.

and singing sounded too Evangelical.[79] Consequently, the association was banned in 1988 with an accusation that its members were following non-Orthodox teaching and had turned heretical *menafiq*. It seems that their tolerance towards missionaries and Evangelical believers was considered a deviation from Orthodoxy. With the banning of Haymanote Abew, Mahbere Kidusan seemed to flourish and assume more and more responsibility in the church's structures and some held it responsible for the banishment of Haymanote Abew.[80] Clearly, the Association was not pleased with the aggressive attitude of members of Haymanote Abew towards ancient traditions of the church.[81]

On the eve of the fall of the Derg in the end of 1980s, however, unprecedented reformation swept through the youth of the church all over the country. The movements were not planned or called for, but were caused by small groups that studied the Bible. The most notable revival was the one at Nazareth town which started among factory workers who gathered to study the Bible. The leaders of the movement, which was accompanied by Pentecostal experiences, were confronted by delegates of the Orthodox Church in the presence of a government appointee. They were asked to renounce their practices or stop using the name of the church. When they refused, they were officially banned by the Orthodox Church as an extension of Evangelicals. Thus they were called, "የቀድሞዎቹ መናፍቃን ቡችሎች፣ አስመሳዮች፣ የመናፍቃን የጥፋት ቡድኖች" stooges of the existing *menafiqan*, deceivers, and agents of destruction.[82]

The leaders applied to be recognized as an association under the church but were denied permission. The group grew in a short period of time and impacted the lives of many youth in the Orthodox Church. In the same period there were similar movements throughout the country, especially in areas where the Orthodox faith was dominant. The determination of the movement to stay in the church and yet keep the charismatic demonstrations

---

79. የገነገም ደጆች፣ *Sem'ea Tsidq* 10, no. 78 (Megabit 1995 Eth. C), 12–13.
80. Melaku, ስውሩ አደጋ, 135–136
81. የገነገም ደጆች (Gates of hell), 11–12.
82. Efrem Beyene, "በአርቶዶክስ ስም የሚነግዱ መናፍቃን በራሳቸው አንደበት ተጋለጡ" (*Menafiqan* exposed), Lisane Tewahdo Ze Orthodox, no. 9 (1987 Eth. C), 46.

resulted in its becoming known as "Ortho-Pente."[83] Especially in the city of Addis nearly every single Orthodox Church was affected by the movement, puzzling the leadership of the church as to how to deal with it.[84]

Initially, the movement was committed to upholding both the Son and the Mother but was against corruption and the marginal status of the Bible. In addition to that, most of them resented the rapid growth of Evangelicals in the country and were determined to stay away from them. When members of the movement were accused of being *Pente*, they were deeply puzzled and tried to argue that they had not abandoned Orthodoxy;[85] in fact, the contrary was true. Some who experienced the gifts of the Spirit belonged to a conservative group which aimed to annihilate *Pente* from Ethiopia. Melese Weyessa was one of such people. He was the chairman of "ጴንቴ መንጠሪ ኮሚቴ" (a committee for eradication of the *Pente*) but he came to know Jesus through his reading of the Bible. Once he understood the truth he used his influence to preach the gospel. He was accused of calling the name of Jesus all the time and preaching only from the gospels without touching on the role of Mary. Eventually he and his friends were expelled from the church.[86]

There was no organized movement in the 1990s but as more and more young people were expelled or left the Orthodox Church they started to look for ways to encourage one another. Many of them were high school students, and those whose parents gave in to the pressure from the clergy

---

83. Their name was compound which was meant to show their belonging to the Orthodox Church and yet demonstrating "Pente" characteristics. Eshete, *Evangelical Movement*, 60. Emphasis by the researcher.

84. Mezgebu, Interview, 23 August 2010, Addis Ababa.

85. Pastor Mesfin Hailu Later on he received Jesus after he was revealed to him while seriously ill and after that he understood the lordship of Christ. He then started to preach and teach about the power of the name of Jesus and the gifts of the Spirit. He was filled by the Spirit of God and started to pray in tongues. He was a teacher in EOC Sunday schools and shared his experience with his friends. Many people were set free from demonic oppression and illnesses through his prayer. The EOC could not tolerate his actions and they drove him out of the church. Up to this point he had no relation what so ever with Pentes but after he was expelled from the church he heard about a group of people who were expelled from EOC and he joined them. They told him that he was Pente. At first he was shocked because he disliked "Pentes." Mesfin Hailu, "ሕይወትና አገልግሎት፣ በተለያየ እስራት ላሉ ጌታ ሸክም ሰጥቶኛል" (Life and ministry: the Lord has given me a burden for those who are in bondage), *Gesame* 2, no. 12 (Tir 2002 Eth. C), 9–11, 24.

86. እግዚአብሔር የተሃድሶ ቀን ቀጥሯል (The Lord has ordained the day of reformation), *Gesame* 2, no. 2 (November 2000 Eth. C), 3–4.

to expel their children suffered from hunger and some of them went to Evangelical churches, desperate for help.[87] Some groups left the church of their own accord even while some priests begged them to stay. Some were expelled because of trivial matters such as making use of modern musical instruments, eating pork, arguing that Mary bore children after Jesus, etc.[88]

Those who left the church or who were expelled wandered in the circles of churches exercising their new found "freedom" from traditional "bondage." They were critical of both the Orthodox and Evangelical churches as spiritually dry. Such a perception of their past experience led many to follow faith preachers who were experimenting with their newfound doctrine learned from faith preachers and healers overseas. Thus, the youth were exposed to all kinds of perverted presentations of the gospel. Disillusioned, some left the faith altogether, and some even committed suicide.[89]

Those were trying times because there was no leader and even no desire to be bound to a given school of thought. There was a thirst to be free from any kind of regulation. They were like newborn calves set free, there was no end to the jumping which blinded some from seeing the ditch ahead into which some fell, not to recover again.[90] Generally speaking, the youth in the movement did not have mature leaders to give them direction, so there was a lot of impulsiveness and action without much thought. They even acted provocatively (praying by kneeling in the Orthodox Church, calling the name of Jesus loudly, exorcising in the church and publicly admonishing the clergy about their lack of knowledge of the Bible and even calling them Orto-Qalicha[91]) leading to their expulsion.[92] Thus, the movement had conviction, but it lacked coherence.

---

87. Mezgebu, Interview, 23 August 2010, Addis Ababa.
88. Informant D, Interview, 18 August 2010.
89. Informant T, Interview 25 February 2011, Addis Ababa.
90. Informant T, Interview 25 February 2011, Addis Ababa.
91. It is to be recalled that the group was called "Ortho-Pente" to imply its resemblance with the "Pente" and the youth called the priests of the Church, "Orto-Qalicha" to imply the involvement of some of the priests in aspects of traditional religion, such as divination. Mezgebu, Interview, 23 August 2010.
92. Informant T, Interview, 25 February 2011.

As the number of those expelled and those who left the church grew, they continued to meet in a number of associations[93] one of which was "Amanuel Menfesawi Mahber" which in 1995 was developed as a separate entity with the name "Amanuel United church." With no strong leadership and little theological engagement with the Orthodox tradition, Amanuel Association found it easier to adopt the existing Evangelical model of church government, worship and lifestyle. Therefore, it has little resemblance to the Orthodox Church, but much to Evangelicals, particularly the Mulu Wongel Church.[94] However, it still uses the term "reformation" widely, perhaps, because many of the members were pushed out while desiring to stay in the EOC. According to inside reformers, the reason that Amanuel United church keeps the term "reformation" is to retain its acceptance among Evangelicals and attract Orthodox adherents.[95]

There are also others who joined Evangelical churches but remain deeply committed to the renewal of the Orthodox Church. Such love and respect for the church surfaces in many ways, one of which being the popularity of choirs of Amanuel United church which make use of the traditional music and dancing of the Orthodox. Some are weary of the lifestyle and worship services of Evangelical churches and deeply miss the Orthodox Church and pray for its renewal, determined to go back when the long-awaited renewal is realized.[96]

6.4. Tension between Reforming and Preserving the Tradition of the Church

There are numerous groups which call themselves reformers, but they do not seem to be well organized or have a common goal in mind; neither do they exhibit a clear vision as to the scope of reformation. From their writings and teaching, one might gather that they are strongly influenced by the Evangelical tradition. Therefore, they tend to evaluate the faith and

---

93. Estifanos Mahber, Medihanealem Mahber, and Kidisina Mahber are some of them. Daniel Teshome, "Implications of the Current Reformation Movement" (2007), 19.

94. Solomon, Abebe, Interview, 25 February 2011.

95. Informant D, Interview 18 August 2010, Addis Ababa; Teshome, "Implications of the Current Reformation Movement," 18–20.

96. Fetha Amlak Eniyew, Discussion held on 11 April 2011, Addis Ababa.

practices of the Orthodox Church against that background. For the sake of discussion, these groups have been divided into three categories. The category includes Mahbere Kidusan because they are at times presented as preservers of traditional Orthodoxy and in attempting to do so, counter the efforts of the other reformers.

6.4.1. The In-Between Reformers

There are groups of people who call themselves reformers but are not active inside the church. They use literature to point out areas which need reformation and what they consider to be pitfalls in the reformation movements. One such groups is "Yemisrach Ministry." The literature produced by this group of people is widely used against reformation movements altogether. Their publication "Hohite *Birhan*" in one of its issues presented the effort of reformation as a spiritual battle and made extensive use of military terminology: "the battle field," "the stronghold of the enemy," "army," "armours," "organized attack," "defence," "fight from inside," "fight from the outside" and so on.[97] Such expressions suggest an intention to take over the church.[98]

Yemisrach Ministry's involvement and publications seem to be resented by some reformers and one of them notes, "They focus on offering training here and there and diligently write reports to their donor organizations outside and to individual donors in the country, even by using old video footage. They are vocal about what they do, so usually, their publications are considered as representative of the reformation movement."[99] The circulation of their publications among Orthodox followers, however, seems to be limited.

There also are other individuals and groups of people who are criticized as using the reformation as a pretext to raise considerable amounts of funds but with little effort towards reformation.[100] Such actions are considered as hindrances to the work of reformation in the church by giving a foothold for

---

97. "የውጊያ ቀጠና," "ምሽግ," "ሠራዊት," "ትጥቅ," "የተቀናጀ ስልት," "ደጀን," "የውስጥ ውጊያ," "የውጭ ውጊያ." የአርቶዶክስ ተዋህዶ ቤተ ክርስቲያን ታሪክና አስተምህሮ, *Hohete Birhan* (Megabit 2002 Eth. C), 15–16.

98. የተሃድሶ መናፍቃን ዘመቻ በኢትዮጵያ ቤተ ክርስቲያን ላይ (The campaign of Tehadiso *menafiqan* against the Church of Ethiopia), 52–53, 59–63.

99. Informant T, Interview, 25 February 2011.

100. Informant T, Interview, 25 February 2011.

faultfinders who present the action of a given group as representative of the whole reformation movement.[101] In this work such people are referred to as "in-between" reformers because they are not part of the inside reformers, nor have they left the church. At times the people in charge of reformation groups are Evangelicals who claim to have a vision to reform the Orthodox Church. This is considered as promoting Evangelicals' subtle agenda of weakening the church.

Mahbere Bekur also falls in the category of the in-between reformers. Of all the reformation groups, this seems to be the most organized. Its writers attempt to engage the Orthodox literature, practices and tradition with the Bible. The convictions of this group are similar to the "silent" reformers except that this group tends to use the erroneous teachings as the springboard to present the truth. Because the founder, Aleqa Meseret Sebhat Leab, was expelled from the church, the publications of Mahbere Bekur are not accepted by the church. Aleqa Meseret Sebhat Leab was expelled from Sewasew Birhane St Paul Theological College, Addis Ababa in 1945 after an allegation of teaching heresy. He came to notice deficiencies in the Orthodox doctrines through his discussions with Aleqa Beyene, one of his mentors. Aleqa Beyene led him to realize that the truth as revealed in the Holy Scriptures was overshadowed by tales which had infiltrated the mainstream over the years.[102]

Aleqa Meseret also noted that he studied *qene* (poems) under Yeneta Awoke Zewoketa, who used the Old and New Testament and the writings of the church scholars (*liqawunt*) as a basis for his *qene* (poems) and reprimanded his students when they quoted from other writings.[103] Such teachers

---

101. Agizachew, Interview, 17 June 2011; Cf. የተሃድሶ መናፍቃን ዘመቻ በኢትዮጵያ ቤተ ክርስቲያን ላይ (The campaign of Tehadiso *menafiqan* against the Church of Ethiopia).

102. "ከአለቃ በየነ ጋር በአደረግናቸው ውይይቶች በዘመናት ውስጥ መቼ እንደገቡ ያልታወቁ የፈጠራ ታሪኮች የቅዱሳት መጻሕፍትን ቃል ሸፍነውብን እንደኖሩና ይልቁንም ከፈደሰ በስተቀር የቃሉን መንፈስ ያጠፋብን፣ ጊዜ የወለዳቸው አዋልድ መጻሕፍት እንደሆኑ በፍጥነት እፐተረዳሁ መጣሁ፡" *Chora*, no. 14: 8–9. Translation by the researcher. *Seme'a Tsidq*, Mahbere Kidusan's newspaper, traced what it called "heretic" teachings of Meseret Sebhat Leab to David Stocks, the missionary of Bible Church Men Society, who trained Aleqa Meseret and sent him to infect the EOC with heresy. *Seme'a Tsidq* 10, no. 78 (Megabit, 1995 Eth. C), 11.

103. Similarly Pastor Amelu Geta, one of the current Pastors of Amanuel United Church in Addis Ababa shared how he went to the priest he chose as his father confessor with his sins written on a piece of paper. But the father tells him "your father confessor is Christ. If you confess your sins, he will forgive you. I cannot pronounce forgiveness to you."

were not encouraged, neither were their students tolerated. Aleqa Meseret was able to realize the lack of coherence in the presentation of reformers. Thus, he saw the need to fill the gap by providing biblically sound teachings in a way which focused on presenting the truth rather than exposing the errors. He also founded Mahbere Bekur.

The publications of Mahbere Bekur are sold in Evangelical stores. Their impact on the Orthodox followers, the association's prime audience, appears to be limited. Some think that the association should revise its strategy because it is not able to reach its audience.[104] Agizachew believes that the distribution of the association's literature, though limited, is impacting Orthodox followers. Mahbere Kidusan definitely reads the works of Mahbere Bekur and presents them as erroneous, although it does not engage their claims with any depth of scholarship.

Mahbere Bekur remains deeply committed to the preaching of the gospel and tackling expressions of popular public reaction by means of the Scriptures. For example, the slogans such as "Without the intercession of the Mother of God the world will not be saved" and "There is no Christianity apart from Mary" are refuted with the teaching of the Bible. Mahbere Bekur argues that the slogans are not supported by the teaching of the church and are contrary to the Bible.[105]

Mahbere Bekur also addresses popular preaching by Memhir Mihretab, one of the Holy Trinity Theological College graduates and a popular preacher in the church, entitled "አልተሳሳትንም" "We are not mistaken." His preaching tries to legitimize with passages from the Bible the tradition of the Orthodox by which rectangular shaped replicas of the Ark (*tabot*) which are named after the angels and saints, are kept in the churches and paraded on major holidays

---

Amelu was perplexed first, then he repented of his sins to Christ and started to follow him. Pastor Amelu, "ከጦር ሜዳ ለወንጌል ጥሪ" (From the battlefield into ministry), *Gesame* 2, no. 10 (Meskerem, 2002 Eth. C), 3. Melese Woyessa also tells how he wanted to enter monastery and a hermit told him that the gospel says "go to the nations and preach the gospel, and not to monastery." Melese Weyessa, "እግዚአብሔር የተሃድሶ ቀን ቀጥሯል" (The Lord has appointed a day of reform), *Gesame* 2, no. 2 (November 2000 Eth. C), 3.

104. Informant T, Interview, 25 February 2011.

105. Editor, "አለቃ ነቅዐ ጥበብና አገልግሎታቸው" (Aleqa Neqe'a Tibeb and his ministry), *Chora*, no. 39 (Hamle 2002 Eth. C), 21–25.

carried on the head of priests.¹⁰⁶ Besides the popular slogans, Mahbere Bekur addresses serious theological issues such as the intercessory ministry of Jesus as spelled out in the Scriptures. The church's current tendency to deny his mediatory role is portrayed as a wolf in the skin of a sheep.¹⁰⁷

The association is concerned that the Orthodox Church has regressed from its ancient foundational theology. According to this group, *tehadiso* does not mean changing the original doctrine or introducing something new but helping the church regain its former, ancient purity of faith.¹⁰⁸ What is meant by "ancient purity of faith" is not clearly articulated. There are some hints in the literature of Mahbere Bekur that the association is against the strong reliance of the church on the law of the Old Testament and has reservations regarding the emphasis laid on righteousness to be attained through works and monastic life. There is an argument in the association's magazine that it is an evil spirit who is at work behind the names of dead saints and different spirits (angels).¹⁰⁹ Although part of what constitutes "ancient pure

---

106. Agizachew Tefera, አልተሳሳትንምን? (Are we not mistaken?) (Addis Ababa: n.p., 2003 Eth. C). Attempting to support different claims and teachings with the Scriptures is growing in the EOC. Formerly, the writings of Saints and fathers were quoted to defend a given conviction, but now the Bible is being quoted although the method of interpretation used is not sound and even contrary to a given interpretation of the EOC itself. It appears as though the Pentecostal's tendency of following a popular preacher with less critical thinking is taken up more and more in the EOC and this is one of the most undesirable legacies of Evangelical Christianity.

107. Editorial, የማንዉክላትን ቤተ ክርስቲያንና አምነታን አናስድብ፣, *Chora*, no. 16 (n.d.), 2.

108. Editor, "ከተሃድሶ ዓላማ" (The purpose of reform), *Chora*, no. 5 (n.d.), 17, 27. Melaku Baweke noted that EOC does not use the term *tehadiso* in reference to faith because according to Jude the apostle, the faith is perfect. Thus faith does not grow old but the life of the believer is to be renewed all the time with repentance, fasting and prayer. Melaku Baweke, ስዉሩ አደጋ (The subtle danger), 122.

109. Nahu Adam, ክርስትና በኢትዮጵያ (Christianity in Ethiopia), 18–19. The writer is strongly against the monastic order which was set by St Antony and refers to Zer'a Ya'iqob's taking of such monastic vows as nullifying his Christian baptism with which he died and rose with Christ. However, according to his hagiography, Aba Estifanos himself took such a vow and was clothed with the skin referred to as "askema" which St. Antony claimed to have received from the angel of the Lord. When Aba Estifanos set himself apart to become a Monk, Aba Samuel, who was the head of the Monastery clothed him with "askema." The hagiography of Aba Estifanos describes the order, "this is the order of our fathers the apostles, and that of their disciples the monastic fathers Antony and Pacomius" "ይህንም የአባቶቻን የሐዋርያትና የተከታዮቻቸው የመነኮሳት አባቶች የአንጦንስና የመቃርስ ሥርዓት ነት." Thus the authenticity of Zer'a Ya'iqob's vow which was questioned by the writer was similar to that of Aba Estifanos. Getatchew Haile, ደቂቀ እስጢፋኖስ:, 62–63.

faith," is indicated by Mahbere Bekur's literature, the question as to how far back into the past of the church one is required to go remains vague.

Mahbere Bekur is thus an "in-between" group because it does not belong to Evangelicals, nor to the "Silent" Reformers. Its current leaders are not expelled from the church although its founder was. With its publications rejected by the church, it continues to voice its concern about the exaltation of Mary and the saints over Christ and the peripheral status of the Bible. However, until its literature reaches the Orthodox, the association is producing the right teaching for the wrong audience.

6.4.2. "Silent" Reformers

The reformation movement inside the church is mostly carried forward by individuals and also associations – more like fellowships. Perhaps because of the nature of their vision, they are not strongly organized.[110] Their convictions are similar to that of the Evangelicals in England as discussed in chapter 4. They believe there are Orthodox adherents who need conversion and others who need renewal. One of the leaders likens their attempt to someone who is renovating his own house from the inside. Such a person will be careful in the tools he uses to repair his house lest the structure collapse on top of him.[111]

These people are determined to bring the Bible to the centre of the life of the church. Like the CMS missionaries, they believe that the reading of the Bible will bring about the desired reformation. They are tolerant in their approach and focus on communicating the truth rather than exposing errors. They are critical of the attempts of both expelled reformers and Evangelicals to work towards the reformation of the church. They are especially at variance with those who have been expelled, whom they consider as having moved far away from the tradition of the church. Moreover, the insiders are critical of the attempt of the expelled to create small groups of their own inside the church structures. They call this "starting a church within a church."[112] According to them, this stems from not recognizing the Orthodox Church as a Christian body. They also do not appreciate the

---

110. Agizachew, Interview, 14 June 2011.
111. Informant D, Interview 18 August 2010, Addis Ababa.
112. Informant D, Interview, 18 August 2010.

involvement of Evangelicals in the process of renewing the church. One of the leaders pleaded with both expelled reformers and Evangelicals to leave the church alone and let them do the work of reformation.[113]

Like the Anglican Evangelicals, the "Silent" Reformers also feel that the clergy are preoccupied with their own business and do not show much concern for the salvation of souls.[114] Evangelicals in the church of England were committed to bringing back the lost fervour for ones faith, but they did not desire to disturb the church of England, nor did they contemplate leaving it. Similarly, the reformers within the Orthodox have no desire to disturb the church. They are also moderate in their approach and wish to appeal to the conscience of people, through the Scriptures. So instead of focusing on the errors they emphasize laying down the truth.[115]

Again similarly to the Evangelicals in the church of England, the "Silent" Reformers of the Orthodox Church recognize the core marks of the reformation: the need for vernacular Bibles, the mediatorship of Christ, justification by faith, regeneration by the Holy Spirit, the efficacy of the atonement of Christ and original sin. They too invite people to be saved, although not publicly, but do the preaching in the context of the church. They too believe that no matter how corrupt or "dead" the church may be, separation is wrong. Therefore, they resent the Evangelicals' act of sheep-stealing and hesitance about recognizing the church. A leader of one one of these "silent" groups asks, "If you recognize the Anglican churches which are ordaining homosexuals, why do you not recognize the ancient Orthodox Church?"[116] They have no desire to leave the church but to work and pray for reformation

---

113. Informant D, Interview, 18 August 2010. One of the leaders of what I called "In-Between" Reformers remarks, "How can we leave them alone? This is not about them or their comfort. We have a divine mandate to preach the gospel to everyone who does not know Christ whether Orthodox member or not. What does leaving them alone mean? Are they asking us to let people perish without coming to the knowledge of their saviour? Besides, they [the 'Silent Reformers'] are not able to reach everyone. They should not look at our work as a hindrance to theirs, but as a complimentary because it is all about Christ's supremacy and the centrality of the Bible." Informant F, Interview, 16 August 2011, Addis Ababa.

114. We recall that numerous unbiblical writings guarantee easy access to heaven and that the clergy do not possess the Bible. Perhaps these are among the reasons for their lack of "converting zeal."

115. Informant D, Interview, 18 August 2010.

116. Informant D, Interview, 18 August 2010.

and renewal. As for the means of reformation, they too believe that it is the Bible that brings the needed reformation.

The "Silent" Reformers view the Bible as central for teaching and preaching, but they do not reject the apocryphal books though they do not hold them as authoritative. Unlike the church of England they do not reject monasticism although they recognize that it needs reformation and strong measures need to be taken against monks who engage in divination and magic.[117] The fellowships or individuals who seek the reformation of the church are not opposed by the leadership of the church but by Mahbere Kidusan which has made them the main focus of its propaganda. The association appears to fear their influence more than that of the other groups.[118]

6.4.3. Popular Preachers and Singers

One of the positive outcomes of the presence of Evangelical Christianity is its influence over the worship style of the Orthodox Church. Some Orthodox theologians and members do not believe that Evangelicals have any meaningful influence over the ancient church, but one of the evidences is not only the increase in number of preachers and gospel singers, but also the content of their songs and sermons over the past twenty years. The Evangelical influence over the Orthodox Church, however, was not a new development. As discussed in the introduction, Evangelicals encouraged Haymanote Abew to practice Bible-centred worship through preaching and singing of the Scriptures.

After the fall of the Derg, when the closed churches were opened, Evangelicals whose number had boomed through tribulation started to practice their faith openly. Most of all, the 1990s revival in the Orthodox Church had wider influence. As discussed above, the revival was sparked through the reading of the Bible. Although many of the youth who were touched by it were expelled from or left the church, their influence over the youth in the church was immense. In particular the choirs of Nazareth and Harar Amanuel United church won the hearts of many with their vibrant gospel songs with traditional musical instruments.

---

117. Informant T, Interview, 25 February 2011. Cf. Agizachew Tefera, የለውጥ ፃሉፃ? (The need for change), 231–233.

118. Informant D, Interview, 18 August 2010, Addis Ababa.

In the ten year period, 2000–2010, another wave of revival broke out, this time with overwhelming numbers of people participating. Opponents in key positions in the church were not able to silence it, nor push it out. The key figures who have massive followings, are young preachers and singers who are committed to the church but brought the Bible to the centre of their life without abandoning the Orthodox tradition of honouring Mary and the saints. Their sermons and songs were so popular that they have overshadowed the songs of both Evangelicals and the expelled *tehadiso* groups alike.[119]

The preachers tried to adopt the Evangelical culture of holding conferences in public halls and the compound of the church by calling it *Gubae*[120] and such gatherings became more and more popular after the 2005 election and its gruesome aftermath.[121] The songs of Mirtnesh Tilahun which included Scriptures in song, gained wide acceptance in 2005 and paved the way for successor singers to do the same. The *Gubae* opened a way for the Orthodox public to hear sermons from the Bible and enjoy gospel songs. It was as though the Orthodox believers, who were critical of some of the church's tradition and did not appreciate the Evangelicals' extreme measures of abandoning it, finally were able to worship in Orthodox terms. The *Gubae* spread like a wild fire throughout the country and a number of preachers and singers emerged as the most popular ones including Begashaw Desalegn and Zerfe Kebede.[122]

The great enthusiasm behind the *Gubae* at times drifted into criticizing the church and its ancient traditions. The preachers were scolded for calling the church "the old Sara" and ridiculing the priests. Similar to the Evangelical trend they openly called people to receive Jesus Christ for their salvation.[123] They also noted their objections to the attitude of the clergy and what they saw as deviation from the Bible. Begashaw laments the state

---

119. የፕሮቴስታንት መዝሙሮች ጉዞ ወዴት? (Where are Protestant songs headed to?) Yohannes Tefera, Qum Neger 10, no. 108 (Tir-Yekatit 2003 Eth. C), 24–25. The Orthodox gospel singers were not only praised for their songs but also their character of humility.

120. "Gubae" means assembly.

121. Agizachew Tefera, Interview, 16 June 2011.

122. The singers, however, do not usually write songs, so they are vocalists. Song writers are deacons and priests in the Church with the gift of writing songs and developing lyrics. The music is carefully done in a way that resembles the music of St. Yared.

123. Zemedkun Bekele, Armageddon Vol. 1, (Audio presentation), Addis Ababa, Gelgela Spiritual Songs House, n.d.

of ministry in the church, "Few ministers serve in the gifts of the Spirit. Instead, they depend on human knowledge and speak of fables rather than the gospel. This has weakened the service of the church." He also notes that calling the name of Jesus makes some people suspicious and causes them to reject those who call his name. On the other hand, there is a practice of using occult and magic for healing.[124]

Needless to say, such an approach was not appreciated by critics, who condemned the whole movement as unorthodox. The revival of Scripture in song and Bible-centred preaching brought significant opposition and resistance as much as support. One of the key figures of opposition was Zemedkun Bekele[125] who was rumoured to be supported by Mahbere Kidusan's leadership. Zemedkun laments:

> These people have taken the believers out of the church in order to expose them to worship in halls. . . . In such gatherings people will not find the church ordinances, nor will they be mindful of the dress codes. . . . They discredit the clergy with false allegations . . . In their preaching they tell people, "believe in Jesus Christ and accept him [as your Lord]." This is not in accordance to the tradition of the Orthodox Church. Their teaching does not give due place to martyrs, Virgin Mary and the saints. . . . In their songs they present the saviour of the world as though he is a personal saviour and thereby plant such feeling in the heart of people.[126]

---

124. "ዘሬ ዘሬ በዕውቀት እንጂ በፀጋ የሚያገለግል አገልጋይ መጥፋቱ ተረትና ምሳሌን እንጂ ወንጌልን የሚገልጥ ደቂ መዝሙር መታጣቱ ምንገስ በነበረው የቤተ ክርስቲያን አገልግሎት ላይ አሾዋ በተነበት እንጂ አሳደገው አልተባለም፡" "የኢየሱስን ስም መጥራት አንዳንዶችን ያስከፋል ጥርጣሬን ያስድራል፡ ጥላቻን ያመጣል።" "በጥንቆላና አስማት ፈውስ ለማምጣት የሚሞክሩ አሉ፡" Begashaw Desalegn, የመስቀሉ ሥር ቁማርተኞች (Gamblers under the cross), 36, 55, 47.

125. His message in Armageddon was that a group of people were out to distort the ancient traditions of the Orthodox Church. Although he did not mention Begashaw by name, the content makes it clear that most of the message was against him. For example, he mentioned Begashaw's book የመስቀሉ ሥር ቁማርተኞች (Gamblers under the cross) in his criticism that Protestant preachers were referred to as "my brothers" but Orthodox Clergy. Zemedkun Bekele, Armageddon Vol. 1, (Audio presentation), Addis Ababa, Gelgela Spiritual Songs House, n.d.

126. "እነዚህ ሰዎች ምዕምኑን ከቤተ ክርስቲያን ወደ አዳራሽ በማውጣት አላማምደውታል . . . ቤተ ክርስቲያን ውስጥ ያለውን ስርዓት አምልኮ በዚህ አዳራሽ አያገኝም አለሰበሱ አይጠነቀቅም . . . ካህናት እንዲጠሉ በስብከት አሳብበው ፕሮፓጋንዳ መንዛት ነው . . . 'ኢየሱስ ክርስቶስን አምኑህ ተቀበል' ይሉ በስብከታቸው፡፡ ይህ ደግሞ የኦርቶዶክስ ተዋሕዶ ቤተ ክርስቲያን አካሄድ አይደለም . . . ሲያስተምሩም ሰማዕታትን፡ ድንግል ማርያምን፡ ቅዱሳንን አያከትብም . . .

Contemporary Reformation Impulses in the Ethiopian Orthodox Church 369

On the other hand, just as the rise of reformers who were expelled turned the opposition away from the Evangelicals, the current Bible movement has called a lot of attention away from expelled insiders. However, the Bible revival is once more blamed on mission organizations through Evangelical agents who train and equip *tehadiso* to pull down the Orthodox Church. The champion of such a perception and the chief opponent of the revival is Mahbere Kidusan. However, the leadership of the church has refrained from expelling the key figures of the revival. Perhaps it fears that their big following would cause a split in the church.

Begashaw likens this group to the Israelites who were not armed but through their shouting demolished the walls of Jericho. He says that this army of holy people is not armed with "explosives or hammer" and yet according to the promise (of the Lord), it has demolished the walls of Jericho. He asserts that this army is yet to cover our land with songs and praise. "ደመሚትና መደሻ ያልያዘ ሠራዊት፣ እንደ ተስፋዉ ቃል ግን ኢያሪኮን ለዘላዓለም ያፈረሰ፣ ገና ምድራችንን በዝማሬና በምሥጋና የሚከድን እንድ ቅዱስ ሕዝብ አለ።"[127]

With the constant allegation of deviating from Orthodoxy made by groups that do not appreciate the ministry of the popular preachers and singers, the key figures of the movement are mindful of their messages. However, their popularity has not decreased and their messages and songs continue to win wide acceptance. Unlike the other reformers, the preachers and singers continue to uphold the glorified status of the saints and also use the Bible extensively.

6.4.4. Mahbere Kidusan: The "Watchdog" of Ancient Tradition

Mahbere Kidusan is a group which looks at itself as being committed to encouraging the younger generation to remain in the church, and preserving the Orthodox tradition from alteration by *tehadiso* movements.[128] The association traces its origin to 1977, in a fellowship of Addis Ababa

---

በመዝሙሮቻቸውም የዓላም መድኃኒትን ወደ ግል አዳኝነት በማዘር ምዕመኑ ውስጥ ስሜቱ እንዲሰርጽ ያደርጋሉ።" Zemedkun Bekele, ቤተ ክርስቲያን አደጋ ላይ ነች (The church is engulfed with danger), *Yanet* 2, no. 19 (2002 Eth. C), 37–38.

127. Ruhama, Songs of Zerfe Kebede, VCD, Veronica Spiritual Songs Shop, Addis Ababa, n.d. Cf. Begashaw Desalegn, የመስቀሉ ሥር ቁማርተኞች (Gamblers under the cross), 1.

128. Informant G, Interview, February 2011.

University students who were Orthodox members.¹²⁹ According to its General Secretary, Mulugeta Haile Mariam, the association has more than twenty thousand members in and outside of the country and forty-three centres in the country.¹³⁰

Recognizing Mahbere Kidusan's work as reformation is debatable. Some call them counter-reformers because of their unwavering stand against any attempt to renew the tradition of the church. However, their efforts to protect the status of the saints, revive the old traditions such as the traditional school system, traditional musical instruments, and observance of strict dress codes implies that they are trying to protect what they consider to be the tenets of ancient orthodoxy. The association also works to promote monastic life and ancient historical sites.

Mahbere Kidusan is open about its chief aim of protecting the status of the saints; in fact, the very meaning of its name, Association of the Saints, speaks for itself.¹³¹ To this end, it follows up the doctrinal position of the clergy in the church, to make sure they are not deviating from the core beliefs regarding the saints. When they are found to deviate, it investigates and reports to the church authorities.¹³²

The association is accused of using the allegation *tehadiso* towards those who oppose its principles in order to get rid of them. If someone gives less emphasis to the role of Mary and angels in his preaching and teaching, he will be suspected of being *tehadiso* and challenged to preach about Mary and refer to apocryphal books. Affirming her elevated status, therefore, serves

---

129. The gathering was strengthened in 1983 Eth. C in Bilate Military Camp while university students were training for compulsory national service. The association was formally established in 1984 Eth. C under the church's structures. የማህበረ ቅዱሳን አመሰራረት ታሪክ (The origins of Mahbere Kidusan) (Addis Ababa, Public Relations Office of Mahbere Kidusan, 2002 Eth. C), 19–27.

130. Mulugeta Haile Mariam, "የዕንቁ እንግዳ" (Guest of *Enqu*) 4, no. 40 (Sene 2003 Eth. C), 12.

131. The publications of Mahbere Kidusan are integral to the name of the Association because most of the columns are primarily committed to promoting veneration of the saints and endorsing numerous traditional writings and their claims. Second, denouncement of "tehadiso" movements as allies of Evangelicals also features on a regular basis. The name of Christ and articles derived from the Scriptures do not feature as much.

132. Asrat, Interview, 30 December 2010, Addis Ababa.

as a "*shibboleth*" of firmly upholding the tenets of Ethiopian Orthodoxy.[133] Needless to say, the scrutiny done by the association has forced many to be apprehensive; looking over their shoulders each time they publicly preach solely from the Bible.[134]

Eshetu Alemayehu, New Testament professor at Sewasew *Birhan* St Paul Theological College remarks, "A particular sermon is identified as Orthodox when it preaches Christ, but with the saints, the righteous and martyrs as branches; with the Old Testament, the New Testament, and monastic literature as the basis – the books of deeds[135] as branches."[136]

Members of the clergy who are suspected of deviating from Orthodoxy as spelled out above, are investigated by delegates of the church, and banned from clerical duties indefinitely when the investigators are not able to agree if punitive measures are to be taken.[137] Many are even banished from their

---

133. Abayneh Kassa in his preaching warns about counterfeit approaches which appear to honour Mary. He noted, "they tell us that our Lady is pure and holy, this is a means to have access into our territory because they will not acknowledge her intercession." He asserted, "The mark [of distinguishing the Orthodox teaching] is Our Lady" "ክርስቶስን አውቃለሁ የሚል፤ ቀራንዮ እሄዳለሁ ለሚል ጥሩ ነው ግን ምልክት እንጠይቀዋለን፤ ምልክታችን፥ እመቤታችን ናት፤ እመቤታችን ንጽሕት ናት ቅድስት ናት ይሉናል ይህ ድንበር ማፍረስ ነው አማላጅ ናት ግን አይሉንም፡" Abayneh Kassa, ድንበራችንን እንደያደርስብን እንጠንቀቅ (The need to protect our distinguishing mark) www.eotc-mkidusan.org, accessed 5 May 2011; Zemedkun Bekele, Armageddon Vol. 1, (Audio presentation), Addis Ababa, Gelgela Spiritual Songs House, n.d.

134. Dereje and Beza, መቅደስ የገቡ መናፍቃን (*Menafiqan* in the temple) (Bahir Dar, 2008), 6–17.

135. The books of deeds are: *Gedil* (Hagiographies of the martyrs), *Dirsan* (Deeds of the angels) and *Tamir* (Miracles of Mary and the saints). Endale Teshi, ቃለ ምልልስ ከመጋቤ ሀዲስ እሸቱ ዓለማየሁ ጋር (Interview with Eshetu Alemayehu), Addis Guday 5, no. 92 (Sene 2003 Eth. C), 20.

136. "አንድ ስብከት ኦርቶዶክሳዊ ነው የሚባለው ክርስቶስን - ግን ቅዱሳንን፣ ጻድቃንን፣ ሰማዕታትን ቅርንጫፍ አድርጎ፣ ብሉይ፣ ሃዲስን፣ መጻሕፍት ሊቃውንት፣ መጻሕፍት መነካሳትን መሠረት - የሠራ መጻሕፍትን ቅርንጫፍ አድርጎ መስበክ ሲችል ነው። እነዚህን አንድ መምህር ጠቅሶ ማስተማር ካልቻሉ እነዚህን አብነት ካላደረጉና ለምሁርት ግብዓት አድርጎ መጠቀም ካልቻሉ ቤተ ክርስቲያኒቱን አላገኙትም ማለት ነው።" Endale Teshi, Interview, *Addis Guday* 5, no. 92 (Sene 2003 Eth. C), 20.

137. Melaku critiques the approach of Mahbere Kidusan as being centred in having people eliminated or expelled. "The current blind extremism is not of the spirit of the Church; neither does it show love. Scholars of the Church are needed to save souls. There needs to be ample time to investigate with a sober mind. But if the purpose is to expel and not restore, the end result will be as though hunting in the forest, chasing and having killed indiscriminately just like the association which calls itself 'Mahbere Kidusan' is doing. Such action, however, is not in accordance to the way or call of the Church." Translation by the researcher. "አሁን የሚታየው ጭፍን አክራሪነት የቤተ ክርስትያን መንፈስ አይደለም፣ የፍቅር መልክም የለውም፣ ነፍስ ለማዳን ሊቃውንት ቤተክርስቲያን ያስፈልጋሉ፡፡ ዝግ ባለ ሁኔታ መመርመር ያስፈልጋል፡ ጉዞ ያስፈልጋል፡ ዓላማው ለማባረር እንጂ ለማዳን ካልሆነ ግን፣ አሁን ራሱን 'ማህበረ ቅዱሳን' እያለ የሚጠራው ማህበር እንደሚያደርገው፡ የሚያስፈልገውን

positions. When the association suspects a group, or a prominent person, to be *tehadiso* it does not refrain from publishing their names on its media. This has resulted in wide criticism of the association.[138] The association continues to write against those who were expelled a long time ago and calls them names. Among these was Aleqa Meseret Sebhat Leab, who was expelled from Siwasew *Birhan* St Paul Theological College on allegations of teaching erroneous teaching/heresy *nufaqe*.[139] Mahbere Kidusan hails his dismissal but regrets that "the poisonous teaching he spread lives to this day."[140]

The association, however, does not accept the allegations against it that it exists primarily to hunt down people with reformed views, but insists that it is only against those whose work jeopardizes the stability of the church and the unity of the nation. "We are not after having people expelled, but when we have evidence about their belief and practice negating the church's Dogma, we report to the church."[141] The association insists, "We care for every single soul in the church. We are misunderstood sometimes, in fact, it is us who usually are accused. We do not look for excuse to have people expelled."[142]

Although the association denies the allegations, there is evidence which suggests that it aims to discredit *tehadiso* movements and also Evangelicals.[143]

አክሩልኝ ግደሉልኝ እያሉ 'የጭካ አደን' ማካሄድ ብቻ ነው፡፡ ይህ ደግሞ የቤተ ክርስቲያን መንፃዋም ተልእኮዋም አይደለም፡ " Melaku Baweke, ስውሩ አደጋ (The subtle danger), 36.

138. Tsigie Sitotaw, ይነጋል (Dawn will come) (Addis Ababa: Raey Publishers, 2002 Eth. C), 111–114; Dereje and Beza, መቅደስ የጉቱ መናፍቃን (Bahr Dar, 2008), 140–141. Cf. የተሃድሶ መናፍቃን ዘመቻ (The campaign of Tehadiso *menafiqan*), 62–85; የገሃነም ደጆች (Gates of hell).

139. See 361–362 above. Mahbere Bekur, the association founded by Aleqa Meseret, noted that he was expelled because he taught "pure Gospel" "ያልተበረዘ ወንጌል" *Chora*, no. 14, n.d., 4.

140. የገሃነም ደጆች, Sem'ea Tsidq 10, no. 78 (Megabit 1995 Eth. C), 11.

141. Asrat, Interview, 30 December 2010.

142. Asrat, Interview, 30 December 2010. Cf. *Hamer*, no. 5 (Tahsas/Tir 1993 Eth. C), 2.

143. For example, the association quotes Paul Balisky's interview with the Christian Science Monitor, in which, in reference to *tehadiso* people, he is quoted as saying, "It is unfortunate they were expelled. Had they remained there, they would have done a lot of good work for us." *Hamer*, no. 5 (Tahsas/Tir, 1993 Eth. C), 2. His actual words were, "That was unfortunate, because they could have done some important work from the inside." Andrea Useem, Evangelicals alter Ethiopia's traditions, Christian Science Monitor, 8 June 2000. Paul Balisky officially wrote to the editor of *Hamer* and copied to the Office of the Patriarch, the General Manager of the Orthodox Church, the Office of Addis Ababa Diocese, and the Head of EOTC Sunday School Departments. In the letter he expressed his disappointment over

Perhaps the growing prominence of Evangelical types of expressions of faith and worship worry the association, causing fear that if they are not put in check, the ancient tradition of the church will be replaced by unpredictable and dynamic Evangelical structures. Mahbere Kidusan refers to *tehadiso* people as "the right hand of the *menafiqan*." As proof of such arguments, it went as far as misquoting an article by Paul Balisky, the former director of SIM in Ethiopia, which appeared on the *Horn of Africa Challenge and Opportunity*. "The objective is not to set up a new church as such, but to introduce reforms within the church." After they published Balisky's words in English, they added their interpretation in the Amharic translation of his words by adding "the objective is to change the church, to convert it into Protestantism."[144]

The association accuses the church of not taking decisive measures against people with *tehadiso* leanings.[145] However, the association itself does not seem to submit to the church authorities. In fact, the major complaint heard from church authorities is that the association uses the church for the sake of credibility and pays lip service to its submission to the church, but in practice it is self-governing.[146]

One of the actions of Mahbere Kidusan which seems to upset the church authorities is its presenting itself as an official medium of the church. This is

---

the way they misquoted him and misrepresented his ideas. His letter was never published by *Hamer*. "እንደራዊ መልዕክት ለማኅበረ ቅዱሳን" (Message to Mahbere Kidusan), Paul Balisky, 10 March 2001. Balisky also wrote a memo to the General Secretary of the Ethiopian Kale Heywet Church expressing his disappointment over the "vitriolic" article published in *Hamer*. Memo to Dr Tesfaye Yacob, from Paul Balisky, "Article in *Hamer* Publication," 14 February 2001.

144. *Hamer* 5 (Tahsas/Tir, 1993 Eth. C), 3.

145. የገሃነም ደጆች (Gates of hell), 12; The association urges that Memhir Leulekal Akalu and Aba Ketsela should be either expelled or watched very closely. Editorial, *Hamer* 5 (Tahsas/Tir 1993 Eth. C), 3.

146. There is a major conflict between the Sunday School Department of the church which structurally is the head of Mahbere Kidusan. The complaint was that the association repeatedly bypasses the Department and takes measures on behalf of the church without the knowledge of the Department. The Head of Sunday School Department complained and the patriarch issued letters in response. Cf. Letter from Head of Sunday School Department registered as 44/70/2002, dated 6/2/2002 was dispatched to Mahbere Kidusan. The head of the Sunday School Department requested Mahbere Kidusan to state its property and accounts throughout the country. The conflict seems to have continued because the Patriarch issued another letter to the same effect: ል/ጽ/ 594/2002, Dated 16/11/2002 Eth. C. www.eotcssd. org, accessed 16 June 2011. Cf. ማኅበረ ቅዱሳን ማስጠንቀቂያ ተሰጠው (Mahbere Kidusan was given a warning), Reporter (Ginbot 24, 2003 Eth. C), 3–4.

not done directly but through interviews conducted and different magazines that publicise the actions of the association.[147] They seem to do this purposely to make it look as though they are the voice of the church or are the protectors of the church.[148] Such views have got the association into trouble with church clergy who do not appreciate the boisterous behaviour of the association (such as illustrated in its printing names of clergy as members of *tehadiso*) and its indiscriminate critique of higher church officials.[149]

There seems to be a power struggle between leaders of Mahbere Kidusan and the leadership of the church who consider Mahbere Kidusan as insubordinate, and even a threat to the church.[150] Such a tension resulted in even a physical clash between its supporters and opponents.[151]

The root cause of the intermittent conflict between Mahbere Kidusan and the church authorities may be its questioning the credibility of the current leadership of the church. The association seems to have problems with both

---

147. ቅድስት ልደታ ለማርያም መንፈሳዊ ማህበር በሚል ስያሜ የሚንቀሳቀሰው ማህበር ስውር ተልዕኮ ተጋለጠ፣ (The conspiracy of the association which calls itself "Qedest Ledeta Lemariam Menfesawi Mahber" exposed), Sem'a Tsidq 18, no. 209, Meskerem 16–30, 2003 Eth. C, 10; Cf. Mulugeta Wolde Gabriel, ማህበረ ቅዱሳን ወይስ ማህበረ ሰይጣን (Association of the saints or Satan) (Addis Ababa: n.p., 2000 Eth. C), 47.

148. Agizachew Tefera, Interview 13 June 2011; Cf. Sime'a Tsidq ZeOrthodox Tewahdo, 18th year 18, no. 209 (Meskerem 16–30, 2003 Eth. C).

149. Wolde Rufael Fetahi, የስልሳ ዓመቱ አዛዉንት በአስር ዓመቱ ሕጻን ተዘለፈ፣ (The sixty-year old elderly scolded by the ten-year kid), Zena Betekristian, 50th year, no. 225, Megabit and Miazia, 1996 Eth. C, 1, 5, 7–8. Some of the clergy members whose names were mentioned as being *tehadiso* pressed charges and the editor was detained for some time. The issue came to a close after he apologized to them. www.dskmariam.org, accessed 10 May 2011; Informant T, Interview, 25 February 2011, Addis Ababa.

150. Cf. አነጋጋሪ ቃለ ምልልስ ከሊቀ ካህናት ጌታቸው ዶኒ ጋር፣ የተደበቀ አጀንዳቸውን አላራምድም (Controversial interview with Liqe Kahnat Getachew Doni: "I will not promote their hidden agenda"), *Maraki* 1, no. 5 (Sene 2003 Eth. C), 7–8, 19.

151. Cf. Begashaw Desalegn, ድንጋይ ወርውረው ሲገቡ በቪዲዮ ተቀርጸዋል (They were videotaped as they went inside after throwing stones) *Maraki* 1, no. 3 (Megabit 2003 Eth. C), 26, 38 –39; የሃዋሳ ጉዳይ 1፤ የእኛ ግዴታ ሲኖዶስ ያወጣውን ሕግ ማስከበር ነው (The issue of Hawassa; our responsibility is enforcing the rules of the synod), T/ Selassie Tsega Kiros, የደቡብ ክልል ርዕሰ መስተዳድር ከምዕመናን ጋር ተወያዩ (The governor of the southern regions held discussion with believers), www.eotc-mkidusan.org, accessed 7 March 2011; Aba Wolde Tinsae was allegedly referred to as anathematized by Mahbere Kidusan, but another group rejects the claim and refers to him as the apostle of our time የዘመናችን ሐዋርያ. Cf. ቤተ ክርስቲያን በገዛ ልጆቿ ስትፈተን 1&2 (The church tried by her own children), Hidar 2002 Eth. C, www.ethiopianorthodox.org, accessed 6 March 2011.

patriarchs.¹⁵² The association's dissatisfaction with the leadership of both synods, the negative remarks of its leaders about the current leadership of the church¹⁵³, and the accusation that it is insubordinate to either synod, perhaps imply that Mahbere Kidusan desires to take over the leadership of the church.¹⁵⁴

Most of those who are *tehadiso* portray Mahbere Kidusan negatively. On the other hand there are those who admire the effort of the association to maintain and promote ancient sites, traditional schools and follow up Orthodox students in higher institutions.¹⁵⁵ Moreover, its efforts to preserve the tradition of the church and teach the young generation to treasure its history and identity are admired by some members of the *tehadiso* movement, and even by Evangelicals, although the association's indiscriminate accommodation of all traditions regardless of their accord with the Bible, is believed to hinder the work of God.¹⁵⁶

A member of one of the *tehadiso* groups comments that the emergence and ascendancy of Mahbere Kidusan has made the clergy of the church serve and live cautiously and not haphazardly, paying attention to what they teach

---

152. Members of Mahbere Kidusan were accused of bypassing the church structures in North America and deliberately causing problem in a way which showed contempt to the leadership there. Moreover, the association's media made a derogatory reference to Melaku Baweke's ordination in North America. የጎሳገም ደጆች, *Sem'ea Tsidq* 10, no. 78 (Megabit 1995 Eth. C), 12; Cf. Daniel Kibret's interview in which he allegedly lamented that the EOC has not found a Synod which would change the course of its history. *Enqu* 4, no. 42 (Tir 2003 Eth. C); see a sarcastic response of Liqe Tiguhan Getachew Doni, ጥቁር እራሱ የሲኖዶስ አባል፣ *Maraki* 1, no. 3 (Megabit 2003 Eth. C), 24–25; www.dskmariam.org, accessed 11 May, 2011. ጥቁር እራስ (Tikur Eras) is an Amharic expression to refer to someone who is not a monk or who could not possibly be a monk (because he is married or is worldly). In the case of Daniel the expression seems to refer to his marital status.

153. Daniel Kibret, የኢትዮጵያ ቤተ ክርስቲያን ታሪክ የሚለውን ሲኖዶስ አላገኘችም፣ (The Church of Ethiopia has not found a synod which will change the course of history), *Enqu* 4, no. 42 (Tir 2003 Eth. C).

154. This could be the reason why the criticisms of leaders and members of Mahbere Kidusan towards the Church are not well taken. Cf. Zena Bete Kristian 60th year, no. 225 (Megabit and Miyazia, 1996 Eth. C), 1, 5–8; Getachew Doni, ጥቁር እራሱ የሲኖዶስ አባል, *Maraki* 1, no. 3 (Megabit 2003 Eth. C), 24–25; Daniel Kibret, የኢትዮጵያ ቤተ ክርስቲያን ታሪክ የሚለውጥ ሲኖዶስ አላገኘችም, *Enqu* 4, no. 42 (Tir 2003 Eth. C). Cf. Getachew Doni, the administrator of the Orthodox Church in Awassa town, remarked that "Mahbere Kidusan has a secret agenda which will soon be exposed by the Church." አነጋጋሪ ቃል ምልልስ ከሊቀ ካህናት ጌታቸው ዶኒ ጋር፣ የተደነቀ አጀንዳቸውን አላራምድም፣ ማራኪ፣ *Maraki* 1, no. 5 (Sene 2003 Eth. C), 19.

155. Informant T, Interview, 25 February 2011.

156. Afework Hailu, Interview, 20 April 2011, Addis Ababa.

and how they conduct their lives. The association, therefore, helped to keep in check the "Protestant" kind of rebellious temperament.[157] Moreover, the association asks legitimate questions as to why the Orthodox Church is the prime mission field for Evangelicals even in areas which are densely populated by Muslims.[158] This may have helped *tehadiso* and Evangelicals alike to re-examine their evangelistic aims and guard against the indiscriminate attempt to target the Orthodox Church as an institution.

6.5. The Evangelicals and Reformation Movements

The Evangelical churches have partnered with reformation movements for a long time by providing Bibles, Bible study materials and training. Although many were accused of using these activities as opportunities to take people out of the EOC, there are some who encourage EOC adherents to remain in their church and serve as agents of renewal.[159] The policy of some of the reformation groups not to encourage Orthodox members to leave their church was not liked by some leaders of Evangelical churches. When admonished to put an end to sheep-stealing, one of the leaders of Evangelical churches allegedly reasoned, "taking people from the EOC is necessary for the numerical growth of our churches."[160]

On the other hand, some Evangelicals are critical of the *tehadiso* groups that established a separate church. The criticism is that they are confused, with one foot in EOC and another in the Evangelical camp. In other words, there are beliefs and traditions which they do not like to give up from their former church, and others that they want to adopt from Evangelicals. The concern is that some of the *tehadiso* groups are helping neither the EOC

---

157. Informant T, Interview, 25 February 2011, Addis Ababa.

158. The association presented an alleged letter sent to Mustard Seed Foundation by Amanuel United Church asking for support to its work in Zeway area which is 65 percent Islam and 30 percent EOC. Amanuel united Church stated its aim, "To reach the Ethiopian orthodox [sic] people In the truth of Gosple [sic]." ሰምዒም ይጽፍ, *Sem'ea Tsidq* 10, no. 77 (Yekatit 1995 Eth. C), 14.

159. There are different opinions among Evangelicals whether EOC needs evangelism or reformation. Nigusse believes that the Church needs both reform and evangelism just like any other Christian body because there are people who are members without personal commitment to Christ and there are those whose commitment is misguided. Nigusse Bulcha, Interview, 30 September 2010.

160. Informant F, Interview, 16 August 2011, Addis Ababa.

nor the Evangelicals through such a posture. They should either remain in the EOC and preach Christ or abandon the EOC tradition altogether and become Evangelicals.[161] Others argue that *tehadiso* only retain the Orthodox name, and in practice have become Pentecostals with very little, if any, trace of Orthodox tradition in their worship, faith statement and lifestyle. They could have retained the songs, the dress code, and the hour of worship. In fact, their example is encouraging the youth in the Orthodox Church to abandon the church tradition, thereby becoming a stumbling block for EOC believers.[162]

However, it should be noted that for the most part the revival kindled the Bible study meetings of factory workers and high school students who did not have theological training. Leaders of *tehadiso* realize the desire of their members to retain some of the EOC tradition but, because they worship in rented houses, they are not able to worship as early as the Orthodox Church does.[163] Afework, one of the former leaders of a *tehadiso* group, believes that this is a lame excuse. He thinks that *tehadiso* could use Evangelical churches for worship early in the morning; after all, most Evangelicals do not go to church before 10:00 a.m.[164]

Afework laments that even after their long encounter with the gospel *tehadiso* did not engage the traditions of the church but continued to focus on the negative things. According to him, they focus on what they do not accept. Had they engaged the traditions such as *degewa* (the songs of St Yared), the liturgy of the church, the apocryphal books, etc., by listing which they accept and why, he believes that their movement would have been fit to be called *tehadiso*. But now, with focusing only on the things they reject and with little theological engagement, he does not think that there is a proper *tehadiso* movement in the EOC; mere opposition does not make one a reformer.[165]

---

161. Bezabih Workneh, Interview, 25 February 2011, Addis Ababa

162. For example some young people are daring to enter the vicinities of the Orthodox Church without "netela" the traditional cloth. Bezabih, Interview, 25 February 2011.

163. Mezgebu, Interview, 23 August 2010.

164. Afework, Interview, 20 April 2011, Addis Ababa.

165. Afework, Interview, 20 April 2011.

Afework cites the intercession of the saints as an example. According to him there are passages in the Bible which hint that the dead saints offer prayers.[166] However, there is no indication that we can address our prayer to them. According to him, mere opposition to the intercession of the saints is wrong.[167] Afework laments that those who call themselves reformers go around listing erroneous beliefs and practices but do not appreciate the numerous commendable indigenous traditions of the church.[168]

However, it would be helpful to keep in mind that the contemporary *tehadiso* movement first arose among the youth, who for the most part were high school students. They could hardly have been able to theologically engage the seventeen-centuries-old church. Now that they have been in existence for over twenty years, and have a number of trained theologians among them, they no longer have this excuse for not engaging the historic and ancient Orthodox tradition on its own grounds instead of attempting to form it in the likeness of Evangelicals.

Conclusion

The concept of *tehadiso* was not foreign to the Orthodox Church but it was discouraged, partly for fear of losing the stability and unity of the church. Moreover, the long isolation of the church from the rest of the Christian world has affected it quite deeply, and the negative experiences it has had with missionaries and their Ethiopian counterparts have made it difficult to accept their proposal for *tehadiso*. Such circumstances appear to have created a conducive environment for some individuals and groups to promote their personal advancement at the expense of the spiritual state of the members of the church.

On the other hand the indiscriminate criticism and the tendency of Evangelical churches to split was a stumbling block for Orthodox followers.[169] As time went by, two kinds of extreme views emerged. The first comprised those who wanted to reshape the church after the likeness of

---

166. Cf. Revelation 6:10.

167. Agizachew strongly disagrees with this notion and looks at it as a statement to please the Orthodox. Agizachew, Interview, 13 June 2011

168. Afework, Interview, 20 April 2011.

169. የጥንግም ይጃች፡ *Sem'ea Tsidq* 10, no. 77 (Yekatit 1995 Eth. C), 14.

Evangelical churches; the second wanted to preserve every single tradition of the church with no critical approach. In the middle of these two extremes lie the "Silent" reformers.

The Ethiopian Orthodox Church's history of isolation and the effect of Zer'a Ya'iqob's strong hand have exposed it to numerous unbiblical teachings. The efforts to correct such perversions were met with strong opposition, partly because of the attitude of agents of change. Moreover the church's conflict with both foreign and Ethiopian Evangelicals has created suspicion towards reformation of any kind. Most of all, however, the reformers' lack of a clear vision has hindered the renewal of the church and the rise of Mahbere Kidusan has ostracized the concept of *tehadiso* altogether.

The scope of the term *tehadiso* appears to be ambiguous in the circle of the Orthodox Church, in "reformed groups," and among Evangelicals. The trouble is that those who use the term "reformation" do not usually differentiate between long-lived dogma of the church as handed down from the church of Alexandria and the later additions which tended to deviate from ancient orthodoxy as upheld by Orthodox churches elsewhere. In other words, there is confusion as to what exactly the term refers to or what the contemporary reformers would like to see changed.

The scope of reform, therefore, varies from group to group. Some long to see structural change, others work towards administrative change. Some were expelled because of insignificant issues. In the course of this study it has been noticed that there is no agreement on the meaning and extent of reformation, but all groups agree on this one thing: that the church needs administrative *tehadiso* (renewal).[170]

Although the desire of nearly all reformers to see "the ancient faith restore" is ambiguous, when they are pressed to unpack it their expectation appears to be duplicating the Evangelical tradition. Mahbere Kidusan's ceaseless accusation towards *tehadiso* groups that they desire to replace the church with Protestant structures, therefore, is not successfully refuted. The association

---

170. Daniel, Interview, 8 September 2010; Mezgebu, Interview, 23 August 2010; Agizachew, Interview, 19 February 2011; Informant G, Interview February 2011; Begashaw Desalegn, የመስቀሉ ሥር ቁማርተኞች (Gamblers under the cross), 1; Mekonnen, Interview, 15 November 2010.

draws such conclusions from the publications of *tehadiso* groups which are far more similar to the Evangelical convictions than to the Orthodox.

For example, one of the vital things which Evangelicals lack in their tradition is respect for the saints. In their attempt to exalt the Bible, Evangelicals have minimized the status of the saints of Christ but the Orthodox reformers seem to walk in the footsteps of Evangelicals. The Orthodox reformers, therefore, are not able to demonstrate one of the marks of Orthodox Christianity, which is the status of the saints. It could be argued that the saints are exalted in the Ethiopian Orthodox tradition. However, the reformers are not able to theologically engage this doctrine and show the proper place of the saints in the Orthodox tradition as opposed to the Evangelical one.

Similar observations could be made concerning the other doctrines that cause conflict. There is a lack of theological engagement. When the movements started, they were not in a position to theologically engage with the doctrines they considered unbiblical because they were basically lay movements. But the question remains; after nearly twenty years, why do the Orthodox reformers still lack coherent arguments which are not copied from Evangelicals?

On the other hand, the structures of the church which have little room for critique have made it difficult for the reformers to address vital issues without being suspected as *menafiqan*. The works of Mahbere Kidusan, which lack depth and theological reflection, but use the saints as a tool for eliminating their opponents, have further complicated the matter. Mahbere Kidusan seems to propagate an indiscriminate accommodation of all doctrines with little critique. This too is far from the Orthodox tradition, which centres on the revelation of the triune God through the Bible and in the incarnation, with appropriate respect for the saints. The time and resources that Mahbere Kidusan devotes to condemning the *tehadiso* movement shows that the association fears the potential of the movement. Had Mahbere Kidusan engaged the reform movements with arguments based on the Bible, history, and the tradition of the Orthodox Church instead of creating apprehension in the minds of people about reformation, it would not have worried as much about the Evangelicals' sheep-stealing.

Currently the scenario is complicated by the tension between the church authorities, including the patriarch, and Mahbere Kidusan. On the one hand

Mahbere Kidusan appears to be moderate in some ways, preaching tolerance but it has not demonstrated it. In addition, its image among *tehadiso* and Evangelicals seems to be damaged beyond repair, so that maintaining trust would be difficult to achieve.

Members of the Orthodox are living in an era marked by internal tension between *tehadiso* and Mahbere Kidusan. The confusion of the people is great when Mahbere Kidusan, which was considered as the protector of the church's tradition, is resisted by the leaders of the church. Preachers and singers whom Mahbere Kidusan opposes as *tehadiso* remain quite popular among the people and are even supported by the leadership of the church. This shows that there is a growing interest in reading the Bible, listening to Bible-centred sermons, reading the available literature both for and against *tehadiso* and the indigenous traditions, and apocryphal books. This provides the public with information they can read for themselves as they contemplate the credibility of the rival groups.

However, the label *menafiq* at times precedes explanation and the needed apologia regarding the doctrines of the church. When one raises questions about a particular long-held doctrine, the priests will be quick to label the inquirer as *menafiq*, thereby causing apprehension in the minds of curious inquirers.[171] Furthermore, there is an inclination on the part of the Orthodox Church's less informed clergy to label Evangelical convictions which appear to differ from those of Ethiopian Orthodoxy as "apostate teachings."[172]

The dilemma seems to remain that even when one of their own brings the message of renewal, official receptivity is limited. Sooner or later people with reformed views are forced out or find themselves in a very difficult situation where it is hard to continue to teach their convictions. The theological controversies which sprang from within and outside have made the church suspicious of any kind of renewal movement, especially because those who attempted to renew the church ended up leaving, either by means of excommunication or because of the difficulty of staying there.

---

171. Bezuayehu Abera, Interview, 14 February 2011.
172. Asaminew Kassa and Zerayehu Sime, የቤተ ክርስቲያን አስተዳደራዊ መዋቅር (The administrative hierarchy of the church) (Addis Ababa: Mahbere Kidusan Educational Section, 1996 Eth. C), 69.

However, the Orthodox Church is introducing reforms. These include increased emphasis on preaching and teaching from the Bible and giving place for educated clergy to preach and teach in the evenings during working days and train the clergy. Moreover, songs with notions taken from the Bible have flourished and preaching from the Bible during funerals and comforting the bereaved with words of the Scripture have increased.[173]

Similar to the Protestant trend, strong Bible study groups have been formed in higher educational institutions, and Bible study materials have been systematically developed and provided. Bible passages are increasingly used to address celebrations such as Epiphany. Graduates from theological colleges no longer struggle to find acceptance in the church, as their counterparts did during Haile Sellassie's regime. They are accepted in the structures of the church and most importantly, the church delegates them to offer systematic training to the traditional clergy of the church.[174]

Such actions could be taken as fruits of reformation in the church although it is not possible to trace them to the effort of a given group or individual. The post-Estifanos reform movements did not have key figures for a long time. The reformation was sparked by the reading of the Bible and brought forth by lay youth movements, thus, it did not have coherence in the beginning but strong conviction that the church needed renewal. The reformers are diverse. Some are against abuse or corruption and others are Biblicist. Others are attracted by Pentecostals.

The current movement mediated by "Silent" Reformers and popular preachers and singers, is progressing steadily, although with increasing opposition from traditional authorities. In the opinion of the members of these inside reformers, the fathers of the EOC are not against them. However, the corporate title *tehadiso* is applied to those who are working for the reformation of the church and also those who use the church for their own personal advancement.

On the other hand, the reform movements are not as strongly organized as they are portrayed by Mahbere Kidusan. They do not seem to pose any

---

173. Fetha Amlak, Discussion held on 11 April 2011.

174. There is tension between the graduates of modern theological colleges and those of traditional schools, but the church is working towards bridging the gap between the two groups. Informant D, Interview, 18 August 2010, Addis Ababa.

threat to the existence of the church, nor to the unity of the nation. Many of them are humble Bible movements with no strong centre or organized leadership, but with strong convictions about the need for the centrality of the Bible in the church. As for the tradition they like to follow, there seems to be no clear vision. Perhaps because the reformers are not exposed to the traditions of other Orthodox churches, they use Evangelical terms, which gives room for their opponents to label them as stooges of Protestants. However, the manner of the presentation of the critique shows the true colour of a given reformer; whether he or she is intent on exposing the wrongs in the church in order to damage its credibility.

It seems that three vital issues are to be considered in discussion of reformation of the Orthodox Church. The first concerns those who feel at home in the EOC, those inside the church. They will be careful while repairing so that the structure might not fall on top of them.[175] In other words, there needs to be an acceptance of the church as Orthodox, instead of toiling to conform it into an Evangelical tradition. Those who have problems with the core Orthodox traditions that distinguish them from other Christian traditions may leave the church and join a tradition which suits them. Second, ignoring cracks in the ceiling or the walls and wishing to retain the structure intact are mutually exclusive options. In other words, resisting change at all cost is not a Christian way. It does not make one a preserver of Orthodox tradition but a counter reformer.

Third, reformers need to mind the guidelines they are using in working towards reformation. To begin with, it is the guidelines that define reformation and evaluate a given doctrine to see whether it is correct or a deviation. The inevitable fact is that the guidelines used in maintaining the structure either move the structure away from the foundation as laid down by apostles and prophets, or firmly establish it on Christ, the cornerstone. Thus, reformers need to check themselves against the Bible as they explore different patterns of reformation.

---

175. Informant D, Interview, 18 August 2010, Addis Ababa

CHAPTER 7

Conclusion

While Nubian Christianity was exterminated and Egyptian Christianity marginalized, Ethiopian Christianity as one of the ancient indigenous Christianities in Africa, survived the worst of all storms and is vibrant. Its unwavering dedication to the Coptic Church and the role of the monarchs in protecting and expanding the faith, played major roles both in its survival and in its fusion with the identity of its adherents.

Over the years, Orthodox Christianity drew its strength from the monastic revival and the subsequent translation of the Bible into Ge'ez. Its doctrinal position was revised by the works of Cyril of Alexandria and developed by the theological controversy among its learned clergy members. Orthodox Christianity also came into contact with foreign influences such as Islam, Catholicism and Protestantism which left a permanent mark on the expressions of Christianity and the attitude of its adherents towards outside forces. However, it was not always open to accommodate changes and renovation and this to some extent contributed to its stability. Its insistence on the use of Ge'ez was meant to stop different kinds of interpretations from entering into the system, because it was feared that such openness would jeopardize the unity of the church.

Despite the church's long isolation from the rest of Christendom, Ethiopian Christianity survived. The isolation, however, had serious repercussions, including opening the way for the acceptance of unbiblical doctrines which contradict each other as authoritative. The undermining of the status of the Bible and the increase in superstitious practices burdened indigenous and outside reformers to attempt to bring the Bible to the centre. The movement of Estifanosites which was quenched, was an example of such attempts, and arose a century before the European Reformation. Missionaries from the church Missionary Society and Swedish Evangelical Mission successively attempted to reform the church with the reading of the Bible in the vernacular. They enjoyed preliminary results with arousing interest in Scripture reading and also won favour in the eyes of the rulers and monarchs who naturally viewed them as channels to European powers. However their core mission was frustrated with the expulsion of CMS from the country and the Bible readers from the church.

On the other hand, the forceful conversions and the subjugation of tribal leaders was so greatly resented in Southern Ethiopia that conversion to Orthodoxy was minimal, but important Christian concepts were introduced. The twentieth-century Protestant missionary movement thus did not labour too long before it saw multitudes respond to Evangelical Christianity. The work of missions prospered, particularly because it enjoyed the support and protection of Haile Sellassie I, because the Orthodox Church had done the groundwork by introducing Christian concepts and because of the "John the Baptist" role of the prophet movements in the south.

However, the Evangelical churches suffered persecution from the Orthodox Church, Islam, adherents of traditional religion and also the political authorities who belonged to one or other of these faiths. The persecution of Evangelicals by the EOC came to a climax with the denial of burial grounds which reflected utter rejection of the Evangelicals. The lifestyle of Evangelicals, Orthodox's rejection of the authenticity of their faith, and the Derg's propaganda against them, combined to earn them the discriminatory title *mete* and they were subjected to unspeakable atrocities. On the part of many Orthodox adherents, the long-standing interaction between Christianity and culture had so fused national and religious identity that they were not willing to acknowledge any other Christian tradition as an authentic Ethiopian expression of Christian faith.

The memory of Christianity's coming from outside and borrowing various theological terms from Syriac Christianity[1] for example, seems to be suppressed. In the case of the EOC, foreign terminologies were adopted in the

---

1. In the translation of the Bible into Ge'ez, some Syriac words were adopted into the Amharic, e.g. *haimanot, gehanem, ta'ot, miswat, qurban*. Sergew Hable Sellassie, *Ancient and Medieval Ethiopian History*, 120.

early years of Christianity. In the case of Evangelicals, however, little effort was made to retain the Orthodox concepts. This could be because Evangelical Christianity thrived in the western and southern parts of Ethiopia among people groups who did not speak Amharic fluently or know Ge'ez. There also was a conscious attempt to dissociate themselves from the Orthodox, which they considered to be part of the oppressive system, in order to develop a separate identity.

The Evangelicals' aggressive evangelism, which targeted traditional believers and Orthodox adherents alike, reached a climax with the coming of Pentecostalism which targeted urban dwellers. The importance they gave to spiritual realities resulted in their being labelled unpatriotic. Most importantly, in addition to the name *Tsere-Mariam* which was given to Evangelicals based on their perception of Mary, *Pente* which was adopted from the term Pentecostal was added as one of the identity badges of Evangelicals.

The Evangelicals are not apologetic regarding their stand on Mary, angels and the saints arguing that the type of veneration offered to them by Orthodox adherents is not commanded in the Bible.[2] This is in accordance with their Protestant tradition. In his attempt to avoid the extremely unbiblical practices of the church of Rome and the papal authority, Martin Luther seemed to have gone to the other extreme of disregarding the saints and their due place in the church. Perhaps following in his footsteps, Evangelicals avoided the tradition of the saints in order to exalt the Bible and seem to have little consciousness of their connection to the church fathers.

The accusation of the Orthodox that the allegiance of Evangelicals is with European Christianity is justified at times.[3] There is little regard for

---

2. There is a growing sense of regret for the way they treated EOC followers as pagans and stole its sheep. Zewde G/Sellassie, who was a popular faith movement leader in the 1990s called taking members of Orthodox "madness." Tertios Ke Vatican, የተዋርያው ዘውዴ አስገራሚ ለውጥና የእንመለስ ጥሪ (The amazing change of apostle Zewde and his call for repentance), *Gesame* 2, no. 11 (Tir 2002 Eth. C), 2, 16–17. I don't think they come. We bring them. We cause them to come. We use different techniques in order to make them uncomfortable to remain in the EOC. Our evangelistic approach is more than invitation. We try to persuade them to join us because we do not consider them as Christians. We make them feel ashamed about their faith and church. We tell them to totally change everything with nearly no trace of EOC's ingredients. Solomon Tilahun, Former Academic Dean of Pentecostal Theological College, Addis Ababa, Interview, 2 September 2010.

3. The way the preachers handle the Bible (folding the other side while reading from the opposite side), preach with one of their hands in their pocket, etc is copied from Western

indigenous Christianity and its scholars. Evangelicals have interacted with Western Christianity more than with the indigenous Ethiopian version. There appears to be little trust of the work of Orthodox theologians and lesser desire to engage them by studying Ge'ez. A tendency of crediting Europeans for the rise of the indigenous movements is perhaps an outcome of such sentiments.[4]

The EOC on the other hand, seems to have gone to the other extreme of glorifying tradition over the Bible; so much so that calling the name of Jesus repeatedly and making extensive use of the Bible is looked at as a mark of Evangelicalism. On the other hand, exalting the Virgin Mary is upheld as the mark of authentic Orthodoxy.

Orthodox reformers and former Orthodox adherents, who have joined Evangelical churches, trace the current exaltation of Mary in the church to the work of Zer'a Ya'iqob. The conflict between EOC and Evangelicals which revolves around the status of the saints and the Bible drew Orthodox and Evangelicals apart to such an extent that some preachers from the EOC used Mary's name for exorcism, whereas, some Evangelicals asserted that Tamre Mariam's Mary has a demonic origin. The mutual antagonism was so alarming that it concerned the government which established the Inter-Religious Council to promote tolerance among people of different faiths and evaluate literature, audio and video messages which have the potential to incite religious conflict.

The conflict between Evangelicals and the Orthodox is also reflected through popular theology which comes in the form of slogans on taxis and private vehicles exalting Mary and condemning the conversion of Orthodox members to Evangelicalism. Evangelicals were also judged based on the impact of secularism in Europe, the home of Protestantism. The argument is that Protestantism is disintegrating because its foundations are faulty.

---

preachers and it is quite offensive to the Orthodox. The message such actions send is that Evangelicals do not seem to show much care for the Ethiopian culture. Getachew Belete, Interview, 18 August 2010.

4. *History of Christianity in Ethiopia with Emphasis on the Ethiopian Evangelical Church Mekane Yesus* (Addis Ababa: MYS-TEE Department, 1989, 1992, 2007), 36. This book makes a historical error and suggests that the fifteenth-century Estifanosites were inspired by the seventeenth-century Peter Heyling. It is hard to understand how such a major historical error was overlooked by Dr Gustav Aren and Dr Emanuel Abraham, who according to the preface to the second revised edition, "carefully checked the whole book."

This reflects the inherent perception that Evangelical faith is not authentically Ethiopian.

However, such an argument backfires on the Orthodox too, whose source, Alexandrian Christianity, declined into a remnant. The truth of the matter is that Christianity does not have a home as such. Palestine was its origin, but it did not thrive in the country of its origin. The power of Christianity is in its potential to be incarnated but this is one of the points of departure between the EOC and Evangelical churches. There is a tension between preserving what is passed on from the fathers, and engaging the tradition in issues pertaining to each generation with its own tongue.

Evangelicals are also highly criticized concerning their ever-increasing splits and the formation of new churches that steal members from each other and worship in tents or public halls. Since Orthodox ecclesiology considers the church building as the abode of God, the gathering of Evangelicals in any other kind of building appears scandalous. On the side of the Evangelicals, there seems to be apparent embarrassment over the numerous factions, especially in the face of the EOC criticism. Therefore, much laying of blame on the new faith movements and their counterparts in Western countries is done in an attempt to save the face of Evangelical faith in Ethiopia. However, it could also be argued that instead of forming mega-churches, planting house churches in every neighbourhood follows the New Testament's model of a local church.

Despite fierce opposition from the established church and the state, Evangelical Christianity has grown tremendously to constitute 18 percent of the total population. A number of factors were behind the growth of Evangelical Christianity. The first is the use of vernacular Scriptures. The EOC had control over the interpretation and application of the Bible, because it was recited in Ge'ez, which was incomprehensible to the common people. The Evangelicals on the other hand, made the Bible an open book. It was translated into vernaculars and any literate person was able to read it and relate to the characters of the stories of the Bible. Even illiterate people were able to hear the words read to them. Evangelical Christianity thus gave the people access to the Bible and in doing so undermined the prestige and authority that the clergy of the EOC had long enjoyed by virtue of their concealing of divine revelation, sometimes, admittedly, out of fear of corruption and misunderstanding on the part of the lay Christians. The availability of mother-tongue Scriptures, therefore, promoted Evangelical Christianity.

Second, the EOC considered entry into its membership as the achievement of higher status. Because it was also associated with civilization and modernity, people were attracted to Orthodoxy. To be identified with the EOC was prestigious, even though many people who are baptized into the EOC and proudly display a baptismal chord around their neck may not have adequate knowledge of the Bible. The Orthodox Church was regarded as the national church; thus, every citizen was expected to belong to it, and even Muslims were forcefully converted because of such expectations. In addition, the peripheral people were discriminated against, regardless of their acceptance of the Orthodox faith. In some cases they were not allowed to go into the church building. When they died their bodies were not put to rest in the vicinity of the church along with northern settlers. Therefore, they felt discriminated against on their own soil, by not being allowed to enter the churches they had helped to build.

Evangelical Christianity on the other hand gave people a new identity, different from the Orthodox one, which did not require them to learn a new language in order to hear and read the Bible. Moreover, it introduced literacy programs which opened the door to higher education for children of marginalized people groups. Many ethnic and linguistic barriers were crossed, thus promoting equality among people groups. People were assured of their acceptance by God and encouraged to practice it with one another despite their social standing. Ethnic and social barriers were usually broken down and brotherhood and sisterhood in the one Lord was promoted.

However, even Evangelical Christians were not fully free from discriminating among themselves. There still are people who are marginalized in social gatherings if not in church worship. These peripheral people (potters, tanners, smiths) are usually discriminated against in marriage and even table fellowship at times.[5] Despising people based on their tradition and

---

5. When I (the researcher) was in Durame, Southern Ethiopia (in the late 1980s), we had a vibrant Bible study group formed by Mr Leslie Winslow, an American SIM missionary who also belonged to the Navigators. In our meetings we used to share one by one new insights we gained from the particular passage we were studying and the practical things we would do out of our understanding of the Scriptures. In one such meeting a fellow Kembatta man told us that he was challenged by the passage (I don't remember what the passage was) and decided to go to the house of "fuga" (potter) that week and have a cup of coffee with them and share the gospel. Members of the group thought that was a sacrificial act. Nearly all of us belonged to the SIM-planted Kale Heywet Church. Even our prominent church leaders were not willing to give their daughters in marriage to men who belonged to one of

ethnic affiliation, therefore, was not unique to the EOC and Amhara.[6] It is interesting to hear the outrage of people groups in southern and western parts of the country towards the Amhara discrimination without giving much thought to how inhumanly they themselves treat artisans of all kinds in their own communities. This would make one wonder if they were doing things any differently from the EOC. Evangelical Christianity itself thus is a victim of the culture of its adherents and cannot shift the blame to the EOC for failing to impartially demonstrate the love of Christ.

Third, the promise of deliverance from physical and spiritual bondage was one of the features of Evangelical Christianity. When the truth of having access to God was communicated to people who were weary of living under the yoke of oppressive *qalicha*, it was liberating news. The Bible also empowered people to stand up for their rights. Now that they were able to read and write they were no longer ignorant of their standing as children of God and also citizens of the country. The translation of the Bible and the literacy program was not always appreciated by some of the clergy of the established church and government officials who for a long time had oppressed the people by exploiting their ignorance of both the teachings of the Scriptures and the law of the land.

On the negative side, what tended to be unhelpful was the prolonged stay of the Protestant missionaries. They tended to manipulate leadership matters and the interrelations between churches of different traditions. When they were left alone with basic instructions of the Scripture and most importantly the copy of the Bible in the vernaculars and their mother-tongues, Ethiopians were able to develop their own indigenous Christianity.[7] At times there

---

the despised groups. In fact, such a union would cut the girl off from her family. Some of the leaders would make peace after a long time but to this day, such a union is not acceptable by the general public who for the most part belong to Kale Heywet and Mekane Yesus churches.

6. A number of groups in the Southern Ethiopia still are utterly despised and marginalized by their own people because of their clans, skills and eating habits. "Conversion to any of the variety of Christian religions, Orthodox, Catholic and particularly Protestant, is supposed to entail abandoning all traditional practices, including traditional craft occupations. Thus all those . . . who have converted, do not practice smithing or tanning anymore, and all those who practice craft occupations do not belong to any of these religions." Dena Freeman and Alula Pankhurst, eds., *Peripheral People: The Excluded Minorities of Ethiopia* (London: Hurst & Co., 2003), 228.

7. Cotterell, *Born at Midnight*, 27ff; Grenstedt, Staffan, *Ambaricho and Shonkolla: From Local Independent Church to Evangelical Mainstream in Ethiopia, the Origins of the Mekane Yesus Church in Kambata Hadiya* (Stockholm: Elanders Gotab, 2000), 19.

was too much coaching on the part of the missionaries and the introduction of the destructive denominational divisions of Western Christianity, to Ethiopians. It was as though they wanted the churches to remain dependent on them. This is what the EOC as an indigenous Ethiopian church had been resisting from the beginning.

The Orthodox Church, on the other hand, has unapologetically and extensively taken up "Jewish" identity into its structures. In fact, true Christianity, is presented as living as the first apostles lived in every way.[8] In the Orthodox Church, indigenous and Jewish consciousnesses are interwoven resulting in a unique Christian identity, and yet there is a strong sense of continuity with the historic church. Ethiopian monks usually drop their indigenous names upon their appointment as bishops and adopt names of the Bible, or names of fathers of Coptic, Greek or Syriac churches.

However, neither the presence of Jewish elements nor the taking of names of church fathers is looked on as foreign but as part and parcel of Ethiopian Christian identity which is continuous with the ancient church. These realities are in the background when Evangelicals are perceived as *mete*. In other words, *mete* also refers to the ethos of Evangelical faith in Ethiopia which turned its back on numerous traditions of the Orthodox Church including the veneration of the saints, monasticism, clerical hierarchy, and the status of apocryphal books. Generally speaking, the Ethiopian Evangelical tradition appears to have little memory of the church fathers and the great church Councils, but the Bible alone. Such a notion makes the EOC people wonder whether the Evangelical faith sprang up in a vacuum. Such things are interpreted by the Orthodox as evidence that Evangelicalism is a deviation from historic Christianity.

Beginning from the 1990s the attention of the Orthodox Church has been drawn to internal reformers whose arguments against EOC's doctrines are not different from those of Evangelicals. The *tehadiso* do not adequately engage with the theological issues pertaining to Mariology and reliance on extra-canonical tradition. This seems to give grounds to opponents to dismiss reformers as mere stooges of Evangelicals. Even though Evangelicals are not the direct focus of official and unofficial writings from EOC's side, nearly all

---

8. Daniel, Interview, 8 September 2010.

reformers are identified with them in one way or another, thereby making it difficult to have a meaningful dialogue with the scholars of the church. In other words, any question raised against unbiblical practices in the church is quickly labelled as *tehadiso* a term that has lost its original positive connotation as a reformer, and now means dissenter and even heretic. Needless to say, some of the *tehadiso* groups lack a clear vision as to what exactly they would wish to see changed, and why.

There is such a strong attraction towards the charismatic/Pentecostal Christian tradition that the reformers are tempted to identify themselves with it and to evaluate the ancient Orthodox Church based on that tradition. In fact, the difference between their Mariology, and understanding of apocryphal books and that of the Evangelicals, is not clear. On the other hand the conservative group, Mahbere Kidusan, is vociferous in its criticism of *tehadiso* groups and likens them to groups like the CMS, which attempted to reform the EOC. However, it too does not engage what it refers to as *tehadiso* sentiments with Orthodox tradition. In other words, Mahbere Kidusan is yet to substantiate how exactly the *tehadiso* groups have deviated from ancient orthodoxy.

If *tehadiso* groups were to present sound and solid theological engagement based on Orthodox tradition, they could successfully challenge the unbiblical developments in the Orthodox Church. In other words, Mahbere Kidusan's role in the church is exaggerated. Apart from blind hatred and appealing to emotion, it does not have strong theological and coherent arguments that could appeal to the enlightened mind of this generation. However, one of its concerns, that the *tehadiso* people are following the Evangelical tradition, appears to be correct.

However, in the Orthodox Church, *tehadiso* groups, and Evangelicals alike, the spirit of teachableness and humility seems to be lacking. Ethiopian Christians are yet to learn tolerance towards people who hold a different opinion. The tendency to stigmatize, insult, and try to expel differing individuals is evident among Evangelicals and Orthodox alike, although the degree may differ.[9]

---

9. In an interview given to *Gesame*, Pastor Dawit Bayou, the former Secretary of the Kale Heywet Church (KHC) in Gofa district, outlined how he and his followers were persecuted because of their doctrinal difference with the KHC. The difference pertained to

Globalization is also playing a major role. The access of urban people to satellite TV is affecting the country for better and for worse. On the negative side, Evangelical pastors struggle to disciple the flock who indiscriminately feed from the table of tele-evangelists and faith preachers.[10] On the positive side, globalization promotes tolerance and mutual understanding. There appears to be a growing openness on the part of the Evangelicals to acknowledge the Orthodox Church and stop sheep-stealing. In fact, it seems that the old dream of the CMS and SEM is returning. Evangelicals who came out of the Orthodox show a great desire to go back to the Orthodox Church and regret stealing its flock. The official stand of the Orthodox Church too is towards ecumenism between the Trinitarians: the Orthodox, Catholic and Evangelical churches. Given the real threat of Islam, the desire to work together is encouraging.

The study of the interaction between the EOC and Evangelicals also shows that there is continuity in the Orthodox's response to Evangelicals – it does not accept the "Sola Scriptura" approach of Evangelicals. The vehement rejection of the status of Mary and the saints also shows continuity in the Evangelicals' perception of the EOC. There are challenges from both sides. It is going to be some time before a proper relationship is achieved. However, the fact remains that whether Evangelicals like it or not, EOC will not be re-formed along Protestant lines. The monarchy is gone, but the church survived and it will continue to exist. Whether the EOC likes it or not, Evangelicals are in Ethiopia to stay. Therefore, Evangelicals and the Orthodox need to continue to find a way of living together. The salutary effort of the Bible Society to bring together the Trinitarians is encouraging and gives hope for a better future of working together.

---

the unity of the church and miraclesand wonders. When his views were rejected Dawit left KHC and started his own church named "the Church of God" but according to him KHC incited the leaders of government to oppose him. Members of KHC who were in government position used their position to press the Church of God. They were accused of false teaching and their credibility was purposely undermined. They were excluded from the community. Eventually they had them arrested with hard labour. The conflict climaxed in KHC refusing to have Pastor Dawit and his followers bury their dead in their cemetery. በነፃነት ዘመን ስደት (Persecution in the time of freedom), *Gesame* 1 & 2, Special issues (Meskerem, 2000 Eth. C), 5, 14.

10. Bekele Wolde-Kidan, (Rev) Senior Pastor of Muluwongel Church, Interview, 25 August 2010, Addis Ababa.

Conclusion

In addition to the efforts of the Bible Society, three vital measures need to be taken towards bringing Orthodox and Evangelicals together.[11] First, the painful past memories need to be dealt with and a conscious decision made to leave them behind. The scars of the painful experiences of persecution and sheep-stealing are there as constant reminders of the past. Pain caused by missionaries also need to be addressed. Although they may not have meant to cause hurt, pioneer missionaries (be they Orthodox or Protestant), and political leaders showed little respect for the culture of the indigenous people they encountered. Such painful memories are not unique to Ethiopia. But if not dealt with, the past will continue to haunt both Orthodox and Evangelical Christians, making it difficult for them to work together and trust one another. In addition to prayer for peace and prosperity in Ethiopia, Christians, who are called to be agents of reconciliation, should make conscious choices to take steps towards mutual tolerance.

In order to move forward, there is the need to let go of the past resentment and anger which has the potential to imprison people in yesterday's hurts. Instead of shifting of blame, there is the need to highlight the positive things in the political and religious history of the nation. In addition to the biblical models, studying traditional models of conflict resolution and promoting tolerance between neighbouring ethnic groups and people of different faiths will also inspire the modern generation.

Second, freedom of expression and worship must be promoted even if the doctrines and practices of each other or the new emerging bodies are unacceptable to Evangelicals or Orthodox. Using forceful measures to exterminate a given movement has no biblical justification. The truth of the matter is that it is impossible and unnecessary to toil to achieve uniformity of doctrine. Otherwise, Christianity loses its uniqueness, which consists in

---

11. Ecumenical move is not new for the Orthodox. When asked why EOC does not have its own higher theological institute like the Catholics and the Lutherans the editor replied, "… ሊጊዜው መሠረት ባትችልም እርስዎ ከመቄዲቸው አብያተ ክርስቲያናት ጋር ተባብሮ ካህናቶችን ለማስልጠን ብትምክር መልካም ይሆንላታል። ይህንን ለማለት የደፈርንው እስካሁን ልጆችን ወደ ውጭ ልከ የምታሰጥነው በ"ሁለት ባርይ" በዮች አርቶዶክሳውያን፣ በካቶሊካውያንና በፕሮቴስታንት ኮሌጆች ስለሆነ ነው። እንዲህ ከሆነ እዚሁ ካለት ጋር የማትተባበርት ምክንያት አይገባንም።" The editor gives examples of theological institutions to which EOC sent her clergy: Lutheran College in West Germany, theological colleges in Russia and Greece, Catholic colleges in Rome and Ireland. It would be best for EOC to open its own college but until then it should cooperate with the other colleges. Zelalem Biresaw, Letter, *Tinsae*, no. 27 (1972 Eth. C), 1.

allowing its adherents to ask questions, to reason out answers and grow in their walk of faith. Needless to say Evangelicals too have shown substantial intolerance not only towards the established Orthodox Church, but also to one another and the new emerging Protestant churches.

Third, theological schools and the Christian media have a vital role to play in promoting understanding and providing platforms for discussion debate. Both Orthodox and Evangelicals seem to have little knowledge of each other's tradition and tend to judge each other from afar. For instance, Evangelicals criticize the Orthodox clergy for not having knowledge of the Bible, but do not seem to realize that the Orthodox do not approach the Bible the way Evangelicals do, verse by verse or theme by theme. Rather, they memorize a whole section, usually in Ge'ez. Neither are the priests trained to support their arguments solely with their personal interpretation of the Bible as an Evangelical would do, but use traditional writings and the interpretation of church fathers as well.

Moreover, even though the legacy of EOC education does not make a distinction between preparing people for church or public service, there is a sharp distinction made between clergy and laity in the church when it comes to religious duties such as teaching and applying the faith, and hearing confession. The lay people are caused to believe that it is the priest who interprets the Bible and holy writings to them. So they do not usually take an active role in reading, interpreting and applying the Scriptures in their daily lives. However, Christian convictions generally remain in the background, informing their decisions. Most of the priests do not have a copy of the Bible for themselves.[12] Carrying the Bible around is not part of the Orthodox tradition. The Bible is to be read in the church by the clergy and not in every location by every believer as the Evangelicals do.[13]

---

12. Liqe Hiruyan, Former Head of the Northern Orthodox churches, discussion held in February 2008.

13. The devout literate adult Christians of the EOC would possess the Psalms in Ge'ez with specific readings assigned for each day of the week. The first section of the little book contains the Psalms and beside that the book has the Songs of the Prophets and Prayer of Moses, the Song of Solomon and the Praises of Mary. Those who read it kiss the book before and after they read the prayer for the day in Ge'ez as the supposed morning prayer. This takes place with mostly no or little comprehension of the meaning. Douglas O'Hanlon, *Features of the Abyssinian Church* (London: SPCK, 1946), 14.

The Orthodox seem to insist on maintaining the old tradition as it is with little critique. This perhaps is one of its major differences with Evangelical tradition. The insistence on protecting old traditions along with ancient languages is one of the marks of Orthodoxy. Fresh ways of looking at the Scriptures are feared as opening the way for alteration of ancient tradition.[14] In fact, Evangelicals are accused of following a dynamic approach to the interpretation of the Bible leading to the mushrooming of numerous factions.

On the other hand, the Orthodox criticize Evangelicals as enemies of Mary, but fail to understand that the Evangelical tradition which has no room for anything apart from the Bible is at play in their perception of Mary. The lack of emotion in the Orthodox presentation of the gospel perplexes Evangelicals who at times interpret this as failing to understand the message. Orthodox preachers do not get as animated as Evangelicals when they preach. On the other hand, Orthodox people feel uncomfortable with the outpouring of emotion at Evangelical gatherings because they are trained to restrain emotions in the church while the gospel is read. Their tradition teaches them to be still in the presence of God. In other words, the Orthodox tradition requires absolute solemnity while listening to the Scriptures read, whereas Evangelicals audibly respond to the word they hear.[15]

In matters of Scripture interpretation, the Orthodox hail the fathers. The fundamental question a devoutly Orthodox person asks towards a given interpretation of a text is, "Who is your father/teacher? Whose arguments are you building on?"[16] Whereas, Evangelicals emphasize one's own reflection on the Bible, prayer and personal relationship with Christ and feel less obligated to check themselves against the centuries-old tradition of the Fathers. An Evangelical seems to be satisfied with his/her understanding of

---

14. Cf. Evangelist Afework Tefera, who was deacon at EOC accepted Evangelical convictions. However, because of his gifts of teaching, he won wider acceptance and to preach, even at Shashemene Orthodox Church. After he preached there several times, the Spirit came upon his listeners in one occasion and they were chased from the church violently with sticks. ልዐግ (Exemplery life), *Mathetes*, no. 4 (May 2007), 2– 3. It could be argued that Afework and his listeners in the EOC were chased away because his identity as Evangelical was revealed, but similar stories are told about Orthodox preachers who had no Evangelical influence but while they preach sings and wonders manifested. They too were kicked out of the Church. እግዚአብሔር የተሃድሶ ቀን ቀጥሯል (God has appointed a day of reformation), *Gesame* 2, no. 2 (November 2000 Eth. C), 3–6.

15. Bekele Wolde Kidan, Interview, 25 August 2010.

16. Agizachew, 13 June 2011. Cf. Getatchew Haile, ደቂቀ እስጢፋኖስ, 95.

the Bible and feels free to fellowship with like-minded people, whereas the Orthodox believes in the national church, emphasizes corporate standing on the tradition of the "great cloud of witnesses" and the living ones. In other words, Evangelicals ask for personal conversion and commitment and assert their personal standing: "I, the Bible and Christ." For the Orthodox "us, the tradition and God" is very important to show togetherness – belonging to the church is understood as belonging to Christ. There seems to be little effort made to differentiate between the assertions of the Bible and traditional writings. Perhaps unconsciously, more emphasis is given to traditional writings and hagiographies of the saints than to the Bible in the EOC.[17]

As for the canon of the EOC, the "Alexandrian canon" of the Old Testament was based on the Septuagint, so is the Ethiopian except for the book of Enoch which is canonized and is retained in its entirety only by the EOC.[18] The Alexandrian canon, therefore, has books that existed in Greek but not in Hebrew. Speaking about the apocryphal books, Jerome, one of the great church fathers of the second century, remarked that the books may not be used to establish an "ecclesiastical dogma," but have ethical value and are suitable for reading in the church.[19]

These books were translated into Latin in the Vulgate and the Roman Catholic Church uses this version today. Protestants usually read only the Hebrew books, taking over the Jewish canon. However, some Protestants use the apocryphal books as "Deutero Canonical" (as second rank to the Scripture). Churches in different parts of the world – Rome, Ephesus, Antioch, Alexandria – often had slightly different canons: not all had Revelation, for instance, and some had Hermas.[20] However, it is not clear that the addition of the apocryphal books made any difference to doctrine. So the dispute about the usage of canonical books in the Ethiopian context is secondary.

---

17. O'Hanlon observes that the Ethiopian church scholars were better acquainted with books which were added to the Bible than the Bible itself. O'Hanlon, *Features of the Abyssinian Church*, 21.

18. Cf. F. F. Bruce, *The Canon of Scripture* (Downers Grove, IL: InterVarsity Press, 1988), 85.

19. Bruce, *Canon of Scripture*, 92–93.

20. Cf. Bruce, 68–97, 117ff.

The real issue, therefore, is in the circulation of massive literature which is not part of the canon of the Orthodox Church, but functions as the hidden dogma. Some of the writings promote Mariolatry by exalting the role of Mary in God's plan of salvation. However, it is doubtful that EOC followers consciously deify Mary. Rather the implications of such texts do not seem to be noticed. Clearly, there is no standard list of authorized books put forward by the Orthodox Church and no centrality in printing and distributing them. The Council of Scholars referred to some books as deviations from Orthodoxy when confronted about their apparent contradiction to each other and to the Bible.[21] Therefore, there is evidence of inconsistency in the traditions which constitute either deliberate additions or scribal errors in the copying. When inconsistencies are pointed out, there seems to be little appreciation on the part of the church.[22] Most importantly, the Council of Scholars is yet to sift the chaff from the wheat by going through the numerous traditions and giving due guidance to Orthodox adherents.

The perceptions of the Orthodox towards themselves are based on the primacy of Orthodox Christian tradition in the country, its connection to historic Christianity and adherence to the apostolic succession. Moreover, in the Ethiopian Orthodox tradition religious and national identities were inseparable. However, inherent belief in the superiority of Semitic languages (especially Amharic and Ge'ez) was evident in the way the church responded to the use of other national languages. The perceptions of Evangelicals towards themselves, on the other hand, are based on their personal relationship with Christ and their belief in the sole authority of the Bible. Generally

---

21. In their reply to Getachew's critique towards contrary traditions, the Scholars of the Church noted that some books have added phrases which were not part of the original writing. The EOTC Council of Scholars, እንዳስትችሁ ተጠንቀቁ፣ 26–27.

22. In response to the critique of Getachew, who pointed out multitudes of hagiographies, the Scholars of the Church asserted, "there are no erroneous books in the Church." To his specific references of perversions, including the one that asserts, "We are saved by the blood of Tekle Haymanot" the Scholars did not offer adequate explanation or open rejection of such traditions. Rather they opted to calling the writer *menafiq*, hired writer, follower of the association of incomplete books, you are of those who have no faith, member of the adulterous generation, instrumental to *menafiqan*, and so on. (መናፍቅ፣ ቅጥረኛ ጸሐፊ፣የባዶሉ መጽሐፍ ማህበር ተከታይ፣ እምነት ከሌላቸው ወገን ነህ፣ ቅጥረኛ መናፍቅ፣ የመናፍቃን መሣሪያ፣ ከሃይማኖት አመንዝራ ትውልድ አንዱ፣ ወዘተ) The EOTC Council of Scholars, እንዳስትችሁ ተጠንቀቁ፣ 10, 28–37. Needless to say Getachew's tactless approach contributed to the defensive and offensive reaction of the Scholars of the Church.

speaking also, Evangelicals consider the Orthodox tradition as an inadequate expression of Christianity. As for their sense of identity, both ethnic consciousness and a sense of unity in faith seem to have primacy over national identity in the Evangelical Christian self-consciousness.

At the heart of the Orthodox-Evangelical divide, therefore, is their sense of identity (who they think they are) and their perception of others (who they think the other party is). If we speak about authenticity strictly in terms of primacy, only the pre-Christian traditions could be taken as authentic, and even then, their form differs among different people groups. Historical primacy and having ancient tradition does not make Orthodox more authentic than the Evangelicals; nor does the dynamism in the Evangelical tradition make it more relevant to the Ethiopian Christian society.

There are conservative people on each side who have extreme views, who demonize the other and have no desire to dialogue with the other party. However, there are also people who long for peaceful dialogue and understanding based on the Bible and the indigenous tradition of the church. The community is mixed. In many cases, both Evangelicals and Orthodox are represented in one family and there is a need to live peacefully together. Despite the presence of people with a militant attitude on both sides, leaders of each group can play a vital role in promoting tolerance and understanding between the two groups by avoiding publicly scolding one another, facilitating platforms for dialogue and demonstrating genuine Christian love towards one another in every way possible. Ethiopian Christian identity, therefore, needs to incorporate diverse expressions but faith in one Lord and unity in the Spirit as attested by the Scriptures.

In view of the significant amount of misunderstanding between the two bodies, theological institutions and the Christian media also ought to play the role of promoting knowledge and understanding between them. On the part of the Evangelicals, early fathers and the saints, especially Mary should be taken seriously and they should reconcile their negative attitude towards the Orthodox Church.

A major Protestant problem is that many Protestants have no Mariology. They have been so afraid of it that they define it in negatives. Such an attitude needs to change in order to have a meaningful dialogue with the EOC. In other words, instead of dismissing EOC's Mariology as unbiblical,

Evangelicals should study the controversy over Mary among the ancient church fathers and also reflect on what EOC is trying to protect by emphasizing the role of Mary. Evangelicals should develop the doctrine of Mary just as it does with other Christian doctrines. Moreover, Evangelicals need to think more clearly about what they are actually asking of people when they offer the gospel. On the part of the Orthodox, the numerous traditions that contradict each other and most importantly the Bible, need to be engaged with sound theological arguments. Theological schools, therefore, are good venues to address such issues and open up their respective bodies.

In addition, both bodies need to encourage ecumenical projects by undertaking joint research projects, exchanging professors, respecting each other's tradition, engaging nominal Christians within their own communities and showing willingness to examine themselves instead of promoting unbiblical practices just to differ from the other. In other words, they need to promote dialogue and aim at promoting understanding, but avoid arguing with an aim of emerging as the winner. Needless to say argumentativeness drives people apart.[23] The media on the other hand would enhance understanding if it were to function more responsibly and refrain from making hasty conclusions regarding the tradition of Orthodox and Evangelicals.[24]

Finally, as an interpretative framework for my identity discussion, I wish to use Andrew Walls' insight concerning the trajectory of world Christian history, in which he discerns three significant aspects: an essential continuity in Christianity, the "Indigenizing" Principle, and the "Pilgrim" Principle.[25]

We have seen that some Orthodox and Evangelical Christians are not keen to recognize one another as authentic Christians. But the history of Christianity shows that Christian faith did not have a single centre. Even though Jerusalem was the initial centre of Christianity and the Christians there desired to lay down the norms and standards for other people, things changed following the work of the apostle Paul and the decision at the Council of Jerusalem to allow Gentiles to become Christians on their own

---

23. Solomon Tilahun, Interview, 2 September 2010.

24. Aemere Ashebir, "ሚዲያና ሕግ" (Media and the law), a paper read at a workshop prepared by the Bible Society of Ethiopia, *Ginbot* 27, (2002 Eth. C, Addis Ababa), 1–7.

25. Walls, *Missionary Movement*, 3–9.

terms and even more so after the destruction of Jerusalem. Subsequently, the centre of gravity of Christianity shifted to different places with different languages emerging as the media of its expansion; Africa is now the continent notable for having the majority of people who profess Christianity.[26]

Even though Christianity's centre has shifted from place to place and its expressions have varied greatly, there are definite signs of continuity: first, the person of Jesus Christ has ultimate significance. Second, all Christians use the same sacred writings, administer the Eucharist and use water in a special way. Third, they consider themselves "as having some community with the others, so different in time and place, and being so obviously out of sympathy with many of their principal concerns." Fourth, each Christian tradition thinks of itself as continuous with ancient Israel.[27]

Thus, despite the vast differences in their expressions of faith, both Orthodox and Evangelical traditions may be seen to belong to the one faith: Christianity. The above listed four themes unify the two groups.

The second aspect of the framework is what Walls calls the "Indigenizing Principle." This is one pole of the tension between two opposing tendencies (the other being the "Pilgrim Principle"), which have their origins in the gospel. God accepts people as they are on the basis of the work of Christ. This means that he accepts them with their group relations and also "dis-relations." There are predispositions, prejudices, suspicions and hostilities which whether justified or not mark the group the people belong to. Thus there is the need for indigenization. There is the need to understand that being in Christ does not mean that the mind of people will become a blank

---

26. The shift in the gravity of the centre of Christianity to Africa calls for action. It is time for Ethiopian Christians to share their indigenous Christian tradition with Christians elsewhere. The ancient literature retained in Ge'ez is not known as much as it should be. If Orthodox and Evangelical theologians are to work together by putting behind their differences, they will contribute greatly to the effort to bring to light ancient Christian tradition of Ethiopia. Ethiopian Christians should join hands with their brothers and sisters in the continent to rise up to the challenge of shaping Christian thinking in this age. The Ethiopian church, as one of the oldest churches in Africa, has so much to offer, especially because Christianity in Ethiopia survived inside and outside aggression. Despite the scarcity of the Bible, inadequately trained clergy, the rampancy of illiteracy and poverty, and having foreign men as its head, the Ethiopian church maintained vibrancy. Such facts and the presence of unique tradition which is not found anywhere else but in Ethiopia, has the potential to impact Christians elsewhere whose faith is being eroded by secularism and materialism.

27. Walls, *Missionary Movement*, 6–7.

table. They will continue to be influenced by their culture, history and past experiences. In other words, Christ makes himself at home in any particular society and culture. "No group of Christians has therefore any right to impose in the name of Christ upon another group of Christians a set of assumptions about life determined by another time and place."[28]

The "Indigenizing Principle" cautions the Orthodox and Evangelicals against attempting to form the one after the likeness of the other. In other words, they are not to impose their assumptions upon the other body and accuse them of being "unauthentic" when the other party refuses or is unable to comply. For example, the Orthodox tradition accepts the apocryphal books and the veneration of the saints but the Evangelical tradition has no room for them. The "Indigenizing Principle" calls for allowing each party to think through its tradition and not uphold abiding by it or discarding it as *the* sign of devotion to Christ. Walls observes that the Jerusalem church might not have realized that the future of the proclamation of the messiah lay "with people who were uncircumcised, defective in their knowledge of Law and the Prophets, still confused by hangovers from paganism, and able to eat pork without turning a hair. . ."[29] But that is exactly what happened and the gospel has come to this age in the hands of imperfect media. It is God who is at work in the good and bad experiences of the Orthodox and Evangelicals to carry out his will and there is no one biblical culture. All expressions of Christianity have defects because they are conditioned by the culture and experiences of the one who proclaims it. However, in the expression of faith which appears to be unbearable for the one, the other feels at home. Thus the "Indigenizing Principle" makes the faith a place to feel at home. This is exactly what many Orthodox say when they are uprooted from their church and placed in Evangelical churches; they do not feel at home.

However, Christianity is not only about having a faith where people feel at home. The "Pilgrim Principle" asserts that God accepts people "in order to transform them into what he wants them to be." This appears to oppose the "Indigenizing Principle." In other words, the "Pilgrim Principle" puts the Christian out of step with his/her society, "not from the adoption of

---

28. Walls, 8.
29. Walls, 8.

a new culture, but from the transformation of the mind towards that of Christ."[30] The Christian is given an "adoptive past" and "is linked to the people of God in all generations;" the race of the faithful from Abraham. Thus all Christians have this common history which they are given; they are adopted into Israel by faith and this "becomes a 'universalizing' factor bringing Christians of all cultures and ages through a common inheritance, lest any of us make the Christian faith such a place to feel at home that no one else can live there; and bringing into everyone's society some sort of outside reference."[31]

The "Pilgrim Principle" challenges the Orthodox and Evangelicals to look at each other from a different angle, as having the same "adoptive past." They belong together. So it is in their best interest (as having a common inheritance), to stop working against each other, but to support and learn from one another by paying attention to what each group brings to the "common table" in Christ for the sake of the maturity of believers and the expansion of his kingdom. Moreover, in spite of belonging to different traditions, Christians are to recognize one another as redeemed by One Lord and partaking from the same Spirit.

It seems to me that greater responsibility falls on the shoulders of Evangelicals to enhance the possibility of coming to a common understanding with the Orthodox. The two vital things Evangelicals are to do towards such a goal are: to develop a positive Mariology and to stop encouraging people to leave the Orthodox Church.

If providing a platform for dialogue, which was part of the Ethiopian Orthodox Church's tradition, were to be practised and if Orthodox and Evangelicals look at each other as belonging to the one faith and not as rivals, Ethiopian Christianity will thrive with its various expressions.

---

30. Walls, 8.
31. Walls, 9.

APPENDIX

Early Attempts at Ecumenism

As the number of Christians with evangelical convictions grew, their life was made more and more difficult by a number of groups one of which was the priests of the EOC in collaboration with government authorities. The evangelicals were either expelled from the EOC or isolated from their communities.[1] Although justice was served at times as illustrated in the dismissal of a case against Protestants, the number of such just rulings was very small and the persecutors were not punished in any way.[2] It was not only the EOC which was opposed to the evangelicals, but also *qalichas* (mediums of traditional religion) incited their people against the evangelicals. Consequently many evangelicals were severely persecuted and some even killed, because of their convictions. During the conquest of Ethiopia by Italy, the fascist regime also persecuted the evangelicals, arrested their leaders and confiscated their properties.

In addition to such external factors, internal needs created a desire for unity among the evangelicals. With the tremendous numerical growth of believers, ecclesiastical, ethical and organizational issues emerged which needed to be addressed.[3] Moreover, the believers needed legal advice as to how to deal with government authorities. These reasons caused the believers to come together. The formal annual meeting had its origin in the informal gathering for consultation and co-operation between missionaries from different traditions and Ethiopian evangelicals in Addis Ababa. Initially the

---

1. Dawit Garoma, "Evangelical Movements in Ethiopia" (MTh thesis, Ethiopian Graduate School of Theology, Addis Ababa, 2007), 55.

2. Engelsviken, "Pentecostal Revival," 161.

3. Dawit Garoma, "Evangelical Movements," 52 ff.

meeting was held every three months and then every six months and later on annually including delegates from other parts of Ethiopia.

After the eviction of Italy the informal meetings became more formal and regular. The denominational background represented by the missionaries did not create a barrier between the Ethiopian Christians. Thus, Christians from Presbyterian, Lutheran and Baptist backgrounds prayed together, mutually encouraged one another and assisted their brothers who came from the countryside for advice. From the consultation a strong desire to unite and form the Ethiopian Evangelical Church emerged thereby raising the need for extending the gathering to include evangelicals from the countryside too.[4]

Consequently, the first formal Conference of Ethiopian Evangelical churches (CEEC) was held in December 1944 in Naqamte, Western Ethiopia in which ten delegates from Addis Ababa and different parts of Wollega were present. Interestingly the conference was an Ethiopian initiative and missionaries were not invited. The first two conferences were attended by delegates from Wollega and Addis Ababa, but the third, which was held in Addis Ababa, was attended by delegates from the SIM-initiated churches of Kembatta and Hadiya in southern Ethiopia, and Society of the Followers of the Apostles which was affiliated with Bible Churchmen's Missionary Society (BCMS). The BCMS had a similar vision to that of the CMS, to see reform in the EOC. "The presence of the Society of the Followers of the Apostles in the Conference is of interest. It shows that at this stage there were people within the CEEC who were open to shape the Evangelical church as a reformed version of the EOC."[5] Interestingly, those attending desired to follow the traditions and practices of the EOC and not that of the missionaries. In addition to the BCMS influence, there were former prominent EOC clergy in the conference such as Qes Badima Yalew who valued the practices of EOC deeply, and wanted only to change unbiblical practices and retain the rest.[6]

---

4. Launhardt, *Evangelicals in Addis Ababa*, 105–107.

5. Launhardt, 108.

6. Launhardt gives two examples of EOC practices which were taken up by the Evangelical Church and a third one which was considered. The first one has to do with baptism. They agreed to baptize whoever comes, and second to administer the Holy Communion early in the morning with the communicants fasting and no observers present. The third EOC practise had to do with ordination. The attendees contemplated on the need

The representation from the SIM-founded churches[7] eventually faded. The CEEC selected the Addis Ababa Evangelical church to represent it before the government and offer advice on legal matters for people from the countryside. The congregations affiliated with Lutherans, Presbyterians and the delegates from BCMS realized the difficulty involved in keeping them together in the absence of a common confessional book and sought to have one. Unfortunately, the CEEC did not achieve the desired goal of bringing the Evangelical Christians together under one Evangelical church and came to an end with the last conference in 1963.

Among the factors leading to the failure of the CEEC to achieve the desired unity is the return of the missionaries after the expulsion of Italy.[8] In the absence of the missionaries the Ethiopians did not have problems with sharing ministers and fellowshipping with one another. The return of the missionaries created denominational consciousness. The coming of Lutheran World Federation is also blamed for the failure of the desired unity, because its initiative naturally led the Lutherans to focus on uniting among themselves.[9] Moreover, the new Imperial decree which indicated areas as open or closed[10] for mission work opened the door for the coming of more

---

for introducing the office of Bishop in order to ordain pastors. Launhardt, *Evangelicals in Addis Ababa*, 108–109.

7. The leaders of the SIM-planted churches in Kembatta were represented in the CEEC five times. They had a strong desire to attend the meetings and unite with the other evangelical congregations but there was SIM's policy that was said to be against their participation. There also was the issue of baptism and alcoholic beverages on which SIM and the other mission organizations held different opinions. But the good relationship between the SIM planted congregations and the Addis Ababa Evangelical Church was demonstrated in practical ways. When the Kembatta church was at the verge of splitting it was the Addis Ababa Evangelical Church leaders who were called in to look into the matter and mediate. The peace was short lived, however, and the splinters decided to join the Lutherans in 1951 and this must have complicated the matter further. There also was a history of competition between SIM and NLM which is described as "the Scramble for Southern Ethiopia" over "boundaries" and evangelists. The fact that NLM paid salary for evangelists from its mission funds attracted evangelists from the SIM side to join the NLM. Grenstedt, *Ambaricho and Shonkolla*, 69, 91, 101–105, 86–88; Launhardt, *Evangelicals in Addis Ababa*, 105ff.

8. The return of the missionaries served for the better as well because the clinics and schools they opened demonstrated to the public that "activities of Evangelicals were permitted in the country." Launhardt, *Evangelicals in Addis Ababa*, 118.

9. Launhardt, 116.

10. Even in areas which were marked as "closed" apart from philanthropic work, missionaries used their relief and development work to preach the gospel. The Mennonites, for example did a lot of evangelism under the umbrella of their educational centres and the

mission organizations, furthering the consciousness of doctrinal differences among the Ethiopians.[11]

At the dawn of the Derg regime, the evangelical church leaders came together to discuss the implications of socialism in February 1975 and discussed the possibility of creating unity. Accordingly in October 1976 the Council for Cooperation of Churches in Ethiopia (CCCE) was established in order to better serve the society and counter the growing influence of atheism in the country and "stave off a possible related attack from the new state." Because of the relentless effort of Qes Gudina Tumsa, the chairman of the EECMY, both EOC and the Catholic Church joined the council. The founding members were EOC, Ethiopian Catholic Church, Kale Heywet Church, Ethiopian Evangelical Church Mekane Yesus, Mulu Wongel, Yehiwot *Birhan*, Berhane Wongel Baptist, Meserete Kristos, and Ethiopian Genet church. The Council uniquely brought together the three major Christian organizations in Ethiopia: EOC, Catholic Church and Evangelical churches. Qes Gudina Tumsa was elected as the chairman. Various seminars and interactive discussions were held by the Council to educate church leaders about the implications of Socialism. The leaders of the church also consulted as to how to respond to the pressures from the new state. Qes Gudina played an active role in exhorting the leaders to maintain a distance in order to be able to criticize those in power and not to be ignorantof the Marxist ideology. He expressed his convictions that the unambiguous principle for the church was formed by the Scriptures and not Socialist ideology.[12] There is no doubt that such a forum was not pleasing to the leaders of the new regime.

Unfortunately, both the EOC and the Catholic Church withdrew from membership without announcing their intent, though there was a rumour that the EOC was pressured by the Derg to do so. The other members could not see the need to keep the Council running in the absence of EOC and the Catholic Church; hence, they decided to blend it with the Council for Evangelical Christians in Ethiopia (CECE) which was born out

---

hospital in Nazareth town. The Emperor Haile Sellassie was eager to give permission for mission organizations even in "closed" areas because he wanted them to expand education and health services.

11. Launhardt, *Evangelicals in Addis Ababa*, 116.
12. Eshete, *Evangelical Movement*, 226–227.

of the pastors' conference in 1976 in the Nazareth Bible Academy of the Mennonite mission. The CECE continued to organize pastors' conferences for delegates of Evangelical churches from all over the country.[13] Eshete notes, "The Pastors' Conference was one of the most important avenues that helped leaders of the various denominations develop strong ecumenical ties throughout the period of the revolution and afterward."[14]

The conference also laid the cornerstone for the establishment of the Evangelical churches Fellowship of Ethiopia in 1976 with nine churches as founding members.[15] But with the continual harassment from the government and the arrest of many leaders, including Qes Gudina, it became very difficult to have the conference and corporate efforts to challenge the government's actions became impossible. Each denomination then tried to look for ways of coping with the unpredictable moves of the new regime.[16]

The leaders of the church tried to maintain unity even while in prison. Upon the fall of the Derg efforts to register and strengthen the fellowship continued and in June 1999 the ECFE was officially recognized by the Ministry of Justice. In the same year it established its head office in Addis Ababa and began its work officially. Currently it has thirty-one denominations with forty-five thousand local churches and more than fifteen million believers. It also has sixty-one para-church organizations under its umbrella. By this profile ECFE represents 99.6 percent of Evangelicals in Ethiopia.[17] Currently 18 percent of the total population is Evangelical, but the strength of the ECFE to influence the government is still overshadowed by the EOC.

---

13. Eshete, 225ff.
14. Eshete, 229.
15. Evangelical Churches Fellowship of Ethiopia, n.d, 11.
16. Eshete, *Evangelical Movement*, 229.
17. The Evangelical Churches Fellowship of Ethiopia (ECFE), n.d., 11–12.

Glossary

Abba/Aba: father, a title given for a bishop in the Ethiopian Orthodox Church

Abesha/Habesha: synonymous to Ethiopian; especially among Orthodox adherents

Abew: fathers (plural form of Aba meaning "father' in Ge'ez)

Abun: title given for the head/patriarch in the Ethiopian Orthodox Church

ahzab: literally nations; the Amharic Bible uses it to translate both nations and gentiles

ager/hager: country

alem: the world

Aleqa: head; a title given to graduates of Qene School, the highest traditional school of the Orthodox Church

amagn: believer. Plural form: *Amagnoch*

amalaj: intercessor

Amlak: God (Ruler, governor)

Andemta: the authoritative commentary of the Ethiopian Orthodox Church

Ato: Mr

awaqi: literally knowledgable; also used in reference to diviners (mediums of the super-natural, seer)

Bete-Israel: house of Israel (the Jewish community in Ethiopia)

Bete Kristian: literally house of Christians; church

beza: redeemer

bezawit: redeemer (feminine)

chelle: beads (also used in reference to beads dedicated to ancestral spirit)

Dawit: the Psalter in Ge'ez

debtera: literally man of books; used in reference to graduates of the highest traditional schools of the Orthodox Church

Derg: the communist regime in Ethiopia 1974 – 1991

diaqon: deacon

dirsan: deeds of angels

Echege: a title of an Ethiopian monk next in rank to the Egyptian patriarch

Edget-Behibret: development through cooperation (literacy campaign of the Derg)

Efeson: Ephesus

Eme: mother of (adjective)

Fandano: the traditional religion of Kembatta and Hadiya people

Felasha/Bete Israel: Ethiopian Jews

feraj: judge

fithat: absolution over the body of the dead

gabar: peasant landholder

Galla: formerly used in reference to Oromo people group; also used to refer to pagans as opposed to Orthodox adherents

gedil: hagiography of saints

Ge'ez: Ethiopic (ancient language which is used as sacred in the Orthodox Church)

Geta: Lord. *Begeta* (adj.): in the Lord

getan meqebel: receiving the Lord (the usual rendering of conversion to Evangelical Christianity)

gubae: assembly

haymanot: faith, religion

haymanote-abew: faith/religion of the fathers

kehadi: apostate

Kelqedon: Chalcedon

Kibre-Negest: literally, Glory of Kings (known for its Solomonic story)

kidus: holy. *kidusan*: (plural form)

Kristian: Christian.

lewut: change.

lij: minor, son; also given as a title for children of the royal family

Magano: God in Kambatisa (Kambata language)

mahber (noun): association. *Mahbere* (adj): association of

Mariam: Mary

mateb: baptismal chord which Orthodox adherents wear on their throat

Medhane-Alem: Saviour of the world

memhir: teacher/instructor

menafiq (noun): doubter, uncertain, someone who questions the faith; *nufaqe* (adj)

Niqiya: Nicaea

mete: foreign, non-indigenous. *metewoch* (plural)

mistir: mystery

Pente: used in reference to Protestants; believed to have originated from the term Pentecostal

qalicha: medium of spirits, diviner

qene: poem; lessons given in the highest of the traditional schools in the Orthodox Church

qes: priest

qesete: he stole (took away). *qesati*: thief (noun). *qeseta*: can mean perversion (adj)

semay: heaven

sigdet: prostration, worship

Tabot: Ark of the Covenant

tamir: miracle

tehadiso: renewal/reformation

tewahdo/tewahido: union

tezkar: memorial rite for the deceased

Tosa: God (in Wolaitta language)

tsebel: consecrated water used for healing and exorcism

tselot bet: house of prayer

tsere Mariam: enemy of Mary

W/ro (Woizero): Mrs

wudassie: adoration.

wuqabi: ancestral spirit

Yasus-Manna: men of Jesus; a title used for early Evangelical Christians in the South

Yesemay Birhan: heavenly light

Bibliography

The University of Birmingham Special Collections
Personal Documents
Gobat, Samuel, A Short Biography of the Abyssinian Hadera, University of Birmingham Special Collections, CMS/B/OMS/C M 028/34B.

Journal of Gobat and Kugler, 20 August 1827, UB SC, CMS/ B/ OMS/ C M O73/13.

Gobat, Samuel, General Remarks on Abyssinia, UB SC, CMS/B/OMS/C M/028/114.

Journal of Rev Samuel Gobat from 25 February 1830 – 16 February 1833, UB SC, CMS/B/OMS/C M/O28/113.

Part of Rev C. Kugler's Journal, 25 February to 24 April 1830, UB SC, CMS/ B/ OMS/ C M O46/24.

Journal of Isenberg, C. W., UB SC, 21 May 1843, Adoa, CMS/B/OMS/C A5 013/21.

Correspondence
Kugler and Gobat to the Secretary of CMS, 26 January 1827, Cairo, UB SC, CMS/ B/ OMS/ C M O28/3.

Gobat to Jowett, 4 September 1827, UB SC, CMS/ B/ OMS/ C M O73/13.

Kugler to Jowett, 1 October 1827, UB SC, CMS/ B/ OMS/ C M O73/13.

Kugler to Rev Mr Bratt, Alexandria, 8 October 1827, UB SC, CMS/B/OMS/ C M O46.

Kugler to Jowett, 15 November 1827, UB SC, CMS/ B/ OMS/ C M O73/13.

Kugler to Jowett, 2 November 1827, UB SC, CMS/ B/ OMS/ C M O73/13.

Jowett to Kugler and Gobat, 11 January 1828, UB SC, CMS/ B/ OMS/ C M O73/16.

Gobat to Jowett, 14 February 1828, UB SC, CMS/ B/ OMS/ C M O73/17.

Kugler to Jowett, 14 February 1828, UB SC, CMS/ B/ OMS/ C M O73/17.

Gobat to Schlienz, 12 March 1828, Alexandria, UB SC, CMS/ B/ OMS/ C M O73/18.

Kugler to Rev E. Bickersteth, 12 April 1828, UB SC, CMS/B/OMS/ C M O46.

Gobat to Jowett, March 1828, UB SC, CMS/ B/ OMS/ C M O73/18.

Kugler to the CMS Committee, 25 July 1828, Islington, UB SC, CMS/ B/ OMS/ C M O46/10.

Kugler and Gobat to D. Coates, 21 May 1829, Cairo, UB SC, CMS/B/OMS/C M/O28/7.

Gobat to Schlienz, 17 October 1829, UB SC, CMS/ B/ OMS/ C M O73/38.

Kugler to Rev C. F. Schlienz in Malta, 6 January 1830, Massowa, UB SC, CMS/ B/ OMS/ C M O73/43.

Gobat and Kugler to D. Coates, Adigrate, 19 February 1830, UB SC, CMS/B/OMS/ C M/ O28/8.

Kugler to D. Coates, Adigrate, 19 February 1830, UB SC, CMS/ B/ OMS/ C M O28/8.

Gobat to his sisters, Gondar, 24 June 1830, UB SC, CMS/B/OMS/ C M/ O28/9.

Kugler to D. Coates, 6 August 1830, Quila, UB SC, CMS/B/OMS/ C M/ O46/22.

Jowett to Messrs Korck, Jetter & Hildner, Malta, 10 August 1830, UB SC, CMS/ B/ OMS/ C M O73/48.

Wolda Girgis to the Christian Society which is in England, 1 October 1830, UB SC, CMS/B/OMS/ C M/O46/23B.

Kugler to D. Coates, 2 October 1830, Quila, UB SC, CMS/B/OMS/ C M/ O46/23A.

Gobat to his parents, Behate, 25 February 1831, UB SC, CMS/B/OMS/C M/ O28/13.

Extract of a letter from Mr Gobat to Miss Hebler, 25 February 1831, UB SC, CMS/B/OMS/ C M/O28/12.

Gobat to his parents, Adigrate, 26 February 1832, UB SC, CMS/B/OMS/ C M/ O28/14A.

Gobat to the Rev E. Bickersteth, Adigrate, 27 February 1832, UB SC, CMS/B/OMS/ C M O73/60.

Extract of a letter from Isenberg to Rev Samuel Gobat, 28 September 1837, UB, SC, CMS/B/OMS/C M/O28/31B.

Gobat and Kugler to D. Coates, UB SC, CMS/ B/ OMS/ C M O28/7.

UB SC, CMS/B/OMS/CM E2/66.

UB SC, CMS/B/OMS/CM E2/67.

Official Letters and Personal Correspondence
Official Letters
Aba Sereqe *Birhan*, Head of Sunday School Department to Mahbere Kidusan: Ref. no. 44/70/2002, Date: 6/2/2002 Eth. C.
Ethiopian Orthodox Tewahedo church, Patriarchate Head Office, Ref no. 354/8717/91, Date: 28/1/91 Eth. C.
Evangelical Churches Fellowship Ethiopia to Inter Religious Council: ኢወአክኅ/554/2003, Date: 4 Tir 2003 Eth. C.
Office of the Patriarch to Mahbere Kidusan ል/ጽ/ 594/2002, Dated 16/11/2002 Eth. C.
Office of the Prime Minister, 14 *Ginbot* 1984 Eth. C, no. ጀ10/55.
Paul Balisky to the Editor of *Hamer* Magazine: "አንጻራዊ መልዕክት ለማኅበረ ቅዱሳን" (Message to Mahbere Kidusan), 10 March 2001.
Paul Balisky, Memo to Dr Tesfaye Yacob: "Article in *Hamer* Publication." 14 February 2001.

Personal Correspondence
Daniel Seife-Michael to Seblewengel Daniel, 10 April 2010.
Daniel Seife-Michael to Seblewengel Daniel, 10 January 2011.
Daniel Seife-Michael to Seblewengel Daniel, 3 March 2011.
Daniel Seife-Michael to Seblewengel Daniel, 29 April 2011.
Staffan Grenstedt to Seblewengel Daniel, 13 and 16 May 2011.
Tamiru Abamo to Seblewengel Daniel, 23 Nehasse 1997 Eth. C.
Zerihun Degu to Seblewengel Daniel, 12 May 2011.

Oral Sources
EOC Clergy/Members
Agizachew Tefera (Deacon), Editor-in-Chief of *Chora*, the Publication of Mahbere Bekur, Date of Interview: 13 June 2011, Addis Ababa.
Asrat Kebede, Editor-in-Chief of Sem'ea Tsidq, one of the publications of Mahbere Kidusan, Date of Interview: 30 December 2010, Addis Ababa.
Daniel Seife-Michael, (Arch Deacon), Teacher at Holy Trinity Theological College, Head Librarian at the Office of the Patriarch, Dates of Interview: 8 September 2010; 30 December 2010, Addis Ababa.
Fire Hiwot, Trader of banners, posters and car decorations, Date of Interview: January 2011, Addis Ababa.
Informant D, Interview, 18 August 2010, Addis Ababa.
Informant G, Interview, February 2011, Addis Ababa.
Informant T, Interview, 25 February 2011, Addis Ababa.

Liqe Hiruyan, Former Head of the Northern Orthodox churches, February 2008, Addis Ababa.

Mekonnen Workneh (Deacon), Teacher at Holy Trinity Theological College, Addis Ababa, Date of Interview: 14 November 2010, Addis Ababa.

Reformed Orthodox

Mezgebu Tsemru (Rev), Pastor of Amanuel United Church (the first organized separatist group from the EOC), Addis Ababa Dates of Interview: 23 August 2010; 25 February 2011, Addis Ababa.

Solomon Abebe, (Rev) Pastor of YeEgziabher Birhan church, Assela. Currently student at Ethiopian Graduate School of Theology, Addis Ababa, Dates of Interview: 24 August 2010; 25 February 2011, Addis Ababa.

Evangelicals

Afework Hailu, Faculty member of the Ethiopian Graduate School of Theology, Addis Ababa. Currently doing his PhD at SOAS, London. Membership: Mulu Wongel Church. Background: Former leader of Bitaniya Menfesawi Mahber (EOC Reformed group). Date of Interview: 20 April 2011.

Alemu Shetta (Rev), Secretary of the Evangelical churches Fellowship of Ethiopia. Membership: EECMY. Date of Interview: 4 February 2011, Addis Ababa.

Bekele Wolde-Kidan (Rev) Pastor of Muluwongel church, Ketena Hulet local church. Background: EOC. Date of Interview: 25 August 2010, Addis Ababa.

Bezabeh Workneh, former board chairman of Mulu Wongel Bible College. Membership: Mulu Wongel Church. Background: EOC, Date of Interview: 25 February 2011.

Bizuayehu Abera, student of Evangelical Theological College. Membership: Gospel Light church. Background: EOC. Date of Interview: 14 February 2011, Addis Ababa.

Desta Birhanu, Secretary of Gamo Kale Heywet Church, Southern Ethiopia. Date of Interview via telephone: 12 April 2011.

Engidash Markos, Secretary of the Evangelical Theological College Publishing Department. Membership: Genet Church. Date of Interview: 18 February 2011, Addis Ababa.

Ermias Mamo, Dean of Students at Ethiopian Graduate School of Theology, Addis Ababa. Membership: Kale Heywet Church. Date of Interview: 1 October 2010, Addis Ababa.

Fitha Amlak Eniyew, Membership: Addis Kidan Baptist Church. Background: Former teacher at the EOC Traditional School (Higher School). Date of Discussion: 11 April 2011, Addis Ababa.

Getachew Belete, Former Head of the Publishing Department of Ethiopian Kale Heywet Church, Currently Manager of Aster Nega Publishing Company, Chairman of elders at Kolfe Kale Heywet Church. Background: EOC. Date of Interview: 18 August 2010, Addis Ababa.

Hailu Letta, General Manager of Agar Microfinance Sc. Co., elder of Ketta Genet Church, Addis Ababa. Background: EOC. Date of Interview: 18 February 2011, Addis Ababa.

Informant F, Evangelical minister. Date of Interview: 16 August 2011, Addis Ababa.

Kedamo Mechato (Evangelist), retired evangelist of the Ethiopian Kale Heywet Church. Converted to Christianity from traditional religion in the South Ethiopia. Date of Interview: 18 January, 2011.

Nigusse Bulcha, Director of Scripture Union, Addis Ababa. Membership: Muluwongel church (Pentecostal). Converted from EOC as a young man. Date of Interview: 30 September 2010, Addis Ababa.

Solomon Tilahun, student of Peace and Reconciliation Department at Mennonite Seminary, USA. Membership: Meserete Kristos Church. Background: EOC. Date of Interview: 2 September 2010, Addis Ababa.

Tesfahun Hatia (Rev), Dean of Students at Pentecostal Theological College, Addis Ababa. Membership: Yehiwot Birhan Church (Pentecostal church). Date of Interview: 5 October 2010, Addis Ababa.

Yared Eshetu (Rev), Pastor and General Secretary of Faith Bible International church, Addis Ababa. Parents converted to Protestantism from EOC when he was a little boy. Date of Interview: 19 January 2011.

Others

Yilma Getahun, Secretary of the Bible Society of Ethiopia. Dates of Interviews: 5 October 2010 and 19 April 2011, Addis Ababa.

Bitew Kassa, Advisor of Religion and Faith Affairs Directorate: Dates of Interviews: 24 February 2011 and 18 April 2011, Addis Ababa.

Zerihun Degu, General Secretary, Inter-Religious Council of Ethiopia. Date via email: 12 May 2011.

Audios and Videos

Begashaw Desalegn, ማጎርሚሳቢብ (Magor-Missabib) (Audiovisual sermon), Addis Ababa, Antsokiya Spiritual Songs House, n.d.

Dawit Molalegn, ቀሉ ስለመጣ አይቅለልባችሁ፣ (Do not take [the humble gospel] for granted), (Audiovisual sermon), n.d.

Dereje Kebede, የአድናቆት ቀን ለእግዚአብሔር, (A day of appreciating God) Vol. 9, Audio Songs, 2009.

Engidawork Bekele, ደጅ ጠናሁ (I waited patiently), Vol. 9, (Audiovisual songs), Addis Ababa, Agape Spiritual Songs Shop, n.d.

Ephrem Ketema, Tekel (Audiovisual presentation), Addis Ababa, n.d.

Mihretab Assefa፣ ፕሮቴስታንታዊ ጂሃድ በተዋህዶ ላይ ሲፋፋም (Protestant jihad against Tewahdo), (Audiovisual presentation), Addis Ababa, Ab Spiritual Songs House, n.d.

Tariku Abera, ክብር ለሚገባው ክብርን ስጡ (Give glory to whom it is due) (Audiovisual presentation), Addis Ababa, Antsokiya Spiritual Songs House, n.d.

Teshome Shiferaw, ተኩላው ማነው? (Who is the wolf?), (Audiovisual presentation), Addis Ababa, Yemelekot Dimts Agelgelot, 2003 Eth. C.

Zemedkun Bekele, Armageddon, Vol. 1, (Audio presentation), Addis Ababa, Gelgela Spiritual Songs House, n.d.

Zerfe Kebede, ሩሃማ (Ruhama), (Audiovisual songs), Addis Ababa, Veronica Spiritual Songs Shop, n.d.

Taxi Slogans

"የጌታዬ እናት ወደ እኔ ትመጣ ዘንድ እንዴት ይሆንልኛል? (But why am I so favoured, that the mother of my Lord should come to me?) Posted on Taxi, 16 February 2011.

"ትውልድ ሁሉ ብፅዕት ይሉኛል." (Generations will call me blessed). Posted on Taxi, 16 February 2011.

"በል አላህ አንድ ነው፣ አይወልድም አይወለድም." (Say it, Allah is one God, he does not give birth, neither is he born). Posted on Taxi, May 2010.

ቅድስት ሆይ አማልጅኝ (Interceed on my behalf, O saint [it calls upon a feminine saint, referring to St Mary]).

"ባጠባሽው ጡትሽ በዚያ በወተቱ፣ ባፈሰስሽው እንባ በግብጽ በስደቱ፣ ከልጅሽ አማልጂኝ የጌታዬ እናቱ." (For you are the one who breastfed him and tearfully fled to Egypt to keep him safe, intercede on my behalf with your Son O mother of my Lord.) Posted on Taxi, 15 December 2010.

"ዓለም ባንቺ ዳነ በልጅሽም ሰላም ሆነ." (The world is saved by you and in your Son it found peace). Posted on Taxi, 19 December 2010.

"እናትና ልጅን የያዘ ምን ይሆናል." (If one has the Mother and the Son, what can he possibly lack?) Posted on Taxi, 19 August 2010.

"ወደድክም ጠላህም እምቤታችን አማላጅ ናት." (Whether you like it or not our Lady is an intercessor). Posted on a Taxi, 3 June 2010.

"ያለ ማርያም ክርስትና የለም." (There is no Christianity apart from Mary). Posted on Taxi, 18 July 2010.

"ያለ ወላዲተ አምላክ አማላጅነት ዓለም አይድንም." (Without the intercession of the Mother of God the world will not be saved). Posted on Taxi, 14 May 2010.

"ድንግል ፈጣሪዋን ወለደችው እርሱም እርሷን ፈጠራት." (The Virgin gave birth to her creator, and he created her.) Posted on Taxi, 7 May 2010.

Electronic Sources

Church Missionary Society: Section III, Part 19, www.ampltd.co.uk/digital_guides/cms_section/, 30 August 2011.

Kevin Knight (ed.). "Robber Council of Ephesus." http://www.newadvent.org, 2 August 2011.

The Battle of Adwa, www.algora.org Accessed 22 April 2010.

Berihun Tefera, ከ400 የሚበልጡ የጉምዝ ብሔረሰብ አባላት ተጠመቁ (More than 400 people from Gumuz ethnic group were baptized), http://www.eotc-mkidusan.org, 25 February 2011.

Dereje Te'ezazu, ከሦስት ሺ በላይ ኢ-አማንያን ዳግመኛ ተወለዱ. (More than three thousand unbelievers were born again), http://www.eotc-mkidusan.org, 1 May 2011.

Fetlework Desta. "ከተለያዩ ሀገረ ስብከቶች የተውጣጡ ሠልጣኞች ተመረቁ." (Trainees from several dioceses graduated), http://www.eotc-mkidusan.org, 7 March 2011.

T/Selassie Tsega Kiros. "አብነት ትምህርት ቤቱ "በእንተ ስማ ለማርያም." ይዘከራል." (The traditional school of the church supported), http://www.eotc-mkidusan.org, 5 May 2011.

ለወጥ(sic) "ለቤተክርስቲያን." (Change for church) http://www.eotc-mkidusan.org, 2 May 2011.

Abayneh Kassa. "ድንበራችንን እንዳያፈርሱብን እንጠንቀቅ." (The need to protect our distinguishing mark), http://www.eotc-mkidusan.org, 5 May 2011.

T/ Selassie Tsega Kiros. "የደቡብ ክልል ርዕሰ መስተዳድር ከምዕመናን ጋር ተወያዩ." (The governor of the southern regions held discussion with believers), www.eotc-mkidusan.org, 7 March 2011.

Official letters, http://www.eotcssd.org, 16 June 2011.

Paulos Fekadu, Brothers, http://www.ethiocross.com, 16 April 2011.

Protoevangelium of James, http://www.earlychurchtexts.com, 12 May 2011.

http://www.dskmariam.org, 10 May 2011.

Country Profile, http://www.bbc.com, May 2011.

Department of Arts of Africa, Oceania, and the Americas. "The Monumental Stelae of Aksum (3rd–4th century)." In *Heilbrunn Timeline of Art History*. New York: Metropolitan Museum of Art, http://www.metmuseum.org/toah/hd/aksu_2/hd_aksu_2.htm, October 2000.

www.uselectionatlas.org, 17 April 2010.

Za Michael Aragawi, http://www.dacb.org, April 2007.

ቤተ ክርስቲያን በገዛ ልጆቿ ስትፈተን 1&2 (The church tried by her own children), Hidar 2002 Eth. C, www.ethiopianorthodox.org, 6 March 2011.

Unpublished Sources

Addise Amado, *Persecution in Ethiopia*. Addis Ababa: Voice of Martyrs [VOM] Ethiopia, 2003.

Aemere Ashebir. "ሚዲያና ሕግ." (Media and the law) A paper read at a workshop prepared by the Bible Society of Ethiopia, *Ginbot* 27, 2002 Eth. C, Addis Ababa.

Alemu Himbaru, ወንጌል ነጻ ያወጣል (The gospel sets free), n.d.

Daniel Seife-Michael. "የመረጃ/የመገናኛ አውታርና ክርስቲያናዊ ሥነ ምግባራት." (Media and Christian ethics), a paper read at a workshop prepared by the Bible Society of Ethiopia, *Ginbot* 27, 2002 Eth. C, Addis Ababa, 14.

Engelsviken, Tormod. "Pentecostal Revival in Ethiopia." Unpublished Manuscript, Oslo, Norway, 1997.

Evangelical Churches Fellowship of Ethiopia (ECFE), Brochure, n.d.

Habtamu Abredew. "የክርስቲያን ሚዲያዎች ሚና ለሰላምና ለልማት." (The role of Christian media for peace and development). A paper read at a workshop prepared by the Bible Society of Ethiopia, *Ginbot* 27, 2002 Eth. C, Addis Ababa, 10.

Nigusse Bulcha. "በሥላሴ አማኞች መካከል ስለሚደረግ ትብብር." (The cooperation between Trinitarians). Paper presented at Trinitarians workshop, Mekane Yesus Seminary, Addis Ababa, 2010.

Nigusse Bulcha. "የክርስቲያን "ሚዲያ." ሜዳ በአብያተ ክርስቲያናት መካከል ባለው ግንኙነት አንጻር." (The Christian media in light of the relationship between churches). A paper read at a workshop prepared by the Bible Society of Ethiopia, *Ginbot* 27, 2002 Eth. C, Addis Ababa, 12.

"The Relief Summary of the Ethiopian Kale Heywet Church," Deputy General Secretary for Development, National Task Force, July 2011.

Tibebu Gashu. "የሚዲያ ሚና በአጠቃላይ መንፈሳዊያን ሚዲያዎች በተለይ ከእምነት ነፃነት እና እኩልነት ሕግ አንፃር." (The role of spiritual media in light of religious freedom, equality and law). A paper read at a workshop prepared by the Bible Society of Ethiopia, *Ginbot* 27, 2002 Eth. C, Addis Ababa, 8.

"የማህበረ ቅዱሳን አመሰራረት ታሪክ." (The origins of Mahbere Kidusan). Addis Ababa: Public Relations Office of Mahbere Kidusan, 2002 Eth. C.

Dissertations and Theses

Abraham Mengesha. "An Evaluation of the Position of the Ethiopian Orthodox Tewahido church on the Eternal High Priesthood of Jesus Christ." MTh diss., Ethiopian Graduate School of Theology, Addis Ababa, 2005.

Afework Hailu. "A Survey of the Ethiopian Orthodox Church Mariology: An Attempt to Understand the Origin, Development, and Teaching Regarding Mary in the EOC." MTh diss., Ethiopian Graduate School of Theology, Addis Ababa, 2002.

Daniel Teshome. "The Current Reformation Movement within the Ethiopian Orthodox Tewahedo Church (1987–2007)." MTh diss., Ethiopian Graduate School of Theology, Addis Ababa, 2007.

Dawit Garoma. "Evangelical Movements in Ethiopia." MTh diss., Ethiopian Graduate School of Theology, Addis Ababa, 2007.

Debela Birri. "History of the Evangelical Church Bethel 1919–1947." ThD thesis, Lutheran School of Theology, Chicago, 1995.

Ermias Guisha Mamo. "Knowing God in Ritual Context in Special Reference to the Hamar People of Southwest Ethiopia." PhD thesis, Fuller Theological Seminary, California, 2008.

Gerimame Yohannes. "The Problem of Proselytism from EOTC to Other Denominations." BTh thesis, Holy Trinity Theological College, Addis Ababa, 2007.

Giday Beyene. "The Impact of Protestantism on the Ethiopian Orthodox Church: Evangelization and Proselytization." BTh thesis, Holy Trinity Theological College, Addis Ababa, 1999.

Melese Atnafu. "The Conversion of Addis Ababa Population from Orthodox Tewahedo Church to Protestant Denominations." BTh thesis, Holy Trinity College, Addis Ababa, 1999.

Shenk, Calvin Earl. "The Development of the Ethiopian Orthodox Church and Its Relationship with the Ethiopian Government from 1930–1970." PhD thesis, New York University, New York, 1972.

Tamiru Zeleke. "The Mission Strategy of the Mulu Wongel Church." MTh diss., Akrofi-Christaller Institute, Akropong, Ghana, 2008.

Published Articles

Aba W/*Tinsae*. "ልሳን." (Tongues) *Hamer* 3. Miyazia, 1985 Eth. C.

Adane, Dechasa. "ስደቱ ለመልካም ሆነልን." (The persecution worked for our good). *Birhan* 29, 1989 Eth. C.

Adugna, Amann. "The Theological School at a Glance." *The Ethiopian Herald*, 26 July 1960.

Afework, Hailu. "ፕሮቴስታንቶች ለማርያም ተገቢውን ሥፍራ ሊሰጡ ይገባል." (Protestants should give Mary due place). *Gesame* 3, no. 9. Nehasse, 1997 Eth. C.

———. "ፕሮቴስታንቶች ለማርያም ተገቢውን ሥፍራ ሊሰጡ ይገባል." (Protestants should give Mary due place). *Gesame* 4, no. 1. Meskerem 1998 Eth. C.

———. "ኦርቶዶክሶች ለማርያም ተገቢውን ሥፍራ ሊሰጡ ይገባል." (Orthodox should give Mary due place). *Gesame* 4, no. 3. Tahsas, 1998 Eth. C.

Afework, Tefera. "ፊለግ." (Exemplary life). *Mathetes* 4, May 2007.

Amare, Chekol. "ምሥክርነት" (Testimony of Amare Chekol). *Gesame* 3, no. 4. Tir 1997 Eth. C.

Amelu Geta (pastor). "ከጦር ሠፈር ለወንጌል ጥሪ" (From the battlefield into ministry). *Gesame* 2, no. 10. Meskerem, 2002 Eth. C.

"Assistant Dean Counters Church's Argument." *The Ethiopian Herald*, 16 April 1971.

Begashaw Desalegn. "ድንጋይ ወርውሬው ሲገቱ በቪዲዮ ተቀርጻዋል" (Videotaped while throwing stones). *Maraki* 1, no. 3. Megabit 2003 Eth. C.

Balisky, E. Paul. "Esa Lale, a Prophet of Religious Innovation in Southern Ethiopia." Baye Yiman et al (eds.), Proceedings of the XIVth International Conference of Ethiopian Studies, 6–11 November 2000.

Belay, Woldeyes. "ሃይማኖት በኢትዮጵያ ላይ ላይን" (An overview of religion in Ethiopia). Yezareyitu Ethiopia. Tir 10, 1967 Eth. C.

Bethlehem, Abebe. "ልጅነቴን ሳላውቀው አደግሁ" (I never enjoyed my childhood). *Gesame* 2, no. 4. Megabit, 2000.

Birhanu, Gobena. "ትምህርተ ሃይማኖት." (Education of faith) *Hamer* 1. Megabit, 1986 Eth. C.

Birhanu, Wolde. "መጽሐፍ ቅዱስ ወይስ ባህል? ይታሰብበት" (Priority to the Bible or tradition?). *Kale Heywet* 25, 1994 Eth. C.

———. "መጽሐፍ ቅዱስ ወይስ ባህል? ይታሰብበት" (Which ones come first: The Bible or culture?). *Kale Heywet* 25. 1994 Eth. C.

Black, Stephanie. "'In the Power of God Christ': Greek Inscriptional Evidence for the Anti-Arian Theology of Ethiopia's First Christian King." In *Bulletin of SOAS* 71, no. 1 (2008): 93–110.

Bosworth, C. E. "Henry Salt, Consul in Egypt 1816–1827 and Pioneer Egyptologist." *Bulletin of the John Rylands Library* 57 (1974): 69–91.

Caulk, R. "Religion and the State in Nineteenth Century Ethiopia." *Journal of Ethiopian Studies* 10 (1972): 30–35.

Chapple, David. "Protestant Missionary Attitudes in Ethiopia: Gobat, Isenberg and Krapf." *Proceedings of the Third Annual Seminar of the Department of History.* Addis Ababa: Addis Ababa University, 1986.

Bibliography

Daniel, Kibret. "የኢትዮጵያ ቤተ ክርስቲያን ታሪክ የሚለውጥ ሲኖዶስ አላገኘችም" (The Church of Ethiopia has not found a synod which will change the course of history). *Enqu* 4, no. 42. Tir 2003 Eth. C.

Dawit, Bayou. "በነጻነት ዘመን ስደት" (Persecution in an age of freedom). *Gesame Special Issue*. Meskerem, 2000 Eth. C.

Dawit, W/Yohannes. "ምሥክርነት" (Testimony). *Gesame* 1, no. 9. Meskerem-Tikimpt 1995 Eth. C.

Deacon Dejene. "በፀጋው መዳን እንዴት ነው?" (What does salvation by grace mean?). *Hamer* 4. Hidar 1988 Eth. C.

Editorial. "መንፈሳዊ ኮሌጅና መንፈሳዊ ትምህርት በኢትዮጵያ" (Spiritual college and spiritual education in Ethiopia). *Addis Zemen*. 13 Miazia 1951 Eth. C.

Editorial. "ማን ማንን ይሰብካል?" (Who is fit to preach?). *Hamer* 2. Ginbot/Sene 1993 Eth. C.

Editorial. "በመንፈሳዊ ኮሌጅ የሚካሄደው ማህበር ክፍ ያለ አገልግሎት በመስጠት ላይ ይገኛል" (The association which is run by the spiritual college is offering a great service). *Ye'Ethiopia Dimts*. 27 Tahsas 1957 Eth. C.

Editorial. "በሀገር ጉዳይ ሃይማኖት አይለያየንም ሴሚናር" (Seminar on the theme: "Religion will not divide us in matters of country"). *Tinsae*, no. 11. 1970 Eth. C.

Editorial. "በኖርዌይ የተደረገው የእምነትና የሥርዓት ጉባኤ የዘር መድልዎን አወገዘ" (The faith and order assembly held in Norway condemned apartheid). *Zena Bete Kristian* 93, 5. Pagume 1977.

Editorial. "በኢትዮጵያ ስደት እንደ ሰደድ እሳት" (Persecution in Ethiopia spread like a wildfire). *Hiwot* 12. Meskerem 1986 Eth. C.

Editorial. "ነህምያና የተሃድሶ አገልግሎቱ" (Nehemiah and his ministry of reform). *Chora* 19 (n.d).

Editorial. "ንቁ፣ ቅድስት ልደታ ለማርያም መንፈሳዊ ማህበር." በሚል ስያሜ የሚንቀሳቀሰው "ማህበር." ስውር ተልዕኮ ተጋለጠ" (Beware, an association that calls itself "Qidist Ledeta Le Mariam Menfesawi Mahber" exposed). *Seme'a Tsidq* 1, no. 209, Meskerem 16–30, 2003 Eth. C.

Editorial. "አለቃ ነቅዐ ጥበብና አገልግሎታቸው" (Aleqa Neqe'a Tibeb and his ministry). *Chora* 29, n.d.

Editorial. "አለቃ ነቅዐ ጥበብና አገልግሎታቸው" (Aleqa Neqe'a Tibeb and his ministry). *Chora* 33, n.d.

Editorial. "አለቃ ነቅዐ ጥበብና አገልግሎታቸው" (Aleqa Neqe'a Tibeb and his ministry). *Chora* 39. Hamle 2002 Eth. C.

Editorial. "አቤት! . . . አቤት! የ. . . . ያለህ!" (Appeal). *Chora* 36, n.d.

Editorial. "እዝራና የተሃድሶ አገልግሎቱ" (Ezra and his ministry of reform). *Chora* 18, n.d.

Editorial. "ከተሃድሶ ዓላማ" (The purpose of reform). *Chora* 5 (n.d).

Editorial. "ክርስትና በኢትዮጵያ፣ የቤተ ክርስቲያን ፈውስ" (Christianity in Ethiopia: Restoration of the church). *Chora* 18, n.d.

Editorial. "ዘሩባቤልና የተሃድሶ አገልግሎቱ" (Zerubbabel and his ministry of reform). *Chora* 16, n.d.

Editorial. "ዘሩባቤልና የተሃድሶ አገልግሎቱ" (Zerubbabel and his ministry of reform). *Chora* 17, n.d.

Editorial. "የተበየነ ፍትሕ የተከለከለ እንዳይሆን" (The need for reinforcement of a ruling). *Seme'a Tsidq* 12, no. 99. Tir 1997 Eth. C.

Editorial. "የዘመን ምሥክር፣ ብጹዕ አቡነ ፊልጶስ ቀዳማዊ የወንጌል እስረኛ (1888–1974)" (Witness through time: His Holiness Abune Philipos, early prisoner of the gospel (1888–1974). *Chora* 39. Hamle 2002 Eth. C.

Editorial. "የዘመን ምሥክር፣ አለቃ ታዬ ገብረ ማርያም (1888–1974 sic)" (Witness through time: Aleqa Taye Gebre Mariam). *Chora* 40. Tahsas 2003 Eth. C.

Editorial. "የጀርመን ሀይማኖት ፕሮቴስታንስ" (The German religion protestants). *Hamer* 1. Tahsas/Tir, 1990 Eth. C.

Editorial. "ጭውውት" (Discussion). *Chora* 5, n.d.

Editorial. "ጭፍን የታሪክ ቅሰጣ" (Deliberate perversion of history). *Zena Bete Kristian* 96. 30 Yekatit 1978 Eth. C.

Editorial. *Hiwot* 10. 1985 Eth. C.

Editorial. *Mathetes* 10. March 2009.

Editorial. *Tinsae* 8. 1970 Eth. C.

Editorial. እያንገላለ (Sifting). *Enqu* 2, no. 19. Miyazia 2001 Eth. C.

Editorial. "ርዕሰ አንቀጽ፣ "ማንም ሰው የሚናገር ቢሆን እንደ እግዚአብሔር ቃል ይናገር" 1ኛ ጴጥ 4፥11 (If anyone speaks, they should do so as one who speaks the very word of God. 1 Peter 4:11). *Chora* 36, n.d.

Editorial. "የማህበሩ መልእክት" (Message from the association). *Hamer* 5. Tahsas/Tir 1993 Year of Merc).

Editorial. *Hamer* 1. Tahsas/Tir, 1990 Eth. C.

Editorial. "የማንወክላትን ቤተ ክርስቲያንና እምነቷን አናሰድብ፣." (Let us not cause to be defiled the church and her faith which we do not represent) *Chora* 16, n.d.

"Editor's Appeal." *Kale Heywet* 15. 1990 Eth. C.

Efrem, Beyene. "በኦርቶዶክስ ስም የሚነግዱ መናፍቃን በራሳቸው አንደበት ተጋለጡ" (*Menafiqan* exposed). *Lisane Tewahdo Ze Orthodox* 9. 1987 Eth. C.

Endale, Teshi. "ቃለ ምልልስ ከመጋቤ ሐዲስ እሸቱ ዓለማየሁ ጋር" (Interview with Eshetu Alemayehu). *Addis Guday* 5, no. 92. Sene 2003 Eth. C.

Endegena, Tadesse. "Interview." *Kale Heywet* 19. 1991 Eth. C.

Esayiyas, Wondimagegnehu. "የሀሳ እስረኛ" (Prisoner of culture). *Tinsae* 22. 1971 Eth. C.

Fantu. "የዕድ አምልኮና አሠራር" (Divination). *Hiwot* 4. Tir/Yekatit, 1986 Eth. C.

Gashu. "Looking Back: The Decayed Monarchical System." *The Ethiopian Herald*, 2 October 1974.

Getachew, Belete. "ከመኪና ጠባቂነት እስከ ጀነራል፣ ሚኒስትርና አምባሳደር ማዕረግ" (From watching cars all the way to becoming a general, minister and an ambassador), *Kale Heywet* 29. 1996 Eth. C.

Getachew, Doni. "አነጋጋሪ ቃለ ምልልስ ከሊቀ ካህናት ጌታቸው ዶኒ ጋር፤ የተደበቀ አጀንዳቸውን አላራምድም" (Controversial interview with Liqe Kahnat Getachew Doni: "I will not promote their hidden agenda"). *Maraki* 1, no. 5. Sene 2003 Eth. C.

Getachew, Doni. "ጥቁር እራሱ የሲኖዶስ አባል" (The non-monk member of the synod). *Maraki* 1, no. 3. Megabit 2003 Eth. C.

Hamer 2. Ginbot/Sene, 1998 Eth. C.

"Help Build Mekele Theological College." *The Ethiopian Herald*, 28 May 1971.

Hiwot, Zefre Kidusan. "ቅዱሳት ሥዕላት በነጻ ገበያ" (Holy pictures on sale). *Hamer* 8. Yekatit 2002 Eth. C.

Hohete Birhan. Megabit 2002 Eth. C.

Interview. "ከአለቃ መሠረት ስብሐት ለአብ ጋር በየጊዜው ተደርጎ ከነበረው ቃለ ምልልስ የተወሰደ" (Taken from interview held with Aleqa Meseret Sibhat Leab over a period of time). *Chora* 14, n.d.

Jarsa, Utta. "አሥራ አራት ቀን የከብት እበት የበላው ሰው ወንጌላዊ ሆነ" (The man who was made to feed on animal dung for fourteen days became an evangelist). *Kale Heywet* 26. 1995 Eth. C.

Jemberu, Bekele. "Letter." *Kale Heywet* 5. 1985 Eth. C.

Joseph, K. C. "Theological College of the Holy Trinity." *The Ethiopian Herald*, 5 May 1966.

Kaplan, Steven. "Ezana's Conversion Reconsidered." *Journal of Religion in Africa* 13, no. 2, (1982): 101–109.

Lesanework, Bezabeh. "የኢትዮጵያ ኦርቶዶክስ ተዋህዶ ቤተ ክርስቲያን በተቀዳሚ ማድረግ የሚገባት" (What the Ethiopian Orthodox Tewahdo Church needs to do first). *Tinsae* 30. Nehassie 1963 Eth. C.

Mamushet G/ Medhin. "ፕሮቴስታንቶች ለማርያም ክብርን አልሰጡም?" (Protestants do not honour Mary?). *Gesame* 3, no. 7. Sene 1997 Eth. C.

Mehaley. "ቤተ ክርስቲያን፣ መሪዎቿና የሕዝብ ድምጽ" (The church, its leaders and the voice of its people). *Kale Heywet* 16. 1990 Eth. C.

Mekbib Atnaw. "የጥንታዊው የሀገር ትምህርት የአማማር አቅድ" (The ancient country education). *Tinsae*. Miazia 1960 Eth. C.

Melese Weyessa. "እግዚአብሔር የተሃድሶ ቀን ቀጥሯል" (The Lord has appointed a day of reform). *Gesame* 2, no. 2. November 2000 Eth. C.

Mersha Alehegn. "አባ ኢየሱስ ሞዓ የመጀመሪያው የኢትዮጵያ ቤተ ክርስቲያን ዩኒቨርሲቲ መስራች" (Aba Yesus Moa, the founder of the first Ethiopian Church university). *Hamer* 2. Nehasse 1988 Eth. C.

Mesfin Hailu. "ሕይወትና አገልግሎት፣ በተለያየ እስራት ላሉ ጌታ ሸክም ሰጥቶኛል" (Life and ministry: The Lord has given me a burden for those who are in bondage) .*Gesame* 2, no. 12. Tir 2002 Eth. C.

Mikiyas Belay. "የክርስቲያን ሚዲያውና ችግሮቹ" (The Christian media and its problems). *Mathetes* 16. July 2010.

Mulugeta, Haile Mariam. "የዕንቁ እንግዳ" (Guest of Enqu) 4, no. 40. Sene 2003 Eth. C.

Mussie, Menberu "የመስተፋቅር ሌላው መጥፊ ገን" (The other side of magic). *Trinity* 9. 2003 Eth. C.

Nahu, Adam. "ክርስትና በኢትዮጵያ፣ የእግዚአብሔር መንግሥት ታሪክ" (Christianity in Ethiopia: The history of the kingdom of God). *Chora* 18, n.d..

Nebiye-Leul, Mengistu. "ከመልካም ሽቱ መልካም ስም ይሻላል" (A good name is more desirable than a good perfume). *Zena Bete Kristian* 37. Hidar 30 1941 Eth. C.

Negussie, Seyoum, and Yimenu Yirdaw. "New School Trains Modern Priests for Rural Areas." *The Ethiopian Herald*, 17 April 1969.

News. "በትግራይ ጠቅላይ ግዛት በ 320,000 ብር መንፈሳዊ ትምህርት ቤት ይሰራል" (The construction of spiritual school is under way in Tigray region with 320,000 Birr). *Addis Zemen* 25 Tahsas 1962 Eth. C.

News. "የመንፈሳዊ ኮሌጅ ተማሪዎች በትያትር ገቢ የድኩማንን ድርጅት ይረዳሉ" (With an income of theatre, students of the spiritual college help the organization for the disabled). *Ye'Ethiopia Dimts* 27 Tahsas, 1957 Eth. C, 5.

News. "ስለ አብያተ ክርስቲያናት አንድነት በብሮክላይን ጉባኤ ተደረገ" (A meeting held in Brooklyn about the unity of churches). Zena Bete Kristian 92. 30 Sene 1977 Eth. C.

News. "ጠንቋዮች ተጋለጡ" (Diviners exposed). *Tinsae* 15. 1971 Eth. C.

News. "የቦረዳው ድንቅ ዋሻ" (The marvellous cave of Boreda). *Hamer* 1. Tir 1985 Eth. C.

News. "የትምህርት ቤቶች ለዕረፍት መዘጋት" (Schools on a break). *Birhanena Selam* 28. 11 Hamle, 1938 Eth. C.

News. "የክርስቲያን ሚድያ ሚና ምን መሆን አለበት?" (What should be the role of Christian media?). *Gesame* 13. Meskerem 2003 Eth. C.

News. "Church Wants Voice in Student Recruitment." *The Ethiopian Herald*, 15 April 1971.

News. "Orthodox Church Conference Opens Here." *The Ethiopian Herald*, 12 May 1967.

News. "In Draft Constitution Church Deplores Some Provisions." *The Ethiopian Herald*, 18 August 1974.

News. "Missionaries Refuse to Comment on Criticism." *The Ethiopian Herald*, 18 May 1967.

Pankhurst, Richard. "The Foundations of Education, Printing, Newspapers, Book Productions, Libraries and Literacy in Ethiopia." *Ethiopia Observer* 6, no. 3 (1960): 241–290.

———. "Menelik and the Utilization of Foreign Skills in Ethiopia." *Journal of Ethiopian Studies* 1 (January 1967): 29–86.

———. "The Role of Foreigners in Nineteenth Century Ethiopia, Prior to the Rise of Menelik." *Boston University Papers on Africa* 2 (1966): 181–214.

Pollak, Karl. "Education and Reform." *The Ethiopian Herald*, 12 August 1946.

Pirouet, M. Louis. "Isenberg, Karl Wilhelm." In *Biographical Dictionary of Christian Missions,* edited by Gerald H. Anderson, 322. Grand Rapids: Eerdmans, 1998.

Rahel, Abayneh. "በአቲዝም ችግር ዙሪያ እስካሁን ድረስ በኢትዮጵያ ውስጥ የተደረገ ጥናት የለም" (No study has been made regarding autism in Ethiopia). *Milja* 15. Tir 1–Miazia 30, 2003 Eth. C.

Rogers, Claudia. "What's a Rasta?" *Caribbean Review* 7, no. 1, (Jan–Mar 1975): 9–12.

Roman, H/Mariam. Interview. *Kale Heywet* 2. 1985 Eth. C.

Samuel, V. C. "The Theological College." *The Ethiopian Herald*, 16 April 1971.

———. "Theology Graduates Not Employed by Church." *The Ethiopian Herald*, 14 April 1971.

Seife, Sellassie Yohannes. "የምሕረት ቃል ኪዳን" (Covenant of mercy). *Tinsae*, no. 29. Yekatit 1972 Eth. C.

Sergew, Hable Sellassie. "The Religious Life in Ethiopia with a Special Emphasis on the Church of Ethiopia." *Education and Culture in Eastern Africa* 1. C. C. Cheseldine Memorial Edition, Report to Institute of International Studies Office of Education, Department of Health, Education and Welfare, Washington DC (18 June 1870).

Sime Taddesse. "ምረጡኝ." (Vote for me) *Kale Heywet* 30. 1997 Eth. C.

Simret Kifle Egzie. "ወቅታዊ ጥያቄዎችና መልሶቻቸው" (Timely questions and the answers). *Chora* 29, n.d.

Solomon Bizuwork. "የማን ቤተ ክርስቲያን አባል ነህ?" (Where is your church membership?). *Birhan* 9. 1967 Eth. C.

Tariku Tedla. "ምስክርነት፣ መንፈሱ በሰው ተመስሎ ይገለጥልኛል" (Testimony: The spirit appears to me in human form). *Gesame* 2, no. 3. Tir, 2000 Eth. C.

Taye Tilahun. "የጀነራሉ ወዳጆች ምስክርነት" (The testimony of friends of the general). *Kale Heywet* 30. 1997 Eth. C.

Teklewold. "መዳን በክርስቶስ ብቻ ነው እንዴት?" (How is salvation in Christ alone?). *Hamer* 6. Hidar, 1986 Eth. C.

Temesgen Sahle. "የአባባ ዳኤሞ እና የአባባ ደዶቦ ምስክርነት" (The testimony of Ababa Daemo and Ababa Dedebo). *Kale Heywet* 25. 1994 Eth. C.

Tertios. "የሐዋርያው ዘውዴ አስገራሚ ለውጥና የእንመለስ ጥሪ" (The amazing change of apostle Zewde and his call for repentance). *Gesame* 2, no. 11. Tir 2002 Eth. C.

Tesfaye Gebre. "ቤተ መንግሥቱ የተታለለበት ጥንቆላ" (Occultism that deceived the state house). *Gesame* 2, no. 5. Ginbot, 2000 Eth. C.

Teshome Zerihun. "የኢትዮጵያ ቤተ ክርስቲያን ዕድገት" (The growth of the church of Ethiopia). *Tinsae* 10 Miazia 1960 Eth. C.

Tigist Tafesse. "ምሥክርነት፤ ተራው የኔ ነው" (Testimony: It is my turn). *Gesame* 2, no. 12. Miyazia 2002 Eth. C.

Walls, Andrew F. "English Neo-Calvinism and the Early Protestant Missionary Movement." In *Calvinism on the Peripheries: Religion and Society in Europe*, edited by Ábrahám Kovács and Béla Baráth. Paris: L'Harmattan, 2009.

Woineshet Assefa. "ቀዳሚዋ ዘያሪ – የዛሪዋ ዘማሪ" (The singer). *Kale Heywet* 29. 1996 Eth. C.

Wolde Rufael Fetahi. "የስልሳ ዓመቱ አዛውንት በአስር ዓመቱ ሕፃን ተዘለፈ" (The sixty-year-old elderly admonished by a ten-year-old). *Zena Bete Kristian* 225. Megabit and Miyazia, 1996 Eth. C.

Wubshet Sahilu. "ምህረቱን ልናገረው" (I proclaim his mercy). *Gesame* 2, no. 13. Tir 2002 Eth. C.

Yared Afework. "ምሥክርነት" (Testimony). *Gesame Gazette* 2, no. 3. Hidar, 1996 Eth. C.

Yirga Haile Mariam. "በሃይማኖት ስም ወጣቱን ከትግል መድረክ ለማዘናጋት በፀረ አብዮተኞች የሚደረግ ደባ" (The conspiracy of anti-revolutionary people). *Addis Zemen* 12 Ginbot 1971 Eth. C.

Yohannes Tefera. "የፕሮቴስታንት መዝሙሮች ጉዞ ወዴት?" (Where are protestant songs headed to?). *Qum Neger* 10, no. 108. Tir–Yekatit 2003 Eth. C.

Zelalem Biresaw. "Letter." *Tinsae* 27. 1972 Eth. C.

Zemedkun Bekele. "ቤተ ክርስቲያን አደጋ ላይ ነች" (The church is engulfed with danger). *Yanet* 42, no. 19. 2002 Eth. C.

Zena Bete Kristian 32, 30 Sene 1940.

"የገሃነም ደጆች" (Gates of hell). *Seme'a Tsidq*, Special issue 10, no. 78. Megabit 1995.

"የገሃነም ደጆች" (Gates of hell). *Seme'a Tsidq*, Special issue 10, no. 77. Yekatit 1995.

Published Books

Aba Gorgorios. የኢትዮጵያ ኦርቶዶክስ ተዋህዶ ቤት ክርስቲያን ታሪክ (The history of the Ethiopian Orthodox Tewahdo Church). Addis Ababa: n.p., 1974 Eth. C.

Bibliography

Abune Paulos. *Brief Life History of His Holiness Patriarch Theophilos: Before and After His Visit to the Western Hemisphere.* Addis Ababa: 1987.

Admasu Jembere. ከኩሃ ሃይማኖት (The foundation of faith). (Addis Ababa: Tinsae Zegubae Printing Press, 1949 Eth. C.

Aemere Awoke. ምኩራብ ጽድቅ (Synagogue of righteousness). Addis Ababa: n.p., 2001 Eth. C.

Agizachew Tefera. የለውጥ ያሉ (The need for change). Addis Ababa: n.p., 2001 Eth. C.

———. አልተሳሳትንም? (Are we not mistaken?). Addis Ababa: 2003 Eth. C.

Archbishop, Yeseḥaq. *The Ethiopian Tewahedo Church an Integrally African Church.* New York: Vantage Press, 1989.

Aren, Gustav. *Evangelical Pioneers in Ethiopia: Origins of the Evangelical Church Mekane Yesus.* Stockholm: EFS Forlaget, 1978.

———. *Envoys of the Gospel.* Stockholm: EFS Forlaget, 1999.

Asaminew Kassa, and Zerayehu Sime. የቤተ ክርስቲያን አስተዳደራዊ መዋቅር (The administrative hierarchy of the church). Addis Ababa: Mahbere Kidusan Educational Section, 1996 Eth. C.

Ayalew, Tamiru. መች ተለመደና ከተኩላ ዝምድና (A wolf is not a friend). Addis Ababa: n.p., 1953 Eth. C.

Ayele, Teklehaymanot. "The Struggle for the 'Ethiopianization' of The Roman Catholic Tradition." In *The Missionary Factor in Ethiopia*, edited by Getatchew Haile, 135–154. Frankfurt: Peter Lang, 1998.

Aymro, Wondmagegnehu, ed., *A Short Introduction to the Ethiopian Orthodox Church.* Addis Ababa: Birhanena Selam Printing Press, 1957 Eth. C.

Bahru, Zewde. *A History of Modern Ethiopia (1855–1991).* Addis Ababa: Addis Ababa University Press, 2002.

Balisky, E. Paul. *Wolaitta Evangelists: A Study of Religious Innovation in Southern Ethiopia, 1937–1975.* Eugene, OR: Pickwick, 2009.

Bakke, Johnny. *Christian Ministry: Patterns & Functions within the Ethiopian Evangelical Church Mekane Yesus.* Oslo: Solum Forlag, 1987.

———. "Models of Leadership in Ethiopia: The Missionary Contribution." In *The Missionary Factor in Ethiopia*, edited by Getatchew Haile et al., 155–168. Frankfurt: Peter Lang, 1998.

Bediako, Kwame. *Theology and Identity: The Impact of Culture upon Christian Thought in the Second Century and Modern Africa.* Oxford: Regnum Books, 1992.

Begashaw Desalegn. የመስቀሉ ሥር ቁማርተኞች (Gamblers under the cross). Addis Ababa: n.p., 1998 Eth. C.

Bekele Wolde Kidan. ሪቫይቫል ኢትዮጵያና የመጨረሻው መጨረሻ (Revival, Ethiopia, and the end of ends). Addis Ababa: Addis Ababa Mulu Wongel Church, 1994 Eth. C.

———. ለዚህ ጊዜ (For such a time as this). Addis Ababa: Bekele Wolde Kidan, 2001 Eth. C.

Birhanu Dido. "Achievements of the First Evangelical Missionaries in Bale." In *Stories of Bale*, edited by Henrik Petersen, 47–53. Addis Ababa: n.p., 2005.

Boyle, Isaac, trans. *The Ecclesiastical History of Eusebius Pamphilus*. Grand Rapids: Baker Book House, 1989.

Bruce, F. F. *The Canon of Scripture*. Downers Grove, IL: InterVarsity Press, 1988.

Bruce, James. *Travels to Discover the Source of the Nile, in the Years 1768–1773*. Edinburgh: George Ramsey & Co., 1813.

Budge, E. A. Wallis. *A History of Ethiopia, Nubia and Abyssinia*. Oosterhout, Netherlands: Anthropological Publications, 1966.

———. *The Legends of Our Lady the Perpetual Virgin and Her Mother Hanna*. Oxford: Oxford University Press, 1933.

———. *The Life of Takla Haymanot in the Version of Dabra Libanos, and the Miracles of Takla Haymanot in the Version of Dabra Libanos, and the Book of the Riches of Kings*. London: Privately printed for Lady Meux, 1906.

Chaillot, Christine. *The Ethiopian Orthodox Church: A Brief Introduction to Its Life and Spirituality*. Paris: Inter-Orthodox Dialogue, 2002.

Chernetsov, Sevir. "Ethiopian Theological Response to European Missionary Proselytizing in the 17th–19th Centuries." In *Ethiopia and the Missions*, edited by Verena Boll et al., 53–62. Munster: LIT, 2005.

Cotterell, Peter. *Born at Midnight*. Chicago: Moody Press, 1973.

Cowley, Roger W. *The Traditional Interpretation of the Apocalypse of St. John in the Ethiopian Orthodox Church*. Cambridge: University of Cambridge Oriental Publications, 1983.

Crummey, Donald. *Priests and Politicians: Protestant and Catholic Missions in Orthodox Ethiopia*. Oxford: Clarendon Press, 1972.

Cumbers, John. *Count It All Joy: Testimonies from a Persecuted Church*. Kearney, NE: Morris Publishing, 1995.

———. *Living with the Red Terror*. Kearney, NE: Morris Publishing, 1996.

Daniel, Kibret. ኦርቶዶክስ መልስ አላት፤ ከፕሮቴስታንቶች ለሚነሱ አንዳንድ ጥያቄዎች የተሰጡ መልሶች (Orthodox replies: Answers given for some of the questions raised by protestants). Addis Ababa: n.p., 2000 Eth. C.

Daniel, Tefera. ዳንዲ የነጋሶ መንገድ (The way of Negaso). Addis Ababa: n.p., 2003 Eth. C.

Dereje and Beza. መቅደስ የገቡ መናፍቃን (*Menafiqan* in the Temple). Bahir Dar: n.p., 2008.

Dibekulu Zewde. *81 ቅዱሳት መጻሕፍትና ምንጮች–ቀኖናት በኢትዮጵያ ኦርቶዶክስ ቤተ ክርስቲያን* (81 Scriptures and the sources of the Ethiopian Orthodox Church's canon). Addis Ababa: self-published, 1987 Eth. C.

Donham, Donald L. "The Making of an Imperial State." In *The Southern Marches of Imperial Ethiopia*, edited by Donald L. Donham and Wendy James, 3–50, Addis Ababa: Addis Ababa University Press, 2002.

Eide, Øyvind M. *Revolution and Religion in Ethiopia*. Addis Ababa: Addis Ababa University Press, 2000.

Ericksson, Bo. et al. *The Gospel of Restoration: Experiences from a Field Study in Ethiopia*. Uppsala: Swedish Institute of Missionary Research, 1999.

Eshete, Tibebe. *The Evangelical Movement in Ethiopia*. Waco, TX: Baylor University Press, 2009.

Esubalew, Belete. የገሃነም ደጆች (Gates of hell). Addis Ababa: n.p., 2004.

Ethiopian Orthodox Tewahdo Church Council of Scholars. ሁቄ ኢያስተካክሙ፣ እንዳያስቱትሁ ተጠንቀቁ፣ መናፍቁ ጌታቸው "ገድል ወይስ ገደል" በማለት ለጻፈው የክህደት ትምህርት ከኢትዮጵያ ኦርቶዶክስ ተዋሕዶ ቤተ ክርስቲያን ሊቃውንት ጉባኤ የተሰጠ መልስ (Beware not to be deceived: A reply from the council of scholars of the Ethiopian Orthodox Tewahdo Church to the apostasy writing of the "menafiq" Getachew entitled "Gedil Weys Gedel"). Addis Ababa: Tinsae Zegubae Printing Press, 1996 Eth. C.

Ethiopian Orthodox Church's Council of Scholars. ሃይማኖት የለያየን መቃብር አንድ አያደርገንም (What a religion has separated a burial site will not unite). Addis Ababa: EOC, 1987 Eth. C.

Fargher, Brian. *The Origins of the New Churches Movement in the Southern Ethiopia 1927–1944*. Leiden: E. J. Brill, 1996.

Fekadu, Gurmessa. *Evangelical Faith Movement in Ethiopia*. Minneapolis, MN: Lutheran University Press, 2009.

Forslund, E. *The Word of God in Ethiopian Tongues: Rhetorical Features in the Preaching of the Ethiopian Evangelical Church Mekane Yesus*. Uppsala: International Tryk AB., 1993.

Freeman, Dena, and Alula Pankhurst, eds. *Peripheral People: The Excluded Minorities of Ethiopia*. London: Hurst & Co., 2003.

Gehman, Richard J. *African Traditional Religion in Biblical Perspective*. Kenya: Kesho Publications, 1989.

Getachew. ገድል ወይስ ገደል. Addis Ababa: n.p., 1995 Eth. C.

Getachew, Belete. ኤሎሄና ሃሌሉያ (Agonies and hallelujah). Addis Ababa: Kale Heywet Church Literature Department, 2000.

Getatchew, Haile, trans. ደቂቀ እስጢፋኖስ፣ በሕግ አምላክ (The disciples of Estifanos: An appeal). Addis Ababa: AAU Press, 2010.

———. *Fikare Haymanot of the Faith of Abba Giyorgis Saglawi*. Addis Ababa: Institute of Ethiopian Studies, Miscellanea 1, n.d.

———. *The Mariology of Emperor Zara Ya'eqob of Ethiopia*. Rome: Pontificium Institutum Studiorum Orientalium, 1992.

———. "The Missionary Dream: An Ethiopian Perspective on Western Missions in Ethiopia." In *The Missionary Factor in Ethiopia,* edited by Getatchew Haile et al., 1–8. Frankfurt: Peter Lang, 1998.

———. *On the Writings of Abba Giyorgis Saglawi from Two Unedited Miracles of Mary.* Addis Ababa: Institute of Ethiopian Studies, Miscellanea 1, n.d.

———. *Religious Controversies and the Growth of Ethiopic Literature in the Fourteenth and Fifteenth Centuries.* Addis Ababa: Ethiopian Studies, Miscellanea 1, n.d.

———. *A Third Supplication for the Reading of the Miracles of Mary, The Cause of Estifanosites: A Fundamental Sect in the Church of Ethiopia,* Appendix V. Addis Ababa: Institute of Ethiopian Studies, Religion Miscellanea 3, n. d.

Girma, Zewde. ኢትዮጲስ (Ethiopis), Vol. 2. Addis Ababa: n.p., 1992 Eth. C.

Gorgorios, የኢትዮጵያ ኦርቶዶክስ ተዋህዶ ቤተ ክርስቲያን ታሪክ (The history of the Ethiopian Orthodox Tewahdo Church). Addis Ababa: Private Printing, 1974 Eth. C.

Grenstedt, Staffan. *Ambaricho and Shonkolla: From Local Independent Church to Evangelical Mainstream in Ethiopia, the Origins of the Mekane Yesus Church in Kambata Hadiya.* Stockholm: Elanders Gotab, 2000.

Habte-Mariam, Worqneh. ጥንታዊ የኢትዮጵያ ትምህርት (The ancient Ethiopian education). Addis Ababa: Birhanena Selam Printing Press, 1970 Eth. C.

Haile, Gabriel Dagne. "Non-Government Schools in Ethiopia." In *Language in Ethiopia,* edited by M. L. Bender et al. 339–370. London: Oxford University Press, 1976.

———. "The School System in Ethiopia." In *Äthiopien: Zeitschrift für Kulturaustausch,* 100–106. Sonderausgabe: 1973.

Halls, J. J., ed. *The Life and Adventures of Nathaniel Pearce, Written by Himself, during a Residence in Abyssinia, from the Year 1810–1819 Together with Mr Coffin's Account of His Visit to Gondar,* vol. 1. London: Henry Colburn & Richard Bentley, 1831.

Hastings, Adrian. *The Church in Africa 1450–1950.* Oxford: Clarendon Press, 1994.

Hawaze Birhan Wolde Michael et al., መጽሐፈ ሚስጢር ዘጉባኤ ጊዮርጊስ ዘጋስጫ (Aba Giorgis of Gascha's book of mysteries). Addis Ababa: Ethiopian National Archives and Library, 2001 Eth. C.

Hege, Nathan B. *Beyond Our Prayers: An Amazing Half Century of Church Growth in Ethiopia (1948–1998).* Scottdale, PA: Herald Press, 1998.

Hennell, Michael. *John Venn and the Clapham Sect.* Cambridge: Lutterworth Press, 1958.

Hiskett, Mervyn. *The Course of Islam in Africa.* Edinburgh: Edinburgh University Press, 1994.

History of Christianity in Ethiopia with Emphasis on the Ethiopian Evangelical church Mekane Yesus. Addis Ababa: MYS–TEE Department, 1989, 1992, 2007.

Isaac, Ephraim. *The Ethiopian Church*. Boston: Henry Sawyer Co., 1967.

Isenberg, C. W., and J. L. Krapf. *The Journals of C. W. Isenberg and J. L. Krapf*. London: Frank Cass & Co., 1968.

Kidane, Mariyam Getahun. ጥንታዊው የቆሉ ተማሪ (The ancient wandering student). Addis Ababa: Birhanena Selam Printing Press, 1954 Eth. C.

Knibb, Michael. *Translating the Bible: The Ethiopic Version of the Old Testament*. Oxford: Oxford University Press, 1999.

Krapf, J. Lewis. *Travels, Researches and Missionary Labours*. London: Frank Cass & Co., 1968.

Knight, William. *The Missionary Secretariat of Henry Venn, B. D.* London: Longmans, Green, & Co., 1880.

Kretschmar, George, "The Councils of the Ancient Church." In *The Councils of the Church*, edited by Hans Jochen Margull, 69–76. Philadelphia: Fortress Press, 1966.

Launhardt, Johannes. *Evangelicals in Addis Ababa 1919–1991*. USA; London: Transaction Publishers, 2004.

Levtzion, Nehemia, and Randall L. Pouwels, eds. *The History of Islam in Africa*. Athens: Ohio University Press, 2000.

Lule, Melaku. የቤተ ክርስቲያን ታሪክ (Church history). Addis Ababa: Tinsae Publishing, 1986 Eth. C.

Mahbere, Kidusan. የተሃድሶ መናፍቃን ዘመቻ በኢትዮጵያ ቤተ ክርስቲያን ላይ (The campaign of Tehadiso *menafiqan* against the Church of Ethiopia). Addis Ababa: Mahbere Kidusan Documentation Unit, 2003 Eth. C.

Malede, Wasyihun. ሐመረ ተዋህዶ (The Ark of Tewahdo). Addis Ababa: Mahbere Kidusan, 2002 Eth. C.

McGrath, Alister. *Reformation Thought*. Oxford: Blackwell, 1999.

Mehari, Choramo. *Ethiopian Pioneer Missionary: Autobiography of Evangelist Mehari Choramo*. Edmonton: Enterprise Publications, 1997.

Mekuria, Bulcha. *The Making of the Oromo Diaspora: A Historical Sociology of Forced Migration*. Minneapolis, MN: Kirk House, 2002.

Melaku, Baweke. ስውሩ አደጋ (The subtle danger). Los Angeles: n.p., 2005.

Menelik, Mered Alemu. መጽሐፍ ቅዱስና ኢትዮጵያ (The Bible and Ethiopia). Addis Ababa: n.p., 1999 Eth. C.

Merid, Wolde Aregay. "The Legacy of Jesuit Missionary Activities in Ethiopia from 1555 to 1632." In *The Missionary Factor in Ethiopia*, edited by Getatchew Haile et al., 31–56. Frankfurt: Peter Lang, 1998.

Merqorios, Arega. ታሪክህን ዕወቅ እንዳትሆን መናፍቅ (Be informed of your history so that you might not become *menafiq*). Addis Ababa: Tinsae Zegubae Printing Press, 1991 Eth. C.

Mihretu, Petros. የንባብ ባህልና ቤተክርስቲያን (General analysis on the reading habits of Ethiopian Evangelical Christians). Addis Ababa: SIM Publications, 2007.

Mulugeta, Wolde Gabriel. ማህበረ ቅዱሳን ወይስ ማህበረ ሰይጣን (Association of the saints or Satan). Addis Ababa: n.p., 2000 Eth. C.

O'Hanlon, Douglas. *Features of the Abyssinian Church.* London: SPCK, 1946.

Pankhurst, Richard. *The Ethiopians.* Oxford: Blackwell, 2001.

Paulos, Gnogno. *Ate Menelik.* 3rd edition. Addis Ababa: n.p., 1999 Year of Mercy.

Paulos, Milkias et al., eds. *The Battle of Adwa.* New York: Algora Publishing, 2005.

Peires, J. B. *The Dead Will Arise: Nongqawuse and the Great Xhosa Cattle-Killing Movement of 1856–7.* Bloomington, IN: Indiana University Press, 1989.

Petersen, Henrik, ed. *Stories of Bale: Religious Development and Evangelical Christianity.* Addis Ababa: n.p., 2005.

Rubenson, Sven. "Consequences of a Colonial Context." In *The Missionary Factor in Ethiopia*, edited by Getatchew Haile et al., 57–70. Frankfurt: Peter Lang, 1998.

Salt, Henry. *A Voyage to Abyssinia and Travels into the Interior of That Country.* London: F. C. and J. Rivington, St Paul's Church-Yard, 1814.

Sanneh, Lamin. *Translating the Message: The Missionary Impact on Culture.* Maryknoll, NY: Orbis Books, 1989.

Scanlon, D., ed. *Ethiopia, Church, State and Education.* New York: Teachers College Press, 1966.

Schaff, Philip, and Henry Wace. *A Select Library of the Nicene and Post-Nicene Fathers of the Christian Church, Vol III, Theodoret, Jerome, Gennadius, Rufinus.* Grand Rapids: Eerdmans, 1979.

———. *A Select Library of the Nicene and Post-Nicene Fathers of the Christian Church, Vol II: Socrates, Sozomenus.* Grand Rapids: Eerdmans 1979.

———. *A Select Library of Nicene and Post-Nicene Fathers of the Christian Church XIV, the Seven Ecumenical Councils.* Grand Rapids: Eerdmans, 1998.

Sergew, Hable Sellassie, *Ancient and Medieval Ethiopian History to 1270.* Addis Ababa: United Printers, 1972.

——— et al., eds., *The Church of Ethiopia: A Panorama of History and Spiritual Life.* Addis Ababa: The Ethiopian Orthodox Church, 1997.

——— et al. *The Church of Ethiopia Past and Present.* Addis Ababa: Ethiopian Orthodox Church, 1997.

Solomon, Tilahun. ደማቆች (The Illuminants). Addis Ababa: n.p., 2000 Year of Mercy.

Sorsa, Sumamo. *Bivocational Missionary-Evangelist: The Story of an Itinerant Preacher in Northern Sidama.* Edmonton, Canada: Enterprise Publications, 2002.

Spitz, Lewis W. *The Rise of Modern Europe: The Protestant Reformation 1517–1559.* New York: Harper & Row, 1985.

Stock, Eugene. *The History of the Church Missionary Society.* London: Church Missionary Society, 1899.

Sundkler, Bengt, and Christopher Steed. *A History of the Church in Africa.* Cambridge: Cambridge University Press, 2000.

Taddesse, Tamrat. *Church and State in Ethiopia 1270–1527.* Oxford: Clarendon Press, 1972.

———. "Evangelizing the Evangelized: The Root Problem between Missions and the Ethiopian Orthodox Church." In *The Missionary Factor in Ethiopia*, edited by Getatchew Haile et al., 17–56. Frankfurt: Peter Lang, 1998.

ታምረ ማርያም ግዕዝና አማርኛ (Tamre Mariyam Geez and Amharic). Addis Ababa: Tinsae Zegubae Printing Press, 1989 Eth. C.

Tesfa, G. Sellassie, ed. ሰኔ ጎልጎታ (Sene Golgotha) Addis Ababa: Tesfa Printing Press, 1984 Eth. C.

Tewodros, Tesfaye. የማስጠንቀቂያው ደወል፤ ማርክሲዝም ዘ ኮምዩኒዝም የሱሳዊ ፋሺዝም ዘ ዲሞክራሲ ጥፋት በሀገረ እግዚአብሔር ኢትዮጵያ (The wakeup call). Addis Ababa: n.p., 2002 Year of Mercy.

Tolo, Arne. *Sidama and Ethiopian: The Emergence of the Mekane Yesus Church in Sidama.* Uppsala: Uppsala University, 1998.

Trimingham, J. Spencer. *The Influence of Islam upon Africa.* London: Longman Group; 1968.

Tsigie, Sitotaw. ይነጋል (Dawn will come). Addis Ababa: Raey Publishers, 2002 Eth. C.

Ullendorff, Edward. *The Ethiopians: An Introduction to Country and People.* London: Oxford University Press, 1965.

Walls, Andrew. *The Cross-Cultural Process in Christian History.* Maryknoll, NY: Orbis, 2002.

———. *The Missionary Movement in Christian History.* Maryknoll, NY; Orbis; Edinburgh: T & T Clark, 1996.

Ward, Kevin, and Brian Stanley, eds. *The Church Mission Society and World Christianity 1799–1999.* Grand Rapids: Eerdmans, 2000.

Willis, John R., ed. *The Teachings of the Church Fathers.* San Francisco: Ignatius Press, 1966.

Wondiye, Ali. የእኩለ ሌሊት ወገግታ (Awakening at midnight: The story of the Kale Heywet Church in Ethiopia 2 [1942–1973]). Addis Ababa: Ethiopian Kale Heywet Church Publishing, 2000).

———. በመከራ ውስጥ ያበበች ቤተ ክርስቲያን (Church out of tribulation). Addis Ababa: Ethiopian Kale Heywet Church Literature Department, 1998.

Yabsira, Girum. ላታምረ ማርያም አትከራከር፣ ክብር ለሚገባው ክብርን ስጡ ለሚለው የመምህር ታሪኩ አበራ ስብከት የተሰጠ ምላሽ (Do not defend Tamre Mariam: A response to Tariku Abera's sermon on the topic "Give Due Honour"). Addis Ababa: n.p., 2003 Eth. C.

Index of Names

A
Abraham, Aba 63, 64
Afework Hailu 292
Aichinger, Christian 64, 139, 152, 154, 156, 161, 164, 181, 182, 189, 190
Alemayehu, Eshetu 371
Alem, Medhane 190, 194, 206, 207, 272, 322
Ali, Ras 66, 148, 153, 159, 160, 182, 201
Aren, Gustav 63, 65, 132, 135, 165, 175, 191, 193, 204, 258

B
Badima Yalew, Qes 406
Bakke, Johnny 50
Balisky, Paul 100, 314, 373
Bediako, Kwame 3, 4, 5
Bell, John 66
Bingham, Rowland 103, 105
Blumhardt, Carl Heinrich, Rev 191, 192

C
Cheleke 99, 101, 102
Coffin, William 137, 139, 141, 145, 146
Crummey, Donald 75, 178
Cyril of Alexandria, Saint 19, 20, 22, 49, 385

D
Dawit, King 31, 285
de Jacobis, Justin 51, 59, 207, 208

E
Edesius 14, 15
Engelsviken, Tormod 115, 117–120, 233
Eshete, Tibebe 78, 112, 113, 168, 244, 263, 264, 315, 316, 353, 409
Estifanos, Aba 38, 181, 237–239, 351–354
Eutyches 19
Ewostatéwos 34
Ezana 14–16

F
Fasiledes, King 59, 65, 234
Flad, J. Martin 209, 210
Frumentius 14, 15, 21, 23, 34, 285, 350

G
Gama, Christovao da 54
Gelawdewos, Emperor 54, 56
George III, King 134, 135
Getatchew Haile 93, 234, 235, 237, 258, 286, 290, 352
Gideon IV, King 51
Girgis 140, 143, 145, 146–147, 157, 164, 173, 187, 214, 215

Gobat, Samuel 62, 64, 91, 138, 139, 141–146, 148, 152–154, 164–190, 192, 198, 201, 203, 205, 206, 208, 209, 211–216, 218–221, 320, 322
Gorgorios, Aba 22, 35, 57, 252, 257, 261
Gragn, Ahmed 46, 53–55, 125
Gragn, Amhed 53
Gragn, Mohammed 39, 52, 252
Gudina Tumsa, Qes 80, 408, 409

H

Haile Sellassie 9
Haile Sellassie I 8, 29, 71–73, 75, 76, 86, 89, 97, 106, 115, 125, 218, 228, 243, 274, 306, 310, 311, 313, 321, 339, 340, 342, 343, 345, 355, 386
Harris, Captain 200, 204
Haymanote Abew 71, 339, 355, 366
Haymanot, Tekle 17, 34–38, 43, 54, 77, 273, 337
Hege, Nathan B. 82, 241
Heyling, Peter 35, 59, 63

I

Isenberg, Carl Wilhelm 65, 95, 186, 189–193, 195, 196, 201, 203–207, 212, 213, 216, 218–220, 253, 320

J

Jesus-men. *See* Yasus-menna
John the Baptist 101, 386
Jowett, William 63, 133, 137, 145–147, 219
Judith (Yodit), Queen 17, 39, 51

K

Kassa Mercha (of Tigray) 67
Kidane Mariam 65, 186, 190–192, 204–207, 221

Krapf, Johann Ludwig 65, 90, 91, 94, 149, 163, 173, 181, 182, 191, 195–204, 207–209, 212, 213, 215–217, 219, 220
Kugler, Christian 62, 64, 139, 141–165, 167, 170, 171, 177–179, 181, 182, 187–189, 191, 198, 202, 205, 212, 215, 320, 322

L

Lalibela, Gebre Meskel 17
Lambie, Thomas 103–107
Leo the Great, Bishop 20
Libne Dingil, Emperor 45, 53
Lundahl 93

M

Mary 38, 41, 60, 61, 143, 159, 173, 174, 182, 184, 205, 206, 216, 219, 238–241, 253, 284–296, 299, 301–303, 353, 354, 357, 358, 362, 368, 388, 400, 401
Mekbib Atnaw, Qes 50, 340, 341
Mendez, Alphonse 57, 218
Menelik 46, 47, 69, 70, 86, 125, 151, 267, 273, 310, 321
Menelik I 17, 25
Menelik II 31, 67, 68, 105
Meseret Sebhat Leab 72, 347, 361, 372
Mikre Selassie G/Amanuel, Qes 345
Mirtnesh Tilahun 367
Mohammed 27, 233
Motolomi, King 36

N

Nestorius of Constantinople 19

O

Omahe, Chacha 116
Oviedo, Andres 56, 57

P

Paez, Pedro 56–58, 218

Pankhurst, Richard 53
Pearce, Nathaniel 137, 180
Plowden, Walter 66

Q
Queen of Sheba 25
Queen of Sidama 52

R
Rosenthal 210
Rosenthal, H. 91
Rosenthal, Mrs 210
Rufinus 14

S
Sabagadis 64, 137, 140, 145, 150–154, 157–162, 164, 173, 177–181, 184–186, 189, 191, 194, 215, 219
Sahle Sellassie 47, 194, 199, 202
Sahle Sellassie, King 181, 197, 198, 201, 203
Salt, Henry 134–139, 145, 153, 162, 171
Sanneh, Lamin 6, 307
Selama, Abune 66, 199, 208, 209
Sergew Hable Sellassie 22, 24, 51, 231
Shewa, king of 166, 191–193, 217, 220
Socrates 14
Solomon, King 25, 26
Spittler, C. F. 209
Stern, Henry Aaron 91, 210
Susinyos, Emperor 57, 58

T
Taddesse Tamrat 25, 28, 59, 173, 178, 220, 235, 320
Tafari Mekonnen 71, 104, 105
Tewodros, Emperor 46, 90, 210
Tewodros II 66–68, 86, 125, 208, 209
Theophilos, Abune 77, 78, 236

Tsion, Amde 30–32, 38, 69, 337

W
Walls, Andrew 5, 276, 401
Wolde Sellassie 134–137, 180, 185
Wubie 166, 184, 185, 189, 191, 192, 200, 204, 205, 207

Y
Yikunno-Amlak 17, 18, 30
Yishak, King 237
Yodit. *See* Judith (Yodit), Queen
Yohannes 125, 308
Yohannes, Hadji 205
Yohannes IV 67, 68
Yohannes, Seife Sellassie 290
Yohannes XIX 71

Z
Zawditu, Queen 71
Zedingil, Emperor 56
Zemedkun, Bekele 368
Zer'a Ya'iqob 30–34, 38, 39, 44, 60, 61, 174, 237–239, 285–287, 290–293, 330, 335, 337, 350, 352–354, 379, 388
Zer'a Ya'iqob, Emperor 44
Zewde, Bahru 62

Index of Subjects

A
absolution 150, 151, 173, 178, 320, 322, 325
Abun 135, 137, 140, 143, 173, 199, 207, 214, 219
Abun of Alexandria 37
Abyssinia 11, 139, 143, 145–148, 166, 176, 181, 182, 185, 186, 188, 193, 195, 197, 198, 200, 204, 205, 212, 213, 217
  Apostle of 172
  Bishop of 172
  church of 127, 142, 143, 203, 205, 208
  kingdom of 127
  king of 135
Abyssinian Frontiers Mission (AFM) 103, 105, 175
Addis Ababa 78, 81, 83, 85, 98–100, 104, 105, 112, 113, 114, 116, 118, 119, 199, 233, 274, 322, 406, 407
Addis Ababa University 117, 369
Adigrate 149
Adwa 65, 74, 92, 189, 191, 192, 194, 201, 204
  church in 190
Africa 68, 90, 176, 402
  horn of 85
  West 91, 103, 137
Africa Inland Mission (AIM) 105
aggression
  Italian 235
  religious and political 225
Ahzab 278, 297, 328
Aksum 12, 13, 15, 17, 23, 47, 52, 167, 191, 285, 342
  centre of power 12, 13
  power of 16
  prosperity of 16
Aksumite Empire 86
alcohol 96, 108, 329
  abstinence from 109
Aleqa 158, 170, 184
Alexandria 15, 60, 137, 139, 141
  church of 18, 21, 22, 75, 85, 187, 188, 234, 284, 303, 340, 379
allies, Turkish 54
alms 149, 155, 156, 169, 197, 215, 254, 289, 322
alms-giving 290
American Grade School and Mission 112
American United Presbyterian Mission (AUPM) 103–105
American United Presbyterian Mission (AUPM) hospital 104
Amhara 17, 99, 100, 180, 218, 229, 273, 274, 277
  political power 251
Amharic 315, 334, 347, 348
amulets 170, 171
ancestors 42, 52, 57, 58, 68, 82, 278
  Orthodox 221
  spiritual 260
Andemta 28, 50, 51, 55, 317, 336

443

angels
  exaltation of 271
  veneration of 387
apocryphal books 125, 129, 318, 351, 366, 377, 381, 392, 393, 398, 403
apostasy 233
apostles 206, 234, 253, 281, 283, 287, 290, 383, 392
  foundation of 383
architecture 23, 158
  Orthodox 24
ark of the covenant 9, 12, 25, 26
army
  British 67, 74, 211
  national 66
artefacts 47
artisans 145, 148, 209
Assemblies of God 112
assimilation 8, 29, 31, 274
attitude
  racist 117
  suspicious 75, 219, 235
authorities, local 104, 313, 324
autocephaly 18, 22, 75, 340
Awaqi 40–42

B

baptism 73, 97, 98, 106, 109, 125, 149, 150, 169, 227, 240
  infant 95, 119
  mass 228, 280, 281
  of the eunuch 8
  of the Holy Spirit 113, 116, 120
Baptist General Conference (BGC) 98
Basel Mission 130, 132, 133, 209
battle, spiritual 360
belief system 314
believers
  Christian ix
  EOC 377
  Ethiopian 117
  Evangelical 82, 282, 356

Orthodox 367
Bible
  Abu Rumi's 64, 65, 134
  Amharic 6, 64, 65, 73, 109, 124–126, 134, 139, 168, 195, 207, 258, 275, 305–309, 312, 314
  Amharic, distribution of 73, 126, 195
  authority of 156, 167, 212, 243, 284, 304, 305, 309, 320, 351, 399
  canon 305
  centrality of x, 221, 226, 317, 318, 366, 383
  courses 116, 308
  Ethiopic 22
  exaltation of 124, 380
  foundation of 304
  Ge'ez 6, 22, 24, 62, 64, 125, 138, 207, 305, 307, 313, 339, 385, 389, 396
  interpretation of 397
  lack of prominence 301
  methods of interpretation 2
  mother-tongue 89, 109, 125, 306, 307, 391
  object of protection 43
  portions of 141
  reading of 319
  sacred tradition 73
  status of 283, 304, 306, 319, 320, 330, 352, 357, 364, 385
  study 92, 112, 260, 314, 356, 376, 377, 382
  translation 22, 23, 63, 64, 76, 89, 138, 141, 306, 309, 313, 316
  vernacular ix, 6, 22, 62, 129, 141, 142, 166, 260, 365, 386, 391
Bible Society x, 73, 133, 134, 201, 333, 394, 395
Bible Society of Ethiopia 255, 333
Bible study, Amharic 355
blasphemy 191

Index of Subjects

body, mortification of 170
body, of believers 228
bondage, spiritual 227, 350, 391
books, canonical 398
brethren 125, 152, 176, 195, 332
Britain 64, 66–68, 91, 134–136, 200
burial 323, 325, 327, 339
   ground 320, 321, 323, 325–327, 332, 386
   Orthodox 322
   place(s) 85, 94, 320
   rites 39
   site 322, 324
Byzantine Empire 20

C

canon
   Jewish 398
   of the EOC 318, 398
care
   medical 103
   pastoral 128, 132
Catholicism 55, 56, 61, 75, 232, 385
Catholocism 56
celibacy
   clerical 129
   vow of 143, 173
centres of reformation 335
Chalcedon creed 20, 23
charms 39, 155, 161, 171, 229
   as protection 39, 43
   for healing 197
   for protection 161, 167, 197
children 43, 48, 132, 138, 172, 182, 234, 284, 313, 322, 326, 329, 390
   Abyssinian 175
   from Sierra Leone 190
   of God 391
   of Luther 265
China, trade with 13
Christ 301, 368
   as mediator 129, 150, 365
   atonement 129

birth of 198, 294
births of 152
centrality of 241, 284, 300, 352
death of 5, 293
deity of 262
devotion to 403
divinity 174
doctrine of 137, 254
exaltation of 296, 300, 302, 364
faith in 317
glory of 284, 298, 304, 353
humanity 302
humanity of 294
in relation to Mary 296
intercession of 255
invoking the name of 297
knowledge of 167
love of 391
miraculous conception 303
nature of 20, 254
one nature 19
on the cross 150
person of 19, 200, 402
profession of 108
redemptive work 212
relationship with 261, 397, 399
representative of God 230
righteousness of 169
role of intercessor 254
saints of 380
significance of x
sufficiency of 153
the cornerstone 383
three births 136, 152, 154, 157
two births 64, 151, 154, 157, 199
two natures 20, 34, 136, 254
work of 402
work of salvation 295
worship of 101
Christianity
   Alexandrian 9, 21, 25, 389
   ancient 52, 230
   European 387
   Evangelical 251

expansion of 15, 22, 27–30, 34, 39, 51, 52, 62, 77, 85, 86, 90, 230, 306, 402
indigenous 2, 5, 6, 8, 56, 65, 109, 158, 216, 307, 309, 331, 385, 388, 391
Latin 52, 55, 60, 61, 86
Nubian 9
origins of 14
Orthodox 86, 87, 171, 184, 227, 229, 234, 268, 277, 385
perversion of 160
preservation of 37
promotion of 335
revival of 37
survival of 52
Syriac 386
Syrian 25
tradition 61
Western 52, 388, 392
Christianization 34, 72, 86, 232
Christians
African 8
suffering for Christ 283
superstitious 171
Christology
Alexandria 19
Antioch 19
church
Alexandrian 18
ancient 34, 55, 62, 114, 124, 229, 233, 256, 257, 263, 331, 338, 366, 392
doctrine of 129
local 319, 389
Lutheran 91
national ix, 87, 93, 97, 98, 127, 129, 131, 144, 218, 227, 228, 248, 263, 264, 390, 398
of Rome 387
reform 69
respect for 229, 359
school system 337
spiritual condition 143
spiritual state of 141, 147
split 247, 254, 369
suspicious 128
Swedish 234
traditional school 338
Church
Armenian 72
Coptic 141, 385
Ethiopian Pentecostal, formation of 116
of England 129
as Evangelical mission field 376
attitude 230
reformation 349, 354, 361, 383
self-perception 230
churches
Abyssinian 131
American 97
ancient 131
Armenian 131
Catholic 84
Christian 120, 131, 328
Coptic 131
European 158
Evangelical 83, 85, 103, 117–119, 123, 251, 254, 261, 266, 271, 272, 274, 306, 347, 358, 359, 376, 388, 403, 409
persecution 386
Greek 131, 146
Greek-speaking 20, 21
indigenous 246
Latin 146
Latin-speaking 20, 21
local 82, 109, 409
Mennonite 98
of Lalibela 17
Oriental 20, 133, 222
Orthodox 84, 225, 358
Pentecostal 83
Protestant 74, 85, 219, 225, 256, 268, 396
status 111
Syrian 131
Western 111, 261
church fathers

ancient 401
teaching of 355
church history 203
Church Missionary Society (CMS)
    ix, 6, 62–64, 66, 90, 92,
    126–132, 143, 146, 148, 149,
    164, 171, 173, 178, 187,
    189–192, 203, 204, 208, 211,
    218, 219, 222, 253, 307, 386,
    393, 394
  leadership 147
  purpose of 218
  school 209
  vision of 406
church splits, Evangelical 389
circumcision 58, 124
  male 26
citizenship
  heavenly 122
  worldly 122
civil war 61, 65, 146, 181, 234, 235,
    336
clergy
  authority of 389
  massacre of 52
  ordained 58
  Orthodox 237, 282
  public correction of 216
  reformation of 163
  spiritual status 189
  trained 72, 168, 188
colleges, theological 76, 342
communities
  Christian 228
  Ethiopian Christian 27
  monastic 37, 168
confession 173, 280
conflict
  Aksumites and Muslims 336
  Christians and Muslims 55
  Orthodox and Evangelicals 283,
    301, 320, 327, 388, 397
  Protestant and Eastern 146
congregation, house 190
consciousness
  Christian ix
  Jewish 392
  social and political 313
consul, British 91, 139
context
  African 4
  African 5
  Ethiopian 6, 123, 136, 160, 307
controversy
  doctrinal 18, 152, 165, 335
  theological 29, 238, 381, 385
conversion 29, 109, 110, 113, 124,
    126, 129, 186, 197, 222, 229,
    274, 364, 398
  Enzana's 15, 16
  experience 271
  fundamentalist theology of 108
  mass 227
  of people 28, 128, 249
  personal 264
  to Catholicism 57
  to Christianity 73
  to Evangelicalism 327, 388
  to Orthodox 261, 273, 386
  to Protestantism 247
converts, indigenous 274
convictions
  Ezana's 16
  religious 321
corruption 38, 46, 143, 269, 306,
    357, 382, 389
  of the gospel 146
Council for Cooperation of Churches
    in Ethiopia 408
Council for Evangelical Christians in
    Ethiopia 408
Council of Boru Meda 34, 68
Council of Chalcedon 20, 254
Council of Ephesus 19, 206
Council of Florence 33
Council of Islamic Affairs 323
Council of Jerusalem 401
Council of Nicaea 18
counter-reformation 338
countries

European 67, 210
Western 243
creatures, exaltation of 292
creeds 129
creeds, ancient 18
criticism
  cultural 212
  doctrinal 212
cross, veneration of 237
cross, the
  controversy 239
  power of 206
  sign of 32
  veneration of 33, 238, 352
  wearing of 154, 216
culture, Amhara 127, 230, 281

D

dancing 108, 359
dead
  burial of 321, 322
  internment of 321
  offering for 325
  prayer for 284, 323
  rising of 120
debates, christological 142
Debre Asbo. *See* Debre Libanos
Debre Libanos 36, 38, 54, 213
debtera 45, 51, 63, 204
deliverance 42, 43, 110, 117, 121, 170, 261, 280, 391
demons 279
Derg, the 76–81, 83, 84, 98, 243, 245, 259, 282, 321, 331, 345, 347, 408
  authorities 84
  fall of 85, 98, 123, 323, 330, 335, 356, 366, 409
  ideology 9, 243
  media of 84
  officials of 82
  propaganda of 386
  revolution 76
  rhetoric of 76
  rise of 259

the coming of 126, 236, 243
development work 96
dialogue
  meaningful 60, 148, 186, 393, 400
  Orthodox and Evangelicals 231, 334
  peaceful ix, 334
  platform for 404
  promotion of 401
  respectful 218
  theological 187
dictionary, Amharic 196, 347
differences
  doctrinal 45, 232, 253, 254, 324, 330, 408
  Orthodox and Evangelicals 324, 325, 402
dirsan 32
discipline, Anglican 133
discrimination 390
discussions, theological 64, 171
disputes
  christological 198
  theological 29, 137
distribution
  of Abu Rumi's Bible 64, 65, 139
  of gospel tracts 113
  of literature 362
  of Pentecostal literature 115
  of the Bible 6, 64, 135, 164, 306, 308
  of the Gospels 166, 195
  of the New Testament 195
divination 39, 41, 44, 279, 366
diviners, consultation of 39, 40, 279
doctrine
  Christian 293, 351, 401
  Tewahdo 66, 68
dominance, political and religious 32
dynamic interpretation method 316

E

East Africa 11
ecclesiology, Orthodox 389

Echege 37, 106, 159, 166, 169, 171–174
ecumenism 394
    creation of 33
education 37, 47, 49, 59, 62, 72, 96, 98, 125, 273, 306, 308, 313, 339, 341, 344, 352, 396
    church 29, 47, 50, 341, 342
    civic 47
    EOC 48
    higher 390
    indigenous 47
    modern 72, 307, 308, 338, 339
    modernization of 268
    moral 78
    mother-tongue 334
    Orthodox 307
    promotion of 86
    religious 48, 343
    theological 340, 343, 396
    Western 339
Egypt 20, 28, 53, 68, 94, 135, 139, 143, 145, 146, 148, 156, 182, 189, 190, 193, 200, 203, 205, 215, 294, 299, 336
    CMS school 209
    Coptic 20
Empress Zewditu Hospital 71
engagement, theological 359, 377, 380, 393
Epiphany 26, 192, 382
Eritrea 92, 338
Ethiopia
    Italian occupation 97
    northern 99, 107, 134, 219, 280
    revival of 62
    the promised land 26
Ethiopians, rescue of 45
ethnic factors 65, 127, 229, 276, 277, 310
Eucharist 44, 128, 303, 402. See also Holy Communion
Evangelical Churches of West Africa (ECWA) 103
Evangelical Church of Eritrea 94

Evangelicalism
    expansion of 315
    founders 267
    public perception of 122
Evangelicals 2, 76, 80, 83, 94, 126–130, 144, 218, 222, 225, 238, 241–249, 251, 253, 255–257, 259–262, 265–267, 269, 270, 276, 278–283, 292–294, 296–298, 303, 304, 316, 317, 321–323, 327–330, 332, 333, 351, 352, 354–357, 359, 364, 366, 367, 369, 372, 375–381, 386–389, 392, 393, 397, 399, 400, 401, 409
    accusations against 81
    Anglican 129, 365
    as "Anti-Mary" 237
    as foreign 243
    as "Mission" 263
    attitudes of 249
    conflict with the EOC 268
    depiction of 284
    foreign 84, 123
    identity of 125, 230
    indigenous 96
    involvement in state matters 250
    persecution of 79, 84, 263, 266, 267
    relationship with the EOC 225, 243, 262
    suffering of 84, 85
    teaching of 226
    treatment of 9, 81
    unity of 228
evangelism 36, 37, 113, 123, 132, 257, 264
    charismatic 36
    Christian 28
    door to door 328
    Evangelical 387
evangelists
    indigenous 227
    Protestant 36
evangelization, strategy 36

evil eye 43, 170
　power of 170
　protection from 171, 202
evil forces 171
evil, protection from 40
evil spirits 36, 41, 42, 43, 213, 229, 279–281, 296, 350, 363
excommunication 32, 157, 206, 211, 273, 282, 321, 381
exorcism 113, 121, 296, 388
expansion
　of the church 37
　territorial 12, 18
expelled ix, 44, 59, 72, 126, 319, 326, 335, 350, 357–359, 361, 364, 366, 369, 372, 379, 405
　children 358
experience
　charismatic 120–123, 356
　spiritual 122, 339
explorers
　European 137
　foreign 11

F

faith 3, 377
　Alexandrian 221, 222
　ancient 65, 70, 75, 86, 200, 379
　Christian 5, 9, 35, 39, 43, 52, 54, 56, 150, 171, 213, 341, 342, 401
　Christian, foundation of 150
　Christianity 402
　Evangelical 82, 128, 225, 226, 230, 281, 282, 322, 365, 389, 392
　Evangelicals 253, 373
　foreign 243
　foundation of 260
　justification by 129
　of the ancestors 235, 265
　Orthodox 66, 76, 99, 127, 134–136, 159, 188, 227, 228, 231, 234, 239, 261, 268, 273, 310, 325, 354–356, 359, 390
　Protestant 178, 272
　superstitious 3, 188
family dependence 39
fasting 95, 106, 117, 123, 133, 149, 153–157, 159, 161, 167–169, 182, 188, 195–198, 202, 212, 219, 254, 284, 331
　rejection of 129
father confessor 42, 319
fathers
　African 4
　Alexandrian 21
　ancestral 324
　ancient 232
　authority of 149, 156
　church 2, 4, 5, 47, 51, 124, 129, 150, 156, 232, 240, 271, 284, 285, 287, 316, 337, 355, 387, 392, 396, 400
　EOC 382
　faith of 204
　Orthodox 304, 389, 397
Felasha (Ethiopian Jews) 25, 65, 72, 210
Felasha Mission 210
fellowship 324, 398
　Christian 285
　table 124, 268, 270, 327
festivals, religious 78
Finnish Pentecostal Mission 113, 114
food 124, 195
forces
　demonic 36, 43
　foreign 346
　indigenous 346
　supernatural 40, 102, 227
foreigners 167, 204
fortune
　bad 47
　good 44
fountain of life 288
freedom

religious 9, 76, 84, 85, 250, 323, 329, 330
spiritual 227

G
gedel 32
Ge'ez commentary 28
Gentiles 401
Germany 89, 90
gifts
 charismatic 98, 316, 350
 of the Holy Spirit 98, 120, 121, 254, 265, 280
globalization 394
God
 access to 391
 blasphemy against 253
 creator 100
 fatherhood of 252
 fear of 318
 glory of 145, 284, 299, 302
 grace of 181, 298
 invoking the name of 78
 kingdom of 193
 knowledge of 167
 mercy of 322, 323
 name of 227
 of Israel 337
 one 99, 330
 peace with 227
 relationship with Christ 18
 triune 380
 word of 142, 156, 162, 164, 165, 182, 195, 198, 203, 215, 314
 worship of 108, 158, 330, 397
Gofa region 99, 101
Gojjam 30, 63, 75
Gondar 65, 66, 152–154, 165, 166, 171, 174, 176, 182, 189, 199, 202, 207, 210
 people of 183
gospel 159
 power of 227, 230
 preaching 6, 35, 38, 86, 89, 90, 113, 117, 130, 158, 193, 203, 209, 214, 218, 265, 273, 277, 308, 311, 313, 337, 340, 357, 362
 presentation of 397
 proclamation of 258
 reception of 105
 sharing of 313
 spreading the 217, 303, 306
Gospels
 Amharic 153, 160, 195, 201
 Amharic, distribution of 168, 185
gospel songs 355, 367
government 117, 332
 central 69, 152, 218
 church 331, 359
 corrupt 115
governors
 local 107, 153
grace
 means of 147
 of God 183, 240, 242
 of Jesus Christ 212
groups
 ethnic 314, 315, 395

H
Habesha 11, 13, 151
habits, ancient 147
Hadiya 30, 53, 82, 111, 274, 406
Hadiya Dynasty 31
hagiographies 32, 262, 289, 296, 318, 398
Haile Mariam Mamo hospital 97
Haile Sellassie I University 72, 113, 114, 117, 342
Hamasen 92, 93, 207
healing 44, 110, 112, 117, 120, 163, 174, 264, 280, 353, 368
 physical 113
healing fountain 41, 162, 213
healing power 41, 162
healing service 113

Heart of Africa (HAM) 104
heathen 64, 90, 130, 131
heaven, kingdom of 222, 286, 289
hell 43, 161
herbalists 40
heresy, Western 308
heritage
   African cultural 3, 4
   Christian 331
   Ethiopian 8
   pre-Christian 4
Hermannsburg Mission (HM) 90, 126
hinterland 12
history
   African 70
   African church 8
   ancient Christian 8
   ancient Ethiopian 85
   Christian 5, 401
   Ethiopian 137, 231
   Ethiopian church 71, 306
   Ethiopian independence 2, 8
   Islam in Ethiopia 53
   kingdom of God 193
   nation 395
   of Christianity 401
   Orthodox Church 241, 375, 379
holiness, promotion of 131
Holy Communion 44, 93, 95, 190–192, 195, 207
Holy Spirit 164, 279
   filling 117
   power of 116
   regeneration 129, 365
   work of 112, 120, 122
homosexuals 260
   ordaining of 365
house churches 389
house of prayer 272
house, worship in 95

I

identity 3–6
   Abyssinian Christian 127
   African 3, 118
   African theologians 4
   Christian 4, 39, 133, 392
   Ethiopian 68, 86, 118, 231, 243, 251, 261, 355, 392
   Ethiopian Christian 204, 400
   ethnic 311, 313
   Evangelicals 10, 230, 263, 316, 331, 387, 390
   in Christ 271
   Jewish 392
   national 232, 264, 313, 386, 399
   of the church 129
   Orthodox 9, 10, 188, 335, 375, 390
   religious 309, 313, 386, 399
identity crisis 4
ideology
   atheistic 122
   Communist 80
   Marxist 408
   Socialist 408
idolatry ix, 124, 146, 158, 161, 201, 297
ignorance
   of people 115, 168, 281, 391
   of priests 141
   of the Abyssinians 151, 189
   of the clergy 143, 269
illiteracy 201
images 129, 143, 146, 147, 155, 157, 160, 161, 171, 223
   of Mary 238
   veneration of 298
immigrants
   Arabian 13
   Jewish 86
impulses
   reform x, 335, 345, 354
   renewal 6
   tehadiso 339
independence
   of Ethiopia 8, 118
India 14, 130, 137, 222, 223
   trade with 13

Indigenizing Principle 5, 401–403
influences, foreign 385
inscription 160
instability, political and religious 140
intercession 206, 239, 242, 294
Inter-Religious Council 332, 388
intolerance 94, 123, 283, 321, 327, 396
  religious 59
invasion
  European 70
  Italian 101, 112
Islam 9, 27, 28, 37, 45, 52–55, 67, 70, 75, 86, 92, 137, 160, 218, 270, 280, 327, 331, 336, 385, 386, 394
  expansion of 30, 33, 52, 268
  rise of 27
  spread of 30
Islamic
  aggression 331
  control 27
  insurgence 59
  invasion 60
  presence 73
isolation 26, 51, 59, 94, 123, 265, 282, 337, 378
Italian conquest 73, 109, 235, 280, 306, 310, 405
Italian War 70

J
Jerusalem 46, 142, 149, 189, 198, 401, 403
  pilgrimage to 17
Jesuits 56, 58, 59, 61, 125, 139, 222, 223, 235, 238
Jesus-men 109
Jihad 52, 53, 328
Judaism 12, 13, 17, 25, 198, 210, 211
  influence of 26
justice 46, 76, 405

K
Kaffa Dynasty 69, 111
Kale Heywet Church (EKHC) 1, 2, 89, 96, 103, 112, 122, 228, 262, 306, 408
Kale Heywet churches 81, 119, 120, 309
Kale Heywet members 327
Kembatta 81, 106, 107, 111, 274, 315, 406
  High God 101
Kibre Negest 25
kingdom
  Aksumite 14, 27, 52
  Christian 17, 31, 52, 55, 86, 235
kings, Aksumite 51
knowledge 50, 51, 64, 131
  of Christ 167
  of salvation 182
  of Scriptures 169, 281, 306
  of the Bible 141, 203, 221, 262, 358, 390
  words of 120, 121

L
Lalibela 107
land
  dark 181
  Ethiopia 330
  fertile 227
  Gafat 210
  mission 191
  Muslim 238
  Oromo 204
languages
  Amharic 8, 29, 62, 85, 138, 139, 189, 306, 307, 310–314, 342, 387, 399
  ancient 51, 133, 255, 305, 313, 397
  Arabic 17
  English 247, 310
  foreign 6, 219, 307
  French 310

Ge'ez 17, 29, 48, 55, 57, 62, 138, 305, 342, 387, 388, 399
Gofa 309
Greek 342
Hadiya 309
Hebrew 342
indigenous 312
liturgical 138
local 95, 310, 312
national 307, 310, 315
of communication 138
of Scripture 86
Oromo 196, 199
pagan 310
sacred 5, 55
Semitic 399
Sidamo 311
vernacular 166
Walayta 312
Wolaitta 311
leaders
  indigenous 120
  political 395
leadership 52, 77, 106, 109, 111, 147, 151, 342, 366, 383, 391
  church 98, 327, 357, 369, 374, 381
  local 83
  traditional 273
Lent 106, 133, 155
literacy 62, 73, 79, 89, 109, 306, 309, 315, 316, 390
literature
  Christian 39
  monastic 50, 371
liturgy 56, 377
  church 33
  divine 15
  Ge'ez 23
  Orthodox 22
Lord's Prayer 202
Lord's Supper 205
Lutheran World Federation 407

M

Magano 101
magic, black and white 41
magic practices 44
Mahadist 69
Mahbere Bekur 347, 349, 350, 353, 361–364
Mahbere Kidusan 222, 248, 249, 252, 254, 258, 260, 261, 272, 303, 334, 346–349, 351, 356, 360, 362, 366, 368, 369, 370, 372–375, 379–393
Mariolatry 399
Mariology 60, 61, 143, 174, 184, 232, 243, 253, 284, 285, 292, 300, 335, 337, 392, 393, 400, 404
  promotion of 33
Marxism 84
Mary
  adoration of 239
  as co-redeemer 60, 284, 285
  as intercessor 254
  as mediator 206
  as redeemer 286
  as saviour 61, 239, 289, 301, 330
  blasphemy against 207
  commemoration of 292
  Cult of 60, 284
  devotion to 266
  disregard of 296
  exaltation of 285, 293, 296, 330, 364, 388
  her sinlessness 174, 241, 284
  honour of 367
  intercession 295
  intercessor 284, 293, 300
  intercessory role 95, 242, 348
  invocation of 186, 220, 289
  motherhood 242
  perception of 387, 397
  picture of 158
  praise of 285
  prostration to 239, 289, 338, 352

providing protection 295
reign of 289
respect for 303
role in salvation 241, 293, 295, 304
salvation through 399
status of ix, 61, 106, 155, 167, 283, 287, 296, 302, 338, 394
teaching 186
veneration of 33, 160, 200, 237, 238, 320, 352, 387
worship of 34, 159, 184, 239, 290, 292, 299, 304, 330
Massawa 54, 146, 149, 177, 182, 185, 186, 189, 202, 207, 215
Red Sea port 92
media, Christian 396, 400
medical work 97, 306
Mediterranean Mission 204
mediums 40, 47, 102, 120, 229, 405
Mekane Yesus Church 1, 9, 80, 83, 89, 94–96, 112, 119, 120, 233, 243, 250, 262, 306, 408
Mekane Yesus Seminary 82
menafiq 251–253, 262, 283, 381
mentorship, spiritual 331
Meserete Kristos Church (MKC) 81, 82, 98, 114, 306, 408
Metshaf Bet 48–50
migrants, Jewish 17
migration, Oromo 55
Ministry of the Interior 263
miracles 32, 36, 110, 112, 120, 213, 264, 286, 287, 297, 303
Miracles of Mary 33, 49, 285, 288, 300
missionaries 64, 76, 109, 112, 153, 154, 160, 162, 171, 175, 185, 188, 216, 217, 227, 233, 241, 247, 249, 306, 309, 311, 312, 315, 343, 407
AOG 112
Catholic 8, 56, 59, 61, 141, 207
Christian 142

CMS 43, 64, 65, 92, 127, 133, 136, 137, 138, 139, 142, 143, 146, 148, 149, 153, 154, 157, 164, 171, 187, 206, 207, 211, 213, 215, 219–222, 226, 305, 308, 364
European 67, 217
expulsion of 67
Finnish 113, 116
foreign 61, 200, 228, 243, 311
German 222
Lutheran 50, 250
North American 87, 97
ordained 90, 132
Orthodox 3
Pentecostal 113
pilgrim 66
pioneer 105, 395
Protestant 3, 8, 76, 86, 207, 218, 241, 272, 391
Reformed 147
SIM 105, 226
Swedish 113, 118
Syriac 24
teaching of 355
Western 83, 263
missions
Catholic 8
foreign 91, 125, 233, 243, 348
Lutheran 89, 90, 95, 96, 111
Protestant 8, 72, 89, 115, 127, 218
Western 126
monastery
Abyssinian 33
Debre Damo 35, 52, 168
Debre Libanos 36
Hayq 35
monasticism 37, 129, 366, 392
revival of 337
spread of 23
monastic life 17, 363, 370
monastic movement, indigenous 34
monastic order 237, 352
monastic vows 35

monks 38, 43, 55, 90, 169, 183, 200, 221, 237, 238, 335, 353, 366
  ancient 230
  death of 54
  EOC 60
  Ethiopian 392
  indigenous 34, 43
  missionary role 38
  Orthodox 229, 273, 281
Mother of God 184, 206, 216, 232, 240, 283, 284, 293, 294, 303, 362
motives, religious and political 281
movement
  Bible 369
  Evangelical 65, 89
  missionary 226
  monastic 39
  Muslim extremists 330
  of Estifanosites 385
  Pentecostal ix, 90, 112–115, 118, 119, 120, 124, 126, 263, 264, 266, 271, 316, 328, 350
  Pentecostal/Charismatic 263
  Protestant 157
  Protestant missionary 386
  reformation 348, 360, 361, 364
  renewal 71, 381
  resistance 74
  revival 96
  tehadiso 375, 378, 380
  youth 263, 358
Mulu Wongel, renewal 122
Mulu Wongel, believers 122
Mulu Wongel Church 81, 90, 96, 108, 113, 114, 116, 118, 119, 122, 246, 359, 408
Muslims 20, 36, 38, 41, 55, 62, 69, 73, 76, 131, 135, 153, 160, 182, 201, 209, 270, 275, 295, 323, 336, 376, 390
  Ethiopian 53, 268, 280
  forced conversion 9

Oromo 53, 312
mystery
  divine 138
  of divine revelation 139
  of religion 168
  of the incarnation 294

N

nationalism, religious 34
nation(s)
  ancient 11
  Christian 134, 136
  Christian, black 70
  EOC's contribution 260
  European 66, 70
  poverty of 259
  spiritual state of 138
  unity of 264, 310, 372, 383
nature of Christ 64, 137
  divine 18, 19, 254
  human 18, 19, 34
Nazareth 97, 366
Nazareth Bible Academy 98, 409
Nebab Bet 48, 49
New Testament 43, 62, 115, 120, 157, 166, 168, 190, 197, 214, 216, 221, 255, 283, 287, 314, 361, 371, 389
  Amharic 63, 141, 144, 185, 194, 202
  as protection 161, 197
  distribution 166
  Ethiopian 49, 194
  Ethiopic 202
  Ge'ez 56
  knowledge of 221
  mother-tongue 307
  translation 309
Nicene Christology 18
Nicene Creed 18, 21, 59
Nine Saints 22–24, 34, 35, 43, 49, 335
Nubia 21

O

obelisks, Aksumite 13
occultism 229
Old Testament 49, 361, 363, 371, 398
  Amharic 144
  Ethiopic 24
  translation 315
one faith 404
oneness, promotion of 311
oppression 20, 227, 268
oracles 46, 47, 103
orientation, other-worldly 245
Oromo 91, 137, 197, 204, 209
  "Germany of Africa" 196
  "pagan" 226
Oromo Liberation Front (OLF) 80
Orthodox 124, 126, 176, 221, 250, 255, 263, 265
  believers 316
  devotion to Mary 266
  mission 65
  persecution of 84
  relationship with Evangelicals 243, 262
  soteriology 264
Orthodox Church 6, 8, 9, 17, 59, 77, 79, 84–86, 89, 93, 95, 97, 99, 103, 104, 107, 110, 112, 114, 115, 118, 124–126, 218, 225, 226, 230, 235, 241, 243, 247, 251, 256, 257, 259, 261, 262, 264, 268, 269, 271–273, 275, 279, 283, 284, 287, 304, 318, 328, 331, 335, 392
  ancient 260
  enmity 278
  foundation of 350
  power 84
  status of 84
Orthodox Church Council of Scholars 61, 239, 253, 257, 296, 354, 399
Orthodox-Evangelical divide ix, 400, 401
orthodoxy
  ancient 220, 370, 379
  Ethiopian ix
Ortho-Pente 357
Orto-Qalicha 358
Othodox Church Council of Scholars 291
Ottomans, the 53, 54, 55
Ourael Mekane Yesus Church 82

P

paganism 13, 23, 38, 43, 67, 403
papal authority 387
Pente 2, 244, 263, 316, 327, 357, 387
Pentecostal 123
Pentecostal experience 116, 117, 121
Pentecostalism, expansion of 328
Pentecostal movement, indigenous 90
Pentecostals
  as "sheep-stealers" 328
  radical 229
  young 120, 263
people
  Abyssinian 203
  Amhara 29
  conservative 400
  Cushitic 53
  educated 339
  indigenous 276, 277, 395
  Kunama 92
  local 36, 100, 273, 277
  Noba 16
  non-Christian 89
  northern 11, 275, 336
  Oromo 90, 92, 196, 280, 309
  Orthodox 85, 241, 269, 303
  pagan 86, 175
  reformers 347
  renewal of 349
  resistant 125

Semitic 12, 86
southern 76, 86, 227
spiritual condition 137, 138, 143, 169
spread of Islam 27
urban 394
young 116, 117, 175, 375
peoples
southern 102
perception 83, 97, 107, 124, 138, 142, 147, 153, 174, 186, 226, 231, 232, 283, 317, 358, 369, 389, 394, 400
of Evangelicals 85
of the EOC 249
Orthodox and Evangelicals 10, 231
persecution 9, 21, 23, 27, 79, 81, 83–85, 90, 93, 94, 110, 120, 121, 126, 225, 237, 245, 260, 263, 264, 266, 267, 282, 327, 328, 331, 352, 386, 395
perversion, protection from 38
Philadelphia Church Mission 116
philosophy 174
athiest 78
secular 78
Pilgrim Mission 209
Pilgrim Principle 5, 401–404
polygamy 38, 96, 108, 208
population
Aksumite 13
Evangelical 7
indigenous 12
Muslims 7
Orthodox 7
Portuguese, the 54, 55, 59
position
christological 20
doctrinal 85, 349, 370, 385
power encounter(s) 43, 227, 230
powers, supernatural 99, 229
practices
Christian 41, 213
non-Christian 278, 301

pagan 41, 43
superstitious 161, 162, 385
prayer
for renewal 129, 365
to Michael 2
praying in tongues 120, 121
preaching 206
Amharic 307, 315
Bible-centred 129, 366, 368
biblical 382
indigenous 230
mother-tongue 6, 308, 334
offensive 230
of missionaries 217, 227, 228
permission 209
role of Mary 370
presuppositions, Western 6, 307
priest(s)
Coptic 205, 211
Orthodox 156, 250
principles
Christian 38
Reformed 132
prophecies 45
proselytism 124, 144, 256, 257
prosperity gospel 258, 259
prostration of honour 330
Protestant. *See* Evangelical
Protestantism, expansion of 268
Provisional Council for the Renewal of the Church 347

Q
Qene Bet (school of poetry) 48, 49, 340
Qiddase Bet 48, 49

R
Radio Voice of the Gospel 80
reconciliation, Orthodox and Evangelicals 395, 396
reform
ecclesiastical 67, 308
educational 342
intolerance of 55

Index of Subjects

of the church 37, 258
Orthodox Church 92, 321, 382
religious 31
theological institutions 345
through translation 63
reformation movements 336, 360, 376, 380, 382
Reformation, the 129, 336
  core values 150, 156
  English 129
  European 93, 125, 386
  Swiss 157
  tradition 211
reformers
  Evangelical 351
  Orthodox 94, 365, 380, 388, 392
Reinhardt Bonkee Crusade 85
relationship
  CMS and EOC 206
  EOC and Alexandrian church 21
  EOC and Evangelicals 123, 226, 394
  Muslims and Axumites 27
  Orthodox and Evangelicals 123, 243, 262
religion
  Christian 59
  European 75
  foreign 324
  isolation 336
  Oromo 228
  primal 7, 95, 96, 235, 272, 283
  traditional 3, 38, 39, 107, 110, 125, 211, 227, 229, 230, 282, 327
    as demonic 227
  traditional African 39
renewal
  church 349, 355, 379, 382
  Orthodox 93, 99, 347, 348, 359
  religious 119
  within the EOC 376
resettlement programs 82
revelation, divine 138, 389
revitalization

Abyssinian church 127
Eastern churches 131
Ethiopian church 65
revival 115, 117, 124, 336, 367, 377
  Bible 369
  church 150
  Evangelical 91, 128, 139
  monastic 34, 349, 385
  Nazareth 356
  of spiritual life 349
  of traditional practices 44
  Orthodox 134, 366
  Pentecostal 90, 116, 119
revolution
  Ethiopian 79
  Russian 79
righteousness 161, 170, 259, 363
  doctrine of 290
rites
  after death 323
  Latin 52
  traditional 108
rituals, pagan 281
Robber Synod 20
Roman Empire 22, 353
rulers
  Amhara 276
  northern 230

S

Sabbath, keeping the 216
Sacraments, the 49, 232
saints
  adoration of 167
  authority of 242
  blasphemy against 207, 253
  commemoration of 124, 292
  devotion to 266
  exaltation of 271, 364
  honour of 367
  images of 146
  indigenous 41
  intercession of 223, 378
  intercessory role 95, 205, 294
  intercessory roll 242

invocation of 143
respect for x, 129, 380
status of 269, 369, 370, 380, 388, 394
veneration of 210, 212, 219, 387, 392, 403
worship of 158, 198, 298
salvation 153
  after death 323
  by faith alone 253
  doctrine of 129
  through Christ alone 154, 317, 352, 367
  through Mary 289, 291
  through works 159
Saviour, exaltation of 131, 292
school(s)
  elementary 82
  EOC 48
  European 51
  Jewish 72
  language 112
  local 48
  modern 69
  modern theological 342, 345
  Orthodox 62, 308
  tension 345
  theological x, 343, 344
  traditional 337, 345, 370
  traditional system 345
school system 341
  EOC 47
Scripture(s)
  Amharic 73
  as a sacred object 168
  as protection 43
  authority of 115, 150, 167, 212, 213, 221
  canon 2
  distribution of 91, 92, 137, 138, 144, 187, 188, 195, 207–209, 221, 222
  in reform 65
  in relation to Mary 290
  in song 367, 368
  interpretation 317, 336, 340, 341
  knowledge of 144, 281, 297
  mother-tongue 6, 227, 307, 389
  object of protection 305
  read by priests 305
  reading of 397
  singing of 366
  status of 147
  study of 131, 355
  sufficiency of 124
  teaching 210
  translation 227, 307
  understanding of 221
  vernacular 22, 62, 64, 133, 144, 146, 148, 167, 185, 209, 308, 340, 389
separation
  from the church 129, 365
  from the world 108
  of church and state 78
Septuagint 255, 398
services
  church 95, 119
  educational 48
  healing 123
  in the house 191
  worship 121, 123, 265, 359
settlers
  Amhara 273
  Christian 35
  Jewish 51
  northern 227, 273, 390
sheep-stealing x, 83, 84, 223, 225, 256, 265, 268, 328, 365, 376, 380, 395
  Evangelicals 394
Shewa 17, 34, 53, 86, 99, 125, 195, 200, 203, 212
  northern 75
shibboleth ix, 371
Sidama. *See* Sidamo
Sidama Dynasty 31
Sidamo 107, 111, 244, 315
sin 129
  freedom from 219

original 365
Siwasew Birhane Kidus Paulos School 320
Socialism 77, 78, 83, 408
social justice 66
sola fide 253
Solomonic Dynasty 17, 30, 37, 71, 76, 337
Son. *See* also Christ
   conception of 241
   glory of 292
   in relation to Mary 160, 241, 284, 286, 292, 302, 357
   praise of 285
   prostration to 289
   relationship with Father 18
   three nativities 136
   two nativities 135
   worship of 200, 237, 330
South Africa 100, 252
Southern Baptists 81, 99
Southern Ethiopia 282
sovereignty
   of Ethiopia 310
   of the country 232
   of the Lord 121
speaking in tongues 113, 120, 247, 254
spirits
   ancestral 42, 262, 280
   evil 297
spiritual growth 282, 343
spirit world 47, 99
   communication with 229
   protection from 162
students, university 71, 76, 79
Sudan Interior Mission (SIM) 1, 82, 89, 90, 96, 103, 105, 109, 111, 119, 125, 218, 306, 311, 312
Swedish Evangelical Mission (SEM) 90, 91, 93, 95, 112, 126, 226, 306, 386, 394
   founders 91
Swedish Evangelical Society 126

Swedish Philadelphia Mission 114, 116
Synod
   EOC 226, 235
   of Constantinople 19
Syria 20
system
   educational 78, 340
   feudal 76
   Gabar 227

T
Tabot 26, 95, 204
tamir 32
teaching
   erroneous 163, 226, 252, 293, 349, 350, 361, 372
   foreign 352
   Lutheran 132
technology 62, 69
   European 67
   modern 47
   Western 71
tehadiso 301, 325, 336, 339, 345–349, 351, 353, 363, 367, 369, 370, 372–382, 392, 393
tenets
   Ethiopian Orthodoxy 371
   Orthodox Church 106
tension 83, 119, 374, 380, 381, 389, 402
   Orthodox and Evangelicals 2, 320
   political 106
   reforming or preserving 359
Tewahdo 57, 199, 200, 261, 323
tezkar 178
theologians 168, 292, 330, 349
   African 4, 5
   church 44
   EOC 248
   Orthodox 238, 257, 269, 297, 301, 302, 304, 366, 388
   trained 378
theological education. *See* education, theological

theological institutions 400
theology
  ancient 363
  indigenous 4
Three Births party 199, 200, 204
Tigray 17, 24, 38, 64, 137, 152, 154, 165–168, 170, 177, 195, 203, 207, 212, 308, 320
tolerance, promotion of 332, 388, 394
Tosa 100, 102
trade 52
tradition(s) 265
  Africa 4
  ancient ix, 356, 367, 373, 400
  authority of 95
  centrality of 281
  charismatic/Pentecostal 393
  Christian 2, 3, 5, 39, 56, 59, 61, 67, 231, 249, 383, 386, 402
  church 65, 124, 144, 188, 211, 271, 304, 305, 364, 367, 370, 375, 381
  contradiction 401
  Egyptian Christian 26
  EOC 285, 316, 377, 392, 404
  establishment of 25
  Ethiopian 337
  Evangelical 267, 325, 354, 359, 379, 380, 383
  extra-canonical 392
  iconographic 298
  indigenous 287, 378, 381, 400
  indigenous Ethiopian 191
  Jewish 283
  of the church fathers 47
  Orthodox 8, 96, 196, 229, 305, 362, 368, 369, 378, 380, 393, 397, 399, 403
  protection of 221, 397
  Protestant 242, 350, 387
  reformed 3, 5, 124
  Syriac 22
  training
    clergy 341
    theological 377
  transformation 119
  translation 315
    Amharic 313, 373
    Bible 62
    Gospel of Mark 309
  translations 6, 73, 125, 141, 167, 306, 385, 391
  treaty 68, 200
    Orthodox and Catholic 33
  tsebel 39, 163
  tsere Mariam 58, 238, 240, 263, 284, 321, 338

U
United Bible Societies 255

V
venereal disease 155
Victory at Adwa 123
villages 82, 110, 116, 230, 276

W
"water-people" 109
weapons
  European 202
  modern 74, 153
Welkayt 168
witchcraft 43, 269, 350
witness, Christian 124, 164
Wolaitta 101, 109, 111, 311, 312, 315
  believers 314
Wolaitta Dynasty 36, 69
Wollega 94, 321, 406
World Council of Churches 84
worldview 176
  African 16, 39
  EOC vs Evangelicals 229
  Ethiopian 163
  European 163
  primal 4
  traditional 41, 43, 281

traditional African 47
worship 82, 83, 100, 122, 132, 219,
    221, 246, 282, 296, 303, 305,
    323, 330, 353, 359, 367, 368,
    373, 377, 389, 395
  ancestor(s) 44, 100, 102
  ancestral 41, 108, 279
  considered demonic 280, 292
  dancing 108
  due to Mary 34
  foreign 350
  freedom of 85, 237, 323
  gospel songs 366
  idol 31, 124
  image 146, 147, 158, 167, 173,
    297, 298
  indigenous 331, 336
  Judaic 26
  Kale Heywet Church (EKHC) 108
  musical instruments 350, 358, 366
  of creatures 186, 220
  of Satan 100, 101
  of Tosa 102
  order of 331
  Orthodox 366
  pagan 12, 44, 337
  Pentecostal 119
  prostration of 330
  solemn 108
  style(s) 90, 121, 126
  use of instruments 108
writing charms 43
Wubie 191
wuqabi 41

X
Xhosa 100

Y
yeqolo temari 49, 272
Yodit. See Judith (Yodit), Queen
youth 76, 80, 99, 112–116, 119,
    198, 244, 292, 355, 356, 358,
    366, 377, 378, 382

Z
Zagwe Dynasty 17, 37
Zema Bet (school of hymns) 48, 49
Zion 61, 181, 285, 350

Langham Literature, with its publishing work, is a ministry of Langham Partnership.

Langham Partnership is a global fellowship working in pursuit of the vision God entrusted to its founder John Stott –

to facilitate the growth of the church in maturity and Christ-likeness through raising the standards of biblical preaching and teaching.

Our vision is to see churches in the majority world equipped for mission and growing to maturity in Christ through the ministry of pastors and leaders who believe, teach and live by the Word of God.

Our mission is to strengthen the ministry of the Word of God through:
- nurturing national movements for biblical preaching
- fostering the creation and distribution of evangelical literature
- enhancing evangelical theological education

especially in countries where churches are under-resourced.

Our ministry

Langham Preaching partners with national leaders to nurture indigenous biblical preaching movements for pastors and lay preachers all around the world. With the support of a team of trainers from many countries, a multi-level programme of seminars provides practical training, and is followed by a programme for training local facilitators. Local preachers' groups and national and regional networks ensure continuity and ongoing development, seeking to build vigorous movements committed to Bible exposition.

Langham Literature provides majority world preachers, scholars and seminary libraries with evangelical books and electronic resources through publishing and distribution, grants and discounts. The programme also fosters the creation of indigenous evangelical books in many languages, through writer's grants, strengthening local evangelical publishing houses, and investment in major regional literature projects, such as one volume Bible commentaries like the *Africa Bible Commentary* and the *South Asia Bible Commentary*.

Langham Scholars provides financial support for evangelical doctoral students from the majority world so that, when they return home, they may train pastors and other Christian leaders with sound, biblical and theological teaching. This programme equips those who equip others. Langham Scholars also works in partnership with majority world seminaries in strengthening evangelical theological education. A growing number of Langham Scholars study in high quality doctoral programmes in the majority world itself. As well as teaching the next generation of pastors, graduated Langham Scholars exercise significant influence through their writing and leadership.

To learn more about Langham Partnership and the work we do visit **langham.org**

www.ingramcontent.com/pod-product-compliance
Lightning Source LLC
Chambersburg PA
CBHW050524300426
44113CB00012B/1943